THIRD EDITION

Teaching in the Middle and Secondary Schools

Planning for Competence

Joseph F. Callahan

Leonard H. Clark

Macmillan Publishing Company
New York
Collier Macmillan Publishers
London

To Jane E. Callahan and Maria A. Clark

Macmillan Publishing Company
866 Third Avenue, New York, New York 10022

Collier Macmillan Canada, Inc.

Library of Congress Cataloging-in-Publication Data

Teaching in the middle and secondary schools.

Includes bibliographies and index.
1. High school teaching—United States   2. Middle
schools—United States.   I. Callahan, Joseph F.
II. Clark, Leonard H.
LB1737.U6T43   1988   373.11'02   87-18515
ISBN 0-02-318210-5

Printing: 3   4   5   6   7   Year: 9   0   1   2   3   4

ISBN 0-02-318210-5

Preface

This volume seeks to provide a basic self-instructional text on teaching methods.

In presenting the material, the authors have been mindful of the rationales for the various techniques used in teaching and have attempted to illustrate how each of the methods named might be implemented in the classroom. They selected the self-teaching module format as their mode of presentation of text in order to encourage reader participation in the learning, reader reaction to the text, and reaction interaction with fellow students to perfect the skills presented.

As progress toward conceptual mastery is experienced it is expected that considerable self-motivation will start operating. There should be a gradual development in confidence as each module is mastered and an increase in self-imposed reading assignments from the lists of sources at the end of each module to augment the sometimes sketchy development in this text resulting from space limitations. It is expected that skill in utilization of the method will ensue after intellectual mastery of the concept has been achieved.

Of course, expertise in methods and techniques comes from practice, particularly guided practice and experience. No one ever became truly expert simply by studying a book and carrying out learning activities. But it is expected that these modules will provide the student with the necessary background and basic knowhow to help make early teaching practice and experience profitable. The modules should serve as effective springboards for laboratory exposures in teaching. We believe that instructors using the modules in methods courses can depend on them to provide some basic instruction so they can individualize instruction and devote their time to higher learning and complicated activities.

Sexist expressions easily find their way into a manuscript. We have tried to avoid them and other marks of prejudice. We have, however, at times used the editorial pronoun "he" to refer to both men and women. This should not be taken as evidence of sexism, but as an effort to facilitate readability. The use of masculine nouns and pronouns makes the writing less awkward.

We, the editors, wish to acknowledge the contributions of colleagues and students who have helped in the preparation of the book. We are particularly indebted to Maria A. Clark and Jane E. Callahan who prepared the manuscript of this Third Edition for publication.

J.F.C.
L.H.C.

iii

Contents

MODULE **10**
Exploration and Discovery   235

MODULE **11**
Reading and Study Skills   271

MODULE **12**
Providing for Individual Differences   303

MODULE **13**
Measurement and Evaluation   337

To the Student

Welcome to an adventure in learning.

Now that you have begun to think seriously about a career in teaching, it is our guess that you will find adventures of this sort very helpful in planning to meet the challenges that await you in the classroom. It seems safe to predict that not only will you increase your background in educational theory and methodology as you work your way through these modules, but also you will improve your chances of becoming an effective teacher when the time arrives to put theory learned into practice.

Probably you have not encountered many books organized as this one, calling for such active participation on your part. From this point forward, you are expected to become a sensitive, self-motivated learner engaged in making frequent and sound judgments about your learning. You will be the one to control the rate of progress through the various modules, and you will decide when you have mastered the knowledge presented in each. We have tried to help by (1) listing the objectives of each module, (2) providing a comprehensive set of questions to test your mastery at the end of each module, and (3) providing an answer key for your use in evaluating progress. Those with little time to spend on study can move through the various modules and finish quickly so long as they study attentively and demonstrate the mastery called for on each test. Slower-paced individuals, who wish to ponder and probe various areas and who decide to read extensively from the selected readings listed in each module, can establish a pace that suits their purposes.

It is not intended that any student will be able to prepare himself for a teaching career solely by completion of this kind of study program. Teaching is a human activity. It deals with people, with children, parents, and fellow professionals. It involves various kinds of knowledge, judgments, and decision making; it requires communications skills, human relations techniques, and a host of other attributes for the cultivation of which human interaction and professional expertise are necessary. But faithful and zealous use of this learning tool will add depth and meaning to your classroom sessions in education courses. Mastery of these modules will carry you beyond the initial steps of preparation so you may place into context more of the campus lectures about education that you hear, and ask questions about schools and students that go beyond the layman's level of significance.

The chapters of the book are called modules, for essentially they are self-contained units that have cognitive values by themselves. Each module contains a rationale, a list of specific objectives, the module text and exercises, a post test, a list of suggested readings, and the answer key to the post test and where appropriate to the exercises.

The rationale attempts to establish the purpose of each module and, in some cases, the link with other aspects of pedagogical knowledge. The objectives inform you very specifically what you should know and be able to do as a consequence of your study of the module. The list of suggested readings points out other sources of information by which to deepen and broaden your understanding of the topic. The test and the key inform you of your progress toward module mastery. The general study plan recommended is as follows:

1. Read the rationale to acquaint yourself with the task you are addressing and, if possible, with how this module fits among the others that you will study.
2. Examine carefully the module objectives. Find out what will be expected of you upon completion of your study.
3. Read through the module, checking back from time to time to see how well you are mastering the objectives. Review what you do not understand. Try the exercises both to check your understanding and to clinch your learning.
4. Try out your knowledge by exposing yourself to some of the suggested readings.

Enjoy the quest!

MODULE
1

Theoretical Considerations

Rationale
Specific Objectives
Module Text
   Introduction
   Teaching as Decision Making
   The Role of Content
   The Nature of the Pupil
   The Nature of Learning
      Learning and the Brain
      Learning as an Individual Matter
      Learning and Brain Orientation
      Learning Style
      Learning and Motivation
      Learning Modes
      Concept Development
      Skill Development
      Attitude Development
      Readiness
      Transfer
      Time on Task
   Direct *Versus* Indirect Instruction

Rationale

This book is primarily aimed at explaining the *know-how* of teaching rather than the *know-why*. Nevertheless, to use methods well requires a basic understanding of the *whys*. Consequently, this module will present some of the considerations that undergird teaching strategies and techniques and their use.

Our reason for presenting these considerations is simple. To be really competent, a teacher must know not only how to teach but also why one approach is likely to be more effective than another for a given purpose or situation. Really professional teachers are not merely craftsmen. They are also creative artists who utilize the best media for the accomplishment of their goals. To illustrate, think of these three teachers described in a speech by Harry Broudy. Teacher A teaches as she does in various situations as a result of intuition; Teacher B teaches as she does because she is following some rule: in such a situation do thus and so; but Teacher C teaches as she does because of theoretical reasons. Teacher C not only does what the others have done but she also knows why she is teaching the various steps. In this example, Teacher C, who knows why, is a professional; Teacher B, who blindly follows the rule, is a craftsman; and Teacher A, who teaches well by following her impulses is, according to Broudy, a miracle.[1] When the chips are down, the teacher you would want for your child would be Teacher C, the professional, who knows not only what to do but also why, when, and how to do it. This module will describe some of the whys.

We cannot go into great detail about theoretical considerations in this module. Such considerations are the province of books and courses in the foundations of education with which you should already be familiar. Instead, we review a few of the more important notions that may help you to select appropriate strategies and tactics and to execute effectively the strategies and techniques you select. Studying these principles will give you a foundation for understanding and applying the content in subsequent modules and becoming more than just an artisan teacher.

Specific Objectives

Specifically, we expect that at the completion of your study of this section you will be able to do the following:

   1. Define teaching.

[1] Harry Broudy, General Session, American Association of Colleges of Teacher Education Convention, Chicago, 1967.

2. Briefly identify the variables that affect a skillful teacher's choice of teaching methods.
3. Describe the role of subject matter in teaching method.
4. Describe the influence of the nature of pupils on teaching method.
5. Describe the influence of the nature of learning on teaching methods.
6. Describe the implications of brain behavior on teaching method.
7. Describe the implications of learning style on teaching methods.
8. Describe the influence of the nature of groups on teaching method.
9. Describe the implications of the differences between direct and indirect teaching or teaching method.
10. Describe the relationship of one's teaching style to teaching method.
11. Describe the characteristics that are typical of effective teachers.
12. Describe the five-step teacher pattern.

Module Text

Introduction

Teaching is helping students learn. It is not merely telling something to a group of listeners, nor explaining some topic, nor demonstrating your mastery of an important topic. Of course, when you are helping students learn, you may engage in telling, explaining, or demonstrating, but you do these only as a means of helping your students to learn. In the final analysis your success as a teacher will be determined by how well the students have learned.

In schools, however, teaching is not simply a matter of helping students to learn. It is a matter of seeing to it that students learn certain designated material. This material is the content that makes up the bulk of the curriculum. Ostensibly this material is arranged so as to facilitate learning. It follows up what has been learned before, and prepares the way for what is to come. Yet in every teaching situation you will be faced with the necessity of selecting from several alternative strategies and tactics the ones most likely to result in the desired learning. Unfortunately, the results may not always be as you hoped, but if the content and methods you select are appropriate, you should have a high degree of success.

Teaching as Decision Making

Although pedagogy is based on scientific principles, classroom teaching is more of an art than a science. There are few hard and fast rules you can depend on in specific classroom teaching situations. In fact, in every teaching situation the teaching content, the instructional objectives, the materials of instruction, the teaching procedures, the evaluation techniques, and instructional follow-ups are basically all the result of subjective judgments. Many of these decisions are made at leisure during one's preinstruction planning. But many of them must be spur-of-the-moment. Once a class has started, there is little time for making carefully reasoned judgments. As far as you can, you will base these decisions on your knowledge of pedagogy, the subject matter, and the boys and girls in your class. Nevertheless, you will also, willy-nilly, be forced to base many judgments on intuition, feeling, impulse, and previous experience. Obviously, the better your understanding of your subject and your students, and the greater your expertise in a large repertory of teaching techniques, the more likely your decisions will result in effective learning.

Still, no matter how well versed you are in pedagogical and academic knowledge, your choice of teaching methods must be subjective. Unfortunately, or perhaps fortunately, there is no one best method of teaching that will always generate a high degree of pupil learning. Rather, there are any number of strategies, tactics, and techniques that may or may not be effective in a particular situation. (Strategy refers to a general approach or plan; tactics refer to the methods used to carry out strategies in particular situations; techniques are the procedures used to carry out the tactics.) The skillful teacher picks the teaching method to suit the teaching-learning situation. In deciding which method to use, you will be influenced by a number of variables.

The first of these variables is the objective of the instruction. The tactics and strategies one uses for teaching information are not necessarily the tactics that one should use to teach concepts, appreciations, attitudes, ideals, or skills. Pupils can and do learn information from teacher presentations, but concepts must be developed by allowing the pupil to look at, feel, handle, and otherwise consider the idea and examples of the idea in a number of contexts. Skills are developed by practice, preferably guided practice, and attitudes are developed slowly by providing models and techniques that enhance their desirability. Among the many tactics and techniques available to you, some are best suited for clarifying ideas, others are better suited for presenting new information, showing pupils how to do things, influencing attitudes, ideals, or appreciations, motivating pupils, evaluating, guiding work in progress, or arousing emotions.

The pupils make up the second consideration. Effective teachers adapt their teaching methods to their pupils. They use approaches that interest the pupils, are not too difficult or too easy, and are, of course, relevant to their lives. This process is complicated by the fact that each pupil is different from every other. They do not all have the same interests, abilities, potentials, or learning styles. As a matter of fact, individuals not only differ from other boys and girls but they tend to differ from themselves from day to day. What appeals to one today may not appeal to one tomorrow. Therefore, as a teacher, you will need to understand not only the nature of pupils in general but also your pupils in particular.

A third consideration is the nature of the groups with which you work. You will need to know something of group dynamics and their application to the structure and processes of the particular groups you teach. Teaching strategies that work well with group A may not be at all effective with group B.

The nature of the subject matter to be taught is also a consideration. Literature meant to be enjoyed should not be taught by the same methods as formulas meant to be remembered. Teachers should select teaching methods best suited to the structure and role of the subject matter to be taught.

Another factor involves the technology and materials available. One cannot use materials, equipment, and techniques that one does not have. Further, some techniques and media suitable for one objective or group may not be suitable in another setting.

Finally, your own skills and preferences influence the appropriateness of teaching methods. Because teachers' styles, personalities, and competencies differ, the approach that works well for you may not work for your colleague in the next classroom.

In short, the strategy and tactics chosen for any given teaching situation should be fitted to the objectives, the pupils, the subject content, the available materials of instruction, and the skills and personality of the teacher. A perfect fit for all these variables is, of course, impossible. Yet they all should be considered when selecting strategies and tactics for a particular teaching-learning situation.

Exercise 1 A

Following is a list of teaching methods. Which ones are familiar to you?

Discussion; small-group work; guided (controlled) discussion; committee; formal discussion, such as debate, jury, and British debate; inquiry, including controlled discussion, Socratic discussion, springboard, and project; questioning, including probing, divergent, evaluative, and convergent questions; role playing, such as simulation or dramatization—with which are you most familiar?

Think back on the teaching of teachers you have known. In what ways did their teaching styles differ? On what strategies, tactics, and techniques did they seem to depend most? Which styles appealed to you most? Which of their qualities would you like to emulate?

Let us now look at some of these variables in more detail.

The Role of Content

Subject content is the substance of teaching. It is what one teaches. Without it there would be no teaching or learning. It cannot really be separated from method. The subject matter of your teaching field consists of facts, concepts, skills, attitudes, and appreciations. It is not solely a matter of information. The skills and appreciations may be more important than the information. If one does not teach pupils the intellectual skills such as critical thinking, problem solving, and clearly expressing one's thoughts, the intellectual value of the instruction may be minimal. Remember, knowing how is as much a part of curriculum content as knowing what.

Much of the content of our academic disciplines is transient. The growth of knowledge is so rapid that what seems basic today may be obsolete tomorrow. Therefore, teachers should select course content, and methods for teaching it, that will give pupils the skill and understanding necessary for assimilating new knowledge and applying their learning to new situations.

All subject matter fields contain so much content that no one can possibly teach it all. Consequently, teachers should select the content that seems most likely to be important to the pupils. This principle is the *doctrine of contingent value*. It implies that thorough coverage of the most important, useful content is more desirable than covering everything superficially. In general, one should regard content not as an end in itself but as a means to knowledge. Learning that is not available for use is not of much value.

Teachers sometimes forget that how a subject is taught, in effect, changes its content. Learning something through lecture is not the same as learning it through experimentation. To an extent, method is content. Therefore, when fitting your methods and content, you should consider what effect methods will have on the pupils' understandings, appreciations, and skills.

The Nature of the Pupil

Middle school and high school pupils are in the process of changing from children to adults. This change is so dramatic in the middle school years that educators call middle school pupils *transescents*. In a dramatic growth spurt transescents change from little boys and girls to gawky adolescents with strange new secondary sex characteristics and all the problems attendant on new growth and the beginnings of new life roles. This growing up continues until the adolescent becomes a young adult—a process not finished until the post–high school years.

During transescence and adolescence, individual differences in physical, intellectual, social, and emotional growth are striking. Not only do individuals differ from each other but they seem to differ from themselves from day to day, for this is not only a period of growth but also a period of instability and insecurity. To establish one's adulthood is not an easy task. Boys and girls, while desiring opportunities to try their wings independently, need and want security and support. Because of their need for both security and escape from adult domination, they tend to band together for mutual support as they experiment with new sociosexual roles. To find security, they often become conformists and susceptible to peer pressure. Nevertheless, they are self-motivated, active, and interested in novelty. Their intellectual growth causes them to be interested in ideas and allows them to cope with formal intellectual operations and abstract ideas. These desires cause some adolescents to adopt idealistic causes. Sometimes they cause adolescents to try adventures and roles that may get them into scrapes. Adolescence, including transescence, is a period of change, of new experiences, of learning new roles, of uncertainty, and instability—undoubtedly one of the most trying times in life. Schools and teachers should provide opportunities for adolescents to explore and experiment in a stable, supportive atmosphere.

Exercise 1 B

Observe a class of seventh- or eighth-graders. What evidences of physical growth do you see? Do you see any evidences of social and emotional development?

The Nature of Learning

Learning and the Brain

Learning is a function of the brain. Obviously, then, it is axiomatic that your teaching should be compatible with students' brain behavior. Unfortunately, if recent research is accurate, much of our present teaching practice is brain antagonistic. For instance, the age-old school routines of sitting still, listening, doing only what one is told to do, and in general being a quiet recipient of imparted knowledge are probably not the most effective ways to learn. Rather, the brain requires an active stimulating environment, not a passive one, because the brain is naturally an aggressive problem solver that creates patterns out of the many inputs provided it by the senses, confusing and complex as these inputs may be. Therefore, the richer the environment, the better are the chances that the learner will develop good concepts, skills, and problem solutions. Furthermore, to work best, the brain needs a supportive climate. Fear and threats tend to shut down the cerebral mechanisms that foster high-level thinking. So we find that, although harsh, overstrict, fear-dominated classrooms may permit learning by rote memorization, they cut off creativity, original thinking, problem solving, and the building and understanding of major concepts. To make your classes most effective, it seems that you must provide a class atmosphere that is rich and challenging, but not threatening.

Learning as an Individual Matter
Pupils differ in their ability to learn, their readiness to learn, their learning skills, and their learning styles. Some of these differences may be innate, but most are the result of how the pupils have learned to learn, for skill in learning is learned. Teachers should take great care to teach the skills of learning—to teach pupils how to learn.

Learning and Brain Orientation
Teachers should also take into account and make adjustments for individual differences in brain orientation and learning style. If the researchers are correct, how one learns is considerably influenced by the differences in the left and right cerebral hemispheres of the brain. Evidently verbal learning, logical thinking, and the academic cognitive processes are the domain of the left hemisphere, whereas affective, spatial, emotional, and visual elements are the province of the right hemisphere. Some people, it seems, tend to be oriented toward their right cerebral hemisphere, and some toward their left hemisphere. Therefore, we find that some students learn better through verbal teaching approaches, whereas others learn better via more visual, emotional, hands-on instruction. As a result, some right-brain-oriented students are turned off by the left-hemisphere-oriented teaching in academic classes and so never progress to their full potential. To prevent this from happening, all teachers in every classroom should include physical and affective as well as cognitive learning in their teaching and attempt to stretch students' brain capacity in each of these areas. All subjects have both affective and cognitive elements. Therefore, although it may be wise to cater to the hemispheric bias of students in early learning, it is best to provide plenty of opportunities for boys and girls to participate creatively and actively in a variety of activities that involve both left- and right-brain-oriented learning.[2]

Learning Style
Left brain–right brain bias is one of the elements that make up learning style. By learning style we refer to the way individuals concentrate on, absorb, and retain

[2] Thomas R. Blakeslee, "Brain Behavior Research," in *Student Learning Styles and Brain Behavior* (Reston, Va.: National Association of Secondary School Principals, 1982), pp. 185–195.

new or difficult information or skills. It is made up of "a combination of environmental, emotional, sociological, physical, and psychological elements that permit individuals to receive, store, and use knowledge or abilities."[3] This combination of elements in one's learning style is different for each individual. Thus we find that some pupils, for instance, are more comfortable in self-contained classes featuring direct expository teaching; others react better in a mix of large-group, small-group, and independent study; still others are best served by small discussion groups; whereas some are most productive alone in independent study. Some pupils learn best in classes that emphasize linear logical presentations, others do better when imagery is stressed. Probably there are as many varieties of learning styles as there are individual students. Silver and Hanson, however, have divided learners according to four types.

1. The sensing-thinking learner who is practical, matter of fact, and work oriented.
2. The sensing-feeling learner who is sympathetic, friendly, and works for group harmony.
3. The intuitive-thinking learner who is theoretical, intellectual, and knowledge oriented.
4. The intuitive-feeling learner who is curious, insightful, imaginative, and creative.[4]

Each of these types of learner needs a different instructional approach to suit his or her variety of learning style. Also each learning style is more effective in certain types of learning situations than in others. When teachers match their teaching styles to students' learning styles, and when students learn to match their learning styles to the learning task, we find that the students' attitudes toward schoolwork and their achievement both improve.

Nevertheless it is not desirable to cater overmuch to student learning style preferences. For instance, some students are scanners, whereas other students are focusers. Scanners are better in English; focusers are better in mathematics. So it seems that students should be taught both styles if they are to be successful in both English and in mathematics. Therefore, the most useful approach you can make in your teaching probably is to:

1. Cater to individual styles as much as feasible, particularly in the early stages of study.
2. Use a mix of teaching styles so that students with different learning styles will have an opportunity to work in their preferred style at least some of the time.
3. Teach students how to use different styles of learning suitable to the teaching situation, subject matter, and learning objectives.

[3] Rita Dunn, "Learning Style and Its Relation to Exceptionality at Both Ends of the Spectrum," *Exceptional Children* (April 1983), **49**:496–506.

[4] Mary Alice Gunter and Phyllis Riley Hotchkiss, "Yuk, Peanut Butter Again: Avoiding Instructional Monotony," in *Action in Teacher Education* (Fall 1985), 7:31–35. Citing H. F. Silver and R. J. Hanson, *Teaching Styles and Strategies* (Moorestown, N.J.: Institute for Cognitive and Behavioral Studies, 1982), pp. 6–7.

Learning and Motivation

Learning also is largely the result of pupil motivation. All learning takes place in relation to some pupil goal. If pupils' goals are not in harmony with the learning we seek to impart, teaching becomes difficult. To make instruction fruitful, teachers must utilize the pupils' natural goals or entice them to accept goals suitable to the instruction.[5]

Learning Modes

The mode of learning determines what is learned. One does not learn to write by parsing sentences. Neither does one learn to swim by listening to a lecture on the Australian crawl. Much school learning is superficial because the teaching methods used are not really appropriate for the understandings, skills, and attitudes desired. Memorizing, for instance, is not the same as understanding. Yet, many pupils do little more than memorize information. The result is verbalism, meaningless mouthing of little-understood words and sentences. To make learning real to pupils, teachers should use direct, realistic experiences, whenever feasible. Vicarious experiences, such as reading about the pyramids, are necessary to bring to pupils knowledge otherwise unattainable; however, direct experience of the real thing is more powerful.

Concept Development

To develop a concept, one should give pupils opportunities to roll the notion over in their minds by providing numerous examples and by letting them see the idea from various angles so as to establish relations and to draw conclusions. Remember, one cannot give concepts to pupils; they must derive their own understandings. So make the experience as full as you can.

Skill Development

Skills also must be learned by experiencing. First the teacher must teach the students how to perform a skill. To do so, teacher explanations and demonstrations can be very effective. In this process show-how procedures are usually more useful than tell-how procedures. But the skill must be learned by guided practice. Teachers can take difficult skills apart so that students can practice the hard-to-master portions separately, but complete mastery can come only with extended practice of the entire skill, under supervision. Only through guided practice can a student eliminate improper procedures and perfect his techniques.

This is true of both psychomotor and cognitive skills. Perhaps, in middle and secondary schools, the most important of these are the academic and thinking skills. It is amazing how much student failure is the result of teachers' neglecting to teach their students how to study, how to take tests, how to do their assignments, and, in general, how to learn. It is most imperative that teachers give students instruction in these skills and develop classes and courses that give students plenty of opportunities to practice the thought processes.

---

[5] Motivational techniques are discussed in Module 6.

Attitude Development

One can teach attitudes by providing a conducive atmosphere and models that pupils can emulate. Developing understanding may enhance the learning of attitudes just as value clarification, role playing, and discussion of moral dilemmas may enhance the development of values and morals. Nevertheless, the changing of attitudes, ideals, and appreciations is a long drawn-out process. It requires numerous experiences favorable to the attitude, ideal, or appreciation to lead pupils to conviction and commitment.

Readiness

No matter what type of learning you are seeking, instruction will be fruitless unless the pupils are ready. Psychologically speaking, readiness is a complex state, but for our purposes we can describe it as the combination of maturity, ability, motivation, and prior learning that makes it possible for a person to learn something. A kindergartner is not ready to read *The Tempest,* for instance. Pupils' lack of readiness creates problems for teachers. In some cases, when lack of maturity is the problem, the only solution may be to direct one's efforts elsewhere until the pupil is ready. In other instances, when the pupil lacks a skill or prerequisite knowledge, one can solve the problem by correcting the deficiency, i.e., by making the student ready.

Transfer

If learning is to be of any value to the learner, it must be retained and transferable. Solid, thorough learning helps one remember what one has learned and transfer or apply it to new situations. So does frequent renewal and reinforcement of the learning. The more one uses what has been learned, the better one can remember and transfer it. Teachers can further facilitate transfer by pointing out its values and uses in different circumstances, both in the initial teaching and later in renewal, reinforcement, or review teaching.

Time on Task

According to an analysis made by John B. Carroll, how much students learn is dependent on

> the time spent on the task;
> the student's motivation;
> the quality of instruction;
> the aptitude of the student for the topic;
> the student's general ability.[6]

Other things being equal, the factor that determines how much a student learns is the amount of time the student is actually engaged in the learning task. In fact, some experts believe that students can learn almost anything if they keep at it

---

[6] John B. Carroll, "A Model of School Learning," *Teachers College Record* (1963), **64**:723–732.

long enough. Therefore, it behooves us teachers to see to it that in our classes students have real learning activities to do and, except for breaks at fortuitous moments, are actually doing them. It is not so much the amount of time allowed for learning activities as the amount of time the students spend really working at the learning activities that counts.

Direct Versus Indirect Instruction

Both direct and indirect (sometimes called experiential) teaching have a place in your teaching repertory. Direct instruction is primarily teacher-centered. It is typically large-group, teacher-directed, highly structured expository teaching focused on academic content. It features lecture and explanation, controlled practice, and question-answer sessions as well as other highly teacher-directed activities. In this type of teaching the teacher provides students with plenty of feedback in the form of criticism, comments, questions, hints, suggestions, and, where appropriate, praise. It covers a large amount of content and aims to keep students actively engaged. Teachers using this type of teaching constantly monitor students' work to encourage an optimum of profitable student time-on-task. In the controlled discussions teachers emphasize questions on factual information—at first simple and later more difficult—followed up with teacher commentary and criticism. In sum, teachers maintain virtually complete control of the content, pace, sequence, and processes of the instruction in direct instruction.

Indirect or experiential teaching is more student centered than direct teaching is (although it includes teacher talk in which the teachers indirectly influence students.) The teachers attempt to get the students to find out and think out things themselves. That includes approaches in which students dig out their own learning. Among these approaches we find open discussions, inquiry and discovery lessons, action learning, individual and small-group work, projects of various types, and numerous multitask activities in which students control, to a large extent, the conduct of their learning activities. In these activities the teachers do not give the students information and knowledge so much as they attempt to guide the students in the search for knowledge.

You should learn to be able to conduct both direct and indirect (experiential) teaching. Direct instruction seems to be most useful for teaching fundamental skills and knowledge, beginners, and so far unsuccessful learners. Higher and affective learning often requires the use of indirect experiential approaches.

The Nature of Groups

In schools almost all teaching is done in groups. It is most effective when the climate of the group is positive; that is when the pupils and teachers know and accept each other and work harmoniously together toward common group goals, because feelings of personal worth, belonging, and security support learning. This condition is most likely to occur when a group is cohesive and diffusely structured. Diffusely structured groups are those free from in-groups and outsiders and in which self-esteem is spread evenly rather than concentrated on a few stars or favorites. Communications in diffusely structured groups are kept open. The class norms allow for a wide range of behavior, thus creating an atmosphere of tolerance and good feeling. Groups with these characteristics tend to develop feelings of cohesiveness or togetherness. When such an atmosphere is coupled with the cooperation of the natural student leaders in the class, teaching and learning usually progress smoothly and efficiently.

Developing a Teaching Style

Every teacher develops a style of teaching that is his or her own and with which he or she feels most comfortable. This teaching style is a combination of personality plus the amount of expertise one has in teaching technology (methods), subject matter, and pedagogical theory. Evidently, the most effective teachers are those who can vary their styles, or whose styles are so flexible that they encompass a great number of strategies and tactics, and are therefore readily adaptable to the different sorts of teaching-learning situations that may develop. Ned Flanders, for instance, found evidence indicating that indirect teachers are usually more effective than direct teachers, not because indirect teachers do not teach in a direct style, but because they can teach both directly and indirectly. Evidently, because they could teach both directly and indirectly, they could select and use the strategy or tactic that is most appropriate under the circumstances and secure more active pupil involvement. Highly effective teaching of this sort requires one to develop a feeling for the appropriateness of various techniques and methods for various kinds of learning situations, and expertise in a large variety of methods, as well as a good command of one's subject matter and an understanding of the pupils one is teaching. This sounds like a large order, but many beginning teachers become adept at all of its facets surprisingly soon.

The implications of all this are at least twofold: You should master a large repertory of techniques so you will be prepared for many contingencies; and you should develop an open style of teaching that allows you to be flexible and adaptable.

In addition you will want to incorporate into your teaching style the characteristics of the most effective teachers. Research indicates that these characteristics typically include the following:

1. The effective teacher knows his students, their styles, their strengths and weaknesses, their knowledge and skills, and how they learn best.
2. The teacher is well prepared. He is a master of content and carefully plans his classes.
3. The effective teacher is well organized. The classes move along smoothly with a minimum of confusion, overlapping, dead spots, irrelevancies, sudden shifts in direction, and inappropriate behavior.
4. The effective teacher is businesslike and conducts a businesslike class in which each student's class time is concentrated on accomplishing learning tasks.
5. The effective teacher manages his classes well. The students know what they are supposed to do and do it because from the very first day the teacher carefully maps out the rules of behavior, and the consequences of inappro-

priate behavior, sets up definite routines for classroom procedures, and makes clear assignments pointing out not only what the students are to do, but also how they are to do it and why.

6. The effective teacher makes manifest by his behavior to the students that he respects each one of them, is concerned about each one's progress and welfare, and confidently expects every one to do well.
7. The effective teacher adjusts teaching methods to his subject matter and to objectives. For instance, he uses direct instruction with whole class or small groups when teaching for basic skill mastery, but uses more indirect experiential discovery or inquiry methods to teach higher-level learning.
8. The effective teacher monitors student performance carefully and continually. In this process he follows up and evaluates the students' various assignments and provides them individual feedback concerning their accomplishments and particularly takes care to recognize and reward good work and progress.

These characteristics make up the bases for most of the content in the remaining modules of this book.

A Pattern for Teaching

You should also incorporate into your teaching style the following five-step pattern that makes up a model for good teaching. The steps of this model are

Diagnosis.
Preparation.
Guidance of learning.
Evaluation of learning.
Follow-up or follow-through.

Diagnosis refers to the initial evaluation or assessment of the teaching-learning situation. In this step, teachers attempt to define the pupils' present state of knowledge and their needs and desires as a basis for determining what should be done.

In the preparation step teachers get ready for the instruction. Preparation includes planning lessons, motivating pupils, gathering materials, and arranging the setting for instruction.

Guidance of learning includes the actual instruction, showing pupils how, presenting information, criticizing their work, and so on.

In the evaluation step teachers assess their pupils' progress and, in so doing, the success of the instruction. Evaluation tells both teachers and pupils where they have succeeded and where not. It is the basis for determining the next steps.

The follow-up or follow-through is the final step. Here the teacher helps pupils fill in what they have missed and build on what they have learned.

These five steps tend to run together. The evaluation and follow-up for one unit or lesson may become the diagnosis, preparation, and guiding-learning phases for the next one. Nevertheless, even when truncated, the five-step sequence is always present in good teaching.

Suggested Reading

Biehler, Robert F., and Jack Snowman. *Psychology Applied to Teaching,* 5th ed. Boston: Houghton Mifflin, 1986.

Blue, Terry W. *The Teaching and Learning Process.* Washington, D.C.: National Education Association, 1981.

Bugelski, B. R., *Some Practical Laws of Learning,* Fastback 9. Bloomington, Ind.: Phi Delta Kappa Educational Foundation, 1977.

Crabtree, June. *Basic Principles of Effective Teaching.* Cincinnati, Oh.: Standard Publishing, 1982.

Dock, Lloyd, *Teaching with Charisma.* Boston: Allyn & Bacon, 1981.

Frymier, Jack R. *The Nature of Educational Method.* Columbus, Oh.: Merrill, 1965.

Gage, N. L., ed. *The Psychology of Teaching Methods,* The Seventy-fifth Yearbook of the National Society for the Study of Education, Part I. Chicago: University of Chicago Press, 1976, chaps. 1–2, 9, 11.

———. *The Scientific Basis of the Art of Teaching.* New York: Teachers College Press, 1978.

Hart, Leslie A. *Human Brain and Human Learning.* New York: Longman, 1983.

Joyce, Bruce, et al. *Flexibility in Teaching: An Excursion into the Nature of Teaching and Training.* New York: Longman, 1980.

Levin, Tamar, with Ruth Long. *Effective Instruction.* Alexandria, Va.: The Association for Supervision and Curriculum Development, 1981.

Lipsitz, Joan, ed. *Barriers, A New Look at the Needs of Young Adolescents.* New York: Ford Foundation, 1979.

Peterson, Penelope, et al. *The Social Context of Instruction, Group Organization and Group Process.* New York: Academic Press, 1983.

Peterson, Penelope, and Herbert J. Walberg, eds. *Research on Teaching.* Berkeley, Ca.: McCutchan Publishing, 1979.

Phillips, D. C., and Jonas F. Soltis. *Perspectives on Learning.* New York: Teachers College Press, 1985.

Reilly, Robert, and Ernest Lewis. *Educational Psychology: Applications for Classroom Learning and Instruction.* New York: Macmillan, 1983, Part I.

Rubin, Louis J *Artistry in Teaching.* New York: Random House, 1985.

Schmuck, Richard A. and Patricia A. Schmuck. *Group Processes in the Classroom.* Dubuque, Ia.: Brown, 1971.

Silvernail, David L. *Teaching Styles as Related to Student Achievement.* Washington, D.C.: National Education Association, 1981.

Student Learning Styles and Brain Behavior. Reston, Va.: National Association of Secondary School Principals, 1982.

Troisi, Nicholas F. *Effective Teaching and Student Achievement.* Reston, Va.: National Association of Secondary School Principals, 1983.

U.S. Department of Education. *What Works: Research about Teaching and Learning.* Washington, D.C.: U.S. Department of Education, 1986.

Post Test

A. Match the statement in column II with the steps listed in column I. All entries in both columns should be used. Some should be used more than once.

I		II	
b,h,c	**1.** Diagnosis.	**a.**	Lesson planning.
a,f	**2.** Preparation.	**b.**	Testing.
e	**3.** Guidance of learning.	**c.**	Pretesting.
b	**4.** Evaluation of learning.	**d.**	Reteaching.
d,g	**5.** Follow-up.	**e.**	Instruction.
		f.	Room arrangement.
		g.	Beginning the next lesson.
		h.	Estimating pupils' prior knowledge.

B. Of the following, check the ones that make correct statements. According to research, effective teachers

(✓) **6.** are masters of the content
(✓) **7.** use a variety of teaching methods
( ) **8.** run permissive laissez-faire classes
(✓) **9.** expect their students to do well
(✓) **10.** monitor performance carefully
(✓) **11.** know their students' strengths and weaknesses
( ) **12.** avoid routinizing classroom procedures
(✓) **13.** use both direct and indirect instruction
(✓) **14.** respect their students
(✓) **15.** adjust method to content~~subject matter~~
(✗) **16.** insist on absolutely quiet classes
(✓) **17.** provide students with individual feedback

C. Place the letter of the "best answer" in the blank provided. If two or more of the choices seem correct, select the one most applicable to the situation.

C **18.** To encourage retention of learning, you should
    a. use memory drills.
    b. use mnemonic devices.
    c. emphasize thorough learning.
    d. emphasize transfer values.

a **19.** One would expect to ascertain a pupil's readiness to learn in which of the following steps?
    a. Diagnosis.
    b. Preparation.
    c. Guidance of learning.
    d. Evaluation.
    e. Follow-up or follow-through.

_a_ **20.** Learning skills are
   a. learned.
   b. innate.
   c. inherited.
   d. instinctive.

_c_ **21.** Transescence is a period of
   a. stability.
   b. self-confidence.
   c. change.
   d. independence from peer pressure.

_a_ **22.** According to the doctrine of contingent value, one should
   a. accentuate the subject matter that is most likely to be valuable to the pupils.
   b. accentuate content that is relevant to pupils now.
   c. accentuate the basics.
   d. accentuate the eternal verities.

_c_ **23.** When selecting teaching methods you should remember that
   a. indirect methods are superior to direct methods.
   b. problem solving is the heart of all good teaching.
   c. the method you use will to some extent determine the content the pupils learn.
   d. exposition is the best type of teaching method.

_b_ **24.** To make the climate of the group positive, try to make the group
   a. centrally structured.
   b. cohesive.
   c. elitist.
   d. teacher-centered.

_c_ **25.** One's teaching style should be
   a. teacher-centered.
   b. pupil-centered.
   c. flexible.
   d. indirect.

_b_ **26.** Indirect teachers, according to Flanders, are usually more effective than direct teachers because
   a. indirect teaching is more efficient than direct teaching.
   b. indirect teachers are usually more flexible than direct teachers.
   c. indirect teachers more frequently aim at the higher mental processes than direct teachers do.
   d. indirect teachers are usually more progressive.

_d_ **27.** It is recommended that you develop a large repertory of teaching techniques so that

a. you can utilize more fully the strategies of direct teaching.
b. you can utilize more fully the strategies of indirect teaching.
c. you can cover the subject more easily.
d. you can better adapt your teaching method to particular teaching-learning situations.

b 28. Middle school pupils are usually
  a. children.
  b. transescents.
  c. adolescents.
  d. young adults.

b 29. Teaching is best described as
  a. forming pupils' minds.
  b. helping pupils learn.
  c. guiding study.
  d. showing and telling pupils.
  e. holding classes.
  f. instructing pupils.

c 30. The real test of one's teachin
  a. the excellence of the plar g.
  b. the degree the lesson int   ts people.
  c. how well the pupils hav   arned.
  d. one's discipline and co   l.

a 31. In selecting teaching met   s it is important to remember that
  a. pupils differ from ea   ther.
  b. pupils prefer easy as   ments.
  c. high school student   nnot think abstractly.
  d. vicarious experienc   preferable to direct experience.

c 32. Time on task refers t
  a. the length of the   son.
  b. time allotted for   arning activity.
  c. time students s   l actually working on a learning activity.
  d. estimated time   complete a unit.

d 33. Which of the following is most typical of indirect teaching?
  a. controlled practice.
  b. teacher-centered methods.
  c. expository teaching methods.
  d. open discussion.

c 34. To make your teaching successful, you should
  a. teach each student in the same way.
  b. match your teaching to each student's learning style.

c. use a mix of teaching styles so as to accommodate different learning styles.

d. emphasize deep-focus learning styles.

a 35. To teach skills one should emphasize
  a. supervised practice.
  b. inductive learning.
  c. indirect teaching.
  d. rote learning.

c 36. The brain responds best when
  a. the input is strict and harsh.
  b. the input is threatening.
  c. the input is complex.
  d. the input is simple.

a 37. To promote higher learning it is best to
  a. make classes challenging.
  b. insist on absolute quiet.
  c. concentrate on right-brain learning.
  d. concentrate on direct teaching.

d 38. In teaching it is best to
  a. concentrate on right-brain learning.
  b. concentrate on left-brain learning.
  c. cater to the student's preference.
  d. teach toward both hemispheres.

d 39. Learning style is
  a. an indication of one's intelligence.
  b. genetic.
  c. unchangeable.
  d. different from individual to individual.

a 40. Students learn best in
  a. a challenging atmosphere.
  b. a very strict repressed atmosphere.
  c. a very permissive atmosphere.
  d. quiet surroundings.

MODULE
2

Principles of Planning

Rationale

Planning is a large part of every teacher's job because each teacher is responsible for planning at three levels: the planning of courses, the planning of units, and the planning of lessons. Throughout your career you and your fellow teachers will be engaged almost continually in the process of planning on one or the other of the three levels. Thus the importance of mastering the process at the very start of your inquiry into the teaching act cannot be overemphasized.

This book defines a course as a complete sequence of instruction that presents to the pupils a major division of subject matter or a discipline. A unit is a major subdivision of a course, comprising planned instruction about some central theme, topic, issue, or problem for a period of several weeks. A lesson is a subdivision of a course to be taught in a single period or, on occasion, two or three successive periods. Courses may be laid out for a year, a semester, a quarter, or, in the case of minicourses, a few weeks. Units are shorter than courses ordinarily; a minicourse is, in effect, a free-standing unit and should be treated as a unit as far as planning is concerned. In many school systems, teachers as members of curriculum committees and workshops also participate in the planning of the entire curriculum.

Although careful planning is a critical skill for a teacher, a well-developed plan for teaching will not guarantee the success of the lesson or unit or even the overall effectiveness of the course. But the lack of a well-developed plan will almost certainly result in failure. Like a good map, a good plan facilitates one's reaching one's goal with more confidence and with fewer wrong turns.

The heart of planning is decision making. For every plan you make, you will have to decide what your objectives or goals are to be, what subject matter and materials of instruction are appropriate, and what methods and techniques you should use to accomplish your objectives, and to evaluate your and the students' accomplishments. This decision making is complicated by the fact that there are almost as many different teaching methods and variations of teaching as there are teachers. It is essential, therefore, that you be familiar with the principles that undergird good lesson, unit, and course planning. The fact that the principles in all educational planning are pretty much the same makes mastering the necessary planning skills somewhat easier. In this module we set forth these principles clearly so as to give you a good base for your classroom teaching.

Specific Objectives

Specifically, we expect that at the end of your study of this section, you will be able to do the following:

1. Explain why planning is so absolutely essential to good teaching.
2. Explain the dangers of ad lib teaching.
3. Describe the two essential elements in any plan: deciding what one hopes to accomplish and how to accomplish it.
4. Describe the purposes of general and specific objectives.
5. Describe the criteria that one should use in selecting learning activities (experiences) to include in one's plans.

6. Identify the principal resources available for use in planning.
7. Explain the purpose and procedures of teacher planning.
8. Explain the rationale for teacher-pupil planning.

Module Text

The Importance of Planning

Careful planning is absolutely essential for effective teaching. It helps to produce well-organized classes and a purposeful class atmosphere since it reduces the likelihood of discipline problems. Also, it helps to ensure that the teacher knows the subject, for, when one plans carefully, one is forced to become master of the material and the methods of teaching it. No one can know all there is to know in the subject matter of any course, but careful planning keeps one from fumbling through half-digested, not clearly understood content and from making mistakes. It is likely to make classes more lively, more interesting, more accurate, and more relevant. Teachers who do not plan carefully are asking for trouble. As Roy Meadows points out, ad lib teaching, that is, teaching with little or no writte preparation, is "the chief weakness of the high school" because in ad lib teachir "the teacher has not zeroed in on the topics to be presented, the examples to used for illustration, or the work to be assigned" and, as a result, tends to te the same old stuff in the same old way day after day and year after year.[1] In sh , teaching without adequate written planning is likely to be sloppy and ineffec , because the teacher has not thought out exactly what to do and how to do i

Essential Elements

Two elements—deciding what one wishes to accomplish and how to g bout accomplishing it—are essential in any planning. They require that you, a acher (and perhaps your pupils as well), ask yourself such questions as the fo wing:

1. What do I want to accomplish?
2. How can I accomplish it?
3. Who is to do what?
4. When and in what order should things be done?
5. What resources are available?
6. What materials and equipment are needed?
7. How will I get things started?
8. How shall I follow up?
9. How can I tell whether I have accomplished my goals?

Exercise 2 A

Review these questions:
   Are these elements important?

---

[1] Roy Meadows, "Adverse Effects of Ad Lib Teaching," *School and Community,* (May 1965), 51:26–27.

If so, why are they important?

Are there other questions that you think you should ask yourself when planning a lesson, unit, or course?

There is at least one important question missing from this list. That question is "why?" Why should pupils learn the content? Why do you want them to achieve these objectives? It is important that you ask yourself "why?" often. When a pupil asks you, "Why do I have to learn this stuff?" you should have at the tip of your tongue a legitimate reason that you have thought out long before. All too frequently, teachers do not have the slightest idea why students should study the content of their courses (except perhaps it is in the textbook or in the curriculum). That is one reason why so much teaching is irrelevant to the lives and needs of both the students and the larger community. To avoid such irrelevancies, for every unit you teach, you as teacher should prepare a rationale statement in which you explain what the students are to learn and why they are to learn it, and, before beginning the unit, share this rationale with your students.

Exercise 2 B

Read a chapter from a secondary or middle school textbook. What, if anything, would you want a student to know as a result of studying that chapter? Then ask yourself why you think a student should learn this material. Be honest. Are your reasons really convincing?

Take your subject field as a whole. What reasons could you give to a boy or girl who wants to know why he or she should study it?

You often hear that the schools should place more emphasis on basics. In general, what do you feel are the basics in your field?

At this stage in your development, this list of questions may well seem formidable and overwhelming. But be assured that as you begin to focus upon them and actually use them in the planning you will do for your classes, they will soon become an automatically functioning part of your professional behavior.

Let us begin our study of planning techniques by considering the first of the two elements cited earlier—objectives, i.e., what one wishes to accomplish.

Objectives and Planning

Just as it is difficult to overestimate the importance of planning, it is also difficult to overestimate the importance of good objectives. In one sense, it is impossible to do any real planning until you have decided what you want to do. In teaching, deciding on the objectives means deciding what you hope the pupils will learn: what facts? what concepts? what skills? what attitudes? what appreciations? what ideals? The objectives are the foundation on which one builds one's plan of action. They provide the basis for your decision regarding the choice of content, material, and methods and techniques that comprise your strategy for teaching the course, unit, or lesson.

A commonplace example will illustrate our meaning. Let us suppose that you are in New York City and want to go to San Francisco. Having this objective in mind, you could then decide on a plan of action. You might decide to leave on

Monday, or Wednesday, or Friday, or maybe next month. You might decide to drive, or go by train, bus, or airplane. You might decide to go by the shortest route possible or take the long scenic route, or even to go by way of the Panama Canal. All of these alternatives would bring you to your objective, San Francisco, but if you did not have that objective, none of the alternatives would be of any value to you.

As another example closer to the teaching profession, let us suppose your objective in a history course is to teach pupils basic concepts underlying democratic freedom. You must decide which course of action would best serve your purpose. You might conclude that your content should include the Magna Charta, the Bill of Rights, and similar documents. Or you might decide that to concentrate on modern examples of freedom and fairness and of rights and responsibilities would be more effective. You might decide that it would be best to lecture, to show films, to use role playing, to use free discussion, or perhaps to combine several methods. You might decide that the pupils ought to study original documents, scholarly discussions, popular reading, textbooks, or learning activity packets. When it comes to deciding what to do to achieve a teaching objective, an effective teacher's options are almost limitless, but they all must be based on achieving that objective.

When you select objectives and the teaching strategies by which to attain them, there are several things you must consider in order to make reasonable decisions. One, of course, is the curriculum. A second is the nature of the learners: are they bright or slow, mature or immature, advantaged or disadvantaged? What are their interests, goals, and general tendencies to behavior? A third consideration is what you have to work with: materials, equipment, software, texts, and reading materials. A fourth consideration is the nature of the community and community expectations. And a final consideration is the nature of the subject matter or discipline to be taught.

Exercise 2 C

Assume that you are teaching a ninth-grade course in your major field. What would you need to know about the curriculum, students, resources, and the like in order to plan the course? Try to be as specific as you can. Talk over your solution with your friends to find out their reactions to your thinking. (Remember that plans go askew if they do not fit the situation.)

One hears a lot about making teaching relevant. What does one have to know in order to make one's teaching relevant? Relevant to what? Argue this one out with your friends.

Generally, educators speak of two broad classes of objectives: general objectives and specific objectives. General objectives or goals are broad concepts, skills, attitudes, appreciations, and ideals, such as "to develop an understanding of the scientific method" or "to develop the habit of reflective thinking in specific situations." Specific objectives are narrow objectives, the achievement of which will bring about the general objectives: For example, at the conclusion of the unit, pupils will be able to demonstrate three techniques for checking the validity of a hypothesis. Course plans are usually built around broad objectives, lesson plans around specific objectives, and unit plans around a combination of the two.

A Plan for Action

As we have already noted, the bulk of any plan consists of the content and procedures that one decides to use to bring about the objectives. The essential element is that the content and teaching procedures be so designed that they really contribute to the achievement of the goal. For instance, if your goal is to teach your pupils to be skillful in thinking scientifically, then you must design course content and procedures that actually give pupils training and practice in thinking. Memorizing formulas and learning the textbook by heart will not achieve that goal because that will not give them a chance to learn to think. Similarly, if you wish to teach pupils to learn to express themselves well in writing, you must provide them training and practice in writing. Learning rules of grammar may help, but it will not do the entire job. Sometimes teachers seem to forget this basic fact: if you want pupils to learn something, your content and procedures must be appropriate for what you want them to learn.

Exercise 2 D

Suppose you want to teach pupils to be good citizens. What types of things would you want them to do? Make a list of ten specific things that you think would actually help make them good citizens. Argue these out with your classmates.

Of course, in selecting your procedures and content there are a number of other important considerations you should keep in mind. Among them are degrees of difficulty, interest levels, suitability for pupils' backgrounds, and feasibility.

Evaluating the Plan

Effective teachers find it helpful to evaluate their plans so as to find out in what ways they succeeded and in what ways they failed. By saving the good plans and the good parts of mediocre plans and by revising (or discarding) the poor plans or poor parts of mediocre plans, you can build a collection of sound plans and a repertory of effective teaching procedures.

Resources for Planning

The planning of courses, units, and lessons is time-consuming work, even if not really difficult. Fortunately, you will not have to do it entirely from scratch, alone and unassisted. You can make your beginning years in the classroom easier by getting together a file of material and ideas for teaching while you are still in college. In addition to the training and practice during your teacher preparation program, when you get on the job, department heads, supervisors, and other teachers are usually ready to give you a helping hand and to give you the benefit of their experience. Some school systems have worked out curriculum guides, courses of study, and syllabuses for the courses offered in their schools. These are, in general, explanations and outlines of the courses in the system's curriculum. They usually suggest the topics to be included in courses, general objectives or goals for courses, general and specific objectives for units, materials and methods that might be used, and a helpful bibliography. Use them. In some school systems, teachers are expected to follow them closely. In others, the guides, courses of study, and syllabuses are suggestions that you may or may not use as you please. You should study them and use what seems to be good for your purposes. Some school systems have adopted standardized curriculums that include course outlines, prepackaged texts, material for study, exercises, assignments, and audiovisual materials and the like. When these are provided, much of your planning has been taken care of. These materials, however, will not teach. Many teachers have found it necessary to change and adapt them. When this is so, supervisors, department heads, and other teachers will undoubtedly advise you. Some school systems have published resource units[2] for particular units of study. These are usually rich in suggestions for teaching the unit. You will find in them, as in courses of study, suggestions for objectives, content, methods, readings, audiovisual, and other teaching materials suitable for that unit.

Some systems provide no guide, syllabus, or course of study. In that case, the neophyte has several options to choose from. One is to use curriculum guides, syllabuses, courses of study, and resource units of other school systems. If you do not use them slavishly, they may be just as helpful to you as to the teachers in the school system for which they were designed. These can usually be found in the central office or curriculum centers of city, regional, county school, or school administrative districts, and at the curriculum libraries of teacher preparation institutions. Other sources usually available in curriculum libraries are the curriculum bulletins and curriculum materials on various topics published by state departments of education, large city school systems, professional organizations, the federal government, and commercial publishing houses. Some of the resource units published by organizations and governmental agencies are especially helpful. The more of these resources you have available to you, the better off you will be. Therefore, if you can, become familiar with the curriculum and teaching resources at your college or in the district where you live now. And begin to collect materials for the day when you will need them in your own classroom.

The most ubiquitous of the resources for course, unit, and lesson planning is the textbook. In addition to its expository role it provides an organized outline of the subject matter field plus such teaching aids as study questions, exercises, and suggestions for learning activities and further study. Many middle and secondary school texts on the market today provide instructor's manuals that can be of great help in the planning process.

Beware, however, of becoming a slave to the textbook. You, the teacher, should be master. Undoubtedly you are more familiar with your own teaching goals and skills, the students' needs, abilities, and inclinations, and the local school requirements than a textbook author living in a far distant environment may be. Use the textbook as a base, but do not let it prevent you from creative, flexible teaching that is suitable to your students and to your instructional goals. Remember: the textbook may be a source of inspiration for your instructional

---

[2] That is a very general plan for the unit on a particular topic designed to be used as the basis for building a teaching unit plan.

objectives, but it is *your* instructional objectives that should determine what you should teach and how you should teach it.

Another resource close at hand is your college textbooks. Although these are likely to be written at a level that is not suitable for middle and secondary school students, they are usually an excellent source of ideas and information that can be adapted for use in your classes.

Exercise 2 E

Visit the curriculum library of your college or a school system nearby. Study several curriculum guides, resource units, state curriculum bulletins, and other materials described in this module. What do they include? How might they be useful to you in planning lessons, units, and courses?

Start your own resource file. A simple cardboard box that you can index as you go along will suffice. Under each heading that you devise, put pictures, diagrams, articles, references that you come across in your daily reading or study that apply to your subject. At some point in the future one of these items you save may be just the thing for turning a routine lesson into a winner because it may be so appropriate.

Cooperative Planning

Team Planning

In some schools teachers plan together in teams. These teams may be teaching teams in which teachers share the teaching of a course. In one Maryland middle school, for instance, four teachers cooperate in the teaching of a social studies course of approximately one hundred pupils. In other middle schools teachers of different subjects collaborate. For example, an eighth-grade team might consist of an English teacher, a mathematics teacher, a science teacher, and a social studies teacher who teach the same students and who meet regularly once or twice a week to plan together and to coordinate activities and assignments. Teams of this type are quite common in middle schools.

Planning procedures in these planning teams, except for the fact that the team members plan together, are about the same as in any other planning. After the team has completed its planning, each teacher must plan specifically for his or her role in the team teaching or for his or her segment of the overall plan. One advantage of team planning is that it makes it easier for teachers to coordinate their teaching activities; another is that it gives one a chance to share ideas. However, successful team teaching may demand even more careful and detailed planning them solo teaching does.

Teacher-Pupil Planning

Many teachers encourage pupils to participate in the planning of their learning activities, units, and courses. Participating in the planning tends to give pupils a proprietary interest in the activities that may cause them to try harder. What pupils have planned themselves seems relevant to them. They like to see their plans succeed. They have good feelings about the plans because they are theirs. Teacher-pupil planning can be an effective motivational aid.

In spite of its merits, teacher-pupil planning can be risky. Therefore one must provide the pupils with much guidance. Beware of asking pupils to make decisions for which they are not equipped.

Suggested Reading

Bedwell, Lance E., Gilbert H. Hunt, Timothy J. Touzel, and Dennis G. Wiseman. *Effective Teaching: Preparation and Implementation.* Springfield, Il.: Charles C. Thomas, 1984.

Clark, Leonard H., and Irving S. Starr. *Secondary and Middle School Teaching Methods,* 5th ed. New York: Macmillan Publishing Co., 1985.

Grambs, Jean Dresden, and John C. Carr. *Modern Methods in Secondary Education,* 4th ed. New York: Holt, Rinehart and Winston, 1979.

Hoover, Kenneth H. *The Professional Teachers Handbook,* abridged 2d ed. Boston: Allyn & Bacon, 1976.

Kim, Eugene C., and Richard D. Kellough. *A Resource Guide for Secondary School Teaching,* 3d ed. New York: Macmillan Publishing Co., 1983, Part II.

Lorber, Michael A., and Walter D. Pierce. *Objectives, Methods and Evaluation for Secondary Teaching.* Englewood Cliffs, N.J.: Prentice-Hall, 1983.

Orlich, Donald C., et al. *Teaching Strategies: A Guide to Better Instruction.* Lexington, Mass.: D. C. Heath, 1985, Chaps. 2–5.

Zapf, Rosalind, M. *Democratic Processes in Secondary Classrooms.* Englewood Cliffs, N.J.: Prentice-Hall, 1959.

Post Test

1. Name two dangers of ad lib teaching.

   Teachers have not thought thru what they're trying to do.
   Dull classes)

2. What are the two most important decisions in planning, according to this module?

   What should my objectives be
   How should I plan to achieve these objectives

3. What questions should you ask yourself when planning, according to this module?

   What do I want to accomplish
   How can I accomplish it
   Who is to do what.
   In what order should things be done.

4. Much teaching is irrelevant. What seems to be the reason for this, according to this module?

Teachers don't ask themselves why should the students have to study & learn this.

5. What considerations are important in the selection of objectives when planning?

Curriculum
Nature of the learners
What do you have to work with
Nature of the community
What does the community expect.

6. What is the most important criterion for the selection of learning activities for a course, unit, or lesson, according to this module?

Will it contribute to the achievement of objectives

7. If you were to test the adequacy of certain subject matter for inclusion in a particular course, unit, or lesson, what should be your chief criterion?

Does it contribute to reaching the objectives

8. What would you expect to find in a course of study?

Suggested contents
,, objectives
,, learning activities
,, reading
,, audio visual & other aids

9. What is one advantage of team planning?

It makes the coordination of learning and teaching activities easier

10. Of what value is a textbook when planning?

It provides content, and a base for planning of sequence & units.

11. How is cooperative team planning different from other planning?

Teams must plan together

12. What is one good argument for using teacher-pupil planning?

promotes favorable attitude & motivation

13. What is a resource unit? *lists objectives, materials, and teaching procedures that can be used to plan a unit*

14. How would you use your textbook as a planning resource? *As an outline and as a guide for basic units.*

15. Point out five reasons why planning is an essential for good teaching.

1. *produces well organized classes*
2. *" " purposeful class atmosphere*
3. *It helps reduce discipline problems*
4. *" insures you know the subject*
5. *It tends to make classes more effective.*

MODULE
3

Setting
Objectives

Rationale

Aimless behavior seldom pays off in any desirable way. To be effective and efficient, when you begin any endeavor you need to have a reasonably clear notion of what it is you wish to accomplish. Otherwise, you have no way of knowing what approach to take; what methods, materials, and tools to use; or how to tell whether or not you have accomplished the task. Teaching is no different from other human activities in this respect. Unless your teaching is well aimed, it will be ineffectual, for neither you nor your pupils will clearly know exactly what the pupils should be learning. Therefore, it is essential that you learn how to formulate clear teaching objectives.

As a rule, in teaching it is best to write out one's objectives. Otherwise the objectives are liable to be too vague, too comprehensive, and too general to provide much guidance to either teacher or pupils. To make your objectives definite and precise, it is recommended that you write them as behavioral objectives. By pinpointing just what behavior you expect as a result of the instruction, behavioral objectives will not only give your teaching direction but also establish criteria for measuring its success.

Therefore, in this module, we attempt to show you how to select and set forth clear teaching objectives. When you have finished this module, you should be able to identify and prepare general and specific objectives in the descriptive, behavioral, and covert categories.

Specific Objectives

Specifically, you should be able to do the following:

1. Define, identify, and construct each of the following.
   a. General objective
   b. Specific objective
   c. Behavioral objective
   d. Simple behavioral objective
   e. Criterion-referenced objective
   f. Covert objective.
2. Explain the role of general and specific objectives.
3. Define and describe the cognitive, affective, and psychomotor taxonomies of educational objectives and their significance.
4. Write objectives suitable for the various levels of the various domains.

Module Text

Ways of Stating Objectives

Teachers can state objectives in a number of ways. One way is to prepare a statement or descriptive phrase in which you describe the skill, concept, appreciation, attitude, or ideal to be learned. Examples of descriptive objectives follow.

> *Concept (or Generalization)*
>   *Weather affects nearly all of people's enterprises.*
> *Skill (or Ability)*
>   *The ability to recognize the difference in spelling of masculine and feminine nouns and adjectives.*
>   *The ability to find synonyms in Roget's* Thesaurus *quickly and easily.*
> *Attitude*
>   *An attitude of respect toward other people.*
>   *A strong desire to look at all sides of an issue before making a decision.*

Descriptive objectives such as these have been and still are commonly used to set forth objectives and goals in curriculum guides, resource units, and the like. They are useful for describing general goals and objectives, but are likely to be too general for pinpointing the specific objectives of units and lessons.

Another common way to write objectives is to use an infinitive phrase, such as the following:

> *To discover the most common cause of accidents in the home.*
> *To appreciate the contribution of immigrants to American life.*
> *To encourage good citizenship.*
> *To develop skill in the use of the micrometer.*

Objectives written as infinitive phrases are usually very general. For this reason their use is discouraged by many authorities on the subject. There is no reason, however, why they should not be used for the most general objectives. A number of statements of the major aims of education are written in this fashion, but infinitive phrases are usually much too vague and general to be useful as course goals or as unit or lesson objectives.

We therefore recommend that you state your goals and objectives as student terminal activity, either as covert or overt behavioral objectives. The following pages are principally concerned with the preparation of behavioral objectives.

Behavioral Objective

A behavioral objective is a statement that describes what the pupil will do, or be able to do, it is hoped, once the instruction has been completed. It is a learning product that the teacher hopes will result from the instruction, whether in a lesson, unit, course, or curriculum. It is the terminal behavior expected from the pupils at the conclusion of a period of learning.

Note that in this definition the behavioral objective describes the behavior of the pupil that results from the instruction. In that sense, the behavior described is terminal behavior for it is the behavior that is expected when the instruction terminates. It is not terminal in the sense that all learning stops at that point. The terminal behavior resulting from one unit of instruction may well be the jumping-off-point for the learning of new or different behavior in the next unit.

Note also that the behavior described is the terminal behavior of the *pupil*. It is not teacher behavior. Behavioral goals do not describe what the teacher is going to do. They describe what the teacher or the school authorities expect the pupil to do or be able to do as a result of being taught. In this sense, behavioral goals are teacher goals. Pupil goals may also be behavioral, but we shall discuss pupil goals later.

Behavioral goals, then, are descriptions of the pupil terminal behavior that it is expected will result from the instruction. If we assume the formula for writing a behavioral objective to consist of these basic words, *At the end of the instruction* (lesson, unit, course, or school curriculum), *the pupils will* (or will be able to) . . . you can easily distinguish behavioral from nonbehavioral objectives. If we examine the following list of objectives, we could easily determine that some describe what pupils will be able to do at the end of the instruction, and some do not. Those that describe terminal behavior of the pupils are behavioral objectives. It does not matter what type of behavior they describe as long as they describe a terminal behavior. One source of confusion is that many writers of behavioral objectives use the present tense rather than the future tense. One would think that objectives would always be written in the future tense, because, after all, an objective is something one hopes to achieve in the future, but educational practices are not always logical.

Exercise 3 A

These objectives were prepared by college juniors for their practicum experience. Which ones describe terminal behavior of pupils and therefore are behavioral objectives?

1. The pupils will understand that the basic issue that resulted in secession was the extension of slavery.
2. Digestion is the chemical change of foods into particles that can be absorbed.
3. To explain what an acid is and what an acid's properties are.
4. Introduction to vector qualities and their use.
5. The pupils will be able to convert temperatures recorded in Celsius scale to Fahrenheit.
6. The pupils will understand that vibrating bodies provide the source of all sounds and sound waves.
7. At the end of the lesson, the pupils will be able to read a bus schedule well enough to determine at what time buses are scheduled to arrive and leave at designated stations, with at least 90 per cent accuracy.
8. Given a number of quadratic equations in one unknown, the pupils solves the equations correctly in 80 per cent of the cases.

9. The pupils will appreciate the problems faced by those who emigrated from Europe to America. ℄
10. A study of the external features and internal organs of the frog through dissection. ℅
11. To discuss the reasons why the field of philosophy was so well developed by the ancient Greeks.
12. Animals' physical adaption to their environment. *Unit*

Covert versus Overt Behavior

You noticed that certain of the behavioral objectives in Exercise 3 A called for the pupils to "understand" or "appreciate" at the conclusion of the instruction. Although such objectives describe terminal behavior, they call for a quite different type of behavior than did the behavioral objectives that require pupils to solve problems, to read the bus schedule correctly, or to convert from one scale to another. Understanding, knowing, feeling, and appreciating are types of behavior that cannot be observed directly. When one understands, he does it inside his head. He may understand perfectly without giving any outward sign. Such behavior is covert. Behavioral objectives that call for covert behavior that cannot be observed directly are called covert behavioral objectives.

The following are stated as covert behavioral objectives:

The pupils will understand that the basic issue that resulted in secession was the extension of slavery.

The pupils will understand that vibrating bodies provide the source of all sounds and sound waves.

The pupils will appreciate the problems faced by those who emigrated from Europe to America.

Behavioral objectives that call for pupils to solve problems, to convert from one scale to the other, and to read bus schedules are talking about overt behavior that anyone can see. To judge whether a person can read a bus schedule successfully, all we must do is to give him a bus schedule and see if he can read it. The behavior itself is directly observable. Other examples of observable behavior include such activities as telling, explaining, describing, writing, running, and spelling. This type of behavior is called overt behavior, and objectives that call for overt terminal behavior are called overt behavior objectives.

The following are stated as overt behavioral objectives:

As a result of the study of this course, the pupil will refrain from making final conclusions until he or she has carefully examined the data.

The students will treat members of other races with respect and consideration.

The students will listen to classical recordings of their own volition.

Both covert and overt behavioral objectives are useful in education, but each has its drawbacks. Because one cannot observe covert activity directly, the only way in which one can judge how well a pupil has progressed toward achieving a covert objective is to observe overt behavior that indicates whether or not the pupil has reached the covert objective. For any covert objective to be useful in a specific teaching and learning situation, one must generate from it overt behavioral objectives that one can use as a basis for determining how well pupils have achieved the covert objective.

For instance, if the objective is, "Upon completion of this unit, the pupils will understand why North Africa and the Middle East are rapidly changing in today's world," one cannot observe directly how well the pupils have achieved the objective, or how well they understand. However, one can estimate how well they understand by measuring their achievement of such overt objectives as, "The pupils will be able to explain the impact that the discovery and exploitation of the Middle East oil fields has had on the development of the area." Frequently, several overt behavioral objectives are needed in order to get a good sampling of the behavior encompassed by the covert behavioral objectives.

The trouble with covert behavioral objectives, then, is that one cannot observe them directly. The trouble with overt behavioral objectives often is that in an effort to find objectives that are readily observable, teachers dredge up trivial objectives. After all, it is difficult to write overt behavioral objectives that adequately describe major cognitive or affective goals. Consequently, writers of objectives tend to concentrate on the less important details and forget the big picture. This tendency to emphasize the unimportant at the expense of the important has been true of teaching throughout all history. That is why in every period of history we find that teachers have concentrated on isolated, unrelated facts rather than on ideas, appreciations, and attitudes. The search for easily observable and easily measurable objectives has made this tendency even stronger. Some lists of behavioral objectives reveal an emphasis on petty and inconsequential learning.

Behavioral Objectives and Evaluation

One of the purposes of setting objectives is to make it possible to determine with some precision whether or not the teaching has brought about the terminal activity desired. This presents no great problem when the terminal activity sought is overt; when the activity is covert the evaluation becomes more difficult. Since one cannot observe covert terminal activity, the only way to tell whether such activity has been achieved is to observe behavior that indicates the presence or absence of the covert terminal activity. Consequently, for purposes of evaluating the success of teaching efforts, it is desirable, insofar as feasible, to state objectives in terms of overt behavior, that is, as overt behavioral objectives. Moreover, it is helpful if the behavioral objective states just what standard of behavior is required to indicate satisfactory performance. Behavioral objectives that indicate the standard of performance expected we shall call *criterion-referenced behavioral objectives*.[1]

General and Specific Objectives

In education, objectives are what it is hoped pupils will learn as a result of instruction. As in other pursuits, objectives may range from the very general to the very specific. What, for instance, can be more general than the following statements of the major purposes of American education?

[1] Sometimes they are called performance objectives.

This concept is becoming of increasing practical importance to teachers. In some school systems the educational goals are set up as competencies that the pupils are supposed to achieve. These goals are divided into specific performance objectives, sometimes called goal indicators. If the pupils can perform the competencies called for by these specific goals, their education is considered successful; if not, it is not. School curricula, teacher performance, and pupil achievement may all be evaluated by these criteria.

Most General	Very General	General		Specific
Education general	Schoolwide goals	Course objective	Unit objectives	Lesson objectives

FIGURE 3-1   *Teaching Objectives Continuum*

As a result of their schooling, American youth will be good citizens;
   think clearly and rationally;
   use their leisure time in a worthwhile manner;
   live a healthful life;
   earn a good living at their vocations;
   appreciate beauty in art, music, nature, and the community.

Or what can be more specific than the following lesson plan objectives?

The student will be able to recite from memory without error the first stanza of A. E. Housman's "Loveliest of Trees."
Given a topographical map of the area, the student will be able to find the altitude of the block house on Signal Mountain to the nearest five feet.

Most teaching objectives fall somewhere between these extremes, for, in teaching, objectives fall in a continuum from the very general to the very specific (Figure 3-1). In thinking of general and specific objectives, it is good to remember that it is not so much a matter of general and specific objectives as it is that some objectives are more general or more specific than others.

In practice you can expect your courses always to be aimed at broad general objectives, and your units to be focused on rather general objectives supported by specific objectives, whereas your lesson objectives will always be specific objectives. (Figure 3-1).[2] (When one sees a general objective in a lesson plan, it is usually a general objective of the unit or perhaps a course goal doubling as a unit general objective.)

Exercise 3 B

On the continuum from most general to most specific, where would you put each of the following objectives?

1. The pupil will appreciate the problems faced by those who emigrate to the United States.
2. The pupil will demonstrate the scientific attitude.

---

[2] Educational authorities have not standardized the terminology to be used for designating the various types of objectives. In the literature the most general objectives of education are often called educational aims; the general objectives of schools, curricula and courses, goals; the objectives of units and lessons, instructional objectives as well as general and specific objectives; and extremely specific and narrow objectives, drill objectives. The implication of this scheme is that educational aims are more general than goals; goals more general than general objectives; general objectives more general than specific objectives; and drill objectives the most specific of specific objectives.

3. The pupil will understand that various species of birds have different types of beaks and that these differences in type of beak are related to what the birds feed on.
   a. The pupils will be able to identify from pictures the beaks of (1) woodpeckers, (2) birds of prey, (3) ducks, (4) seed eaters (finches, grosbeaks), (5) insect eaters, (6) pelicans, (7) herons, (8) crossbills, (9) sandpipers.
   b. The pupils will be able to explain the functions of each type of beak listed.

Furthermore, in a well-ordered school systems, the more specific objectives combine to support the more general ones. Thus we may find that the learning required by the specific objectives of several lessons combine to bring about the learning that makes up a general unit objective, or that several unit objectives may combine to build a course objective, or that certain course objectives combine to produce a schoolwide goal. For instance, the schoolwide goal

The students will become good citizens

might be supported by such subordinate curriculum or course goals as

The students will understand their duties and responsibilities as citizens.
The students will understand the legislative process and how it works.
The students will take an active part in community affairs.

In planning one's courses one should first select the general objectives that are to be the course goals, then break down these course goals into the general objectives that are to be the unit goals, and then divide these into the specific objectives for the lessons in the unit, so that the specific lesson plans will support the general objectives of the unit, the unit objectives will support the course goals, and the course goals will support your schoolwide objectives. See Figure 3-2.

Since, as we have seen, teaching objectives describe the terminal behavior that teachers expect of students at the end of their instruction, they may be written in terms of covert or overt activity. As a rule, however, although broad curricula and course goals may be written as covert behavior, unit and lesson specific objectives probably should always describe overt behavior. As a matter of fact, since there seems to be a tendency for teachers to emphasize petty inconsequential behavioral objectives, it may be wise to write your general objectives or goals as covert objectives, supported by several more specific overt behavioral objectives (Figure 3-2). For example, in a unit, one of the general objectives might be the following:

The pupil understands the difference between common and proper nouns.

Subordinate, specific objectives whose achievement would result in attaining this general objective might be

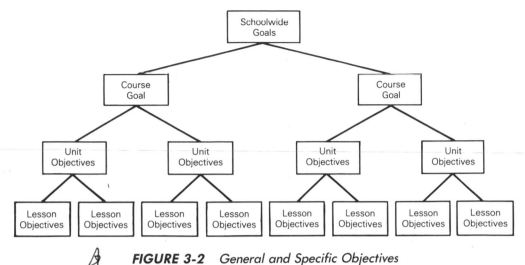

FIGURE 3-2 *General and Specific Objectives*

1. *The pupil can define both proper and common nouns.*
2. *The pupil can pick out the proper and common nouns in a passage with 90 per cent accuracy.*
3. *The pupil capitalizes proper nouns but not common nouns when he writes.*

In practice, it is best to set one's general objectives or goals first and then generate a sampling of subordinate specific objectives that together would accomplish the goals. It may then be necessary to build a sampling of still more specific objectives to accomplish the specific goals that then become lower-level general objectives.

For example, you might select the following as a unit objective:

The pupils will understand the difference between the two temperature scales: Fahrenheit and Celsius (centigrade).

You might decide that a good way to get the pupils to understand the difference between the two scales would be to teach them to convert from one scale to another and to interpret the meaning of readings on the two scales. You then set up the following subordinate goals:

1. *The pupils will be able to convert from Fahrenheit to Celsius.*
2. *The pupils will be able to convert from Celsius to Fahrenheit.*
3. *The pupils will be able to give the formulas for converting from Celsius to Fahrenheit and from Fahrenheit to Celsius.*
4. *The pupils will be able to interpret verbally the temperature as indicated on either a Celsius or Fahrenheit scale.*

If you choose your subordinate objectives well, presumably the pupils will have achieved the general understanding you seek once they have achieved the subordinate objectives. However, some worthwhile goals are so elusive that it is almost impossible to write specific behavior that truly indicates whether or not the pupils have really achieved the goal.

We therefore recommend that you write most of your cognitive and affective course goals and unit general objectives as covert objectives and reserve your behavioral objectives for the specific objectives of your units and lessons and for psychomotor skills objectives.[3]

Affective objectives may be either behavioral or covert, but attitudes and feelings are probably too difficult to change to warrant setting specific behavioral objectives at the unit or lesson level, especially when it is so difficult to judge attitudes and feelings from overt behavior. There can be no fixed rule about any of this, however. As in almost everything in teaching, you must learn to adjust your choice of objectives to the circumstances.

Exercise 3 C

a. To be sure that you understand, try to set up a sequence of objectives from most general to most specific in which every specific objective supports a more general objective.

b. Following are some general goals for courses in various fields. Can you think of specific objectives that must be achieved before these general goals can be attained? Discuss your conclusions with your colleagues.

1. Pupils will be able to distinguish the major characteristics of tragedy and comedy.
2. Pupils will write clear, expository prose.
3. Pupils will understand the place of the planet earth in the galaxy.
4. Pupils will be able to discuss differences that exist among microorganisms, plants, and animals.
5. Pupils will understand that the basic nature of society is rooted in its values.
6. Pupils will understand that man's need for sociality is a factor in implementing change.

Simple or Criterion-referenced Behavioral Objectives

Behavioral objectives may be either *simple* or *criterion-referenced*. The difference is that a simple objective states only what the pupil will be able to do after the instruction while a criterion-referenced objective states not only the terminal behavior expected but also what standards of performance pupils should attain.

"At the end of the lesson the pupil will be able to read a bus schedule" is a simple behavioral objective. It states what the pupil should be able to do at the end of the instruction. To make it a criterion-referenced behavioral objective one would have to add the standard of performance to be attained, for example:

---

[3] One can also use criterion-referenced behavioral objectives (i.e., behavioral objectives that specify how well the students should perform) as goal *indicators* (competencies) for school and curriculum goals, but ordinarily these will be established by curriculum committees and workers.

At the end of the lesson, the pupil will be able to read a bus schedule well enough to determine at what time buses are scheduled to arrive and leave designated points with at least 90 per cent accuracy.

The criterion-referenced objectives may also give the conditions under which the pupil is expected to meet the standard required, as in the following:

Given an interurban bus schedule at the end of the lesson, the pupil will be able to read the schedule well enough to determine at what times buses are scheduled to arrive and leave designated points with at least 90 per cent accuracy.

Notice that the conditions and, consequently, the severity of the standards of this criterion-referenced objective differ from the conditions set forth in the following example:

Given excerpts from a bus schedule, the pupil will be able to read the schedule well enough to determine at what time buses are scheduled to arrive and leave the points contained in the excerpts with at least 90 per cent accuracy.

Presumably, reading excerpts from the bus schedule would not be as difficult as reading the bus schedule itself.

Criterion-referenced behavioral (or performance) objectives set forth at least three essentials:

1. Some observable, and therefore measurable, behavior that the pupils will be able to perform at the completion of instruction,
2. The standard at which the pupils are expected to perform,
3. The conditions under which the pupils are expected to perform in order to meet the standard.

Some critics think that these three essentials tend to make the objectives too trivial so that instruction is likely to emphasize bits and pieces of information at the expense of large understandings and appreciations. No doubt this is a danger, but the wary teacher can avoid such pitfalls. With care, you can make the performance standards and conditions broad and strong. Furthermore, understandings, appreciations, and attitudes are made up of clusters of smaller behaviors. By selecting a good sampling of subordinate (criterion-referenced) instructional objectives for each understanding, attitude, and appreciation that you wish to teach and by achieving them, you can attain the larger goals and tell when you have done so. For these reasons, the specific objectives that we use in our teaching probably should be criterion-referenced behavioral objectives.

Because criterion-referenced behavioral objectives call for much more specific terminal behavior than do simple behavioral objectives, and because they provide the test builder and evaluator a definite standard by which to judge pupil performance, they are more useful for test building, evaluation, diagnosis, and feedback than are other types of objectives. This type of objective has become quite popular with educational experts, particularly those whose interests center on tests and evaluation, programming, and systematizing instruction.

Cognitive, Affective, and Psychomotor Objectives

Objectives may be cognitive in nature (for example, concepts, ideas, factual knowledge, or intellectual skill), affective (appreciation, ideals, attitudes, or morals), or psychomotor (motor skills such as piano playing, basket weaving, and swimming, that involve the intelligent use of motor functions). In each of these areas, or domains, objectives may range from those calling for the simplest of activities to those requiring the most complex ideas, skills, or reactions. Several authorities have attempted to arrange the objectives in each of the domains (cognitive, affective, and psychomotor) into taxonomies, according to the complexity, intensity, or sophistication of the activities involved. These taxonomies are most useful for judging the depth of teaching.

The Cognitive Domain.   In their taxonomy of objectives in the cognitive domain, Bloom and his associates[4] attempted to arrange cognitive educational objectives into classifications, according to the complexity of the skills and abilities embodied in the objectives. The resulting taxonomy portrays a ladder ranging from the simplest to the most complex mental processes.

1. Knowledge (the recognition and recall of information).
2. Comprehension (the understanding of the meaning of the information).
3. Application (the ability to use the information).
4. Analysis (the ability to dissect knowledge into component parts and see their relationships).
5. Synthesis (the ability to put the parts together to form new ideas).
6. Evaluation (the ability to judge the worth of an idea, notion, theory, thesis, proposition, information, or belief).

A more complete outline of the taxonomy is shown in Table 3-1. Studying it may clarify your understanding of the taxonomy. This module, however, is not particularly concerned about the subcategories.

1. Knowledge.

The basic category in Bloom's hierarchy of educational objectives in the cognitive domain concerns the acquisition of knowledge, i.e., the ability to recognize and recall information. Although this is the lowest level of the hierarchy, the information to be learned well enough, to be recognized, recalled, or remembered is not necessarily low level. In fact it may be of extremely high level. In their taxonomy, Bloom and his associates include at this level such complex and sophisticated knowledge as knowledge of principles, generalizations, theories, structures, and methodology, as well as knowledge of specifics and ways and means of dealing with specifics. (See Table 3-1.)

[4]Benjamin S. Bloom, ed. *Taxonomy of Educational Objectives, Handbook I: Cognitive Domain* (New York: David McKay Co., 1956).

TABLE 3-1
*Taxonomy of Objectives: The Cognitive Domain**

Knowledge

1.00 Knowledge
    1.10 Knowledge of Specifics
    1.11 Knowledge of Terminology
    1.12 Knowledge of Specific Facts

1.20 Knowledge of Ways and Means of Dealing with Specifics
    1.21 Knowledge of Conventions
    1.22 Knowledge of Trends and Sequences
    1.23 Knowledge of Classifications and Categories
    1.24 Knowledge of Criteria
    1.25 Knowledge of Methodology

1.30 Knowledge of the Universals and Abstractions in a Field
    1.31 Knowledge of Principles and Generalizations
    1.32 Knowledge of Theories and Structures

Intellectual Abilities and Skills

2.00 Comprehension
    2.10 Translation
    2.20 Interpretation
    2.30 Extrapolation

3.00 Application

4.00 Analysis
    4.10 Analysis of Elements
    4.20 Analysis of Relationships
    4.30 Analysis of Organizational Principles

5.00 Synthesis
    5.10 Production of a Unique Communication
    5.20 Production of a Plan, of Proposed Set of
           Operations
    5.30 Derivation of a Set of Abstract Relations

6.00 Evaluation
    6.10 Judgments in Terms of Internal Evidence
    6.20 Judgments in Terms of External Criteria

The following are examples of objectives in the knowledge category:

The student will be able to list the principal parts of speech.
The student will be able to conjugate the Latin verb amare.
The student will be able to name the logical fallacies.
The student will be able to repeat the Pythagorean theorem.
The student will remember which criteria are recommended for testing certain hypotheses.
The student will be able to recall the formula for sulfuric acid.

The student will be able to define the following: axiom, reflexive, symmetric, transitive substitute theorem, equivalent.

Given a selection of common working tools, the student will be able to identify each by name and purpose.

The student will be able to describe the procedure for diagnosing the cause of a stalled motor.

Given a picture of a skeleton, the student will correctly label the various bones listed.

The other categories of educational objectives in the cognitive domain have to do with using knowledge. They include those educational objectives aimed at developing intellectual skills and abilities. According to Bloom and his associates, these abilities and skills include those of comprehension, application, analysis, synthesis, and evaluation of information. (See Table 3-1).

2. Comprehension.

The skills and abilities next higher than simple knowledge are those of comprehension. According to the taxonomy, these include the ability to translate or explain knowledge or information, to interpret it, and to extrapolate it to new situations. Examples of objectives at this level follow.

The student will be able to explain the Pythagorean theorem.
The student will be able to identify transitive verbs.
The student will be able to describe mitosis in his or her own words.
The student will be able to explain the general functions of the cerebrum.
The student will be able to interpret relationships among the elements depicted in a bar graph.
The student will be able to explain the concept represented by $E = mc^2$.
The student will be able to define electric current in his or her own words.
The student will be able to factor a perfect trinomial square in the type form $a^2 + 2ab + b^2 = (a + b)^2$.

3. Application.

Next higher on the scale are the skills of application. Once students can understand the information presumably they should be able to apply it. Doing so represents a somewhat higher level of cognitive ability than comprehension. Samples of objectives at the application level might include:

The student will be able to translate simple word problems into algebraic equations.
Given the length of its sides, the student will be able to determine the area of a right triangle.
The student will be able to apply the appropriate formulas for determining the area of a woodlot.
The students will be able to convert yards to meters accurately.

Given the necessary data, the students will be able to construct an appropriate bar graph.

4. Analysis.

The category next higher than application includes objectives that require students to utilize the skills of analysis. According to Bloom, these skills include analysis of elements, analysis of relationships, and analysis of organizational principles. Some examples of educational objectives at the analysis level follow.

The students will be able to spot inconsistencies in television commercials.

The students will be able to identify the major themes of a novel.

The students will be able to spot slanting in a news story.

Confronted with an inoperative small engine, the student will be able to diagnose the difficulty.

Given a short essay to read, the student will be able to determine logical fallacies in an argument.

5. Synthesis.

The synthesis level of the cognitive objectives includes objectives involving such skills as producing a unique communication, producing a plan or a proposed set of operations, or deriving a set of abstract relations. Examples of objectives at this level of the taxonomy might include:

The student will be able to write clear directions for performing a simple task.

Given an unknown, the student will be able to propose a suitable method for determining its chemical consistency.

The student can create a logical outline of a proposition preparatory for writing an essay.

Given the necessary data, the student will be able to construct a graph showing the rise and fall of the GNP in the past decade.

The student will be able to design a plan for a community survey.

The student will be able to write an acceptable term paper.

Given a hypothesis, the student will be able to design an experiment suitable for testing the hypothesis.

Given the necessary information concerning income, exemptions, deductions, and withholding tax, and the appropriate IRS 1040 instruction booklet, the student will be able to fill out an IRS Form 1040 correctly.

6. Evaluation.

The highest cognitive level of the taxonomy, according to Bloom, is evaluation. This includes the ability to make judgment according to internal criteria and external criteria. Following are some examples of educational objectives aimed at this level of cognitive ability.

The student can distinguish between a well-developed character and a stereotyped one.

The student will be able to write a critique of a television drama showing merits and faults in its plot and characterization.

The student will be able to judge which form—1040EZ, 1040A, or 1040—is appropriate in a given situation of tax reporting.

The student will be able to determine which picture best meets the stated criteria.

The student will be able to distinguish between decision making and problem solving.

Exercise 3 D

The following cognitive objectives are taken from plans prepared by college students doing their senior student teaching. At what level of the Bloom taxonomy of the cognitive domain does each of these objectives belong? If you do not agree with the key, turn back to the taxonomy and study it again. Then if you still disagree, discuss the matter with your instructor. These classifications are sometimes ambiguous. It may be that your answer is as right as that in the key.

1. The pupil will be able to detect faulty logic in advertising propaganda.
2. The pupil will be able to differentiate fact and opinion in news stories.
3. Given the facts of a political situation, the student will be able to draw reasonable hypotheses concerning the causes of the situation.
4. The student will be able to devise a workable plan for investigating a social phenomenon.
5. The pupil will be able to write clear directions.
6. At the end of the lesson, the pupils will perceive the moods of melancholy and retreat in Byron's *The Ocean.*
7. You will be able to define corporation in your own words.
8. Given the requisite tools and materials, electric drill and bit, knife, screwdriver, ruler, soldering gun, wire strippers, solder, and flax, the pupil will be able to construct a portable testing device for repair of motors and sealed-in units.
9. Given a list of five solids, five liquids, and five gases, pupils will be able to describe the physical and chemical properties of each.
10. You will be able to devise a method to prove a ray to be the bisector of an angle.

The Affective Domain. Krathwohl, Bloom, and Masia[5] arranged the objectives of the affective domain into categories from highest to lowest according to

---

[5] David R. Krathwohl, Benjamin S. Bloom, and Bertram B. Masia. *Taxonomy of Educational Goals, Handbook II: Affective Domain* (New York: David McKay Co., 1964).

the degree of internalization each of the objectives required. The following main levels of the taxonomy are from least internalized to most internalized:

1. *Receiving (awareness of the affective stimulus and the beginning of favorable feelings toward it).*
2. *Responding (taking an interest in the stimulus and viewing it favorably).*
3. *Valuing (tentative belief in the value of the affective stimulus becomes commitment to it).*
4. *Organization (organization of values into a system of dominant and supporting values).*
5. *Characterized by a value or value complex (determination of one's conduct, beliefs, and, finally, one's character or philosophy of life).*

The following paragraphs describe the types of objectives that fit these categories somewhat more fully. However, as Figure 3-3 shows, the categories overlap considerably. Still, they give one a basis by which to judge the quality of objectives in the affective domain.

1. Receiving (awareness of the affective stimulus and the beginning of favorable feelings toward it).

At this, the least internalized, level the student exhibits willingness to give his or her attention to particular phenomena or stimuli, and the teacher is able to arouse, hold, and direct that attention. Some examples of objectives at the receiving level are:

The student pays close attention to the directions for extra activities.
The student listens carefully to the classroom lectures.
The student shows sensitivity to the concerns of others.

2. Responding (taking an interest in the stimulus and viewing it favorably).

At this level, students respond to the stimulus they have received. They may do so because of some outside pressure or voluntarily, because they find it interesting or because responding gives them satisfaction. Some examples of objectives at the responding level follow.

The student shows interest in the subject by doing extra reading.
The student volunteers in classroom recitation.
The student participates wholeheartedly in classroom discussions and projects.
The student seeks out examples of good art.
The student reads for recreation.
The student selects high-quality classical music to listen to.
The student willingly cooperates in group activities.
The student finds pleasure in studying nature in the field.

3. Valuing (tentative belief in the value of the affective stimulus becomes commitment to it).

Objectives in the valuing category have to do with students' beliefs, attitudes,

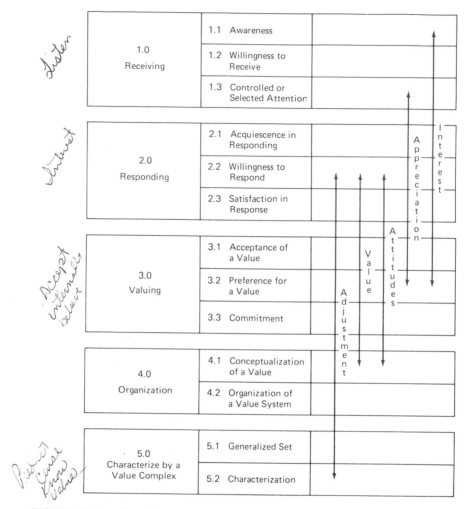

FIGURE 3-3 *The Affective Domain (From* Taxonomy of Educational Objectives Handbook II. Affective Domain *by David R. Krathwohl et al. Copyright © 1964 by Longman Inc. Reprinted by permission of Longman Inc., New York.)*

and appreciations. The simplest of these have to do with student acceptance of beliefs and values. Objectives at higher level in this category have to do with student learning to prefer certain values and finally becoming committed to them. Examples of objectives in this category are as follows:

The student shows concern about racial injustice.
The student recognizes the value of the freedom of the press.
In class discussions the student shows concern about the need for a more pollution-free atmosphere.
The student demonstrates problem-solving attitudes.

The student withholds judgment until he has considered evidence pro and con.

The student shows his concern for language by trying to speak and write precisely.

The student shows his appreciation of poetry by selecting poetry for recreational reading.

The student attempts to consider data on different sides of an issue before committing himself to a position.

The student exhibits willingness to change his position when faced with new evidence.

4. Organization (organization of values into a system of dominant and lesser values).

The fourth category in the affective domain hierarchy, organization, concerns the building of a person's value system. At this level the student begins to conceptualize values and arrange them into a value system that recognizes priorities and relative importance of the various values one faces. Examples of objectives at this level follow.

The student forms judgments concerning proper behavior in school and society.

The student decides what values are most important to him.

The student forms judgments concerning the type of life he would like to lead in view of his abilities, interests, and beliefs.

The student forms judgment concerning what his life work should be.

The student sets up standards of behavior that he or she intends to be guided by.

5. Characterization by a Value or Value Complex.

The topmost category in the affective domain hierarchy is called characterization by a value or value complex. At this level "the individual acts consistently in accordance with values he has internalized." These controlling tendencies are so much a part of the person's behavior as to describe the sort of person he is and make up his "total philosophy or world view."[6] Examples of objectives at this level follow.

The student regularly cooperates in group activities.

The student is always meticulous about his grooming.

The student works independently and diligently.

The student tries to live up to a well-defined ethical code of behavior.

The student shows desire to be precise in his speech by attempting to be accurate in his use of language expression and thought.

When confronted by a word he is not sure how to spell, the student usually looks it up in a dictionary.

---

[6] Ibid. p. 165.

The Psychomotor Domain. A taxonomy of objectives in the psychomotor domain probably is really unnecessary. In this domain the goal is simply to develop proficiency in skills. Consequently, the objectives are simply steps enabling one to move from unskillful to most skillful. However, several persons have constructed taxonomies in the domain. Among them is the following hierarchy developed in a graduate class. Perhaps it may serve as a guide as you develop objectives suitable for the various steps in skill development.

1. Familiarization.

The first step in this progression is to make the student familiar with the skill to be developed. At this level the student learns about the skill but as yet has not learned the skill. For instance,

> *The student can describe the procedure for approaching the high hurdles.*

2. Fundamentals.

At this level the student learns the basic rudiments of the skill. For instance,

> *The student will be able to demonstrate the basic positions for fingering the keyboard.*
> *The student will be able to play the scales on the piano.*
> *The student will be able to execute procedure for heading a soccer ball.*
> *The student will grasp the golf club correctly.*
> *The student assumes the proper stance at the plate.*
> *The student can properly finger the violin.*

3. Development.

At this third level the student develops his or her skill until it becomes smooth and automatic. For example,

> *The student will be able to run the 100-yard dash in 12 seconds.*
> *The student can swim fifty yards.*
> *The student can play the B-flat scale on the violin.*

4. Adjusting and Adapting.

The student at this level continues to develop his or her skill by learning to adjust and adapt his or her techniques to meet situations. By practice and experience he or she learns to control his behavior so that it is more expert and suitable to variations and changes in conditions and requirements. For instance,

> *The student will be able to set up laboratory equipment quickly and correctly.*

5. Perfection and Maintenance.

At this level the student becomes expert. He or she not only achieves and maintains a high level of skill but also arrives at the point where he can invent and modify techniques and create new procedures and combinations. For instance,

The student will be able to create new dance patterns.
The student can draw an accurate map of the local area.
The student can sing tonefully and accurately.
The student can perform on the piano professionally.
The student can operate a saw safely and skillfully.

Using the Taxonomies.   Theoretically, the taxonomies are arranged so that it would be necessary for learners to achieve each lower level before being ready to move to the higher levels. However, this theory probably does not hold in practice, particularly in the affective domain in which categories overlap greatly (see Figure 3-3). Attempts to arrange instruction so that pupils move in order up through the categories are likely to be self-defeating. However, the taxonomies are important in that they point out the various levels to which instruction should aspire. If education is to be worthwhile, teachers must aim at and achieve objectives in the higher levels of the taxonomies as well as in the lower ones. If you aim at these higher objectives sufficiently often, your teaching will not be trivial. Unfortunately, most teachers do not include enough objectives in the higher categories of the domains when they form their objectives. If in your teaching you build higher learnings on a firm base, your students' learning should be really worthwhile.

In writing your objectives, however, remember that the point is not so much to write objectives at any particular level as it is to formulate the best objectives you can for the job you have to do. Use the taxonomies to make sure that your teaching is not completely trivial.

Writing Objectives

Writing Criterion-referenced Objectives

To write good criterion-referenced behavioral objectives is difficult, so difficult, in fact, that some critics feel that writing them is not worth the effort. However, they do make for precise objectives, especially as a basis for evaluation and feedback. Perhaps we should always use them for specific objectives of units and lessons. We can use other types of objectives for larger units perhaps, although criterion-referenced objectives may serve there too. If we keep the taxonomy of educational objectives before us and bear in mind the need for some objectives from the higher categories of the domains, we can avoid criterion-referenced objectives that make the teaching content petty and trivial.

As we have seen, a complete criterion-referenced behavioral objective consists of a statement that tells us

1. Who will perform the behavior.
2. The overt behavior that will be performed.[7]
3. The standard of performance expected.
4. The conditions under which the behavior will be performed.

---

[7] Some authorities divide this into two categories: the act or behavior and the product. Thus in the objective "The student will be able to write an essay describing the causes of the revolution," *write* is the behavior and *an essay describing the causes of the revolution* is the product, We think that combining the two is preferable.

1   Therefore, in writing out the criterion-referenced objectives, first you must designate the person who is going to do the performing called for by the objectives. That is the pupil, student, learner, or candidate (see examples, p. 46). If the objective is addressed to the learner, use "you." Even when the words are not written down, one should assume that every objective begins, "At the conclusion of the instruction, the student (or you). . . ." If you wish, there is no reason that you cannot use the plural (e.g., pupils, learners, students), if the instruction is not going to be individualized.

2   Second, describe what the behavior or performance will be. To do this you will need an action verb and its object, such as the following: *will write a poem; will describe the plan; will run the mile; will build a desk.* In this type of behavioral objective, the verb must be an action verb that describes overt action which can be observed and measured. Action that is covert is useless to you when you are preparing criterion-referenced objectives.

    We have seen examples in the overt behavioral objectives of such verbs as *solve, convert, read, explain,* and *describe.* Covert objectives use less active verbs such as *understand, appreciate, feel, think,* and *believe.* The test by which one determines whether behavior is overt or covert is to check whether or not the verb describes action that can be observed directly.

Exercise 3 E

See if you can pick out the verbs used in overt behavioral objectives from the list that follows. (It is possible, of course, that, sometimes because of different contexts, a verb may have both an overt and covert meaning.)

apply	design	select
cov appreciate	*cov* enjoy	solve
cov comprehend	explain	state
compute	identify	summarize
create	*cov* know	*cov* understand
define	outline	
demonstrate	predict	

3   Next, describe the conditions under which the behavior will occur. These conditions include the information, tools or equipment, and materials and supplies that will or will not be available to the pupil; limitations as to time and space; and other restrictions that may be applicable. In writing this portion of the objective, it would be wise to try to visualize what conditions would be present in a "real life" performance and to try to duplicate them as nearly as you can in the objective.

    Examples include such introductory phrases as *in a 30-minute written multiple choice test; given a ruler and protractor; given excerpts from the interurban bus schedule; completely without notes; in a new and strange situation;* or *from a set of pictures.* These conditions should be clear enough so that conditions are standard for everyone. If they are vague and fuzzy, one pupil may have a considerably more difficult task to perform than another, although the basis for behavior and standards set may seem the same.

4   Finally, the standard of performance is the last part of the objective to write. Here you state what will be the level of behavior you will accept as satisfactory. Your criterion may be the minimum number acceptable *("at least five reasons," "All ten reasons");* the per cent or proportion acceptable *(with 90 per cent accuracy, in eight of ten cases);* acceptable limits of tolerance *(within ±5 per cent);* acceptable limits of time *(within a period of fifteen minutes);* or some other standard. Usually, this standard is set rather arbitrarily on the basis of one's experience and expectations.

Exercise 3 F

a. In the following objectives, identify the parts of the objectives:

Objective 1—You will write a 500-word account of the battle between the forces of Gondor and its allies against those of Mordor and its allies, as related in *The Lord of the Rings,* completely from memory. This account will be accurate in all basic details and include all the important incidents of the battle.

Objective 2—Given an interurban bus schedule, at the end of the lesson the pupil will be able to read the schedule well enough to determine at what time buses are scheduled to leave randomly selected points, with at least 90 per cent accuracy.

b. Now try to make up some criterion-referenced objectives for each of the following hypothetical situations:

1. You are a teacher of typewriting. You think that by the end of the semester each pupil should be able to type at least 40 words per minute with no more than one error per minute.
2. You are teaching map reading, and you hope that at the end of the unit your pupils will be able to locate places on the practice globe by giving latitude and longitude to the nearest degree ±3 degrees in at least 75 per cent of the examples you set for them as a test.
3. You are teaching English literature. At the end of the unit you hope that at least half of your pupils will like Shakespearean comedy enough so that they will read some on their own.
4. You are teaching mathematics. You expect that at the end of the unit each person will be able to do simple multiplication and division on the slide rule with reasonable accuracy at least nine-tenths of the time.
5. You are teaching French. You expect all your pupils to be able to read and translate simple high-school level-three French prose at the end of the semester.

Writing Simple Behavioral Objectives

Simple behavioral objectives are much easier to formulate than criterion-referenced objectives. You must state what has to be done and who has to do it. The procedure for writing simple behavioral objectives is the same as that for writing criterion-referenced behavioral objectives except that steps three and four are omitted and you may use the less active verbs such as *know, understand, apprehend, appreciate,* and *enjoy.* Remember that simple behavioral objectives may be covert objectives; criterion-referenced objectives may not. Use them when formulating general objectives and goals.

Exercise 3 G

a. Now try to make up some simple behavioral objectives for each of the hypothetical situations described in the preceding exercise.

b. Of the following, which examples are criterion-referenced behavioral objectives? Which are simple behavioral objectives?

1. The pupil will be able to solve equations in one unknown.
2. Given examples of the type X^5/X^3, the pupil will solve the examples correctly by subtracting exponents in at least nine out of ten cases.
3. The pupil will be able to describe the differences between the policies followed by Lincoln and Johnson and those followed by the Radical Republicans in Congress.
4. Given a paper triangle, the pupil will be able to determine the center of gravity of the triangle by the paper-folding technique.
5. The pupil will be able to spell correctly each of the common contractions: *doesn't, wouldn't, he's, you're, isn't, aren't, I'd, what's, hadn't, there's, they're, hasn't, you'll, don't.*
6. Given a new and strange situation, the pupil usually attempts to examine all the available relevant data before making a conclusion.
7. The pupil can accurately define both common and proper nouns.
8. Given an unassembled machine gun, the pupil can quickly and unhesitatingly assemble it.
9. The pupil can run a hundred yards in twelve seconds.
10. Given a dozen examples of rocks, the pupil can identify each of them without making more than three errors.

Writing Affective Behavioral Objectives

As we have already suggested, to write behavioral objectives in the affective domain is difficult because attitudes and feelings are covert. One cannot always tell how people feel from their behavior. Often, people's behavior does not represent their real feelings. Quite frequently they dissimulate—whistle a happy tune so no one will know they are afraid. If persons could not hide their real feelings, social relations would soon break down. Moreover, sometimes people do not know what their real attitudes are. Under periods of stress, attitudes carefully hidden from ourselves suddenly reappear. Also, one's attitudes and feelings may be transitory and selective. The scientist who is carefully objective in the laboratory may be emotional, prejudiced, and irrational when making social judgments. Another consideration is that the development and changing of attitudes, ideals, and appreciations is usually a long process of months and years rather than of lessons and units. Finally, pupils often say and do outwardly what they think the teachers want to hear and see but keep their real feelings, attitudes, and beliefs to themselves.

For these reasons, writing behavioral objectives for the affective domain may be gilding the lily. Covert objectives may serve our purposes just as well in the average classroom situation. Nevertheless, it is possible to write useful affective behavioral objectives. In doing so, one uses the same procedures as when writing other behavioral objectives except that adding a note stating what effect (feeling, attitude) the behavior is supposed to indicate may make the objective clearer. The following example illustrates the suggested format.

> *The student illustrates his growing interest in operatic music by regularly listening to the weekly radio programs of the Metropolitan Opera Company for recreational purposes.*

In this objective, the elements are

Who? The student.
Will do what? Listen to the radio programs of the Metropolitan Opera Company.
Under what conditions? For recreational purposes.
How much? Regularly.
For what purpose? To illustrate his interest in opera.

Here are some other examples of affective domain behavioral objectives.

> *The pupil exhibits a willingness to revise his conclusions on the basis of new evidence.*
> *The student shows an interest in history by borrowing and reading library books on history.*
> *The pupil exhibits civic responsibility by participating in civic projects.*
> *The student keeps meticulous records of his spending.*
> *The student reads Shakespearean plays for recreation.*
> *The student associates freely with his peers without regard for race or class.*

Writing Covert Objectives

To write covert objectives one uses the same formula as for simple behavioral objectives: i.e., who does what. The difference is that the activity described is not observable and the verb used is not an action verb. Verbs that might be used in covert objectives include *know, understand, appreciate, recognize, feel, like, believe, think, enjoy,* as we have already seen. They are most useful for describing emotional or instructional goals and affective objectives.

Matching Taxonomic Levels

The Cognitive Domain. When formulating behavioral objectives, you should pick out those you believe to be the most important and relevant to the subject and to the more general goals set for the course, curriculum, or school. At this point you should not worry too much about their level in the taxonomy of educational objectives. However, you should check your objectives to be certain that you have included a reasonable sampling of objectives at the higher mental levels, wherever pertinent. Following are examples of action verbs that are suitable for stating objectives at the various levels of the cognitive domain.[8]

Level 1. Knowledge.
   Define, describe, distinguish, identify, list, match, outline, recall, recognize, reproduce, state.

Level 2. Comprehension.
   Change, compare, conclude, contrast, convert, differentiate, estimate, explain, generalize, give examples, illustrate, infer, interpret, paraphrase, predict, prepare, read, rephrase, represent, restate, translate.

Level 3. Application.
   Apply, choose, classify, compute, demonstrate, develop, employ, generalize, operate, organize, predict, prepare, produce, relate, restructure, show, solve, transfer, use.

Level 4. Analysis.
   Break down, categorize, classify, compare, contrast, deduce, diagram, differentiate, discriminate, distinguish, identify, illustrate, infer, outline, point out, recognize, relate, separate, subdivide.

Level 5. Synthesis.
   Arrange, categorize, classify, combine, compile, constitute, create, design, develop, devise, document, explain, formulate, generate, modify, organize, originate, plan, produce, rearrange, reconstruct, revise, rewrite, summarize, tell, transmit, write.

Level 6. Evaluation.
   Appraise, argue, assess, compare, conclude, consider, contrast, criticize, decide, discriminate, explain, evaluate, interpret, judge, justify, rank, rate, relate, standardize, support, validate.

The Affective Domain.   Affective behavioral objectives may be written at each of the taxonomic levels. Following is a list of verbs typical of the action verbs that are useful at the various levels of the affective domain taxonomy. Remember, however, that because the divisions between the various categories of the affective domain are so indistinct, the usefulness of action verbs in this domain may spread over several categories.

Level 1. Receiving.
   Ask, choose, describe, differentiate, distinguish, hold, identify, locate, name, point to, select, recall, recognize, reply, use.

Level 2. Responding.
   Answer, applaud, approve, assist, comply, command, conform, discuss,

---

[8] Note that some verbs may be used to state objectives at two or more levels.

greet, help, label, perform, play, practice, present, read, recite, report, select, spend leisure time in, tell, write.

Level 3. Valuing.

Argue, assist, complete, describe, differentiate, explain, follow form, initiate, invite, join, justify, propose, protest, read, report, select, share, study, support, work.

Level 4. Organization.

Adhere, alter, arrange, balance, combine, compare, defend, define, discuss, explain, generalize, identify, integrate, modify, order, organize, prepare, relate, synthesize.

Level 5. Characterization by a value or value complex.

Act, complete, discriminate, display, influence, listen, modify, perform, practice, propose, qualify, question, revise, serve, solve, use, verify.

Exercise 3 H

Try to write both a behavioral and a covert objective for each of the major categories listed in the following. In doing so, do not limit yourself to any one topic or subject. Not all topics lend themselves to the writing of objectives at every level.

Cognitive Domain	*Affective Domain*	*Psychomotor*
1. Knowledge or memory	1. Receiving	1. Familiarization
2. Comprehension	2. Responding	2. Fundamentals
3. Application	3. Valuing	3. Development
4. Analysis	4. Organization	4. Adjusting and adapting
5. Synthesis	5. Characterization	5. Perfection and maintenance
6. Evaluation		

Putting It All Together

As we have seen, objectives may be (a) overt or covert, (b) general or specific, (c) simple or criterion-referenced. Also, in some cases these categories tend to overlap (for example, some general objectives are more general than other general objectives), and the categories may be combined in a number of ways (for example, a general objective may be either overt or covert and either simple or criterion-referenced).

Objectives range from the very general to the very specific. Course goals, for instance, are usually quite general, while unit and lesson objectives represent specific elements of the course goals. These fairly specific objectives should be behavioral in form. Ordinarily course goals and broad educational aims should be written as covert objectives, as should affective objectives for classroom use. Specific unit and lesson objectives should be behavioral, sometimes simple, sometimes criterion referenced.

You will have to use all the possible combinations of characteristics in the behavioral objectives you will need to prepare for your courses, units, and lessons when you teach.

When you write the objectives for your courses, units, and lessons, you will want to follow a procedure similar to the following:

1. Set up your course goals. Usually, these will have to be quite general; therefore, you will probably need to make them simple, and in many cases you will find it easier and more rewarding to make them covert. (Can you see why general, simple, covert statements may be most useful as overall course objectives?) Behavioral objectives, simple or criterion-referenced, may also be useful. In some cases criterion-referenced objectives are a necessity. This is particularly likely to be so in skill subjects and under accountability systems.

2. Once the course objectives have been formulated, you should set up the general objectives for each of your units. When doing so, be sure that these unit objectives, together, make up the course objectives. No necessary ingredient should be left out or short-changed. These objectives may be behavioral or covert, simple or criterion-referenced, depending upon your evaluation of what is most desirable.

3. Now you need to set the specific objectives for the unit. These may be objectives for specific lessons if the unit is organized on a day-by-day lesson basis, or they may be simply unit subdivisions if you are using the laboratory or module approach. In any case, these objectives should all add up to the learning products called for in the general objectives. Remember, the specific examples can only be a sampling of all the subordinate objectives that could be combined to make up the general objectives. The general objectives can be broken down into many specific objectives, but you can select only a limited number, so you must try to get a good sampling of specific objectives for each and every general objective. Usually you will want to make these specific objectives both behavioral and criterion-referenced. However, simple objectives may seem preferable at times. Covert objectives are seldom useful for specific objectives.

When writing objectives you should remember to:

1. Try to get a good spread among the various levels of the three domains: cognitive, affective, and psychomotor. It is much too easy to get caught up with trivia. To build specific, criterion-referenced behavioral objectives that call for use of the higher mental processes and affective responses is particularly difficult. Perhaps the list of action verbs will help you as you try to write specific objectives that call for important learnings.

2. State each goal as a statement that describes the behavior sought, in general terms such as understands, comprehends, knows, appreciates.

3. State each behavioral objective, general or specific, in terms of pupil performance rather than teacher performance.

4. Describe the terminal behavior of the pupil rather than subject matter,

learning process, or teaching procedure in each behavioral objective, general or specific.

5. State each behavioral objective at the proper level of generality.

6. Define each general objective or goal by a sampling of specific behavioral objectives that describe terminal behavior and that show when the objective has been reached.

7. Provide a sufficient sampling of relevant specific behavioral objectives to demonstrate that each of the more general objectives or goals has been achieved.

8. Include in your objectives an adequate sampling of the complex, high-level cognitive and affective goals that are frequently omitted because they are so difficult to write.

9. Limit each specific behavioral objective to only one learning product rather than a combination of learning products.

Exercise 3 I

Following are some general objectives taken from a high school social studies unit. Each of the objectives selected is elementary enough in nature so that any college student should be informed on it. However, unless you are a sociologist, we expect you to answer only on the basis of common knowledge and common sense rather than sociological principles. For each of these objectives, write two or three specific behavioral objectives. Try to make your objectives non-trivial and, if possible, criterion-referenced. Discuss your solutions to this exercise with your instructor and friends.

1. Concepts.
   a. The student will understand that social problems have many causes;
   b. The student will understand that man is a social animal;
   c. The student will understand that solutions to social problems involve effecting changes in society and in the individual.
2. Skills.
   a. The pupil attacks problems in a rational manner.
   b. The student gathers information effectively.
   c. The student organizes and analyzes information and draws conclusions.
3. Attitudes.
   a. The student is skeptical of panaceas.
   b. The student values human dignity.
   c. The student has a sense of responsibility for taking informed action about problems confronting the nation.

Student Goals

Although so far in this module we have talked only of the objectives formulated by teachers, these objectives are likely to be fruitless unless the pupils adopt the same or similar ones. Pupils act not to fulfill the teacher's objectives but their own objectives. Therefore, you must take steps to ensure that pupils adopt objectives that will lead them to your objectives. One way to do this is to inform the pupils early in the course, unit, or lesson of what you hope they will learn. If they consider these learnings to be desirable and decide to accept them as goals for which they will work, you will be well on your way toward success. For that reason, it may be wise to select goals that are attractive and also to try to sell them as worthwhile to your pupils. In addition, in many courses, pupils have a good notion of what learning they would enjoy and profit from most. Research indicates that pupil participation in the selection of objectives can be highly motivating. Knowing the goals set for courses and having good feedback concerning one's progress toward these goals are strong motivating devices. When the pupils know clearly what they are supposed to do, and why, and can see that they are making progress, they will usually try. That is why, if teachers set clear behavioral objectives that seem reasonable, pupils will accept them as their own objectives and work toward them.

Suggested Reading

Clark, D. Cecil. *Using Instructional Objectives in Teaching.* Glenview, Il.: Scott Foresman, 1972.

Grambs, Jean Dresden, and John C. Carr. *Modern Methods in Secondary Education,* 4th ed. New York: Holt, Rinehart and Winston, 1979, chap. 7.

Gronlund, Normal E. *Stating Objectives for Classroom Instruction,* 3d ed. New York: Macmillan Publishing Co., 1985.

Kibler, Robert J., Donald J. Cegala, Larry L. Barker, and David T. Miles. *Objectives for Instruction and Evaluation.* Boston: Allyn & Bacon, 1974.

Lorber, Michael A., and Walter D. Pierce. *Objectives, Methods, and Evaluation for Secondary Teaching.* Englewood Cliffs, N.J.: Prentice-Hall, 1983.

Martin, Barbara L., and Leslie J. Briggs. *The Affective and Cognitive Domains.* Englewood Cliffs, N.J.: Educational Technology Publications, 1986.

Popham, W. James, and Eva L. Baker. *Establishing Instructional Objectives.* Englewood Cliffs, N.J.: Prentice-Hall, 1970.

Tanner, Daniel. *Using Behavioral Objectives in Classroom.* New York: Macmillan, 1972.

Thompson, Duane G. *Writing Long-Term and Short-Term Objectives, A Painless Approach.* Champaign, Il.: Research Press, 1977.

Exercise Answer Key
Exercise 3 A

If you understand the principle that a behavioral objective is one that describes pupil terminal behavior, the answers to this exercise become obvious.

Objective 1 is a behavioral objective. Understanding is a kind of behavior and, in this case, understanding that slavery was the basic issue that brought about secession is the terminal behavior the teacher expects of the pupils.

Objective 2 is not a behavioral objective. It is a description of a concept. It does not describe terminal behavior.

Objective 3 is not a behavioral objective. It describes teacher behavior rather than pupil terminal behavior. It is more a teaching procedure than an objective.

Objective 4 is not a behavioral objective. It is a topic or title. It is not an objective of any type.

Objective 5 is a behavioral objective. It describes what the pupils will be able to do at the end of the lesson; it describes the pupils' terminal behavior.

Objective 6 is also a behavioral objective. Understanding is a kind of terminal behavior. The objective is very broad, but it is still behavioral.

Objective 7 is a behavioral objective. It describes pupil terminal behavior somewhat more specific than that described in Objective 6.

Objective 8 is also a behavioral objective. It is similar to Objective 7 except that it uses the present tense to describe the pupil terminal behavior.

Objective 9 is a behavioral objective. The terminal behavior described is vague and general, but it is terminal behavior.

Objective 10 is not a behavioral objective. Rather, it is the title of a topic. It describes no behavior of any kind.

Objective 11 is not a behavioral objective. It is not an objective at all, but a description of the teaching procedure to be used.

Objective 12 is not a behavioral objective. It is a title of a topic. It describes no behavior and no objective.

Exercise 3 B

According to our thinking, in this list Objective 2 is very general, Objective 1 is quite general, Objective 3 is fairly specific, and its subordinate objectives are more specific. Do you agree?

Exercise 3 D

Following are our answers to the exercise. Do you agree? We have indicated in parentheses the subheads of the taxonomy as listed in Table 3-1 under which we think the objective falls, to show our reasoning.

1. 6 (6.20)
2. 4 (4.10)
3. 5 (5.30)
4. 5 (5.20)
5. 5 (5.10)
6. 2 (2.20)
7. 2 (2.10)
8. 3 (3.00)
9. 1 (1.23)
10. 5 (5.20)

Exercise 3 E

Of this list, *apply, compute, create, define, demonstrate, design, explain, identify, know, outline, predict, select, solve, state, summarize* are overt action verbs. The others, *appreciate, comprehend, enjoy, know, understand,* describe covert behavior. Remember the verbs in this list, which verbs are overt "action" verbs, and which describe covert behavior. The information may come in handy later on.

Exercise 3 F

The parts of Objective 1 are (a) you; (b) will write a 500-word account of the battle between the forces of Gondor and its allies against those of Mordor and its allies, as related in *The Lord of the Rings;* (c) completely from memory; (d) this account will be accurate in all basic details and include all the important incidents of the battle.

The parts of Objective 2 are (a) the pupil; (b) will be able to read the schedule; (c) given an interurban bus schedule; (d) well enough to determine.

Exercise 3 G

Of the ten sample objectives you should have concluded (a) that items 2, 9, and 10 are unequivocally criterion-referenced; (b) that items 6, 7, and 8 are also criterion-referenced although the criteria, *usually, accurately, quickly,* and *unhesitatingly,* are subjective and liable to interpretation; (c) that items 4 and 5 are not criterion-referenced (unless the writer means that the goal is 100 per cent errorless performance); and (d) that items 1 and 3 are not criterion-referenced and therefore presumably items 1, 3, 4, and 5 are simple behavioral objectives.

Post Test

1. In the following, mark the overt behavioral objectives B; the covert objectives, C; other objectives, D; and items that are not objectives, X.
   (C) **a.** The pupils will realize that Romanticism was and is sentimental. C
   (B) **b.** You will be able to read altitudes by the use of contour lines on a topographical map. B
   (D) **c.** To encourage pupils to be neat and accurate in their work. X C
   X (B) **d.** To discuss the reasons for the Protestant Reformation. X B
   (X) **e.** In this course we will examine the great works of Renaissance art. X
   (C) **f.** An appreciation of modern music. C
   X (C) **g.** To cultivate the scientific attitude. C
   (B) **h.** The pupils will be able to type at least thirty words a minute with no more than five errors. C-R D B

2. Of the following, mark those verbs that describe covert activities A; those that describe overt behavior, B.

_A_ a. Appreciate. A   _A_ b. Comprehend. A
_B_ c. Define. B   _B_ d. Estimate. B
_B_ e. Identify. B   _B_ f. Organize. B
_B_ g. Predict. B   _A_ h. Realize. A
_A_ i. Recognize. A   _B_ j. Solve. B
_A_ k. Understand. A   _B_ l. Write. B

3. Which of the following are general objectives? Which are specific objectives? Mark the general objectives G; the specific objectives S.

(S) a. You will be able to speak French well enough to carry on a simple conversation.

(G) b. The pupil will develop salable vocational skills.

(S) c. Given an appropriate sample of verse, the pupil will be able to identify the alliteration in it.

(G) d. The pupil will appreciate the role economics plays in our national life.

(S) e. The pupil will be able to define ionization.

(S) f. The pupil will be able to convert yards to meters.

? G (S) g. The pupil will speak correct idiomatic English.

4. Which of the following objectives are covert? Which are overt behavioral objectives? Mark the covert objectives C; the behavioral objectives B.

(c) a. The pupils will realize the contributions of the various ethnic groups. C

(c) b. The pupils will enjoy listening to good music. C

(B) c. You will be able to identify correctly the tools in an ordinary woodworking laboratory.

(B) d. The pupils will be able to use the card catalog easily and accurately.

5. Check (√) each complete criterion-referenced objective in the following list.

(   ) a. You will be able to write a summary of the plot of *The Wife of Bath*.

(✓) b. Given a diagram of an internal combustion engine, the student will be able to label at least 80 per cent of the components.

(✓) c. You will be able to list the steps for troubleshooting a Tecumseh motor without error.

(✓) d. Given a right triangle with the length of sides indicated, the student will specify the sine of one of the acute angles as a fraction in four out of five cases.

6. Rank the following in correct order from lowest to highest mental processes according to the Bloom taxonomy.

(4) a. Analysis. 4

(3) b. Application. 3

(2) c. Comprehension. 2

(6) d. Evaluation. 6

(1) e. Knowledge. 1

(5) f. Synthesis. 5

Kn
Comp.
App
An
Sy.
Ev

Multiple Choice. Place the letter of the best answer in the space provided.

(C) 7. What is the major relationship between general and specific objectives?
    a. A general and specific objective is necessary for every lesson plan.
    b. General objectives must be written as overt behavioral objectives; specific objectives should not be.
    c. Specific objectives should always support a general objective.
    d. Specific objectives should be written as descriptive objectives; general objectives should not be.

(d) 8. Descriptive objectives are most useful for describing
    a. Drill objectives.
    b. Performance objectives.
    c. Specific lesson objectives.
    d. General aims and goals.

(b) 9. The purpose of the taxonomies, according to the module, is to point out
    a. proper teaching strategies.
    b. levels to which instruction should aspire.
    c. standards for curriculum improvement.
    d. standards for pupil evaluation.

(a) 10. Covert objectives describe
    a. unobserved terminal activity.
    b. terminal behavior.
    c. performance standards.
    d. terminal pupil competencies.

11. The following is a list of elements that may or may not appear in objectives. Mark elements that according to the module may appear in (1) behavioral objectives, B; (2) covert objectives, C; (3) affective objectives, A; (4) psychomotor objectives, S; (5) cognitive objectives, X; (6) criterion-referenced objectives, R. Note: Each element may appear, probably does, in more than one type of objective.
    ( ) **a.** Who will perform the behavior (activity). 1 – 2 – 3 – 4 – 5 6
    ( ) **b.** The behavior (activity) to be performed.
    ( ) **c.** The standard of performance to be accepted.
    ( ) **d.** The conditions under which the behavior (activity) will be performed.
    (a) **e.** The purpose of the behavior (activity).

12. Define a criterion-referenced behavioral objective.

    Specifies the performance level expected

13. Give two arguments for using behavioral objectives.

    They provide a clear objective for ones teaching.
    "   " definite basis for evaluation.

14. Define terminal behavior.

The behavior expected of the learner at the end of the instruction period.

15. What is a covert objective?

One in which the learner cannot be directly observed to tell if they learned.

16. What is the value of a taxonomy of objectives?

Provide a framework to which you can structure your important parts of your teaching.

17. A complete criterion-referenced objective consists of four parts. What are they?

Who? Does what? How well? Under what conditions

18. What fifth part is usually added to an affective objective?

For what purpose

19. It is sometimes recommended that objectives in the affective domain not be written as overt behavioral objectives. Why not?

It is impossible to observe activity directly in the affective domain.

20. Of what value are descriptive objectives?

General aims & Goals

21. What relationships should specific objectives have to general objectives and goals?

specific objectives should support general objectives & goals

22. A broad objective, such as to understand the scientific method, is called a _____ objective.

General Objective

23. Planners sometimes write objectives as infinitive phrases; sometimes as statements describing the learning product (the skill, concept, attitude, appreciation, or ideal to be learned); sometimes as covert objectives, and sometimes as overt behavioral objectives. Which of them is preferable for specific objectives according to this module?

Behavioral objectives usually are best.

Indicate the taxonomic category level of each of the following.

24. The student will be able to play the piano well enough to perform professionally.

#5- Perfection & maintenance of the psychomotor domain.

25. The student shows concern about racial injustice by his treatment of others.

#3 — Valuing of the affective domain

26. When listening to a debate, the student can distinguish between valid and invalid arguments.

#4 — Analysis of the cognitive domain

27. The student will be able to describe the meaning of the web of life.

#2 Comprehension of the cognitive domain

28. The student shows his love of fine literature by his choice of recreational reading.

#3 Valuing of the affective domain

29. The student will be able to read and interpret the stock market reports.

#2 Comprehension of the cognitive domain

30. Given the topographic map of an area, the student will be able to identify the drainage system of the district.

#3 Application in the cognitive domain.

MODULE
4

Unit and Course Planning

Rationale
Specific Objectives
Module Text
  Units
    General Unit Planning Procedure
    The Ordinary Unit
      Preparing the Ordinary Unit Plan
    The Laboratory-type Unit
      Introductory Phase
      Laboratory Phase
      Sharing Phase
      Evaluating Phase
    Planning the Laboratory-type Unit
      Step 1. Selecting the Topic
      Step 2. Writing the Unit Objectives
      Step 3. Planning the Unit of Work
      Step 4. Preparing the General Study and Activity Guide
      Step 5. Preparing Special Study and Activity Guides
      Step 6. Developing a Scheme for Evaluation
      Step 7. Preparing a List of Readings for the Students' Use

Rationale

This module deals with the planning of units and courses. It will show how to carry out the two essentials of planning—determining suitable goals and objectives, and selecting learning activities that will accomplish these goals and objectives—at the unit and course levels.

Unit and course planning have a much greater scope than lesson planning. A course plan lays out the objectives, content, and organization for a whole year or semester. Unit plans lay out the objectives, content, and organization for course subdivisions of several weeks' duration. They set forth the major goals toward which the instruction will be directed. Lesson plans, on the other hand, lay out only the daily objectives and activities by which the teachers hope to bring about the learning that makes up the course or unit objectives. For this reason the direction and validity of the specific immediate objectives and content of daily lesson plans are determined by the general goals and content outlined in the unit and course plans. In short, unit and course planning determines pretty much what students should study in their daily lessons and what the impact of the entire curriculum should be, while the specific objectives and procedures of the daily lessons lead to the ultimate achievement of the long-term goals of the unit and the course. So while lesson planning sets forth what teachers and pupils will do in their daily sessions, unit and course planning determines the overall learning.

Specific Objectives

It is expected that at the completion of the module you will be able to explain and demonstrate the procedures for building effective units and course plans, and for carrying out teacher-pupil planning. Specifically you should be able to:

1. Identify the four types of units described in this module.

2. Describe the distinguishing characteristics of each of the four types of units.
3. Describe the procedures for planning each of the four types of units.
4. Explain what considerations one should keep in mind when selecting (a) goals, (b) activities, (c) content, (d) materials, and (e) evaluation procedures.
5. Describe the basic procedures of course planning.
6. Explain what is meant for a course to be psychologically organized.
7. Describe the five principles of course organization set forth in this section of the module.
8. Explain what steps one can take in course planning so as to increase the course's value for retention and transfer.
9. Describe a procedure for building a plan for a continuous progress course.
10. Describe how to conduct teacher-pupil planning in units and courses.

Module Text

Units

As a rule, courses are divided into units. Each unit is in effect a long assignment in which, for a period of several weeks, the instruction centers on a central topic, theme, or major concept. By centering on a theme or topic, units serve to organize the course into manageable divisions that bring cohesiveness and focus to pupils' learning. They facilitate the development of general principles and understandings and avoid the fractionalization and trivialization of course content that would result from a succession of unrelated lessons. They also serve to center the course on its important elements and to bring out the relationships between these elements. Course content divided into units is more usable and more meaningful than it would be if divided only into lessons. From our point of view, units can be organized in four basic ways:

1. An ordinary unit.
2. A true or laboratory type unit.
3. A learning packet or module.
4. A learning contract.

These are discussed in more detail later. Basically, however, an ordinary unit consists of a series of lessons centered on a topic, theme, major concept, or block of subject matter; a true or laboratory unit consists of a variety of learning experiences centered around long-term assignments rather than a series of separate lessons; learning activity packets are units designed for individualized, modulized self-instruction. Contracts are individualized unit plans in which students agree to carry out certain activities during the unit.

General Unit Planning Procedure
The steps for planning units are much the same for all types of units.

1. Select a suitable topic or theme. Often these are already laid out in your course of study or textbook.
2. Select the unit's general objectives. We recommend that the objectives be stated as an overview or rationale stating what the unit is about and a general description of what the students are to learn. However, they may be stated as descriptive or behavioral objectives as described earlier in Module 3.

When you plan these objectives we suggest that you:

   a. become as familiar with the topic and materials on the topic as you can;
   b. consult courses of study, curriculum guides, curriculum bulletins, and resource units for ideas;
   c. decide what you feel the pupils should learn from the study of the topic and how you should approach it;
   d. write out a general statement or overview in which you summarize what you hope the pupils will have learned about the topic at the completion of the unit;
   e. make sure that your unit objectives contribute to the course objectives.

3. Select suitable specific learning objectives. In doing so
   a. include understandings, skills, attitudes, appreciations, and ideals;
   b. be specific. Avoid vagueness and generalizations;
   c. use behavioral objectives whenever feasible;
   d. be sure that the specific objectives will contribute to the major learning described in your general statement or overview.

4. Lay out the instructional procedures by which you will teach the topics. These procedures will include the subject content and the learning activities. This may be set up as a series of lessons or as a unit of work. In either case no matter which approach you take, you will have to follow the same general steps in your initial planning.
   a. Gather ideas for learning activities that might be suitable for the unit. Refer to curriculum guides, curriculum bulletins, textbooks, and the like.
   b. Check these learning activities to make sure that they would actually contribute to the learnings that are your objectives. Throw out any activities that do not contribute directly to your goals.
   c. Check to make sure that the learning activities are feasible in your situation. Can you afford to give them the time, effort, and expense necessary? Do you have the necessary materials and equipment? Are they suited to the maturity level of your pupils?
   d. Check the resources available to be sure that they support the content and learning activities.
   e. Decide how to introduce the unit of work. Provide for introductory activities that will
      (1) arouse the pupils' interest;

     (2) inform the pupils of what the unit is about;

     (3) help you learn more about your pupils—their interests, their abilities, and their present knowledge of the topics;

     (4) show the relationship with preceding units and courses;

     (5) give pupils opportunities to plan what they will do during the rest of the unit.

  f. Plan developmental activities. Try to provide activities that will

     (1) keep up interest;

     (2) provide for individual differences;

     (3) develop the learnings cited in your specific objectives.

  g. Plan culminating activities. Try to include activities that will

     (1) summarize what has been learned;

     (2) tie together any loose ends;

     (3) apply what has been learned to new situations.

5. Plan for the evaluation of students' learning. Evaluating student progress should go on throughout the unit. Make plans to gather information in several ways: informal observation, pupil performance, paper and pencil tests, and so on. Be sure that your plan for evaluating the progress of your pupils is actually keyed to the specific learning products or terminal behavior that were your unit objectives.

6. Provide for the materials of instruction. Your units cannot function without materials. Therefore, you must plan for audiovisual materials, bibliographies, reading matter, reproduced materials, community resources, and the like long before the unit of work begins. Reading matter that is not available to the pupils is not much help to them, even if it is in your bibliography.

The Ordinary Unit

As we have seen, an ordinary unit is a series of lessons centered on a topic, theme, major concept, or block of subject. This series of lessons hangs together because the lessons are all aimed at accomplishing the unit objectives and because each of the lessons is related to the others. In this type of unit each lesson builds on the previous lesson by contributing additional subject matter, providing further illustrations, and supplying more practice or other added instruction, which, it is hoped, will bring about mastery of the knowledge and skills on which the unit is centered. Usually these lessons are teacher-centered, expository, and supplemented by student recitations, reports, projects, and the like.

Preparing the Ordinary Unit Plan. To prepare a plan for an ordinary unit is quite simple. The procedure consists of the following steps.

Step 1. Select a topic, such as Water, the Civil War, or Introduction to Equations. This should be easy to do as the topics for the course should already be laid out in your course plan.

Step 2. Select general and specific objectives that represent what you hope the students will learn about the topic. These unit objectives should be such that they contribute to the course objectives. As a rule, they are general in nature, pointing out the major concepts, skills, attitudes, and appreciations at which the unit is aimed. Specific objectives are usually reserved for lesson plans in this type of unit.

These general unit objectives may be stated as major concepts to be learned, e.g.,

Scientific methods are more accurate, reliable, and valid than other methods of study,

or as covert behavioral objectives, e.g.,

The students will realize the difficulties the pioneers faced as they moved westward,

or as infinitive phrases, e.g.,

To develop in students an understanding of the essential ingredients of a short story: plot, character, and ending, or as an overview or rationale such as these described in the discussion of the laboratory-type unit in the next section of this module.

Step 3. Concoct a sequence of daily lesson plans that will cause pupils to reach your objectives. You do not have to build the lessons in their entirety now, but you should note what you expect their content and procedure to be. These lessons make up the "procedure" of the ordinary unit. They include the following:

(1) Introductory lessons, i.e., lessons that tie this unit to the preceding ones, point out the objectives and reason for studying this unit, provide for preassessment and diagnostic activities, set the tone for the lessons to follow, and in general motivate the students.

(2) Developmental lessons, i.e., lessons that build the learnings that make up the unit objectives and content. In most ordinary units the learning activities in these lessons are largely of the teacher-centered expository type although not necessarily so. Small-group work, seatwork, discussion, practice sessions, and inquiry exercises may all be included in the lessons of the developmental section of the ordinary unit.

(3) Culminating lessons, i.e., lessons that tie together what has been learned in the developmental lessons and clinch the learning. These may include teacher recapitulations, review lessons, student reports, and other similar activities, and usually end in a teacher-built unit test.

Step 4. Decide on any major activities, projects, or other assignments, e.g., field trips, written assignments, and the like, and incorporate them in your lessons.

Step 5. Provide some sort of scheme and instrument(s) to evaluate student progress. Usually this includes the teacher-built unit test mentioned earlier. Since the purpose of the unit test is to determine how well the students have mastered the unit's content, the test questions are based on that content. Successful completion of this test indicates that the students are ready to move on to the next unit.

Step 6. Provide for the necessary materials of instruction.

Exercise 4 A

Try out the steps just outlined for practice. Imagine yourself invited into a classroom to substitute for a while. Pick some topic in your major subject that you especially like. Outline a sequence of daily plans that you think would be adequate for that topic.

The Laboratory-type Unit

A laboratory-type unit, sometimes called a true unit, differs from an ordinary unit in that it is much more cohesive and, at the same time, allows for much more individualization. Most of the teaching takes place in an individualized, problem-solving, laboratory fashion rather than in daily lessons. The bulk of the teaching is of the inquiry rather than of the expository type so that during much of the unit the student is more seriously engaged in active personal research than in listening to the recitation of the teacher. In such a unit not all the activities and experiences are required of each pupil. Some of them are, but in addition there are a number of optional activities that pupils can choose to do, or not, as they please in view of their interests, needs, and goals. The required activities or experiences we call *core* or *basic activities*. The optional activities we call *optional related activities*. In this type of unit the pupils do a considerable amount of the planning themselves. So that they can have freedom to proceed at their own speed and in their own direction, the pupils are provided a study guide that allows them to begin and to carry out activities, under supervision, without being tied to the teacher. The following description of a unit in action may clarify what teaching via the laboratory unit approach encompasses.

A Laboratory Unit in Action

Mr. Jones teaches Problems of Democracy at Quinbost High School. In his course outline he has listed a unit on minority groups. Mr. Jones always tries to make his course interesting and challenging, stimulating and motivating to his students. On the day he was to begin the unit, he came to the classroom seemingly in an angry mood, tossed his books on the desk, and glared at the class. He then began a tirade on a particular minority group, telling the class of something that a member of this group had done to him the day before, and concluding by saying that all members of that particular group were alike.

Immediately, his class began to challenge him, disagreeing, telling him he was unfair to generalize about one incident and that he shouldn't talk like that. Seizing upon this reaction, Mr. Jones then asked the class whether or not they had ever expressed such feelings toward any group. As the animated discussion continued, the class members began to see what the teacher was doing. Almost as one body they said that they wanted to discuss minority groups as a class topic.

The stage had been set! The teacher had fired their interest; the students' desire to study the topic was keen, He, then, set the class to discussing what subject matter should be discussed and what outcomes there should be. This led to general teacher-pupil planning. Soon pupils were choosing committees and projects on which to work. Then, with the aid of study guides and their committee and project assignments, individual pupils completed tentative plans for their roles in the unit.

The study guide they used consisted of three parts:

1. The first part noted questions and problems for which everyone was to find answers and also suggested where the pupils might look to find these answers.

2. The second part listed a number of readings and activities that the pupils might find interesting. All were expected to do some of these, but no one had to do any particular one. These activities were optional. In none of these activities or the required problems and questions was the pupil held to any prescribed reading or procedure. All he was asked to do was to carry out the activity, solve the problem, or find the information; he had free choice of ways and means.

3. The third part of the study guide was a bibliography.

Once the teacher and pupils had finished the planning, they began to work. Except for two periods that Mr. Jones used for motion pictures, the next two weeks were devoted to laboratory work. The committees met; the researchers investigated; the pupils carried out their plans.

Then the committees and researchers began to report. Some of the groups presented a panel discussion. Another group presented a play. Another conducted a question-and-answer game. In all of these activities pupils tried to bring out what they had learned. In between these reports, Mr. Jones and the pupils discussed the implications of the findings and other points they thought pertinent and important.

Finally, the unit ended with everyone's setting down his ideas concerning the treatment of minority groups, and with a short objective test, based on the teacher's objectives as shown in the questions of the study guide.[1]

Thus, after a little over three weeks, the unit was finished.

A close examination of this unit will show you that it was actually divided into four phases. First, Mr. Jones introduced the unit to his students and tried to "fire their interest" in it. Second, the pupils worked individually and in small groups in laboratory fashion. Third, the committees and individual researchers reported on what they had accomplished and discussed their findings. Finally, Mr. Jones tried to assess the pupils' growth by means of evaluative devices and evaluative procedures. These four phases we shall call (1) the introductory phase; (2) the laboratory phase; (3) the sharing phase; and (4) the evaluating phase. They may appear in order or they may not. When a unit is successfully individualized, all the phases of the unit may be going on at once.

Let us now consider the role and procedure for each of these phases.

Introductory Phase. In the introductory phase your purpose is to get the unit off to a good start. If your introductory activities work well, they should arouse

---

[1] Leonard H. Clark and Irving S. Starr, *Secondary School Teaching Methods,* 4th ed. (New York: Macmillan Publishing Co., 1981), p. 144.

the pupils' interest; inform the pupils of what the unit is about; help you learn more about your pupils, their interests, their abilities, and their present knowledge; show how the unit relates to earlier units and courses; and provide an opportunity for the pupils to plan how they will study the unit. The introductory phase of the unit should be well done because it sets the tone for the whole unit. A bright, breezy, stimulating start may make all the difference. Therefore, the teacher should strive to find introductory activities that will challenge the pupils' curiosity, arouse their interest, and set them to thinking. Since it is expected that pupils will plan their work cooperatively, the teacher must see to it that the pupils have the necessary backgrounds. Introductory teacher talks, moving pictures, recordings, and tapes may give pupils just the orientation they need. For the actual planning of their own activities, probably the best method is to give out a study and activity guide or list of possible activities and let the students choose and organize for themselves under your guidance. Once they have decided what to do, individual pupils could fill out a plan such as that shown in Figure 4-1.

Laboratory Phase. During the laboratory phase, the pupils carry out the plans they have made, both the required activities and the optional activities they have selected. Most of the work in this phase is done individually or in small groups, at the pupils' own speed and in his or her own way. Nevertheless, the teacher reserves class time for whole class activities that may be necessary or seem advantageous. Sometimes, pooling and sharing activities are interspersed through the laboratory phase. During this phase, most of the pupils' direction for carrying out their learning activities comes from their study and activity guides and from special study guides provided for optional related activities. Although the pupils will not all do the same activities in the same way during the laboratory phase, the pupils will learn the same things, the learning products set forth in the objectives. For this reason, the required activities are usually set up as problems that all pupils must attempt to solve in one way or another, and the optional activities are related to them. In this way, pupils should achieve the same objectives even though they do not read or study the same books or solve the problems in the same way.

NAME _____ CLASS_____

UNIT _____ DATE _____

Activities I plan to do

Committees I plan to work with

Materials I plan to read

Things I plan to make

FIGURE 4-1 *A Form for a Work Plan*

Sharing Phase. The pooling and sharing of experience phase consists of opportunities for pupils to pool what they have learned. This does not mean a series of reports although there should be some reporting. Since the activities have all been aimed at the same set of objectives, the pupils' learning should have much in common. Therefore, there should be much meat for group discussion and debate on the problems in which pupils pool their ideas and share what they have found out. In addition, the pupils might share their experiences through panels, dramatizations, demonstrations, exhibits, class newspapers, jury procedures, and similar techniques.

Evaluating Phase. Effective teachers evaluate continually, as we have said. Nevertheless, the end of the unit makes an excellent occasion for taking stock. At this point, the teacher needs to know how well the pupils have done so as to estimate the success of the unit, to prepare for whatever remedial follow-up seems necessary, and to move smoothly into the next unit. To be of most practical value, the measurement devices you use in the evaluation should be diagnostic.

Planning the Laboratory-type Unit

When you plan a unit of the laboratory type you must provide for the following elements:

1. Introduction, including topic, time duration, course title, grade level, justification, and place in the course or curriculum.
2. The general objective, often written as an overview or rationale, telling what the unit is about and what pupils are expected to learn.
3. The specific objectives, skills, understandings, attitudes, ideals, and appreciations it is expected that the pupils will learn. These should be expressed as learning products or as behavioral objectives. Current opinion seems to favor behavioral objectives.
4. The unit of work or unit assignment, the required and optional related activities in which your pupils engage. Frequently, these activities are categorized as introductory activities, developmental activities, and culminating activities. The introductory activities are used, of course, in the introductory phase, the developmental activities in the laboratory and sharing phases, and the culminating activities in the sharing and evaluating phases. Note that the activities of the sharing phase can be either developmental or culminating. Culminating activities are activities that tie things together and bring the unit to an end in high style. Activities in which pupils pool and share experiences and learning are excellent for this purpose; so is an end-of-unit test. The idea is for the unit of work to start with a bang and end with a boom. A calendar scheduling when various activities and films are to occur is a handy tool for implementing the unit of work.
5. The study and activity guide, which will contain the instructions for carrying out the core activities to be done individually and in small groups.
6. Special study and activity guides, which contain the instructions for carrying out the optional related activities and special activities, such as field trips.

7. Procedures and instruments for measuring and evaluating pupil progress and the success of the unit. These should adequately test both the general and specific objectives.
8. A list of readings for the pupils to use.
9. A list of the materials needed.
10. A short bibliography for the teacher's use.

Some teachers also include an outline of the subject matter content. In order to provide for each of these elements adequately, it is recommended that you use the following procedure.

Step 1. Selecting the Topic. As we have seen in the discussion of the ordinary unit, the topic of the unit is, for all practical purposes, the name of the unit. It is usually a section of subject matter, but it might be a problem or a theme. Ordinarily, it is one of the topics in the sequence already outlined in the course plan. To be usable it should (a) center around some major understanding, problem, issue, or theme; (b) fit the course objectives and further the course plan; (c) be relevant to pupils' lives and to the society in which they live; (d) be manageable, not too difficult, too big, or too demanding of time and resources; and (e) be suitable to pupils' abilities and interests.

Step 2. Writing the Unit Objectives. The general objective can be written as an overview describing the major concept that the pupils should learn. For example, the overview for Mr. Jones' unit on minority groups was that:

> *Every citizen should understand what our minority problems are. Citizens should analyze their feelings about different minority groups. All should evaluate the contributions of each of these groups to the development of America. We must try to understand the importance of cooperation among all the groups.*

Other examples of unit overviews follow.

> *Overview: The learning products sought for each pupil are (1) the ability to make a screwdriver involving the use of those common hand tools peculiar to the machine shop; the ability to operate the engine lathe, drill press, and milling machine with the dividing or indexing head; (2) some understanding and appreciation of the source, characteristics, and properties of tool steel (water quench), machinery steel, and hard maple from the standpoint of the consumer; (3) some understanding and appreciation of the place of the metalworking industry in present-day civilization from the standpoint of materials and processes employed, products produced, and the effect of these materials, processes, and products on the worker and on the consuming public; and (4) some understanding and appreciation of the work performed by those employed in a variety of occupations in the metalworking industries and related shops from the standpoint of the opportunities and requirements for employment in these industries.*

Overview: Well-written adventure stories appeal to seventh-grade readers because of their exciting, suspenseful plots, their heroic characters, and interesting settings.

The purpose of the overview or general objectives is to give the unit a focal point (examples of overviews can be found in the rationale sections of many of the modules in this series). In addition, the general objectives section of the unit should list the general skills, attitudes, appreciations, and ideals that it is hoped pupils will acquire from studying the unit.

The specific learning products may be written as descriptions of the concepts, attitudes, or skills to be learned, for example

Concept to be learned—The guilt for starting World War I was shared by many nations;

but they are probably best written as behavioral objectives, as in the following example:

Behavioral objectives—The pupils will be able to determine the perimeter of (a) triangles, (b) squares, (c) rectangles, (d) parallelograms, (e) trapezoids, and (f) general polygons.

The important concerns are that the specific objectives must contribute to your larger goal, and that they must be specific enough and clear enough for you, the teacher, and the pupils to understand what the objectives are. In addition, the objectives must be achievable in the time allotted and with the resources available; be worthwhile in the eyes of the pupils and, in fact, be neither too difficult nor too easy to achieve; and allow for differences in pupils' abilities, interests, needs, and goals. Teachers seem to find it helpful to list the different categories of specific objectives (concepts, skills, appreciations, attitudes) separately. Note that in this type of unit the specific objectives cannot be relegated to lesson plans as in an ordinary unit.

Step. 3. Planning the Unit of Work.   Once the objectives are ready, it is time to prepare the plan for the unit of work. The first step in this procedure is to identify potentially good activities. To gather activities that might be useful, search curriculum guides, curriculum bulletins, textbooks, books on teaching in the field, and professional periodical literature. Then the activities must be culled. Are they really suitable for the objectives? If not, can they be adapted so as to make them suitable? Are they feasible in view of the time, material equipment, and other resources available? Are they worth the time and effort? Are they too difficult or too easy? Which will do the job best? At this point, it would be good to check the resources available and list them. The list should include audiovisual media, library resources, equipment, and supplies. It is embarrassing after concocting elaborate plans to find that you don't have the materials and supplies you need.

Now divide the activities into two categories: those that should be required of all pupils and those that should be optional. In each unit there should be enough optional work to give every boy and girl a chance to do something he or she can enjoy and do well.

Next decide how to introduce the unit. Try to find introductory activities that will tell the pupils what the unit is about and arouse their interest. If you intend to have pupils cooperate in planning, include cooperative planning in your introductory activities.

Next plan the developmental activities and culminating activities. These should include (1) provisions for committee and individual problem-solving laboratory types of work; (2) opportunities for pupils to share what they have learned with each other; and (3) whole class activities, such as films, guest speakers, field trips, and teacher talks. Schedule activities that need scheduling for definite, even if tentative, times. In your scheduling, remember to allow pupils enough time to complete both their required and optional work.

Then prepare a study guide for the pupils to follow during the laboratory phases when they are working alone or in small groups. In addition to using this study guide in the laboratory phase, the pupils will find it helpful in the introductory phase for their personal planning. Finally, plan how you will evaluate the pupils' work. Build tests, quizzes, rating scales, and other instruments and devices that you will need in your evaluating.

The following is an excerpt from the plan for a unit of work designed for the industrial arts unit for which the overview was presented during the discussion of Step 2 earlier in this module.

Unit of Work: (Tentative time allotment is five forty-four-minute periods per week for five weeks. Four periods each week are given to manipulative and observational experiences in the machine shop; one period each week to witnessing demonstrations, listening to brief lectures and illustrated talks, participating in discussions, and in other forms of individual and group activity in the industrial arts related laboratory.)

  A. Introduction: Illustrated lecture, discussion, test, and demonstration.

   1. Explain the threefold nature of the unit study: (a) to learn how to make a useful and practical screwdriver from both wood and steel in preparation for doing more advanced work which permits the learner to select, under the guidance of the instructor, those projects which best meet immediate and anticipated needs of the students; (b) to learn about the various branches of the metalworking industry, related industries, and their services to society through readings and through visual aids, such as the films, "The Tool and Diemaker," "The Drama of Steel," "Grits That Grind," "Magnesium," and "Files on Parade"; (c) to learn how to buy and care for the tools and products of metalworking and related industries.

   2. Demonstrate the correct and safe use of each tool and machine in the elementary situations in which the pupils will use it.

   3. Give a test of multiple-response, completion, matching, and identification questions to discover what the pupils already know about the meanings and insights to be developed.

   4. Hand out the "List of Readings and References" and activity guide (Job Breakdown) for the Screwdriver Ferrule, and explain the uses of the list of readings and references and the more detailed activity guides (Job Breakdowns) to follow.

B. Laboratory work.
　*1. Make a useful screwdriver with a wooden handle as per assembly print to be furnished by the instructor.
　　*a. Study the sample screwdriver, completed component parts, and the assembly print submitted by the instructor, and develop the necessary working detail sketches, scale of two to one, of the screwdriver ferrule, blade, and handle. (Ask the teacher for a special study and activity guide showing good sketches and giving suggestions for making them.)
　　*b. After the sketches for the screwdriver have been completed and initialed by the instructor, prepare a bill of materials needed for making the project. (Ask the teacher for a special study and activity guide for making out a bill of materials.) Figure how much the article will cost to produce. Get the teacher's approval on your bill of materials and estimated cost.
　　*c. Select and cut to length on the power hacksaw the stock which you will need for making the screwdriver. (Ask for the special study and activity guide.)
　　*d. Machine the stock to overall finished length and break all sharp edges. (Ask for the special study and activity guide or breakdown.)
　　*e. Machine and fabricate screwdriver ferrule and blade to blueprint (B/P) specifications. (Ask for the special study and activity guides or job breakdowns.)

Step 4. Preparing the General Study and Activity Guide. The purpose of the general unit study and activity guide is to give the pupils the information they need to do the required activities and to select the optional activities they want to pursue. The activities should be largely of the problem-solving or inquiry type. The instructions should be explicit enough so that the pupils can guide themselves through the activities without undue dependence on the teacher. They are useful because they give the pupil (1) a source to which he can refer if he forgets his assignment; (2) a picture of what activities he might want to do so that he can pick his choice of activities and the order in which he wishes to do them; (3) a definite assignment so that he can go ahead to new activities on his own without waiting for a new assignment from the teacher; and (4) definite instructions that should eliminate misunderstandings about assignments and excuses for incomplete or unattempted assignments.

Following are excerpts from a general study guide accompanying the unit on adventure stories for which the overview was presented earlier in this module.

> *1. Read Jack London's story, "The Lost Poacher" (1:312–321). [Read pages 312–321 of the first reference appearing at the end of the study guide.] What chance has "Bub" Russell to become a hero in the eyes of his mates? What makes a person a hero? Study the questions appearing in 1:380–381[2] as a basis for class study.*

---

* All items marked with asterisks will be made part of a general study and activity guide or job breakdown.

[2] These references are keyed to the Bibliography furnished with the study guide. The number preceding the colon refers to a book; the numbers following the colon are the page references.

3. *Read Jeannette Eaton's story of David Livingstone's life (1:176–186). As you read, think how Livingstone's life differs from that of "Bub" Russell. If you could change places with either of these people, which would you prefer to be? Write a short paragraph explaining why. Be prepared to discuss the story using the questions appearing in the study guide.*

5. *Read "Old Slewfoot" from* The Yearling *by Marjorie Kennan Rawlings (2:109–120). What sort of person is Penny to the other people and animals in the story?*

6. *Prepare an adventure poem to recite to the class as a committee. Part of the poem might be recited in chorus. Examples of poems your committee might recite are "Casey at the Bat," "Clara Barton," "The Cremation of Sam McGee," and "The Highwayman." Be prepared to show why the selection is a good adventure poem.*

8. *Read "Treasure," by Mark Twain (1:65–75) and "Mafatu Stout Heart," by Armstrong Sperry (1:91–100). Which had the more exciting existence, Mafatu or Tom Sawyer? Back up your answer with evidence from the story.*

10. *Read "One Minute Longer," by Albert Payson Terhune (1:240–249). How does the author build suspense in this story?*

11. *Read Stephen Meader's "Escape from the River of the Wolves" (1:250–260). Notice how the excitement is carried through the story. How does the author maintain this excitement?*

Step 5. Preparing Special Study and Activity Guides. The study and activity guides you prepare do not need to follow any particular form. Just be sure that they explain to students how to carry out the study or activity concerned. Some of the things you might want to include in a special study or activity guide are:

The purpose of the activity.
Background information.
Directions for carrying out the activity.
Exercises and drill material.
Fact and/or problem questions.
Problems to solve.
Suggested readings.
Self-correcting tests and exercises.
Follow-up activities.

Following are examples of special study guides for a discussion and a record.

Sample Special Study Guide

12th Grade Social studies.
Factors in the consideration of Means and Ends.

1. Can necessity create its own law?
2. Can "ends" be judged without previous standards of judgment?
3. Who decides, or how is it decided, that an "end" is good?
4. Are the "means" employed toward marking an "end" good?

5. When is necessity "real," when is it "imagined"?
6. Can we separate 'means' from 'ends'?
7. Are the "means" to be judged before or after the "ends" are achieved?
8. Is the question of the "ends" justifying the "means" for both individuals and states?
9. Do the means determine the ends?
10. Does the pinch of necessity preclude any national consideration of means?
11. How do we consider degrees of 'necessity'?
12. How can we determine whether some "ends" are better than others?
13. Are certain types of "means" and "ends" peculiar to specific aspects of society?
14. Are certain 'means' improper, criminal, etc., even when they are not employed?
15. Can "means" and "ends" ever be considered amoral?
16. Is law only a fact when it can be enforced?
17. Can evil "means" be employed toward a good "end"?
18. How can we evaluate abstract ends?
19. How is the concept of what constitutes an "end" to be reached?
20. Can "ends" exist independent of the individual?[3]

Listening Questions for The Phoenician Traders

1. What seems to be the major business of the Phoenicians?
2. What seems to be the relationship between Tyre and Carthage?
3. What can you learn about the trade routes of the Phoenicians?
4. What was life like on a caravan?
5. What can you note about Phoenician ships and seamanship?
6. What did you learn about Phoenician trade? How did they carry it on? How did they keep accurate accounts and so on? In what way did they trade?
7. How nearly accurate is the reconstruction of Phoenician life? If you do not know, how can you find out?
8. Prepare a list of questions that would emphasize or bring about the important idea expressed in this recording.[4]

Step 6. Developing a Scheme for Evaluation. Because the evaluating of pupil progress must take place continually throughout the unit, it is necessary to incorporate evaluating procedures and devices into the unit of work. Reports, papers, classwork, and progress tests are among the types of activities that make up this continual evaluation. In addition, probably each unit should culminate in a diagnostic test. Such a culmination will help tie together the various threads in the unit and reveal how well you have achieved your teaching goals. It is essential for determining what you should do next.

---

[3] From a Cheltenham (PA) 12th Grade Social Studies Unit.
[4] These questions are illustrative of the type of questions one might use in a special study guide for use with this record. They represent different levels and types of questions. In using such study guides one must guard against merely mechanical exercises.

Step 7. Preparing a List of Readings for the Students' Use. Here you should list the important references for the students' study. Number the works listed so that they may be keyed to the exercises, problems, and other activities listed in the unit of work or unit assignment. Check to be sure the readings are available. This list should be duplicated and issued to the students for their own use.

Step 8. Deciding and Noting Down What Instructional Materials Will Be Needed. Long before the unit of work begins, it is essential that you know both what audiovisual materials, reproduced material, community resources, and the like you will need, and that these materials will be available. In some instances information concerning necessary materials and their availability should be attached to the students' study guide.

Step 9. Preparing a Special Teacher's Bibliography. Here note down references that you might find helpful for reference, information, ideas, and the like, as the unit proceeds. This list is for your use, not the students'.

The Learning Activity Packet

A learning activity packet (also called a learning packet, learning activity package, or instructional packet) is designed for independent, individual study. It consists of instruction, references, exercises, problems, self-correcting materials, and all the other information and materials that a student needs to carry out a unit of work on his own. Consequently, students can work on learning packets individually at their own speed and different students can be working on different packets at the same time. Students who successfully finish a packet can move on to another unit without waiting for the other students to catch up. Such packets are essential ingredients of continuous progress courses. To prepare a learning activity packet, you should follow about the same procedures as for other types of units. The principal difference is that the learning packet is designed for independent, individual self-instruction. The process consists of the following five basic steps:

1. Assuming that the course has already been divided into a sequence of topics or modules as described in the following section, the first step is to set up the module objectives. The process is essentially the same as in any other unit. The general objectives can be presented as an overview, commonly called the Rationale, in which you give a general description of (a) the terminal behavior to result from studying the module; (b) why anyone should study the module; (c) the relationship of the module to other modules and courses; and (d) any other information that you think necessary for the pupils' orientation and motivation. The specific objectives are usually expressed as behavioral objectives. They may be either simple or criterion-referenced, depending upon your preference and the exigencies of the situation. They, of course, should be pertinent to the general objectives. Because these objectives will be used by the students as guides in their studying, it is usually helpful to write these goals in the second person, as follows:

At the conclusion of your study of this unit, you should be able to construct a learning packet with reasonable ease and effectiveness.

At the end of this module, you should be able to locate the principal oceanic streams on the globe.

2. Select the content activities to be included in learning packets. These include all the readings, problems, and exercises that the pupil will do in the module. Take care that the activities and content are pertinent to the goals.

3. Develop a plan for evaluating the pupil's progress. Ordinarily this plan should include self-correcting tests—pretests, progress tests, and post tests. The pretest can be used by pupils to ascertain their present strengths and weaknesses, what they know and what they do not know. They can also be used by pupils to prove that they have already learned what is in the module and so should be excused from studying it at this time. The progress tests can be used by pupils to evaluate their progress as they move through the module. The post test can be used to measure the students' final progress. Probably this should be a teacher-corrected, criterion-referenced test to be practical in the middle and secondary schools. Some teachers make provisions by which the pupils can check off each of these behavioral objectives when they have mastered the required behavior.

4. Prepare the instructional materials to be used in the module.

5. After you have developed and gathered together all the materials described in steps 1 through 4, prepare and run off the study guide. The purpose of the study guide is to orient the pupils and give them the directions they will need to work independently. It should make clear to the pupils what they are to learn, why they are to learn it, what they should do to learn it, where to find the materials they need to learn it, and finally how to judge how well they have learned it. To that end it should include
   a. The topic.
   b. The rationale prepared in step 1.
   c. The specific objectives prepared in step 1.
   d. Directions for carrying out the activities selected in step 2. These directions should include:
   (1) General directions: agenda, time limits (if any), and options.
   (2) Specific directions: that is, the directions and explanations for specific activities. For example,
      (a) Problem to be solved: What the problem is, what the background of the problem is, what requirements must be met to solve the problem successfully.
      (b) Reading: Purpose of the reading, what information is to be learned, what is to be done with the information, questions on the reading, exact citations.
      (c) Information to be learned.
   (3) Where to go for materials and information.
   e. Bibliography.

6. Finally, assemble the entire learning activity packet. It should include
   a. The study guide.
   b. The instructional materials that you have prepared for the module. (These may be included with the study guide or distributed separately.)

c. The self-correcting and other testing and evaluating materials. These should include a pretest, a post test, and perhaps an intermediate progress test or two. Note, however, that teacher-corrected mastery tests should be distributed separately as needed, not in the original packet. Mastery tests should be administered separately under supervision and corrected by the teacher. Progress tests are more useful when they are self-correcting.

Planning a Learning Contract

The contract is another variation of the unit. The procedure for a plan for a contract is about the same as that for any other unit except that in the learning contract plan the pupil agrees to fulfill certain requirements during the unit.

The basic procedure for planning a contract is as follows:

1. Set up objectives and activities whereby pupils may achieve the objectives.
2. Decide what activities will be required.
3. Decide which activities will be optional.
4. Decide what the unit requirements will be.
5. Provide a written study and activity guide describing the activities.
6. Let each pupil decide how to meet the requirements.
7. On the basis of these decisions have the pupil make out a contract in writing.

All contracts involve an element of *quid pro quo*. Some contracts are simply pupil-teacher agreements of what the pupil must do and the teacher accept for satisfactory completion of the unit. Other contracts have a marking agreement built into them. The sample contract shown as Figure 4-2 does not contain such an element. It could be made to do so by adding the requirements for a certain mark. (Figure 4-3).

Another system for planning a contract is to decide what activities and quality of work will be required for each of the grade levels A, B, C, and D, and to specify these requirements on the study guide. For example:

```
                          CONTRACT

Jacques C.                              To be completed by Nov. 1

    During the unit, I will
        Read Chapter III of the text.
        Do the problems on Worksheet A.
        Participate in the panel on the Panama Canal.
        Pass the unit test.
        Demonstrate that I can perform all the requirements in Group C.

                          signed    PUPIL

                          approved   TEACHER
```

FIGURE 4-2 *A Sample Contract*

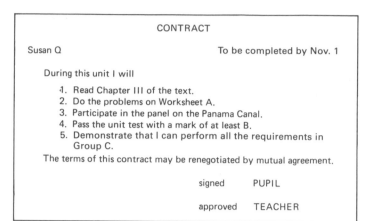

FIGURE 4-3   *A Sample Contract*

To pass with a D, you must complete activities 1–10 and pass the post test.

For the grade of C, you must complete activities 1–10, receive at least a C on the post test, and do two optional related activities satisfactorily.

For the grade of B, you must complete activities 1–10 plus perform four of the optional related activities very well, and receive a grade of at least B on the post test.

For a grade of A, you must complete activities 1–10 plus perform six of the optional activities excellently, and receive a grade of at least B on the post test.

Planning the Course

The responsibility for what goes on in your course is yours as teacher. In some schools, as you know, you will be provided with courses of study, syllabuses, and curriculum guides that provide suggestions concerning course objectives, content, sequences, procedures, and materials of instruction. In some schools, you may be expected to give pupils a major role in charting the course. In others, you will be left alone to cope as best you can. No matter which policy the school follows, the responsibility for the course and what the pupils learn from it is still yours.

Even when the course plans are rigidly laid out by the school authorities, it is the teacher who determines what is really taught. As teacher, you determine emphases, interpretations, and methods of presentation. It is also you who adapts the course so that it suits the pupils. You put your stamp on the course by such procedures as changing the unit sequence, modifying the time to be spent on topics, using different teaching methods, supplementing the prescribed content, and providing for individualized projects and papers. Even such a simple thing as the way you field questions makes a difference in what you teach in your course.

This section will discuss some of the principles of course planning and a procedure for planning a course.

Basic Principles

The procedures for planning a course are not difficult. In general, they consist of the following basic steps:

1. Determine the overall course goals (what it is you hope the pupils will learn) and principal supporting objectives.
2. Determine what content to incorporate into the course in view of your objectives. This step includes selecting the topics to be studied, arranging them into an appropriate sequence, and deciding how much emphasis to place on each topic.
3. Decide how much time to spend on each topic.
4. Determine your approach including basic strategies, major assignments, references, texts, and so on, in view of the goals and topics you have selected.
5. Determine procedure for assessing student attainment of course objectives.

In carrying out these steps one should keep in mind several important principles:

1. The course should be psychologically organized.
   a. Its organization should be based on the nature of the pupils and how they learn.
   b. It should pick up pupils at their own levels of maturity and be relevant to their present needs, interests, and concerns.
   c. It should allow for the differences in pupils, recognizing that pupils do not all have the same needs, interests, and concerns. Neither are an individual's needs, interests, and concerns constant. Consequently, effective teachers not only try to select topics that have intrinsic interest for the pupils, but they also try to provide variation for individuals within the topics by providing ways in which pupils may skip, add, or substitute topics if it should seem desirable.
   d. It should be selective. It does not try to cover all of the subjects, which no course could really do, but it includes the content most valuable and relevant to the student and to the course goals, and leaves out content not necessary for those purposes.
   e. It should encourage the development of logical memory as opposed to rote memory, skill in the use of the tools of learning, and the ability to think and solve problems.
   f. It should use a combination of both vicarious and direct learning experiences in proportions suitable to the ability levels of the learners. Ordinarily, younger, less able, less experienced, and less sophisticated pupils will profit more from direct experiences, and older, more able, more experienced, and more sophisticated students learn well from vicarious experiences, such as lectures and reading. In any case, the course does not limit itself to book learning.

2. The course should be compatible with the resources available. If you do not have, or cannot get, the things you need to carry out your plans, they will be fruitless.
3. The course content organization and approach should be selected because of their value in securing transfer and retention. Unless the content stays with the learner and can be used by him in new situations, it is not of much value. Retention and transfer are most likely when
    a. The learner sees the value of the learning and how to use it in other situations and the learning situation is similar to the using situation.
    b. The learning is thorough.
    c. The learning is reviewed by frequent use in which the learner applies what has been learned and adds the new learning to previous learning.
    d. The learner draws generalizations that help point out the application of the learning to new situations.

    Effective teachers try to plan courses that meet these conditions.
4. The course content, organization, and instructional approaches should contribute to achieving the course objectives. This is such an obvious requirement that it seems hardly worth repeating, but teachers often ignore it. You must plan your course so that it contributes to your objectives. For example, if your objective is to create skill in writing, your course must give plenty of practice in writing. Practice in reading may be excellent for some things but it cannot take the place of writing if the goal is excellence in writing. It is surprising how much course content has nothing to do with what the teachers claim to be their objectives.
5. The course content, organization, and teaching strategies must reflect the nature of the discipline or subject matter. Not all subject matter can be learned in the same way. The structures of disciplines, and portions of discipline, differ. In planning courses, it is necessary to respect these differences and to reflect the structures of the disciplines we teach in the organization of our courses and the strategies for teaching them.

Selecting the Goals

In many school districts, the course goals are established by the school authorities in a course of study, curriculum guide, or syllabus. When this is true, the teacher should make use of the goals provided. But even so, you must think out what it is you would like the pupils to learn. It may be that you want them to master certain subject matter and believe that other subject matter is relatively expendable. Or it may be that you believe the most important goal should be the development of certain skills or attitudes. The important thing is that you should know *what you want the pupils to learn* and *why you want them to learn it.* All too often what we teach in school has little value to the learners. (This fact has always been true; the Roman philosopher Seneca complained about it in Nero's time.)

Your overall course goals should be, and of necessity will be, quite general. This is not the time to make up specific objectives, although some general objectives may refer to rather specific criteria. Specific objectives should be used for the planning of units and lessons. What form the course goals should take is not so very important at this point, either. Whether or not they should be behavioral or criterion-referenced is a matter for your individual decision. Ordinarily, general descriptions of the learning will suffice.

Following are a few examples of course objectives gleaned from courses of study:

Advanced Biology II

Objectives:
1. *To achieve a working knowledge of the skills, mental and physical, necessary to perform scientific experimentation safely and correctly.*
2. *To learn the use of statistical analysis in the study of experimental results.*
3. *To learn the use of scientific literature when attempting to solve problems.*
4. *To achieve a deeper knowledge in some areas of biology studied in previous courses.*

Creative Writing I

A. *To learn to tighten sentence structure.*
B. *To learn to use concrete sensory words.*
C. *To express feelings about experiences.*

French III

To develop reading and writing skills (in French) to the point that the student can read and write anything he or she can express orally.

Latin I

To develop the ability to recognize, define, and use English derivations from Latin encountered during Level I.

Exercise 4 B

Examine the course objectives listed. How much guidance does each give the teacher who is about to plan the sequence of topics, subject matter content, and instructional approaches?

Examine some courses of study. What are the objectives? What objectives would you think most desirable for these courses? Specify what you consider to be the ten most important general concepts that pupils should learn in a course you might teach.

For a course in your major field, decide exactly what the course objectives should be.

Planning the Sequence of Topics

After you have decided on the objectives for the course, it becomes necessary to select the basic content and teaching approaches. Probably the best way is to outline the content and divide the course into broad topics that you expect can be covered in two to four weeks. Then arrange these topics into a logical, psychological sequence and allocate the amount of time to be given to each. At this time you should also decide on the general teaching approach you expect to use for the topics. This is important because your teaching approach may make a considerable difference in the amount of time you will need for teaching the topic. In setting up the time schedule for the course, you should give yourself a leeway of ten days or so to allow for assemblies, examinations, storms, miscalculations, and so forth. You should also decide on any major assignments, such as term papers and projects, so that you can provide time for them in your calendar.

Of course, the basic criterion in deciding the sequence of topics and approaches is whether or not they contribute to the course objectives. You must also consider other criteria such as transfer value, interest level, and relevance. These topics are, in effect, the titles of the units that will make up the course.

As a neophyte you will find that you need assistance in setting up a sequence of topics. You can usually find all the assistance you need in courses of study, curriculum guides, syllabuses, teacher's manuals, and textbooks. A Wisconsin teacher's manual for a single semester senior high school psychology course, for instance, outlines the following sequence of units with commentary on how each should be taught.

I.	The Science of Psychology	2 weeks
II.	Learning	3 "
III.	Understanding Human Behavior	3 "
IV.	Patterns of Behavior	3 "
V.	Mental Health	4 "
VI.	Family and Small Group Behavior	2 "
VII.	You and Society	1 "

Some schools and districts do not provide outlines or, if they do, do not suggest time allocations in them. If you do not have such an outline provided by your own school or district, do not hesitate to consult the courses of study of other school districts. Another aid is the table of contents of a good textbook. Following a textbook has the advantage of giving you a carefully built structure on which to lean until you become more expert and confident. If you select to go this route, however, you should remember that all the topics (chapters or units) included in the text are probably not equally important and that to follow a text too closely reduces your chances to make your course creative, flexible, innovative, and relevant to your pupils' needs. It seldom pays to "marry" the text. If you find that you have to plan this way at first, you should try to divorce yourself from it as soon as you can. It is particularly important to remember that it is not necessary to cover everything just because it is in the text. Remember, *to cover everything in a subject is impossible.*

You should also keep in mind that all course plans are of necessity tentative. Therefore, make your plans in outline. You can and should fill in the details later when you plan your units. However, if you plan to order films or similar aids, you ought to have firm dates in order to get them when you need them.

Exercise 4 C

Map out a sequence of topics for a course in your major field. Be sure that (a) all the topics necessary for fulfilling your course objective are covered; (b) enough time is allocated for each topic (assume a

180-day school year); (c) the sequence of topics makes sense logically and psychologically.

Take your time with the assignment. It may take some juggling before it satisfies you. Then have your friends criticize it. Will it really do what you want it to do?

Continuous Progress Course Planning

In continuous progress courses pupils continue through courses at their own speeds and according to their own needs. A pupil who finishes a module is free to go on to another; a pupil who is having trouble with a module may keep at it even though other pupils move on. Pupils who demonstrate that they have already mastered the content of a module may be excused from that module; students who demonstrate they need more help may be steered into additional modules in the area in which they need help. In short, continuous progress courses provide a mode for individualizing pupils' course work according to their demonstrated abilities and needs.

The only difference between preparing a continuous progress, individualized course and an ordinary course is that when preparing the continuous progress course one must divide the course into modules and give the pupils self-instructional packets or learning activity packets so they can guide their own learning. The procedure we recommend for teaching such courses is as follows:

1. Divide the course into modules and try to make the modules of fairly equal length.
2. Prepare behavioral objectives with standards of competence performance.
3. Prepare a learning activity packet for each module. As we have already stated, each packet should contain (1) the rationale for studying the module; (2) the objective of the module stated as behavioral objectives; (3) the materials necessary for pupils to have as they work on the module, or directions for getting the materials and equipment needed; and (4) the directions they need to carry out the activities called for in the module.
4. Prepare a plan for evaluating the pupils' learning for each module. This plan should provide for pretests, progress tests, and final mastery tests. Provisions should be made so that pupils can "test out" of modules or parts of modules in which they are already competent.
5. Set pupils to work on their modules in laboratory fashion.
6. Supervise the pupils as they work on the modules.
7. Determine when the pupils are ready to move on from one module to another. Pupils who fail to achieve the standards of performance in the mastery test should be asked to restudy the module and take another mastery test until they can meet the standard. For this reason each pupil should take a diagnostic pretest before beginning a module. Note that the mastery tests should be criterion-referenced but do not need to be written tests. Often performance tests are more satisfactory. Note also that in many instances there is no need for pupils to follow the same sequence. Pupils may be allowed to select which module they will do and when they will do it, as long as you agree that their selection is a reasonable one that will allow them to meet the criteria set by you in step 2.

Work with individuals as they progress through the module. Pupils should not have to stand around waiting to find out what they should do next; neither should they have to struggle along trying to do work they do not understand. When pupils need help, they should get it! Consequently, plan to give all your class time to supervising and guiding while pupils are working on the modules. In order to save time, it may be helpful to gather pupils who are having the same or similar problems or who are doing the same activities in a particular module for small group instruction.

In such a sequence, pupils can work through the modules at their own speed, selecting or omitting modules, under guidance, as seems most desirable. This freedom makes it possible for each person to have, in effect, an individual course of study.

Teacher-Pupil Planning

Pupils should enter into the planning of units, lessons, and courses. But no matter how much pupils enter into planning, the responsibility for the plan is the teacher's.

There are two approaches to teacher-pupil planning. In the first approach the teacher does the basic planning, but provides options for the students who then plan their own work by selecting those options they will undertake. The simplest form of the pupil option approach is the standard practice of encouraging pupils to select and carry out, in their own way, projects, reports, outside reading, and similar independent activities. Another version of this approach is the type of unit plan in which pupils must select what they will do from a study guide that lists required and optional activities. In the second teacher-pupil planning approach, the class participates in the formulating of the original plan. They may go as far as to select the goals, the content, the procedures, the sequences, and the materials to be studied, although usually they do not have that large a role. There are also various combinations of these two approaches.

Whichever plan you use, you should approach teacher-pupil planning cautiously. Pupils should not be expected to take on their planning role without instruction and practice. We recommend that you introduce it gradually. The following briefly describes the sort of procedures you might take in introducing teacher-pupil planning to your class.

Begin teacher-pupil planning slowly. Start off by such minor questions as, Would you prefer to have the test on Monday or Tuesday? or, Which story would you like to read next? or by letting pupils select which activities they prefer from a list of activities. Another beginning approach to teacher-pupil planning is to issue study guides that call for pupils to plan and complete their learning activities in laboratory fashion.

After these types of beginning you can gradually increase the pupils' roles in planning units. At first the pupils might be encouraged to set up their personal learning objectives and plans for achieving their objectives. Later pupils might work together to plan unit goals, content, and learning activities and to establish standards for their own work until finally they are ready to take major responsibility for unit and course planning. If you carry out the introduction of teacher-pupil planning in a step-by-step fashion and show pupils how to carry out each step before going on to the next, you have a right to expect gratifying results.

Teacher-Pupil Unit Planning

The laboratory unit approach to teaching allows pupils to do a considerable amount of their own planning. In laboratory learning pupils decide which of the options they will elect, what activities they will do first, what groups they will join, and so on.

Some teachers have been very successful with almost entirely teacher-pupil planned units in which the pupils decide with the teachers' help what they want to learn, what materials to study, what activities to include, and how their learning should be evaluated.

This approach is illustrated by the following description of a class, planned and conducted almost entirely by pupils in a Massachusetts high school. In this school, the teacher was working with a preselected unit prescribed by the course of study. The teacher also had carefully worked out an overview and objectives. In her introduction, she asked the pupils to develop the kind of things they would like to learn about most in the unit. On the basis of this discussion, a list of problem questions was drawn up and the class was divided into committees to prepare a bibliography of available material for use in answering the various questions. The committees then proceeded to investigate the topics and to prepare plans for reporting their findings and conclusions. For a few meetings, the class met as a club with a pupil presiding to make decisions about the scheduling and reporting phase of the plan. An ad hoc committee, selected by the pupils in their club meeting, worked out the details. Each committee planned its own reporting technique in accordance with the general plan proposed by the ad hoc committee and approved by the class. After the presentations, the class discussed them both as to technique and to content.[5]

Notice that in carrying out this process the teacher made ample use of discussion techniques. The class began with a discussion of what the pupils would like to learn; then the pupils discussed how to learn it and in discussion laid out a plan for the learning activities, and finally the group decided through discussion what procedures should be adopted for the scheduling and reporting phase of the unit. Discussions of this sort can be very productive, but until pupils become expert in the process, they will need much guidance by the teacher.

When you attempt to build units in this fashion, we suggest you keep in mind these five major steps recommended by Zapf. The steps and criteria for judging the excellence of their execution are as follows:

> 1. *A clarification of the limits of choice.* How far am I, the teacher, able and willing to carry out pupil-teacher planned procedures? What are the subject-matter limits? What are the procedural limits? Must I use a text-book? How much freedom in the use of a text do I have? Do the pupils understand these limits?

---

[5] Leonard H. Clark, *Teaching Social Studies in Secondary Schools: A Handbook* (New York: Macmillan Publishing Co., 1973), pp. 60–61.

2. *Establishment of criteria for topic selection.* Did the pupils have a major part in establishing the criteria? Are the criteria developed for a previous problem still satisfactory? How can they be improved so that better choices will be made? Are they being used?

3. *Development of a list of possible problem areas.* Was every pupil involved in building the list? Is it representative of the pupils' concerns? Has every item that pupils feel to be important been included? Have the items been checked against the criteria? Were the suggested topics discussed by the class with respect to possible specific problems for study, and to opportunities for activities such as field trips, hand work, etc.? Has the list been organized so that topics that belong together have been placed under common headings?

4. *Selection of one or more problem areas.* Did the method of choice focus attention on the values of the problem areas? Were the available resources checked before final choices were made? If a single area was selected, was the decision reached by consensus rather than by majority vote?

5. *Definition of problem.* Were all group members involved in the process of stating the problem? Is the statement of the problem broad enough to cover the major items the group wants to know, but specific enough to limit the study to a particular part of the entire topic area?[6]

Teacher-Pupil Course Planning

Courses can and should be planned cooperatively by teachers and pupils. The following outline illustrates how Zapf's five-step procedure might be used in the cooperative planning of a course in *Problems of American Democracy.*

1. Begin by introducing the pupils to the course and to the notion that it is to be planned cooperatively.
2. Set up limits, e.g.,
   a. The course will be limited to major problems of the United States, particularly problems having to do with government.
   b. We may consider any topics that really concern the class as long as these topics are important problems of American democracy, and the resources for studying them are available.
   c. School regulations require that during part of the year certain aspects of local and state government must be studied.
3. Set up criteria for selection of the topics, e.g.,
   a. Conduct buzz sessions in which each buzz group makes a short list of criteria to present to the class.
   b. Conduct a whole class session in which all the criteria recommended by the groups are listed on the chalkboard and discussed.

[6] Rosalind Zapf, *Democratic Processes in the Secondary Classroom* (Englewood Cliffs, N.J.: Prentice-Hall, 1959), p. 197. Copyright © 1959. Reprinted by permission of Prentice-Hall, Inc., Englewood Cliffs, N.J.

    c. By common consensus, develop a final list of criteria.

4. Select the topics, e.g.,
   a. For homework, pupils individually make lists of the topics they would like to suggest.
   b. In class discussions, the pupils decide on a list of topics.
   c. Before the class makes its final choice, committees should check the availability of materials for the various topics proposed, and compile a bibliography.
   d. Choices should be made by consensus. Never take a formal vote, if you can help it, before a consensus of opinion seems evident; if you do, you can split the group into armed camps or be forced to accept a topic palatable to only a bare majority.

5. Use a similar plan to select specific areas to be studied in the various units, e.g.,
   a. Have pupils make lists of what they would like to learn about. You will have to give them help, because they may not know enough to realize the possibilities. These can be listed as a series of questions from which pupils can choose the areas they particularly wish to learn. At this point, it is very important for you to help the pupils fix clearly in their mind what they are trying to do. If their understanding of their task is not clear, probably the understandings they glean from their study will not be clear either.
   b. Use discussion and consensus procedures to make the final selections.

Exercise 4 D

Turn back to the example of cooperative teacher-pupil unit planning. Prepare an outline of the steps the teacher used in her procedure.

Now outline a plan for using teacher-pupil planning procedures for a unit in a course you might teach.

Suggested Reading

Alcorn, Marvin D., James W. Kinder, and Jim R. Schunert. *Better Teaching in Secondary Schools*, 3d ed. New York: Holt, Rinehart and Winston, 1970.

Berenson, David H., Sally R. Berenson, and Robert R. Carkhuff. *The Skills of Teaching: Content Development Skills*. Amherst, Mass.: Human Resource Development Press, 1978, Chaps. 2, 3–4, and 5.

Gayles, Anne Richardson. *Instructional Planning in the Secondary Schools*. New York: David McKay, 1973, Part IX.

Grambs, Jean D., and John C. Carr. *Modern Methods in Secondary Education*, 4th ed New York: Holt, Rinehart and Winston 1979, Chap. 7.

Henson, Kenneth T. *Secondary and Middle School Methods*. Minneapolis, Minn.: Burgess Publishing, 1987.

Hoover, Kenneth H. *The Professional Teacher's Handbook*, abridged 2d ed. Boston: Allyn & Bacon, 1976, Chap. 3.

Lorber, Michael A., and Walter D. Pierce. *Objectives, Methods, and Evaluation in Secondary Teaching.* Englewood Cliffs, N.J.: Prentice-Hall, 1983.
Meyen, Edward L. *Developing Instructional Units for the Regular and Special Teacher,* 3d ed. Dubuque, Ia.: Brown, 1980.
Stewart, William J. *Transferring Traditional Unit Teaching.* Boston: American Press, 1982.
———, *Unit Teaching: Perspectives and Prospects.* Boston: American Press, 1983.

Post Test

Place the letter of the "best" answer in the space provided.

(*a*) 1. In an ordinary unit one would expect to find, according to this module,
    a. A series of lessons centered on a topic.
    b. A laboratory plan.
    c. A contractual agreement between teacher and pupil.
    d. A packet of learning materials.

(*a*) 2. According to the module, a true unit differs from an ordinary unit in that it
    a. is more cohesive and allows for more individualization.
    b. does not provide a scheme for pupil evaluation.
    c. sets up wider general objectives.
    d. does not provide optional activities.

(*d*) 3. In preparing the objectives for a unit, what types of objectives would be acceptable?
    a. Criterion-referenced objectives.
    b. Covert objectives.
    c. Simple behavioral objectives.
    d. Any or all of the above.

(*d*) 4. In a true unit all pupils must engage in the required activities
    a. at the same time.
    b. in the same way.
    c. in sequence.
    d. as need and interest dictate.

(*d*) 5. In the laboratory phase of the unit students engage in
    a. individual activities.
    b. small group activities.
    c. whole class activities.
    d. any or all of the above.

(*a*) 6. Which of the four unit plans discussed gives pupils the least freedom?
    a. Ordinary unit.
    b. The true unit.
    c. The learning activity packet.
    d. The contract.

(*b*) **7.** To introduce cooperative teacher-pupil planning to your classes it is recommended that you
  a. run a wide-open class from the very first.
  b. initiate teacher-pupil planning in small steps.
  c. do not interfere with pupils' planning; let them learn from their mistakes.
  d. start with a discussion in which you plan the course objectives.

(*c*) **8.** Zapf lists five steps for teacher-pupil planning, including which of the following?
  a. First make clear to the pupils that the selection of topics is their decision without restrictions.
  b. Select the topics by majority vote.
  c. Set a clear limit of choice.
  d. Set up a committee to decide the sequence of topics.

(*b*) **9.** Ultimately, who decides what is actually taught in a course?
  a. Pupil.
  b. Teacher.
  c. Principal.
  d. Superintendent of schools.

(*c*) **10.** In a psychologically organized course
  a. the course sequence is based on the structure of the disciplines.
  b. the course covers the subject.
  c. the course allows for differences in pupils.
  d. the course centers around direct experiences as opposed to vicarious experiences.

(*d*) **11.** To give the course transfer value you should
  a. provide complete coverage of the subject.
  b. provide for much extrinsic interest.
  c. provide variation by giving pupils opportunities to skip, add, or substitute topics.
  d. provide opportunities for applying the learning to new situations.

(*a*) **12.** The basic criterion for selecting unit topics is
  a. whether or not they contribute to course objectives.
  b. whether or not they are interesting.
  c. whether or not they have transfer value.
  d. whether or not they follow logical course organization.

Short Answer

13. In preparing the objectives for an ordinary unit, what types of objectives should you use, general or specific?
_____ *both* _____

14. Is it necessary to set up a time schedule when planning a unit?

yes

15. Should a plan for an ordinary unit contain provisions for tests and other major assignments?

yes

16. Should the specific objectives for the true unit be written as statements describing the learning products or as behavioral objectives?

Either

17. Name four criteria for the topic of a unit.

Is it pertinent to the course
It centers on some major underlying theme or topic
It is relative to the students lives & the communities
It suits the students interests & abilities

18. What are four criteria for good, specific unit objectives?

They contribute to the general obj. of the unit
They should be clear to you & to the students
"   "   " specific enough
They should be & seem worthwhile.

19. Ordinarily, what type of activities would you hope to find in the introductory phase of a unit?

Planning activities
Activities that tie in rest of the course
"   " motivate

20. Do all the required activities in the unit have to be done by all pupils
  a. at the same time?
  b. in the same way?

_no_
_no_

21. What is the principal difference between a learning packet and a laboratory unit?

LAP's are designed more for, the individual learning

22. What are the essential differences between writing objectives for a unit and a learning packet; for a unit and a contract plan?

None

23. What is the simplest way to set up a learning contract in a contract plan?

List the obj— then have the student decide which level they are going to shoot for.

24. What would you expect to find in a study guide for a laboratory unit?

Problems to solve
Activities to do
Directions for finding info
Optional related activities to choose from
Info concerning readings & materials

25. What would you expect to put in a learning packet you constructed?

Specific objectives
Directions for carrying out the activities
Rationale for carrying out the obj.
Materials needed & how to obtain them
Measuring Devices, tests etc.

26. What are the five principles one should keep in mind when carrying out the steps for course building, according to this module?

The course should be psychologically organized
"   "   should be compatible with available resources
The course plan should lend itself to retention & transfer
"   "   should reflect the discipline.
Everything should contribute to the cost course objectives

27. According to this module there are five basic steps in planning a course. What are they?

Determine the objectives

" " content.

Decide on the time allotment

Determine strategies, assignments & materials

28. Unless a course plan facilitates pupils' retention and transfer of what is studied in it, it will be unsuccessful. In general, what can you do in planning the course to aid retention and transfer? You should be able to name at least three possibilities.

The value of the learning needs pointed out.
The ways the learning can be used should be pointed out.
There should be opportunities for renewal of
learning.

29. Outline the procedure recommended for building a continuous progress course.

Prepare overall course obj.
Determine the sequence of the modules
Prepare general & specific obj. for the modules
Select content & learning procedures for the modules
Prepare LAP for the modules.

30. Outline the procedure recommended for cooperative teacher-pupil planning of courses.

¹Set up limits – ²set up criteria for topic selection
³ Select topics.

MODULE
5

Lesson Planning

Rationale
Specific Objectives
Module Text
  The Daily Lesson Plan
    Assumptions
    Written Plans
    A Continual Process
    The Problem of Time
    The Plan Book
  Constructing a Daily Lesson Plan
    Components of a Daily Lesson Plan
    Control and Identification Data
    General Objectives
    Specific Objectives
    Content
    Key Point
    The Procedure
      Introduction to the Lesson
      The Lesson Development
      Conclusion or Culminating Activities
      The Timetable
    Materials to Be Used

The first edition version of this module was written by William J. Meisner, Jersey City State College. It has been revised and updated by the editors of this third edition.

Rationale

It is a rare teacher who can step before a class unprepared and yet teach effectively. Spur-of-the-moment teaching seldom results in forceful, meaningful, interesting, logically presented lessons from which students develop clear understanding of the knowledge, skills, or concepts underlying its inclusion in the curriculum. Such lessons require careful thought. The teacher must decide which aspects of the subject should be the focus of a lesson, how the topic is to be adapted to a particular audience, how the lesson will follow up on preceding lessons, and how a lesson will prepare students for lessons to come. Without careful attention to these matters, lessons tend to be dull and drift aimlessly.

This module is designed to acquaint you with the basic components and procedures necessary for developing effective lesson plans. It includes both examples and suggestions that should prove helpful. Ultimately, however, it will fall on you, as teacher, to adapt, alter, modify, and adjust these suggestions to meet the needs of your students and to find a lesson plan style that is comfortable to you and usable in your classroom.

Specific Objectives

Specifically, when you complete the module you will

1. Be familiar with the various formats for lesson plans.
2. Be able to explain the role of the daily lesson plan.
3. Describe the basic components of the daily lesson plan and their functions.
4. Construct a daily lesson plan.

Module Text

The Daily Lesson Plan

Good teachers are always planning. For the long range they are involved in the planning of the scope and sequence of courses, and the development of the content of courses. Within courses they develop units and within units they design the activities to be used and the tests to be given. They familiarize themselves with textbooks, resource materials, and innovations in their field. Yet, despite all this planning, the daily lesson plan is still the pivotal point in the planning process.

Assumptions

Not all teachers need elaborate written plans for every lesson. Sometimes skilled teachers need only a sketchy outline. Sometimes they may not need *written* plans at all. Old hands who have taught the topic many times in the past may need only the presence of a class to stimulate excellent teaching in a pattern of presentation that has often been successful before (although frequent use of old patterns may lead one into the rut of dull, unimaginative teaching).

It is apparent, therefore, that from the onset certain assumptions should be made about planning lessons.

1. Not all teachers need elaborately written lesson plans for all lessons.

2. There is no particular pattern or format that all teachers need to follow when writing out their plans.

3. Some subject matter fields and topics require more detailed planning than others do.

4. Some experienced teachers have clearly defined goals and objectives in mind even though they have not written them into lesson plans.

5. The depth of knowledge a teacher has about a subject or topic influences the amount of planning necessary for his lessons.

6. The skill a teacher has in following a trend of thought in the presence of distraction will influence the amount of detail necessary when planning activities.

7. A plan is more likely to be carefully plotted when it is written out.

8. All effective teachers have a planned pattern of instruction for every lesson whether that plan is written out or not.

You should keep these assumptions in mind as you consider your role in lesson planning.

Written Plans

Well-written lesson plans have many uses. They give one an agenda or outline to follow as one teaches a lesson. They give substitute teachers a basis for presenting real lessons to the class they teach. They are certainly very useful when one is planning to teach the same lesson in the future. They provide one with something to fall back on in case of a memory lapse, an interruption, or a distraction such as a call from the office or a fire drill. Above all they provide beginners security for, with a carefully prepared plan, a beginning teacher can walk into a classroom with the confidence gained from having developed, in an organized form, a sensible framework for that day's instruction.

For this reason, as a beginning teacher you should make considerably detailed lesson plans. Naturally, this will require a great deal of work for at least the first year or two, but the reward of knowing that you have prepared and presented an effective lesson compensates for the effort. Since most teachers plan their daily lessons no more than a day or two ahead, you can expect a busy first year of teaching.

Some prospective teachers are concerned with being seen using a written plan in class, as they think it may suggest that the teacher has not mastered the field. On the contrary, a lesson plan is a visible sign of preparation on the part of the teacher. It shows that prethinking and planning have taken place, and that the teacher has a road map to guide him through the lesson whatever the distractions. Most experienced teachers believe that there is no excuse for appearing before a class without evidence of careful preparation.

A Continual Process

Whereas experienced teachers may not require plans as detailed as those necessary for beginning teachers (after all, experienced teachers do develop shortcuts to lesson planning without sacrificing effectiveness), lesson planning is a continual process even for them, for there is a constant need to keep materials and plans current and relevant to present needs. Because no two classes are ever exactly the same, today's lesson plan most probably will need to be tailored to the peculiar needs of each class. Also as the content of a course may change, and as new developments occur or as new theories are introduced, your objectives and the objectives of the students, of the school, and of the staff will change.

It is for these reasons that lesson plans should be in a constant state of revision. Once the basic framework is developed, however, the task of updating and modifying becomes minimal. The daily lesson plan should be flexible and provide a tentative outline of the class period. A carefully worked out plan may have to be set aside because unforeseen circumstances, such as a delayed school bus, an impromptu assembly program, or a fire drill, interfere with its implementation. A daily lesson planned to cover six aspects of a given topic may end with only three of the points having been considered. These occurrences are natural in the school setting, and the teacher and the plans should be flexible enough to accommodate them.

The Problem of Time

The lesson plan should provide enough materials and activities to consume the entire class period. Since exact planning is a skill that only very experienced teachers master, it is wiser for the beginning teacher to over-plan rather than run the risk of running short. Beginning teachers may find that they have lost control of the class and that discipline problems are developing when the lesson plans do not provide enough activity to take up the class period. Students are very perceptive when it comes to a teacher who has finished the plan for the period and is attempting to bluff through the last ten minutes.[1]

---

[1] *Note:* Should you ever be unfortunate enough to get caught short, as most teachers do at one time or another, one suggestion that avoids embarrassment is to tell the class that you have completed all the *new* material planned for today, and now you would like to review the material considered during the past thirty minutes or past several days.

a. To develop an understanding of the reasons for the division between the strict constructionist and loose constructionist points of view at the Philadelphia Convention in 1787.

b. To appreciate the effect that the life-style of Edgar Allan Poe had on his writing.

c. To understand the differences between the laws of probability and random choice.

Specific Objectives

Specific objectives should briefly indicate the major aims of the daily lesson plan. Ordinarily these objectives should be specific enough for accomplishment within the class period, although sometimes the development of a specific objective must be stretched over several days. When writing them you should consider as outcomes, understandings, appreciations, attitudes, special abilities, skills, and facts. Both teacher and student objectives should be included. Frequently, specific objectives are stated in behavioral terms, but this should not preclude your striving for attitudinal change. There has been a great educational war raging for a number of years that has resulted in a swing toward behavioral objectives more easily measured by student performance than are the objectives that deal with attitude and opinion. You might consider your own philosophical bent when developing such specific objectives as the following:

a. The student will be able to add, subtract, multiply, and divide two-digit numbers using the slide rule. (Behavioral.)

b. The student will be able to identify the major internal organs of a common pond frog. (Behavioral.)

c. The student will appreciate the symbolism in Lord of the Flies. *(Covert, affective.)*

d. The student will understand the underlying cause of the Civil War as it relates to the stated causes. (Covert, cognitive.)

Setting specific objectives is a crucial step in any lesson plan. It is at this point that many lesson plans go wrong. Teachers say they intend "to cover the next five pages" or "to do the next 10 problems" and fail to focus on what their objective for asking students to perform these activities truly is. When you approach this step in your lesson plan, ask yourself "What do I want these students to learn from these lessons?" Your answer is your objective!

Content

To make sure that your lesson actually covers what you want it to cover, you should note down just what content is to be covered. This matter may be included in a separate section or combined with the procedure section. The important thing is to be sure that your information is noted down so that you can refer to it quickly and easily when you need to.

If, for instance, you are going to introduce new material, using the lecture method, you will want to outline the content. It should be noted here that the word *outline* is not used casually. You should not have pages of notes to sift through nor should you read declarative statements to the class. You should be familiar enough with the content so that an outline (in detail if necessary) will be sufficient to carry on the lesson as in the following example.

    I. *Causes of Civil War*
       A. *Primary causes.*
          1. *Economics.*
          2. *Abolitionist pressure.*
          3. *Slavery.*
          4. _____ .
       B. *Secondary causes.*
          1. *North-South friction.*
          2. *Southern economic dependence.*
          3. _____ .

If you intend to conduct the lesson through discussion, you should write out the discussion questions. For example:

    What do you think Golding had in mind when he wrote Lord of the Flies?
    What did the conch shell represent? Why did the other boys resent Piggy?

Since it is presumptuous to assume that you can remember all the aspects of a topic while in the midst of responding and reacting to student discussion, be sure that these aspects are well noted in your content. If there are opposing sides to topics, for instance, your plan should include the pros and cons of each in order to prompt student discussion as in the following example.

   III. *Capital punishment.*
        Pro
     A. *Deterrent.*
     B. *Saves money.*
     C. *Eye for eye.*

        Con
     A. *Not a deterrent.*
     B. *Rehabilitation.*
     C. *Morally wrong.*

Similarly, if activities such as debates or simulations are to be used, your plan should spell out the details of the activity as the following illustration shows.

   IV. *Simulation: War and Peace.*
     A. *Read directions.*
     B. *Break class into nation groups.*
     C. *Elect spokesman.*
     D. *Read directions for Phase 1.*
     E. *Begin Phase 1.*

Key Point

Not every lesson has a key point. Ask yourself if you had to select one thing in the lesson that you most want the students to retain, could you identify it? If not, then there is no need to include this component in the plan. On the other hand, if there is a key pivotal point around which the entire lesson centers, you may wish to identify it, not only for yourself, but for the class as well. This key point could be effectively used as an introduction or as a conclusion. It could also be emphasized in the content of the lesson. Examples follow:

> *Key Point:* Although there were many causes, primary and secondary, for the Civil War, the main cause for this as for all wars was economics.
> *Used as an introduction:*
> Today we shall see that. . . .
> *Used as a conclusion:*
> Today we have seen. . . .

The Procedure

The procedure is that part of the plan in which you set forth what you and your students will do during the lesson. Ordinarily you should plan the procedure portion of your lesson as an organized entity having a beginning, middle, and an end to be completed during the lesson. This is not always needed, because some lessons are simply parts of units or long-term plans and merely carry on activities spelled out in the long-term plans. Still most daily lessons need to include in their procedure

an introduction;
a development section;
a conclusion;
and probably a timetable.

Because a written lesson plan can serve as a ready reference, not only should the procedure section of your plan be written down, but it should be written in a format you can easily follow. Therefore, write down your lesson development so you can read it easily and quickly find the place. Usually this means to write large, and outline.

Introduction to the Lesson. Like any good performance, a lesson needs an effective introduction. In many respects the introduction sets the tone for the rest of the lesson. It alerts the class to the fact that the business of learning is to begin. If it is exciting, interesting, or innovative, it can create a favorable mood for the class. In any case, when well done it serves as a solid indication that you are thoroughly prepared. Although it is difficult to develop an exciting introduction to every lesson, there is always a variety of options available by which to spice up the launching of a lesson. You might, for instance, begin the lesson by briefly reviewing yesterday's lesson. This serves the twofold purpose of introducing today's work and reinforcing yesterday's. A second possibility is to review vocabulary words from previous lessons and to introduce new vocabulary. A third approach might be to review a concept developed in the previous day's lesson. Still

another possibility, is to use the key point of the same day's lesson as an introduction and then again as the conclusion of the same lesson. Examples follow.

> a. *"As we have seen by yesterday's demonstration, the gravitational
> pull on the earth's surface affects the tides . . . Today we will consider
> different types of tide. . ."*
> b. *"Johnny, what is meant by factor?" "Suzy, what do we mean when
> we say interpolate?"*
> c. *"We have seen that despite the claims of national unity, the period of
> the 1820s was actually a time of great regional rivalry."*

In short, you can use the introduction of the lesson to review past learning, tie
the new lesson to yesterday's lesson, introduce the new material, point out the
objectives of the new lesson, or, by showing what will be learned and why learning is important, induce in students a psychological set favorable to the new
lesson.

The Lesson Development.   The developmental activities make up the bulk of
the lesson plan. These are the activities by which you hope to achieve your lesson
objectives. They include activities that present students with information, demonstrate skills, provide opportunities to develop understanding and skill, and so
on. These activities should be described in some detail so that you will know
exactly what it is you plan to do. At this point generalities usually do not help.
Often teachers think that as long as they have determined the principal line of the
lesson development, they have done enough. Not so. Simply to decide that in a
certain lesson we shall "discuss the XYZ affair", for instance, will not be very
helpful. You will need also to know what principal points should be considered,
what key questions should be used, what sequence should be followed, and what
conclusions the discussion should focus on. Otherwise the class is liable to drift
aimlessly.

To be sure that plans for these activities are clearly laid out, ordinarily they
should be carefully written out. Again in some detail. This ensures that you have
a firm plan of action (too often plans that are not written out are only dreams
without substance), and it also serves as a reminder or reference. During the stress
of a class it is easy to forget details of your plan and of your subject. For this
reason it is wise to note the answers to the questions you intend to ask and the
solutions to the problems you wish your students to solve.

Conclusion or Culminating Activities.   It is as important to have a clear-cut
conclusion as it is to have a strong introduction. This activity should summarize
and bind together what has gone on in the developmental stage and drive home
the principal point. One way to do this is to restate the key point of the lesson.
Another is to briefly outline the major points of the lesson development. Another
is to repeat the major concept that was your objective. In any case, this concluding activity should be short and to the point.

The Timetable. To estimate the time factors in any lesson is difficult. A good procedure is to gauge the amount of time that you will need for each learning activity and note that time alongside the activity in your plan. For example:

Introduce film   10 minutes
  a. Why was Ghandi popular?
  b. What was Ghandi trying to do?
  c. Why were his methods successful?
Show film   25 minutes.

Another technique is to allocate time allotments to the various methods of instruction to be used. For example:

  a. Teacher introduction (10 minutes);
  b. Class discussion (15 minutes);
  c. Review (10 minutes);
  d. Go over homework assignment (5 minutes).

Do not, however, place too much faith in your estimate. Frequently beginning teachers find that their discussions and lectures do not last as long as was expected. In order to avoid being embarrassed by running out of material, try to make sure that you have planned enough work to take up the entire class session. If you plan too much, you can use it for the next day's class. Sometimes it is wise to plan an extra activity which you can use, if your lesson runs short. Also, of course, if your lesson runs short, you can spend some time on review, or on introducing the next day's lesson.

Materials to Be Used

This section of the plan is simply a reminder that you should have certain materials ready for the class. It is not a big task. Use it to remind yourself that, for instance, for this class you must obtain an opaque projector and certain pictures. There is no point in listing materials here that are already and constantly in your classroom. The purpose of this section of the plan is simply to make sure that you know what material you need for the lesson and have it ready when you need it. An example follows.

Materials: Opaque projector, pictures from Rise and Fall of Rome, *pp. 29, 47, 137, 540.*

Assignment

If a homework assignment is to be given, you should be certain to include it somewhere in your lesson plan. When to present it to the class is optional, except that it should never be an afterthought as the students are leaving. Some teachers prefer to place the assignment on the board at the beginning of the class and to draw the students' attention to it early. Some prefer to wait until the end. Either method is acceptable; however, doing it at the beginning of a class period minimizes the chance of your forgetting it.

Whether you decide to present the assignment at the beginning or end of the lesson, or at a propitious time during the lesson development, you should allow enough time to develop the assignment clearly and make sure that the students understand what they are supposed to do and how to go about doing it. In preparing the assignment you should make sure that it

a. is clear;
b. is definite;
c. is reasonable, neither too long nor too difficult;
d. gives the pupils background necessary for them to do it successfully;
e. shows the pupils how to do it sufficiently well so that they will not flounder needlessly;
f. provides for individual differences.

However, in the written plan usually it is necessary to include only a short notation concerning the assignment, e.g., *Assignment:* Read pp. 234–239, and answer questions 1, 5, 8.

Special Notes

We recommend that you leave a special place in your lesson plan for special notes and reminders. A good share of the time you will need no such reminders, but when you do, it helps to have a special place for them so that you can refer to them readily when they are needed. In this spot you can place reminders concerning such things as special announcements to be made, school programs, makeup work for certain students, and so on. They may, or may not, be important, but they do need to be remembered.

Evaluation

This component is reserved for the teacher to make any notes or comments regarding the lesson. It is particularly useful if you use the plan again. When you take it out the following year or two, it is unlikely that you will recall if the lesson was dull, or if you had too much material, or your overall reaction to it. If you jot down a few notes such as the following, it may help to make the second presentation more effective than the first.

1. Evaluation: Fairly good, dragged near end, and kids got bored.
2. Evaluation: Bombed out, too technical, pep it up.
3. Evaluation: Fantastic, into the national archives with it.

Criteria for evaluating lesson plans are listed in Figure 5-1.

Exercise 5 A

Prepare several trial lesson plans for classes you might teach using different types of teaching strategies such as teacher talk, discussion, and simulation.

Lesson Plan Formats

As stated in the preceding section, there is no mandatory basic lesson plan format and no irreplaceable list of lesson plan components. You should select a format that you find easy to work with and adapt it to the various types of lessons you

Does your lesson plan:
    Provide a tie-in to previous lessons?
    Provide for adequate set induction?
    Point out the objectives to the students?
    Provide for a clear presentation of the learning content?
    Provide for adequate demonstration and illustration?
    Provide for checking student understanding?
    Provide for preparing students for their homework assignment?
    Provide for adequate summing up and follow up?
    Provide for the elimination of dead spots?
    Make adequate provision for any individual or small group activities?
    Provide adequately for materials of instruction and equipment?
    Provide a lead-in for the next lesson?

FIGURE 5-1   *Lesson Plan Checklist*

teach. We favor an outline such as that in the following example. In this format the content of the lesson is incorporated into the procedure, although the major concept or key point is listed separately.

Sample Lesson Plan Format[2]

United States History   Grade 11
Unit: The New Nation
Topic: Hamilton's Financial Plan
Unit objective: The students will understand the major problems faced by the new nation.
Specific objective: The students will be able to explain the financial dilemma faced by the new nation.

Key Point: The diversity of means of exchange helped confuse financial matters in the United States during the Revolution and under the Articles of Confederation.

Procedure:
1. Brief introduction by teacher to set scene. Make following points and show samples of each. (8 min.)
   a. Back country and West—barter system
     (1) Put word "barter" on board
     (2) Ask "What does it mean"?
   b. After 1764 no paper money could be printed but some still in circulation.
   c. British, French, and Spanish coins in demand.
   d. Virginia—tobacco warehouse receipt used as money.

---

[2] This plan was prepared by a senior student teacher for one of her student teaching classes.

  e. IOUs to soldiers from Continental Congress.
  f. Promisory notes to European creditors.
  g. Each state had own paper money under Articles of Confederation.
2. Role Playing. (20 min.)
  a. Have pupils play parts of:
    (1) Merchants (three students)
    (2) Soldiers (three students)
    (3) Continental Congress officials (six students)
    (4) European creditors (three students)
    (5) Residents of different states (ten students)
  b. Merchants sell to Continental Congress.
  c. Soldiers receive pay from Continental Congress.
  d. Continental Congress go to European creditors (who sit at a distance).
  e. Residents of different states go back and forth trying to buy or sell.
  f. Easterners go to Kentucky and try to use his cash where only barter is used and vice versa.
  g. *In all cases*—each uses his own money and much trouble develops over various forms of currency.
3. Enter Alexander Hamilton (played by bright pupil). (5 min.)
  a. Speech outlining financial policy.
    (1) Debts of previous government ($12 million foreign, $44 million domestic, $25 million state).
    (2) Where get money for new government?
    (3) How to strengthen credit?
4. Discussion. (12 min.)
  a. Ask individuals what they learned from role playing.
  b. What were characteristics of system? (List on board)

Elicit from class
{
(1) Confusion
(2) Diversity
(3) Separateness of each political entity
(4) Animosity among people
(5) Much debt
}

  c. What effect would Hamilton's program have on these characteristics? (List on board)

Elicit from class
{
(1) Clear up confusion.
(2) Unify nation.
(3) Sound credit.
}

Materials:
  Play coins, play paper money, replicas of colonial and Revolutionary currency, handmade IOUs, promissory notes, tobacco warehouse receipt, and objects for trade.

Assignment:
  Read Thomas Jefferson's reaction to Hamilton's plan. What was his position and why?

Note: Speak to "Alexander Hamilton" before class.

Alternative Formats

You or the school system for which you work may prefer other formats. Illustrations of other commonly used formats of lesson plans follow.

Alternative Format 1. The first of these alternative formats follows the outline form described earlier, except that it lists the content and procedure separately.

Lesson Topic   Date
Unit   Grade
1. Lesson Objective
2. Content
3. Procedure
4. Instructional Materials
5. Evaluation

FIGURE 5-2 *Alternative Lesson Plan Format 1*

Alternative Format 2. The second alternative format is virtually the same as the first, except that it provides a column for notes concerning the items in the content and procedure sections. It also has a special section for evaluation and questions. The evaluation referred to is the test or other evaluative devices of the students' work, whereas the questions refer to the questions one would use in the class recitation or discussion.

Teacher   Course Topic   Date
Unit
Objectives

        Content   Notes
_____

Procedures

Evaluation and Questions

_____

Assignment

Materials of Instruction

FIGURE 5-3 *Alternative Lesson Plan Format 2*

Alternative Format 3.   The third alternative format is most suited to a recitation or lecture-question type of lesson. In this format, following a space for noting the introductory activities, one writes down the content in outline form, and in a second column one writes the key questions one would ask in connection with the various items of content. This section is followed by a space for a summary. Although the word procedure is not mentioned, this format provides for a procedure section of three parts: introduction, development, and conclusion.

Unit   Course   Date

Lesson Topic

Objective

Introduction

Content	Key Questions

Summary

Materials

Assignment

FIGURE 5-4   *Alternative Lesson Plan Format 3*

Alternative Format 4.   A fourth type of format commonly used lists the objectives in one column and the activities that are to bring about these objectives in another column. This format has the advantage of pointing out which activity is designed to bring about each objective, and thus incidentally ensures that each activity is designed to bring about some objective. However, to at least one teacher, the format seems to be harder to use in class because it does not lend itself to the step-by-step outline of the procedure as well as the format recommended earlier. An example of this format follows.

Lesson   Course   Date

Objectives	Activities
1. Bargain and compromise were the principal methods of solving political difficulties about 1850.	1. Map Study. Review the new territory added to United States. 2. What was slave? What free? 3. On map find slave states.
2.	4. 5. 6. 7.
3.	8. 9.

Materials of Instruction Needed

Assignment

FIGURE 5-5   *Alternative Lesson Plan Format 4*

Alternative Format 5. The fifth illustration of an alternative lesson format is one used in a large metropolitan district, partly as a supervisory device. It provides for detailed identification data as well as spaces for aims, understandings, special notes, and assignment, plus columns for one's timetable, outline of content, and the methods to be used to teach the content. Although the form seems complicated, the fact that the three columns of the "procedure" are listed according to time sequence makes the format easy to follow during the class.

School _____

Grade _____   Date _____ Day _____

Period(s) or Mod(s) _____ Room(s) _____ Week Ending _____

Daily Lesson Plan

Day's Aims and Objectives *Major Understandings:* *Skills to Be Developed:* *Attitudes:*	Routines (general housekeeping reminders)
	Student Assignment(s) (for one or more days)

Chronological Time Sequence (Minute by minute or number of minutes to be used in each part of outline)	*Outline of Content to Focus Upon in Order to Achieve Aims and Objectives* Content should be arranged so as to begin with *Initiatory Activities:* interest getters, previews, or previous unit work; move to *Developmental Activities* (those that expand understanding of what is known); and end with *Culminating Activities*, which can include summary, review, and evaluation.	*Teaching Methods Techniques* (and needed materials). Student involvement is prime consideration for choice of method.
	(Continue on additional paper if needed)	

FIGURE 5-6 *Alternative Lesson Plan Format 5*

Summary

The preceding pages attempt to outline, in some logical order, the fundamental components that go into the development of a daily lesson plan. It must be emphasized again that there is no single best way to prepare a daily lesson plan; no fool-proof formula that will ensure a teacher of an effective lesson or guarantee that students will absorb the materials or concepts that are being considered. With experience and increased competence in the field, you will develop your own style, your own methods of implementing that style, and your own formula for preparing a "teaching map." This teaching map charts the course, places markers along the trails, pinpoints danger areas, highlights places of interest and importance along the way, and ultimately brings the journeyer to the successful completion of the objective.

It is important for the beginning teacher to note the various aspects of the daily lesson plan as mentioned in this module. Some components will bear more strikingly on certain subject matter fields. Some can be modified to relate more specifically to a given subject, topic, or even different intelligence levels. The essential point to remember, however, is that a daily lesson plan should be a flexible instrument that can be used by the classroom teacher. It is valueless if it is simply prepared to meet an administrative requirement that plans be prepared and filed in the main office. Similarly, it is valueless if it is prepared so rigidly that departures are impossible. Examples of lesson plans in various formats follow.

Examples of Lesson Plans

Lesson Plan #1
Algebra I, Grade 9
1. Course: Algebra I.
   9th grade.
   Average group.
2. Topic: Factoring polynomials having common factors. unit NAme
3. Content:
   a. Vocabulary: Old: Factor, product, polynomial, monomial.
      New: Common factor, greatest common factor.
   b. Concepts: Old: Distributive law.
      New: Factoring polynomials that have common factors is the inverse process of multiplying a polynomial by a monomial.
   c. Skills: Old: Using the distributive law, multiplying a polynomial by a monomial.
      New: Finding the greatest common factor.
4. Method of presentation: Teacher-pupil discussion.
   Time Schedule: 10 min.—review homework.
   15 min.—present new material.
   15 min.—supervised study.
   Assignment: Read pp. 244–245, p. 245, 1–29 all odd numbers.
5. Objectives:
   a. Pupils will be able to demonstrate that factoring polynomials having common factors is the inverse process of multiplying a polynomial by a monomial.
   b. Pupils will be able to find the greatest common factor.

Procedure:
1. Review:
   a. What is a product?
   b. What is a factor?

2. Given the problem: $3a + 4b$ what are the factors?
   $\times\ 4a$ how do we find the products?
                    what is the product?

3. Can we write this problem another way?
   $4a(3a - 4b) = 12a^2 - 16ab$.
   What gives us the right to do the problem this way? (Dist. Law).
   What is the Distributive Law?

4. Give examples: $2a(m + 3n)$, $3x(2x - 1)$, $a^2(a^2 + b^2)$.

5. $a(x + y + z) = ax + ay + az$.
   What law is this?
   When multiplying a polynomial by a monomial, what may be said about the product? (The monomial is seen in each term of the product.)
   We may say that a is what to each term in the product? (common).

6. In $2ax + 2ay =$ what is the common factor? $(2a)$.
   Where do you think we would put the common factor?
   What do we do to each term in the product? (divide it by the common factor and put quotient in parentheses).
   Just as division is the inverse of multiplication, what can we say the relationship between factoring polynomials and the process of multiplying a polynomial by a monomial is? (the inverse).

7. $6m + 6n = 6(m + n)$.   ⎰ What is the common factor?
   $mn_2 + m1 = m(n + 1)$. ⎱ Where do I put it?
   $3a_2 - 3a = 3a(a - 1)$.   What do I do to each term in the product?

8. $4a + 12a = 4a(a + 3)$.
   Could I write $4a^2 + 12a = 4(a^2 + 3a)$? Why?
   What is $4a$ called? (greatest common factor).
   What is the greatest common factor in these problems?

9. $6xy - 3x^2 = 3x(2y - x)$.   ⎧ What is G.C.F.?
   $2_\pi r - 2_\pi R = 2_\pi(r - R)$.   ⎨ Where do I put it?
   $2a + 4ab + 2ac = 2a(1 + 2b + c)$. ⎩ What do I do to each term in product?

10. Given the example: $6a^2b - 15ab^2 =$? $3ab(2a - 5b)$.
    This check would still be valid if G.C.F. had not been chosen, ex. $3a$ instead of $3ab$. Therefore, what should we do to check for G.C.F.? (Inspect each term in the polynomial to make sure no single number or letter is seen in each term.)

Lesson Plan #2

Social Studies II: United States History and Problems.
Unit: "Evolving a Foreign Policy."
Topic: The Changing Relationship of Puerto Rico to the United States in the Twentieth Century.

Objective: Pupils will be able to:
1. Outline the evolution of the political and economic ties between Puerto Rico and the United States.
2. Appreciate the unique role of Puerto Rico in current inter-American affairs.
3. Relate current problems to their historical antecedents.

Procedure: Teacher Activity

1. Conclude some unfinished business: an oral report comparing life in Maryland suburbia with life in the rural Dakotas.
2. Review by means of puzzle.
3. Establish purposes for listening to oral reports by offering listening guide questions.
   Present reports sequentially to trace the changing relationship of Puerto Rico to the United States.
   a. "The Island of Puerto Rico Before 1898."
   b. "Political and Economic Change, 1898–1940."
   c. "Luis Muñoz Marin and Operation Bootstrap."
   d. "Puerto Rico: The Cultural Bridge Between the Americas."
   e. "Teodoro Moscoso and the Alliance for Progress."
4. Summarize by means of a special assignment, which the pupils will copy from the chalkboard upon entering the classroom.

Assignment: Read "Crisis in Latin America," a speech made by the governor   LACKS Time Limit
of Puerto Rico. Keep these questions in mind:

1. Why does the author caution us about the use of political "labels"?
2. In what ways is the term "Latin America" really an unsuitable expression?
3. What are the particular problems that Latin America faces?
4. In the Alliance for Progress, what roles does the author hope the United States will play?
5. Why is there stress on the phrase "Operation Seeing-Is-Believing"?
6. What unique function does the governor feel his own island can play in the Alliance for Progress?

Lesson Plan #3
Sophomore Biology Class, Advanced
The Microscope and Its Use

Objective: Pupils will be able to identify the parts of the microscope and to describe its proper use.

Procedure:

1. Assign one microscope to every two students, and record the microscope numbers.
2. Inform the class of the proper manner in which to carry and hold a microscope so as not to damage it.
3. Show the prepared diagrams of the microscope on the overhead projector, and point out the various parts and their functions.
4. Point out the parts on the prepared diagrams and have the students locate the parts on their microscopes.
5. Pass out the mimeographed material on the proper use of microscopes. This information is as follows:
   Skill in using the microscope can be developed only by following all steps correctly. Read and perform each step in the order given.
   a. Place the microscope on the table with the arm toward you and with the back of the base about one inch from the edge of the table.
   b. Adjust your position and tilt the microscope so that you can look into the eyepiece comfortably.

    c. Wipe the top lens of the eyepiece, the lens of the objectives, and the mirror with lens paper.

    d. Turn the disk to the largest opening so that the greatest amount of light is admitted.

    e. Turn the low-power objective in line with the body tube.

    f. Place your eye to the eyepiece and turn the mirror toward a source of light, but never directly toward the sun. Adjust the mirror until a uniform circle of light without shadows appears. This is a field. The microscope is now ready to use.

    g. When you receive the prepared slide, place it on the stage, clip it into place, and move the slide until the object is in the center of the stage opening.

    h. Watching the bottom lens, turn the low-power objective down as far as it will go, using care not to touch the slide.

    i. Place your eye to the eyepiece, and as you watch the field, turn the coarse adjustment slowly toward you, raising the body tube. Watch for the material to appear in the field.

Go through each step with the class, making sure that the students understand the procedure of using low magnification.

Ask for volunteers to describe the slides they are examining.

When they have grasped the procedure of using low-power magnification, instruct the class to turn the high-power objective in line with the body tube, and use the fine adjustment slowly until the object comes into the field. Go around the room and help individuals who are having difficulty.

Ask for volunteers to compare the differences between low power and high power. Instruct the students to place the microscopes in the cabinets and prepare for leaving.

Exercise 5 B

Examine the sample lesson plans. What do you think of them? How do they measure up to the criteria listed in Figure 5-1?

Suggested Reading

Berenson, David H., Sally R. Berenson, and Robert R. Carkhuff. *The Skills of Teaching: Lesson Planning Skills.* Amherst, Mass.: Human Resources Development Press, 1978.

Grambs, Jean Dresden, and John C. Carr. *Modern Methods in Secondary Education,* 4th ed. New York: Holt, Rinehart and Winston, 1979. Chap. 7.

Henak, Richard, M. *Lesson Planning for Meaningful Variety.* Washington, D.C.: National Education Association, 1980.

Henson, Kenneth T. *Secondary and Middle School Methods.* Minneapolis, Minn.: Burgess Publishing, 1987.

Hoover, Kenneth H. *The Professional Teacher's Handbook,* abridged 2d ed. Boston: Allyn & Bacon, 1976, Chap. 3.

Kim, Eugene C., and Richard D. Kellough. *A Resource Guide for Secondary School Teaching,* 4th ed. New York: Macmillan Publishing Co., 1983, Part II.

Lorber, Michael A., and Walter D. Pierce. *Objectives, Methods, and Evaluation for Secondary Teaching.* Englewood Cliffs, N.J.: Prentice-Hall, 1983.

Orlich, Donald C., et al. *Teaching Strategies: A Guide to Better Instruction,* 2d ed. Lexington, Mass.: D. C. Heath, 1985, Chap. 5.

Romiszowski, A. J. *Producing Instructional Systems: Lesson Planning for Individualized and Group Learning Activities.* New York: Nichols Publishing, 1984.

Post Test

True-False If you consider the statement false or iffy, explain why.

1. _F_ A good daily lesson plan ensures a good lesson.

2. _T_ All teachers, regardless of their experience, should have daily lesson plans.

3. _F_ It is quite acceptable for beginning teachers who are firm in their grasp of subject matter to keep their lesson plans in their heads.

4. _T_ Each teacher should develop a personal style of lesson planning that is appropriate for his or her needs.

5. _F_ Students should never see a teacher using a lesson plan.

6. _F_ Most teachers develop the knack of perfect timing after several ~YEARS months; that is, they can bring a class right up to the bell with a lesson plan. ~overplan!

7. _T_ Lesson plans should be in a constant state of revision.

8. _F_ Lesson plans are the single most important element in all the planning a teacher does.   IS NO single Imp element

9. _T_ General objectives usually refer to larger goals than those sought in the daily lesson.

10. _F_ A lesson begins when the bell rings and ends when the bell rings. when you begin It & end It

11. _F_ A teacher should never use the same plan twice. IF Good why Not

12. _T_ Formats for lesson plans should be tailored to meet student and teacher goals.

13. _F_ If the lesson plan falls short of the time limit, giving the class a study hall is really the best remedy.   think other Activity

14. _T_ A lesson plan should be flexible: it should lend itself to sudden unforeseen occurrences.   Never marry It.

15. _T_ A strong introduction to a lesson sometimes sets the tone for the entire class period.

16. _F_ Every lesson plan should stress a key point. Not All need them

17. __F__ The general objectives in the lesson plan should be stated as criterion-referenced behavioral objectives. *usually not behavioral*

18. __F__ The content of your lesson plan should be written out in long, detailed paragraphs. *Outline more usable*

19. __T__ The content of your lesson plan should spell out details you might not remember. *That's reason for!*

20. __T__ Your plan should provide for a strong conclusion. *yes, can clinch*

21. __F__ To be acceptable, your lesson plan must contain an outline of the content in the procedure section of the plan. *Yes have, not necess. here*

22. __F__ Every lesson plan must identify the key point of the lesson. *May not be one*

23. __T__ A principal purpose of a written lesson plan is to remind one of things one might otherwise forget. *Easy to forget detail*

24. __F__ As a beginning teacher you should prepare an elaborately detailed lesson plan for every lesson you teach. *Some just simple outline*

25. __F__ You should avoid allowing students see you following a written plan. *why not*

26. __T__ A plan book is ordinarily little more than a layout sheet. *overview week or term*

27. __T__ In some schools, teachers are required to submit their lesson plans to their supervisor or principal.

28. __F__ Ordinarily the procedure section of a lesson plan should be written in general terms. *Just what plan to do*

29. __F__ All lesson plan objectives must be stated as behavioral objectives.

30. __T__ Good lesson plans should be saved to be used again. *yes,*

31. __F__ Every lesson plan should follow the same format. *no*

32. __F__ Your lesson plans should be written out in detail in your plan book. *no room outline.*

33. __F__ Every lesson plan should contain an introduction, a lesson development section, and a conclusion. *Some just parts of units or long term plans*

34. __T__ When writing out a lesson plan, it is better to outline the procedure than to write it out in text form. *Easier to follow*

35. __T__ It is wise to include the answers to important questions and problems in your lesson plan. *May forget.*

Short Answer

36. What relation should the learning activities of the lesson have to the specific objective component?

The activity method should help achieve those objectives

― concept

37. What is the role of the key point in the plan?

Should be the key issue that ties the whole issue together

38. Give two reasons for writing out your lesson in some detail.

In case of a substitute teacher
To form a firm base for your lesson

39. What might you do if your class lesson proves to be too short?

Review & introduce next unit

40. When should you give the assignment for the next day?

At the best time

MODULE
6

Motivation

Rationale

A key to effective classroom management, and consequently to effective teaching, is motivation. Pupils who are well motivated to learn usually do learn if lessons are reasonably well designed. If pupils' attitudes are antagonistic toward school, school learning, or classes, teachers' efforts are not likely to be fruitful. Therefore it behooves teachers to persuade pupils that learning well in their classes is the thing to do. Teachers have a better chance of persuading them if they know the individual pupils well enough to adapt the lessons and courses to their needs and interests and to tempt them by making the course seem valuable to them personally.

This module offers you some methods and techniques that will help you as you learn, to know your pupils, to make their motivation favorable to your coursework, and to gain good discipline and control in your classes.

Specific Objectives

Specifically, by the completion of this unit, you should be able to do the following:

1. Describe resources and devices teachers can use to learn more about pupils. Specifically, you should be able to tell how to use the cumulative record, observation, pupil conferences, parent conferences, pupil assignments, questionnaires, and test results.
2. Describe a dozen general procedures for improving students' motivation toward their schoolwork.
3. Describe how one might use principles of reinforcement for school motivation.

Module Text

Getting to Know Your Students

If your classes are to move forward smoothly and efficiently, they should fit your students' abilities, needs, aptitudes, interests, and goals. Therefore, you need to know your students well enough to provide classroom learning activities that they will find interesting and valuable.

To help you do this, prepare a seating chart. (See Fig. 6-1). A good technique for making a chart is to prepare slips of paper bearing the names of the pupils, and then as you call the roll, place the name slips into the proper spots in a pocket-type seating chart. If the school does not provide pocket-type charts, you can make them very easily. You can also make a blank seating chart on which you write in the names during roll call or when the pupils are doing seat work. Then work at learning names and faces just as soon as you can. While pupils are working at their seats, some teachers spend the time trying to associate names and faces and fixing them in their memory. Addressing pupils by name every time

			Ross Bernard		Chinsky Christine
	Westerman Kathaleen	Healy Thomas	Ghirlanda Ann		Casey Noreen
	Anderson Keith	Wyles Henry	Gallagher Maureen	Matta Theodore	Bush Eleanor
	Pear Constance	Donovan Gayle	Gaffney Edward	Dobrowolski Maryann	Wozniak Helene
	Szper Richard	Kubrak James	Foley Patricia	Debski Christine	Berriz Carmen
	Niedzinski Michael	Adamkiewicz Geraldine	Eyles Janette	Donahue Richard	O'Donnell Sharon

FRONT OF ROOM

ROOM NO. __33__   PERIOD __1st__

TEACHER __J. Sullivan__   SUBJECT __W History__

FIGURE 6-1 *Seating Chart*

you speak to them will help you remember their names. (Be sure to learn to pronounce the students' names correctly if you wish to make a good impression on them.)

Then, as soon as you can, learn to know the students as people. Learn as much as you can about their personalities, characters, and ability levels. The best way to learn to know anyone is to spend a lot of time with him; to talk together, to socialize together, and to work together. Unfortunately the structure of secondary (and to a lesser extent middle) schools makes it difficult to know students well. The daily teacher load is often quite heavy (for example, 100–150 students per teacher) and the teacher's time is very limited. Consequently, it will be necessary for you to utilize shortcuts, tips, clues, and techniques such as those described in the following paragraphs. However, remember that the most useful measures for learning about your students are records, conversations and conferences, observation of the students' behavior, and analysis of their work.

These and other information-gathering devices and techniques are described in the following paragraphs.

1. Cumulative Record Folders. These can be found in the school office or guidance department. They include data recorded annually by teachers, administrators, and guidance personnel and contain all sorts of information about the pupils' academic background, standardized test scores, and extracurricular activities.
2. Observation. Watching the pupils in class, on the playing field, and at lunch may give you information about their personalities and potentialities. For instance, you may find that a pupil who seems phlegmatic, lackadaisical, or uninteresting in the classroom is a real fireball or leader on the playing field or at informal student gatherings.
3. Conferences. Conferences with the pupils are usually the best way to find out their interests, ambitions, problems, hopes, and other things that would

help you to fit your instruction to their personalities, abilities, and needs. Conference sessions can be formal, structured, face-to-face interactions set up by you in accordance with a schedule you have mapped out for this purpose. As a rule, though, more significant information is picked up in informal sessions consisting of a few minutes with the pupil now and then on no particular schedule, but when the time and mood are right. In either type of conference, it will be helpful if you follow these suggestions:

   a. Ask only open-ended questions. Encourage the pupil to talk freely. Listen to what he or she says.
   b. Don't moralize, judge, or condemn, but accept a pupil's opinions and values as what they are, his or her opinions and values.
   c. Record your observations soon after the conference. Your personal file concerning the students you teach should, by year's end, contain hunches about actions you have seen and direct quotations of statements you have heard that seem to have some bearing on the pupils' behavior. Failure to record such revelations shortly after you obtain them may result in your forgetting them or, worse yet, remembering them incorrectly.

4. Parent Conferences. Parent conferences can tell you a lot about the pupil, and his or her interests, abilities, and goals. This information may be volunteered directly by the parent or be obtained in answers to your questions. 'ust as often, though, you may be able to draw conclusions from uninten-ι nal clues. Parents' speech defects, for example, may reveal causes of stu 'ents' mispronunciations. Aggressive or meek behavior by the parents may uggest reasons for their children's behavior mannerisms.

5. Autoɒ graphies, Themes, Reading Reaction Sheets, and Value Sheets, and sin. 'ar assignments.

6. Question ires, such as the following:
   a. Interest nder. An interest finder asks such questions as "What type of television rograms do you like best? Do you like sports? Which sport do you like the most?" See Figure 6-2.

Exercise 6 A

Figure 6-2 is an interest finder made by a senior interne. How could it be used in your teaching? Are there other questions you would add to this interest finder?

   b. Autobiographical questionnaires. Autobiographical questionnaires can give you many ideas about how to tailor assignments for individual pupils. Include such questions as the following:
   (1) What do you plan to do when you finish high school?
   (2) Do you have a job? If so, what is it? Do you like it?
   (3) How do you like to spend your leisure time?
   (4) Do you like to read? What do you like to read?
   (5) Do you have a hobby? What is it?

7. Test results. Both standardized and teacher tests will help you match the learning activities to present knowledge and capabilities of the pupils. Di-

1. When talking to your friends in the cafeteria, what do you usually discuss?
2. Do you like to read?
3. What kind of books do you read in your spare time?
4. Do you read the daily newspaper?
5. If so, which section do you read the most?
6. What kind of movies do you enjoy seeing?
7. Do you watch television very often?
8. If so, what type of programs do you like?
9. Do you have any hobbies?
10. If you had your choice, would you take a course in American History or Political Science?

FIGURE 6-2   *Interest Finder*

agnostic tests are especially useful for this purpose. Many excellent ones are available commercially. However, it is quite possible to build useful diagnostic tests of your own. Unit tests should almost always be diagnostic, unless they are end-of-term tests. To build such a diagnostic test, proceed as follows:

a. Establish the specific learning products, information, concepts, skills, attitudes, ideas, and appreciations for which you wish to test. Probably these will be most useful if they are written as specific behavioral objectives.

b. Write test items that test each of these objectives. To utilize such tests for diagnostic purposes, it is necessary to analyze the test results so as to find where the pupils do well and where they do not. This analysis can be done by inspection sometimes, but often it is essential to use some form of test analysis, as in the item analysis illustrated in Fig. 6-3. In this type of analysis, simply check off which items each pupil answered correctly and which incorrectly. You can assume that pupils who answered the items having to do with an objective correctly have achieved that objective and that pupils who missed those items did not.

Exercise 6 B

Assuming that the small sample of an item analysis in Figure 6-3 is typical of the entire analysis, what, if anything, needs to be retaught? Do any of the pupils need any remedial work? If so, what?

8. Use sociometric devices. Sociometry is "the measurement of attitudes of social acceptance or rejection through expressed preferences among members of a social group."[1] By the use of sociometric devices, it is possible to learn much about the social structure of a class and the interrelationship among the individual pupils in the class. During the past years, social scientists have developed a number of sociometric instruments that can be used in school. In this module we shall discuss only two of them, the sociogram, and the Guess Who Test.

---

[1] *The Random House Dictionary of the English Language,* unabridged ed. (New York: Random House, 1966).

Objective	Item	Abel	Bill	Charles	David	Ellen	Etc.
	1	√	0	√	√	√	
1	2	√	0	√	√	√	
	3	√	0	√	√	√	
	4	0	0	0	0	0	
2	5	0	√	0	0	0	
	6	√	√	0	0	0	
	7	√	√	√	√	0	
3	8	√	0	0	√	0	
	9	√	√	√	√	√	

Etc.

√ = correct answer   0 = incorrect answer

FIGURE 6-3   *Sample Item Analysis*

a. Sociogram. A sociogram is a diagrammatic representation of the structure of a group. By examining a sociogram, one should be able to find clues to group leaders, isolates, cliques, friendships, and the like. A procedure recommended for constructing a sociogram follows.
(1) Ask the pupils to answer in secret such questions as, Which two pupils would you like to work with on a topic for an oral report? If we should change the seating plan, whom would you like to sit beside? Or, with whom would you most like to work on a class committee on planning? Sometimes one might also ask, With whom would you rather not work?
(2) Tabulate the choices of each pupil. Keep the boys and girls in separate columns.
(3) Construct the sociogram.
   (a) Select a symbol for boy and another for girl.
   (b) Place the symbols representing the most popular pupils near the center of the page, those of the less popular farther out, and those of the least popular on the fringes. It may be helpful to place the boys on one side of the page and the girls on the other.
   (c) Draw lines to represent the choices. Show the direction of the choice by an arrow. Show mutual choices by a double arrow. Dislike may be shown by using dotted or colored lines.[2]

[2] Leonard H. Clark and Irving S. Starr, *Secondary and Middle School Teaching Methods,* 4th ed. (New York: Macmillan Publishing Co., 1981), pp. 91–92.

professionals. Remember also that for you as a teacher the most useful of these sources are records, conferences, observation, and analyses of students' work.

Exercise 6 E

The Case of Mike

The following case study is excerpted from a report by a Jersey City State College junior practicum student. It is based upon observation of Mike, an American History Student in his junior year at a New Jersey high school.

If you were to teach Mike, what more information would you want to have? What sources could you use to get this information? Is the information in this student teacher's practicum report of any value? Does it give you any clues you might use to make your teaching of Mike more effective? Do you agree with the college student's diagnosis? Do you have enough information to make a valid diagnosis?

The student I studied was a 16-year-old black male. He is 5 feet, 8 inches tall, weighs about 145 pounds, and is a very neat dresser. He has one brother and two sisters, and lives in the downtown area of_____. His father is a service station mechanic and his mother works part-time as a waitress. He has a very active mind and can't stay interested in one thing too long, but once something does interest him, he becomes very inquisitive. Most of the time he is very well mannered.

Mike is in the second period American History class, which is a slow group with a few discipline problems. Mike is passing history through his efforts in class and his performance on tests. Speaking to Mike before class one day, I asked what he wants to do after he graduates, and he told me that he wants to join the army and make it his career. I asked why he wanted to join the army, and he said he thought a soldier's life was very exciting and filled with adventure. I said I certainly agreed with him and I wished him success in attaining his goal. At least Mike has some sort of constructive aspiration for his future and seems determined to achieve his goal. Most people his age are confused and undecided about what they really want to be in life.

Observations of Mike:

4/16—I went to the cafeteria to buy a container of orange juice, and I found out that Mike helps out in the cafeteria before the lunch session starts. When he saw me in the cafeteria he asked if I ate alone, and I told him I ate in the teacher's room with the other teachers. He said he was glad when I told him this, for, he said, the teachers around here are too snobby to new people to sit at their tables. I thought he was being very thoughtful to ask and decided to make him the student I would do my case study on because he has a very interesting personality.

4/17—I was giving out answer papers for the test the students were about to take, and Mike was the only student to say thank you after I handed him a piece of paper. After the test the teacher asked for the answers to the homework questions, and Mike was exceptionally anxious to answer the questions.

4/21—This wasn't a good day for Mike. Mike didn't have any paper to write answers to reference questions with, and he was clowning around so much that the teacher had to scold him. He asked me a question about the slave issue in the South when the answer was right in the textbook, but he said he could not find it. Then he made a paper airplane and the teacher found it on his desk and accused him of being the one who was throwing paper airplanes around the classroom two weeks ago. He said he made it a month ago and just found it in his book now. The teacher took it from him and threw it away.

4/23—Mike had no homework because he was absent the day the assignment was given. The teacher asked why he did not come to him for the questions, but Mike had no excuse. He has no cover on his text so the teacher told him get the book covered for the following day or penalties will be dealt to him and to others who did not cover their books.

Mike didn't fail any subjects the past marking period, and he received a C in history, and that is what he was working for.

My opinion of Mike is that he wants to learn but his mind is too active and he is unable to direct his thinking in a scholastic direction. In order to teach Mike, you must always make your lectures and discussion periods very exciting and interesting.

Motivation

One of the primary concerns in classroom management is motivation. Motivation, discipline, and control are all facets of the same teaching problem. If pupils' motivation is favorable to your classes and teaching, then their behavior will also be favorable and your classes will be well disciplined and effective. If pupils' motivation is not favorable, the chances are that your control and your effort to teach will also fail. Obviously, then, you should do whatever you can to see to it that your pupils are favorably motivated toward your classes and their content. Ultimately, a primary objective of your teaching should be to so motivate students that they will endeavor to use their own resources in their learning rather than rely on spoon feeding from their teacher. Pupils who can attain such intellectual independence can go on to educate themselves when they have left school and no longer have a teacher to fall back on. Pupils who have been spoon-fed cannot.

The experienced teacher knows that to motivate pupils one must teach many things besides book studies. In our public schools, there will always be some pupils who have not learned to read with understanding, and without understanding there is no interest. Such pupils must depend upon the teacher for the interest they take in school. There are many ways for the teacher to catch pupils' interest. The silent demonstration, role playing, games, and simulation are a few examples of the devices that can be used.

The teacher who is patient enough and willing to explore may discover that each pupil has a special proclivity. On the surface, this may appear unrelated to the subject matter being taught. Yet, with some ingenuity on the teacher's part, it may well be the means by which to involve the pupil. For example, in one science class at the secondary level, a teacher became aware of John's doodling in the back of the classroom. After an informal conversation, the teacher learned that John loved to draw. The teacher gradually drew John out by having him make charts for the class. These charts were displayed prominently. Drawing them helped John to better understand what the class was learning, and the fact that he was playing such an important role in what they were doing gave him the recognition and feeling of adequacy for which he thirsted. This incident is but one example of how boredom and apathy can be turned into enthusiasm and motivation for further inquiry. It is important to keep in mind that this is a most critical period of the pupils' lives, the potential turning-off period in their education. Whatever impression is made upon them now may be final. If pupils become disgusted with the boredom and confinement of school and associate learning with pain and repulsiveness, injury done to their attitudes toward education may be irreparable. If, on the other hand, the teacher is really skillful, and excites in pupils a spirit of inquiry and curiosity, leading them to observe, to think, to explore and to feel that school is a stimulating experience, all will be enriched in the process.

Now let us consider some strategies for managing classes and classroom instruction so as to arouse and support student's motivation.

Exercise 6 F

Think back over your own high school days. Which courses and teachers do you remember as being interesting and worthwhile? Why were they so? What was there about them that caused you to be motivated favorably toward them? Now think of courses that have turned you off completely. What was there about them that caused your motivation to be so negative?

Creating A Positive Atmosphere

To promote motivation and learning "accentuate the positive." Teachers who foster a pleasant, positive atmosphere in their classes find that their pupils learn and behave better than do those teachers whose classes are harsh and repressive. Following are some suggestions for making the atmosphere in your classroom supportive to motivation, learning, and good discipline.

1. Pay attention to your classroom's physical appearance. A pleasant, neat, comfortable, and bright classroom helps to provide a climate that is favorable to good discipline. When things look nice, one usually does not wish to mess them up. Therefore, it pays to keep the classroom as attractive as possible. It is surprising how much you and your pupils can do to make even the most drab classroom a pleasant place if you put your minds to it.

The first thing to do to improve the classroom's appearance and pupil attitudes is to keep the classroom neat and orderly. Provide a place for everything and try to keep everything in its place. Tidy up, clean up, and put things away after using them. Improve the classroom atmosphere by brightening it up. Use displays, murals, bulletin boards, posters, and pictures. If you lack tackboards or display areas, extemporize. Use the new adhesives that allow you to fasten things directly to the wall without marring it, or cover the wall with murals drawn on wrapping paper. Cover the walls with wrapping paper and let your grafitti artists decorate them (be sure not to use paint or ink that will stain through and mark the wall). Use lots of pictures. Preferably, these should all be pertinent to what you are teaching, and should be changed every few weeks so as to keep the classroom bright, interesting, and up to date. But purely decorative pictures are better than no pictures at all.

Exercise 6 G

Most college classrooms are quite drab. Plan how you could brighten up a drab classroom in your college in order to make it more attractive.

2. Watch out for students' creature comforts. Students find it difficult to study when they are uncomfortable. Pay attention to the light, heat, and ventilation in the classroom. A hot, stuffy classroom can destroy motivation and control. So can classrooms that are too dark or in which pupils are facing a glare. Young adolescents particularly are not built to sit still for long periods of time. Try to vary their instruction so that they will not have to sit and listen quietly too much of the time.

3. Be supportive. In your teaching try to emphasize the dos, not the don'ts; the rewards, not the punishments; the joy of learning, not the pain of studying or the fear of failure. Let the pupils know that you want them to do their best. Do not "put them down." Give them time. Support their attempts. Award their successes and honest attempts. Especially avoid punishing a pupil who tried but did not succeed.

4. Try to run a happy ship. Try to make what you have to teach seem attractive. A little fun or humor once in a while seldom hurts.

5. Try to encourage students' high levels of aspiration and self-esteem. Success raises students' aspirations, whereas failure lowers them. Therefore try to see to it that your students have large measures of success in your classes. Provide challenging but reasonable assignments. Treat mistakes positively, and use them as opportunities to teach the students how to avoid future errors. But do try to see to it that your students succeed more than they fail. They need real success so that they will not become discouraged and give up. Set high standards, however. (Don't give the students baby food.) Be sure that the students know what your standards are and that you are confident of their ability to meet these standards. Take time to make your expectations clear and help the pupils achieve these goals by showing them what they do well and what they should be doing better so that they can be proud of their work.

6. Diffusely structure your class. Try to build group cohesiveness in your class by encouraging students' involvement and participation. Utilize learning activities and teaching procedures that get all your students into the act. Do not allow any in-group to dominate the class. Avoid recitations and other activities in which a few of the better students dominate. Insofar as feasible, involve all the students in democratic leadership and decision-making roles. Your class should act as a group working for a common cause with shared responsibilities rather than as a bunch of individuals.

7. Try to use interesting strategies and tactics. Examples of the many different teaching strategies that can be used to arouse interest and sharpen productive motivation include,

    a. Special projects, both individual and group.
    b. Real-life situations in which pupils do real things.
    c. Simulations and role playing.
    d. Games (adaptations of "Hollywood Squares" and "Jeopardy," for instance).
    e. Mock trials, courts, elections, and the like.
    f. Problem solving and action (attempts to solve a real community problem).
    g. Building real things.
    h. Use of overhead projector, maps, globes, charts, pictures, and other audio-visual aids, and media.
    i. Real discussions on real topics.
    j. Silent demonstrations.

Exercise 6 H

List specific techniques by which your teachers made their classes interesting to you. What techniques might you use to make your classes interesting?

8. Personalize your teaching. Treat the pupils as individuals. Call them by name, chat with them about their personal interests and extracurricular life. Compliment them when they look good or do well, both in class and out. Follow their lives outside class as much as you can. Try to build their self-concepts, show them that you are interested in them and respect them, and aim your teaching at their individual needs, interests, and goals by adjusting your courses and lessons for them and providing special experiences for individual pupils. Try never to let any pupil get lost in the crowd.

Providing Good Examples

Pupils of school age learn most of their behavior by imitating others. If we as their teachers can provide them with good, prestigious models that they will pattern themselves after, we shall do much to achieve the kind of behavior we seek. It may be possible to harness pupils' admiration for older students, highly regarded pupils, natural peer group leaders, and such admired personalities as stars of sports, screen, and television, and world figures. Unfortunately, such personages are not always available or reliable. However, fictional and historical characters are always available in books and other media, and it may be possible to use such characters to great advantage in your teaching.

Exercise 6 I

What characters in television might one harness as models for creating the type of behavior you wish in your classes? What could you do to harness these models? Discuss your selection with your colleagues. You, yourself, may be the most influential model.

Probably the most influential example is a pleasant teacher whose classroom personality is characterized by "empathy, warmth and genuineness"[3] and who does not take himself too seriously. Self-centered teachers, who worry about how they will appear and how classroom incidents will affect them, are much more likely to have difficulty than are teachers whose interests center on their pupils and on how classroom incidents will affect their pupils. Therefore, go in there and teach the best you can. Act with confidence but without arrogance, and everything will probably go well. If you concentrate on teaching well and if your plans and procedures are reasonably good, discipline may take care of itself. Also, you would do well to develop an active interest in your pupils, a friendly attitude, an interesting personality, and a sense of humor if you wish to avoid discipline problems. Above all, show that you enjoy teaching, studying, and working with pupils. Attitudes are contagious. If you show that you are enthusiastic about what you teach and teach joyously, your pupils may become enthusiastic too. Approach your teaching with pleasure and with confidence. If you concentrate on teaching in a businesslike, confident manner, you will probably be well on the road to having the kind of classroom control you desire.

Although every teacher should be friendly with pupils, it does not pay to become too chummy with them. Avoid entangling alliances, teacher's pets, and boon companionship. Teachers should be adults, behave as adults, and socialize with adults. Pupils will like them better that way, and then there is no danger of playing favorites or of pupils attempting to take advantage of friendship.

In the final analysis, what we are trying to say is that you should set a good example. If the pupils realize that you are trying really to serve them well and that you really care for them as people, they will probably respond well to your teaching.

Inducing a Favorable Set

When you begin a lesson, unit, or activity, try to induce in your students an appropriate set, that is, a predisposition or receptive mood that will generate interest and attention and, it is hoped, spur students to attack their work enthusiastically and diligently. For instance, one teacher used the following approach to launch the study of the Constitutional Convention of 1787.

> Teacher: Suppose you were setting up a colony on a distant planet. Since this colony will be self-governing, the colonists have to draw up some kind of rules for governing themselves. For tonight I want each of you to pretend that you are a colonist on a planet, and that tomorrow you will begin discussions to draw up some sort of constitution. Think about who will do the ruling, how the ruler will be chosen, and what kinds of rights each individual will be guaranteed. Also consider what the colony will do when its population expands to over a million people. Each one of you should answer these questions and be prepared to discuss them tomorrow.

After spending a subsequent class period discussing these and related questions, the teacher assigned appropriate reading and conducted discussions about the problems that confronted the Founding Fathers in 1787. In this way the teacher tried to stimulate her students and prepare them for the learning activity.

---

[3] Duane Brown, *Changing Student Behavior: A New Approach to Discipline* (Dubuque, Ia: William C. Brown Company, 1971), p. 12.

Similarly, to introduce a lesson on density and specific gravity, another teacher put an ice cube into each of two beakers. In one beaker the ice floated; in the other it sank. Then the class discussed why this happened.

In yet another instance, a teacher introduced a chapter on the American Civil War by asking the students to think about how they would have tried to prevent the war had they been President. Such set-inducing tactics would be appropriate for almost any learning activity. For example:

1. At the start of a unit.
2. Before a discussion.
3. Before a question and answer period.
4. When assigning homework.
5. Before hearing a panel discussion.
6. Before student reports.
7. When assigning student reports.
8. Before a film or filmstrip.
9. Before discussion following a film.
10. Before a homework assignment based on a discussion that followed a film-strip.

Making the Learning Seem Worthwhile

Be sure the learnings and activities seem worthwhile. Show the pupils how what they are studying can be useful to them now. Provide an assortment of activities, materials, and content that will appeal to the variety of tastes and interests present in the class. Find special things for special individuals to do. Encourage pupils to cooperate with you in the planning of their own learning activities. Above all, select content that is relevant to their lives and to the needs of the community, and be sure they know why it is important and relevant for them personally. Never start them off on an activity without being sure they know why they should do it.

Utilizing Pupils' Present Motives

Take advantage of the pupils' motives. Use their interests, ideals, goals, and attitudes. Appeal to their curiosity, pride, desire for fun, need for achievement, and social interests. Try to use the concerns of your students as vehicles of teaching. Focus on the present and future, more than on the past. Utilize job-related applications of the content you teach. Take advantage of situations that occur outside the classroom. In this connection remember that intrinsic motivation is usually more powerful than extrinsic motivation. People will often work harder to learn something because they want to learn it than they will merely to earn some extrinsic reward or prize.

The more you know about your students, the better you will be able to harness their prior motives, inclinations, and interests. Use the procedures described earlier in the module to find out such information.

Making Clear Assignments

Your new assignments should not only motivate your students, they should also clearly tell them what to do and how to do it. For instance, the teacher who wished to introduce the study of the Constitutional Convention of 1787 might say: "Now, class, for tomorrow I want all of you to read Chapter Six on the Constitutional Convention of 1787." Normally such a weak assignment would produce a weak response. The next day the teacher might discover that half the class had not read the assignment, and that the other half, although claiming to have read it, was unable to discuss it in any depth. A better approach might have been for the teacher to say: "For tomorrow I want you to read Chapter Six in the text and come to class prepared for a discussion." This assignment is an improvement over the other. It gives the students more information about the instructional goal; they are to prepare for a discussion. But the students need a good deal more information before they will be able, or disposed, to prepare themselves for an interesting, stimulating discussion. Exactly what will be discussed? What points should they consider as they read? What should be the focus while they read? How should they use previously learned material? Should they study facts or principles? Should they compare? Should they contrast? Both? Neither?[4]

By so clearly defining the assignment, you can be relatively sure that the students know what to do. Sometimes it will also be necessary for you to demonstrate to them how to do it. Many times the reason students do not do their assignments is that they do not understand what they are supposed to do or know how to do it. So be sure your directions, assignment, and time schedule are clear. Teach and show the students what to do, and how to do it, and set standards so that they will know when they are doing well.

Exercise 6 J

Criticize the following assignment and rewrite it to meet your specifications: Assignment: Finish Chapter 18, paying special attention to the Radical Reconstruction Program as compared to President Johnson's.

Mrs. Jones taught twelfth-graders in an American History II class. No lesson plan was used, and a problem arose during a unit dealing with the Eisenhower administration. Mrs. Jones doesn't even write out general goals to be accomplished. One day she distributed as a homework assignment mimeographed copies of an article by Archibald MacLeish discussing the "Swing Right." There were seniors in the class, some about to leave for a work-study program, and only about five were interested in what Archibald MacLeish had to say about conservatism in America. Mrs. Jones tried to start a discussion, and when, in frustration, she asked how many had read the article, only two students raised their hands. After about five minutes of scolding, she said that she would attempt to carry on a discussion with the two who had read the article.[5]

How could Mrs. Jones have avoided this fiasco? What could she have done to salvage the situation? Discuss your solutions with your colleagues.

[4] Adapted from course materials developed by Janice Boone for the Jersey City State College Junior Secondary Education Block.
[5] From a student's junior practicum observation report.

Introducing Variety and Novelty

Variety is the spice of life, so we are told. Varying the teaching approach may make rather uninteresting subject matter seem more interesting. Teachers spice up their courses by making lessons active, investigative, adventurous, and useful. Tactics that meet these criteria are field trips, library visits, laboratory work, role playing, contests, and individual study. Whatever you do, do not let yourself get stuck in the same rut of teaching by the same procedures, in the same manner, day after day. Remember, boredom is the enemy of learning!

On the other hand, do not switch your procedures too much or too rapidly. Changing activities, content, or method too frequently is liable to be confusing to your students. Students, particularly low-ability students, need the security and directions of established patterns. However, changes in tempo, vivid illustrations and demonstrations, switches from teacher-dominated to student-centered activities (e.g., from lectures to small-group work or discussion), can relieve the humdrum. So bring in new material, change the seating arrangement, put up new displays on the bulletin board, use unusual activities, play music, show pictures—in short, do anything that will make your class sprightly and profitable, and avoid the deadly rehashing of the text day after day. This is all too common in many classes.

Keeping Up the Pace

Keep things lively. Do not let them drag. Keep the pupils informed of their progress. Involve them in their own learning. Utilize active rather than passive activities. Be sure the work is difficult enough to be challenging, but not too difficult. Do not baby pupils, but do not frustrate them either.

Using Reinforcement Techniques

Reinforcement Theory and Motivation. One of the theories of modern psychology holds that people tend to behave in ways that have paid off in some sort of reward that they find valuable. This is called reinforcement theory because it is based on the belief that rewards or gratifying results strengthen a tendency to behave in a certain fashion, and lack of reward weakens the tendency to act in that fashion. For instance, if a girl is allowed free time for her own purposes when she works well for a certain period, she may work for that reward and develop higher standards for work in the future. This theory seems to hold many implications for the motivation and control of student behavior.

Unfortunately, this theory has been honored in the breach in all too many cases. Teachers frequently unintentionally reinforce the wrong behavior. When the boy who is seeking attention misbehaves, we reward him by reprimanding him, thus giving him the attention he craves, but when he behaves well, we ignore him. We reinforce the bad behavior and neglect the good behavior and, as a result, strengthen his tendency to misbehave and weaken his inclinations to behave well. Therefore, take care to reinforce the type of activity you want to encourage. Try not to reinforce untoward behavior, but accentuate the positive. Look for successful efforts to comment on rather than failures to berate. Try to catch your students doing well, then praise or reward them.

Do not put too much faith in grades and marks for student reinforcement. They are not dependable for several reasons.

1. Not all students place much value on high grades.
2. Not all students can expect to receive high grades. High-ability students who try usually receive high grades, but low-ability students who try seldom do.
3. Because the efforts of low-ability students so seldom pay off in high marks no matter how hard they try, "those students who need to try hardest are given the least incentive to do so."[6]

Rather than depending too much on using grades to provide motivation, it would ordinarily be more profitable to adjust the lessons and the curriculum so that they would appeal more to pupils' intrinsic motives or to use such techniques as computer-assisted instruction, continuous promotion, or pass-fail marking.

Exercise 6 K

There are several types of rewards that can be used to reinforce desirable student behavior. Among them are tangible rewards (such as athletic passes), social rewards (such as being assistant coach or teacher), activities (preparing a bulletin board or doing free reading), and intrinsic rewards (deriving pleasure from doing the activity). List examples of rewards in each category that you think would be suitable for a course you might teach.

Observe a class or think back over your own classroom experience. What behaviors were rewarded? What were not? Do you find examples of pupils being rewarded for being quiet, for being cooperative, and so on? Do you find examples of pupils being rewarded for misbehaving? Remember, sometimes a punishment can be a reward. From your own experience can you think of examples when this has been so?

Following are some principles of reinforcement that may be helpful to you in motivating and controlling pupils.

Reinforcement Principles.
1. Try to reinforce new desired behavior by rewarding it every time it occurs.
2. Then, once the behavior has been established fairly consistently gradually reduce the frequency of reinforcement until finally the reinforcement occurs only occasionally at haphazard intervals. Such intermittent reinforcement is much more effective for maintaining an established behavior than frequent or regular reinforcement.
3. At first, reward the behavior as soon as it occurs. Then, as the pupil becomes more confident, you may delay the reward somewhat.
4. Try to use rewards that are suitable for each pupil. Remember that what is rewarding for one pupil may be punishing to another. (Also, what may be a punishment for one pupil, or what you may think to be a punishment may be rewarding to another.) Remember also that performing the act

---

[6] James W. Michaels, "Classroom Reward Structure and Academic Performance," *Review of Educational Research* 47:95 (Winter 1977).

or improving one's competency may be its own reward. Probably a mix of tangible rewards, social rewards, rewarding activities and feedback, and success activities will prove the most satisfactory. If possible, try to see to it that the performance itself is rewarding.

It is, of course, advantageous if the pupils can select their own rewards. For this purpose, the reinforcement menus described in a later section of this module can be very helpful.

5. In using rewards with recalcitrant pupils, you may have to start small. Sometimes, it is very hard to find anything really commendable in a pupil's work at first. Therefore, you should reward such pupils when they do better and keep rewarding small improvements until the pupil achieves the behavior desired.

6. Utilize contingency contracts.

Contingency Contracts. Contigency contracts were first developed by L. E. Homme[7] from the common practice that he calls Grandma's law: if first you do this, then you can do that, or have that. Most of us remember this law as, "You don't get any ice cream until you finish eating your vegetables." Clarizio describes contract categories as follows:

> In the school setting, the contract specifies that the student can engage in an enjoyable high preference task, for example, art activities, or will receive a very desirable tangible or social reward, if he first engages in a low preference task, for example, a math assignment. To be effective, the contract must offer a reward that is, (a) highly attractive and (b) not obtainable outside the conditions of the contract.[8]

When the pupils find it difficult to meet the terms of the contingency contract or it becomes evident that their motivation is slipping, teachers should feel free to renegotiate the contract.

Reinforcement Menus. The reinforcement menu is a close cousin of the contingency contract. It consists of a list of activities a pupil can do if he completes a certain assignment according to certain conditions. These activities may be purely recreational or strictly educational, but they must be of high value to the pupils if they are to be effective. Reading a comic book might be a useful activity for this purpose.

Exercise 6 L

1. Set up a contingency contract that you could use in your course. Use rewards that you could offer in the course or classroom without impinging on the time or prerogatives of other teachers.

[7] L. E. Homme, *How to Use Contingency Contracting in the Classroom* (Urbana, Ill.: Rescard Press, 1969).

[8] Harvey F. Clarizio, *Toward Positive Classroom Discipline* (New York: John Wiley & Sons, 1971), p. 42.

2. Complete the following reinforcement menu:

   a. Read a comic book.

   b. _____.

   c. _____.

   d. _____.

   e. _____.

   f. _____.

   g. _____.

Building Trust

Try to build pupils' trust in you. Careful preparation, hard work, good teaching techniques, empathy, respect for your pupils, fairness, and justice will help you here. Trust is something you cannot create; it is given only to those who appear to deserve it. Try to earn it for trust is probably the greatest resource you can have when it comes to generating desirable student motivation and furthering excellent classroom management and discipline.

Suggested Reading

Ball, Samuel, ed. *Motivation in Education*. Orlando, Fla.: Academic Press, 1977.

Biehler, Robert F., and Jack Snowman. *Psychology Applied to Teaching,* 4th ed. Boston: Houghton Mifflin, 1982, Chap. 8.

Emmers, Amy Pyeth. *After the Lesson Plan: Realities of High School Teaching*. New York: Teachers College Press, 1981, Part II.

Frymier, Jack R. *Motivation and Learning in School*. Bloomington, Ind.: Phi Delta Kappa Educational Foundation, 1974.

Gage, N. L., and David C. Berliner. *Educational Psychology,* 3d ed. Boston: Houghton Mifflin, 1984.

Gnagey, William J. *Motivating Classroom Discipline*. New York: Macmillan Publishing Co., 1981.

Paris, Scott G., and Gary M. Alson, eds. *Learning and Motivation in the Classroom*. Hillsdale, N.J.: Lawrence Erlbaum Associates, 1983.

Reilly, Robert R., and Ernest L. Lewis. *Educational Psychology*. New York: Macmillan, 1983.

Rubin, Louis J. *Artistry in Teaching*. New York: Random House, 1984.

Schwartz, Lita Lenzer. *Educational Psychology*. 2d ed. Boston: Holbrook Press, 1981, Chap. 4.

Silvernail, David L. *Developing Positive Student Self-Concept*. Washington, D.C.: National Education Association, 1981.

Wlodkowski, Raymond J. *Motivation, What Research Says to the Teacher*. Washington, D.C.: National Education Association, 1977.

———. *Motivation and Teaching*. Washington, D.C.: National Education Association, 1978.

Post Test

Which of the following are recommended for use in motivating one's students? Mark those recommended in this module, R; those not recommended, X.

1. Give clear instructions.

2. Provide a variety of activities.

3. Be enthusiastic yourself.

4. Emphasize deferred values.

5. Emphasize marks and grades.

6. Try to fit your teaching to the students' present goals.

7. Allow students complete freedom.

8. Utilize real-life situations in which students do real things.

9. Diffusely structure your class.

10. Set high standards.

11. Reward and reenforce desirable behavior.

12. Utilize individual projects.

13. Threaten punishment for inappropriate behavior.

14. Make your assignments challenging.

15. Treat students as individuals.

16. Be a buddy of each student.

17. Try to provide students with success.

18. Be very strict.

19. Come down hard on students who make mistakes.

20. Run a happy ship.

21. What would you expect to find in a cumulative record folder?

_____

_____

22. In a pupil conference, is it usually preferable to ask open-ended or closed questions?

_____

23. What is the purpose of an interest finder?

_____

24. In a sociogram you noticed the following:

(In this sociogram circles indicate girls)

What would you interpret this as meaning?

_____

25. In a sociogram a large number of arrows point to △M. What does this probably mean?

_____

26. According to reinforcement theory, which is usually preferable, to reward or to punish?

_____

27. When using rewards in early reinforcement, which is preferable, immediate or deferred reward?

_____

28. What is a reinforcement menu?

_____

29. Plutarch, the Roman writer, tried to build character in boys by providing models for them to imitate. According to modern theory, was his basic idea sound?

_____

30. When should you record what you have learned in a student conference?

31. Basically, how would one prepare a teacher-made diagnostic test?

32. When would one use a set-inducing activity?

33. What is a contingency contract?

34. What does the following excerpt from an item analysis of a diagnostic test tell you?

Objective	Item	Student				
		George	Joe	Jane	Betty	John
	1	√	√	√	0	√
1	2	√	√	√	0	√
	3	√	√	√	0	√

35. In what way might a student's autobiography or answers to an autobiographical questionnaire help you as a teacher?

MODULE
7

Classroom Management and Discipline

Rationale

In order for your teaching to be effective, you should strive for a well-organized, businesslike classroom in which well-motivated students work diligently at their learning tasks free from distractions and inappropriate behavior. Providing such a setting for learning is what we call classroom management.

A principal aspect of good management is the maintaining of discipline and control. This aspect of teaching is the most worrisome to beginning teachers. And they have good cause to be concerned. Even more experienced teachers find discipline and control difficult, particularly at the junior high school and high school levels where teachers have so many pupils each day that it is difficult to know them all well, and where so many pupils have been turned off by unfortunate school experiences in earlier years.

Another aspect of good management is good organization and administration of the classroom activities and materials. In a well-managed class students know what to do, have the materials to work with, and keep on task; the class atmosphere is supportive, the assignments clear, the materials of instruction readily available, and the classroom proceedings businesslike. At all times the teacher is in control seeing to it that students are spending their time on appropriate tasks. If your teaching is to be efffective you must develop skill in classroom management.

Specific Objectives

At the end of this module you will have a firm understanding of the principles underlying good classroom management and control. Specifically, you will be able to:

1. Describe the modern concept of good discipline.
2. Define permissiveness, democratic discipline, and self-discipline.
3. Explain several strategies and tactics that should help create self-discipline in your pupils.
4. Show how each of the following contributes to good classroom control: a positive approach, well-planned classes, a good start, classroom rules, enforcement of rules, correcting misbehavior, and classroom management.
5. Describe specific procedures for establishing the conditions and carrying out the action necessary to establish and maintain classroom control pertinent to each of the headings listed in Objective 4.

Module Text

Introduction

Classroom management is the process of organizing and conducting a class so that it is efficient and effective and results in maximum student learning. To manage your classes successfully, you need to carefully plan your classes, provide students with a pleasant supportive climate for learning, create interest and a desire to learn and achieve, establish control, avoid disciplinary disturbances, and, in general, promote effective student learning.

What is a well-managed, well-disciplined class? In the schools of today, the classroom atmosphere is more likely to be, in the words of the lyricist, "more free and easy," and teachers, "more bright and breezy" than they were in the days of our grandparents when "reading and writing and 'rithmetic" were "taught to the tune of a hickory stick." Nevertheless, this swing toward pleasantness and "permissiveness" does not mean that students are free to behave as they wish. Even though silence is no longer a *sine qua non* and repressive classes are considered taboo, every teacher is charged with the responsibility of seeing to it that the classroom atmosphere is favorable to learning. Learning does not usually occur in disorderly, noisy classes. The degree of quiet and kind of order necessary depend somewhat on the type of class. Laboratory sessions allow for a great amount of conversation and movement; lecture sessions require quiet attention; and discussions, purposeful conversation. Work sessions in schoolrooms resemble work sessions in business or industry, periods in which many things are happening, most of which, it is hoped, will be productively directed toward the job at hand.

Sometimes, beginning teachers misunderstand the new philosophy of classroom atmosphere and assume that the permissive classroom atmosphere means that anything goes. Such teachers are way off base; the pupils will soon tag them out. Orderliness is essential. Permissiveness, as used in this context, merely means that the teaching should support the pupils in their efforts to learn and not clamp them down tightly in a pattern that would keep them from thinking for themselves. In a permissive class, pupils are encouraged to seek out and express their own ideas without fear of reprisals because of honest mistakes, but misbehavior should not be tolerated any more than it would be in a traditional class. It would be better to think of them as supportive classes.

Another belief that seems to confuse young teachers is that correction and strict control will be harmful to the mental health of pupils. Quite the contrary is true. Pupils evidently benefit from the maintenance of high standards and strict discipline; laissez-faire teaching, in contrast, can be downright harmful. Evidently, mental health is best fostered by democratic teaching in strictly controlled classes. This is known as democratic discipline.

In short, you, as the teacher, must establish yourself as the boss. Students should not have any doubt that you are the person in charge and that their behavior is governed by your parameters or parameters that have been set up with your approval. Your classes should be democratic, not anarchistic.

Getting Organized

In classroom management a good beginning may make all the difference. Therefore, you should appear at your first class, and every following class, as well prepared and as confident as possible. Perhaps you will feel nervous and apprehensive, but being ready and well prepared will probably help you at least to look confident. Then, if you proceed in a businesslike, matter-of-fact way, the impetus of your good, well-prepared start will cause things to proceed well.

Planning

Since a good start is so important, you should take great care with your planning. Poorly planned classes that wander, or classes in which pupils have nothing to do, or that seem worthless, or that are dull and drab have the seeds of discipline problems in them. Ad lib teaching is sloppy teaching, and sloppy teaching leads to control and learning problems. To prevent or minimize problems of this sort, the teacher should take care in planning. The following suggestions should help:

1. Furnish the pupils with enough purposeful activities to keep them busy and active. The devil makes work for idle hands, so be sure the pupils have plenty of worthwhile things to do.
2. Avoid dead spots. Be sure you have something worthwhile planned for every minute of the entire period.
3. Beware of scheduling too much time for lectures or teacher talk. One fifth of the class time is usually about all of the time that should be given to such activities. Most classes get restless after more than twenty minutes of straight lecture. If you must lecture, and sometimes it may be the only practicable procedure, then plan to lighten your lecture with key questions, audio-visual aids, or some other interest-catching tactic.
4. Provide for individual differences in your planning. Be sure pupils know what to do and how to do it. If necessary, provide instruction in how to

study the lesson, how to use the equipment or reference, and how to do the assignment. Plan the lesson so that it keeps the class moving quickly with no dead spots. Furnish plenty of all the necessary materials. Be sure they are ready for use at the time they can be used. Allow for pupils' predispositions. Let your plan fit the nature of the pupils but, if for some reason their mood is not what you expected, be ready to adjust your plan to meet the occasion if it seems necessary. Any plan that combats the natural inclinations of the pupils is likely to go down in defeat. Unreasonable expectations, such as absolute quiet from an excited student body, will lead only to complications.

5. Provide for good motivation. The lesson planned should seem interesting, challenging, and valuable to the pupils. Avoid planning classes that repeat the same deadly routine day after day after day. This is the type of class that so often results from ad lib teaching.

6. Routinize the organizational and administrative details of classroom management so as to eliminate dead spots and to avoid disorderly breakdowns in classroom decorum. The routines should be part of your plan.

7. Spice up your assignments. Be sure that you tell the pupils clearly what to do and how to do it. It may be necessary to go into great detail, give examples, and demonstrate proper procedures to make everything clear. When pupils are not clear on what they should do or how to do it, they tend to give up easily. In addition, the assignment should seem worthwhile, interesting, relevant, and challenging.

8. Make sure that you have plenty of materials and that the materials are readily available to the students.

To make your planning and management easier, have a standard plan or ritual for your lesson organization. This does not mean that you should use the same strategies and tactics in all your classes. Quite the contrary. But you should check to see which of your standard plan components are necessary for a particular lesson and whether you have adequately provided for each of these necessary components.

Components you should consider when you are organizing your lesson are:

1. Set induction.
2. Clarification of objectives for the students (what they are to learn and why).
3. Tie-in with previous classes.
4. Presentation of new content. (Lecture, demonstrations, audiovisual illustrations, and the like)
5. Presentation follow-up. (Checking students' understanding, guided monitored practice, independent practice, discussion, and the like)
6. Small group and independent laboratory-type study.
7. Summing up.
8. Materials of instruction and equipment.

9. Lead-in to next class.
10. New assignment.

It is most important that in preparing for your lesson you double check to be sure that you have the proper instructional material ready for each lesson component and the elements of your lesson follow in a logical psychological order. The checklist presented in Figure 5-1[1] may help in this regard.

Setting Rules

Part of your preclass preparation should be the determination of your classroom rules. Even, just, compassionate but objective enforcement of rules will improve the tenor of your classes if the rules seem reasonable. But sometimes the rules can be a cause of trouble. To avoid this difficulty, you should set up only a few rules. Too many rules may confuse pupils and make the classroom atmosphere too repressive. Ordinarily, these rules should be quite definite and specific so that pupils will know just what is acceptable and what is not. However, a few general principles such as, "rowdy behavior which interferes with other people will not be acceptable," may serve just as well. Whatever rules you select, it is best not to make them too rigid at first. Rigid rules, particularly when there are too many of them, seem to encourage misbehavior. Besides, they may compel you to enforce rules when you really do not think it wise. By sticking to a few rules or principles, you can leave yourself a little room for maneuvering.

Obviously, the rules you decide on should be reasonable ones. Not many people, young or old, will comply with rules that seem unreasonable to them, except under duress, but they will usually accept rules that seem to be reasonable. One of the key words in this statement is *seem*. Pupils will resist reasonable rules if they do not think them to be reasonable. Rules that do not seem reasonable create tension and dissension when one tries to enforce them. For this reason, it may be wise to talk over the reasons for establishing and enforcing these particular rules. At this time, and in this way, one can also make sure that the pupils understand just what abiding by the rules entails.

When you decide on what your classroom rules will be, you should also decide what the consequences for violating those rules will be for the offending student, and how you will carry out these consequences. Do not paint yourself into a corner, but do know what you will do in the face of inappropriate student behavior. Completely extemporaneous decisions, not based on prior thought, may lead to unnecessary, undesirable complications.

At no time should your students be in doubt about what the rules are and what the consequences for inappropriate behavior will be. Explain these matters to the students early in the course—preferably on the first day. Then, until you have complete confidence in your abilities to control your class, be quite strict and keep movement in your class at a minimum.

Exercise 7 A

Make up a list of rules that you feel you should insist on when you teach. Discuss this list with your colleagues.

[1] See Module 5.

FIGURE 7-1 *Seating Arrangements*

✎ Organizing the Classroom

When it is time for the class to start, you should be all ready to go. Get together all the instructional material you will need, ahead of time. Have the room and materials arranged for orderly and efficient use. Be sure the bulletin boards are set, any boardwork ready, all needed equipment set up, and any necessary supplies at hand.

In most classrooms the seats are arranged in rows. This is a good arrangement for lectures and audiovisual activities, but rows discourage discussion and student involvement. You may find it more satisfactory to arrange your class in a circle, hollow square, or double horseshoe, if you plan to use that type of activity frequently. If you plan to use committee or small-group work, small circles usually work best. Although it is, in general, important to adjust your classroom seating arrangements to the type of class activity, it may be better to go along with an existing seating arrangement rather than to cause a large commotion by moving furniture once a class has started.

Conducting the Class

As soon as the bell rings, you should start your class without delay, confusion, or dead time. Experts generally recommend that you require students to report to their assigned classroom stations at the beginning of the class period so that you can take attendance and perform other routine administrative tasks quickly. Once these details are completed, the students can move to ad hoc work stations that are suitable for the day's learning activities.

Keeping Things Moving

Once the class has started, it should move forward steadily. The pace should be vigorous enough to keep the students alert, but not enough to lose students who are trying. Each student should feel some pressure to do well. This pressure should not be oppressive, but everyone should realize it exists. So let it be known by word and by your actions that you expect everyone to do his best and that you will not tolerate dawdling, disturbances, time wasting, or other inappropriate behavior. To promote a businesslike atmosphere try to make sure that everyone has something worthwhile to do and that the students all know how to do what they are supposed to be doing, and have the materials they need. At no time should any student be standing around with nothing to do or be kept waiting for equipment, materials, or attention.

Movement Management

To keep things moving smoothly, and to minimize distractions, utilize the principles of movement management.[2] Movement management is basically the process of keeping the class moving forward at a good pace without sidetrips or interruptions. The first of these principles is that by starting your class the moment the bell rings you can eliminate fooling around and time wasting before they start. The second is that the class should move forward steadily and purposefully. Transitions from one activity to the next should be natural and unobtrusive. Each activity should start promptly without confusion and continue briskly to a definite, planned conclusion. Movement around the class should be controlled, orderly, and routinized. In short, movement management is keeping the class on track.

To ensure that your movement management is effective, be careful not to interrupt the smooth progress of the class yourself. For example,

Do not interrupt pupils with orders, statements, or announcements when they are busy doing something else.

Be sure the pupils are ready to hear you before you make announcements, issue orders, or make statements.

Be sure the first activity is finished before you start on the next one. Don't leave pupils dangling on an unfinished activity while you start off in a new direction. Be sure they know when you end one thing and begin the next.

Don't interrupt yourself. Avoid getting off the topic. If you start discussing one thing, keep to it until you are finished. Don't jump around from one topic or activity to another and then back again.

Don't let yourself be distracted by the irrelevant. Never interrupt the class's progress by harping on matters not pertinent to the activity at hand. Avoid all harangues.

Don't make mountains out of molehills. Avoid talking an activity to death. When you have said what you have to say, stop.

Don't go into too much detail. If something can be done in a few steps or explained in a few words, don't expand unnecessarily.

Keep to a logical sequence. (An outline can be a help. Put the outline on a transparency or on the chalkboard and let the students follow it.)

Try to involve the students in your teaching.

Avoid the overuse of workbooks and other humdrum seatwork. (Workbooks and seatwork exercises are best reserved for reinforcing and assessing skills that have already been taught.)

Pay particular attention to small-group work.

Small-group Work

Small-group activities are useful for teaching students to handle ideas and for helping students to learn from each other. Brainstorming; oral reports; sharing, editing, and reacting to each other's work; and joint projects are examples of activities that lend themselves to small-group work. However, unless they are

---

[2] Jacob S. Kounin, *Discipline and Group Management in the Classroom* (New York: Holt, Rinehart and Winston, 1970), pp. 102–108.

well managed and monitored, small groups may bog down and become time wasting.

In order to make group work move smoothly, you should carefully structure groups. Groups should probably be based on interest, or perhaps specific skills, rather than on students' general ability. Further, the makeup of the groups should be flexible. Group membership should change from time to time according to group task. No group or committee should become a permanent clique.

To keep things moving, you should be especially careful to ensure that the group members understand their tasks, procedures, routines, and responsibilities. It may be also helpful to appoint a monitor to check the group's progress and to answer questions about the assignment, and to require students who have questions to consult with other students before questioning you. You should also have several standing assignments ready for students who finish their group work early.

Clarifying by Routinizing

Routinizing the humdrum day-after-day tasks will ease movement management. Pupils are more likely to do things without argument or disruption when they are used to doing them and doing them in a certain way. If you set up routines for various everyday functions, pupils will always know what they are supposed to do. In this way, you can reduce fuss and confusion. Just what routine you select does not really matter, as long as it seems reasonably efficient. Among the common tasks that need routinizing are taking attendance, issuing equipment and supplies, collecting and passing papers, starting class, and stopping class. Therefore, take time to ensure that your students understand the classroom procedures and behavior that are expected of them. Be sure your students know proper routines to be followed when they first enter the classroom for obtaining supplies, for giving oral reports, for passing out and collecting papers, for issuing equipment and other materials, for completing written assignments, for obtaining permission to leave the room, for conducting small-group or laboratory work, for closing up shop and putting things away at the end of a class, and for carrying out other housekeeping and administrative details. Ordinarily the time to teach such routines occurs when the routine is first introduced. Soon these routines should become so automatic that students follow them without prompting.

"Withitness"

You should also develop skill in the techniques Kounin calls "withitness." We used to call it "having eyes in the back of your head."

Keep all of the class under surveillance all the time. Look around the room frequently. Move around.

Keep pupils alert by calling on them randomly, asking questions and then calling on an answerer, circulating from group to group, and frequently checking on individual progress.

Keep all the pupils in the act. Don't let yourself become overinvolved with any one pupil or group. Avoid the temptation to concentrate on those pupils who seem most interested or responsive.

Above all, keep pupil interest at a high level by introducing variety and sparkle into your classroom activities.

Monitoring

Above all monitor. Effective classroom management is dependent on monitoring. If your classes are to run smoothly, efficiently, and effectively, you must monitor unceasingly. This requires more than movement management and withitness. It requires constant checking and feedback. Among the things to check are:

Is everyone attending to business?
Does everyone have something to do?
Does everyone understand the assignment?
Does everyone understand how to proceed?
Does everyone have the materials to work with?
Are your directions clear?
Is the content too difficult?
Is the work challenging enough?
Are the physical conditions all right?
Does everyone understand your standards of behavior and workmanship?
Are the students progressing as well as they should? Are they using the proper procedures? Are they making mistakes?

It is absolutely imperative that you continually check students' work and provide feedback. By so doing you can catch errors and correct them before they become a problem, and find opportunities to praise good work. Careful monitoring can prevent both present and future problems, and ensures a businesslike learning climate. It is much better for a student to learn things right today than to have to unlearn bad practices tomorrow.

In short, you should see to it that your class moves briskly from the first to the final ringing of the bell. To achieve this goal, you should pay particular attention to your preparation, organization, movement management, "withitness" and, above all, to monitoring.

Maintaining Discipline

Most beginning teachers find discipline their most worrisome problem. As a rule, however, teachers who establish good motivation and classroom management are not greatly troubled by discipline problems. Even in the "worst" schools in the "worst" neighborhoods we find teachers who run efficient, effective classes with hardly any discipline problems at all.

Why Students Misbehave

Pupils misbehave for many reasons. One is the sheer deviltry of it. Classroom situations are somewhat unnatural, restrictive situations, so pupils like to relieve the tension. Other reasons for misbehavior may stem from their family and community backgrounds or their emotional life. Some misbehavior is simply the outburst of the restlessness, rowdiness, and exuberance of youth. But much of pupil misbehavior is school-caused and teacher-caused. Classes are tedious and boring. The curriculum seems worthless and irrelevant to anything that is important to youth. When their schooling is often so far removed from the pupils' lives, it is no wonder that they lose interest, become inattentive, and direct their energies into what to them seem more productive, fulfilling activities. Furthermore, many teachers and their classes are unpleasant, repressive, and abrasive. Irrelevance, tedium, unpleasantness, repression, and boredom all contain the seeds of mis-behavior.

Preventive Discipline

In view of what has just been said, it would seem that the most fruitful steps you can take to achieve well-disciplined classes are preventive. We have considered these steps in our earlier discussions of motivation and classroom management. Basically our premise is that if motivation and classroom management are well taken care of, discipline problems will be minimized.

Self-discipline

The best discipline, of course, is self-discipline. If you can teach pupils to take over the responsibility for their own learning and to carry out this responsibility, you will have done much. Some of the ways teachers work to help pupils become self-disciplined include the following.

1. Help pupils establish a code of conduct for themselves. Doing so has the advantage of acquainting pupils with what acceptable behavior is and why such behavior is necessary for the success of the group or of society. This code should not be dictated by the teacher, but worked out together to the mutual satisfaction of all concerned if it is to be successful.

2. Help pupils improve their own standards of conduct. This must be a slow process. It is done by making pupils aware of the advantages to them of high standards and the disadvantages of the lower standards. Techniques such as value-clarifying questions and discussions should be helpful in the process.

3. Use the enforcement of rules as a tool. Sometimes, enforcing rules helps pupils learn to discipline themselves. Proper enforcement of rules and making pupils follow the rules tend to make desirable behavior habitual. Teachers also have had good success by talking out behavior problems with the pupils so they can see why the behavior is unacceptable, what the pupil should do about it as penance, and the remedy to the fault. In some classes pupils enforce many of the rules themselves. This procedure may work well for mature groups, but it is likely to throw too much burden on the pupils. Probably it is best for the teacher to assume all the responsibility for rule enforcement.

Enforcing Rules

No matter how well motivated, managed, and self-disciplined your classes are, problems will arise. Therefore, you should be particularly attentive to rule enforcement. What you do when someone breaks the rules is more important than the rule breaking.

Reasonably strict enforcement of rules can have a salutory effect on the class and the classroom atmosphere. One reason for this is that enforcement has a ripple effect. When pupils see that you take swift, firm action against infractions by other pupils, they are less likely to misbehave. The ripple effect is especially powerful when you show that you can control pupils who have high status in their peer group. Conversely, when pupils see that others are getting away with break-ing the rules, they lose respect for the rules and for the teacher. To gain the most advantage of the ripple effect, you should start a policy of strict enforcement on the very first day. Being lax in the beginning is to court disaster. It is much easier to relax a policy of strict enforcement later than it is to turn a class around.

In any case, rule enforcement should be consistent and fair. Fairness and consistency in enforcement does not mean mindless conformity to an enforcement pattern. Sometimes justice should be tempered with mercy, and sometimes the nature of the punishment should be adjusted to the nature of the offender as well as to the nature of the offense. But when this is done, the action taken should seem reasonable to all concerned. Ordinarily, measures such as the following will be more effective than negative ones.

Let the students know what you expect of them and make them understand that they must ante up or else.

Correct inappropriate behavior at once. Don't let the students get started on inappropriate behavior or on disregarding rules.

Use nonintensive corrective measures: move toward the source of the trouble; use hand signals, eye contact, and dirty looks; tell the culprit to stop what he is doing and then see that he stops; ask the inattentive student a question.

Expect to handle all minor problems and punishments yourself.

Treat the problem rather than the person. Avoid making corrective actions personal.

If at all possible, use alternatives rather than punishment, but, if necessary, punishment should be swift, sure, and impressive.

Try to relieve tensions. Talk things over with the students. Tell them how to improve. Point out what they are doing well. Inject a little fun and good feeling.

When the class becomes restless, switch assignments. Switching to a written assignment may be particular effective for turning off incipient misbehavior.

If a student is a consistent rule breaker or show off, it may pay to isolate him by changing his seat. Sometimes giving such a student a minor responsibility may redirect his behavior.

If you must deny a student request, explain why.

Keep movement in the classroom to a minimum at least until you are sure of your control.

Have an alternative plan ready in case your original plan goes wrong.

On the whole, negative methods of rule enforcement are not every effective. Avoid using such methods as the following:

Nagging. Continual or unnecessary scolding or criticizing of a pupil succeeds only in upsetting the pupil and arousing the resentment of other pupils.

Threats and Ultimatums. Avoid painting yourself into a corner. Once you have made a threat or given an ultimatum, you are stuck with it if the pupils call you. In maintaining discipline, threats become promises. Once made, they must be carried out, or you will lose control. If pupils learn that your threats are impotent, they will disregard them and you.

Hasty Judgment and Action. Although your responses to behavior problems should be prompt, don't be overly hasty. Impulsive reactions may lead to complications rather than solutions.

Overreacting. Avoid treating minor incidents as major ones. Otherwise they may develop into real problems.

Arbitrary, Capricious, Inconsistent Disciplining. If you are inconsistent, students will test you to see what they can get away with. Inconsistency also causes student resentment and confusion.

Yelling and Screaming. Yelling and screaming simply add to the commotion. Teachers who yell and scream are part of the problem; yelling and screaming seldom solve anything.

Harsh, Unusual, Inconsistent Punishment. Flogging, beating, tongue-lashing, and humiliation are seldom effective. Although some pupils may occasionally need to be told off, hurting or humiliating them may do much more harm than good. Punishment is discussed in more detail in the next section.

Exercise 7 B

Observe good middle and high school classes. How do the teachers maintain good discipline? Often it seems as though the best teachers do not have to do anything to maintain discipline. What is it about their teaching that seems to keep their classes free from discipline and control problems?

Think back to your high school days. What did the best teachers do to establish and maintain good control and discipline?

Correcting Misbehavior

The goal of classroom control is to so motivate and shape the pupils that they do not create discipline problems. Positive motivation is a preventive measure that is the real key to classroom control. When pupils are working well, control and discipline take care of themselves. Nevertheless, even in the best of classes, the behavior of some pupils is less than desirable and needs to be turned into new directions.

Theoretically, there are four basic methods to stop anyone from behaving in an undesirable way. One is to keep the offender at it until he gets sick of it. A second is to make sure that the undesirable behavior is not rewarded in any way and so dies out. A third approach is to provide an alternative that is incompatible with the undesirable behavior, and to see to it that the alternate behavior is rewarded but the undesirable behavior is not. The fourth method is to create an aversive situation that the person can relieve only by giving up the undesirable behavior. The principles on which these methods are based are called, respectively, the satiation principle, the extinction principle, the incompatible alternative principle, and the negative reinforcement principle. A fifth principle calls for punishment or results supposedly so unpleasant that the person will not willingly repeat the misbehavior again.

Satiation and extinction are seldom practicable measures for correcting unseemly behavior in schools. Therefore, teachers can depend only on incompatible alternatives, negative reinforcement, and punishment to correct misbehavior. The incompatible alternative and the negative reinforcement methods are likely to be more successful than punishment.

In the incompatible alternative method, the teacher sets up an alternative behavior that is so rewarding the pupil forsakes the misbehavior. To find extremely strong, usable rewards suitable to the classroom situation may be difficult, but they do exist, as we pointed out in the discussion of the reinforcement menu. The catch, of course, is that the reward for the alternative behavior must be very powerful so as to overshadow the reward derived from the misbehavior.

The negative reinforcement method is much more subtle. In this method, the teacher sets up an aversive situation designed to plague the pupil as long as he misbehaves. As soon as he stops misbehaving, then the plaguing stops. The pupil who stops misbehaving is rewarded by relief from pain or annoyance. This approach is a much more effective way to correct student misbehavior than is punishment.

At times it is necessary to fall back on punishment in attempts to cure a malefactor. When this time comes, a teacher should attempt to make the punishment appropriate to the misdeed and also swift, sure, and impressive. The pupil should have no doubt that he is being punished, why he is being punished, and the types of behavior that will prevent his being punished again. Among the punishments often used are isolation, reprimands, extra work, deprivation of privileges, and detention. None of them is very effective in the long run. In the short term, however, they may shake up the pupil enough so that more positive measures can be used with greater chances of success. We now consider some of the punishments available to us.

Verbal Punishment

You will often have to reprimand a student. When you do, make it short and matter of fact. When it is necessary to explain in some detail why a student's behavior is unacceptable, do it in private. Avoid shouting, yelling, and nagging. Loud, frequent reprimands do not create a favorable learning environment. In fact, frequent reprimands seem to foster misbehavior. If you must call students to task, point out their inappropriate behavior and spell out corrective action. But there is no point in hurting their feelings, causing resentment, and building an unpleasant atmosphere unnecessarily by injudicious use of your acid tongue. Continual beratement of a student will get you nowhere.

Detention

Although detention is not particularly effective, keeping students after school is one of the most common types of punishment. Since it does have a mildly unpleasant effect on students, it is of some value as a deterrent. However, for many students, detention is such a mild inconvenience that they take it in stride. (For other students who work it may be a major concern, sometimes causing the student distress out of proportion to the initial misbehavior.) Besides, if the students just sit around during the detention period, detention can be a complete waste of time for everyone concerned. In order to make it profitable, detention probably should be combined with individual conferences, makeup work, extra help, or some other educational activity.

Loss of Privileges

Loss of privileges seems to be one of the most effective of all the punishments. It probably works best when it is combined with a system that grants rewards for good behavior. Then, if the privileges lost seem valuable to the student, loss of privileges demonstrates to the student that inappropriate behavior is costly, while appropriate behavior pays off.

Restitution and Reparation

A time-honored belief in the Anglo-American tradition is that "the punishment should fit the crime." This notion is the basis for the use of restitution and reparation as punishment. Punishment of this type has several advantages. It associates the punishment with the offense in a natural way. It teaches malefactors that they are responsible for their misdeeds, and that willful damage should be compensated for. It can be dealt fairly with impartiality. Most importantly, it teaches offenders that their actions affect the welfare of others and so they must accept the responsibility for making things right and paying back others for inconvenience and expense caused by their inappropriate behavior.

Punishing the Group

At times teachers punish the entire class for the misbehavior of one student. Usually, in these incidents, the teacher does not know just who the miscreant is. Although this type of punishment may sometimes be useful in arousing student disapproval of misbehavior, it generally does more harm than good. It tends to align the class against the teacher and create a hostile climate. You would be wise never to use it.

Assigning Extra Work

Assigning extra class work to offenders is another punishment you would do well to avoid. It seems to have no worthwhile advantages. All it does, evidently, is to create a dislike for school work and so, for school teachers, is self-defeating.

Lowering Academic Marks

To lower students' marks as a punishment is a misuse of the marking system. Academic marks should be only an indicator of academic achievement. To mark a student down for his behavior when he has learned well gives a false index of the student's progress.

Corporal Punishment

In spite of being dramatic and impressive, corporal punishment has not proven to be very effective in the long run. It humiliates students and creates feelings of resentment and hostility, and so generally disrupts one's attempts to build a favorable classroom climate. In addition, it is fraught with danger. Corporal punishment may arouse the entire class against the teacher. Further, it may lead to legal problems. In some states and school districts striking a student is illegal. Sometimes this type of punishment has resulted in student injury and in a subsequent suit against the teacher. In other cases students have reacted violently and injured the teacher. In short, using corporal punishment is liable to put the teacher in a no-win situation.

To protect yourself from legal actions, any teacher who uses corporal punishment should:

Make absolutely certain the culprit is guilty beyond all doubt.
Know and abide by the local laws and regulations concerning corporal punishment.

Administer the punishment in private with witnesses.

Do not strike a pupil's face, ears, or head.

Never punish while angry.

Record the punishment and the offense and file the record in the principal's office.

A safer policy is: *Never use corporal punishment. Never strike a student. Never push, shove, or manhandle any student in any way. If such drastic punishment must be used, turn the matter over to the principal. Do not do it yourself, ever!*

When a Class Is Out of Control

If a class gets out of control, the first thing to do is to stop the disturbance. Later, you can take affirmative action to set things right. The following tactics should help.

1. Get the students' attention. Shout, if you must, but not much. Don't add to the confusion.

2. Try to get everyone in his seat or at least standing still and quiet.

3. If this does not work, single out individuals and give specific instructions, e.g., "You, come here now and sit down."

4. If the disturbance continues, do not say anything humiliating or unfriendly, but do show that you are impatient. Avoid threats, but do let the students know you expect corrective behavior.

5. Whatever happens, keep calm. If you feel panicky, keep quiet for a while. If you feel the situation is dangerous, get help.

6. As soon as things seem to be coming under control, move into affirmative learning activity.[3]

Handling Major Offenses

If you are ever confronted with a major offense, such as students' carrying weapons, using drugs, vandalism, leaving the room without authorization, or fighting, try to stop the misbehavior. Then report it immediately and let the principal take it from here.

Remember, you are neither a law enforcement officer nor a psychiatrist. Major problems require outside assistance from a professional. Refer!

Exercise 7 C

Assume that one of the girls in your class is a continual talker. Can you think of a high-status reward activity that might cause her to keep quiet?

Can you think of an aversive situation you might set up as a basis for negative reinforcement? Discuss this with your friends.

[3] After Edward T. Ladd (with John C. Walden), *Student Rights and Discipline* (Arlington: Va.: National Association of Elementary School Principals, 1975), pp. 47–48.

Therapeutic Techniques

Recently expert teachers have been turning to the use of various therapeutic techniques in their campaign against misbehavior and the reformation of disruptive pupils. Among these approaches are reality therapy, the life-space interview, and creative listening techniques.

Reality Therapy

Glasser recommends that one should correct misbehavior by applying the techniques of reality therapy to disruptive pupils. Basically, these procedures are as follows:

1. Pick a student whose behavior is troublesome but not hopeless. Note the measures you are taking to curb his disruptive behavior.
2. Analyze the measures you are taking. Discard any that do not seem to be working.
3. Do something special to show that you care for the offender, for instance, give him some responsibility. If the offender feels that you are treating him well, his behavior may improve.
4. If the pupil is disruptive, ask him what he is doing. Then ask him to please not do it any more.
5. If disruptions continue, ask, "What are you doing?" Then ask, "Is it against the rules?" Finally, ask, "What should you be doing?" The object of this interchange is to suggest that you expect him to do what he should be doing from now on.
6. If these interchanges are not effective, repeat step five, but instead of asking what he should be doing, ask him to devise a plan that will result in his following the rules. Then the two of you together should work out a simple, short-term plan for improved behavior that the pupil accepts. The more the pupil is involved in forming this plan, the better it is.
7. If the pupil continues to misbehave, isolate the pupil and bar him from class activities until he is ready to behave well.
8. If the pupil's misbehavior persists, refer the pupil to the principal or disciplinarian. At this level the administration presumably will resort first to in-school suspension, followed by out-of-school suspension and a showdown with the pupil's parents if the in-school suspension fails, and finally, as a last resort, permanent explusion from school.[4]

Life-Space Interview

William C. Morse recommends the use of the life-space interview for dealing with disruptive pupils.

1. Begin the process by asking the pupil to tell what happened. If two or more pupils are involved, be sure to "balance" your listening. At this time try to listen empathetically so as to establish trust and to learn the pupils' perception of what happened.

---

[4] William Glasser, "10 Steps to Discipline," *Today's Education* 66:60–63. (November-December 1977).

2. Try to find out the central issue. The incident and what pupils say is the problem may be only symptomatic of some deeper problem.
3. Ask the pupil what he thinks should be done about it. Often at this stage the problem may be resolved through reasonable discussion.
4. If it is not resolved, discuss with the student what will likely happen if such behavior continues. Be careful at this point not to oversell. Be straightforward when describing what the penalties, punishments, and other results might be.
5. Find out from the pupil how the pupil thinks he may be helped and how you may be able to help him with his problem.
6. Develop a follow-through plan with the pupil in which you work out with the pupil what will happen if such an incident occurs again. This plan must, of course, conform to school policy.[5]

Creative Listening

Creative listening techniques are useful for carrying out such interviews. Essentially, creative listening consists of encouraging pupils to express their ideas and feelings by repeating the person's statements and by asking for clarification when it becomes obvious that the person will not continue talking on his own. Creative listening is completely nonjudgmental and nondirective. It is simply a technique to encourage people to talk out their feelings. Sometimes after a problem is out in the open, it solves itself. Pupils, in effect, talk themselves into rational feelings and behavior once the pressure is off. Following is an example of the kind of reacting and questioning one might use in creative listening.

> Pupil: I hate history.
> Teacher: You hate history?
> Pupil: It's a lot of junk. Who cares what happened a hundred years ago?
> Teacher: You don't care what happened long ago?
> Pupil: No. What's it to me?
> Teacher: You don't think what happened long ago has any relevance to you?

If repetition fails to draw the pupil out, you might ask such clarification questions as

> "What is it about history that makes you dislike it?"
> "Why do you think it is boring?"

If the conversation seems to be drying up, you might refer to something the pupil said earlier, either repeating it or asking for a clarification. For example,

> "A little while ago you said you thought history was a lot of junk."

[5] William C. Morse, "Working Paper: Training Teachers in Life-Space Interviewing," *American Journal of Orthopsychiatry* (July 1963), 37:727–730. Described in Laurel N. Tanner, *Classroom Discipline for Effective Teaching and Learning* (New York: Holt, Rinehart and Winston, 1978), p. 68.

Similarly, you might ask the pupil to expand on something he said as in the following:

"You say that history is a lot of junk. What do you mean by that?" or "Would you like history if it were about things that are happening today? Tell me about something you studied you thought was really irrelevant to you," or "Tell me more about why you hate history."

The objective of the creative listening technique is to draw the pupil out by being supportive and empathetic without encouraging undesirable attitudes and behavior. Although this type of listening, which was developed by Carl Rogers as a basic technique for nondirective counseling in client-centered therapy, can be very successful, it is not an approach to use lightly. Before you attempt to use it with secondary or middle school pupils, you should master the technique by practice sessions with your college friends and colleagues in a small group. Ask a friend to act as a subject and have other friends observe and criticize your technique as you engage in a creative listening session. If you can tape-record or videotape the session, you can observe and criticize yourself. You may find it most enlightening.

Exercise 7 D

We have a young person—small, different from the rest of the class—who tends to monologue. The other children seem to dislike her. She wants to answer all the questions. When she does, the other pupils make remarks to each other and make faces. The student teacher does not interrupt her because he is afraid of hurting her feelings. Neither does he speak to the other pupils. This is an eighth-grade class.

How would you handle this girl and others in the class?

Suggested Reading

Alschuler, Alfred S. *School Discipline.* New York: McGraw-Hill, 1980.

Canter, Lee, and Marlene Canter. *Assertive Discipline: A Take Charge Approach for Today's Education.* Los Angeles: Canter and Associates, 1979.

Center on Evaluation Development and Research. *Discipline* Hot Topics Series 1984–1985. Bloomington, Ind.: Phi Delta Kappa, 1984, pp. 79–228, 287–331.

Charles, C. M. *Building Classroom Discipline.* New York: Longman, 1981.

Clarizio, Harvey F. *Toward Positive Classroom Discipline,* 3d ed. New York: John Wiley & Sons, 1980.

Congelosi, James S. *Cooperation in the Classroom: Students and Teachers Together.* Washington, D.C.: National Education Association, 1984.

Conners, Eugene T. *Student Discipline and the Law,* Fastback 121. Bloomington, Ind.: Phi Delta Kappa Educational Foundation, 1979.

Discipline in the Classroom, 2d rev. ed. Washington, D.C.: National Education Association, 1980.

Duke, Daniel L. *Helping Teachers Manage Classrooms.* Alexandria, Va.: Association for Supervision and Curriculum Development, 1982.

———. *Managing Student Behavior Problems.* New York: Teachers College Press, 1981.

Duke, Daniel L., and Adrienne Maravich Mickel. *Teachers Guide to Classroom Management.* New York: Random House, 1984.

Emmers, Edmund T., Carolyn M. Evertson, Julie P. Sanford, Barbara S. Clements, and Murray E. Worsham. *Classroom Management for Secondary Teachers.* Englewood Cliffs, N.J.: Prentice-Hall, 1984.

Gervais, Robert L., and Delos A. Dittburner. *What to Do When. . .? A Handbook for Classroom Discipline Problems with Practical and Positive Solutions.* Lanham, Md.: University Press of America, 1985.

Harvey, Karen. *Classroom Management.* Glenview, Ill.: Foresman, 1985.

Ladd, Edward T. (with John C. Walden). *Student Rights and Discipline.* Arlington, Va.: National Association of Elementary School Principals, 1975.

Laslett, Robert, and Colin Smith. *Effective Classroom Management.* New York: Nichols Publishing, 1984.

Long, James D., Virginia Frye, and Elizabeth W. Long. *Making It Till Friday: A Guide to Successful Classroom Management,* 3d ed. Princeton, N.J.: Princeton Book Co., 1985.

Mann, Lester. *Discipline and Behavioral Management.* Aspen, Colo.: Aspen Publications, 1983.

Rich, John Martin. *Innovative School Discipline.* Springfield, Il.: Charles C. Thomas, 1985.

Rinne, Carl H. *Attention: The Fundamentals of Classroom Control.* Columbus, Oh.: Charles E. Merrill, 1984.

Tanner, Laurel N. *Classroom Discipline for Effective Teaching and Learning.* New York: Holt, Rinehart and Winston, 1978.

Wolfgang, Charles H., and Carl D. Glickman. *Solving Discipline Problems: Strategies for Teachers,* 2d ed. Boston: Allyn and Bacon, 1986.

Post Test

A. Mark practice recommended in this module R; practice not recommended X.

1. At the first class do a great deal of teacher-student planning.

2. Make your classes completely nondirective.

3. Provide for individual differences.

4. Plan to lecture at least half of the period during each lesson, if possible.

5. Routinize ordinary administrative procedures.

6. Talk over the reasons for the various rules you establish.

7. Avoid setting rules until you are sure that you have the students under control.

8. Start classes immediately when the bell rings.

9. If you plan to use audiovisual media, arrange the class in a hollow square or circle.

10. Keep the class moving swiftly enough so that every student feels some pressure.

11. Base small-group membership on students' general ability rather than on their individual interests.

12. Change the membership in small groups from time to time.

13. Monitor your classes constantly.

14. Accent self-discipline.

15. Turn the responsibility for rule enforcement over to the students.

16. Encourage students to participate in establishing classroom behavioral standards.

17. At first keep movement in your classroom to a minimum.

18. Isolate show-offs.

19. Give troublemakers some small responsibility to encourage their cooperation and better behavior.

20. When in doubt about who the miscreant is, punish the entire class.

21. Punish persistent misbehavior by lowering the student's grade.

22. If corporal punishment seems advisable, turn the student over to the principal.

23. Punish malefactors by assigning them additional classwork.

24. Direct questions at nonattentive students.

25. Take care of all minor discipline problems yourself, but do not hesitate to call the principal's aid in case of major problems.

B. Answer the following questions briefly in the spaces provided.

26. Why do we advise teachers to avoid laissez-faire teaching?

   _____

   _____

   _____

27. Name one strategy that might help pupils to improve their own standards of conduct.

   _____

   _____

   _____

28. What is probably the most common cause of pupil misbehavior?

   _____

29. A new teacher was told never to smile in her classes until she has established firm control. Is this sound advice?

_____

_____

30. Would you advise a new teacher to set up a long list of rigid rules?

_____

_____

31. According to this module, which is the better technique: to be very strict at first and then relax when you have established control, or to be relaxed at first and become strict later if pupils misbehave?

_____

_____

32. What is negative reinforcement?

_____

_____

_____

33. What is the incompatible alternative method of control?

_____

_____

34. Is it better to have the classroom discipline strict or relaxed?

_____

_____

_____

35. What do we say is the key to good discipline?

_____

_____

_____

36. What is the difference between permissive and laissez-faire teaching?

_____

37. When should you, as a teacher, use harsh punishment?

_____

38. What can you do when planning to minimize discipline problems?

_____

_____

39. What are the six steps of the life-space interview?

_____

_____

_____

_____

_____

_____

40. Explain the movement management concept in classroom discipline.

_____

_____

_____

MODULE
8

Teacher-Centered Techniques

The first edition version of this module was written by William B. Fisher of Jersey City State College. It has been somewhat revised and updated for this edition.

Rationale

Today, teachers have entered a period of "professional competency." As professionals they know what they want and ought to do and how to do it. Therefore, if you are to become a professional, it is all-important that you have well-defined educational goals at which to aim. Basically, those aims should be to arouse your pupils to think for themselves and to awaken their power to observe, to remember, to reflect, and to combine.

To achieve these basic objectives, you must develop skill in teaching because, in spite of clichés, most master teachers are made, not born. Aptness for teaching, the cliché tells us, is a native endowment, a sort of instinct—an instinct such as that which guides the robin, though hatched in an oven, to build a perfect nest just like that of its parent without ever having seen one. Nonsense! Instincts in man are rare. Ability to teach, like the ability to do anything else, is usually an acquired power derived from a correct knowledge of what is to be done. If there are exceptions to this rule, they are very uncommon. Of course, teachers vary in their ability to execute instructional plans effectively, and to some extent these variations derive from differences in innate skills. However, seeming variations in innate ability are more likely the product of the personal skills and personality traits that a teacher has developed during the normal course of growing up. Therefore, the only safe way for most humans to become master teachers is to study carefully the how and why of the educational processes and to practice diligently, according to the best theory. Each teacher can most effectively harness whatever innate skills and character traits he or she may possess only through careful definition of objectives, thoughtful planning, and effective execution of those plans.

Knowledge of these procedures can be learned. And so it is imperative that you master the skills required for preparing and giving interesting, informative lectures, for using questions to build concepts and to stimulate thinking, and for carrying out lessons that will both drive concepts home and increase pupils' skills.

In this module we shall consider teaching methods that are basically expository in nature. These are the time-honored methods used by teachers to impart knowledge to neophytes. We shall also briefly discuss methods used in skill development and in fixing knowledge. All these methods are largely teacher-centered. Their basic technique is to give learners information and then insure remembering. Their role is to provide students with knowledge that will provide a foundation for higher thinking. At the conclusion of your study of this module, you should be able to demonstrate how various methods, specifically the lecture, the question, the practice activities, and the recitation, can be used to help pupils learn and to further the fundamental educational aims: to arouse pupils to think for themselves and to awaken their power to observe, to remember, to reflect, and to combine.

Specific Objectives

More specifically, upon the completion of this module, it is expected that you will be able to do the following:

1. Describe a general strategy for expository teaching.
2. Explain how to use the lecture method effectively.
3. Describe techniques for improving recitations.
4. Explain how to conduct an open-text recitation.
5. Explain how to conduct show-how teaching activities.
6. Explain how to conduct effective practice and drill.
7. Explain how to help pupils memorize effectively.
8. Explain how to carry out effective classroom questioning.
9. Describe the Socratic technique.
10. Describe the use of broad, narrow, cognitive memory, convergent, divergent and evaluative questions.
11. Show how to handle pupil questions.
12. Describe recommended procedures for conducting review.

Module Text

Expository Methods

Of all the teaching methods available, probably the most commonly used in middle and secondary schools are the expository techniques: informal teacher talks and their more formal cousins, the lecture.

According to Ausubel, "verbal exposition is the most efficient way of teaching subject matter and leads to sounder and less trivial knowledge than when pupils serve as their own pedagogues."[1] Be that as it may, there is no doubt that telling activities, i.e., lecture and informal teacher talks, will be among your most valuable tools.

However, you should be aware of two risks associated with teacher-telling strategies. One is that you will be tempted to talk too much. Of course, you will need to explain and describe things on many occasions, but do not overdo it.

---

[1] David P. Ausubel, *Educational Psychology: A Cognitive View* (New York: Holt, Rinehart and Winston, 1968), pp. 86–87.

Instead, ask questions, pose problems, seek comments, and solicit questions. When pupils seek out and discuss the explanations, they may learn more than they would from your telling.

The second risk to be aware of is that you must not let yourself believe that the pupils have learned something just because you have explained or described it. A pedagogical rule that has the force of eternal law is that whenever it is at all possible, pupils will misunderstand, misinterpret, or miss altogether what teachers tell them. Follow up your talks with questions designed to check the pupils' understanding.

A General Strategy

When you use lectures and other teacher talks, you may find it helpful to proceed along the following lines.

Begin by presenting an advance organizer, that is a brief presentation outlining the main ideas you hope to get across in your talk. This may, or may not, be in writing. Use this to introduce your topic and to orient the students. Then proceed with the body of your talk. As you do so, explain unfamiliar terms. Writing them down on the chalkboard or on a study guide sheet so that the pupils can see them will help them recognize and understand them. In giving your talk try to move forward easily and smoothly. Proceed in an orderly fashion making the relationship between the various facts and ideas clear and avoiding unnecessary verbiage, frills, and embellishments.

As your talk progresses, require students to participate actively. Ask occasional questions to make students think about what you have said. These questions should cause students both to recall information and to organize and discriminate among the facts and ideas you have presented. Provide immediate feedback to the student answers and comments so that they will know where they are right and where wrong, thus by comparison and contrast building better understanding. As you talk, try to ensure your effectiveness by carefully monitoring for signs of confusion, misunderstanding, and mind wandering and by building redundancy into your talk. Remember, the advice of the famous speaker. Tell them what you are going to tell them; tell them; and then tell them what you told them.

Then, when you have finished your talk, follow up with some other activity that will help clinch the learning.

Informal Teacher Talks

Most of your teacher-telling activities should be short, informal extemporary explanations or descriptions rising out of the needs of the occasion—the course of class discussion, pupil questions, the making of an assignment, and the like. They are usually most effective when they are interwoven with questions and discussion in what we sometimes call the lecture demonstration.

Talks of this sort will probably be one of your most common modes of teaching. Learn to use them well. Because of their short length and informality, they need not be planned so carefully as the lecture, but they should be planned. Be sure to get all the important points down in your lesson plan and provide for supporting aids that might be helpful.

Formal Talks and Lectures

In the lecture method the teacher tries to give to the learner by word of mouth knowledge he or she possesses but the learner does not. Although this definition is true as far as it goes, it is something of an oversimplification. The lecture, when done well, is not only a matter of the teacher's telling learners things they do not know. Skillful lecturers use it to arouse pupil interest, to set pupils to thinking and wondering, to open up new vistas, to tie together loose facts and ideas, to summarize and synthesize quickly, and to review.

Unfortunately not all lecturers are skillful. Consequently their pupils do not learn as much as they might. One reason for these failures is that lectures tend to make students passive. Although physical passivity does not necessarily indicate mental inactivity, unless one interjects opportunities for interaction into one's lecture, the students may just sit there. (Sometimes they don't even listen.) Besides, unless the lecturer takes special precautions, most lectures provide little reinforcement by which to drive home understanding. Consequently such lectures result in only superficial learning. The result is that ordinary lectures are often not very effective for changing attitudes, or for leading pupils to the attainment of higher cognitive goals.

Planning the Lecture.   In spite of these difficulties, the lecture can be a most valuable tool in your teaching arsenal. To be so, it must be carefully planned. Well-made plans for lectures

1. Clearly state the purpose and major theme or themes of the lecture.
2. Develop the lecture in a logical fashion that the pupils can follow.
3. Adjust the content and style to the situation and the audience.
4. Include clues that point out the logical development of the concepts step by step.
5. Avoid attempting too much. The lecture is the quickest way to present material that cannot be given in writing or by film, but if the lecture rushes on too fast, its impact will be lost. To include only a few important points is usually quite enough. Too often, especially with the inexperienced teacher, lecturing consists of pouring into the pupils every fact that occurs to him. Such lectures are focused on bringing to the pupils as many facts as possible in a limited time. Such lecturing is analogous to forced-feeding which can cause resistance and loathing for the food. It may result in lack of receptiveness, and the turning off of pupils' intellectual curiosity.
6. Begin with some interest-catching device. Often, experienced lecturers say, it is good to puzzle the listeners a little at first in order to catch their interest and to entice them to listen carefully.
7. Provide for the repetition of important points. Repetition is about the only means of reinforcement available to the lecturer.
8. Provide for questions, both real and rhetorical, to check pupils' understanding and to revive their interest at strategic points.
9. Encourage pupil questions and reactions.
10. Make the lecture as short as you reasonably can.
11. Include humor and the excitement of the unexpected.

12. Provide concrete examples.
13. Provide for audiovisual aids.
14. Follow an outline. Let the students have copies to follow or put the main points on the board.
15. Provide some sort of forceful summing up.

Giving the Lecture. During the lecture, the transfer of knowledge should produce an exhilarating experience. It should develop in the learner a sense of putting things together. To produce this feeling, the skillful lecturer learns to read his audience, feel its reaction, and adjust himself to the response. Therefore, when you lecture you should

1. Be alert to signs of restlessness, boredom, or confusion, and provide some sort of change of pace when such signs occur.
2. Include recapitulation as an aid to the pupils.
3. Point out clues that will help the listeners follow the steps in the development of the concept.
4. Use your voice to emphasize and dramatize. Remember that the teacher who lectures is on stage and must use any device that will captivate his audience.
5. Use other methods to complement the lecture. Study guides and outlines that the pupils may follow during the lecture may help, for instance. Any device that you can use to capture your pupils' attention and put across your concepts is legitimate. On occasion, you may wish to use a silent demonstration to bolster your lecture presentation, as in the following example: For a lecture on the relationship of gas volume to temperature change, a lecturer prepared a system consisting of a Bunsen burner heating a retort to which a balloon had been attached. He did not explain the purpose of this system. However, as he lectured on the concept that the heating of a gas tends to increase its volume, the size of the balloon attached to the heated retort increased until finally the balloon burst. By this technique, the lecturer hoped to give the pupils a visual example of the concept he was developing verbally. This technique not only concretized the concept, but also dramatized it. The bursting of the balloon particularly brought forth a strong class response to what might otherwise have been an obscure abstraction.
6. Use incomplete outlines that the pupils complete as the lecture goes on so as to make an active learning situation out of a passive one.
7. Throw in a question, real or rhetorical, from time to time to whet pupils' interest and to start them thinking.
8. Whenever feasible, use audiovisual aids. The use of the chalkboard, the overhead projector, pictures, maps, and graphs not only adds life to your lectures but usually also makes your ideas clearer. It is easier to understand what you can both see and hear than what you can only hear.
9. Keep your language clear, concise, and as simple as you reasonably can. Avoid pomposity.
10. Try to keep to the point. Digressions, reminiscences, and trivia obscure the message.

11. To be sure that your message is getting across, ask a few check questions once in a while.
12. In your lecture notes, mark those things that you wish to stress by writing them in capital letters, by underlining, or by placing a large star in the margin.
13. Above all, try to excite a spirit of inquiry and create in each pupil a desire to know and, when possible, to discover by himself. Therefore, you must not think for the pupil or give him results before the pupil has been given the opportunity to explore the concepts himself. A teacher who does that makes the mind of the pupil into something resembling a two-gallon jug into which he can pour two gallons, but no more. The mind, so far as retention is concerned, will act as the jug; that is, what is poured in today will be diluted by a part of that which is poured in tomorrow, and that again will be partially displaced and partially mixed with the next day's pouring until, at the end, there will be nothing characteristic left. The jug may be as good after such use as before, but the mind suffers by every unsuccessful effort to retain in this manner. This process of lecturing pupils into torpidity is altogether too frequently practiced, and it is hoped that intelligent teachers will pause and inquire before they pursue it further.

Following Up the Lecture.   After you have completed a lecture, you should follow it up with other related activities in order to bind the learning. Hold the pupils responsible for the content of the lecture. Make sure that they take notes and study them. Check their notes and check their knowledge. Utilize follow-up discussions, projects, themes, tests, quizzes, and other activities. Have someone summarize the main points in the next class session. It does not matter so much what you do as long as you do something that will help pupils to fix the important ideas in their heads and build these ideas into larger concepts through thought and inquiry.

Note Taking.   One reason that students do not learn from lectures as well as they might is that no one has ever really taught them how to listen and take notes. To be sure that your students learn these skills, you should monitor their note taking. If it seems that they do not do well, teach them how.

When to Use the Lecture.   Lectures have limited usefulness in middle and secondary school classes. They give pupils little opportunity to inquire or explore. They are not very effective for changing attitudes. They seldom exercise pupils' higher mental faculties or lead pupils directly to the attainment of the higher cognitive goals.

Yet, lectures do have many uses, and you should learn to use them to (1) establish a general point of view; (2) run over facts quickly; (3) arouse interest (if you are a good lecturer); (4) fill in basic or background information; (5) introduce new units, assignment, or content; (6) summarize; and (7) provide information otherwise not available to the pupils.[2]

---

[2] Leonard H. Clark, *Teaching Social Studies in Secondary Schools: A Handbook* (New York: Macmillan Publishing Co., 1973), p. 84.

Exercise 8 A

As a summary and review, consider each of the following questions. If you cannot answer any of them readily, you should turn back and review the pertinent section.

1. The lecture, although a useful technique, should not be overused in junior and senior high school classes. Why is it not as useful as some other techniques? For what might you use the lecture?
2. What can a lecturer do to arouse and maintain interest in his lecture?
3. How can one encourage the inquiry process when he lectures?
4. What principles should you keep in mind when planning a lecture?
5. What can you do to make your lecturing successful?

Think back to the classes given by the best lecturer in your college experience. What did this professor do that made his or her lectures better than average?

Listen to a lecture or teacher talk given by one of your professors or colleagues. What use of aids did the lecturer use to spice up the lecture? What devices might have been used? If you were the lecturer, would you have handled it differently?

Prepare a major behavioral objective for a topic in your subject field. What points would you try to make and how would you try to get the points across in a lecture to support that major objective?

Questioning

Questioning is probably the key technique in most teaching. It can be used for so many purposes that it is hard to see how a teacher can persevere unless he is a skillful questioner. Therefore, you, as a new teacher, should learn the rationale for different questioning techniques and should practice these techniques.

As we have already noted, questions may be used for many purposes. Among them are the following:

1. To find out something one did not know.
2. To find out whether someone knows something.
3. To develop the ability to think.
4. To motivate pupil learning.
5. To provide drill or practice.
6. To help pupils organize materials.
7. To help pupils interpret materials.
8. To emphasize important points.
9. To show relationships, such as cause and effect.
10. To discover pupil interests.
11. To develop appreciation.
12. To provide review.

13. To give practice in expression.
14. To reveal mental processes.
15. To show agreement or disagreement.
16. To establish rapport with pupils.
17. To diagnose.
18. To evaluate.
19. To obtain the attention of wandering minds.[3]

Effective teachers try to adapt the type and form of each question they ask to the purpose for which they ask it. Consequently, the questions they ask to find out whether pupils know something may differ considerably from questions designed to start pupils thinking.

Types of Questions

Questions may be either narrow or broad. Narrow questions usually seek recall of fact or specific correct answers. The answer may consist of a single word or phrase. The answers to broad questions, on the other hand, are more complicated. Seldom can such questions be answered by a single word or a simple correct answer. Rather, these questions require the answerer to arrive at his own conclusions. By causing students to think and provide original answers, they broaden the scope of the learning situation and stimulate interaction and involvement among the pupils.

Questions can also be categorized as cognitive memory questions, convergent questions, divergent questions, and evaluative questions.[4] According to this classification, cognitive memory questions are those that test one's memory. They are narrow rather than broad and require little or no thinking—just remembering. Convergent questions are also quite narrow. In answering this type of question, the pupil should respond with the correct answer. The question may require quite a lot of thinking but, once thought out, there is a correct answer and usually only one correct answer. For example, the question "If the radius of a circle is 10 feet, what is the circumference of the circle?" requires one to respond with a specific correct answer even though it may require some thinking. Many questions in logic call for quite complicated thinking and close analysis, but can result in only one correct answer if one accepts the premises. In convergent questions then, the correct answer can be predicted.

Exercise 8 B

Try to formulate some convergent questions that would be appropriate for your subject field. Remember that you are trying to ask questions that require considerable thinking but have a predictable correct answer.

[3] Leonard H. Clark and Irving S. Starr, *Secondary and Middle School Teaching Methods,* 4th ed. (New York: Macmillan Publishing Co., 1981), pp. 172–173.
[4] James J. Gallagher and Mary Jane Aschner, "A Preliminary Report of Analyses of Classroom Interaction," *The Merrill-Palmer Quarterly of Behavior and Development,* (July 1963), 9:183–194.

Divergent questions are wide-open questions. No one can predict exactly what the answers will, or should, be. Divergent questions do not have correct answers. They are the type of questions that open pupils up, that get them to thinking and imagining. Some examples follow. Suppose that the thirteen American colonies had not separated themselves from England, what would the map of North America look like today? or, What steps might the United States government take to improve the economic situation? What course would you advise the government to take?

Exercise 8 C

Try to prepare a few divergent questions that would be suitable for a course you might teach.

Evaluative questions ask the pupil to put a value on something. In a sense, this is a special case of the divergent question because, as a rule, values are very subjective. As the Romans used to say, "There is no accounting for taste."[5] However, some evaluative questions may be convergent, because if we start with similar assumptions, presumably we should all arrive at the same or similar conclusions. Examples of evaluative questions are (1) Which do you consider to be the better practice? (2) Should Mr. Nixon have been impeached? (3) What kind of a character was Othello?

Exercise 8 D

Try to construct some evaluative questions suitable for classes you might teach.

Remember that one must allow pupils to arrive at their own answers to convergent, divergent, and evaluative questions. If you have given pupils ready-made answers that they cough up on call, your questioning is not convergent, divergent, or evaluative, but is the cognitive memory type. So are most fact questions whose answers one can find in the textbook.

You should also remember that in your teaching you will have to use all of the types of questions. There will be times when your questions should be broad and times when they should be narrow. There will be times when you should use memory questions and times when you should use convergent questions just as there will be times when you should use divergent or evaluative questions. The point is that *you should always try to use the type of question best suited to your purpose.* Usually, this means that you should use divergent and evaluative questions much more frequently than most teachers do.

---

[5] *De gustibus non disputandum est.*

Exercise 8 E

Look at the following questions. Which do you find narrow and which broad? Which are cognitive memory, convergent, divergent, or evaluative? Compare your answers with those listed at the end of the module.

1. Do you agree with Mary, John?
2. Do you believe that argument will hold up in the case of Switzerland?
3. What must I multiply by in order to clear the fractions in this equation?
4. How does the repetition in the Bolero affect you?
5. Did O'Henry's trick ending make the story more interesting?
6. How would you end the story?
7. Who came out of the door, the lady or the tiger?
8. How do the natural resources of the United States compare with those of the USSR?
9. If you were setting up the defense of the colonies, where would you put the forts?
10. In view of all the information we have, do you believe the union's sending out seventy thousand letters asking voters to defeat the six assemblymen was justified?
11. What difference will an Equal Rights Amendment make?
12. Who was Otto Jespersen?
13. Should a teacher who earns $20,000 a year be entitled to unemployment benefits during the summer months when school is not in session and when he does not get paid?
14. What would you do in this situation if you were the governor?
15. What would have happened if Washington had decided to attack New Brunswick rather than Quebec?
16. What would happen if you used H_2SO_4 instead of HCl?
17. How would you set up the equation?
18. Why did you like this poem better?

Note learning situations that are likely to occur in a course you expect to teach in which you would use cognitive memory questions, convergent questions, divergent questions, and evaluative questions.

Build some questions for situations of each type.

Thought Questions

Thought questions may be convergent, divergent, or evaluative. They differ from cognitive memory questions only in that the pupils must supply the answers from their own thinking, not their memory. You should use them frequently as a means for involving pupils in their own learning and to set them thinking. Use convergent questions to make pupils figure out the solutions to problems with set answers. For example,

> *To treat an elm for Dutch elm disease, one should use one gallon of the inoculant mixture for each six inches of the tree's diameter at chest height. You have a tree three feet, six inches in circumference at chest height. The formula for the inoculant mixture is one quart of "Noculant" to one gallon of water. How much "Noculant" and how much water should you mix together to treat your tree?*

Use divergent and evaluative questions to open up discussions and to widen pupils' thinking about the topic at hand.

> *Should the United States take on the role of peacekeeper in the Middle East?*
> *When is it appropriate to use the sediment dating of fossils?*
> *In what ways might we test our hypothesis concerning the genesis of this phenomenon?*

Probing and Socratic Questions

Probing questions are the type used to follow up pupil responses, to force them to think more thoroughly, to firm up flimsily thought out answers or notions, to ferret out solid answers to half-answered questions, and the like. One type of probing question helps pupils to clarify their ideas. For instance, if a student states that everyone in a democracy must speak the same language if the country is to remain viable, you might ask, "What about Switzerland?" Other examples of such questions are, "Is that fact or opinion?"; "Can you cite specific instances?"; "What is the factual basis of such a belief?" and so on.

Other types of probing questions simply go further into the topic. If, for instance, a girl states that every American has the right of free speech, you might ask her, "What gives them the right to free speech?" "Does the right of free speech include spreading malicious, libelous gossip?" and so on.

Still another type of probing is the Socratic question. The ancient Greek philosopher Socrates used this approach to try to get his pupils to think. Socrates' idea was that one should never tell a pupil what to think but that by means of questioning one should act as a midwife assisting at the birth of pupils' ideas. In general, the procedure for Socratic questioning is to

1. Elicit from your pupils a statement of belief or opinion. This can be done by using some sort of simple expository statement or one of the various springboard techniques, or by asking pupils to express their belief or opinion.
2. Examine this situation, belief, or opinion by the use of probing questions. In your questioning you should
   a. Try to bring out certain answers.
   b. Challenge pupils to examine their own ideas and beliefs.
   c. Ask your questions in a logical sequence.
   d. Attempt to aid pupils to develop their own idea as a result of your questioning.
   e. Lead the pupils to your predetermined goal, concept, or belief.

Probing and Socratic questioning are important tools in discovery teaching, and thought and value clarification. They will be discussed further in Module 10.

Levels of Questions

In his *Questioning Strategies and Techniques,* Francis Hunkins[6] shows how questions can be adjusted to the taxonomic levels of Bloom's taxonomy of cognitive objectives.[7] You will remember that in this taxonomy the levels run from the lowest, simple understandings, through comprehension, application, analysis, synthesis to evaluation, of the highest level. Examples of questions at various levels follow.

Knowledge of facts. *What is the formula for water?*
Knowledge of ways and means. *How do you find the area of a circle?*
Knowledge of universals and abstractions. *Basically, what is gravity?*
Comprehension. *What does market value mean? What did Lincoln mean by "a government of the people by the people and for the people"?*
Application. *According to the map, what bearing would one have to take to fly straight from New York, N.Y., to Rome, Italy? In the Northern Hemisphere in which direction should your heat-energy gathering device face?*
Analysis. *In view of the terrain at what three points would efforts to prevent an invasion be most effective? Why? In what ways does this advertisement violate common sense?*
Synthesis. *What steps would you recommend the city take to reduce violence in the streets? How could we correct the traffic problem at Thomas Jefferson Junior High School?*
Evaluation. *In view of the arguments presented by Senator Merlino and the National Rifle Association do you think that the Legislature should ban Saturday Night Specials? Which of the two film strips seems to be most effective? What advantages and disadvantages do you find in the plan?*

Presumably, if the taxonomies are correct, one should ask questions at the higher levels only after one is sure that the pupils understand and can perform at the lower levels. In practice this may be difficult and even impractical, but there is no doubt that teachers should attempt to use questions both to expand pupils' understandings and to lift them to higher cognitive levels. Do this by following up exposition and low level questions with higher level questions that expand the students' knowledge. For instance, after you ask the provisions of a decision you might follow up with additional questions on what impact these provisions would have and whether they would be beneficial or not. This can be done both by asking pupils to elaborate on their own answers or to comment on or expand other

---

[6] Francis P. Hunkins, *Questioning Strategies and Techniques* (Boston, Mass.: Allyn & Bacon, 1972), Chap. 2.

[7] Benjamin Bloom, et al., *Taxonomy of Educational Objectives: Handbook I. The Cognitive Domain* (New York: David McKay Co., 1956), pp. 201–207. See Module 3 for an outline of this taxonomy.

pupils' answers. Questions at the synthesis level are usually a little difficult to carry off in the ordinary class discussion. Ordinarily they are best reserved for committee work, projects and the like. Nevertheless sometimes they can form the nucleus for a rousing class discussion as when a Jersey City high school class brought forth numerous suggestions on how one might rejuvenate a decaying downtown area.

Guidelines for Questioning Techniques

Obviously, as a teacher you should have a well-digested plan of operation that you know beforehand you can successfully execute. If you first identify the concepts you wish to develop, you can easily select your texts and orchestrate your procedures so as to keep your students thinking and alert. A useful tool in this pursuit is the divergent question described earlier. This type of question inquires "how" rather than "what" and encourages greater inquiry. For this purpose it is more useful than leading questions that pupils can barely fail to answer, and other pouring in and regurgitative procedures. Let your objective be to excite inquiry and thought by asking questions that pupils cannot answer without thought and observation. Questioning is a dynamic process. Like a chemical reaction it contains both movement and reaction. Questions cause the movement of information from pupil to teacher, and, it is to be hoped, from pupil to pupil. The result is that all participants become involved and interaction occurs. Real learning comes from interaction and involvement.

To develop good skill in questioning is not difficult, but it does require attention to detail. Perhaps the following guidelines will prove useful as you try to build your skill in questioning.

A. General Guidelines.
  1. Questions should be clear.
  2. Questions are to be used to stimulate thinking and to produce an extended answer.
  3. A question should not contain the answer
  4. Questions should not suggest the correct answer.
  5. Questions should rarely call for a simple yes or no answer.
  6. Questions should lead pupils toward the development of the concept.
B. Guidelines for Presenting Questions.
  1. Ask the questions first, and then call on some pupil to answer it.
  2. Ask the question and provide time for thought. Do not use the machine gun approach.
  3. If a partial answer is given, pose another question to expand the answer.
  4. Involve as many pupils as possible. Do not fall into the habit of calling on only those who you know will give the correct answer.
  5. Praise a good answer.
  6. Handle wrong answers positively. Do not use sarcasm! Try to rephrase the question in such a way that the student will arrive at the correct answer or at least a partially correct answer. Reinforce the correct part of partially correct answers.
  7. Encourage pupils not to accept an answer that they believe to be incorrect. This calls for listening and thinking.

8. Evaluate your own questions as to clarity, level, and relevancy.
C. Guidelines That May Help You Develop Proficiency In the Use of Thought Questions.
   1. Use developmental questions emphasizing how and why rather than who, what, where, and when.
   2. Follow up leads. Build on pupils' contributions. Give pupils a chance to comment on each other's answers; for example, "Do you agree with John on that, Mary?" or "Do you think this argument would hold in such and such case, John?" *[handwritten: TOO PERSONAL]*
   3. Be sure the pupils have the facts before you ask thought questions about them. One way is to ask fact questions first and then follow up with thought questions. Another way is to lead in by means of good summary questions. Other ways are to incorporate the facts in the question itself or to give the pupils fact sheets that they can consult as they try to think through suitable answers to the question. Similar results can be gained by putting the facts on the blackboard or on the overhead projector, by allowing pupils to refer to their texts, or by simply telling the pupils the facts before beginning the questioning.
   4. Remember that the best thought questions usually do not have correct answers. In such cases, the thinking concerned is much more important than the answer derived. Be sure pupils back up their answers by valid, logical reasoning. Insist that they show their evidence and demonstrate why this evidence leads to their conclusions. *[handwritten: divergent]*
   5. Encourage pupils to challenge each other's thinking and even that of their teacher. Good use of thought questions leads to true discussion rather than simple question-answer teaching.[8]
   6. Try to sequence your questions so as to use higher level questions to build on and expand what has been established by lower order questions.

Handling Student Questions

To create the proper atmosphere for interaction and involvement, you must be careful not only how you ask questions but also how you handle pupils' questions and answers. There is an old proverb that says, "What I hear, I forget. What I see, I remember. What I say and do, I understand." What pupils say and do can also cause them to think in an inquiring manner. They may question each other; they may question the teacher, who should be able to respond with other questions that can guide pupils in the right direction. This approach should help pupils reach some conceptual conclusion. Therefore try to build a classroom atmosphere in which students are encouraged to ask relevant questions.

Student questions present teachers with a persistent dilemma: How much should you as teacher help the pupils versus how much should you as teacher require students to work things out on their own? The nature of teaching seems to indicate that students should be taught to depend on their own resources. Therefore, it is not wise to let students acquire the habit of running to you as soon as a slight difficulty presents itself. Neither is it wise to discourage students who need assistance and clarification. Oftentimes the best procedure is to suggest clues

---

[8] Clark, op. cit., pp. 80–81.

that will help students solve their problems themselves. Refer the pupil to the principles which he previously has learned and of which he now may have lost sight. Perhaps call his attention to some rule or explanation previously given to the class. Go just so far as to enlighten him enough to put him on the track. Then leave him to achieve the victory himself. There is a great satisfaction in discovering the solution to a difficult problem for one's self.

Some additional hints on handling pupil questions and promoting pupil interaction might include the following:

1. Use pupil questions as springboards for further questions and discussion.
2. Consider all relevant questions that pupils ask. Some you may answer yourself; others you may refer to the class or to specific classmates; others you may have to look up or have someone look up.
3. Encourage pupils to ask questions that challenge the text or other pupils' statements, such as "What was the authority or basis for that statement?" or "Can you prove that to be true?"
4. Turn off trivial and irrelevant questions kindly and courteously, but firmly.
5. Avoid allowing particular pupils to dominate. Counsel pupils who dominate. Counsel privately pupils who take up too much time.

Exercise 8 F

Figure 8-1 presents two patterns of classroom interaction when questions are being used. Which do you believe to be preferable? Why? Compare your answers with those given at the end of the module. Do you agree?

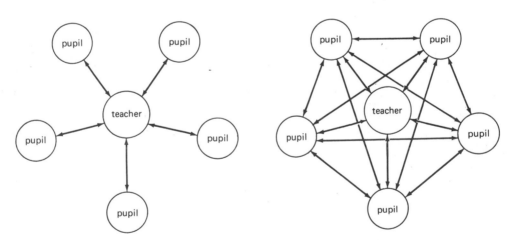

FIGURE 8-1 *Patterns of Classroom Interaction, Questioning*

In the following exercise evaluate the questions by checking the appropriate columns for each question. Use the following code letters to indicate your reasons.

A—Calls for no answer and is a pseudo question.
B—Asks for recall but no thinking.
C—Challenging, stimulating, or discussion-provoking type of question that calls for thinking and involves reasoning and problem solving.

Questions	Poor	Fair	Good	Why?
1. In what region are major earthquakes located? B		✓		
2. According to the theory of isostasy, how would you describe our mountainous regions? C			✗	
3. What mineral will react with HCl to produce carbon dioxide? B		✓		
4. What kind of rock is highly resistant to weathering? B		✗	✗	
5. Will the continents look different in the future and why? A C	✗		✗	
6. Who can describe a continental shelf? A		✗		
7. What caused the Industrial Revolution? A C				
8. What political scandal involved President Harding? B				
9. This is a parallelogram, isn't it? A				
10. Wouldn't you agree that the base angles of an isosceles triangle are congruent? A				
11. In trying to determine the proof of this exercise, what would you suggest we examine at the outset? C				
12. What conclusion can be drawn concerning the points of intersection of two graphs? C				
13. Why is pure water a poor conductor of electricity? B				
14. How do fossils help explain the theory of continental drift? C				
15. If Macbeth told you about his encounter with the apparitions, what advice would you have offered? C				
16. Who said, "if it were done when 'tis done, then 'twere well if it were done quickly"? B				
17. In the poem, "The Sick Rose," what do you think Blake means by "the invisible worm"? C				
18. Should teachers censor the books which students read? C				
19. Explain the phrase, "Ontogeny recapitulates philogeny." C				
20. What are the ten life functions? B				
21. What living thing can live without air? B				

Questions	Poor	Fair	Good	Why?
22. What is chlorophyll?				
23. Explain the difference between RNA and DNA.				
24. Who developed the periodic table based on the fact that elements are functions of their atomic weight?				

Recitation

The old-fashioned recitation method still continues very much in vogue, perhaps because it is one of the simplest teaching methods to understand. Theoretically, it should be one of the easiest to conduct, for essentially it consists of only three steps.

1. The teacher assigns pupils something to study.
2. The pupils study it.
3. The teacher asks the pupils (in a whole class situation ordinarily) about what they have studied to see if they have got it right.

The method has considerable merit. Because of its long history, it is pretty well known and accepted by pupils. The question-and-answer technique provides reinforcement for what has been learned and gives pupils feedback concerning its accuracy. The expectation of having to face questions in class has motivational value as well. Finally, it provides opportunities for pupils to learn from each other.

Unfortunately, as practiced in many classes, the recitation seems to have more faults than merits. Too much of the questioning is simple cognitive memory. As a result, it tends to yield only skimpy understanding and often to discourage the development of the higher mental processes and the development of favorable attitudes, appreciations, ideals, and skills. It tends to be boring and to create an unfriendly, anti-intellectual class atmosphere.

Recitations do not have to be stifling, however. To liven them up, center them around interesting thought questions. Present these thought-provoking questions to the pupils in the assignment so that they can have them before them as they study. Then use the thought questions, rather than memory questions, as the basis for the recitation. Plan your questioning procedures in advance of the class so that they will focus on thinking and the sharing of ideas rather than only remembering. Because of the deemphasis on rote memory and the emphasis on using the higher intellectual processes, the pupils can be, and perhaps should be, allowed to consult their texts as the recitation is carried on.

Open-Text Recitation

The open-text recitation is really a discussion in which the pupils may consult their texts and other materials to back up their arguments and justify their opinions. The procedure for conducting an open text recitation is basically the same as that outlined in the preceding paragraphs. The teacher first makes a study assignment that includes suggestions and questions designed to encourage pupils to think and draw inferences about what they are to read and study. Then in class, the recitation is centered around open-ended, thought questions of the Socratic, divergent, or evaluative type. Cognitive memory and convergent questions must be used too, of course, but ordinarily they do not play as important a role as broad, open-ended questions. As the recitation proceeds, the teacher encourages pupils to challenge and respond to others' statements and to put forth their own interpretations, inferences, and conclusions. At any time the pupils are free to consult their texts, notes, or other material to bolster their arguments. Finally, someone, the teacher or a pupil, sums up. In many instances no final decision or argument is necessary or desirable. The summary simply cites the positions and arguments taken. At other times, the facts of the case and the nature of the subject matter may require a definite conclusion.

This technique has many advantages. It frees the class from overemphasis on remembering facts and opens it up to thinking. It helps students to realize that facts are means to ends—the ends being concepts, ideas, understanding, and the ability to think. It gives pupils practice in checking and documenting, and, it is hoped, shows them the importance of getting facts straight. All in all, this procedure is an excellent means of teaching pupils to use their higher mental faculties, because the basic technique is to use broad divergent and evaluative questions and to bounce follow-up questions around the class until the group begins to discuss the question freely. It is an excellent technique for use in the approaches discussed in Module 10.

Show-how Techniques

So far this module has been concerned with telling and questioning, but one of the most important methods of teaching is showing learners how. As we pointed out earlier, pupils do not always learn from what we tell them. Often showing them how or running through a practice session may be much more effective. That is why we must take sufficient time to show pupils how to study, to show them how to conduct experiments, to show them how to set up equations, to show them how to use the library, and so on, and then give them sufficient practice to master the learning.

Show-how teaching deals mostly with skill development. It is necessary for teaching both intellectual and physical skills. Usually a show-how operation starts off with an introduction describing the procedure, its purposes, its merits, and warnings against any potential risks or problems. This introduction is usually followed by a demonstration. The demonstration may be by the teacher, an aide, or by film, videotape, or a sequence of still pictures. In any case the presentation should be accompanied by a verbal explanation of what is happening. Ordinarily, it is best if the demonstrator runs through the complete procedure first and then demonstrates the steps in the procedure separately. Thus, in teaching a library skill, it might be advantageous, after a short introduction, to show a film clip of the procedure to be learned, then to go through the procedure step by step. In carrying out the demonstration, the following guidelines should be helpful.

1. Be sure everyone can see. A demonstration one cannot see is not much help.
2. Go slowly. If you go through it too quickly, pupils will not be able to see how the procedure goes. Sometimes, if pupils are to understand the procedure, it may be best to go through the procedure at normal speed and then repeat it in slow motion.
3. If the procedure is complex, after demonstrating the complete procedure, break it down into steps and demonstrate the steps separately.
4. Repeat the demonstration or portions of it as necessary until pupils understand what is to be done. Repeating demonstrations after pupils have started practicing is usually effective.
5. In demonstrating, remember that when one is facing the pupils, right and left are reversed. Try to assume a position that will allow pupils to see the demonstration in proper perspective.

After the demonstration, it may be advantageous to have the pupils walk through the steps "by the numbers" as you explain and demonstrate. Thus, in teaching a dance routine you might explain the first step, demonstrate how to do it, and then have pupils do it under your supervision. Then do the second step in the same fashion. And so on at each step you or an aide should check to see that pupils are performing correctly. Similarly, when teaching map-reading skills, one might begin by explaining contour lines, demonstrate their use, and then give the pupils a simple exercise in reading contour lines, checking to see that they are on the right track.

Then, once the students seem to understand the procedure, start practice activities. Use the guidelines outlined in the following section.

Drill and Practice

Sometimes we learn things quite thoroughly in one attempt. More frequently, repetition is needed if learning is to be thorough or lasting. That is why we must count on drill and practice to master skills and to increase understanding. Use them to consolidate, clarify, strengthen, and refine what pupils have already learned and to give them additional opportunities to learn thoroughly. The procedures for using drill and practice activities described in the section on show-how techniques are equally useful for teaching and reinforcing the learning and the retention of cognitive skills, facts, and understandings. The procedure outlined in the following guidelines should be useful for teaching and reenforcing the learning and retention of both psychomotor skills and cognitive skills, facts, and understandings.

1. Be sure that pupils have the proper tools and work under good conditions.
2. Keep practice highly motivated.
   a. Eliminate unnecessary drill and practice.
   b. Vary the kind of practice to make concepts fuller and practice less boring. Early practice should be concrete; later sessions can become increasingly more abstract.
   c. Use short practice periods. As pupils improve, the periods can become longer with longer spaces between them.

    d. Keep the practice intense. Be sure pupils have goals and standards to work toward. Keep the practice moving swiftly, but do not sacrifice accuracy for speed.

    e. Use some pressure.

    f. Use such devices as games and contests.

    g. Include only pertinent and important material so the practice lesson will not become dull.

    h. Make practice meaningful. Be sure the pupils understand what they have to do, why they have to do it, and how to do it. Be sure they have a goal and standards of excellence to shoot at. Point out why the drill is needed.

    i. Let the pupils contribute to the planning and evaluating of their own practice activities.

    j. Provide pupils with knowledge of their progress. It is an excellent motivator.

3. Keep practice as real and lifelike as possible. Simulations are useful for this purpose.

4. Carefully supervise practice. Point out errors and show how to correct them but avoid harsh criticism. Encourage pupils to criticize and evaluate their own work.

5. Structure the practice sessions. It is often necessary to pull skills out of context for formal practice. Use the part-whole method; that is, practice the whole operation, but take difficult parts out of context and practice them separately when necessary.

6. Individualize practice. Use diagnosis as the basis of each pupil's practice. Focus practice on individual pupil's weaknesses and gaps in learning. Use materials that can be automated. Self-correcting material, either purchased or homemade, is very useful. Exercises in which pupils work in pairs or small groups to help each other and correct each other can be excellent.

7. Make practice part of the regular work. Do not separate it for special instruction unless necessary. Use the regular schoolwork for practice material. Keep it simple. In the beginning it may be necessary to take practice out of context and concentrate on it alone for short periods. Practice tends to get lost in the regular class situation, but keep such practice to a minimum.

8. Use a variety of materials. Homemade mimeographed, or dittoed material, workbooks, and other purchased exercises are all useful. Make a bank of such materials by saving exercises, items, workbook materials, programmed materials, and so on.[9]

Memorization

Sometimes pupils just have to memorize things. There is even a time for memorization without understanding. For example, in the study of chemistry, it would be advantageous to know the symbols and valences of the common elements. These symbols must be memorized. They are tools. In mathematics, certain as-

---

[9] Ibid., p. 87.

sumptions must be memorized before other concepts can be developed. In fact, in all of the disciplines there are some basic points that we must memorize so that we can understand other concepts.

Exercise 8 G

What in your discipline must be memorized before one can move on to the development of other concepts?

When teaching through memorizing, remember that in effect memorization is really a special case of practicing. In general, the techniques suggested for conducting practice sessions hold for memorizing sessions. Nevertheless, perhaps the following five guidelines will prove to be of service:

1. Avoid overuse of memorizing. Have pupils memorize only those things it is essential that they memorize.
2. Be sure there is a purpose for the memorizing and that the pupils see what that purpose is.
3. If possible, have pupils study for meaning before memorizing. As we have seen, some things we must learn, meaningful or not, such as German word order or Cyrillic or Greek letters which do not have any real reason for being as they are. They just are as they are, so we must memorize that Σ is sigma and that in mathematics it stands for the sum of. These are tools of the trade and we must master them. However, it is much easier to memorize those things that have meaning if we understand the meaning. For instance, it is probably much easier to remember the phrase "There is no accounting for taste," than "De gustibus non disputandum est," if we are not versed in Latin.
4. When pupils are memorizing long pieces, they should use the part-whole method. Otherwise, it is probably better to memorize by whole units. The part-whole method consists of learning parts separately and then incorporating them in learning the whole, just as in practicing you work on the hard parts and then practice the whole operation.
5. Utilize the recall method. Pupils should study and then try to recall without prompting.

Review

In the development of learning within any class of pupils, frequent reviews are necessary. This is so because memory is aided by repetition and by association, and because understanding is improved by review. In the sciences, for instance, many concepts cannot be fully understood in isolation. Neither can all the scientific terms be fully appreciated until they are seen in the context of later topics. Frequently, notions that were understood only dimly the first time they were studied become much clearer when "re-viewed" later in connection with later topics.

In conducting reviews, the teacher must be aware of the character of the pupils and of the discipline being pursued. In mathematics, where so much depends upon every link in the great chain, very frequent reviews are generally necessary. It is profitable to recall, almost daily, some principles which were previously studied. In several disciplines, where the parts have less intimate connection, as in geography and some others, the reviews may be given at greater intervals, although daily review helps to keep pupils on their toes.

Here again, the techniques of questioning come into play. As far as possible, the review should lead from facts to concepts and principles applied to practical life. Experience in thinking is often more profitable than the knowledge itself.

It is always advantageous to have a general review at the close of any particular study. This enables you to detect any false conceptions that the pupils entertained during the original process. You now can present the subject as a whole, and view one part in the light of another. In physiology, much more understanding is gained about the process of growth after one has studied absorption and secretion, for instance. Similarly, the economy of respiration is much clearer when viewed in connection with the circulation of the blood.

A general review is an enlightening process and is always profitable, with perhaps one exception: when the review is instituted solely as preparation for a written examination. Then, review may degenerate into a mere device for getting by at exam time. The object of reviewing should be to master the subject for its own sake, not for the purpose of being able to talk about it on one special occasion.

In summary, a review is an opportunity for the pupils to look at a topic again. It is a "re-view" or second look. It is not the same as drill or practice, although sometimes one can use the same methodology. Review is useful every day as a means for tying the day's lesson to preceding lessons. At this time you can summarize the points that should have been made and establish relationships with past and future lessons. End-of-unit and end-of-term reviews are also useful, but it is usually unwise to put off reviewing for such a long time. Frequent reviews are more effective. Besides, end-of-unit and end-of-term reviews tend to become preparations for examinations.

Almost any technique can be used in review classes, although the common oral quiz in which the teacher goes around the room asking fact question after fact question can become pretty boring. If you do use this type of review, use some scheme to mix up the questions so as to keep students alert. Tactics that you might profitably use are pupil summaries, reteaching the lesson, quiz games, dramatizations, pupil-constructed test questions, application problems, discussion, and broad questioning. Among the techniques used by social studies student teachers recently observed by the writer are (1) a Hollywood Bowl quiz game featuring questions drawn up by the student audience; (2) a British-style debate on the reconstruction period; (3) role playing of a congressional debate on slavery; (4) a spelling bee in which each side attempted to answer questions posed by the teacher; (5) a round table gathering that discussed the items considered most important in the unit; and (6) a panel featuring students' summaries of different areas of the unit, followed by a general discussion.

Techniques that require pupils to use what they should have learned are good because they may not only serve as review but also open up new vistas for the pupils.

Exercise 8 H

Teaching is primarily the ability to develop awareness. In each of the following three statements, identify and elaborate the concept relevant to the educational process in view of what we have discussed.

1. No man can reveal to you aught but that which is half asleep in the dawning of your knowledge.[10]
2. If the teacher is wise, he does not bid you enter the house of wisdom, but rather leads you to the threshold of your own mind.
3. Find that the vision of one man lends not its wings to another man.

The concepts about teaching just mentioned are frequently quoted to teachers. The words have had little effect upon the behavior of many teachers. Why?

Explain why students often do not understand what college professors are talking about.

Suggested Reading

Broadwell, Martin M. *The Lecture Method of Education.* Englewood Cliffs, N.J.: Educational Technology Publications, 1980.

Devine, Thomas G. "Listening in the Classroom," in *Teaching Study Skills: A Guide for Teachers.* Boston: Allyn and Bacon, 1981.

——. *Listening Skills Schoolwide: Activities and Programs.* Urbana, Il.: ERIC Clearinghouse on Reading and Communications Skills, 1982.

Dillon, J. T. *Teaching and the Art of Questioning,* Fastback 194. Bloomington, Ind.: Phi Delta Kappa Educational Foundation, 1983.

Friedman, Paul G. *Listening Processes: Attention, Understanding, Evaluation.* Washington, D.C.: National Education Association, 1983.

Gage, N. L. and David C. Berliner. *Educational Psychology,* 3d ed. Boston: Houghton Mifflin, 1984, Chap. 19.

Hunkins, Francis P. *Involving Students in Questioning.* Boston: Allyn & Bacon, 1976.

Hyman, Ronald T. *Strategic Questioning.* Englewood Cliffs, N.J.: Prentice-Hall, 1979.

Judy, Stephen N., and Susan J. Judy. *The Teaching of Writing.* New York: Wiley, 1981.

McLeish, John. "The Lecture Method," in N. L. Gage, ed. *The Psychology of Teaching Methods,* The Seventy-fifth Yearbook of the Society for the Study of Education. Chicago: University of Chicago Press, 1976, Chap. 8.

Orlich, Donald C., et al. *Teaching Strategies: A Guide to Better Instruction,* 2d ed. Lexington, Mass.: D. C. Heath, 1985, Part VI, Chap. 6.

Sudman, S., and N. M. Bradburn. *Asking Questions.* San Francisco: Jossey-Bass, 1982.

Tchudi, Stephen N., and Margie C. Huerta. *Teaching Writing in the Content Areas.* Washington, D.C.: National Education Association, 1983.

Tchudi, Stephen N., and Joanne M. Yates. *Teaching Writing in the Content Areas: Senior High School.* Washington, D.C.: National Education Association, 1983.

Wilen, William W. *Questioning Skills for Teaching.* Washington, D.C.: National Education Association, 1982.

Wolven, Andrew D., and Carolyn Gwynn Coakley. *Listening Instruction.* Washington, D.C.: National Education Association, 1979.

[10] Kahlil Gibran, *The Prophet* (New York: Alfred A. Knopf, 1923, 1968).

Exercise Answers
Exercise 8 A

The answers to these questions can all be found in this module. In brief, they all point out that you should make your lectures short, interesting, and pointed and that you can arouse and maintain interest in your lecture by such techniques as the following:

1. Open with a challenging question, problem, or fact.
2. Puzzle them a little.
3. Tell them what you intend to do.
4. Relate the content to things they already know and like.
5. Use questions (both real and rhetorical).
6. Use demonstrations, projectors, flannel boards, and other instructional aids.
7. Utilize humor.
8. Give plenty of examples—the more specific and concrete the better.[11]
9. Keep up the pace. Don't let the lecture drag or the audience relax.
10. Make use of dramatic effects—pause, ask questions, change tempo, inject humor, cite concrete examples, illustrate with forgettable detail, take time out for short discussions and teacher-pupil exchanges, introduce pertinent anecdotes—anything to avoid monotony.

Exercise 8 E

The following are suggested answers to the exercise on questioning. Compare them to your own answers and consider the reasons for whatever differences may exist.

These are the classifications of the questions.

1. Broad. Divergent.
2. Broad. Divergent.
3. Narrow. Convergent.
4. Broad. Evaluative.
5. Broad. Evaluative.
6. Broad. Divergent.
7. Broad. Evaluative.
8. Narrow. Convergent.
9. Broad. Divergent.
10. Broad. Evaluative.
11. Broad. Divergent.
12. Narrow. Cognitive.
13. Broad. Evaluative.
14. Broad. Divergent.

[11] Clark, op.cit., p. 84.

15. Broad. Divergent.
16. Narrow. Convergent.
17. Narrow. Convergent.
18. Broad. Evaluative.

Exercise 8F

The second pattern of interaction in Figure 8-1 would ordinarily be preferable, because interaction of this sort involves more pupils, stimulates thought, and binds the pupils into a cohesive group.

What follows are suggested answers to the question evaluating items. Compare them to your own answers and consider the reasons for whatever differences may exist.

Questions	Poor	Fair	Good	Why?
1. In what region are major earthquakes located?		X		B
2. According to the theory of isostasy, how would you describe our mountainous regions?			X	C
3. What mineral will react with HCl to produce carbon dioxide?		X		B
4. What kind of rock is highly resistant to weathering?		X		B
5. Will the continents look different in the future and why?			X	C
6. Who can describe a continental shelf?	X			A
7. What caused the Industrial Revolution?			X	C
8. What political scandal involved President Harding?		X		B
9. This is a parallelogram, isn't it?	X			A
10. Wouldn't you agree that the base angles of an isosocles triangle are congruent?	X			A
11. In trying to determine the proof of this exercise, what would you suggest we examine at the outset?			X	C
12. What conclusion can be drawn concerning the points of intersection of two graphs?			X	C
13. Why is pure water a poor conductor of electricity?		X		B
14. How do fossils help explain the theory of continental drift?			X	C
15. If Macbeth told you about his encounter with the apparitions, what advice would you have offered?			X	C
16. Who said, "if it were done when 'tis done, then 'twere well if it were done quickly"?		X		B

Questions	Poor	Fair	Good	Why?
17. In the poem, "The Sick Rose," what do you think Blake means by "the invisible worm"?			X	C
18. Should teachers censor the books which students read?			X	C
19. Explain the phrase, "Ontogeny recapitulates philogeny."			X	C
20. What are the ten life functions?		X		B
21. What living thing can live without air?		X		B
22. What is chlorophyll?		X		B
23. Explain the difference between RNA and DNA.			X	C
24. Who developed the periodic table based on the fact that clements are functions of their atomic weight?		X		B

Post Test

Check List Items Check each item that answers or completes the initial statement.

1. In the following list check the techniques that are recommended for use in reviewing.
    ( ) **a.** Use review to prep for a specific examination.
    ( ) **b.** Emphasize end of unit and end of term reviews.
    (✓) **c.** Use pupil summaries as review techniques.
    (✓) **d.** Conduct a general review every time you complete a topic.
    (✓) **e.** Review daily.
    ( ) **f.** Emphasize drill techniques.
    (✓) **g.** Use review to tie today's lesson to yesterday's.

2. According to the module, the lecture is useful for
    (✓) **a.** Summarizing.
    ( ) **b.** Carrying out depth study.
    (✓) **c.** Arousing pupil interest.
    ( ) **d.** Concept building.
    ( ) **e.** Changing attitudes.
    (✓) **f.** Giving pupils background information.

3. In planning for a lecture try to provide for
    (✓) **a.** Repetition of important points.
    (✓) **b.** An introductory statement of the purpose of the lecture.
    (✓) **c.** Concrete examples.
    ( ) **d.** The inclusion of many major points.
    (✓) **e.** Humor.
    (✓) **f.** Rhetorical questions.

4. When conducting practice activities
   ( ) **a.** Use long intensive practice periods.
   (✓) **b.** Individualize the practice.
   (✓) **c.** Use self-administering self-correcting materials.
   ( ) **d.** Be sure pupils practice each part of the skills separately.
   (✓) **e.** Use regular classroom materials whenever feasible.
   (✓) **f.** Use a variety of materials.
   (✓) **g.** Use the part-whole method.
   ( ) **h.** Avoid the use of pressure.

5. Of the following check those that are true of memorization.
   ( ) **a.** Memorization has little or no place in the modern secondary school.
   (✓) **b.** The part-whole method is recommended.
   (✓) **c.** Pupils should study and then try to recall what they have studied.
   (✓) **d.** Pupils should learn what something means before memorizing.
   ( ) **e.** Teachers should never use rote memorization.

6. Of the following check those which are recommended as show how operations.
   (✓) **a.** Use a film or filmstrip showing the operation.
   ( ) **b.** Explain the procedure and then let the pupils go to it.
   (✓) **c.** Walk pupils through the procedure by the numbers.
   (✓) **d.** First demonstrate the whole procedure then demonstrate the difficult parts.

7. Of the following check those that are recommended as questioning guidelines.
   ( ) **a.** Call on pupils before asking the question.
   ( ) **b.** Scold pupils who give wrong answers.
   (✓) **c.** Use probing questions to follow up incomplete answers.
   (✓) **d.** Use probing questions to build up pupil concepts.
   (✓) **e.** Try to sequence questions so that higher level questions build on the answers to lower level questions.
   ( ) **f.** Avoid cognitive memory questions.
   (✓) **g.** Encourage pupils to comment on other pupils' answers.
   (✓) **h.** Ask pupils to give reasons for their answers to thought questions.

8. Of the following check those that can be used as thought questions.
   (✓) **a.** Broad questions.
   (✓) **b.** Evaluative questions.
   (·) **c.** Cognitive memory questions.
   (✓) **d.** Divergent questions.
   (✓) **e.** Convergent questions.
   (✓) **f.** Analysis questions.

Multiple Choice   In each of the following place the letter of the "best" response in the space provided.

(d) 9. The Socratic method of teaching uses
   a. Lecture
   b. Drill

c. Simulation
d. Probing questions.

(*a*) **10.** In conducting an open-text recitation you should center the discussion on
    a. the use of open-ended questions
    b. memory questions
    c. drill questions
    d. fact questions.

(*c*) **11.** When memorizing a passage pupils should try to
    a. memorize the passage piecemeal
    b. concentrate on mnemonic devices
    c. use the recall method
    d. use the a b c approach.

(*a*) **12.** Authorities criticize the frequent use of lectures because
    a. lectures provide little reinforcement
    b. lectures are too time consuming to present new material
    c. lectures tend to divert pupils' attention from the most important aspects of learning
    d. lectures overemphasize student inquiry.

(*b*) **13.** Most teachers
    a. overemphasize problem solving
    b. talk too much
    c. worry too much about motivation
    d. ask too many broad questions.

(*c*) **14.** A divergent question calls for
    a. a set answer
    b. the recall of specific facts
    c. a creative or thoughtful answer
    d. knowledge of generalizations.

(*b*) **15.** When conducting a demonstration it is recommended that you
    a. go through the procedure slowly step by step at first, then run through it quickly
    b. after showing the procedure in its entirety, walk through the procedure step by step
    c. always face the students
    d. emphasize the use of high level questions as one conducts the demonstration.

(*d*) **16.** Which type of questions would be most useful for starting a discussion?
    a. Narrow
    b. Convergent
    c. Memory
    d. Divergent.

(**a**) **17.** Practice is best conducted in
  a. a number of short practice sessions
  b. long tough practice sessions
  c. out of context situations
  d. large group sessions.

Short Answer

18. Why is the lecture considered to be one of the least effective methods of teaching secondary school pupils?

Because students are receivers instead of doers

19. Name six suggestions for the lecturer's plan made in the module.

State Purpose
Be Logical
Include clues to development
Avoid attempting too much
Begin w/ interest catcher
Provide for repetition

20. What can the lecturer do to excite a spirit of inquiry in his students?

Let listeners think before giving them the ans. ask Q's

21. Name five of the more important uses of the lecture.

Establish a general point of view
Present facts quickly
Arouse interest
Fill in Background info
Intro new route info
Summarize

22. What are the distinguishing characteristics of cognitive memory questions, convergent questions, divergent questions, and evaluative questions?

Cognitive memory test ones memory
Convergent Q's have 1 distinct ans.

Divergent Q's are broad, open-ended Q's

Evaluation Q's ask pupils to put a value on something.

23. What does the module recommend that you do when the pupil answers your question incorrectly or superficially?

Reword, rephrase & come back again

24. Should you encourage pupils to ask questions that challenge the text?

Yes

25. What is the basic principle in Socratic questioning?

To lead the pupils to discover the correct ans.

26. Is it ever permissible to allow pupils to use their books during a class recitation or discussion?

Yes

27. When pupils practice a skill, is it better to provide special materials or the regular materials they would ordinarily use? Why or why not?

Regular

28. Which is preferable, broad or narrow questions?

Broad

29. Is it best to avoid low-level questions and focus on high-level questions?

No - should use both

30. Name three things that one can do to improve the effectiveness of recitations.

Make Q's interesting
Keep content meaningful
Follow Q's with discussion

31. Explain how to conduct the part-whole method.

Should be whole - part - whole theory.

32. How would you conduct an open-text recitation?

Utilize discussion based on upper level Qs, in which students should refer to the text.

33. One of the problems with lectures is that they lack reinforcement. What can one do to remedy this lack?

Utilize repetition of key points.

34. When would you use divergent questions?

to arouse original thinking

35. When would you use probing questions?

When pupils ans. are superficial

36. The module points out two risks associated with teacher-telling strategies. What are they?

teacher tempted to talk too much
" may think because he said it, students now know it

37. What is an advance organizer?

A brief presentation (written or oral) describing main theme of lesson, lecture or talk

38. How might one liven up one's recitations? *Use interesting thought Qs*

39. How did Socrates conduct his teaching? *He ask a series of leading Qs*

40. Is it proper to encourage students to ask relevant questions of each other as well as of the teacher? *Yes*

MODULE
9

Discussion and Group Techniques

The first edition of this module was written by Louise E. Hock of New York University. It has been revised and updated by the editors for this edition.

Rationale

In recent years, as in earlier ones of this century, many theorists and practioners have attempted to make what goes on in the classroom more consonant with the reality of the world outside the classroom. They urge us to give greater recognition to the various skills needed to function in society as human being, worker, citizen, consumer, and parent, to develop a more sophisticated awareness of the uses of knowledge, and to become concerned not only with knowing about but also in knowing how.

These theorists and practitioners also urge us to accept the principle that learning is an active process. The goals of education, they tell us, encompass not only the acquisition of knowledge but also the guidance of the individual to his or her fullest potential. The latter involves the development of a multitude of skills—skills of critical thinking, of independent inquiry, of group participatory behavior, for instance. They also urge us to consider the role of the school as a humanizing experience and to move toward more openness in the educative process—openness of objectives, of curriculum, of methodology, of evaluation, of environment. In many ways, these twin currents of openness and humanism can be traced to an earlier era when some progressive educators were suggesting that the educational experience is not preparation for life, but rather that learning is living here and now.

As these progressive ideas have gained new support and fresh interpretation, the nature of teaching itself has undergone critical scrutiny with a resultant broadening of the processes, techniques, and procedures used by many teachers, as they try to cope with new priorities among vastly expanded objectives. Illustrative of this trend to mesh process with goals is a growing interest in developing skills of active participation in group endeavors and of active involvement with others in life's ongoing activities. It is obvious to all that life is not a solitary existence but must be lived in and with the company of others. Group living is a fact of life and a realistic aspect of existence.

Even cursory reflection reveals the extent to which group activity is prevalent in one's life—in the circles of one's family and friends, as well as in the civic, religious, economic, governmental, and social recreational realms. In one way or another, at one time or another, we are all involved in activities with others, either as participants or observers. To call the roll of such activities would be to cite, among others, legislative committee operations, collective negotiations in business and labor, radio and television talk shows, discussion and round-table sessions, religious and club activities, various symposia, panels, and Town Hall meetings on the cultural circuit, and many more.

It is readily evident that participants in such group activities assume multiple roles, depending upon the nature and purpose of the activity and the personal predilection of individual participants. In addition to the obvious leader-follower dichotomy, participants' roles in group activity include those as questioner, clarifier, problem solver, compromiser, advocate, facilitator, catalyst, evaluator, and synthesizer.

The past dozen years have seen a growing awareness of the need for more and more sophisticated skills in participatory behavior and deeper insights into such phenomena. We have only to witness the proliferation of human relations workshops, group dynamics training sessions, encounter groups, sensitivity training, and similar efforts to recognize the drive for increased skill in human interaction.

Such efforts are vivid testimony to the fact that group participatory skills are learned skills, not innate skills. As a result of this and other testimony, it is increasingly evident that the school has a role to play in the development of social skills, both by encouraging cognitive awareness and analysis, and by experiential approaches. More and more teachers, therefore, are adding to their repertoire of instructional strategies a variety of techniques and procedures that provide students with opportunities to interact with one another. Such procedures also provide experience in analysis of group behavior and human interaction, and the development of individual skills along those lines. The range of possibilities is wide and varied; to name only a few, there are debates, forums, panels, symposia, committee work, buzz sessions, small-group activities and role playing.

The task of the prospective teacher is threefold: (1) to acquire skills of functioning in such participatory endeavors oneself; (2) to comprehend the principles and theory underlying effective use of such activities; and (3) to develop skill in the use of such group experiences with learners and ability to guide students toward effective functioning in and understanding of participatory activities.

The techniques and procedures described in this module are ones that teachers can use, whatever the character of their educational enterprise. In other words, teachers in relatively traditional classroom situations would find them useful as part of their overall instructional repertoire, and teachers in more innovative, open educational settings would find them especially appropriate to the participatory nature of such learning situations.

Specific Objectives

In studying this module, your goal is to become familiar with the wide range of possibilities for student participation in the learning process through discussion and group experiences. You should be able to identify those most relevant to your subject area and to conceive of various possible uses of them. The following objectives should guide your study of and reading for this module.

Upon conclusion of your study of this module, it is expected that you will be able to do the following:

1. Describe the varieties of techniques for discussion and group work available for instructional purposes.
2. Analyze the advantages and disadvantages of each technique.
3. Show how to conduct each of these techniques.
4. Select the specific discussion or other group work technique appropriate for your specific purposes and content.
5. Describe the roles of the teacher and various participants in group activities.

Module Text

The American school has long accepted as a major function the socializing of the human being—the guidance of the child from a self-centered, immature, dependent state to that of a mature, self-directive, interdependent individual able to live and work with others in responsible fashion. This function assumes greater significance as participatory democracy becomes a pervasive characteristic of all phases and segments of our society. The increased sophistication of such participation requires the use of highly developed skills of communication, cooperation, self-direction, critical judgment, and problem solving. Such skills can and should be taught in our schools.

Fortunately, as a teacher you will have at your disposal a wide and varied range of techniques of a participatory nature. These procedures can be formal or informal. The purposes can be of an information-giving nature or can be opinion-sharing or value-clarifying in character. The participants can number two or many times that number. The time involved can vary from a few minutes to many sessions continuing over a period of days or weeks.

Exercise 9 A

Here is a list of participatory activities.

Discussion	Forums	Role playing
Panels	Committees	Simulation
Symposia	Small groups	Brainstorming
Debates	Sociodrama	Fishbowl
Round tables	Buzz sessions	Jury trial

With which are you familiar? Which of these have been used effectively by your teachers? Which did you enjoy as a student? Consider how you might use such activities in your own classes.

As you pursue your study of this module, try to engage in various group activities with your college classmates. Assume various roles. Keep records of the involvement and interaction. Ask someone to serve as observer and help you analyze the process and its effectiveness.

Total Class as a Group Enterprise

Perhaps the most helpful way to start thinking about processes of participation and group interaction is to view the total class as a group. In their efforts to provide discussion and group experiences for learners, teachers frequently overlook the opportunity to make the total class sessions more interactive in nature. You should not find it difficult to move from a lecture or teacher-dominated type of classroom to one involving various discussion approaches.

Consider for a moment some readily evident characteristics of the two instructional approaches. The stereotypic, yet still prevalent, recitation-type strategy suggests (1) teacher-led and teacher-dominated sessions; (2) a questioning approach of a relatively superficial information-seeking nature; (3) repeating or restating (re-citing) that which was learned, studied, memorized; (4) the "hearing" of lessons to detect right and wrong answers; (5) teacher checking to see if students have done their work; (6) a one-to-one relationship between the questioner and hearer and the teller and answerer; (7) all decision making in the hands of the teacher regarding purposes, content, process, and participation.

A flow chart of participation in such a session would probably reveal a significant number of tallies for the teacher, with a smaller number distributed over a relatively small number of students selected by the teacher to participate. The major mode of operation would tend to be question and answer with occasional comment relative to accuracy or character of student response. There might be occasional lecture or minilecture.

On the other hand, consider the possibilities inherent in the concept of such total class activity viewed as genuine discussion, with student interactive participation and the focus not on hearing lessons but on inquiry and discovery. When viewed this way, class sessions are characterized by (1) the probing exploration of ideas, concepts, and issues; (2) building upon student responses in a developmental flow; (3) interaction among all participants; (4) shifting leadership among participants; (5) questioning, sharing, differing, conjecturing on the part of all; (6) student participation in decision making; (7) hypothesizing and problem solving.

The essential difference between the two types of classroom is that the first seems to view knowledge as consisting of a series of correct answers, whereas the latter tends to view knowledge as the product of creative inquiry and active student participation in the learning process. Only through genuine student involvement and interaction can hypotheses be tested, views expressed, questions raised, controversy examined, and insights developed, along with other desirable cognitive processes.

A helpful way to begin analyzing the differences between the two approaches is to use an interaction analysis system, such as the Flanders approach or the

Amidon-Hunter Verbal Interaction Category System or other similar ones. These systems attempt to record in easily recognizable and quantifiable ways the nature of classroom interaction, providing a clear indication of the relative proportion of teacher-talk and student-talk, along with varying degrees of analysis of the nature of the interaction and exchange. Any teacher wishing to move toward more participatory discussion might well start with such analysis to determine the present character of the classroom sessions. Steps can then be taken to improve the amount and quality of student involvement. See Module 17 for a brief discussion of the Flanders interaction analysis system.

Exercise 9 B

Identify the various groups to which you belong or in which you participate; also indicate all of the group experiences in which you have participated in the past week or two. Reflect on the kinds of skills needed to function effectively in them, and consider what you can learn from them that may be of value in your teaching.

Analyze your own participation in a recent group activity:

a. What was the nature of your participation?
b. What role did you perform?
c. How effective was your participation?
d. How might it have been more effective?

Select three talk shows currently on television (or radio). Analyze and compare them in terms of the nature of the group interaction, the form of the discussion, the roles of participants, and other relevant characteristics.

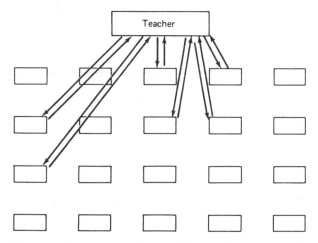

FIGURE 9-1 *Diagram Showing the Type of Flow of Interaction Found in a Typical Recitation.* **Note that the interaction is between the teacher and individual pupils only. There is no cross flow between pupil and pupil.**

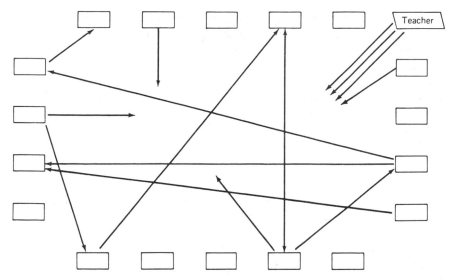

FIGURE 9-2 *Diagram Showing the Type of Flow Interaction in a Whole Class Discussion.* In this class, pupils have been arranged in a hollow square. Arrows pointing to the center of the square indicate that the person was speaking to the group as a whole. Arrows pointing to individuals indicate the person the speaker was addressing. Note that the conversation includes much cross talk between pupil and pupil, and much talk addressed to the group as a whole. The teacher's role in the discussion is minimal.

Various Techniques of Interaction

In addition to total class discussion, teachers have at their disposal a varied repertoire that provides many opportunities for students to participate actively in the learning process. The tactics and strategies can be broadly classified into two types: the relatively formal, planned, short-term presentation-type technique; and those group strategies that involve more student interaction and work of a long-term nature with varied purposes, including the analysis of the group process itself.

Presentation-type Techniques

The first category of group discussion techniques includes the use of panels, symposia, debates, forums, round-table discussions, and similar ways of involving students in their own learning. All these possibilities provide opportunities for student presentation of ideas, opinions, and information and for the expression of differing viewpoints. They all involve a degree of structure and the need for some planning. However, they vary in the degree of formal preparation involved, as the following definitions show.

Round table—a quite informal group, usually five or fewer participants, who sit around a table and converse among themselves and with the audience.

Panel—a fairly informal setting in which four to six participants, with a chairman, discuss a topic among themselves, and then there is a give-and-take with the class. Each participant makes an opening statement, but there are no speeches.

Forum—a type of panel approach in which a panel gives and takes with the audience.

Symposium—a more formal setting in which the participants present speeches representing different positions and then open up for questions from the floor.

Debate—a very formal approach consisting of set speeches by participants of two opposing teams and a rebuttal by each participant.

British-style debate—a modification of the debate format in which the class is divided into two parties, and party members, other than the presenters, may ask questions, make comments, and the like; as in a parliamentary debate.[1]

Symposia, debates, and forums require thoughtfully prepared and well-organized material, whether in the form of written papers or outlines, or in the form of well-conceived remarks. Panels and round-table discussions, while usually benefiting by advance preparation, can be utilized along more informal lines, permitting the chance for spontaneous exchange of views, free-flowing exposition of ideas, even rap sessions of a wide-open character.

Such techniques are widely adaptable to a variety of subject areas. As you read the examples of the varying uses of these methods in various subjects, try to think of how you could utilize these or similar tactics in courses you expect to teach.

A symposium might be held in a science class to present and discuss various current developments of a scientific nature or to present differing viewpoints on certain controversial issues. In a home economics class or home and family living course, a panel of students could discuss views on family roles and responsibilities. A variation on this could have each student reacting in a particular role, as parent, child, peer group friend, or nonparental adult. Or a panel might consist of a group of invited participants, parents, community leaders, and law enforcement representatives, who would exchange views on the meaning and character of family life today.

In a social studies class, students could engage in a panel discussion of the causes and manifestations of racism in society and in their own lives and experience. Or a symposium could examine the problem of racism from several aspects, historically, economically, socially, morally, and ethically. Or a debate could be held on a topic such as, "There is less racism in the 1980s than there was in the 1960s."

An interesting variation of such approaches is that of adapting a "Meet the Press" or "Face the Nation" format for exploration of important ideas and developments. Students could take turns playing the expert, or the interviewers; the entire class could be involved in the questioning as well.

Other examples should come readily to mind for English and foreign language classes, as well as other areas of the curriculum. There are manifold opportunities throughout the instructional program for the use of such techniques for student participation.

It should be pointed out that all of these techniques also permit development of some specific skills, such as exposition, discussion, or analysis. For example,

---

[1] Based on Leonard H. Clark and Irving S. Starr, *Secondary and Middle School Teaching Methods*, 4th ed. (New York: Macmillan Publishing, 1981), p. 195.

debates require skills of critical analysis, the art of persuasion, rapid rebuttal skills, and the ability to suspend judgment until all points are heard. Panels, forums, and symposia provide opportunity for learning how to organize material, as well as the listening and communication skills necessary to any informal interaction following the original presentation. Round-table discussions provide experience in effective exchange of ideas, opinions, and viewpoints, active listening and responding, and rapid, spontaneous, and responsive interaction.

These techniques are helpful one-shot approaches to be used whenever appropriate to the given content and purposes. Teachers should not take for granted that students know how to handle such procedures. The skills involved in individual preparation and presentation are acquired and can be taught, as should the skills of working with others in such enterprises. Students need to be taught how to gather information, take notes, select major points, organize material, present a position succinctly, and engage in dialogue and debates with one another. These are skills that can be taught by the teacher, sometimes in class sessions as a whole, sometimes with individual guidance, as students begin to participate in a variety of such activities. The use of such techniques helps students learn to avoid verbatim copying of material and memorization of presentations, which should be eliminated from the classroom.

These techniques can be used effectively for many purposes.

1. To report the findings of committees, research, and investigation. This is perhaps the most common use of formal discussions. Panels may consist of representatives of several committees or a single committee.
2. To present the findings of individual investigations.
3. To add a measure of pupil participation to large group instruction.
4. To vary the pace of the class.
5. To furnish springboards for beginning a discussion or class investigation.
6. To get differing viewpoints and information before the class. Formal discussions are excellent when they are used as a strategy for making pupils aware of the many sides of an issue, or for presenting the different points of view, beliefs, or opinions on matters of all sorts. They are very useful for presenting a fair picture of the various positions concerning a controversial matter.
7. As a culminating activity that reviews and ties together what has been learned in a unit or course.

In general, all of these methods follow a similar pattern. The common procedure of this general pattern is that first, several participants present positions, arguments, points of view, or reports, and then the other members and the audience ask questions and discuss the matter. In large groups, this discussion is usually only a question-and-answer period, but in smaller groups, it may be a truly free discussion.

Exercise 9 C

Investigate in some detail the distinctive characteristics of debate, forum, round-table discussion, and symposium. Suggest some appropriate uses for each, relative to specific content in your subject area.

Panels, Symposia, Round Tables, and Forums. Suggestions for conducting presentation-type discussions, panels, symposia, round tables, and forums include the following:

1. Let the pupils cooperate in selecting the topic with your help and guidance.
2. Select the panel members. They may be representatives of small groups, persons having special interests, self-selected persons, or persons who would do well or need the experience.
3. Help the pupils to prepare the presentation.
   a. If the panel members are committee or group representatives, supervise the committee or group work as you would any other committee. Otherwise, treat the gathering and organizing of material as you would in any other report or research study.
   b. Help panel members develop their presentations. Work with them as they build their presentation plans, prepare their notes, and so on. In some cases you should rehearse the pupils and coach them in their delivery.
   c. Brief pupils on their procedures and their roles. Be sure they know what to do. Let them talk their plans over, but there should be no rehearsal of the entire panel (except in the case of formal presentations at assemblies, PTOs, and the like).
   d. Be sure the chairperson is well briefed and knows how to
      (1) Introduce the topic, prepare the audience, and explain the procedures.
      (2) Introduce the panelists.
      (3) Ensure that the panelists do not talk too long.
      (4) Solicit questions from the audience. Pupils can also be assigned to make up questions for homework.
      (5) Accept questions and refer them in such a way as to encourage more questions.
      (6) Sum up when necessary.
      (7) Redirect the flow of discussion when necessary.
      (8) Close the discussion.
4. Conduct the presentation. To involve pupils, ask them to take notes on the panel and the discussion following, to summarize the major points taken, pro, con, and in-between, and to evaluate the arguments and logic of the panel members (but not their manner or skill of presentation).
5. Follow the presentation with a class discussion. Call for questions from the floor, additional comments, criticisms of the positions taken, and the like. Sometimes it is wise to have questions planted in addition to the questions and comments that should naturally arise.
6. Follow up and tie up loose ends. Have the chairperson or members of the class summarize the important points and positions.

Formal Debate.   The most formal of all discussion techniques is the debate. It is so formal that many teachers doubt its effectiveness in ordinary classrooms. Other teachers advocate it, because debate (1) provides depth study of a controversial matter; (2) gives two sides of an issue; (3) can be very interesting; and (4) clarifies the controversy at issue. On the other hand, these advantages are offset by its formality, its emphasis on black and white thinking, its involvement of only a few pupils, and its tendency to focus on skill in debating rather than on discovering the truth.

To conduct a debate, it is necessary to have a proposition, such as Resolved: that the entire cost of public schools in every school district should be borne by the state; two teams of debaters, one arguing for the proposition and one arguing against it; and a formal procedure in which each team member makes a formal presentation for a set number of minutes and later a rebuttal to the arguments of the other team. The order of presentation and rebuttal is first speaker for; first speaker against; second speaker for; second speaker against; first rebuttal for; first rebuttal against; second rebuttal for; second rebuttal against. After the final rebuttal, there is usually a general discussion. This discussion is conducted by a moderator who also introduces the topic of the debate, introduces the speakers, and closes the meeting. Because most formal debates outside the classroom are held as contests between debating teams, it may be advantageous to have the class or a panel of judges decide which team presented the better case. Many teachers, however, feel that this competition detracts from the classroom atmosphere and therefore do not recommend it.

British-style Debate.   Some of the disadvantages of the formal debate are avoided in the British-style debate. This type of debate is patterned after procedures made famous by the British Parliament. Briefly, it consists of having principal spokespersons on each side to present their cases pro and con, and then to invite questions and comments from the other members of each team alternatively. When you use this technique, we recommend that you do the following:

1. Select a question or proposition to be debated.
2. Divide the class into two teams, one for the proposition, the other against it.
3. Select two principal speakers for each team.
4. Direct the first principal speaker of each team to present the team's argument in a five-minute talk.
5. Direct the second speaker for each team to present the team's argument in a three-minute talk.
6. Throw the question open to comments, questions, and answers from the other team members. In order to keep things fair, alternate between members of the pro and con teams.
7. Let one member of each team summarize its case. Often this is done by the first speaker, but if a third principal speaker does the summarizing, it makes for better class participation.
8. Follow up with general discussion.[2]

[2] Ibid., p. 197.

Class Discussions

Among other things, class discussions can be used in problem solving, developing and changing attitudes, value clarification, development of communication skills, and building sensitivity to other people's viewpoints. They directly involve pupils in their own learning by making them responsible for their learning. They give pupils opportunities to develop self-confidence, self-reliance, and poise as they learn to organize, present, and defend their own views.

To carry out a class discussion, you should first prepare for the discussion. Be sure that the topic selected is discussable. The best topics are controversial problems or issues that can be resolved or clarified through discussion. Make up a plan for the discussion to follow. Include an agenda, time limits, and topic boundaries. Be sure the pupils are well informed on the topic. In an opening statement, brief the students on the purpose of the discussion and its ground rules. Try to create a pleasant physical environment.

Next, start off the discussion with some lively springboard such as an anecdote, role playing, a series of open-ended questions, a film, or a contrived incident.

Once the discussion has begun, try to keep it moving. Keep it on track by restating the problem, summarizing, redirecting the course of the discussion, and stopping inefficient, immaterial, impertinent, or emotional discussion when necessary. Use open-ended questioning. Throw questions around to involve many class members. Use questions such as, "Do you agree?" and "Would you like to make a comment?" Sometimes such questions will draw out the shy, reserved pupils. Encourage cross discussion.

Try to elicit a high order of thinking. Challenge inconsistencies, faulty logic, and superficiality by careful questioning. Ask students why they say what they say and believe what they believe. Make them consider consequences of their position. In other words, force them to examine their own ideas and the ideas of their colleagues critically. Do not allow unexamined opinions to go unchallenged. See to it that mistakes in fact are corrected. If necessary, supply the correct information yourself.

Finally, try to bring the discussion to a conclusion. Keep the discussion open-ended, but try to stimulate the pupils to integrate and synthesize the point discussed into logical conclusions. These conclusions should be theirs, not yours. End the discussion with a good summarizing activity. The following checklist provides guidelines for conducting discussions and evaluating your discussion techniques.

> *Checklist for Discussion Leader*
> 1. Did I lead rather than monopolize?
> 2. Did I introduce the topic well?
> 3. Did I keep the discussion moving?
> 4. Did I keep the group on the topic?
> 5. Did I give everyone a chance to participate? Did I encourage everyone to participate?
> 6. Did I draw out the shy ones? Did I keep the atmosphere permissive?
> 7. Did I prevent anyone from monopolizing?

8. Did I handle the overtalkative tactfully and kindly?
9. Did I keep the discussion open? Did I encourage fresh new ideas?
10. Did I discourage time-wasting side issues?
11. Did I clarify issues and questions?
12. Did I summarize as needed?
13. Did I close when we were finished?
14. Did the group accomplish its objective satisfactorily?
15. Was it a good discussion?[3]

Exercise 9D

Identify several topics, issues, or problems in your subject fields suitable for genuine class discussion.

Committees and Small Groups

The use of small group work for a particular task requires longer involvement of perhaps two, three, or even more sessions. Sometimes these groups are considered committees and may function for a week or two or longer. Whatever the length of time, such group work is distinguished from the buzz group techniques discussed later in the module by the specific task orientation, a planned involvement of all, and a more formal outcome in the form of an activity, project, or presentation.

Such group work can be used for (1) planning activities for various purposes, such as a party or field trip; (2) cooperative project work; (3) actual study of a specific unit of work.

The background experience of the students should guide the teacher in determination of the nature and extent of group work. With students who have had little or no experience in working together, it is wise to start with activities of interest that have an immediate or early visible result. For example, students might work in small groups on the planning of party or music activities. In classes where field trips are involved, whether to museums, theaters, civic centers, or historical monuments, the various aspects of planning can be handled by the students in small groups, each of which is responsible for one aspect of the trip.

Another early type of experience might involve discussion and decision making about matters of genuine interest to the class. For example, as students become more experienced in working together, they might engage in developing criteria for grading in their particular class situation or actually prepare evaluative instruments for various aspects of their course work.

With more experience, students can accept responsibility for projects that span a longer time period but still are of a direct nature and involve visible progress. In a science class, for example, small groups can be established for (1) the care of terrariums; (2) fish raising; (3) care and study of hamsters and mice; (4) care and study of various plants, among other possibilities. Students can take care of their respective projects, study various aspects of growth and development, ob-

---

[3] Leonard H. Clark, *Teaching Social Studies in Secondary Schools: A Handbook* (New York: Macmillan Publishing, 1973), p. 91.

serve, and make regular progress reports to the entire class. Similarly, students can work together in small groups on various ecology projects, or activities focused around study of nutrition vis-á-vis cost and advertising, or any number of consumer education projects. In such projects, there are usually clearly defined goals and clear-cut procedures for achieving them. The results of such study will have meaning for the entire class.

In English and social studies classes, group work can be used to help students acquire knowledge of the mass media—especially newspapers, radio, and television—including the various kinds of writing and production involved and the roles of various personnel. Students could engage in the actual production of a class newspaper or magazine. In such an endeavor, the class could be so organized that certain pupils would be made responsible for editing, reporting, editorializing, writing columns, obtaining and writing advertisements, and similar duties. Students could specialize in reporting and writing about medicine, education, leisure activities, national and international affairs, or local and state issues.

A variation of the activity could be the production of a television news program or a documentary focusing on a specific issue of current interest. As with the class newspaper, students will gain rich insights into the processes of news gathering and reporting, as well as much knowledge about the substantive matters being reported.

As students gain more experience with group procedures and acquire more sophisticated skills, they can begin to handle more substantive aspects of course content through working together in genuine inquiry. More advanced skills of planning, hypothesizing, decision making, investigating, organizing, sharing, and reporting are involved. In addition to providing opportunities for inquiry and genuine interaction on important content areas, small-group work makes possible the study of a wider variety of topics, issues, and problems than does a course conducted along more typical lines of total class attention to the same content.

Several examples of more substantive topics will help illustrate the value of such group involvement. In a study of transportation in a science class, groups might be formed according to the various means of transportation. One group studying the development of the automobile could investigate the internal combustion engine, the Wankel engine, and electric cars. A group investigating air travel could study the various types of lighter or heavier than aircraft—balloons, prop and jet planes, and rockets. A study of sea travel could involve analysis of the use of wind, steam, diesel, atomic power, and various types of seacraft.

In a social studies class, groups organized along similar lines might focus on the historical development of the various means of transportation and their social and economic impact, with critical analysis of various issues related to transportation today. History teachers wishing to develop a sophisticated insight into the nature of revolution might set up several groups, each of which could develop broad guidelines in advance so that the separate groups will proceed in ways that will yield common bases for comparison at the conclusion of the group investigations. Thus, each group's investigation and report might be designed to include such considerations as long-term causes, immediate causes, class of people who instigated the revolt, method of revolt, and results.

Sociodrama and Role Playing

Another type of experience in participation and interaction is that of sociodrama and role playing. Examples of this type of activity include mock trials and portrayals of town meetings, United Nations sessions, Congressional hearings and similar types of civic portrayals. A more imaginative form of dramatic involvement would be acting out "You Are There" types of scenes in which students portray various figures from history or fiction. Reference has already been made to the possibilities of role-playing adaptations of various television programs, such as "Meet the Press."

Such dramatic role-playing activities have several advantages. They permit students to use information in the light of the particular perceptions of the role being played. They make it possible to examine concepts and ideas from different viewpoints expressed in the role playing. They help promote understanding and deepen insights through the necessity of thinking as the character being portrayed. They can provide opportunity for greater understanding by having students act out roles and positions different from those they would tend to favor and approve. Such reversal of roles helps to deepen the awareness of the complex, controversial nature of much knowledge and of many issues. Suggestions for conducting role playing and simulation can be found in Module 10.

Buzz Sessions and Group Work

Another broad category of student involvement includes strategies of buzz sessions, group work of a relatively short-term span, and committee work of longer duration. The buzz session can serve many useful purposes and functions as the name implies. It is an opportunity for students to meet together briefly in relatively small groups of four to seven to share with each other opinions, viewpoints, and reactions. These sessions rarely last more than fifteen minutes and require no advance formal preparation or lengthy follow-up.

A teacher can use the buzz session at the beginning of the school year to help students get to know each other. In such situations, the students can talk about themselves, their interests, hobbies, travel, and other matters of concern to young people. There need be no reporting back to the class from such a session, although a brief summary of the group activity might occasionally be desirable.

Buzz sessions can be used for informal discussion of certain aspects of the course content. In an English class, students can meet in small groups to discuss various short stories, essays, or books that they have read on an individual basis. In this way, they not only share reactions and opinions but also become acquainted with a wide variety of literary material. Similarly, buzz sessions can be used to discuss comparisons of two or three literary works that have been studied by the entire class. In a foreign language class, buzz sessions can be used to give students practice in conversing and communicating in the specific language under study. The substance of the sessions will depend on the purposes desired and the content under study. The ideas and topics being discussed can range from opinions on certain films to discussions of travels at home and abroad, and critiques of literary works in the language being studied.

Buzz sessions in a social studies class could be used in such situations as the following:

1. After a study of a given problem or issue, students could share views as to the single most effective way of coping with the problem, whether it be pollution, transportation, or any similar matter of current importance.
2. Students can share their reading of newspapers and newsmagazines to provide exchange of views on current events.
3. Sessions can focus on hypothetical thinking: what would have happened if. . .? or what would happen if. . .?

Whatever the substantive nature of such discussions, these buzz sessions serve many other purposes. They provide an opportunity for all to participate in a way that is not possible in a total class situation. They help students learn the skills of listening as well as of talking. They can be used to let off steam when students seem restless, bored, or are in some way not responsive to the larger class session of the day. They help students learn to think in action while interacting with each other.

Guidelines for conducting buzz groups include the following:

1. Form buzz groups arbitrarily by some such procedure as counting off, drawing cards, or simply "you six in the rear right-hand corner," "you six in the first three seats of the first and second rows," and so on.
2. Appoint a leader and recorder for each group.
3. Brief the group on what they are to do. Be sure they understand.
4. Let them discuss for five to ten minutes or so. It is better if the discussion is too short than too long.
5. Follow up with a whole class exercise—a class discussion, a fishbowl-type panel by the group representatives, a panel of recorders, or the like.

Brainstorming

Another technique for generating ideas and stimulating meaningful discussion and problem-solving activity is called brainstorming. In this technique the leader introduces a topic or problem and asks group members for their ideas, solutions, or comments. Group members respond with whatever comes to mind. No holds are barred. All comments, no matter how farfetched, are accepted and recorded, anonymously, on the board or on a transparency. No discussion or comments on the various contributions are allowed until all the group members have expressed every idea that they can think of, for the purpose of the brainstorming session is to get as many ideas as possible on the floor. Later in a discussion the members may cull the responses and decide next steps, but during the brainstorming there should be no restraints except those of decency and decorum. The ideas generated make excellent springboards for discussion, research, problem solving, small group, and other inquiry and discovery techniques.

The Fishbowl Technique

A form of group technique sometimes used in group decision making or conflict resolution and to develop skills in participation is the fishbowl technique. Guidelines for conducting the fishbowl technique include the following:

1. Confront the class with a problem, issue, or conflict that requires a solution or decision.
2. Divide the class into subgroups and arrange the groups around a circle.
3. For each group, select or have them select a representative who will argue the group's position.
4. Give the group members five or six minutes to discuss and to take a position on the problem, issue, or conflict under consideration.
5. Have the representatives of the various groups meet in the center of the circle and argue the case in accordance with their instructions. No one else can talk, but group members may pass instructions to their representatives by written notes.
6. Allow any representative or group to call a recess for group-representative consultation, if it seems necessary.
7. End the fishbowl after a set period of time or when the discussants have reached a decision or resolved the conflict.
8. Follow up the discussion with a critique.

Jury Trial Technique

Jury trial technique combines elements of group work, research, study, and panel presentation. It uses simulated courtroom procedures to discuss an issue or problem. Examples are, Should the draft be re-established? or Should there be mandatory 55 mile per hour speed limit? Guidelines for conducting this procedure follow.

1. Select an issue or problem to judge.
2. Have all pupils research the issue or problem.
3. Select pupils to act as lawyers, researchers, and writers, both pro and con.
4. Have the lawyers, witnesses, and researchers prepare arguments and plan for arguing the case.
5. Conduct the trial.
   a. Let the teacher, an administrator, or a visiting teacher act as judge. If you elect to have a student judge, you must plan to act as the judge's coach.
   b. Let the attorneys present their opening statements.
   c. Call the witnesses pro and con to testify.
   d. Attorneys question and cross question. Researchers feed the attorneys information and questions that they can use.
   e. The attorneys from each side interpret the evidence and argue that it favors their side in a final statement.
   f. As the trial proceeds, the judge points out fallacious arguments, errors in fact, and other obvious errors.
   g. The class, acting as the jury, votes to see who won the case.
   h. Follow up with general discussion, if it seems desirable.

Role of the Teacher

Whatever the activity or project, it is important to keep in mind the need to teach the skills of group functioning. The process of guiding student growth in participatory experiences is a major responsibility of the teacher. The teacher must come to know each student well, must be constantly aware that participatory skills must be learned, and must be perceptive in guiding group activities.

The teacher's role is significant at every stage of the process. It begins with a commitment to the value of and need for group instructional procedures. The attitude of teachers is important. The effective teacher knows that skills of group work must be taught, and so builds upon students' present levels of experience and skill. The effective teacher understands the difference between the kind of verbal noise that signifies purposeful group activity and the type of noisy interaction that suggests group disintegration. The effective teacher is aware of the many decisions involved in the use of group techniques and has the data and insights upon which to make such decisions.

For example, your first decision will have to do with the appropriateness of a particular group procedure to the content under study and the purposes to be achieved. Subsequent decisions have to do with the readiness of students for group work, the size of the groups, the placement of students in particular groups, and the degree of help and guidance you must provide. For students who have had little or no experience with group activities, you should begin with frequent buzz-group sessions of short duration to help students become familiar with verbal interaction among themselves. You can then move toward the establishment of groups or committees for relatively easy, direct, clearly defined tasks. As students gain experience and expertise, more sophisticated involvement can be expected of them.

The degree of direction and help you supply should vary from student to student, from group to group, and situation to situation. Again, if group work is a relatively novel experience, you may have to set specific guidelines at first, such as requiring the selection of a leader and recording secretary, and provide alternative suggestions regarding procedures and division of responsibility in the groups. It is helpful to circulate from group to group, assuming whatever role seems appropriate at any given time—observer, resource, mediator, or participant—until students gain experience and confidence in handling group strategies. Of course, you will have a variety of materials and resources available, as well as a fund of possibilities to suggest when asked.

An important responsibility of the teacher has to do with the placement of students in group situations. For group work to be most effective, you should use a variety of approaches to such placement.

When buzz groups are set up, it is wise to use different techniques of student assignment so that over a period of time students will get to talk and work with all classmates. You might ask the five people in the corner to make up a buzz group on one occasion; on the next occasion, the five people in the row next to the board; or the next, every fifth pupil as we "count off" around the room.

Membership in groups or committees might be based on student choice of classmates they would like to work with, or the task, responsibility, or topic they would like to work on, as well as teacher assignments. If you decide to make the assignment yourself, you should always keep in mind student preferences, abilities, and inclinations.

Under most circumstances, the results of group work will be more productive if students can participate in groups of their own selection. However, there will be times when you will wish to assign students on the basis of some criterion. A student's self-selection over many months may not have included a certain kind of group process or project. To provide a breadth of experience, you may decide to assign the students to a specific type of group. In other instances, you may believe it wise to break up certain pairings or clustering of students to broaden their contacts with other pupils, to avoid or break down dependency relationships, or to find out more about a student's ability to function with different people.

Throughout the group work experience, you as teacher have a valuable role to perform. It is helpful at the very beginning to circulate from one group to another to be available for questioning, to provide necessary guidance, or to get a "feel" for the interaction and progress within each group. After group plans are underway, individual students may need teacher advice and guidance relative to their particular responsibilities. Keeping in close touch also permits you to detect any potential difficulties or trouble spots and makes possible wise decisions regarding occasional shifting of students from one group to another.

There are many skills involved in group procedures—planning skills, research skills, search for appropriate materials and references, note-taking and reporting techniques—for which you can be an ever-ready resource. Reporting techniques can be the kind of sharing with fellow group members that helps keep all abreast of progress, and the kind of sharing in which pupils report the result and products of their group endeavor to the entire class. For students who have had no experience in such group reporting, you may have to suggest a number of possibilities or meet with the group frequently as students explore their own thinking.

For group work of relatively long duration, two weeks or more, the use of student progress reports can be very helpful. Use them to help students become aware of their use of time, to assess the degree of accomplishment, to reappraise their plans, and to share with the rest of the class various problems encountered or bring helpful suggestions to the attention of other groups. The progress report can be oral or written and can vary in form in relation to the nature of the group work. A simple statement reporting how the group is getting along may be quite sufficient.

An important aspect of group work is the evaluative process that should accompany it at all stages, but especially at the conclusion of the endeavor. Not only results and accomplishments but also the process engaged in throughout the group work need assessment. In such appraisal sessions, students can identify areas of weakness and think through ways of improving group activities another time. The role of the teacher in helping students evaluate effectively and purposefully is crucial. During pupils' initial experience with group activities, the teacher will have to assume strong leadership in guiding evaluative sessions and procedures. As students gain experience in group work, they will be able to assume more and more responsibility for evaluation, as well as for all other aspects of group processes.

Some Caveats

It would be misleading to give the impression that once a decision has been made to use a particular discussion or group technique all will go well. Often that is not the case. As with all other learning activities, there will be successes and failures, progress and retrogression. It is during times of trouble that the role of the teacher becomes crucial.

Most problems arise as a result of unwarranted and exaggerated expectations of teachers relative to students' ability to handle group procedures and processes of inquiry. Teachers tend to overestimate the level of skill, degree of competence, and background of experience of the students. As a result, the teacher often does not provide for gradual involvement in such work, moving from the relatively easy to the more difficult. Frequently, the teacher does not provide sufficient help at the start of any such study or the continuous guidance students need as the work proceeds.

It is important to recall that students in all likelihood will confront two types of problems, those associated with the processes of working together, and those involving the substantive aspects of an inquiry approach to learning. The first set of problems will require the teacher's help in guiding toward consensus and compromise, in helping to resolve personality differences, and in coping with overt behavior problems.

The second kind of problem requires constant attention to the many aspects of the discovery or inquiry approach—locating information, effective use of materials and resources, note-taking and organizational skills, and effective communication. You should not assume that once the rudiments of these skills are taught little more needs to be done. Rather, as students confront different and more complex challenges in their discussion and group work, their prior learnings need to be reinforced and more sophisticated insights and skills need to be taught. Teaching, therefore, becomes a continuous, ongoing process.

A helpful procedure you might follow is to involve the students in direct discussion of such problems as often as seems appropriate and desirable. One of the objectives of participatory experiences is that of guiding students toward skill in analysis and evaluation of their own functioning and accomplishments. The more students can analyze and assess the problems they face, the more likely they will be to arrive at sensible solutions. Such evaluation is part of the process of learning to work with others.

Another kind of problem likely to arise is that of individual students who in one way or another pose difficulties. There will be the reluctant student, the loner who prefers to work alone, who cannot or will not engage in group endeavors. There will be the aggressive, dominating type of student, ever eager to impose his will upon others. There will be the retiring, reserved student, content to do what is asked, but not likely to exhibit initiative or imagination. There will be the student whose abilities are of such a low order that much understanding, direction, and help will be required of fellow group members and of the teacher.

There is, of course, no one way to cope with any of these problems. You will have to be guided by your knowledge of the individual involved (as well as of the other students), by the nature of any given situation, by the past record of performance, by the objectives to be achieved, and by many other factors that will contribute to wise handling of problem cases.

Some Guidelines

In summary, the following guidelines may be helpful:

1. Start where the students are, assess their readiness for group activity, and plan accordingly.
2. Be alert throughout the process, and be ready to vary your own involvement as the occasion requires, at times being a dominant figure, at other times a retiring one.
3. Assume a variety of roles—leader, resource, guide, mediator—as needed.
4. Have a multitude of materials and resources available and be ready to suggest others.
5. Provide a variety of opportunities throughout the year for student participation in discussion and group activities.
6. Keep helpful records of the nature of the group work used during the year and of each student's participation. Anecdotal records about individual students may be especially helpful.
7. Encourage students to keep records, perhaps even a diary, of their experiences throughout the year in discussion and group work.
8. Be an active observer at all times, diagnosing, assessing, appraising, evaluating, and planning for improvement and progress.

Exercise 9 E

Investigate the nature and use of the *sociogram.* Indicate ways in which you might use it vis-á-vis group work.

Investigate various ways by which teachers can discover students' (as a class and as individuals) readiness for discussion and group activities.

Means and Ends

The uses of discussion techniques and group procedures can be viewed in terms of means and ends, for they serve both purposes. As means, they are processes and strategies used to achieve some specific instructional objective related to course content or substance. As ends, they are valuable learning experiences in themselves, providing their own rationale for use and analysis.

Means

As has been pointed out earlier, the use of various discussion techniques serves a number of purposes in the teacher's overall instructional strategy. They can be an appropriate *means* of achieving specific content knowledge and comprehension. They can provide variety in learning activity and a needed change of pace. They can serve to reduce tension or resolve conflict. They can promote independent thinking and help to clarify beliefs and values. They provide opportunities for cooperative action as well as for independent study.

You should view the use of the various techniques as a continuum that provides opportunities ranging from the relatively elementary to the highly sophisticated. For example, panels and buzz sessions can make possible the sharing of a wide range of opinions and views, and can provide a setting for the conveying of information, telling about, or exposition. Forums, debates, and round table discussions are appropriate techniques for highlighting controversy and for expression of differing viewpoints. A science class could utilize them effectively in probing an issue, such as the ecology movement vis-á-vis traditional concepts of progress in technology and society.

Small groups and committees can operate at a more sophisticated level in exploring, probing, and examining complex issues, such as the morality of nuclear energy or nerve warfare, or various solutions to the energy crisis. As students acquire skills in group action, they can engage in problem-solving and research activities of an advanced nature through small group and committee planning and activity.

Ends

As *ends,* the process dimension of discussion and group work takes priority. The techniques and procedures can be viewed as ends in themselves, as learning experiences utilized to acquire skills of participation and cooperative action. Learning the ways of discussion is an important aspect of education. As such, the experiences help students acquire skills in expression, argumentation, exposition, planning, execution of plans, and cooperation. Direct appraisal and evaluation are important in helping students gain insights relative to participant roles, their own functioning, their typical tendencies, strengths, and weaknesses. Skillful use of discussion and group work provides many opportunities for self-knowledge and self-actualization as an integral part of the participatory experience.

Exercise 9 F

Develop three behavioral objectives for a specific instructional unit. Indicate which type of discussion techniques would be appropriate for the achievement of each objective.

Analysis of Student Roles

In order to conduct discussion and group work well one needs to understand the nature of the various roles assumed by participants. Already familiar are the formal roles of leader, whether as moderator, chairman, or designated leader of a small group endeavor, and the informal role of leadership assumed by various participants as discussion, planning, and sharing shifts from one student to another. Similarly, the role of cooperative participant or follower is a familiar one to all of us who find this often more comfortable than exerting leadership. Then, there is the frequent role designation of recording secretary for certain types of group sessions.

Even a cursory observation of group process reveals a multitude of other roles, reflected either subconsciously as an outgrowth of individual traits and characteristics, or assumed deliberately in an effort to facilitate or block group process.

Several such roles can be readily identified. There is the facilitator, the group member whose contributions generally try to move forward the discussion or planning. There is the blocker, who tends to object, challenge, hold back, disrupt, or in other ways interfere with orderly progress. There is the mediator or compromiser, who attempts to help the group out of an impasse or controversy. There is the loner, who can be either a nonparticipant, or one who seeks to do his or her own thing and rarely engages in general cooperative action. There is the observer type who participates little but, at appropriate times, comments on the procedures of the group. The observer can help to clarify for the group its particular stage of development and progress, as well as the ways in which it has been functioning.

Many more roles could be identified, but several important points might well be made, whatever the number and types of roles delineated. If students are to be guided toward effective, cooperative activity, they need to be helped toward an understanding of these roles and of their own type of participation. They need to be encouraged to try different positive roles and need to be helped to change more negative behavior. Especially to be noted are the dangers inherent in assuming dependency roles, whether the student becomes dependent on the teacher, on a specific classmate, on the leader, or on the entire group. One of the values of group techniques is the opportunity for growth in independent functioning. As teacher, therefore, you must be a perceptive observer at all times in order to help students move in positive directions toward positive, effective, and productive roles.

Desirable Outcomes

Involvement in group work seems to result in greater participation when all students come together again in the total class situation. The participation in small groups seems to build confidence, develop verbal skills, and promote thinking and doing. As a result, these characteristics seem to carry over to behavior in large class situations.

Another promising aspect of the use of these processes is their contribution to growth in various affective realms. Group activities seem conducive to developing openness to ideas, acceptance of others, and sensitivity to people and beliefs, all qualities for which education claims to accept some responsibility.

A third desirable outcome is the generally more cooperative atmosphere in the classroom as a result of the more cooperative attitude of students. Genuine discussion and group work tends to promote a *we* feeling, a willingness to work together on common goals and projects. Such attitudes become a welcome substitute for the more usual competitive *I* versus *you* atmosphere of much of educational practice.

Some Concepts to Be Explored

It should be obvious that there is more to participatory activities than mere verbalization. In fact, there are many areas of inquiry devoted to rigorous study of key aspects of effective participation. Two that might be noted here are in the realm of group dynamics and in communication theory.

Group dynamics, or the study of behavior in groups, is a provocative area for investigation, and one which pays rich dividends for teachers and other educators. The teacher who wishes to become skillful in the use of discussion and group techniques could gain much help from the principles of group dynamics and the research that has been done in that area.

Similarly, an understanding of communication theory offers rich insights into the complexities of the act of communication. The current saying, "I know you think you heard what I said, but . . . ," illustrates the complex relationship between sender, message, and receiver. If discussion and group work are to reach their full potential in classroom practice, teachers must bring to their work with students the insights and understandings to be gained from serious investigation of communication theory. Students need to be helped to acquire these same insights as they increasingly participate in an active way in the entire educational process.

Suggested Reading

Gage, N. L. *Educational Psychology,* 3d ed. Boston: Houghton Mifflin, 1984, Chap. 20.

Gall, Meredith D., and Joyce P. Gall. "The Discussion Method," in N. L. Gage, ed., *The Psychology of Teaching Methods,* The Seventy-fifth Yearbook of the Society for the Study of Education. Chicago: University of Chicago Press, 1976, Chap. 6.

Hill, William Fawcett. *Learning Through Discussion: Guide for Leaders and Members of Discussion Groups.* Beverly Hills, Cal.: Sage Publications, 1969.

Hock, Louise. *Group Discussion.* New York: Holt, Rinehart and Winston 1961.

Howes, Virgil M., *Informal Teaching in the Open Classroom.* New York: Macmillan, 1974.

Johnson, David W., et al. *Circles of Learning: Cooperation in the Classroom.* Alexandria, Va.: Association for Supervision and Curriculum Development, 1984.

Orlich, Donald C., et al. *Teaching Strategies: A Guide to Better Instruction,* 2d ed. Lexington, Mass.: D. C. Heath, 1985, Part 7.

Schmuch, Richard A., and Patricia A. Schmuch. *Group Processes in the Classroom.* Dubuque, Ia.: W. C. Brown, 1971.

Shaw, Marvin E. *Group Dynamics: The Psychology of Small-Group Behavior,* 2d ed. LaJolla, Cal.: Learning Resources, 1976.

Stanford, Gene. *Developing Effective Classroom Groups: A Practical Guide for Teachers.* New York: Hart, 1977.

Weil, Marsha, and Bruce Joyce. *Social Models of Teaching: Expanding Your Teaching Repertoire.* Englewood Cliffs, N.J.: Prentice-Hall, 1978.

Post Test

Multiple choice Select the most appropriate response to each of the following:

1. The major justification for helping students develop skills in discussion and group process is
   a. the inclusion of speech in the language arts curriculum.
   b. the failure of parents to accept responsibility for teaching these skills.
   c. the necessary respite that such activities provide from the more cognitive aspects of the instructional program.

d. the prevalence of group activity and human interaction in everyday life and experience.

2. The use of small group or committee work techniques is most appropriate in relation to
    a. acquisition of specified information.
    b. development of psychomotor skills.
    c. promoting individual creative talents.
    d. an inquiry approach to learning.

3. All but *one* of the following are characteristic of total class sessions involving student interaction and an emphasis on inquiry:
    a. student involvement in decision making.
    b. teacher checking of lessons to determine right and wrong answers.
    c. probing analysis of concepts and issues.
    d. shifting leadership roles among the participants.

4. Fundamental to the importance of teaching group skills in the classroom is the view that the school
    a. exists solely for the transmission of knowledge.
    b. is intended to provide salable skills and career preparation.
    c. has a major responsibility to help socialize the individual.
    d. should concentrate on teaching students how to think.

5. The least formal of the following group discussion techniques is
    a. round-table discussion.
    b. symposium.
    c. debate.
    d. forum.

6. The greatest value in role-playing activities lies in
    a. enhancing the acting skills of talented students.
    b. permitting ego gratification on the part of some students.
    c. promoting the creative instincts of students.
    d. deepending insights and understandings relative to the issues and personalities involved.

7. To gain skill in spontaneous conversation in a foreign language, the most appropriate technique would be
    a. panels.
    b. debates.
    c. buzz groups.
    d. simulated TV programs.

8. The least important purpose of buzz sessions is
    a. acquisition of specific information.
    b. greater participation of all students.
    c. the opportunity for a change of pace and reduction of tension.
    d. sharing of many individual views and opinions.

9. Committee work differs from the buzz group techniques largely on the basis of
   a. involvement of more students.
   b. greater focus on expressive skills.
   c. well-organized outcome relative to a specific task.
   d. more direct teacher involvement.

10. For students inexperienced in small-group work, the best type of activity to start with would be
   a. production of a class magazine.
   b. planning of a field trip to a local museum.
   c. a survey of community consumer habits.
   d. committee study of several different revolutions.

11. In group work activities, it is important for the teacher to be an active observer at all times in order to
   a. assess and guide individual and group growth in participatory skills.
   b. prevent errors and misjudgment on the part of students.
   c. select appropriate leaders.
   d. direct student plans for class presentations.

12. The least likely outcome of small group and committee work is
   a. increased confidence on the part of individual students.
   b. increased competition among students.
   c. increased skill in self-direction.
   d. increased sensitivity to others.

13. Which of the following would be most useful in presenting the research of individuals or committees?
   a. A buzz session.
   b. A brainstorming session.
   c. A panel.
   d. A fishbowl.

14. Which of the following would you recommend as a means for group decision making?
   a. Panels.
   b. Symposia.
   c. Formal debate.
   d. Fishbowl.

15. In what way does the British-style debate differ from the formal debate?
   a. There must be more than two sides.
   b. Each side has a chance for rebuttal.
   c. Team members other than presenters may ask questions or make comments.
   d. Each side presents its case by set speeches.

16. To make small-group work productive the teacher should
   a. keep rigid control of the group process.
   b. teach pupils how to work as groups.

    c. let pupils do as they will.

    d. limit small-group work to committee projects.

17. Which of the following flow chart diagrams best pictures an excellent discussion?

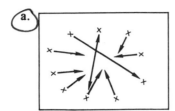

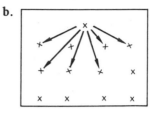

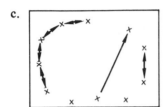

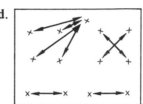

18. One virtue of group techniques is that they

    a. tend to foster an openness to ideas and acceptance of others.

    b. are teacher centered.

    c. present facts more vividly.

    d. save time.

19. The discussion leader can stimulate discussion by

    a. asking open-ended questions.

    b. using a springboard.

    c. asking divergent questions.

    d. all of the above.

    e. none of the above.

20. Which of these roles should the teacher assume when conducting discussions and group activities?

    a. Resource person.

    b. Guide.

    c. Mediator.

    d. All of the above.

    e. None of the above.

MODULE
10

Exploration and Discovery

Rationale

This module examines a number of teaching strategies, all of which have elements of problem solving or discovery learning that is here combined under the heading of inquiry or discovery teaching methods. The principal common factor in these teaching methods is that the pupils are expected to draw conclusions, concepts, and generalizations from some form of induction, deduction, observation or application of principles. The premises behind these methods are that one learns to think by thinking and that knowledge one figures out for oneself is more meaningful, permanent, and transferable than concepts that teachers attempt to give to pupils ready-made.

Specific Objectives

This module is designed to familiarize you with strategies and tactics used in the discovery or inquiry methods and with techniques used in building and clarifying values and morals. When you have finished it, you should be able to describe the following:

1. The procedures advocated for teaching by each of the following techniques: discovery, problem solving, project, research project, case study, Socratic discussion, open text recitation, role playing, simulation, springboards, value discussions, problem-solving discussions, moral dilemma discussions, and value clarification techniques.
2. The advantages and disadvantages of using each of the methods listed.
3. General procedures common to teaching by any discovery, inquiry, or problem-solving technique.
4. The procedures for conducting the study of controversial issues, as recommended in this module.
5. Traditional and newer procedures for building morals and values.

Module Text

Behind the methods described in this module is the assumption that pupils should actively seek out knowledge, rather than having it handed to them by some such expository teaching procedure as the lecture, demonstration, or textbook reading and reciting. Ordinarily, methods of the inquiry, discovery and problem solving persuasion have several advantages over the expository methods. They offer good motivating activity. They give pupils opportunity to learn and practice the intellectual skills, to learn to think rationally, to see relationships and the disciplinary structure, to understand the intellectual processes, and to learn how to learn.

Inquiry, discovery, and clarification methods also have several disadvantages. Usually they are costly in time and effort with no guarantee that the cost will pay off. Sometimes the truths that pupils discover for themselves are far removed from the truths the teachers have in mind. Slipshod thinking and investigating is difficult to eliminate and to correct. When pupils reach erroneous conclusions, reteaching may be more difficult than expository teaching would have been. Although teaching by inquiry and discovery when done well is usually more effective, it is not always more efficient. How much time one should take to rediscover well-known facts and principles is problematical, particularly in a time when there is so much to learn.

Inquiry and Discovery Teaching

The notion that pupil learning is more meaningful, more thorough, and therefore more usable when pupils seek out and discover knowledge, rather than just being receivers of knowledge, has been held by educational theorists for centuries. It is implicit in what we know of the teaching strategies of such master teachers as Socrates and Jesus of Nazareth, and in the theories of more modern thinkers such as Rousseau and Pestalozzi, not to mention twentieth-century educational philosophers such as John Dewey. Many practitioners today are convinced that these theories are true and they use discovery teaching as the heart of their teaching approaches. Experience over the years indicates that, to an extent, they are right. If teachers will give pupils opportunities to draw conclusions from data that are provided or that they seek out for themselves, the pupils will benefit. Pupils also can learn from being shown, told, or conditioned. It is neither necessary nor wise for teachers to insist that pupils rediscover all the knowledge encompassed by the curriculum. Some of that knowledge can best be learned by expository methods. Effective teachers use a mix of the discovery and expository strategies that seems most suitable to a particular teaching-learning situation.

The essential element in discovery learning is the pupils' drawing conclusions or generalizations or applying them to new situations. One method of doing this is to supply the pupils with information from which they draw conclusions. For instance, you might show the pupils an experiment or a series of experiments that illustrate a generalization and then let the pupils infer the generalization by means of logical thinking. The thinking may be deductive or inductive (in this example, inductive, no doubt). Another approach would be for the pupils to conduct an experiment and then draw the generalization from the results. This method differs from the cookbook laboratory method in that the pupil discovers the generalization rather than being told by the teacher or the laboratory manual what to do, what to see, and what the finding signifies. This type of discovery teaching is truly inquiry teaching, because the pupils do their own inquiring and research. It can also be problem solving if the pupils are allowed to go through the entire laboratory process themselves. Once the pupils understand the generalization or principle, either having discovered it or having been told it, they may discover how to use it in specific applications.

Actually much discovery teaching must be a combination of inductive and deductive teaching. If one understands the principles of map reading and the difficulty of pulling a wagon over steep mountains, map study will show a pupil why the pioneers took the Oregon Trial by South Pass and Bear Lake and through Idaho to Oregon rather than by the Lewis and Clark route. The basic model for conducting discovery learning consists of the following steps:

1. Select the generalization or generalizations.
2. Set up a problem situation.
3. Set up experiences that will bring out the essential elements, such as problem solving, questions, demonstrations, and so on.
4. Set up experiences that will bring out contrasting elements.
5. Draw generalization or concept.
6. Apply the generalization or concept.[1]

There are many ways to introduce discovery into your teaching. Among the most common examples are Socratic and guided discussions, research and other projects, case studies, and the various types of action learning and community involvement activities.

---

[1] Leonard H. Clark and Irving S. Starr, *Secondary School Teaching Methods,* 3rd ed. (New York: Macmillan Publishing Co., 1976), p. 231.

Teacher's Role in Inquiry and Discovery

Since inquiry connotes seeking and discovering rather than learning from exposition, your role in inquiry teaching will be to guide learning rather than to direct or dictate. In this role you must raise problems, issues, and questions designed to catch the pupils' interest, start them thinking, and encourage them to investigate. While the pupils are investigating, you should guide their search by helping them clarify their problems, map out their procedures, order their thinking, come to logical conclusions, and, finally, test and apply their conclusions. In this process you should

1. Be supportive and accepting.
2. Accentuate the positive.
3. Provide clues.
4. Encourage the exchange of ideas.
5. Accept legitimate hypotheses.
6. Warn and rescue pupils when they seem to lose their way.
7. Encourage pupils to make informed guesses.
8. Help pupils to analyze and evaluate their ideas, interpretations, and thinking.
9. Foster free debate and open discussion, and urge pupils to try to think things out with no threat of reprisals when their thinking does not conform to the expected or to the norm.

In addition, to stimulate independent, resourceful thinking you should also:

1. Check the pupils' data-gathering techniques.
2. Ask thought questions.
3. Ask for interpretations, explanations, and hypotheses.
4. Question the interpretations, explanations, and hypotheses at which the pupil arrives.
5. Ask pupils what their data and information imply.
6. Ask pupils to check their thinking and their logic.
7. Confront pupils with problems, contradictions, fallacies, implications, value assumptions, value conflicts, and other factors that may call for a reassessment of their thinking and positions.[2]

In some types of discovery lessons, such as the controlled discussion, however, the free inquiry element of discovery teaching is likely to be minimal. In these lessons, the teachers are more often directors of learning than guides.

Exercise 10 A

Take a basic generalization in your field. What are some ways that a person could discover it?

A person builds notions or concepts by becoming familiar with

---

[2] Ibid., p. 225.

things (ideas, beliefs, artifacts, or objects) that are examples of a category and those that are not. A child, for instance, by observation learns that certain characteristics signify an animal to be a dog and that other characteristics signify that an animal is not a dog by observing dogs and not dogs, or that certain characteristics signify being free and others signify being not free by seeing and hearing about instances when people or animals are free and not free. Pick a generalization or concept in your own major field. What experiences could you give pupils so that they could discover from examples of positive and negative characteristics what the concept is and what it is not, and so define the concept or generalization in their own thinking?

The Use of Thought Questions

All of inquiry and discovery teaching relies on skillful use of thought and probing questions. You should practice these questions until their use becomes second nature. These techniques have already been described in Module 8. Essentially they are:

1. Emphasize how and why.
2. Follow up leads. Develop ideas through additional probing, clarifying questions.
3. Be sure the pupils have the facts before they venture into flights of fancy.
4. Ask questions that have no right answers.
5. Let pupils discuss each other's thinking.
6. Utilize Socratic techniques.

Springboards

Springboard techniques are excellent media for launching inquiry, discovery, and problem-solving strategies. These techniques include anything that lends itself to such questions as "How come?" "So what?" "If so, then what?" Examples of such techniques are role playing, movies, dramatizations, pictures, and models. Among the most impressive are contrived incidents, such as Mr. Jones' tantrum described in Module 4. The great teachers of ancient and modern times used parables to stimulate original thinking. In this method those teachers told a simple story, such as the story of the good Samaritan, and then asked their pupils to use this story as a jumping-off point for building conclusions or generalizations.

Problem Solving and Inquiry

Most inquiry, both in school and in the real world, is carried out by some variety of problem solving. The problem at hand may be exceedingly complex, requiring great skill and effort for its solution, or it may be so simple that solving it is almost automatic. But, in any case, the problem-solving activity is one that requires thought and a search for a solution. Examples of problem-solving approaches include such diverse activities as writing term papers, attempting to identify an unknown chemical, preparing an oral report, composing a menu, balancing a budget, or repairing a gasoline engine. Essentially, any learning activity in which the learner has to hunt for or think out answers is a problem-solving activity. However, one should not dignify an activity with the name problem solving if one can find the answer by the process of simple recall.

The steps in problem solving have been described differently by different theorists, but essentially the process is as follows:

1. We become aware of a problem (it may be started by the occasion, by someone else, or by ourselves), isolate it, and decide to do something about it.
2. We look for clues for the solution of the problem.
   a. We think up possible solutions (hypotheses) or approaches to take in solving the problem.
   b. We test the tentative solutions or approaches against criteria that will help us evaluate them adequately.
3. We reject the tentative solutions or approaches that do not meet our requirements and try new ones until we find one that is suitable, or we give up. In making our conclusions, we may accept the first solution or approach that appears adequate, or we may test all hypotheses to find the best one.[3]

This is essentially the process that John Dewey called a complete thought. In short, we must become aware of what the problem is; look for a solution; and check the solution to see if it is any good.

The ability to solve problems, particularly academic problems, does not seem to come naturally to most people. Excellence in problem solving is a skill that must be learned, so must be taught. If you supervise pupils carefully at every stage of the problem-solving process, you may be able not only to help the pupils solve the problems but also to help them improve their problem-solving techniques.

One of the perplexing truisms about problem solving is that often the reason no one has solved a problem is because no one has realized exactly what the problem is. In 1729, young Benjamin Franklin conducted a now famous experiment to find out the relation of color to heat absorption and thermal conductivity. According to Crane,

> From a tailor's sample-card Franklin detached broadcloth squares of different colors and shades, laid them on snow in bright sunshine, and measured the relative depth to which they sank as the snow melted. It was a simple test; a schoolboy, it has often been said, could have done it. But Franklin was the first to define the problem and to devise the experiment.[4]

Any schoolboy could have done it, but it took Franklin to think up the question, define it, and follow through.

Pupils need help in finding questions to ask and investigate. You may be able to help them by suggesting problem areas or specific problems to them by either directly or indirectly setting the stage. Here is where springboard techniques come in handy.

---

[3] Leonard H. Clark, *Teaching Social Studies in Secondary Schools* (New York: Macmillan Publishing Co., 1973), p. 28.

[4] Verner W. Crane, *Benjamin Franklin and a Rising People* (Boston: Little, Brown, 1954), p. 42.

You must also see to it that the problems pupils select are suitable for their purposes. Among the criteria they can use to test the suitability of the problem are the following:

1. Is it pertinent to the course objectives?
2. Is it relevant to pupils' lives and to community life?
3. Is it feasible? Do we have the necessary resources? Can we complete it in the time available? Can the pupils handle it?
4. Is it worth the effort?

Exercise 10 B

What would be interesting problem areas in your major field? Set up a list of eight or ten problems that pupils might investigate in the study of a topic in your major field. Why would each of these problems be good for pupils to investigate? Or why would it not be?

It is sometimes said that all secondary school learning must, or should be, problem-solving learning. Do you agree? Justify your position.

In selecting the problem, it is necessary to define it so as to set up the limits of the problem and to decide what must be done. Franklin's breakthrough in the study of heat absorption and thermal conductivity was caused because he was, evidently, the first person to define the problem. If one does not know exactly what the problem is, it is difficult to solve it. It is also difficult if the problem is too large and so impossible to focus on. Defining the problem by making it clear and giving it clear limits makes the solving of a particular problem a more reasonable task than it would be if it were not defined.

Once the problem has been isolated and defined, we begin to search for ways to solve it. This process involves gathering the data we need to make tentative hypotheses concerning ways to solve the problem, and trying out or testing these proposed solutions.

The last step in the process is to accept or reject the proposed solution. If the first idea seems to be satisfactory, we may end our search right there; otherwise we may try out other hypotheses or resume our search for more data and ideas in hope of finding new hypotheses. It may even be necessary to redefine the problem. Finally we find a hypothesis that we do accept or we give up trying to solve the problem. These steps—getting the data we need, making hypotheses, and testing them—do not necessarily occur in a particularly orderly fashion although, of course, one has to think of a hypothetical solution before he tries it or rejects it. The hypothetical solution may come out of the data we have accumulated, or the data may be gathered as a way of testing or developing a hypothesis.

Projects

In the field of education, the word *project* has come to mean any unit of activity, individual or group, involving the investigation and solution of problems, that is planned and carried to a conclusion by a pupil or pupils under the guidance of the teacher. Originally, it was conceived as being of significant practical value and resulting in some tangible product of personal value to the learner, such as the raising and marketing of a calf. To be worthy of the name, a project must be truly a problem-solving activity. In a true project the student plans, executes, and evaluates the entire undertaking. The teacher's role is simply to help, advise, and guide the learning.

Although ideally all projects should derive from pupils' interests, usually pupils have trouble finding and selecting suitable projects. You can help them at this point in several ways; you can provide lists of suggestions or try to stimulate ideas by class discussion. Sometimes telling pupils what others have done in the past or having last year's pupils come to the class on a consulting basis to describe successful projects of the past work well. No matter how the pupils get the idea, when they finally pick out their projects, they should check them for suitability. The criteria that should be met are that (1) the project should make a real contribution to a worthwhile learning objective; (2) it should result in a worthwhile end project; and (3) it should be reasonable insofar as time, effort, cost, and availability of resources are concerned.

To conduct a project requires a combination of restraint and guidance from the teacher. The pupils need to accept most of the responsibility for their projects, but they should not be allowed to flounder. The teachers must make themselves available to assist the pupils when necessary and from time to time to check their progress without interfering. Taking the middle course between too much and too little requires both tact and good judgment.

Exercise 10 C

Think up a half dozen projects in your subject field that would result in a product really valuable to the students who do them. Would they be really practicable in time, costs, materials, and abilities of the average middle school student? High school student?

Research Projects

The research project is an interesting variety of the genre. In this type of project, the pupil, independently or as a member of a committee, investigates some matter and then reports on it. As a rule this type of project is best done by the more academically talented pupils. Yet although pupils with little academic talent or interest usually do not take to this type of activity well, they can accomplish appropriate projects reasonably well when the projects are interesting enough to them, when they have the necessary guidance, and when the roles given to them are not unreasonable for persons of their abilities. Often they can also make significant contributions to group research projects; however, less able pupils should not be forced to do research projects. They can usually gain more benefits from other types of activities.

The process used in a research project is that of any problem-solving activity, as follows:

1. Decide exactly what it is that one is to try to find out.
2. Define the problem so that it is manageable in the time available and with the materials and personnel available.

3. Decide on what tasks must be done to get the necessary data and who will do each job.
4. Gather the materials and equipment necessary.
5. Perform the data-gathering tasks.
6. Review and analyze the data gathered.
7. Draw conclusions and generalizations from the data gathered.
8. Report the findings and conclusions.[5]

Perhaps, as applied to research projects, these steps need some elucidation. Selecting a topic for research can be somewhat bothersome. Most students find it difficult to select a problem on which they can really focus. To be worthwhile, the research should be aimed at a specific problem. Large, diffuse, ill-defined topics seldom result in anything worthwhile. Help pupils select topics of manageable proportions. Gathering the information requires that the pupils have mastered certain skills and are cognizant of certain materials. Too many research projects are simply data and information cribbed from an encyclopedia. Help pupils develop skill in looking up and finding pertinent references. They also need help in developing research techniques. Few students take adequate notes unless teachers instruct them in the art of note-taking. Pupils also have great trouble with such research skills as use of scientific equipment, sampling, analyzing data, testing for fact, and interpreting statistics unless they receive special instruction and supervision. Research is not easy, and proficiency in the use of scholarly procedures and intellectual tools is difficult to attain unless students are carefully schooled and supervised in their use. Students also need help in seeing the significance of their data and in drawing valid conclusions and generalizations from their research. Special class sessions for teaching these intellectual skills are helpful and should be utilized, but most of the skill development in this area must be taught by supervising the individual efforts of student researchers.

Research projects usually are best conducted as individual or small group activities. Very few of them are truly successful when conducted as whole class activities, although sometimes projects such as community surveys or the investigation and preparation of a report on a community problem can be very rewarding. The pupils in one New Jersey high school class, for instance, were concerned about racial prejudice in that school and community. As a class, they studied a number of references on the problem of prejudice, developed a questionnaire, gave the questionnaire to citizens in the community, analyzed the findings, and published the results. Some of the data and conclusions resulting from this study may be suspect in several ways (after all the study was the work of beginners), but the students found out much about race prejudice, about their community, and developed some familiarity with research techniques. Because the teacher carefully supervised the project and frequently criticized the pupils' efforts, errors were kept to a minimum, and the pupils learned through their mistakes as well as their successes.

[5] Clark and Starr, op. cit., p. 229.

Surveys

Surveys of the community or of the school population are among the most interesting types of research projects. If well planned and well conducted, they can teach the pupils much, but if poorly conceived and executed, they can lead to confusion, miseducation, and an upset community. Before launching into a community survey, be sure that the pupils know well both the topic they are to investigate and the procedures they are to use. This can be achieved by direct teaching and practice in the class.

Gathering the Information. There are many ways to conduct the gathering of data: interviews, questionnaires, and observation, for instance. It is, of course, important to pick the right data-gathering technique and to aim it directly at the correct goal. To be sure that the technique is suitable and well aimed, you and your pupils must carefully examine the problem to see exactly what data is needed for its solution. Then the pupils, under your guidance, must design a strategy to obtain that information. If this strategy involves a questionnaire or opinion sampling this is the point at which one designs the instrument. Although the development of an instrument may not be so necessary if the strategy adopted involves interviewing or observation, probably the results will be more profitable and dependable if a data-gathering instrument such as a rating scale or checklist is used. The pupils, of course, must be instructed and practiced in the use of these instruments so they will not waste the time of the respondents and also so the data gathered will be what was wanted. We discuss the construction and use of this sort of instrument later.

Processing the Data. Once the data have been gathered, they must be interpreted. This part of the research can be somewhat tricky. Most persons are tempted to make generalizations and conclusions that are not justified by the data. You should help pupils set up criteria by which to distinguish between significant and insignificant data. In some cases, to interpret the data, one may have to use simple statistics, but usually for class use careful inspection will suffice. The important point is to extrapolate cautiously. It is much safer to say that of the people we asked, 10 per cent said yes, 70 per cent said no, and 20 per cent did not answer, than to say that the people of the community reject the proposition. In this regard, pupils should be made aware of the difficulties of sampling and the need of an adequate sample as well as techniques for analyzing and interpreting their data. It is probably best to record and report the data in tabular form without comment. For example: Question 1. Do you prefer Plan A or Plan B? Total, 50 (100 per cent). A, 5 (10 per cent). B, 30 (60 per cent). No Answer, 15 (30 per cent).

Publishing the Results. Publishing the results of a survey usually should be reserved for classroom use only. Only exceptionally good surveys rate publishing more widely and even they should not be published until cleared by school officials. There is no reason to publish anything that will not enhance the school's image or reputation as a scholarly institution.

Building the Instrument. As many college and university graduate students have found out to their sorrow, to build an effective questionnaire or opinionaire is not an easy task. The following suggestions may help pupils who attempt to use questionnaires or opinion samplings in research projects.

1. Be sure to include in the questionnaire only those things that are needed. If you can find the information in another way with reasonable ease, do so.
2. Be sure the questions are clear. Check them for ambiguities. To be sure that they are unambiguous, try them out on other pupils and teachers. You may find that you ought to rewrite many of them or explain the terms or references you are using.
3. Be sure the questions are easy to answer. Yes-no, one word checklists, or multiple choice questions are the easiest and quickest both to answer and to interpret. However, be sure to give the respondent a chance to comment. It is maddening to a respondent not to be able to say that the answer is "yes, but . . ." or "well, it depends on . . ." Forced choice items have no place in questionnaires written by public school pupils; they should be reserved for use by professionals or by graduate students.
4. Be sure to set up the questionnaire so that it will be easy to tally the answers. For instance, if the answers can be arranged so that they appear in a column on the right (or left) side of the sheet, it makes tabulating much easier. Additional remarks and comments cannot be made easy to tabulate, but space should be provided for them. Be sure to give the respondent room enough to write a reasonably long, but not too long, comment.

Interview Procedure. To be sure that pupils conducting interviews ask the questions they should without taking up too much of the interviewee's time, or garbling the questions, or omitting necessary questions, the interview questions should be planned and written out before the interview. A written plan is necessary also because, if one hopes to get comparable data from the interviews, the pupils must ask all the respondents the same questions in the same way. Therefore, it is wise to develop a formal procedure, such as the following suggested by Popkewitz:

My name is _____ . My class is doing a survey about student participation. I will be speaking to many students in your school and other schools. I would like to ask you a few questions.

    A. Do you often discuss school issues with
        1. Friends?
        2. Class officers?
        3. School officials?
    B. Have you ever attended a meeting (church, school board, union, etc.) in which school policy was discussed?
    C. Have you ever taken an active part regarding school issues, such as writing a letter or presenting a petition?[6]

---

[6] Thomas S. Popkewitz, *How to Study Political Participation*, How to Do It Series No. 27 (Washington, D.C.: National Council for the Social Studies, 1974), p. 5.

This format makes it easy for pupils to record answers to their questions. They should record the answers of the respondent immediately. If they try to depend on memory, they will get mixed up, forget, and, therefore, bring in incorrect data.

Observation Techniques. If research involving the use of observation techniques is to be successful, the pupils must be well prepared to observe carefully and profitably. The observation must be planned and the observers trained so that they see and report the data in the same way. For this purpose, the pupils should decide exactly what it is they must look for. In some instances, this means that they will have to decide upon the standards for establishing the presence or absence of the phenomenon, or for deciding the criteria for such categories as *much, some, little*. They will also need to devise sort of instrument on which to record their observations. Frequently this instrument should be a checklist in which the observers merely note the presence or absence of phenomena, as in the following:

> 1. Check the applicable item.
>   a. Pupil selected a hot dish.
>   b. Pupil selected a dessert.
>   c. Pupil selected a coke.

Or the instrument may be a rating scale in which the pupil records his judgment of the amount or quality of the phenomenon present, as in the following:

> The pupils' conduct in the cafeteria line was
>   very orderly   fairly orderly   disorderly
> The pupils' conduct at their tables was
>   very orderly   fairly orderly   disorderly

In the constructing of these devices, teachers should try to help pupils concoct procedures that make observing, recording, and interpreting the data as simple and as easy as possible. When observing, recording, or interpreting becomes unnecessarily complicated, the devices are usually accompanied by unnecessary errors.

Case Study Method

The case study is a special type of problem-solving method. It consists of a searching, detailed study of a particular situation, institution, decision, or issue from which pupils draw generalizations concerning the type. The case study can give pupils considerable understanding of difficult, complex matters.

Although the procedures for conducting case studies are quite simple, they are usually difficult to carry out. In general, they include the following steps:

1. Select and define a topic or problem to investigate. The topic should be a specific case so typical of a larger area that studying it would throw light on the entire area.

2. Identify, collect, and make ready the materials needed for studying the case in depth. Usually, most will be reading material, but do not forget that sometimes films, pictures, or audio and video tapes may be better for your purpose. So may laboratory or field work.

3. Now that you have the things to work with, you are ready to begin the case study. Start with any good introduction. In the introduction, the pupils should get an understanding of the problem or issue before them, what they are attempting to find out, and the method of attack. This is the time when you sell the case study to the pupils so make your introduction persuasive. At this point, it may be wise to give out a study guide that the pupils can use as they investigate the case. The bulk of the study of the case can be done individually by pupils investigating individually with the study guide for a base. If one wishes, it is possible to proceed on a group or whole class basis through the use of discussions and the like. But the really important part of this phase of the case study approach is to study the particular case in depth, learn as much as one can about it, and draw conclusions.

4. Now the pupils share their findings and conclusions. They can do this in many ways; perhaps the most profitable is the free discussion. Role playing, panels, and symposia may also prove very useful. In these discussions, the pupils should be encouraged to draw inferences from the case study, as they have been doing right along about the class of things the case study represents.

Exercise 10 D

Think of a case study that you might use as a means for teaching your subject. How might a presentation technique be used as a motivating device for the case study? What type of presentation would you select? Why?

Field Trip

One of the very best ways to make instruction real is to take the pupils out in the field to see and do things, such as to go to the theater to see a production of *Macbeth,* to go down to the swamp to gather specimens, to see ecological problems firsthand, to go to the museum to see the works of great art, or to visit the site of a battle. Field trips, carefully planned and executed, can pay off in increased motivation and meaningful learning, but they require careful planning. In fact, of all the possible instructional activities, they probably require the most careful planning. Among the items one may need to consider in preparing for a particular field trip are the following:

1. Talk over the trip with your principal and department head.
2. Take the trip yourself, if feasible, to see how to make it most productive and to see what arrangements should be made.
3. Arrange for details at the place to be visited. These arrangements include a schedule; the briefing of the host, or tour personnel, on what you want and what type of group you are; provisions for eating and rest rooms; and so on. Get clear information about fees.

4. Arrange for permissions from the school authorities and parents.
5. Arrange for schedule changes, excuses from other classes, and so on.
6. Arrange for transportation.
7. Arrange for the collection of funds, payments, and so on.
8. Arrange for the safety of pupils.
9. Arrange the itinerary, including all stops—rest stops, meals, and so on. Do not plan to rush. Allow plenty of time. Figure that someone will get lost, or be late, or something!
10. Establish rules of conduct.
11. Brief the pupils. Give them directions: what to do if lost or left behind, what to take along, what they are going to do, what they should look for, what notes they should take, what materials they should bring back. Give them a duplicated study guide.
12. Provide for follow-up activities. Taking along tape recorders and cameras will allow you to bring back a record of what you did and saw. Tape record interviews, talks, questions and answers, and take pictures of the people, places, and things seen as the basis of a class follow-up.
13. Take steps to see that no one is left out because of lack of money, race, religion, or ethnic background.
14. Arrange for other teachers and parents to help you.[7]

Figure 10-1 (pages 250 and 251), is a worksheet used for planning and reporting field trips at a New Jersey junior high school. Notice the meticulous detail that the board of education expects of teachers who conduct field trips. As you examine this form, ask yourself why the school board and school administrators have required each of the items they have listed.

Another type of field study is field work in which students go into the field to gather or collect materials (as in life science, biology, or geology class, for instance), to record observations, or generally to gather data useful for their class assignments. Field work of this type tends to tie one's instruction to reality as well as making it more active and interesting.

Action Learning

Field trips and surveys are examples of community involvement activities. Such activities allow students to observe and study realities outside the schoolroom. Action learning activities tend to carry such learning a step further. In these activities students actually become involved in community affairs or community service projects. In Jersey City (N.J.), for instance, students participated in a local political campaign, and in a Vermont village a science class investigated and brought to the attention of the selectmen a problem concerning water pollution. Such activities effectively extend the classroom into the community. By so doing they quite often get at objectives that other learning activities fail to reach. In action learning, what in the classroom is academic becomes real and vivid. To prepare students for such activities, use the techniques suggested for community involvement and research projects discussed in preceding paragraphs.

[7] Leonard H. Clark, *op. cit.*, p. 321.

Date _____

Teacher's Worksheet on Field Trip

This worksheet is intended both as a teacher's guide and a report. It should be handed in after the completion of the trip. Check applicable items as completed.

Trip to _____

Teacher _____ Subject _____ Date of trip _____

Group or section _____ Alternate date _____

Planning on Part of Teacher

_____ Are the educational values of the proposed trip definite and clear? State them briefly:

_____ Figure the cost: Transportation $_____

Admissions $_____

Meals $_____

Total $_____

_____ Is the total cost figure sufficient, reasonable, and within the reach of most of the group?

_____ Secure approval of the principal and turn in Permission for School Excursion (Form 132).

_____ Check school calendar with vice-principal and sign for date.

_____ Make arrangements with bus company, after securing at least two bids.

_____ Have the places you intend to visit been "scouted," either by you or someone you know?

_____ Chaperones to be secured: two adults per bus, one of whom must be a licensed teacher.

_____ If the trip takes two hours or more, is a bathroom stop available enroute?

_____ Have teachers made arrangements with the vice-principal for students left behind or for teachers' duties left "uncovered"?

Preparation of the Class

_____ Discuss purposes of trip with the class.

_____ Each child who is going must have Field Trip Permit signed by parents (Form 126).

_____ Discuss proper clothes to be worn by the students.

_____ Discuss conduct on bus, including:
_____ No arms or heads to be out of windows.
_____ Remain in seats except by permission.

FIGURE 10-1

_____ Trash to be placed in paper bags.

_____ Nothing to be thrown out of bus windows.

_____ Pupils remain in seats on bus at destination until teacher gets off first.

_____ Listen to teacher's directions for dismounting at destination.

_____ Discuss the method of control which is to be used during the trip:

_____ "Buddy System"—students are paired up and given numbers (1A-1B, 2A-2B, etc.) The pair must remain together. If they leave the main group, they must tell another pair where they are going. Students must immediately report the loss of a "buddy." Each chaperone will supervise so many sets of buddies.

_____ Or "Group system"—divide a busload into two or three squads, with a student leader *and* a chaperone in charge of each. Attendance to be taken by each group frequently.

_____ Or other system of control as planned by teacher and approved by principal.

_____ Eating arrangements to be explained to pupils. Need for staple foods, rather than a day of candy and soda, should be discussed.

_____ On day before trip, class should make a list of things to be looked for on trip.

On the Morning of the Trip

_____ Proper attendance taken in homeroom or classroom.

_____ Correct absentee cards sent to office.

_____ Correct list of those remaining behind turned in to office.

_____ Permission slips (Form 126) filed in main office.

_____ Students reinstructed on bus safety rules.

_____ Take first-aid kit; also empty paper bags for car sickness.

_____ Check attendance *on the bus* immediately before leaving. Teacher in charge reports discrepancies to the attendance secretary in main office.

Follow-Up

_____ Has the trip been followed up by the class with evaluation—either written or oral—of ideas and facts learned?

_____ Write a brief evaluation of the trip: What were its values? Would you take a group on it next year? Other comments. Use space below.

_____

Signature of Teacher

FIGURE 10-1   (Continued)

Discussion and Discovery

Socratic Method

Socratic questioning has been treated in an earlier module of this series. It is one of the very oldest of discovery methods of which we have any record. According to Plato, Socrates' method was to ask a series of questions by which he hoped to cause his pupil to examine his beliefs, upset his preconceptions, and then draw new conclusions. The secret of the method was in the use of questions that were both challenging and leading. This questioning requires a great amount of skill and a thorough knowledge, because the questioner must be ready to follow with a new appropriate question wherever the pupil may lead him. When you use Socratic questioning, think out beforehand the type of questions you should ask. In fluid situations, it is impossible to anticipate what the answers will be and to be prepared for all contingencies. Probably that was why Socrates depended so much upon leading questions, such as, All people want to be happy, don't they? Handled by an expert, such as Socrates was, the Socratic method can be a superb instrument for examining and discovering ideas as the following excerpt from the *Meno* illustrates.

> SOCRATES. Now boy, you know that a square is a figure like this?
> (*Socrates begins to draw figures in the sand at his feet. He points to the square* A B C D.)

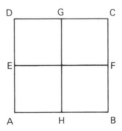

> BOY. Yes.
> SOCRATES. It has all these four sides equal?
> BOY. Yes.
> SOCRATES. And these lines which go through the middle of it are also equal? (The lines EF, GH.)
> BOY. Yes.
> SOCRATES. Such a figure could be either larger or smaller, could it not?
> BOY. Yes.
> SOCRATES. Now if this side is two feet long, and this side the same, how many feet will the whole be? Put it this way. If it were two feet in this direction and only one in that, must not the area be two feet taken once?
> BOY. Yes.
> SOCRATES. But since it is two feet this way also, does it not become twice two feet?
> BOY. Yes.
> SOCRATES. And how many feet is twice two? Work it out and tell me.
> BOY. Four.
> SOCRATES. Now could one draw another figure double the size of this, but similar, that is, with all its sides equal like this one?
> BOY. Yes.

SOCRATES. How many feet will its area be?

BOY. Eight.

SOCRATES. Now then, try to tell me how long each of its sides will be. The present figure has a side of two feet. What will be the side of the double-sized one?

BOY. It will be double, Socrates, obviously.[8]

Controlled or Guided Discussion

The controlled or guided discussion is an attempt to adopt the Socratic method to the exigencies of large classes found in most schools. Basically it consists of the following three steps:

1. Select certain generalizations to be learned.
2. Furnish the pupils with information by means of lectures, reading, film, or other expository devices or techniques.
3. Utilize probing questions to guide the pupils as they draw principles and generalizations from the information they have been given or have found in their reading or study. This method is not a true discussion or a true inquiry. As usually conducted, it is very teacher-centered and seldom open-ended. In carrying it out, the teacher continually asks pupils challenging, thought-provoking questions, designed to arouse their thinking in an attempt to persuade them to arrive at the conclusions or generalizations he has set up as his goals.

For an example of how one might use a guided discussion to develop a generalization, let us return to the Oregon Trail example to which we referred earlier. Let us suppose that we wished to have the pupils realize that the terrain has considerable impact on the location of routes. We could then initiate a lesson in map study and perhaps a reading, describing travel along the trail. Then, in discussion, we could ask questions such as (1) What seems to be the most direct route from Missouri to Oregon? (2) What are the disadvantages of this route? (3) In setting out to select a route to Oregon, what factors would you, as a pioneer, look for?

As a result of this type of questioning, it is hoped that the teacher will be able to draw the conclusion that, in setting out a route, one must consider such elements as slope, water, and attitudes of the natives. To reinforce these ideas, one might compare the route selected for the Oregon Trail with the routes selected for super tankers bringing oil from the Arabian oil fields to the East Coast of the United States.

Open-text Recitation

In the controlled discussion, there is no reason that the pupils should not have before them the information to be used in drawing their conclusions. Controlled discussions should not be exercises in remembering, but in discovering. In the lesson we have just seen, the maps and written information provided are resources that can make the lesson more meaningful and productive if the pupils can refer to them during the class. This sort of class is often called an open-textbook recitation. It has already been discussed in Module 8. The point in this type of

[8] From *Plato: Protagoras and Meno*, translated by W. K. C. Guthrie (London: Penguin Books, 1965), pp. 133–137. Reprinted by permission of the publisher.

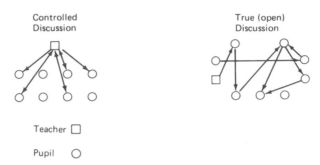

FIGURE 10-2 *Flow of Conversation in Discussions*

lesson is to develop a discussion in which pupils can defend their ideas, justify their contributions, and check on proposals while the class is in progress. Such discussions may or may not be open-ended. Although the open textbook recitation is ordinarily conducted as a controlled discussion, there is absolutely no reason why textbooks and references should not be used in true discussions. Probably it would be preferable in many instances if many open-textbook recitations were conducted as true discussions rather than as controlled discussions.

Problem-solving Discussion

Discussion can be used both as a means of inquiry and intellectual discovery if the problem under discussion is important to the discussants and if conducted so that it is free and permissive, yet also disciplined and orderly. Rap sessions or bull sessions will not suffice, but well-conducted discussions are excellent for solving problems, because they bring out so many ideas from so many different people. Group members usually have many differing values, biases, insights, standards, conclusions, and beliefs. Open discussion reveals these differences and frees group members to examine, or at least to defend, their own values and beliefs and consider the values and beliefs of others. Because it is difficult to maintain narrow stereotypic thinking in such circumstances, the discussion tends to open group members to new ideas, to stimulate new thinking and, perhaps, to create answers to the problems to be solved. In this connection brainstorming and the fishbowl technique discussed in the preceding module can be especially useful.

The procedures for conducting a discussion that is aimed at solving a problem are just about the same as those for carrying on any other type of discussion. Although they, or other discussions, seldom hew strictly to the line prescribed by the most logical development, they should follow the general patterns of the problem-solving process. As adapted for discussion groups by Burton, Kimball and Wing, these procedures include the following points:

1. The group becomes aware of a problem that it believes can be solved by talking it out.
2. The group defines the problem. This defining process may be quite difficult and time-consuming.
3. The group analyzes and explores the problem so that all will understand it.

The process includes (a) determining what the facts are; (b) becoming acquainted with the values, backgrounds, and levels of maturity of the various group members; and (c) discovering the hidden objectives, if any, of individual group members.

4. The group thinks the problem through together. This process will undoubtedly be slow and orderly. Errors will be made and time consumed, but the procedure is necessary.

5. The group brings resources to help explore the problem. A pooling of ignorance solves no problems, so the group seeks out the information it needs from whatever sources promise to be most fruitful.

6. The group develops the "machinery and organization" necessary for cooperative thinking as it goes along. These are not set up in advance.

7. The group continually summarizes, casts straw votes, and projects tentative solutions as the discussion goes along, so as to delay making premature final conclusions and to bring about the consensus of all its members.

8. The group continually evaluates its progress, both as to process and to substance.

9. The group comes to a tentative conclusion which it tries out in an actual situation.[9]

You recognize, of course, that these are the procedures used by all successful committees, society meetings, town meetings, and the like to solve problems brought before them.

Exercise 10 E

As a group discussion leader, how does your role in a controlled discussion differ from that in a problem-solving discussion?

Formal Discussion

The formal discussion methods discussed in Module 9—panels, forums, symposiums, debates, British-style debates, and the like—are not so much inquiry methods as they are methods for reporting and clarifying what has been inquired into and discovered. The procedures that lead up to these presentations are ordinarily inquiry or problem-solving techniques. Panels, forums, round tables, and British-style debates can be the capstones for projects and case studies, for example. They can be used to give a project or case study a visible reason for being. See Module 9 for procedures for carrying out these strategies.

Developing Values and Morals[10]

It is becoming increasingly evident that the lay people of the community hold the schools responsible for teaching pupils the morals and values that they perceive to be essential to the good life in a democratic country.

---

[9] Adapted from William H. Burton, Roland B. Kimball, and Richard L. Wing, *Education for Effective Thinking* (New York: Appleton-Century-Crofts, 1960), p. 328.

[10] This section has been adapted in part from Module 11, "Teaching Values," *Teaching in the Elementary School* (New York: Macmillan Publishing Co., 1977), Joseph F. Callahan and Leonard H. Clark, eds. The original module was written by John C. Turpin of Baldwin-Wallace College.

Traditional Approaches

For years the methods used by teachers to help students adopt certain values have been as follows.

1. Models and Modeling. Either by their own behavior or by selecting outstanding examples of virtue among the adult world, living or dead, the teachers drew attention to the practice of values that they looked upon as acceptable.

This was the purpose behind Plutarch's *Lives* and the numerous biographies of exemplary Americans such as George Washington who never told a lie and Honest Abe Lincoln. It was also the reason that in decades past townspeople expected exemplary behavior of teachers, preachers, and other professional persons.

The force of this strategy should not be downgraded. Modeling is the source of a major share of our beliefs and attitudes. We tend to imitate those we admire. Therefore, you should try to provide students with admirable exemplars to pattern after.

2. Persuasion. By presenting their arguments carefully, teachers traditionally hoped to prevail upon students to accept selected sets of values that were approved by segments of the adult population. In short, they tried to sell certain beliefs and attitudes to the pupils. This is the approach used by the advertisers and propagandists in the press, radio, and television. It works well when it is sufficiently convincing and alternatives are not too enticing.

3. Limiting Choice. By eliminating attractive but unacceptable value choices from the options offered to students, teachers attempted to provide practice in judgment making. They offered, for example, two "goods" so that despite the selection made, no conflict with society resulted. Or they stacked the deck and offered choices, one of which was so obnoxious as to leave little doubt about the option exercised.

4. Inspiration. Through the use of fable, myth, biography, and history, teachers highlighted and made attractive the values they wished to inculcate. We have already mentioned the influence of examples set by historical characters. It remains only to mention the influence of song and story. Youths' behavior, beliefs, and attitudes are frequently the direct result of what they have read, what they have seen on stage, screen, or television, or what they have heard in the songs of the times.

5. Rules and Regulations. The intent of these rules was the control of behavior by rewards and punishments until the stage of automatic "correct" response had been reached. The influence of these approaches can be seen in some of the modern behavior modification techniques discussed in the modules on discipline and control.

6. Tradition and Religious Dogma. Acceptance of values was encouraged on the grounds that holy people or heroic people of the past had practiced them. Many people behave the way they do because they have been convinced that that is the way one ought to act. That is why for years so many men rigorously followed a code of honor. The power of religious dogma and historical tradition can be seen in the behavior of members of various religious groups and societies.

7. Appeal to Conscience.   By indicating the shame or guilt associated with one way of behavior, teachers cultivated behavior of the opposite sort in accordance with the values they supported.

8. Indoctrination.   Using their position of esteem and authority gained from their training, and superior knowledge, teachers informed their students what values, beliefs, and behavior were important with the expectation that students would accept their dictates without much debate.

Recently, two additional strategies for teaching values and moral development have become popular. These strategies are value clarification and the discussion of moral dilemmas. Some teachers and theorists have come to the basic belief that these approaches are much more effective than the traditional ones and should therefore be used by teachers. However, one should not be too quick to give up the traditional techniques and their modern counterparts. They have worked well in the past and are working well now all over the world. Now let us look briefly at value clarification.

Value Clarification

As described by Raths, its principal proponent, value clarification "is a way of interacting with a student so that he considers what he has chosen, what he prizes, or what he is doing. It stimulates him to clarify his thinking and behavior and thus to clarify his values."[11] Its purpose is to help students to accept, and become committed to, proper high level values. The basic method is to question, to challenge, and without moralizing, to help students look at what they have chosen, or are prizing, or are doing. The object is not to dictate values, but to encourage each student to look at his or her own behavior and make decisions from the alternatives that exist, and by so doing create a mood in which students have an opportunity to modify the direction of their lives.

Of course, if no acceptable options for students are available, value-clarification techniques are not appropriate. In such situations you should specifically direct the students concerning how they should behave. When, however, options are available, you must avoid trying to influence the students to accept particular values. Thus, in matters when no choice is permissible, such a setting a fire in the classroom wastebasket, or using profane language during class, you should be clear and forceful in denying choice to students, because an unwise choice cannot be tolerated by the policies that govern the group behavior. After all, some behavior is proper, and some behavior is wrong, and students should understand which is which. But in matters that are less crucial, when choice is possible you must be willing to give children the freedom to choose, if values are to result.

The use of value clarification has other limitations also. John Stewart complains that value clarification is too much dependent on peer pressure and so

---

[11] Louis E. Raths, Merrill Harmin, and Sidney B. Simon, *Values and Teaching, Working with Values in the Classroom* (Columbus, Oh.: Charles E. Merrill Publishing, 1966), p. 51.

"may possibly cause more harm than good." Stewart is also concerned that, in his opinion, value clarification being based on moral relativism may be "inadequate, ineffective, and possibly even dangerous."[12] Is it not possible that when a teacher has students clarify their own values without making a value judgment about the correctness of that judgment he is as much as saying, "Whatever you believe is all right"? And, of course, that simply is not true. In fact, the student may be adopting a value that is destructive to himself as an individual. In some cases citizens have objected strenuously to the use of value clarification and moral dilemma techniques—even to the extent of going to court to protest their use.

Nevertheless, value clarification has a number of strengths. Raths, for instance, believes that value clarification will be beneficial to pupils having manifestly idiosyncratic behavior patterns—apathy, flightiness, drift, overconformity, underachievement, for instance—that may be caused by confusion of values. Another strength of value clarification is that much of the time it is a personal and private prodding of pupils to look at themselves, their attitudes, their behavior, and their ideas that helps them to a better understanding and, possibly, a reshaping of themselves. Because of its supportive nonjudgmental aspect, it creates an atmosphere conducive to learning and change. Because of its emphasis on choosing, it helps to develop skill in decision making.

Now let us look at a number of the techniques used in value clarification.

Clarifying Response.   Clarifying responses are short, informal interchanges, mostly spur of the moment, in which the teacher asks the pupil to reconsider what he or she has said or has done. They consist of such teacher questions as, "Do you really believe that?" "What makes you take that position?" "Does your remark apply to everyone?" "Would it apply in such and such a situation?" The teacher tries to raise questions in the pupil's mind and to cause the pupil to think further about the bases of what he or she has said or done.

Value-Clarifying Discussions.   Short, informal discussions of the discovery type are also useful for helping pupils discover and understand values, for they give pupils a chance to examine their own views and compare them with those of other pupils. Frequently, value-clarification discussions can arise naturally out of the class situation. At other times you may wish to use a springboard that will present a value judgment or a conflict. Possible springboards include provocative questions, anecdotes, cartoons, pictures, tape recordings, news items, and the like. As in problem-solving discussions, the teacher should encourage pupils to think freely. To create and maintain a supportive class climate that will stimulate thought, you should avoid the use of leading questions, preaching, informing pupils that their opinions are wrong, and other tactics that cut off thinking, or force pupils into giving lip service to positions that they may not believe in, or that impede the consideration of alternative positions. Insofar as possible, keep the value clarifying discussion open-ended, nonjudgmental, and pressure-free, for your purpose is to enhance understanding, not to sell a belief.[13]

---

[12] John S. Stewart, "Clarifying Values Clarification: A Critique," *Phi Delta Kappan,* (June 1975), 684–688.

[13] Raths, op.cit., p. 115.

Value Sheets. A value sheet consists of a series of questions about an issue. The issue may be presented on the value sheet, or by a role-playing incident, a simulation, a dramatization, a film clip, a tape recording, a reading selection, or some other manner. After the pupils have seen, heard, or read the presentation of the issue, have them write answers to the questions on the value sheet. Then follow up with one of the following procedures.

1. Have the pupils discuss their answers in small groups without your being present.
2. Have pupils turn in their completed value sheets to you. Read selected portions to the class aloud. Do not identify the writers of the papers unless they want you to.
3. Have pupils turn in their completed value sheets to you. Read them privately. Return them with comments but without grading them.
4. Have pupils turn in the papers to a committee that will select papers representing various positions for posting or to be read aloud.
5. Use the value sheets as a basis for a class discussion.[14]

Moral Dilemmas. Discussions of moral dilemmas are used to develop a high standard of intelligent moral behavior in students. In this procedure the teacher tries to raise students' moral levels by facing them with challenging moral problems or dilemmas by means of an anecdote, a story, a news item, a parable, or the like. Then one asks the students to consider what one ought to do in a given situation and why. Their responses and their implications can be worked into an open discussion of what is the right and proper thing to do under the circumstances.

Role Playing and Simulation

Role Playing

Role playing and simulation can be used effectively in inquiry and discovery teaching. By attempting to simulate a real problem, students may get real insight into the nature of a problem situation. Role playing may be used to clarify attitudes and concepts; demonstrate attitudes and concepts; deepen understandings of social situations; prepare for real situations (such as practicing the interview procedures to be used in a survey); plan and try out strategies for attacking problems; test out hypothetical solutions to problems; and practice leadership and other skills. Role playing has a number of drawbacks, however. Role playing is slow; is often not realistic enough so that false concepts result; and although serious business, is often thought of as entertainment.

As you already know, role playing is an unrehearsed dramatization, in which the players try to clarify a situation by acting out the roles of the participants in the situation. To carry out a role-playing session, the following procedures are recommended:

[14] Ibid., pp. 107–109.

1. Pick a simple situation, not a complicated one, to role play. Two to four characters usually are quite enough.
2. Select a cast who will do the job. Use volunteers, if feasible, but only if the volunteers are equal to the task. It is preferable to sacrifice self-selection for effectiveness. Sometimes it is helpful to select several casts and run through the role playing several times, each time with a different cast. Different interpretations of the parts should give the audience more data from which to draw their inferences and make their discoveries.
3. Be sure that the characters in the cast understand the situation, the purpose of the role playing, and their roles. To this end, brief the players well and then discuss their roles with them. Sometimes it is helpful to outline the general line they should follow and to rehearse the first few lines. However, too much direction and too much warmup can ruin the role playing by stereotyping the interpretations.
4. Brief the audience. Be sure everyone understands what the players are supposed to be trying to do.
5. Stage the role playing. Let the role players interpret freely. However, if they get hopelessly lost, it may be necessary for you to stop the role playing and reorient the players.
6. If it seems desirable, repeat the role playing with reversed roles or with different role players.
7. Follow up the role playing with a discussion about what happened in the role playing and its significance. At this point, the teacher should encourage pupils to come to some conclusions and make some generalizations (although it may be more satisfactory to leave the discussion open-ended). Sometimes the discussion may reveal new or different interpretations and concepts that warrant a replaying of the roles and further discussion and analysis.

Simulation

Basically a simulation differs from role playing. It is an enactment of a make-believe episode as much like the real thing as possible, but with some of the dangerous and complicating factors removed. The embryonic truck driver does not suffer dire results from his mistake if he pulls in front of a speeding bus when he is driving his driver education simulator; the beginning aviatrix crashes with impunity when the plane she stalls is simulated; and the soldier who mishandles his new weapon in a dry run without live ammunition kills no one. Simulations of this sort, although in our examples largely aimed at developing skills, can be useful for helping pupils to gain insights into difficult matters. The young, aspiring lawyer who tries a case in a simulated courtroom not only gains skill in legal practice but also gains insight into the law of the case being tried. In the social studies classroom, the pupils simulating the management of a business are learning what happens when they overbuy, overprice, and make strategic errors.

In these simulations, students go through the process in what they were learning in a real way. That is the value of simulation. By taking roles in the simulated activity, the pupils, it is hoped, will come to understand the real situation and how to act in it.

Simulations differ from role playing in that the scenarios must be carefully drafted. In these scenarios the pupils are assigned definite roles that require them to take specific action in a well-defined situation, and the pupils are confronted by simulated, real-life situations that require them to take actions just as they would have to in real life (or at least as close to real life as feasible). These actions may lead to new predicaments that require new actions. In taking action, the players are not free but must stay in character and keep their actions within the limits prescribed by the roles they have assumed and by the realities of the simulated situation.

If you are to produce a simulation, the following procedure may prove to be useful:

1. Prepare the material, equipment, and props that will be needed.
2. Introduce the plan to the pupils. Explain the purpose of the simulation. Give the directions for playing it.
3. Assign roles. Probably it is best to pick the players yourself. Accepting volunteers or selecting pupils by chance may result in disastrous miscasting.
4. Brief the pupils in their roles. Be sure they understand them.
5. Conduct the simulation. Follow the scenario to the letter.
6. Follow up with a critique in which pupils have a chance to discuss what they have done and to draw generalizations.

Controversial Issues

The content of topics most suitable for the methods described in this module may sometimes be controversial. Teaching controversial issues can be something of a problem. Pupils, parents, and the local public often feel very strongly about them. It is wise to treat them gingerly or your teaching may do more harm than good.

In the first place, because controversial issues can be so touchy, you should be careful to select topics that will throw more light than heat. There is no point in introducing into your courses topics so controversial that they upset your effectiveness. Therefore, before you commit yourself to any controversial topics consider the following criteria.

1. Is the topic pertinent to your course and your course goals?
2. Are you knowledgeable enough and neutral enough to handle it fairly and impartially?
3. Is it worth the time and effort?
4. Are the pupils sufficiently mature and informed to cope with it?
5. Is there sufficient material available to allow pupils adequate consideration of the various points of view?
6. Can it be discussed without overemotionalism? Will it be upsetting to the people in the community?

After you select a controversial topic, you must be careful to teach it fairly and honestly. Controversial issues are open-ended questions and so should be treated as such. Ordinarily they do not have "right answers" or "correct solutions", otherwise there would be no controversy. Therefore your focus, when teaching controversial matters, should be on process rather than content. Your goal should be to show pupils how to deal with controversial issues so as to make wise decisions on the basis of carefully considered information.

To achieve this end you should teach your pupils what the issues are, how to sort out facts from propaganda and myth, how to evaluate the positions of the various sides, and how to draw their own conclusions. To do this you will have to teach pupils how to check out sources of information and facts, to identify sources of information, and to test these sources for authority, accuracy, objectivity, and timeliness by using such questions as, "What is the basis for this statement?" "Is this 'authority' really in a position to know?" "Is it corroborated by other evidence?" "Is the information current?" To build reasoning skills provide pupils with questionable statements and show them how to prove or disprove them. To help pupils separate fact from opinion, keep a fact-opinion table on the chalkboard. (See Fig. 10-3.) You should also help pupils from getting hung up on the meaning of words. Often the emotional connotations of words obscure their meaning and prevent logical evaluation of facts and arguments. So do pupils' values. Such techniques as value-clarifying responses, value sheets, and value discussions help pupils discover and evaluate their own values. So that the pupils may understand just what community value conflicts are involved in the issue being studied, it is sometimes helpful for pupils to conduct an opinion survey on the topic. In any case you should encourage the pupils to use research-type activities to dig out facts, opinions and values, and to place them on the table for all to see and evaluate.

When teaching controversial issues, you should try not to become too involved in the controversy. Certainly you should not advocate one position or another. This is another reason for using research or problem solving activities as a basis for the study of controversial issues. Nevertheless, at times you may find that in order to give pupils a chance to look at all sides of the controversy, you may have to present some aspects of the topic yourself. Otherwise pupils may never understand the complexity of the issue, the variety of positions, the divergence in values, or the moral, ethical, political, financial implications, and the like. Sometimes it may be necessary to play the devil's advocate. When you do, try not to

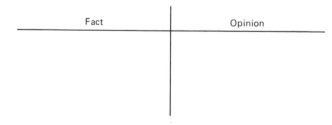

FIGURE 10-3 *Fact-Opinion Table*

give the impression that you are advocating one side or another. Use expressions like "some people say" . . . "other people believe . . .," and so on.

Everyone in a class should have the right to express an opinion on the issue to be studied. Problem solving, research type activities followed by discussion activities provide good media for obtaining nearly universal pupil involvement. Debates, panels, dramatics, role playing, simulations are other examples of activities that let pupils present their points of view. Simulated town meetings, jury trials, council meetings, legislatures, or party conventions can be especially useful.

When using such discussion modes for teaching controversial issues, you should first establish some ground rules. For example,

All facts must be supported by authority.

Everyone must be given an opportunity to be heard.

No one should interrupt (except perhaps the leader to keep the discussion on track).

Personal remarks are forbidden.

To get the study of the issue started and to arouse interest, sometimes a free-for-all introductory discussion in which pupils may express themselves without restraint is helpful, but ordinarily you should apply the ground rules so as to promote orderly thinking and to keep the discussion from getting too hot. To keep rash opinion statements under control, sometimes teachers ask pupils to present arguments contrary to their own point of view. Doing so may help pupils to understand and respect the opinions of others and to realize the complexity of the issue.

In short, to teach controversial issues well, you must see to it that pupils learn how to identify what is the basis for the controversy, what is at stake, what value conflicts are involved, what the facts are, and what their own values and beliefs are so that they can make informed decisions and take intelligent stands now and in the future.

Teaching Thinking Skills

One of the principal goals of education is to develop skill in thinking. Unfortunately skills in thinking do not appear full-blown in boys and girls. They must be cultivated. Consequently educators have invented numerous programs for sowing and cultivating thinking skills. Many of these programs are set apart from the standard school curriculum. If you are to use any of these programs, it may be necessary to obtain special training in the techniques and strategies of the program.[15]

Fortunately, however, thinking skills can and should be taught in regular classes. Skillful use of discovery, approach, and problem-solving approaches allows teachers to teach and students to learn and practice skills essential to reflective thinking such as

---

[15] Examples of such programs include the CoRT (Cognitive Research Trust), the Thinking Skills Program, the Instrumental Enrichment Program, the Philosophy of Children Program, and the Strategic Reasoning Program.

Finding, recognizing, and defining problems.

Finding evidence.

Observing accurately.

Interpreting and reporting correctly.

Detecting faulty arguments, polemics, bias, prejudice, poor logic, and other evidences of faulty reasoning.

Detecting relationships, seeing parts in relationship to the whole, tying elements together, recognizing similarities and differences.

Choosing between alternatives.

Making inferences and drawing conclusions.

Analyzing.

Separating facts from fiction.

Using knowledge as a jumping-off point for building new knowledge, ideas, and thought.

Unless students develop skills in such thinking skills, they are doomed to be prejudiced, ill-informed, and narrow-minded. If students are ever to become good thinkers, courses should not only include thought-provoking content but direct interaction in various teaching techniques as well. Examples of techniques that can be taught directly include, but are not limited to, the following:

Teaching oneself through a problem.

Trying to imagine what is being described as one reads or listens.

Paraphrasing what one reads or hears into one's own words.

Trying to solve complex problems by breaking them into parts and then combining the solutions of the parts, or by trying to solve a simpler version of the problem and then applying this solution to the original, more complex problem.[16]

To teach these skills one should begin by teaching them directly. To do so one can, of course, explain and demonstrate the procedure and provide examples of the skill well done. For example, a teacher might model the skill herself, or point out an excellent use of the technique employed by one of the pupils, or show an example of proper execution of the skill in a film or recording. Teachers might also use such techniques as probing questions to shape students' abilities to think logically, to find and solve problems. If the teacher can, he should stimulate the students to think about their behavior and try to adopt new, different, and presumably more effective ways to proceed. To do so, one might have the students examine their procedures, list the strategies and tactics they use, and describe changes that might improve them.

Once the students have caught on to the how and why of the thinking skills, they then should have plenty of practice in using it. At first, of course, this practice should be limited to comparatively easy problems with plenty of instructional aids to help them remember what to do and how to do it. Here the teacher can take advantage of propitious moments to prompt the students to select and execute improved thinking procedures. For this purpose many teachers recommend the use of dyads or small groups in which one student goes through the process while others provide feedback. If students take the opportunity to examine their own

---

[16] "Teaching Thinking," *NASSP Curriculum Report* (May 1986), 15:5, p. 3.

behavior, especially in the light of feedback from their peers or teachers, they should be able to sharpen their thinking skills considerably.

Finally, students should reinforce their learning by applying their thinking skills in a variety of assignments so as to increase their proficiency and to be able to transfer their thinking skills to other situations. In this phase of learning, as in the practice phase, the students need plenty of feedback so as to better capitalize on their successes and errors.

To introduce the teaching of specific thinking skills into their courses, some teachers recommend an approach similar to the following:

1. *Select the skill to be taught.* Presumably, as in the teaching of any other skill, one should build the "greater skills" on "lesser skills." The implication is that the building of thinking skills in any curriculum or course should follow a planned sequence. When you teach thinking skills in your courses, you should make sure that the students in your classes are equipped with the skills and knowledge necessary to provide a foundation for the new skill.

2. *Identify the main attributes of the skill to be taught.* In this step you make sure that you understand what the skill is, what its purpose is, what skills and knowledge are prerequisite, how to carry out the skill step by step, and so on. This step may require of you some hard thinking and studying.

3. *Introduce the skill.* The skill should be introduced when it will be a meaningful addition to the course content. If the skill is not relevant to the course at this point, it will not help. To introduce the skill, first explain what the skill is and why it is important to learn it. When you are sure they understand, explain how to carry out the skill step by step, and then demonstrate the whole procedure and its steps. Once they have caught on to what is expected and how to do it, put the students to work using the procedure. As they work, let them analyze their procedures and provide them feedback on their progress.

4. *Provide practice.* Students should have opportunity to practice until they attain mastery. At first, practice sessions should be guided and rather carefully monitored. At this stage, peer criticism, as well as teacher guidance, may be beneficial. Later, as soon as students seem ready, independent practice should prove profitable.

5. *Continue review and practice sessions throughout the course.* After the skill has been pretty well mastered, it should be used as occasions demand throughout the school year. Skills that are not practiced from time to time soon disappear. Such practice sessions should of course be closely tied to normal course content.[17]

Suggested Reading

Aronstein, Laurence W., and Edward G. Olsen. *Action Learning: Student Community Service Project.* Washington, D.C.: Association for Supervision and Curriculum Development, 1974.

Frankel, Jack R. *How to Teach About Values: An Analytic Approach.* Englewood Cliffs, N.J.: Prentice-Hall, 1977.

[17] Roberta M. Jackson, "Thumbs Up for Direct Teaching of Thinking Skills," *Educational Leadership* (May 1986), 43:33–36 describes how teachers in a Virginia middle school are using this type of procedure to teach thinking skills directly.

Grambs, Jean D., and John C. Carr. *Modern Methods in Secondary Education,* 4th ed. New York: Holt, Rinehart and Winston, 1979, Chap. 9.

Heitzman, William Ray. *Educational Games and Simulation, What Research Says to the Teacher.* Washington, D.C.: National Education Association, 1974.

Hersch, Richard H., John P. Miller, and Glen D. Fielding, *Models of Moral Education: An Appraisal.* New York: Longman, 1980.

Hoover, Kenneth H. *The Professional Teacher's Handbook: A Guide for Improving Instruction in Today's Middle and Secondary Schools,* 2nd ed. Boston: Allyn & Bacon, 1976, Chaps. 10, 14, 27, 28, and 29.

Kurfman, Dana G., ed. *Developing Decision Making Skills,* Forty-seventh Yearbook of the National Council for the Social Studies. Washington, D.C.: The Council, 1977.

Ohrlich, Donald C., et al., *Teaching Strategies: A Guide to Better Instruction,* 2d ed. Lexington, Mass.: Heath, 1985, Parts 8-9.

Raths, Louis E. *Teaching for Thinking.* Columbus, Oh.: Merrill, 1973.

Raths, Louis E., Merrill Harmin, and Sidney Simon. *Values and Teaching,* 2d ed. Columbus, Oh.: Merrill, 1978.

Seidner, Constance J., "Teaching with Simulations and Games" in N. L. Gage, ed. *The Psychology of Teaching Methods,* The Seventy-fifth Yearbook of the National Society for the Study of Education. Chicago: The University of Chicago Press, 1976, Chapter VII.

Shaftel, Fannie, and George Shaftel. *Role Playing for Social Values.* Englewood Cliffs, N.J.: Prentice-Hall, 1968.

Thompson, John F. *Using Role Playing in the Classroom,* Fastback 114. Bloomington, Ind.: Phi Delta Kappa Educational Foundation, 1978.

Zeleny, Leslie D., *How to Use Sociodramas: Practical Exercises in Role Interpretation,* How to Do It Series No. 20. Washington, D.C.: National Council for the Social Studies, 1964.

Post Test

1. List two advantages of inquiry over expository methods.

_____

_____

2. List two disadvantages of inquiry over expository methods.

_____

_____

3. Should pupils be free to challenge each other's thinking?

_____

4. Should pupils be allowed to challenge the book?

_____

5. Describe the steps in problem solving.

_____

_____

_____

6. Name two criteria that can be used to test the suitability of a problem, according to this module.

_____

_____

7. Pupils have difficulty finding projects to do. Give at least two suggestions for helping them find them.

_____

_____

8. Is it ordinarily good policy to publish class survey results outside the school?

_____

9. What devices can one use to make objective the recording of observations?

_____

_____

_____

10. What techniques are recommended in order to standardize interviews?

_____

_____

11. Tell how to conduct a case study.

_____

_____

_____

_____

12. Tell how to conduct a Socratic dialogue.

_____

_____

_____

_____

_____

13. What is the difference between a controlled discussion and a true discussion?

_____

_____

_____

14. How does conducting a value-clarifying discussion differ from conducting a controlled discussion?

_____

_____

_____

_____

_____

15. Outline the procedure for conducting role playing.

_____

_____

16. Why use simulations?

_____

_____

17. What procedures would you use for launching and carrying out student research projects in your classes?

_____

_____

_____

_____

_____

18. Describe the distinguishing characteristic of discovery teaching.

_____

_____

19. Describe the procedure for carrying out a moral dilemma discussion.

_____

_____

_____

20. Name three procedures used in traditional approaches to teaching moral values.

_____

_____

_____

21. How would you use a value sheet?

_____

_____

22. List four questions to consider before you select a controversial issue to teach.

_____

_____

_____

_____

MODULE
11

Reading and Study Skills

The first edition version of this module was written by Leo Auerbach, Jersey City State College. It has been revised and updated by the editors of this third edition.

Rationale

Why bother to teach reading? This challenge from our media-oriented students makes us reexamine the need and importance of reading. Part of the answer is that reading is one key to educational success. Aside from strictly physical activities, virtually every aspect of learning uses reading as a major component. Even when demonstration and imitation are necessary, the written word is turned to for explanation and elaboration. So far, no other medium equals books as the repository of culture, the storehouse of information and ideas, the source of enlightenment and pleasure. Books can be used repeatedly and without restriction of time. Properly used, books can propel us to new levels of understanding and mastery, both of ourselves and of the world. They can enrich our personalities, expand our horizons, provide us with varied experiences, help organize our thoughts and feelings, stimulate our creativity, and contribute to our social and vocational effectiveness. Actually, full, democratic participation in this complex and rapidly changing world demands ever higher levels of literacy. To help every student become an effective reader is clearly a major responsibility of the schools. As we become convinced of this, we, in turn, can convince our students.

Mastery of reading is a significant problem in today's schools. Research indicates that from one quarter to one third of secondary school students cannot read their textbooks. Furthermore, we know that when reading skills are inadequate or minimal, time is wasted, frustration can become overwhelming and the loss of interest may start the cycle which blocks further learning. Data on school dropouts reveal that more than three times as many poor readers as good readers drop out of high school before graduation. The public is rightly concerned, since stories about reading scores and comparison of results make front-page stories in our largest newspapers. Families know that reading achievement is used as a predictor of success in academic work, on college-admission examinations, on civil-service tests, and in career placement and upgrading. The ongoing Right to

Read program is based on the recognized gap between student needs and student accomplishment. As educators, we must accept this challenge to help all our students develop functionally adequate reading skills. At the same time, recognizing the value of reading, we must work to increase every student's performance to the highest possible level. We must help them to continue on a lifelong process, making a major contribution to their growth and development, and to the richness of their lives.

This module will discuss the reading process, elaborate on some techniques and activities designed to improve reading, and hopefully provoke you to further thought and study on what more you can do to help your students achieve reading competency.

Specific Objectives

As a result of working through this module, you should be able to do the following:

1. Identify the major features of the reading process.
2. Describe the subject matter teacher's responsibility for teaching reading.
3. Describe activities for building vocabulary.
4. Describe the major aspects of reading comprehension.
5. Characterize good homework assignments.
6. Describe procedures for the use of textbooks and study guides.
7. Identify the features of good questions to accompany reading.
8. Describe the steps in effective study.
9. Explain scanning and skimming and describe their uses.
10. Distinguish recreational reading, critical reading, and imaginative reading.
11. Describe the features of critical reading and problem solving.
12. Identify the special features of reading maps, charts, graphs, and diagrams.
13. Distinguish among various types of problem readers.
14. Plan activities to include directed reading, supervised study, and diagnosis of reading difficulties.
15. Describe the reading inventory and Cloze procedures.

Module Text

What Kind of Reader Are You?

In an important sense, you already know a good deal about reading. Yet, before you undertake to help others, it should be useful to examine your reading habits as well as your general ideas about reading. What kind of reader are you? Slow and plodding or rapid and superficial, word-for-word or idea-to-idea, absorbed or impatient, easily distracted or off in another world? You have been reading for many years. Within each day you may read a considerable variety, notes, signs, letters, information on boxes, a newspaper or two, a magazine, part of a book. Because you take reading for granted, you may never have stopped to evaluate yourself as a reader. This preliminary test will not measure your reading ability, but will help you explore your habits, experiences, knowledge, and ideas before you read the rest of the module. Before you commit yourself to a mental answer, reread the set of questions. Stop at each numbered set and let your thoughts wander in many directions before continuing with the next set.

1. When you first picked up this book, did you look through the table of contents? Did you see how the entire book was organized? Did you read the module headings? Were you curious about any special features?

2. Did you open the book at random or choose a section in which you were interested? Did you sample any of the module's content? How quickly did you read it? How carefully and how critically? On the basis of your first impressions, did you decide how much you would get out of this book? Do you always rely on your own judgment or sampling, or do you usually consider someone else's opinion, a friend's, a teacher's, a librarian's?

3. Do you read everything at the same speed or with the same attention to individual words? Have you ever tried to speed up your reading? What were the results? Have you tried to read mainly for ideas, rather than for specific facts to remember?

4. What happens when you come across words of which you may not be too sure? Do you skip them and expect to figure out the gist of what you are reading from the parts that you do know? Do you look up unfamiliar words in a glossary or dictionary? Do you try to fit the meaning in the passage?

5. When you finish reading a new selection, passage, or chapter, do you think over what you have read or do you just go on to the next reading? If you stop to think it over, do you jot down notes on what you have read or discuss it with other people?

6. Are you satisfied with the way you have done homework? Are you efficient or are you slow and impatient with yourself? Do you have good study habits or would you like to improve them? How would you try to achieve higher stages of self-discipline?

7. When you encounter statistics, graphs, or charts, do you skip them or do you spend time studying them? What is their real value to you? What was the author's purpose in using them?

8. Do you continue serious reading mainly in the area of your school major? Are you satisfied with your present reading interests?

9. How well do you read instructions on tests, in books, on recipes, on hobby materials, or similar sets of directions?

10. Have you enjoyed reading fiction, poetry, plays, and other forms of imaginative writing? Have any books had an effect on the way you think or feel about life, other people, yourself, the world, or the future?

11. How quickly do you find numbers in a directory, dates and events of a person's life, specific facts in newspapers, reference books, or textbooks?

12. Are you easily distracted when you read, or do you concentrate enough to forget the place or time or your other responsibilities? What factors can make the difference?

13. Where do you look for the main ideas in books, newspapers, and magazine articles? What makes it possible to remember more content more readily?

14. Do you review for tests by reading over the entire material for which you are responsible? Does reviewing make you nervous or pressured, or are you reassured by refreshing your memory?

15. Have you read material with which you disagreed? Were you bothered by the facts, the author's opinions, his bias, his tone, his language, his attitudes, values, and beliefs? How did it affect your reading? Did you take any action? Did you work out your own viewpoint, using evidence collected through research? Have you ever changed your mind as a result of reading?

16. How would you sum up your own purposes in reading? Should teachers read in special ways, for themselves, for preparing their teaching materials, and procedures for anticipating their students' reactions?

Since there are no right or wrong answers for this exercise, there is no score. However, the areas touched on and the problems raised in this survey will give you insight into the discussion and procedures that follow. The way you explored your own habits, experience, and knowledge will help you apply your answers to the problems of reading and study techniques. It should be clear from the items included that all of us can continue to improve our reading for the rest of our lives.

Every Teacher Is a Reading Teacher

Consciously or unconsciously, every teacher is a reading teacher. No reading takes place without content, and the content that teachers must use is their own subject matter area. Although severe problems require the help of a reading specialist, the subject matter teacher will be thwarted in reaching the learning goal if students are unable to read the textbook used or the written materials assigned for study. The subject matter teacher as the resident expert in the content field has learned the concepts and specialized vocabulary to be mastered, the materials and activities to be used, the sequences of growth and maturation and the kinds of learning to be measured and evaluated. However, if the subject matter teacher fails to help all students unlock the messages contained in the written words, his students will be condemned to rely solely on the oral presentations in class and ultimately emerge as impaired learners.

Different content requires different reading styles and approaches, a fact that becomes especially apparent when the student leaves the elementary grades. Within a single school day, the student may confront equations, diagrams, and problems of mathematics, the technical vocabulary, detailed data, and causal explanations of science, the chronological or thematic presentation of events and the interpretations of social studies, the imaginative or expository literature of English, and a host of other specialized reading materials. No one teacher handles them all, but all teachers must be prepared to make their contributions to students' progress in the context of their own disciplines.

Some misguided teachers have been known to exercise this obligation as teacher of reading with considerable reluctance. They have exhibited the attitude that the teaching of skills, like reading "that should have been learned in the lower grades," is beneath their dignity and beyond the call of duty. Such teachers eventually find themselves flying in a tiresome holding pattern with many of their students in great need. They have failed to learn a significant fact about educational systems which is that not all students make identical progress each year. It should have been impressed early upon them that when children start grade one there is a minimum of three years of difference among them in readiness for learning. Some are on target at age six, and ready. Some are precocious and already one year or more advanced in their skills. Some, too, are slower in maturing and are at least one year or more in arrears. From grade one onward, the amount of separation in achievement among these groups progresses annually so that by grade five, for example, there may be five years of difference among those who started at the same age and same time. Consider this: "By the junior high school years this overall spread is estimated to be approximately two thirds the mean age of the grade group. A group entering the seventh grade is approximately twelve years of age. Two thirds of this figure is eight. Consequently, the spread in achievement is from third grade to the eleventh."[1]

The Reading Process

Reading is an active process; it does not happen to the student and it is not done for him. Since it requires attention or a favorable attitude or set, it is not mechanical. An aroused interest or a felt need starts it and keeps it going. The reader's feeling of purpose is the motivating and effective sustaining force. Most basically, reading is a thinking process, since its central aspect is extracting meaning from print. The essential unit of meaning is the idea, the concept, the thought, the image, the statement. Meaning does not emerge from an arbitrary string of words, but from words in relationship. The sum total of these relationships makes up the context of the reading material, and only within a context do words (or other symbols) have meaning. Understanding and enlarging contexts is the reader's major goal. Finally, reading is a developmental process, changing with the ideas, concepts, or operations that increase in depth and scope with the reader's life experience.

Reading is not an isolated skill. It is one of the four major communication skills: listening and speaking (oral skills), and reading and writing (written skills). Only after he has achieved success in the oral realm can the child learn to read. Of course, all the language skills are related and in this hierarchic scheme reading becomes the third component of language mastery.

The organization of the reading program in the elementary school, after the readiness stage has been reached in kindergarten and early first grade reflects the organization of this hierarchy. Developmental programs are begun that provide systematic instruction to classes, to small groups, and to individuals. Functional programs that use resource materials from all parts of the curriculum are scheduled. Recreational reading programs are devised that focus on reading for personal enjoyment. Enrichment reading programs are explored in an effort to further expand reading experiences to other language arts areas. Remedial programs are developed to keep pace with the needs that are revealed as students progress through all of these programs.

[1] John I. Goodlad, *School Curriculum and the Individual.* (Waltham, Mass.: Blaisdell Publishing, 1966), p. 6.

In the middle and upper elementary grades there is special emphasis on cultivating study skills such as locating information (e.g., through an index or table of contents, in reference books and in tables and charts) and organizing ideas (e.g., with notes, outlines, and summaries). These developmental programs are sequentially arranged to (1) reinforce and extend those desirable reading skills and appreciations acquired in previous years and (2) develop new skills and appreciations as they are needed to comprehend and enjoy advanced and complex forms of written communications. Among the abilities included in those developmental reading programs extended into the secondary schools are:

Getting the central idea
Selecting the significant details
Understanding words in context
Following directions
Answering specific questions
Determining relationships
Drawing conclusions
Predicting outcomes
Outlining and summarizing
Determining the author's purpose and mood
Understanding figurative language
Evaluating ideas
Understanding graphic material
Increasing speed
Adjusting speed to purpose and content
Using reference material.

Whether or not a highly structured developmental reading program in which the entire faculty becomes involved during specified periods in reading instruction will exist in your school, you should feel responsible for attending to the reading and learning needs of your students in your subject at least in the areas of vocabulary development, improving comprehension, and in developing reading flexibility.

Remedial classes in most schools are usually taught in special sessions or in reading laboratories—generally by a reading specialist. The focus of this instruction is usually upon individual difficulties experienced by individual students. Some students may be just latent learners who need a little more time for mastery while others may be plagued by deepseated and serious blockages that require the expertise of the skilled practitioner to root out.

Building Vocabulary

Success in working with vocabulary building often hinges upon the interest in word growth and development shown by the teacher. Enthusiasm exhibited by you for an apt phrase or a descriptive adjective can be "caught" by your students especially if the student response is acknowledged and rewarded. It helps to condition students to savor the language to which they are exposed so that their progress can be accelerated rather than merely result by incidental accretion.

Direct and indirect student experiences are major sources of new words for students. Drawing upon such experiences in the classroom, encouraging students to use the vocabulary that they hve already mastered, and to listen to and appropriate what they hear others use, enables students to apply new meanings to words already known.

A major hurdle for beginning teachers is the finding of the middle way in introducing new words. To be avoided is the gratuitous assumption that everyone knows every word: knows what it looks like, what it sounds like, what it means in the particular context used in the text and what it means in other contexts. Also to be avoided is the pedantic belaboring of definitions of words beyond the appreciation of anyone except the belaborer, the elaboration of refinements and nuances beyond the current need for study.

Effective teachers are accustomed to using the following techniques in their systematic attempt to expand knowledge of vocabulary:

1. Provide appropriate context for new words. The dictionary defines only certain limits within which a word may range. Selecting the appropriate meaning is the skill that has to be developed. Note how the context brings out the meaning in each of the following sentences:
   a. Jake is a *pugapoo*. His mother was a cute little black poodle, his father a feisty, sandy-haired pug.
   b. He was a *rock hound* who loved to wander through the desert hunting for interesting rocks and semiprecious stones.
   c. The *savannah,* a flat grassy plain, stretches from here to there.
   d. He was a true hero—a *Lochinvar* out of the west.
   e. *Orcs* are nasty, despicable, foul-mouthed, foul-breathed, dirty, murderous goblins.
   f. He drove forward about a *league,* five miles in our reckoning. [2]

2. Teach key words. Key words or "stopper" words to be encountered by the student in new assignments or units should be taught by the teacher prior to the assignment. These may be precisely the words with multiple meanings so that the specific meaning in the new material must be gleaned, obviously from the context. Attend to both the oral and visual mastery of these stopper words you are focusing on. Use the blackboard to list such words and get all students to attend to the configuration of the word. Skip about the class with the questions you ask which require oral pronunciation of stopper words. Above all, provide positive reinforcement with your commendation for students who attempt to use words under study in oral responses to questions in the classroom.

3. Utilize word-attack devices: To develop understanding of word meanings, various word attack devices can be used. If there are roots, prefixes, and suffixes that can be pinpointed, these can be separated and analyzed. Long words can be divided into easy-to-manage syllables. Sounding out the words, placing the proper stress, hearing and recognizing the audi-

[2] Leonard H. Clark, and Irving S. Starr, *Secondary and Middle School Teaching Methods,* 5th ed. (New York: Macmillan Publishing Co., 1986), p. 275.

tory components call into play other senses used in learning. Syntactical clues such as the ending *ed* that probably indicates a verb, or *ly* which usually indicates an adverb or *ist* which generally indicates a person who does or is something can be clarifying aids. Marks such as capital letters, articles, auxiliary verbs, and prepositions are also helps to decide the function of words. The way a word is used in a sentence, or in its relationship with other words, often will supply a broad hint to its meaning.

4. Teach the use of printed aids to reading—marginal notes, parenthetical definitions, headings, footnotes, summaries, and punctuation marks such as commas, periods, and the like.

5. Encourage and teach use of the dictionary. "When a student learns to make appropriate and frequent use of the dictionary, he is strengthening his power to keep his vocabulary growing for life."[3] Perhaps the key word in this statement is "appropriate." The dictionary is a resource with which students need help. Among the necessary dictionary-use skills for vocabulary growth are the following:

   a. Using guide words.
   b. Selecting the best fitting meaning.
   c. Recognizing differences in meaning.
   d. Figuring out pronunciation by proper use of the key.
   e. Syllabication, stresses, and blending.
   f. Relating the meaning to word derivation.
   g. Using information about nuances of meaning among synonyms.

   The teacher who provides experience with any or all of these skills, to a whole class, to small groups, or to individual students, contrasts sharply with the one who merely says, "Look it up in the dictionary." Of course, there are times when students must be told to "Look it up" when the inquiries about the same word are repeated often, or when the request appears to indicate a laziness on the part of the student. The teacher response should be based upon the goal of developing a self-sufficient inquirer rather than on the petulance of the instructor, though. A quick way to kill a budding interest in word growth is to make the quest too tedious or time consuming.

6. Utilize word slips or vocabulary notebooks. Recording words on a word slip or in a vocabulary notebook, if the practice is connected with the other activities, may be the task that sets the student on the road to independent vocabulary growth. On small slips of paper or in a notepad, he or she records the word and the sentence in which it was used. When convenient, he or she looks it up and lists the meaning that fits the context. The pronunciation should be recorded if it presents a problem, and the derivation may be helpful in remembering the meaning. Some find 3 × 5 index cards useful, while others use bookmarks to write down the

---

[3] Ellen Lamar Thomas and H. Alan Robinson. *Improving Reading in Every Class*, abridged ed. (Boston: Allyn & Bacon, Inc., 1972), p. 33.

word, which they later transfer with the sentence to a notebook for full treatment.

Some teachers who use this technique fail to carry their efforts far enough. The goal is the absorption of the new definition into the oral vocabulary of the student. Often, the quantum leap is not made from notebook to mind and mastery is never quite insured. To avoid such a fate for your efforts, make use of the work that is done by students:

1. Periodically, examine their collections of words and volunteer appropriate commendation.

2. Occasionally, schedule a quiz on contextual meanings of several of the words that have been recorded.

3. Conduct short sessions, such as the last ten minutes of a class before the bell, devoted to contests in word recognition, word spelling, word definition or words collected in the notebook.

Encourage Wide Reading

"The most important means of vocabulary development is wide reading. This is at once the most painless and the most rewarding way of building one's vocabulary. In wide reading the student not only meets many new words in different fields but also becomes familiar with their different meanings in a variety of contexts."[4] With increments of contact or meaning at repeated encounters, the students gradually incorporate the words into their vocabulary. The competent reader who practices this independently can be encouraged or praised by the teacher for acquiring unfamiliar words. The reluctant reader needs the teacher's help in finding books or magazines that deal with his interests. He needs to be shown the delights and freedom that are potentially his when he gains the power to unlock the message of the book.

Sanford Patlak, a physical education instructor and coach, succeeds in involving students in reading all kinds of books on sports. He learns the students' reading levels and discusses their individual interests. From his large, carefully acquired and readily available supply, he recommends books appropriate in content and reading ease. When students return books, he manages to chat informally, a practice they carry over to their own interaction. His encouragement, guidance, and enthusiasm make reading continuous and habit-forming for some otherwise reluctant readers.[5]

Have you, college student, future teacher, always been or ever been a wide reader? Did any teacher ever take the time to find out where you were on the reading scale or endeavor to interest you in some special book that he treasured? It's not so difficult a project to adopt and it is loaded with benefits for the caring teacher who tries it. More than anything else it reveals to a student a caring

---

[4] Ruth Strang, Constance M. McCullough, and Arthur E. Traxler, *The Improvement of Reading,* 4th ed. (New York: McGraw-Hill, 1967), p. 241.

[5] H. Alan Robinson and Ellen Lamar Thomas, eds., *Fusing Reading Skills and Content* (Newark, Del.: International Reading Association, 1969), pp. 81–88, and Ellen Lamar Thomas and H. Alan Robinson, *Improving Reading in Every Class,* abridged ed. (op. cit., pp. 301–307).

attitude on your part and hence works toward ameliorating your student toward efforts to improve.

If you have not been an extensive reader, begin now. Your "reluctance" may have stemmed from the difficulties you have had with the printed medium. Now that you are older and are focusing on material designed for early youth, some of the previous difficulty may have lessened. Enjoy it! Profit from it! Remember your experiences as you emerge from your previous alienation to print so that you can recapture your feelings and delights as you work with "reluctants" whom you discover in your classroom.

It has been said that there is more new vocabulary to learn in a first course in high school biology than in a first course in high school French.[6] Although one must approach a statement such as this with a jaundiced eye, there is enough apparent accuracy in it to give any teacher pause for thought. The plaguing part about assuming responsibility to change the situation is the paucity of time: there just are not enough minutes in any period to attend to all the words you could possibly dwell upon. The solution of this problem for you will depend upon your ability to select judiciously the most salient, or significant, or prevalent, or key words in the context of your goal.

Improving Comprehension

We read in order to understand, regardless of what we read and whether we read for information or for pleasure. Some writers distinguish three levels of comprehension: (1) reading the lines, (2) reading between the lines, and (3) reading beyond the lines.[7] This is a useful analysis which we shall follow in this module.

Reading the Lines

Reading the lines refers to the literal meaning of the material, clearly the most basic level, without which no other is possible. When we noted earlier that about one third of secondary school students could not read their textbooks, we meant that they could not comprehend the material, even on this literal level. Whether the words, sentence structure, concepts, or any combination of these create the problem of comprehension, or whether the students' training, ability, or background is involved must be determined by the teacher. Through direct and indirect questions, the teacher informally diagnoses pupils' problems and checks the diagnosis by experimenting and observing responses. Then the teacher can use alternate texts, varied reading assignments, and different guide questions to assist students with this level. Prereading and postreading discussions are essential to provide stimulus and reassurance. Reading the lines is usually tested by questions such as, What is the author telling us? What evidence is he giving for his statements? What does the sentence (paragraph, selection, chapter, book) mean?

Beginning teachers must be aware of the necessity to adjust their thinking to the array of abilities in any group that they address. They must avoid making the

---

[6] Clark and Starr, op cit, p. 273; Connie Muther, "Where to Get Help If the Science Textbook Fails," *Educational Leadership* (October 1986), 44:86–87.

[7] Strang, McCullough, and Traxler, op. cit., pp. 11–12.

error sometimes made by teachers, referred to earlier, of assuming that all students are at grade level on all topics and with all skills. Although students may be on step in some areas, the chances of finding this situation as a regular routine are slim.

Textbooks present special difficulties for those students who may not be quite ready when particular topics arise for study. No one text can meet the reading needs of all students at the same time. Therefore it seems only sensible for each teacher to exercise good judgment in making assignments in the classroom.

Experienced teachers often resort to the use of multitexts and differentiated assignments when suitable materials are on hand. Beginners will work toward this end and begin early the collection and cataloging of materials to facilitate an early attempt at following in this direction.

Reading Between the Lines

The second level, reading between the lines, is one in which the reader "recognizes the author's intent and purpose, interprets the thought, passes judgment on his statements, searches for and interprets clues. . . , distinguishes between fact and opinion, and separates his own ideas from the author's."[8] The reader also judges the merit of the author's evidence or sources. This is obviously a mature level of reading, requiring thinking and experience. Reading between the lines involves answering such questions as, Why do you think the author wrote this? What does this mean to you? Do you agree or disagree with it? Why? Can you separate the facts from author's opinions? Do the opinions seem to follow logically from the facts? Are you convinced by the author's facts, evidence, and judgments, or do you have opinions which are different? In what ways are your sources of evidence different from the author's?

The most prevalent error-point regarding the teaching of this skill appears to be in making assignments. Students are not prepared by the teacher to perform the task that is set for them. The purpose for the activity is not clearly established and hence the reading is done without adequate orientation, without the proper motivation, and without the stimulation that should accompany the start of an interesting activity. One activity (among a host of others) that has proved helpful calls for teachers to elicit predictions about the content to be read. Each student records what he thinks is about to happen, or what he feels the main idea of the author will be, or what the supporting data for the generalization of the chapter will be. After the reading the accuracy rate of each student is arrived at by contrasting their own predictions against the concensus of the class resulting from the study.

Reading Beyond the Lines

Reading beyond the lines "involves deriving implications, speculating about consequences, and drawing generalizations not stated by the author."[9] The process of analysis also leads to a new synthesis by the reader whose initiative and originality lead to new insights and to reflection on the significance of the ideas. This goal is perhaps the highest and most difficult to attain; yet, some aspects of it are

---

[8] Ibid., p. 12.
[9] Ibid.

within reach of the more mature pupils. As teachers, we can offer such questions as, If what the author says is true, what additional conclusions not mentioned in the selection can we draw? What other reactions can we or other people have to the same material, and why? If things had been different from ways mentioned by the author, how would this have changed our viewpoint? What changes can be expected to occur if things continue as the author predicts? What changes would you like to see, and why? How would they become possible? Why are these alternatives important? To whom? What new directions of thinking has this reading started for you? (Reading imaginative literature, especially drama and poetry, commonly involves reading beyond the lines.)

Methods for Improving Comprehension

Devices that will help students improve comprehension include the following:

1. Provide background experience. The same kinds of experience listed under Building Vocabulary apply here with great force. The nonreading experiences—trips, talks, films, records, and television—may help supply a background of concepts, of familiar information, of prior learning, which makes new learning easier and more enjoyable. "To achieve full comprehension, the reader must know not only the semantic and structural meaning, but he must have had some experience related to the author's ideas."[10] In practical classroom terms, this quotation signifies that the teacher must investigate the students' backgrounds—in life experience as well as in reading—before assigning new reading. Besides specific vocabulary, the students need a preview of the basic concepts to be encountered and assistance in recognizing the value and relevance of the new material. What themes they will meet and what importance they may have in their lives—as students, as adolescents, as citizens, as human beings—are a natural introduction. Questioning to elicit background and to establish direction and purpose is part of the teacher's contribution to the students' success in reading.[11]

2. Give fully developed homework assignments. You may remember assignments of the type, "For tomorrow, read Chapter 14 and answer questions 1–4 at the end of the chapter." Whether the assignment was on the board or was dictated by the teacher, it was assumed that all or most students would read the material, write full answers to the questions, and be adequately prepared to participate in the next lesson. The teacher may have been relying exclusively on these assumptions for the next day's activities. In the light of our knowledge of the reading process and of student needs and abilities, let us evaluate this kind of assignment.

No reason is given for doing the assignment. Presumably, the teacher knows the sequence, or this may be the next chapter in the text. Since no subject or topic is mentioned, no frame of reference is suggested. No stimulus to thinking, especially the problem-solving variety, no arousal of curiosity, no attention-grabbing or interest-generating activity appears. The only student experience tapped by this assignment is the knowledge that the routine requires simple obedience. If the material were interesting in itself, students might be self-motivated. Yet,

[10] Ibid., p. 11.
[11] David L. Shepherd, "Reading in the Subject Areas," in *Reading For All*, ed. by Robert Karlin (Newark, Del.: International Reading Association, 1973), pp. 173–179.

only a few minutes of class time and some imagination are all that is needed to develop a dramatic, challenging, provocative, or stimulating start to the homework assignment. For a long-term assignment, such interest-stimulating motivation is indispensable. Similarly, assistance with major concepts, varied sources of material, and suitable problems for projects should be included when needed as integral parts of assignments and assignment making. Assignments should also anticipate problems in reading and provide for them in matters such as student interest, background or experience, new concepts, vocabulary, structure, and tone. Differentiated assignments can individualize learning. By imaginatively adopting the student's point of view and building assignments creatively from there, the teacher can really reach the learner. Attention paid to the manner of making assignments will pay dividends, indeed. Make sure the student knows why he should do the assignment, i.e., how it fits into the ongoing study and what he can expect to be able to do with the new knowledge once he gains it. Intelligence of this sort can serve as a motivation for completion of the study and also as a self-testing procedure when he tries to determine if he has completed the assignment.

3. Teach pupils how to use their textbooks. In the subject matter areas, some schools still use a single textbook for all students on the same grade level, although in recent years more schools have begun to vary the books according to ability levels of students and other considerations. Whether or not your school uses one or many textbooks, though, most of the time the books you must use have been selected by others. Having inherited these hand-me-downs, you will be obliged to determine how well they will serve your classes. Is the material organized in a way best suited to inform or satisfy the students? Is the presentation readable, comprehensible, and adequate? We can say one textbook is better than another only when we apply these questions to specific classes and students. Hence, some teachers use different textbooks for different groups within the same class. So long as areas of common learning are included, there is a basis for whole-class discussion. There may be other advantages. If different groups or individuals have undertaken supplementary work, different sources are essential.

Spending time on cooperative examination of textbooks pays dividends to the teacher and to the class. A review of the textbook prior to any assignment can include the following:

a. The table of contents, for overall scope of treatment, organization, and for detail.
b. The preface, foreword, and introduction for statements of purpose and use as well as acknowledgment of assistance.
c. The major parts, chapter headings, introductions, and summaries.
d. Problems for solution or study.
e. Special aids, such as illustrations, diagrams, footnotes, and reference materials.
f. Appendices, glossaries, and indexes.

Because these features are underutilized by most students, you should plan to teach the parts of a book, making use of available textbooks. The skills needed for mastering this material appear later in this module in the discussion of flexibility. Planning a session on problems of the organization and features of textbooks is both natural and rewarding.

4. Utilize study guides and questions. A valuable device for the detailed reading of chapters is the study guide. In some respects, a study guide is an elaboration of the assignments, with questions as the core and suggested readings as aids to finding answers. Organized according to content—thematic, chronological, conceptual, logical—the guide should include both easy and difficult reading, basic and enriched materials. The questions set one or more of the following tasks for the student: (a) following directions; (b) grasping details or facts; (c) finding the main thought; (d) recognizing relationships of time, place, cause and effect, motives and reactions; (f) drawing inferences or extracting implied meanings; (g) anticipating outcomes; (h) recognizing tone, mood, and intent; (i) drawing comparisons and contrasts; (j) making generalizations; and (k) evaluating or judging according to acceptable criteria.

As in all questioning, whether oral or written, used in class or in connection with outside reading, the teacher must make sure that

a. Questions are definite and clear.
b. Questions aim at recognizable, meaningful, and attainable goals.
c. Questions are challenging and thought provoking.
d. Questions are adapted to the background, abilities, needs, and interests of the students.

Formulating good questions is worth all the time and effort a teacher can give. Eventually, the students learn to develop their own questions, the stage at which purpose and direction reflect the concerns close to them. For further discussion, see Module 8 which treats questioning. It is the study guide, with its major questions, allowance for a selection of specific subdivisions, and provision for varied resources, including multiple readings, that is an ideal vehicle for individualizing education.

5. Use directed reading lessons. Sometimes, textbook material is difficult because of the nature of the topic, the age and relative inexperience of the students, the vocabulary and concepts, or some combination of these factors. The teacher may plan a directed reading lesson in which the techniques discussed in the Building Vocabulary and Improving Comprehension sections of this module are combined with the experience of reading the selection in class. To conduct a directed reading lesson:

1. Prepare the pupils by going over new vocabulary and ideas, and reviewing old material and experiences so that they can see the relationships between the new and the old.
2. Have pupils skim the selection and look at pictures, headings, and so on.
3. Help pupils formulate questions about the selection to be read, for instance:
   a. What should a pupil try to find out when studying the selection?
   b. Is this the kind of selection that must be studied carefully?
   c. How does this selection connect with other lessons studied in the past?
      Three or four questions are quite enough. Too many questions may confuse and discourage the pupils. The questions should be pupil made rather than teacher made, if at all possible.
4. Let the pupils read the selection to themselves.

5. Discuss the reading. By using questions, help them see the relationships among the facts presented and also relationships to what has been learned previously.

Teaching How to Study

Writers who for many years have observed and experimented with students' study habits have generally agreed on the main features of efficient study skills. The list of admonitions about how to study, that have resulted from their efforts, however, is as long as your arm. It contains almost as many different entries as the number of researchers who have looked into the process of study. The most widely circulated list contains suggestions such as the following:

1. Establish a study routine for yourself. Make a schedule indicating time and place and on cue assume your study position in the study environment.
2. Start working immediately. Have your study materials all ready to go before you start your routine.
3. Space your learning prudently. Take short breaks when fatigue sets in or your attention begins to stray.
4. Study actively. React to your reading. Recite orally to yourself.
5. Vary your study technique to suit the subject you are studying and the purpose of your study.
6. Avoid rote memorization. Strive instead for comprehension and put recall into your own words.
7. Put the brief notes that you write into your own words. Avoid rewriting the text.

One group of researchers distilled its findings until it emerged with a system made up of five basic steps. The researchers named it the PQ4R system. "PQ4R is a package of techniques that should be effective in improving the reading of chapter-length materials when the student's purpose is thorough understanding of the content. . . . The steps in the procedure are Preview, Question, Read, Reflect, Recite, and Review."[12] Studies have shown that even top honors students benefit from studying and using these techniques. Since study skills are usually the haphazard result of trial and error, all students need help. Expository, informational materials in any subject area can be the basis for "how to study" sessions, with steps being worked on separately before the total approach is attempted. Let us examine each of the steps more closely.

Preview

This step provides for an overview or survey of the material. "How does an author help you learn in just minutes what a chapter will contain? How can you make the best use of these clues? What are the advantages in making an advance

---

[12] Thomas and Robinson, op. cit., p. 70. The authors acknowledge their debt to Francis P. Robinson, Donald E. P. Smith, and Thomas F. Stanton. (This procedure is a refinement of the *SQ3R*. In SQ3R the steps are Survey, Question, Read, Recite, and Review. They correspond closely to the PQ4R steps—Preview, Question, Read, Reflect, Recite, and Review.)

survey?" Brief practice under teacher guidance can help make this step automatic. Experience with the parts of a textbook can serve as a useful preliminary. Headlines, subtitles, introductory paragraphs, and summaries are invaluable for a picture of overall content. Questions that students prepare independently, mentally at least, may touch on their own background, their expectations, the type of material, its relative difficulty, the sequence and structure of presentation, and the author's purpose and main ideas. Since different subject areas have special features, some flexibility is needed, but all study materials should be treated with this overview, survey approach. The five minutes spent previewing an easy chapter or the fifteen minutes spent on a difficult one are well spent. They provide the student with "an accurate map of the rugged terrain."

Question

As in all reading comprehension, this is the crucial step. Ways of helping students acquire this skill include turning headlines into questions, formulating main ideas as questions, searching for deeper, more probing questions than the surface ones, and pretending to be the teacher and asking questions which might be used in class or on examinations. Anticipating possible answers is frequently helpful in both the actual reading and in leading to more and deeper questions.

Read and Reflect

When students start with questions, they must read to find answers. This involves looking for meaning with full attention and at a speed adapted to the difficulty of the passage, sometimes pausing completely. The tasks enumerated in the section on textbooks cover the kind of reading vital to effective study. All aspects of reading the lines, reading between the lines, and reading beyond the lines are important. Reflecting is not a separate step but an essential component of the reading step. Since study is more than memorization, more than preparing for a class discussion or a test, this emphasis makes information "the *foundation* for higher-level thought."[13] Recognizing how important and useful the knowledge is, the student becomes a "studier," a thinker rather than a repository of facts.

Recite

This step is really a self-reciting operation. No matter how many times a student rereads a difficult chapter or passage, he does not understand until he can answer in his own words: What have I read here? Some experts advise looking away from the printed material or covering it, at least half the time. One suggestion to students from Thomas and Robinson: "'See it! Say it! Hear it! Draw or write it!'" is a four-way reinforcement. The variety itself helps you recall. The change of pace—eyes, voice, ears, pencil—keeps you alert and increases absorption."[14] Through this technique, instead of a semipassive memorization, the student turns half-learned to fully-learned material. He selects because he understands what is important. Only as an aid does he make notes, choosing one or more of the marking and note-making techniques; marginal lines, underlining, see-through coloring, marginal mininotes, numerals, asterisks, question marks, check marks,

[13] Ibid., p. 79.
[14] Ibid., p. 94.

capsule summaries, quick outlines in his own shorthand, notebook jottings, and others. Whatever keeps the student mentally active, not copying absentmindedly or semiautomatically, may be helfpul. If to his note making he adds the processes of his own reflections, interpretations, and evaluations, his own brainstorming, he is making full and meaningful use of the self-reciting step. Since developing good habits in this area requires work and students may have acquired such ineffective methods as repeated rereading and excessive underlining, the teacher must teach this step directly and provide sufficient practice.

Review

Think of your own experiences with forgetting, or perhaps consult a psychology textbook with material on short-term memory, long-term memory, retention, and recall. Whatever shape the curve of forgetting takes, we all personally experience the decay of learning. To counteract some of this, we reread both immediately after completing a chapter and after a period of time. Review helps us regain a broad, overall view of the chapter and helps check on important details. Spacing review over a day or a longer period dramatically increases retention, yet requires shorter times for each successive rereading. Only this arrangement makes "quick review" an effective, meaningful exercise.

In the beginning of the year, it is a salutary practice to walk your students through a study session or two. Begin by selecting a section in your text on which to focus. Having preread the section yourself, determine just what you would want your students to learn from their study of it. Note the caliber of the words used in the text and mark for further explanation or attention those words which might prove difficult for various groups of students in your class.

When your exploration has been completed, set the stage for the work of your students. Lead them to see how the section you intend to start will fit into the scheme of learning they have been following. Announce the purposes for their reading and give some direction to their quest. Have them skim through the section, look at the pictures, paragraph headings, and so on. Supplying a study guide at the outset that tells the student what to do and how to do it will be a great boon for all, but especially for slower students.

The post-reading discussion of the section should reveal many things to you about the quality of reading your students are capable of and the nature of some of the difficulties which will stymie their future study efforts. You should be able to develop a clearer picture of those most ready for independent study and those still needing some kind of crutch and you should discover what kinds of problems are most disconcerting to those who have difficulties in performance. Conclusions about differentiating future assignments are often the result of this kind of post-mortem analysis of study. Sessions of this sort should be repeated frequently throughout a semester as you pass from one unit to the next. Your judgment about the difficulties inherent in upcoming lessons or units should be juxtaposed to your knowledge of the study-potency of the various students in your class and help determine the frequency and nature of future supervised study periods. At some point in the year it may be necessary for you to conduct ten-minute supervised periods such as this on almost a daily basis until you are sure that your students have gotten the hang of how to get to where they want to go.

Supervising Study

Since studying is individual, some teachers neglect to plan for it in class, the library, laboratory, or resource center. Yet that is the only way to supervise it. On the basis of observation of students' habits, the teacher recognizes their individual needs, provides appropriate materials and assignments, offers help with questions and procedures, checks on understanding, and evaluates progress. The time spent on this kind of individualized, supervised study is a major contribution to students' reading skills and their learning.

Developing Flexibility in Reading

Look through a typical page of a textbook in social studies, science, mathematics, English, business education, music, and a foreign language. You can recognize the need for building vocabulary and improving comprehension. Consider the students as they move from one classroom to another or undertake homework assignments. Besides adjusting to diverse content, they must also shift gears in their rate and style of reading. In these, the teacher must help by direct teaching and providing varied practice. Obviously, textbooks cannot be read as though they were light fiction; yet, some people are taken in by the national obsession with record-breaking reading speeds. Since speed reading is definitely not for most schoolwork, our question should be: In what ways and for what purposes should reading speeds be varied?

Scanning

Scanning is the most rapid reading method. It is used to locate specific items of information: a name, an address, a date, a phrase. Used with directories, dictionaries, indexes, tables, maps, and columns, this form of search involve having an image or word clearly in mind, so that an entire body of material can be scanned or reviewed quickly, without the reader having to understand or to perceive all the words. Sometimes the single words or facts for which one is looking seem to pop out of the context. Exercises in any subject matter area can be easily devised by the teacher. Use the simple experience involving class examination of a textbook. Since students must consult many resources quite rapidly, this skill is essential.

Good readers will naturally adapt their reading approach to the type of reading they are asked to do and the purpose they have in mind. Poorer readers tend to read everything in the same fashion, slowly, laboriously, inefficiently. Teachers must supply specific practice and instruction if they hope that such students will learn how to vary their rate.

Skimming

Skimming, another rapid form of reading, is used to survey the content of a book, chapter, or article, for such purposes as getting the heart or gist of the material, its general structure or plan, or the points of view or facts bearing on a particular problem. The eyes seem to float down the page, lighting on main ideas or significant phrases or key words. Besides its usefulness as a rather close sampling during initial reading, skimming is also useful for quick review. The preview step in the study skills procedure lends itself to skimming. Teacher-created exercises for finding answers to questions about main points are a typical use of this technique.

Recreational or Light Reading

Recreational or light reading is the fairly rapid form of reading one uses when the material is easy or fast-moving and the main purpose is entertainment or passing the time pleasantly. Readers have no problem recognizing the type of material or situation for which this technique is appropriate. Most frequently this category includes the reading of narrative, biographical, or journalistic material. The humorous and the sentimental also fall within its range.

Self-starters will have no difficulty in your class with this kind of reading. All others, though, will need your guidance, encouragement, enthusiasm, participation, and leadership. Lacking assurance about what to read and, perhaps, unsure of their power in reading, some students don't know where to begin. Like adults, though, who hear about and then read best-sellers for pleasure, students will try to get on the bandwagon that has been set rolling by an interesting or respected teacher. "Being-in-the-know" will form the motivation for some students who want to be able to respond to teacher's queries about books that he has highlighted.

For other students, reading recommended books will supply topics for conversation with a teacher they admire and like. Some adolescents are fearful of conversation with adults, especially teachers, because they are unsure about what topics to address. For many students, a teacher who is willing to talk about the reading they have done is a delightful person. Without such a person around, they have almost nothing to do with the reading they have done and almost no reason for spending time doing it.

Close Reading of Imaginative Literature

Close reading of imaginative literature is sometimes confused with recreational or light reading, both traditionally lumped together as Reading or Literature and assigned by the English or language teacher. Although enjoyment remains the major aim, the more artistic or more complex material requires mature response, depending on "imaginative entry"[15] into fiction, drama, or poetry. Among other tasks, close reading develops perception of meaning, interpretation of character motivation and interaction, and evaluation of structure and effect. Learning to read better is a lifelong activity, since the fusion of emotional and intellectual responses and the cultivation of sensitivity and insight remain a challenge to even the most highly skilled readers. Its special problems are perhaps best handled by English and language teachers. Ideally, the abilities involved should become the property of all students.

---

[15] Dwight L. Burton, "Teaching Students to Read Imaginative Literature," in *Teaching English in Today's High Schools,* ed. by Dwight L. Burton and John S. Simmons (New York: Holt, Rinehart and Winston, 1970), pp. 90–105.

Critical Reading

Critical reading is another example of the slow, careful reading that requires mature cognitive processes. Since its main purpose is developing independent thinking and skills in analysis and judgment, the process has numerous components. The reader first has to recognize what the author is saying. Then the reader weighs the evidence for reliability, accuracy, and representativeness, tries to separate opinion from fact, and identifies the viewpoints and biases of the writer. In analyzing the material, the reader checks the author's assumptions and logic and traces the relationship between the evidence, assumptions, and conclusions. The critical reader detects fallacies and recognizes the way the author intends him to draw inferences. He is alert to propaganda devices or emotional appeals. Sensitive to tone, style, and diction, the reader is critical in the most alert and positive way. Through reading experiences in the subject matter areas, the student meets the challenge of the open marketplace of ideas and grows in intellectual maturity.

Some Special Aspects of Reading

Research

No new reading skills or rates are needed for research, but it does require an effective use of scanning, skimming, study, and critical reading.

Problem Solving

This involves a combination of skills and rates similar to reference work. It may be required in almost any subject matter area. In science, mathematics, and social studies it may be especially necessary to focus on a problem, separate the relevant from the irrelevant, make the problem manageable, attack it with appropriate resources and processes, work out the pattern of explanation, and present the solution. Most careful reading and rereading are essential at every stage.

Reading Maps, Graphs, Charts, Tables, Diagrams, and Illustrations

A procedure to use when dealing with these aids to learning is to insist upon the reading by the students of the title and any legend that is attached. This procedure is placed first because it appears to be the prime stumbling-block in students' quest for understanding of information contained in such visuals. Preparation for this step will, of course, include the teaching of such concepts as latitude and longitude, scale, finding directions, reading elevations, recognizing key symbols, and the like. Student focus can be enhanced by supplying pointed questions that will give them some reason to examine the aid and track down the information requested. For example: How many inches represent a hundred miles on this map? What two countries border Spain? How many state parks are shown? Where is Cleveland in relation to Cincinnati? How many miles is Chicago from Denver?

Graphs and tables will have to be taught in a similar basic way. Students tend to skip devices of this sort because they do not know how to use them. Demonstrations by you on the vast amount of information that can be gleaned from such devices will help some to lay the groundwork. Thereafter, until conviction sets in, motivation to attend to such data should be supplied by your pointed questions to which students must search for answers.

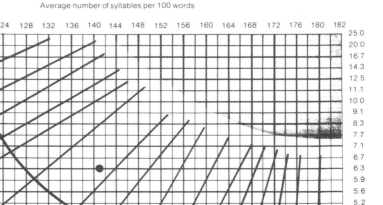

Average number of syllables per 100 words

FIGURE 11-1 *Fry Readability Graph*

DIRECTIONS: Randomly select 3 one hundred word passages from a book or an article. Plot average number of syllables and average number of sentences per 100 words on graph to determine the grade level of the material. Choose more passages per book if great variability is observed and conclude that the book has uneven readability. Few books will fall in gray area but when they do grade level scores are invalid.

Count proper nouns, numerals and initializations as words. Count a syllable for each symbol. For example, "1945" is 1 word and 4 syllables and "IRA" is 1 word and 3 syllables.

EXAMPLE:

	SYLLABLES	SENTENCES
1st Hundred Words	124	6.6
2nd Hundred Words	141	5.5
3rd Hundred Words	158	6.8
AVERAGE	141	6.3

READABILITY 7th GRADE (see dot plotted on graph)

Readability Formulas

As a rule none of these procedures will be effective unless the reading level of the textbook matches the reading level of the students. Use a technique such as the Dale-Chall readability formula or the Fry readability graph to estimate the grade level of the text. To use these formulas is not difficult. For instance, the procedure for the Fry technique is to

1. Determine the average number of syllables in three 100-word selections taken one from the beginning, one from the middle, and one from the ending parts of the book.

2. Determine the average number of sentences in the three 100-word selections.

3. Plot the two values on the Fry readability graph (Figure 11-1). Their intersection will give you an estimate of the text's reading level at the 50 per cent to 75 per cent comprehension level.[16]

Exercise 11 A

Compute the reading level of a text in which you find that three 100-syllable passages contain 130, 145 and 149 words and 7, 9, and 11 sentences.

Since these formulas give only the technical reading level of the book, you will have to temper the results by subjectively estimating the conceptual reading level of the work. To do so, consider your pupils' experience with the subject, the number of new ideas introduced, the abstraction of the ideas, and the author's external and internal clues. Then raise or lower the estimated level of difficulty.

To tell how well your students can read the text, use the Cloze technique, or an informal reading inventory. The Cloze technique which was first described by Bormuth[17] in 1968 and has since appeared in a number of versions, is really quite simple. From your textbook select several typical passages so that you will have a total of 400 to 415 words or so. Delete every eighth word in the passage except for the words in the first and last sentences, proper names, numbers, and initial words in sentences. It will be helpful if you eliminate 50 words. Duplicate the passages with 10 to 15 space blanks replacing the eliminated words. Pass out these "mutilated" readings to the pupils. Ask them to fill in the blanks with the most *appropriate* words they can think of. Collect the papers. Score them by counting all the words that are the exact words in the original text[18] and by dividing the number of correct responses by the number of possibles. (Fifty blanks makes the division easy.)

$$\text{Score} = \frac{\text{Number of correct responses}}{\text{Number of possibles}}$$

You can assume that pupils who score better than 50 per cent can read the book quite well; pupils who score between 40 and 50 per cent can read the book at the instructional level; and pupils who score below 40 per cent will probably find the book frustrating.

To conduct a *silent reading inventory,* ask the pupils to read four or five pages of the text, and then give a ten-item quiz on what they have read. You can consider the text too difficult for any pupil who scores less than 70 per cent on the

[16] Edward Fry, "A Readability Formula That Saves Time," *Journal of Reading* (April 1968), 11:587.

[17] J. Bormuth, "The Cloze Readability Procedure," *Elementary English* (April 1968), 45:429–436.

[18] Some persons recommend that only exact words be counted; others would allow exact synonyms. We suggest that you not count synonyms or verbs of different tense. See N. McKenna, "Synonymic versus Verbatim Scoring of the Cloze Procedure," *Journal of Reading,* (November 1976) 20:141–143.

quiz. Similarly, to conduct an *oral reading inventory,* have the pupil read a 100-word passage. The text is too difficult for any pupil who stumbles over and misses more than 5 per cent of the words.[19]

Problem Readers

Types of Problem Readers

All teachers should know about the different kinds of problem readers, to recognize those who can be helped in regular classes and those who need special treatment. Readers have numerous individual differences, but almost all can be helped to improve. Therefore, subject matter teachers along with reading specialists and English teachers share the responsibility for helping problem readers.

1. Slow readers may be slow learners who, because of a below-average rate of maturation, need relatively easy materials with which they can cope. These materials should contain the basic or common learnings agreed upon as essential to the subject. Instruction should feature spaced repetition and adequate explanation. Work should be planned for small groups or individuals who need encouragement. Slow pupils respond to teachers who show patience and understanding. Pupils can overcome the social or emotional problems acquired as a result, perhaps, of unfavorable comments by previous teachers or of their recognition that other students work on more difficult material.

2. Able retarded readers work below their capacity for some reason. Building interests is fundamental and can be done by connecting reading with activities in which they are successful. Within the subject matter area, practice in skills that are inadequately developed can move them from present levels to higher levels of performance. Variety of materials (textbooks, supplementary resources, homework assignments, and individualized projects) plus encouragement can help build their confidence and achievement. Such readers can recognize their problems, set their own purposes, and increase their voluntary reading.

3. Culturally different, economically impoverished, or educationally disadvantaged readers may have difficulty because of language or language variety differences, home or environmental conditions, or previous educational experiences. Since most school materials are sources of difficulty to these students, special programs offer the best remedy. To be sure, building vocabulary, improving comprehension, and developing flexibility are the same reading objectives as for all readers, but special knowledge, training, and expertise are needed for effective teaching of these students. The subject matter teacher should work with the reading specialist in order to outline the concepts, which should be handled sequentially, and to identify materials that will stimulate progress by these students.

4. Although bright or gifted students may not be thought of as problem readers, many have poor reading and study habits. Frequently, they need help overcoming boredom or distraction by being offered materials that are varied, absorbing, intellectually challenging, and rewarding. The rapid readers can benefit from instruction in study skills, from critical and imaginative reading which requires

[19] See M. S. Johnson, and R. A. Kress, *Informal Reading Inventories* (Neward, Del.: International Reading Association, 1965).

interpretation and evaluation, and from creative reading. Encouraging them to plan a balanced program with reading, social experiences, outdoor and recreational activities, and unscheduled time helps them place their reading progress in a reasonable perspective and enables them to reach a higher level of achievement.

5. Retarded students with emotional, visual, auditory, and neurological problems require individual diagnosis and treatment. Teachers should be alert to the need to identify such students and to guide them to those specialists who can provide help.

Helping Retarded Readers

Often the difficulty with problem readers is not so much that they cannot read as that they will not read. If you can stimulate these students to want to read, some of your problems will be solved. Try to sell reading in your subject to them. Do everything you can to make reading assignments exciting and inte᠎ sting. Read interesting assignments to them. Discuss the reading with them. Pr᠎ ide variety.

Many pupils can read much better than their class performance a᠎ their opinions of themselves indicate. Moreover, they may know much m᠎ ᠎ about the subject than you realize or they think they do. Try to discover and ᠎ ᠎rness these abilities and knowledge. Utilize discussions in which they tell of ᠎ ᠎ir own experiences. Initiate brainstorming sessions in which pupils tell you a᠎ ᠎nany words about the topic to be studied as they can think of. Ask pupils to pr᠎ ᠎ict what the author will say about the topic, and then let them read the selection ᠎ see if they were right. Provide study guides that show pupils what to look for ᠎ the assignment before they start reading. In the guide use easy recognition q᠎ ᠎stions. The more successes you can provide the pupils, the sooner they will le᠎ ᠎ to read on their own.

Show pupils how! Teach the vocabulary and how to decipher tl᠎ ᠎meaning of new words. Show them how to locate the main ideas and supportin᠎ ᠎deas in their reading. Demonstrate how to identify and use the author's organiz᠎ ᠎on pattern.

In short, arouse their interests, encourage them, and show them ᠎ow.

Summary

This summary will briefly touch on the main points of the preceding text. As you read try to fill in the details of the various points that are raised.

This module attempts to show you how to improve your own reading skills, but primarily how to help pupils learn to read and study more effectively. After all, it points out, everyone who teaches must be a teacher of reading.

Reading is an active process in which people attempt to extract ideas, concepts, thoughts, or images from the pattern of words set forth on the printed page. The reader's major goal is always to understand and enlarge contexts. It is to this end that all must direct their reading skills and activities. To help pupils become proficient, you as the teacher must be able to help them with each of the major subdivisions of reading skills and activities: building vocabulary, improving comprehension, and developing flexibility.

To build pupils' vocabulary it is recommended that you (1) provide pupils with many experiences, (2) encourage wide reading, and (3) teach vocabulary directly. Direct teaching of vocabulary requires you to (1) provide appropriate contexts,

(2) teach the key or "stopper" words, (3) utilize word attack devices, (4) encourage and teach the use of the dictionary, and (5) utilize word slips or vocabulary notebooks.

There seem to be three levels of comprehension: reading the lines, reading between the lines, and reading beyond the lines. To help pupils learn to read at the highest level, you should (1) provide background experience, (2) give fully developed homework assignments, (3) teach pupils how to use their textbooks, (4) utilize study guides and questions, (5) use directed reading lessons, and (6) teach pupils how to study by the PQ4R method (Preview, Question, Read, Reflect, Recite, and Review) or SQ3R method (Survey, Question, Read, Recite, and Review).

To develop flexibility in their reading, you should teach pupils to adjust their speed and style of reading to their reading objectives and the type of material to be read. Some reading should be scanned, some skimmed, some read lightly, some read closely, some studied, and some read critically. Frequently, a combination of methods is desirable or necessary.

You will find that problem readers in your classes will include slow learners; able retarded readers; culturally, economically, or educationally disadvantaged pupils; bright pupils who do not read as well as they should; and pupils with physical or emotional problems. Each of these should be treated in a special way in order to give them optimum help.

Suggested Reading

Barr, Rebecca, and Marilyn Sadow. *Reading Diagnosis for Teachers*. New York: Longman, 1985.

Brunner, Joseph F., and John J. Campbell. *Participation in Secondary Reading: A Practical Approach*. Englewood Cliffs, N.J.: Prentice-Hall, 1978.

Burnmeister, Lou E. *Reading Strategies for Middle and Secondary School Teachers*, 2d ed. Reading, Mass.: Addison-Wesley, 1978.

Chall, Jeanne. *Reading 1967–1977; A Decade of Change and Promise*, Fastback 97. Bloomington, Ind.: Phi Delta Kappa Educational Foundation, 1977.

Collins-Cheek, Martha. *Diagnostic-prescriptive Reading Instruction: A Guide for Classroom Teachers.*, 2d ed. Dubuque, Iowa: W. C. Brown, 1984.

Cunningham, James W., Patricia M. Cunningham, and Sharon V. Arthur. *Middle and Secondary School Reading*. New York: Longman, 1981.

Danks, Joseph H., and Kathy Pezdek, ed. by Frank B. Murray. *Reading and Understanding*. Newark, Del.: International Reading Association, 1980.

Early, Margaret, with the help of Diane J. Sawyer. *Reading to Learn in Grades 5 to 12*. San Diego: Harcourt Brace Jovanovich, 1984.

Fogan, Harry W., and Charles T. Mangrum II. *Teaching Content Area Reading Skills: A Modular Preservice and Inservice Program*. 2nd ed. Columbus, Oh.: Charles E. Merrill, 1981.

Gordon, William MacGuire. *The Reading Curriculum: A Reference Guide to Criterion-based Skill Development in Grades K-8*. New York: Praeger, 1982.

Herber, Harold L. *Teaching Reading in Content Areas*, 2d ed. Englewood Cliffs, N.J.: Prentice-Hall, 1978.

Hill, Walter R., *Secondary School Reading: Process, Program, Procedure*. Boston: Allyn & Bacon, 1975.

Purvis, Alan C., and Olive Niles. *Becoming Readers in a Complex Society*. Chicago: National Society for the Study of Education, University Chicago Press, 1984.

Robinson, H. Alan. *Teaching Reading and Study Strategies: The Content Areas*. Boston: Allyn & Bacon, 1975.

Rubin, Dorothy. *Reading and Learning Power.* New York: Macmillan Publishing Co., 1980.

Shuman, R. Baird. *Strategies in Teaching Reading: Secondary.* Washington, D.C.: National Education Association, 1978.

Thomas, Ellen Lamar, and H. Alan Robinson. *Improving Reading in Every Class,* abridged, 2d ed. Boston: Allyn & Bacon, 1977.

Thomas, Ellen Lamar. *Reading Aids for Every Class: 400 Activities for Instruction and Enrichment.* Boston: Allyn & Bacon, 1980.

Exercise Answer Key
Exercise 11 A

(Solution: Your answer should be grade 6.

$$\frac{130 + 145 + 149}{3} = \frac{424}{3} = 141 \text{ syllables}$$

$$\frac{7 + 9 + 11}{3} = \frac{27}{3} = 9 \text{ sentences}$$

By plotting 141 and 9 on the graph, we find that the intersection of the two falls in the area designated as approximate grade level 6. Presumably, then, the book would be suitable for most sixth-graders.)

Post Test

In the following test, select from each group of four statements the one that is m̤ t accurate. State the reasons you believe your choice is best. Then explain the shortcom̤ s or inadequacies of the other statements.

1. **a.** Reading is most important for impressing people socially.
    b. Reading is essential to success in every subject matter area, except strictly hysical activities.
    c. Reading is valuable because it may help in getting better jobs in later lif
    d. Reading is the major means for controlling the environment.

    _____
    _____
    _____
    _____
    _____
    _____

2. **a.** Reading is the responsibility of the English teacher.
    b. Reading can only be developed by reading specialists.
    c. All subject matter teachers are responsible for reading improvement.

d. Reading skills cannot be taught because they depend mainly on the native ability of students.

_____

_____

_____

_____

_____

_____

_____

3. a. Repeated drill on graded word lists is the best way to learn new vocabulary.
  b. Acquiring vocabulary depends mainly on understanding the contexts in which words appear.
  c. Key words should first of all be looked up in a dictionary.
  d. The meaning of words is more clearly explained by roots, prefixes, and suffixes than by their use in sentences.

_____

_____

_____

_____

_____

_____

_____

4. a. Unlike other reading, textbook mastery mainly involves "reading the lines" and memorizing them.
  b. All textbooks are equally satisfactory for learning study skills.
  c. When a school uses a single textbook for each grade, all students should be expected to learn the same content.
  d. A variety of textbooks should be used to allow for individual differences among students.

_____

_____

_____

_____

_____

_____

_____

5. **a.** If a teacher wants to discuss a subject in class the next day, every student has to do the same homework assignment.
   b. Homework assignments should be varied according to the abilities of students.
   c. Long homework assignments are a good way to make students read rapidly.
   d. Good homework assignments do not have to involve student interests.

   _____
   _____
   _____
   _____
   _____
   _____

6. **a.** Reading with numerous questions in mind is the best way to check on comprehension.
   b. Questions to guarantee comprehension should keep close to the literal meaning of the reading material.
   c. The most helpful questions are those that appear at the end of each chapter in a book.
   d. Questions in study guides are needed mainly by the slowest students.

   _____
   _____
   _____
   _____

7. **a.** Almost all students need help in developing effective study skills.
   b. As long as students pass tests, we can assume that they know how to study.
   c. Study skills develop naturally over a period of time as a student matures.
   d. All the steps in studying can be mastered with one good explanation by the teacher.

   _____
   _____
   _____
   _____
   _____

8. **a.** Scanning means reading very carefully to seek out each important word.
   b. Scanning is reading quickly with the mind set on finding specific information, such as a date, a formula, or any important fact.

    c. Scanning is very quick reading which helps the reader decide whether to reread the material more carefully.

    d. Scanning is done by sweeping the eyes back and forth over the words to test speed or eye movements.

_____

_____

_____

_____

_____

_____

9. a. Skimming involves looking for phrases to underline or to memorize.

    b. Skimming means reading very quickly to pick out a word or idea here and there.

    c. Skimming allows for reading every other sentence.

    d. Skimming uses "floating down" the page to find main ideas and key phrases.

_____

_____

_____

_____

_____

_____

10. a. Critical reading means judging how much fact and how much opinion an author has included, how much bias and how much fairness he shows.

    b. Critical reading involves deciding whether an author's style is appropriate to his material.

    c. Critical reading refers to judging whether one writer or one book is better than another.

    d. Critical reading means using personal taste to decide what the student would like to read and report on.

_____

_____

_____

_____

_____

_____

11. a. Maps, charts, graphs, tables, and illustrations are included to help people who cannot read the text.

   b. Maps and other graphic aids are used to decorate pages so that they do not have only straight text.

   c. Maps and other graphic aids usually include material that is not in the text.

   d. Maps and other graphic aids are usually important additions to the visual and conceptual content of a text.

_____

_____

_____

_____

_____

_____

12. a. Except for a few special cases, ost people read as well as they are able.

   b. Every reader can learn to becom a better reader by applying interest and effort.

   c. Because we do a great deal of rea ng to succeed in school or to get along in life, we automatically learn to become tter readers.

   d. By continuing to increase our read rate and the variety of reading material we become better readers.

_____ _____

_____ _____

_____ _____

_____ _____

_____ _____

_____ _____

13. a. A pupil who scores 60 per cent on a silent ading inventory can be considered a capable reader.

   b. A pupil who stumbles on no more than 10 pei nt of the words in an oral reading inventory can be considered a capable reader.

   c. A pupil who scores better than 60 per cent on Cloze procedure can be considered a capable reader.

   d. A pupil who scores better than 145 on the Fry chart is a capable reader.

_____

_____

_____

_____

_____

_____

14. **a.** To help slow readers, use very challenging materials.
   b. To help slow readers, concentrate on intensive drill.
   c. To help slow readers, feature spaced repetition and adequate explanation.
   d. To help slow readers, concentrate on critical reading and problem solving.

_____

_____

_____

_____

_____

15. **a.** When reading maps or charts, one should first preview the materials to ascertain their general nature and relevance to other material.
   b. When dealing with able retarded readers, it is usually best to concentrate on a single textbook approach.
   c. When building a study guide for slow readers, you should emphasize probing questions.
   d. When teaching pupils research skills, you should abandon the PQ4R approach and substitute the SQ3R approach.

_____

_____

_____

_____

_____

MODULE
12

Providing for Individual Differences

Rationale

No one is exactly like anyone else. Even identical twins are not identical. In spite of the similarity in their genetic background, environmental factors beginning even before birth shape each twin differently. And for other people, the differences in genetic structure make the chances of anyone's being an exact duplicate of anyone else completely nil. Brothers and sisters may have family resemblances; tenth-graders may have some traits in common, as do members of honors sections, secondary education majors, and college professors; yet each one is an individual and looks and behaves differently from everyone else.

   The ways in which individuals differ are manifold. Not only are there differences in physical appearance but also in personality traits. Some of your pupils will be quick, some slow; some academically intelligent, some stupid; some socially skillful, some socially inept; some eager, some phlegmatic; some interested in your subject, some not; some male, some female; some friendly, some hostile.

Some of these differences may be of no importance as far as school is concerned. Whether a girl's eyes are blue, grey, or brown does not really matter (except perhaps to certain boys and even then the boys' reaction is only incidental to a combination of other, more powerful influences). Others are extremely important for teaching, because what is good education for one person may not be good for another. Therefore, in this module we shall present some of the differences in pupils that you should consider in your teaching; some ways of finding out important characteristics of individual pupils; some of the curricular and organizational schemes that have been invented by school administrators to provide for differences in pupils; and strategies and tactics that you can use in your own classes, not only to cope with the problems of individual differences, but also to use these differences to enhance your effectiveness as a teacher.

Specific Objectives

Specifically, at the completion of this unit you should be able to do the following:

1. Describe ways in which administrators attempt to provide for individuals. Among the plans you should be able to describe are (a) curriculum tracks; (b) tracks, streams, and homogeneous groups; (c) promotion schemes including continuous promotion, minicourses, half-yearly and term promotion, and nongraded plans; (d) curriculum provisions including electives, minicourses, and extracurriculum; and (e) the use of teaching aides, learning centers, and modular schedules. You should also be able to summarize the arguments for and against the use of plans featuring the principle of homogeneous groups.
2. Describe how to conduct such strategies and tactics as differentiating the assignment; using homogeneous groups within the classroom; conducting the class as a laboratory; units; contracts; learning activity packets; special assignments; individualizing instruction; special help; laboratory classes.

   Also, continuous progress plans; self-instructional devices; study guides; self-correcting material; machines for teaching; correspondence and television courses; use of small groups and committees; independent study; accelerating brilliant pupils; and projects.
3. Describe methods by which one can make time for individual instruction.
4. Describe approaches for teaching certain homogeneous groups, such as (a) academically talented pupils; (b) academically incompetent pupils; (c) children of poverty; (d) handicapped pupils; and (e) pupils of different ethnic origins.

Module Text

Necessity of Providing for Differences in Pupils

As we have already observed, pupils differ in many ways: physical characteristics, interests, intellectual ability, motor ability, social ability, aptitudes of various kinds, background, experience, ideals, attitudes, needs, ambitions, dreams, and hopes. Furthermore, all persons learn in their own ways and at their own rate.

Their interests, their prior background, their innate and acquired abilities, and a myriad of other personal and environmental influences shape how and what they learn. That is why no two pupils ever learn exactly the same thing from any particular learning experience.

That these statements represent a basic condition of humanity carries with it at least one profound implication for teaching: *It is ridiculous to believe that any teaching strategy or school organization that treats pupils as though they were all alike can succeed.* The fact of individual differences in pupils requires that teachers find teaching strategies and tactics that accommodate individual differences.

As Keuscher points out, individualized instruction is imperative.

I. Philosophically, it is consistent with the principles upon which our form of government, which spawned our educational system, is based.

II. The very nature of our democratic system and the way it functions demands knowledgeable, thinking participants.

III. Assembly-line methods are tending to produce mass-produced, standardized citizens at the expense of individuality.

IV. As society grows increasingly complex, there is a greater demand for a diversity of talents and skills.

V. It is probably the most efficient way to educate if one focuses on the product rather than just the process.[1]

Therefore, you ought to develop skill in techniques that will allow you to capitalize on pupils' differences so that your teaching may become more thorough, efficient, and effective.

Unfortunately, in practice, most schemes for individualizing instruction do not approach the ideal. Most of the techniques now used to provide for individual differences in pupils are simply techniques by which teachers (1) manipulate course content so that it is easier for some pupils and more difficult for others; (2) give some pupils more work than they give others; (3) allow some pupils to progress more or less rapidly than others do; or (4) combine these techniques.

True individualization of instruction requires a quite different approach. Its emphasis is on the development of each different individual to his or her fullest potential with the accent not so much on the differences as on the development. Therefore, individualized teaching goals and subject matter vary from individual to individual, according to personal needs, activities, and aspirations. Difficulty and speed are also considerations, but the principal thrust should be on providing all pupils with the curriculums best suited for them individually.

Knowing the Student

In order to provide for individual differences adequately, it is really necessary to know something about your students' strengths and weaknesses, their interests, goals, backgrounds, and attitudes. You cannot expect to provide for differences you know nothing about. To find out the information you need to know about

[1] Robert E. Keuscher, "Why Individualize Instruction," In Virgil Howes, *Individualizing of Instruction* (New York: Macmillan Publishing Co., 1970), p. 7.

pupils, you have a great number of tools available. Among them are the cumulative record folder; observation; conferences; and questionnaires such as interest finder, autobiographical questionnaire, test results, and sociometric devices. These are described in Module 6. If you are not conversant with them, review Module 6.

It is important to remember in this quest for knowledge about the student that there are different styles for learning that each has. Evidence is lacking as to which style is better than which, but it is vital to keep in mind that each student will select the style for himself that fits most comfortably with his way of performing. Principally, some students prefer to use a visual style of learning, to read in the subject or about the topic in pursuit of mastery of a goal. They read easily and often rapidly. They enjoy the reading process and can recall most readily what they learn in this fashion. They most naturally opt for this activity if given some task to master. Another great category of students is made up of those who prefer the listening style of learning. It may be that they are not as facile with reading as they might be. It also may be that they can't tolerate the silence, or can't sit still long enough to concentrate on unlocking the message contained in the written word. They enjoy learning by listening; they remember what they hear; they become so engrossed in listening that they forget that they are sitting still. Of course, others do their best learning by becoming physically active—they touch objects and learn about them; they feel shapes and textures; they try to construct the object they are trying to learn about.

Most of us become somewhat proficient with each of these learning styles and can switch from one to the other as the mood is upon us. Since many of your students will not have reached this point while they are under your supervision, it will be necessary for you to know which style they prefer most often, and to provide opportunities for them to learn using the mode that suits them best in the learning activity of the day.

Often the best thing for you to do is to get out of the way of the learner and let him set up a pace and a gait. Since the student is the agent of his own learning, the more actively engaged he becomes, the more effective a producer of learning he will become. Teachers in the past have been known in the cause of uniformity to impede learning by insisting on the utilization of the established classroom learning mode. They have adopted a teaching procedure and have felt threatened if students deviated from this pattern. Of course, good judgment must be used, for sometimes it is imperative for a teacher to interpose. The intention here is solely to free newcomers to the field from the compulsion that creeps in to pontificate more than to teach, to control more than foster and create learning situations.

Some students are very comfortable in beginning their learning in the abstract while others feel the need to begin with the concrete. Some prosper easily working in groups while others prefer to work alone. Some are quick in their studies and others are slow and methodical and cautious and meticulous. Some can sustain attention on a single topic for a long time, becoming more absorbed in their study as time passes without feeling the need for a break. Others are slower starters, more casual in their pursuits, capable of shifting with ease from subject to subject, or to take a break. Some can study in the midst of music, noise, or people movement and others need quiet, solitude, and a desk or table.

The trap for civilians and teachers alike to avoid is that of regarding all students who do poorly in school as being alike. In a pragmatic culture, such as ours, oriented as it is toward quantity, speed and measurement, it is easy to conclude that being a *slow learner* is synonymous with being a *poor learner.* It takes some studied perception to discover that slowness may be simply another style of learning with potential strengths of its own. Slowness can reflect many things—caution, a desire to be thorough, a meticulous style, a great interest that may constrain one from rushing through a problem. To begin ignoring the slow student, without close inspection, or to begin treating all slow students as though they were victims of some deficiency is to risk discouraging those who have deliberately opted for slowness and putting a lid upon their learning incentives and opportunities.

Administrative Provisions

For years, school administrators have been trying to provide for the differences in pupils administratively. In the earliest times, they provided different types of schools for persons with different goals. For example, in medieval times, the clerk-to-be was educated in a monastery or church school, but the would-be knight was apprenticed as a page to an influential knighted lord, who trained the aspirant to knighthood. In seventeenth-century Massachusetts, the minister-to-be went to Harvard for his academic training, but the tradesman was schooled in his trade in a private venture school, or as an apprentice. Women were trained at home.

Curriculum Tracks

Today, the practice of providing different routes for pupils with different vocational and academic aims continues. Some school systems provide different schools for youths planning for different vocations, but in most school systems, beginning at the high school level, these differences are accommodated by offering a variety of curricula in comprehensive high schools. By a judicious selection of courses or curricula, students can prepare themselves for college entrance, or for a specific vocation, or, if they wish neither college nor vocational preparation, they can select a general program. The offering of a choice of curricula is probably the most common administrative or organizational method of providing for individual differences at the high school level. It is not used so frequently at lower grade levels, however.

Tracks or Streams

Some school systems are set up on the basis of pupil ability. For instance, one sequence might be for honors groups, a second sequence for college preparatory students, a third sequence for general students, and a fourth sequence for slow learners. These different sequences—sometimes called tracks or streams—may differ from each other in difficulty and complexity of content, rate of pupil progress, and methods of teaching. Thus, the pupils in a mathematics honors group move through to the study of calculus in the twelfth grade, but a slow group might never go beyond the development of basic computational skills.

Homogeneous Groups

Tracks or streams are, in effect, a type of homogeneous grouping. Homogeneous groups are formed by dividing the pupils into class sections, according to some criterion or combination of criteria. Usually the criterion is ability. However, it might be sex (boys' physical education) or educational-vocational (Business English or college preparatory English), or even interest. In any case, the reasons for forming homogeneous groups are to provide for the differences in pupils and to make teaching easier. Theoretically, when classes are grouped homogeneously, it is easier to select content and methods that will be suitable for all pupils in that group.

To a degree, homogeneous grouping works. When all the pupils in an advanced mathematics class are bright and interested, teaching them is easier. There is no doubt of that. It is easier to find content and methods suitable for everyone if the group is homogeneous. Nevertheless, homogeneous grouping is not necessarily the answer to the problem of individual differences in pupils.

In the first place, homogeneous groups are not truly homogeneous. They are merely attempts to make groups similar, according to one or two criteria. Girls' physical education classes are homogeneous in that they are limited to girls, but the girls are not all alike, physically, mentally, emotionally, or socially. Even if one were to have a section of girls' physical education in which all the girls were interested in sports, there would still be great differences in the characteristics and capabilities of the girls. *All homogeneous grouping does is to reduce the heterogeneity of classes; it makes certain aspects of the problem of providing for individual differences in pupils a little more manageable.*

It is most important that you remember this point. Many teachers teach as though they thought their classes really were homogeneous. Do not be one of them. Always keep in mind that a homogeneous class is one in which your school administrators have tried to reduce the spread of one or more pupil characteristics. The other characteristics run the full gamut just as in the heterogeneous classes. In classes grouped according to ability, although the range of academic ability may be reduced, the range of interest, ambitions, motivations, and goals is probably just as wide as in any other class. Even the range of ability in a high ability class may be quite large; a thirty-point range in IQ in such a class would be quite usual. Similarly, a slow class may consist of pupils who cannot learn, presumably because of lack of innate ability, pupils who cannot learn because of gaps in their background or poor preparation in earlier classes, and pupils who could learn easily if they ever tried. No matter how much one attempts to homogenize classes and no matter what plan of grouping is used, you as the teacher will always face the problem of providing for differences in individuals. Homogeneous grouping can reduce the problem, but it cannot eliminate it.

Homogeneous grouping brings with it several built-in problems of its own. One of these is the danger that, in ability grouping schemes, the less talented pupils may be shortchanged. Teachers who teach "slow classes" often feel frustrated. Many of them seem to feel that being asked to teach classes of slow learners is somehow demeaning. After all, they are subject matter specialists and, they believe, to spend their talents on the less-than-bright is to waste those talents. Such teacher attitudes defeat the purpose of ability grouping. If you feel this way, perhaps you should not go into teaching. All who wish to teach should be willing to adapt their teaching to the talents of the students with whom they must work.

Another danger is that the content and methods used will not be those best suited for the students being taught. Frequently, classes of bright students are hurried through their courses without any real mind-stretching experiences. Of course, bright students usually learn more quickly, but just learning more of the same is hardly the way to develop their talent to the full. Perhaps even more dangerous is the common practice of watering down academic courses for slow students. The result is dull, drab, boring teaching day after day. If you teach homogeneously grouped classes, you should adjust your content and your teaching strategies and tactics to the pupils so that the classes will be productive experiences that result in expanding pupils' minds and their mastering skills and concepts worthwhile to them now and in the future.

In practice, the less academically inclined students are more often short-changed than are other students. When their courses are merely watered down versions of academic courses, their classes may not only be a waste of time but actually harmful to them. The courses are seldom structured so that students can capitalize on the strengths they have. Instead, the assumption is that these students cannot learn. Since little is expected of them, they do little. There is little fun, or success, or relevancy to anything important to them to motivate them. In the classes in which students most need challenging and motivating, there is no challenge and little motivation. Furthermore, these students do not have a chance to learn from the help and the example of their more talented peers. Students learn a great deal from each other. Consequently, slow youths benefit from associating with talented pupils, and bright youths can learn from slow pupils. It is unfortunate that in so many instances the classes for slow students have become educational ghettos. There is no boy or girl in a public school who cannot learn if given the proper opportunity and encouragement.

One of the practices that helps to perpetuate the problems inherent in teaching is the division of students into classes. For administrative purposes, students are divided into categories based upon age and designated as classes. Teachers are appointed to instruct so many classes daily. Unconsciously, such teachers begin thinking in terms of the entire number in each group. Progressive sequences are designated for study and specific levels of mastery are earmarked for those subjects that are developmental in nature. Expectations are established for each student in each class for quarterly or annual achievement based on the amount of content in the subject and the time to be allocated for its mastery. The teacher who forgets that individuals differ will fall easy prey to the *class* dilemma and tend to transgress in the direction of group achievement.

Exercise 12 A

Review the material on homogeneous grouping and recall your own school experiences. Do you favor homogeneous grouping? Many people claim homogeneous grouping to be undemocratic. Do you think it is? Can you think of any reasons why bright pupils should be required to sit in the same classes as slow pupils? Is it fair to them to be in such classes? Is it fair for slow pupils to be relegated to slow sections? Is there any way to establish levels of achievement for a single class that are at the same time not too low for the gifted and not too high for the slow learner?

Promotion Schemes

The old-fashioned techniques of "skipping grades" and "keeping pupils back" are also administrative devices used to provide for differences in pupil ability. Years ago, in order that the period skipped or repeated might not be too long, city systems instituted half-year courses. Under this sort of plan, pupils were promoted every half year. Nowadays, some systems schedule half-year and quarterly courses and even short minicourses. One of the most promising developments is the movement toward continuous promotion schemes in ungraded schools.

Continuous Promotion. Continuous promotion plans consist principally of dividing the course work of the curriculum into short modules. When the students complete one module, they are ready to go on to another. Usually, the students are issued learning activity packets, which contain the instructions and materials for studying the module so that individual pupils can work through the modules alone, at their own time, and at their own speed. Theoretically, at least, continuous progress plans are an excellent means of providing for individual differences. Students who find that they are not ready to move on when the class moves on are not forced to do so, and students who finish the unit quickly are not forced to wait for others to catch up. Furthermore, it may not be necessary for all students to follow the same order of units. Not only may one be able to change the order of the modules, but one can, in effect, build a personal sequence or course by electing to skip certain modules, or to select additional modules different from those laid out for the other pupils. Although it seldom happens in practice, in theory, the students by their choice of modules, can have courses and curricula specially tailored to meet their own needs in continuous progress programs.

Nongraded Schools. In another type of nongraded program, courses are offered at various levels. Students are not placed in courses because they are in the tenth or eleventh grade, but because they have reached a certain level of academic proficiency. In such a program, quite possibly a course would not be a tenth-grade course, but, rather, the class might consist of pupils from all of the secondary school grades proficient at that level.

Curriculum Provisions for Individual Differences

In addition to the various curricula, tracks, or streams that one finds in the ordinary high school, curriculum builders try to provide for differences in interest and goals by providing a diversity of courses, extending from the humanities through the fine arts and the practical arts, to the vocational subjects and into the extracurriculum. To give pupils an adequate opportunity to study in areas that appeal to them, the curriculum builders provide electives in the program. A good selection of electives allows students to pursue special interests and to explore special bents. They allow pupils to add both breadth and depth to their course selection. Even further variety is offered by the extracurriculum, which allows pupils to elect activities for the fun of it.

Minicourses are another way to add still more variety to the school curriculum. These short courses that may extend from a few weeks to a full term, depending upon the school, may be offered for credit or they may not. Some of them are offered as a result of pupil requests. Pupils may or may not be permitted to co-operate in the planning and carrying out of the courses. Minicourses may vary from the depth study of an academic problem to the discussion of youthful problems, to the development of hobbies, or to the serious study of contemporary trends in music. When the courses are concerned with viable content and provide a large enough choice of attractive alternatives, minicourses can be really valuable tools for individualizing instruction.

Further study by you in this area will reveal a host of pros and cons about this method of trying to satisfy individual differences. Psychologically, for example, the short-term length serves to motivate those students who seem antipathetic to the concept of interminably long semesters. For students who have serious ups and down for one reason or another, it enables them to recoup previous successes after a short period of failure instead of giving-up-the ghost for the year after a down period. The usual problems associated with this kind of project, e.g., keeping track of the progress of each as he passes through the various mini courses, are ever present and need to be resolved.

Use of Teacher Aides

Three other innovations provided by the administrations of some schools may make it easier for teachers to provide for individual differences. They are the introduction of teacher aides, the establishment of learning centers in the schools, and the adoption of flexible, modular daily schedules.

Teacher aides can make it easier for teachers to provide independent and individualized study. By using aides to do time-consuming chores, teachers have more time to work with individuals and small groups. Among the things that the aides can do to help individualize instruction are the following:

1. To help pupils as they practice.
2. To help pupils as they work at their desks.
3. To help follow up.
4. To tutor.
5. To supervise and help small groups.[2]

Learning Centers

Learning centers are places where pupils can go to study under supervision. When these centers are provided with adequate facilities, pupils can do a great deal of independent study away from the lockstep of the traditional classroom. Flexible modular schedules give pupils time in which to engage in independent work. In such schedules, students meet with their teachers in regular classrooms at specified times. At these times, the students receive their assignments, which they do independently in the learning center under the supervision of a teacher assistant.

[2] Gertrude Noar, *Individualized Instruction* (New York: John Wiley & Sons, 1972), pp. 66–67.

Frequently, the independent study is outlined in a learning packet, a contract, or a study guide. At other times, the students' time is not structured so that they can be free to get to the learning centers to do their independent study.

Flexible Schedules

Schools that have adopted flexible modular scheduling have found themselves generally stymied by the rigidity of the five-, 6- or 7-period day. They have concluded that the usual 45-, 55-, or 60-minute periods in such a scheduled day are both too short and too long. Such periods often provide many more minutes for instruction each hour than are reasonably usable for the teaching goals for that hour. At other times such time allotments are too short to permit goal satisfaction as when committees need to do research, or take a field trip, or view a long film. For their period length, modular schools have established as a base an amount of time that represents the smallest number of minutes that can be effectively utilizable. In such a schedule, for example, a period can be as small as one mod (say, 15 minutes) and students can meet for such things as attendance taking in the homeroom, and the like. Periods can be extended by linking together as many mods (3–4–5–6) as the goals for the instruction intended seem to indicate as necessary. In a similar fashion can the size of the student group be modified from 3–10 students (known as small group) to 10–20 (middle group) to 60–120 (large group) determined by the nature of the instruction planned. During the day, or during the week not all periods have the same length or meet in the same sequence.

In the schedule that follows, the school day is divided into 15–minute modules. According to this schedule, on Monday the seventh-graders are free to go to the learning center during modules 1–3, and also during modules 16–19, their lunch hour. During modules 4–6, 7–9, and 13–15 they meet in regular class-size groups, but in modules 10–12 and 20–22 they all meet together for large group instruction in science or language arts. On other days the pupils follow much the same pattern, except that they meet in regular size classes for science and language arts and have large-group instruction for social studies on Thursday. Unstructured time for independent study in the learning centers is available to them every day.

Monday	Mods 1–3	Unstructured or unassigned time. The student has the option of reporting to any of the six learning centers. In addition, the library is available, as well as the student center.
	Mods 4–6	Social Studies Middle Group
	Mods 7–9	Spanish
	Mods 10–12	Science Large Group
	Mods 13–15	Math Middle Group
	Mods 16–19	Unstructured (lunch included here)
	Mods 20–22	Language Arts Large Group
	Mods 23–26	Clubs and Activities
Tuesday	Mods 1–3	Science Middle Group
	Mods 4–6	Unstructured
	Mods 7–9	Spanish

	Mods 10–12	Phys. Ed.
	Mods 13–14	Math Small Group
	Mods 15–18	Unstructured (includes lunch)
	Mods 19–21	Language Arts Middle Group
	Mod 22	Unstructured
	Mods 23–26	Clubs and Activities
Wednesday	Mods 1–2	Social Studies Small Group
	Mods 6–9	Unified Arts
	Mods 10–12	Music
	Mods 13–15	Math Middle Group
	Mods 16–18	Unstructured (includes lunch)
	Mods 19–20	Language Arts Small Group
	Mods 21–22	Unstructured
	Mods 23–26	Clubs and Activities
Thursday	Mods 1–3	Unstructured
	Mods 4–6	Social Studies Large Group
	Mods 7–9	Spanish
	Mod 12	Unstructured
	Mods 13–15	Science Middle Group
	Mods 16–18	Unstructured (includes lunch)
	Mods 19–20	Language Arts Small Group
	Mods 21–22	Unstructured
	Mods 23–26	Clubs and Activities
Friday	Mods 1–3	Phys. Ed.
	Mods 4–6	Music
	Mods 7–9	Science Middle Group
	Mods 10–12	Math Middle Group
	Mods 13–19	Unstructured (includes lunch)
	Mods 20–22	Language Arts Middle Group
	Mods 23–26	Clubs and Activities[3]

Differentiating Assignments

In the ordinary lesson, even though the lesson objectives may be the same for everyone, there is usually no reason why everyone should have to do exactly the same activities. Consequently, one can provide for differences in ability and interest by differentiating the assignment, such as specifying different learning activities for different pupils or groups of students. Pupils who do not read well may be asked to read in works that are less difficult than those required of the better readers. Or students more able in mathematics might be assigned the difficult problems while the less able do the easier problems. Or the bright and quick students might be given longer, more demanding assignments.

[3] Fred S. Wien, "Flexible Modular Scheduling," *New Jersey Association of Teacher Educators Journal,* (Spring 1974), 17:11–12.

Differentiating Length and Difficulty

One way to carry out the differentiating of assignments according to length or difficulty of the work is to divide the class into groups or committees. You might, for instance, divide your class into three groups. One group might be assigned readings in a rather difficult text. It might also be asked to solve or react to some quite difficult problems. The second group might read selections that are somewhat less demanding and work on easier problems. The third group's reading assignment might be extremely easy with no real problems to confront it at all. In this case, all are studying the same thing, but at different levels of difficulty. Usually such grouping of a class is done after completion of the first 3–6 weeks of school on the basis of achievement in the first unit of study. It is not foisted upon the class as an outside judgment about student ability but is agreed upon after discussion concerning the most appropriate way to achieve upcoming goals. Each student exercises responsibility for selecting the group to which to belong based on record achieved. Errors made in judgment about placement should be readily rectifiable as the unit progresses by the availability of flexible movement from one group to the next.

Differentiating Type of Work

You can differentiate your assignments by allowing pupils to do different types of work to achieve the learning objectives. Capitalize on the different interests and abilities of the pupils. Perhaps some pupils might learn best through art, some through reading, and others through acting things out. There is no reason why everyone should do the same thing. What is important is that pupils achieve the understandings, skills, and attitudes that are the learning objectives.

> For example, not everyone needs to express his understanding of the ante-bellum South by writing essays and answering questions about it. Many other media are available. Talented youngsters might produce illustrations of life in the South; a boy interested in mechanical drawing might draw a layout of a plantation; a girl interested in homemaking might investigate the menus of the era, or run up a costume appropriate to the period; a young engineer might construct a cotton gin; a young choreographer might score and dance a ballet in the *Gone with the Wind* motif; a poet might contribute some lyric poetry, perhaps an ode or two.[4]

Although differentiating assignments by giving different ones to small groups and committees is a relatively easy way to do it, there is no reason why differentiation cannot be done on a more individualized basis. For instance,

> in the study of Ancient Man, pupils with low reading ability might read such easy reading material as the Abramowitz pamphlet, *World History Study Lessons,* while others read such difficult and esoteric material as the final chapter of Von Koenigswald's *The Evolution of Man.* Others might be reading in such varied works as Chapters 2 and 3 of Van Loon's *The Story of Mankind,* Ashley Montagu's *Man: His First Million Years,* a *National Geographic* Magazine article (e.g., Cynthia Irwin, Henry Irwin, and George Agogino, "Ice Age Man vs. Mammoth," June 1962, **121**:828–836, or Thomas R. Henry, "Ice Age Man, the First American," December 1955, *Life* Mag-

[4] Leonard H. Clark and Irving S. Starr, *Secondary and Middle School Teaching Methods,* 4th ed. (New York: Macmillan Publishing Co., 1981), p. 103.

azine articles on Ancient Man, or the Dell Visual paperback *Prehistory*). Or they might be reading the first unit "Days before History" in Hartmann and Saunders' text, *Builders of the Old World,* or Chapter 1 of Black's textbook, *Our World History.*[5]

Usually, the procedure to follow is to give pupils a number of options from which they select their own individual activities. You will probably find it best to offer these options in a study guide that you issue to the pupils before they start their work.

You can also differentiate single lessons. For example, in a mathematics lesson, you might assign certain pupils examples 1, 4, 5, and 8, while others do 2, 3, 6, 7, 9, and 10. Frequently, math teachers add some difficult exercises to challenge the brighter students. Usually, however, you will find that in order to differentiate your classes in any meaningful way, you need a longer period of time. Ordinarily, the differentiated assignment should be a long assignment covering a period of several days or even weeks.

Homogeneous Groups Within the Classroom

Another way to differentiate work in a class is to set up homogeneous groups within the classroom. This practice is very common in the elementary schools. There is no reason why it should not be very common in secondary schools. Grouping can be accomplished in several ways, as follows:

1. Divide the class into groups on the basis of scholastic ability or ability in the subject.
2. Divide the class in accordance with pupil interest.
3. Divide the class according to goal. Pupils who are interested in the same or similar goals can work together.
4. Divide the class according to needs; for instance, pupils requiring remedial work will work together.

You can differentiate class assignments to meet the needs of these various groups by varying the length, difficulty, and content of the assignments. There is no need for groups with different interests or different goals to study the exact same content, for instance. To conduct several groups in one class is hard work, but then all good teaching requires hard work. Actually, using groups is often less arduous than is endeavoring to teach the unready in an en masse situation something that they cannot learn or trying teach the uninterested something they are not willing to give their attention to. The practice of trying to teach the entire class at one time compounds the problems inherent in group teaching and only exacerbates a teacher's problems the longer it is continued.

For many years rural schools have conducted multigrade classes with good results. The essentials are (1) to be sure that everyone has something worthwhile to do; (2) to encourage pupils to participate both in planning and in implementing plans for group work; (3) to supervise the group carefully, always being sure that every group gets its share of attention, guidance, and help. The use of written assignment sheets and study guides may help the groups keep to their tasks.

[5] Ibid., p. 240.

You should remember to keep such homogeneous groups fluid and flexible. Access to and egress from any group should be based upon ongoing conclusions regarding subject mastery, learning goals, and student personal development. Groups that are constituted once per year and which then congeal are stultifying to learners who catch on, who achieve the learning goals for particular sessions of instruction, and who become motivated and receptive to further learning but who cannot break out of the grouping into which they were previously placed.

Conducting the Class as a Laboratory

Another way to differentiate the work in the class is to conduct the class as a laboratory. This type of approach is best served by long-term assignments, as in the unit plan. In the laboratory, pupils work in small groups or as individuals under the guidance of the teacher. No student is necessarily working on the same project as any other student at any particular time. Rather, one group may be working on a group report; another group may be setting up a demonstration; some individuals may be doing research for their projects; and others may be studying required or optional readings. The laboratory period is a work period.

When you conduct a laboratory, try using a procedure similar to the following. There is no set procedure for teaching by the laboratory method, however.

Give out a general study guide, unit of work, or learning packet that outlines what is to be done in the unit. The activities may be required or optional. Let the pupils select the activities they plan to do from the study guide or suggest activities themselves. Once you have approved their individual plans, let the pupils execute their plans. They may look things up in pamphlets, books, and magazines. They may play tapes and records or look at films, filmstrips, or slides. They may do these activities as individuals or as committees and usually in any order they choose. They may confer with each other and help each other. As the pupils execute their plans, help, guide, and supervise them.

1. Observe pupils to diagnose their study habits.
2. Show pupils where to find information.
3. Show pupils how to use the tools of learning.
4. Clarify assignments.
5. Help pupils form goals for study.
6. Suggest methods for attacking problems.
7. Point out errors and incorrect procedures.
8. Help pupils summarize.[6]

As a means of providing for individual differences, laboratory classes have many merits. When properly done, they allow the pupils to work on individual learning sequences that are theirs alone. The loose structure of the laboratory allows pupils to work at different speeds. The swift, or more able, can move as quickly as they wish without waiting for the slow, and the slow do not have to push themselves unreasonably to keep up with their swifter colleagues. There is no need for all students to do the same things in a laboratory setup. The students, under guidance, can select the activities that they feel will be most useful. It is

---

[6] Based on Leonard H. Clark, *Teaching Social Studies in Secondary Schools: A Handbook* (New York: Macmillan Publishing Co., 1973), p. 125.

quite permissible for students to learn in different ways. However, unless the laboratory method is given form, as in the unit, contract, or modular approach, the laboratory can become chaotic and the learning experiences of the pupils meaningless.

For the laboratory method to work best, the classroom should be set up as a laboratory. The more fully equipped the room, the better. The students should have easily available a classroom library of pertinent books and other reading matter, audiovisual materials, and plenty of work space and material with which to work. Most of this material should be kept in the classroom permanently. Overhead projectors, filmstrip projectors, tape recorders, for instance, should either be assigned as permanent equipment or, if that is not feasible, on long-term loan. Books can be borrowed from the main library for the duration of the course or unit. All of this material and equipment should be set up so that it is readily available to pupils when they need it. Figure 12-1 shows an example of a classroom laboratory in a suburban New Jersey high school.

Special Assignments for Special Students

Another way to differentiate the assignment is to give special assignments to special students. These special assignments may be done as part of the regular classwork, in addition to the regular classwork, or instead of regular classwork. For example, in one English class, it became evident that one of the boys, although quite bright, was having a great deal of trouble with the ordinary classwork because he had not learned basic writing skills. So the teacher found special materials that were aimed at correcting his problem, wrote out a special study guide for him to follow, and put him to work on correcting his problem on a part-time basis. In that same class, a truly brilliant pupil obviously found the work too easy. The teacher took him off the ordinary course work and substituted a series of assignments from the syllabus of a literature course given in a nearby liberal arts college. The boy did very well at this college-level work that took the place of the ordinary high school work for an entire term. Pupils should be expected to work on such special assignments both during class time and out of class as homework. You can work with these students during the class period if you conduct the class as a laboratory or have small group and individual study sessions. You can also work with them during free periods and during the hours before and after school.

Units, Contracts, and Learning Activity Packets

Units, contracts, and learning activity packets are specialized versions of long-term differentiated assignments. They differ from each other only in detail. In spite of the surface differences, they are all versions that have been in use by educators for more than a half century.

Unit Teaching

In many schools, a unit is simply a topic about which a number of lessons are grouped. For instance, an inexperienced teacher of English, who has been teaching lyric poetry for a couple of weeks, might say that she is teaching a unit on lyric poetry, even though her teaching consists of nothing more than a series of

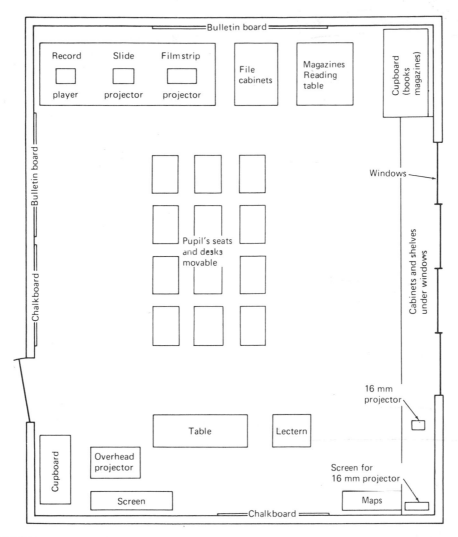

FIGURE 12-1 *A Classroom Laboratory.* [*Source:* Leonard H. Clark, *Teaching Social Studies in Secondary Schools: A Handbook* (New York: Macmillan Publishing Co., 1973), p. 126.]

nonrelated lessons having to do with lyric poetry. More sophisticated teachers would not consider such a series of lessons on a topic as a real unit. Rather, they believe the unit to be a "method of organizing subject matter, teaching techniques, and teaching devices so as to facilitate individualization of instruction, motivation, pupil planning, pupil responsibility for their own learning, and teaching emphasis on the higher levels of psychomotor, cognitive, and affective learning."[7] This type of unit has been described in Module 4. Combined with laboratory work, it is one of the most useful ways to provide for individual differences.

---

[7] Clark and Starr, op. cit., pp. 113–14.

Learning Activity Packets

Learning activity packets (also called instructional learning packets, learning modules, instructional modules, or learning packets) are developed in much the same way as are units. They are really an adaptation of the unit idea to meet the demands for individualized instruction, independent study, pupil acceptance of the responsibility for much of their own learning, and continuous progress promotion plans. They differ from units in that they place more emphasis on the individualized aspects. The procedures for building learning activity packets are included in Module 4.

The learning activity packets are best used in continuous progress plans in which pupils proceed at their own speeds and in their own direction under teacher guidance. Learning activity packets may also be given to pupils for independent study in traditional courses. They then would be handled just as any other independent study assignment or project. The implementation of a continuous progress plan is explained in a later section of this module.

The Contract Plan

Both units and learning modules can be set up as contracts. In a contract, the pupil agrees to do a certain amount of work of a certain quality during a certain period of time. Teachers frequently forget to specify that the pupil must meet both the requirements of *quality* and *quantity*. Quality control is sometimes quite difficult when teaching with the contract plan.

The procedure for setting up and using the contract plan is explained in Module 4.

Individualizing Instruction

The ideal way to provide for individual differences would be to provide each pupil with a tailor-made curriculum and lessons. Since every pupil is different, ideally every pupil should have a different curriculum and different learning experiences. At present, this is beyond our means. The differentiated assignments, units, and modules that we have described so far provide only partial differentiation for individuals or small groups, although modules may offer a good approach to the ultimate goal. In this section, let us consider some techniques that allow the teachers to concentrate on individual instruction.

Exercise 12 B

Review the uses of such techniques as the unit, the laboratory class, the learning activity packet, the module, the contract, and special assignments. In what ways could you individualize instruction when using these techniques?

Special Help

Undoubtedly, the most usual way to individualize instruction is to teach pupils on a one-to-one basis through the special help that most teachers give to pupils who need assistance for one reason or another. Teachers have always given special help to those who seem to need it and probably always will continue to do so, no matter how sophisticated teaching methods become. Students who are having difficulties and students who are doing well both need special help. At times, just inspecting a girl's work and giving her a pat on the back, or encouraging her to continue, or suggesting a new line of attack may be all that is needed. Often, to be of any real benefit, the special help will entail tutoring, or devising special instruction aimed specifically at correcting a student's faulty learning, or helping a student with some task he or she finds difficult. Perhaps the most interesting type of tutoring occurs when you help a pupil work on a difficult, advanced, independent project. To really help the boy who is having academic difficulty or the girl who needs special guidance as she forges ahead independently requires that you give them individualized assistance. The teacher, either as a tutor or as a guide, must teach pupils individually.

Continuous Progress Courses

The continuous progress course combines the use of learning activity packets or learning modules with a laboratory approach. Even if a school is not set up according to the continuous progress plan, you can arrange your own courses according to the plan. The procedure recommended for a continuous progress course has been presented in Module 4.

Use of Self-instructional Devices

Learning activity packets are self-instructional devices. They consist of the materials to use, instructions on how to use them, and self-correcting exercises and tests so that the students can instruct themselves. Self-administering and self-correcting materials of this sort make it much easier to individualize instruction. The fact that each student has directions, materials, and self-correcting tests and exercises frees the students and the teacher from the necessity of lockstep education. A teacher need not spend so much time telling what to do, how to do it, or giving and correcting exercises and tests. The time saved can be given over to individual instruction, tutoring, or special help. Homemade self-administering, self-correcting materials can be gleaned from a teacher's own experience and from old workbooks, textbooks, and tests. Although a teacher would not want to use an outdated text, its exercises might be easily adapted for self-correcting exercises.

Study Guides. Study guides are useful for individualizing instruction whether or not they are part of a module, unit, or contract. Special study guides that provide explicit instructions on how to carry out individual assignments or special projects can be very effective. Keep them on file. When students are ready to start a project or assignment, they can go to the file, draw out the study guide, and go to work. A good special study guide will inform students how to start, what some of the objectives are, present questions and problems to help them think, and point out things to look for. Exactly what it should contain, of course, depends upon the activity for which it is designed, but it should enable the student to function for varying periods of time without direct assistance from the teacher. Special study guides are discussed more fully in Module 4.

More general study guides have been described in discussion of the unit. In the study of philosophy, for instance, perhaps the study guide might consist of a series of questions for the pupil to consider; in science, it might point out selections to read, experiments to conduct and how to conduct them, what to observe, exercises to be done, and ideas to be considered.

Self-correcting Materials. Self-correcting materials, exercises, and tests can relieve a teacher of much busy work. Use them for diagnosis and practice. Do not use them for casting up term marks or for deciding whether a pupil has passed a unit or module. Mastery tests and similar teacher-administered and corrected, evaluative instruments should be used for that purpose. If self-administered, self-correcting materials are used for marking, it places too much responsibility on the pupils and tempts them to be dishonest.

In making self-administering, self-correcting exercises and tests, put the answers on a separate sheet of paper, or print them upside down on the test, or place them in the teacher's file. Even when it makes no difference, few people have enough willpower to resist the temptation to peek when the answers are easily available. Whatever arrangement you decide on, be sure that the students write their answers on separate sheets. Do not let them write on the test or exercise paper; then you can use the exercises or tests for other students and other classes. Some teachers believe that the best procedure is to keep all test and exercise papers on file so that students can obtain them whenever they need them; others pass them out with the study guide.

Machines for Teaching. Many of the new media devices are useful as self-instructional devices. The language laboratory, for instance, which is little more than a tape recorder or combination of tape recorders, is used for practice of pronunciation and pattern drills in a foreign language. There is no reason that this machine cannot be used for practice in oral English, dictation in business courses, and similar exercises. Some of these machines can play a number of tapes at once so that different pupils can practice different exercises at the same time or exercises in different languages.

The most sophisticated of self-instructional devices are computers and computer programs. By means of computer-assisted and computer-managed instruction it is quite possible to adjust students' instruction to their peculiar needs, abilities, and rates of learning. The use of teaching programs and computers is described in more detail in Modules 15 and 16.

But such sophisticated equipment is not really necessary. One can get much the same effect by giving tapes to all the pupils and letting individuals use the tape recorder whenever it is free. Tape recorders can be used for any number of other individualized lessons. Pupils can listen to different tapes, just as they read different books and articles. Exercises and lessons can also be put on tape for individual consumption. Teachers can dictate lessons and instructions to the tape recorder. The resultant tape can be played by individual students in class or during free or unscheduled periods. The tape will tell them what to do, ask them questions, and give them information. If they find the assignment difficult, they can repeat the playing of the tape or portions of the tape until they are satisfied. In order that the recorders be not too noisy, insist that pupils wear earphones while listening to them.

Many English departments have resorted to the tape recorder for help in critiquing composition efforts. Teachers discovered that covering student papers with red pencil markings served to create negative feelings about writing. They also discovered that writing at length their critical reaction or constructive suggestions for improvement on each student paper was time consuming and impersonal. Many, however, found out that dictating their commentary to the tape device was not only less onerous for them but much more intimate and rewarding to the students who listened to the playback, privately, before the following class period on composition. They discovered that many students who previously had not bothered to read the written critique were willing and eager to listen to the teacher observations when they were delivered orally.

The eight-millimeter, self-loading, individual viewing, motion picture projector can be used in the same way except that, ordinarily, the film to be used must be purchased rather than homemade. Homemade lessons can be prepared for the 35-mm slide projector, however. Prepare a sequence of slides that tells your story. If you wish to go to the trouble, you can make captioned slides or tape a commentary to go with the slides. Otherwise, you can ditto a commentary for the pupils to read as they look at the slides. Individual viewing of slides can be arranged easily by placing a screen of white cardboard close to the projector. With a little experimenting, you will be able to project a small but clear image that makes for very fine individual viewing. If possible, use a machine that allows you to preload your slides in trays for automatic or semiautomatic viewing. Be sure the slides are numbered so that the pupils will not get them mixed up. Also mark the slides at the top right corner so that pupils will load them into the machine right-side up.

Filmstrip and motion picture projectors will probably require that you use commercial materials rather than your own tailor-made lessons. Procedures for individualizing the use of these devices are described in Module 15.

The most sophisticated self-instructional devices are teaching machines and computers that use automated teaching programs. These devices, particularly in their most sophisticated versions, computer-assisted and computer-managed instruction, have tremendous potential for individualizing instruction. Because they are "autoinstructional," they make it possible for pupils to proceed at different speeds and in different directions. With a good computer-based program, there seems no reason why instruction could not be almost entirely individualized. Machine teaching, however, got off to a poor start because of poor programming and cost. Computer time is both expensive and difficult to provide to the ordinary classroom, although the new microcomputers may solve this problem. If you have these devices available to you, use them as you would other self-instructional devices. They are described in Module 16.

Correspondence and Television Courses. Perhaps the best tested of all self-instructional devices is the correspondence course. It has been used with great success for many years. Television and radio courses are also available. Many of these are excellent. Correspondence and television courses can be used to offer individual pupils instruction that otherwise would not be available to them. Pupils with special needs should be encouraged to make use of these kinds of courses. Use them just as you would any other learning activity packet.

Using Small Groups and Committees for Individualizing Instruction

To individualize instruction, a teacher may divide the class into groups or committees according to ability, interest, need, or task to be completed. The groups may or may not all study the same topic. Perhaps it is better if they do not.

When the deadline agreed upon for the termination of the activity has been reached, each of the groups or committees will perform the culminating activity it has prepared. In this fashion all students will experience the psychic satisfaction of having contributed to the overall growth of the class.

The following steps provide an outline well suited for most committee work. Not all of the steps will apply to all small-group committee work, however. Feel free to adapt them as necessary.

1. Pick a leader and a secretary.
2. Define the task.
3. Set the objectives.
4. Set up a plan.
   a. What tasks must be done?
   b. What material and/or equipment must be secured?
   c. How will information be shared among the committee members?
   d. What records or notes need be kept?
   e. Who will do each of the various tasks? When will the tasks be done?
   f. What are the time limits?
5. Implement the plan.
6. Share the results with each other.
7. Plan how to report the findings.
8. Make the report.[8]

Independent Study

One of the goals of education is to help students to learn to work independently; consequently, students should have practice in working independently. Independent study is one way to teach students to become self-sufficient, self-directing, and responsible. When the independent study concerns things that are important and interesting to the student, as it always should in secondary schools, it has an excellent motivating effect. To conduct independent study well, however, is quite difficult. One has to steer a course between too much guidance and consequent hampering of the student's independence, and not enough guidance and consequent chaos.

In conducting independent study, you should take the following precautions:

1. Be sure that the independent study is appropriate. Pupils tend to bite off too much, or to wander off into irrelevant areas. Sometimes they wish to do things for which the school does not have the proper facilities, equipment, or material. Try not to let pupils elect to do studies that they are going to have to give up before they finish. Study guides and learning activity packets eliminate much of this danger, but they also confine pupils

[8] Clark, op. cit., p. 96.

to preplanned topics that sometimes may not be appropriate for the needs of individual pupils.

2. In the beginning, have the pupils map out quite definitely what they hope to accomplish and how they hope to accomplish it; at this point, it may be wise to require each pupil to prepare a written agenda or plan for your approval. If the independent study plan follows a study guide or learning activity packet, much of this problem can be alleviated, although it may still be wise for the student to decide on a time schedule or agenda.

3. Keep a running check on each pupil's progress. All of us know how easy it is to put off term papers and other independent study. By checking, you can also catch potential difficulties, correct errors, and help misguided pupils to get back on the track before it is too late. Schedule conferences with the pupils so you will be sure that you check on everyone sufficiently and do not neglect anyone. Also take pains to be available to pupils and to let pupils know you welcome their requests for advice and guidance.

Acceleration

Some individuals can move more rapidly through courses than other pupils. This is possible if a teacher prepares units or learning packets in advance. It is also possible to allow pupils to accelerate in traditional classes by giving them special assignments or, more frequently, by letting pupils move through the ordinary assignments more rapidly. If you do not have the year's work entirely mapped out, there is probably no reason why the pupil should not follow last year's course work. If you have a syllabus or curriculum guide, then the planning for accelerating the exceptional student is relatively easy. Another easy way is to let pupils work through the readings and exercises of a good textbook or workbook plus supplementary work. Or you might draw upon items and exercises from other textbooks or workbooks.

Evaluating accelerated students' work may be something of a problem. The work these students are engaged in doing is beyond the call of duty. If they tried, they could devise ways of avoiding it by doing what the rest of the class is doing—and for top grades! And yet, to acknowledge shoddy work with high grades is not only to encourage poor scholarship but also the strengthening of study habits that will enhance the students' academic growth very little. Procedures for grading accelerated work should be carefully explored with students before the work is begun. The stress should be placed upon the quality of the work done as well as the quantity, with the due dates clearly delineated as well as the penalties for failure to meet clearly stipulated deadlines. To save building extra tests, you might have students demonstrate what they have learned by writing summaries of the topic. Test banks also can be very helpful in this situation.

Projects

The project is a form of independent study in which an individual or a small group attempts to produce something—e.g., a map, a model, a booklet, a paper, or a report. At one time the term project referred primarily or solely to something having tangible value such as a vase, or a lamp, or some article made for one's own pleasure and use, or as a present. The motivational power of this form of study was thought to derive from its similarity to real life, that is, adult life, where the need for the product supplies the motivation for the work to be done.

Pupils should do projects because they want to and because the product to be completed seems valuable to them. Therefore, they should decide whether to do a project, what project to do, and how to do it. You, as a teacher, should limit yourself to advising and guiding pupils so that their projects will be successful. Projects laid out by teachers are not really projects; they are assignments.

When you use projects in your teaching, the following procedure is recommended:

1. Stimulate ideas by providing lists of things pupils might do, asking former pupils to tell about past projects, suggest readings that might give pupils ideas for projects, or use class discussion to explore possible projects.
2. Let pupils select a project or not. Pupils who do not wish to do a project should be allowed to do something else.
3. Let the pupils plan the procedure they will follow. Help them with their planning.
4. Guide the pupils as they proceed with their plan. The worth inherent in this form of study derives not only from individual contributions to the tangible product but also in the group learnings that can result from the experience.
5. Evaluate the pupils' work.

Making Time for Individual Instruction

Individual instruction is an extremely time-consuming way of teaching. Unless one is willing to relinquish the center of the stage and allow pupils to accept much of the responsibility for their own learning, it is an impossible task. To help pupils to make the right decisions, you will have to provide them with self-instructional materials, study guides, learning packets, and self-administering and self-correcting tests and exercises. With these materials, the pupils can move ahead without waiting for you. Without them, you will never find time to do all the work that needs to be done with each individual.

In addition, arrange for pupils to help each other. Young people often learn better from their peers. Bright students can help the slower students, but more effective perhaps is to let the average or slow student, who has mastered a concept or skill, help students who have not yet done so. Be careful that you do not exploit your successful students, however.

If you keep your classes informal, as in the laboratory approach, you will find that you have much more time to do important things than if you keep to formal classes. Still, no matter what approach you use, you will be busy.

Accepting Different Evidence of Accomplishment

If, in order to provide for individual differences, you arrange for students to learn in different ways, you must also allow for different evidences of pupil progress. Of course, everyone should attain the essential learnings. However, if you allow some pupils to learn through the dance, and some to learn by making models, then you should consider the special learnings that are concomitant with these learning activities in estimating pupil achievement.

Need for a Variety of Materials

To provide for individual differences one must have things to do it with. The single textbook course will no longer suffice. You need material to suit a variety of interests and different ability levels. Not only do you need a variety of materials but also you need them to be where the pupils can get them when they need them. The classroom suitable for truly individualized instruction must be full of attractive, usable materials, readily available for pupil use. Such a classroom would in itself be a resource center—truly a laboratory for learning.

The time for you to start preparing for the creation of an appropriate resource-center type of classroom is now. To wait until you meet your first class of students in your first teaching position will unnecessarily inhibit you from reaching your goal. If you have not already started a filing system to preserve pictures and charts and handouts, start now. In a simple cardboard box preserve and catalogue those items you come across in your study or in your daily living that may some day prove of value for your purpose. Down the road you may need to edit your collection to keep it at manageable size. However, it is easier to delete, later, some of the items you have saved than it is to find the precise one that will meet your needs which you neglected to preserve.

Teaching Homogeneously Grouped Classes

In many schools, pupils are grouped homogeneously, either by a deliberate plan of ability grouping, or by incidental selection as the more academically talented pupils select the more academically rigorous courses, or by a combination of both these influences. In these circumstances, varying your course content and methods of teaching according to your type of class will make your teaching much more effective.

The Academically Talented

You can use all of the secondary school teaching methods in classes for the academically talented, because most of them were first invented with academically talented pupils in mind. The important thing is to make the work interesting and challenging and to give the pupils plenty of opportunity to use their talents. The following suggestions may help you:

1. Encourage the talented to think. Use problem solving, inquiry, and open-ended assignments. Insist that pupils dig into the subject. Hold them to a high level of analysis and critical thinking.
2. See to it that the talented keep to high academic standards. Do not accept sloppy thinking or sloppy work. Force them to discipline themselves and their thinking.
3. Don't hold them back. Give them a chance to move on to the new, the

interesting, and the challenging. Don't make them repeat what they already know.

4. Be sure they become well grounded in the academic skills.

5. Give them lots of responsibility for their own work. Let them plan and evaluate. Encourage independent study and research.

6. Use high-level materials: original sources, college textbooks, and adult materials.

7. Use the seminar discussion strategy in which students present and criticize original papers or reports and discuss topics in depth. Be sure that their discussions hew to a high level of criticism and thinking.

The Academically Slow

The slow sections cause teachers problems because the students, as a rule, find most schoolwork difficult and unappetizing. Because it seems difficult for them and they often fail, most academically slow students develop an aversion to schoolwork. Your job, when you have a section of these students, is to try to make the work interesting to them, to build their skills so that they can perform reasonably well, and to make the school situation less distasteful to them.

Among the things you can do are the following:

1. Try to make the work seem important and relevant to their own lives. Use subject matter that has meaning and significance to them personally. Show them how their learning will pay off in personal benefits.

2. Diagnose. Find out what their difficulties are and help them overcome them. If they do not have the necessary skills or background, try to find a way of remedying any difficult situation.

3. Emphasize the development rather than the remedial aspects. Review and summarize frequently. As much as possible, apply new learning to practical situations.

4. Avoid infantile materials. If a pupil has not learned something in five years, going over it in the same way once again will not correct the deficiency. Try to use lively new approaches. Keep the material to be learned adult even if it must be simple. Keep problems and activities short and easy.

5. Take your time. Avoid rushing the pupils. Present new work slowly. Move forward in short steps. Don't take shortcuts. Teach the details. Be sure students have the basics before you move on. Show them how to do the assignments. Be sure your explanations are simple, clear, and thorough.

6. Encourage, praise, and help. Build up the students' confidence and self-esteem as much as you can.

7. Use concrete subject matter. Keep abstractions at a minimum. Let students work with things rather than with words.

8. Give plenty of individual attention. Help students with their study skills and with subject matter. Be patient, understanding, and helpful, but not bossy.

9. **Use lots of audiovisual materials.** They should be simple and clear, but of high-interest level.
10. **Give plenty of practice in thinking.** Slow learners need to learn how to think logically just as much as the bright students do. Use the same discussion techniques as you would with bright students except that with the slow learners you will probably have to provide the basic data.
11. **Let students learn from each other.** They may gain much, both intellectually and socially, from helping each other. Besides, it makes the learning process less threatening.
12. **Give such students plenty of opportunity to do their assignments in class.** Do not count on their getting much accomplished as homework. In supervised study sessions, you can help them and they can help each other.

Disadvantaged Students

The children of the poor are bright, slow, and average, just as other students are. The bright ones should be treated just as any other bright students, and the slow ones as any other slow students. However, because of the concomitants of poverty and life experiences in poor neighborhoods, there are some special considerations that you should keep in mind even though they may not apply to specific students.

Poor youths are likely to be disaffected and suspicious of school. Much of the schoolwork they have had has seemed irrelevant to their lives. They may feel that in the school situation the cards are stacked against them. Sometimes, at least, they are probably right. Their past schooling may have been inadequate and they may have been slow in performing traditional intellectual tasks. Consequently, they may have been deemed to be academically incompetent despite being actually potentially brilliant. Their customs and life-styles may be considerably different from those espoused by the school. Often, the language that is native to them is not the standard English that the school believes to be requisite for scholastic success. (Do not mistake, as many have done, language differences for an inability to express oneself. The children of poor parents are usually fluent in a rich but nonstandard English dialect or a foreign language. The language may be deficient in words by which to express abstractions, however.)

The characteristics we have just pointed out tend to be dysfunctional in the ordinary secondary school class. To some extent, then, one makes adjustments in curriculum and methods when teaching poor youth. Still, on the whole, the same tactics and strategies should be used for both poor and affluent youth, due allowance being made for the differences in each particular situation. Courses for poor youth should not be watered down. Neither should course requirements. Poor youth have the same potentials as rich youth. To water down the courses and requirements is to demean them and to deprive them of the benefits of a good education. Intensive remedial work should be provided whenever needed, and every effort should be made to make the course work relevant to the lives of the pupils.

Following are twelve suggestions that may help you when teaching the children of the poor.

1. Respect the pupils as people. If their culture is different learn their taboos and mores; respect their culture just as you hope they will learn to respect yours.

2. Pay great attention to motivation. Fight anti-intellectualism by showing pupils that the subject matter is worthwhile. Point out its practical value. Pick topics to study that have obvious importance.

3. Be sure the course content has meaning to the students and relates to their lives and interests. Be sure the content helps the students to understand themselves and their role so that they can learn how to function in society. Do not put this at a low how-to-do-it level, but at a high enough level so that they can understand what is really involved. Give them real work. Do not feed them pap. If the pupils cannot do the work required of them, substitute work they can do, but make it something respectable.

4. Give students opportunities to succeed. Praise them when they do well, but avoid gushiness. Make it evident that you expect them to learn just like everyone else, that you see no reason why they cannot, and that you intend to see to it that they really get their money's worth out of the course. Recognize that students from minorities may have unrealistically low aspiration levels and consequently may have little interest in classwork. The first task for you is to help such individuals see themselves in a more favorable light.

5. Be firm, strict, and definite, but not harsh. Harsh measures may seem to work on the surface, but, as a rule, they make it more difficult to carry out any meaningful communication or real learning. The basic rules that you establish must be kept simple and reasonable and be fully explained. Once established the rules must be enforced firmly but without humiliation of the offender. Challenge students who enter class late or who fail to complete assignments; insist upon quiet rather than try to speak above the noise; discourage aimless wandering from place to place. Some individuals are accustomed to meet hostility with more hostility. Avoid creating an audience situation by engaging in argument in front of the class.

6. Use laboratory techniques, individual instruction, and individual help on basic skills. Adjust the subject content to the needs of the pupils. Because many of the pupils are physically oriented, they enjoy working on concrete projects. Begin at the pupils' level and then move toward the more abstract and academic.

7. Use simple language in the classroom. Worry less about the words pupils use and the way they express themselves and more about the ideas they are expressing. Let them use their own idioms without carping on grammar, syntax, and the like. Give only one instruction at a time making certain that it is executed before another is made. Disadvantaged students are often easily confused.

8. Use unstructured discussions of real problems. Unstructured discussions

may help you understand the pupils and help them learn how to express themselves. In selecting problems to study,

a. Be sure the problems seem real to the pupils.

b. Be sure to pick problems they will accept.

Sometimes they do not recognize problems as problems. Sometimes they do not want to. In such cases you may get them to see the truth by challenging their thinking. The Socratic method is useful for this purpose. Use it to pursue the faulty thinking of individual pupils. However, in doing so, be careful to let each pupil keep his self-respect. On the other hand, do not force pupils into discussions they would rather avoid. There is no point in discussing what they already know too much about.

9. Use inductive approaches. Students seem to respond better to open-ended questioning than they do to memorizing, for instance.

10. Sometimes students greatly enjoy and profit from role playing and dramatization. Simulations like *City 1, Consumer,* and *Poor People's Choice* seem to go very well. Students appear to be able to work out mental problems best when they can do things.

11. If students have not learned basic skills because of failures in the elementary school grades, help them learn those skills.

12. Use a variety of reading materials. Use multiple readings in laboratory fashion rather than the single textbook. Use adult material of low reading level. Use materials other than reading matter for pupils who cannot read: tapes, recordings, video, films, and pictures. Where no suitable reading matter is available, prepare your own.[9]

Handicapped Students

In Public Law 94-142, the Education for All Handicapped Children Act, the Congress mandates that all students have the right to a full and free public education. The legislation requires the least restrictive environment for special students—the hard of hearing, the deaf, the speech impaired, the visually handicapped, the mentally handicapped, the emotionally disturbed, and the orthopedically impaired. It has placed emphasis on mainstreaming and a normalized environment for all students.

In effect, this means that you must be, part of your time, a special education teacher. Basically, special education teaching is not so very different from ordinary teaching except that it requires more care, better diagnosis, greater skill, more attention to individual needs, and greater understanding of the pupils. Yet, the challenges of teaching handicapped persons in the regular class are great enough so that to do the job right, you need additional specialized training far beyond the scope of this book. Before you get far into your teaching career, you should take courses in teaching the handicapped in regular classrooms.

Because of its concern for problems of the handicapped, Congress has decreed that an Individualized Educational Program (IEP) be devised for each handi-

---

[9] Clark, op. cit., pp. 133–134.

capped pupil. According to law, each IEP should be made up by a team of specialized personnel, parents, and classroom teachers yearly. It should contain (1) a statement of the pupil's present educational levels, (2) the educational goals for the year, (3) specifications for the services to be provided and the extent to which the student should be expected to take part in the regular program, and (4) the type, direction, and evaluative criteria for the services to be provided. Consultation by special and skilled support personnel becomes essential in all mainstream models. The consultant works directly with teachers or with students and parents. You should have an active role in the preparation of these specifications for the handicapped students assigned to your classes as well as the major responsibility for carrying them out.

Some general guidelines for working with handicapped students within the framework of the regular class are:

1. Maintain a consistent approach. Students find themselves very frustrated when they can't depend upon teacher reactions to their responses.
2. Define objectives in behavioral terms.
3. Adapt and modify materials and procedures to the special needs of the handicapped. Children with cardiac conditions can be umpires in baseball games. A child who cannot sit still for longer than ten minutes might require a change in learning activity every ten minutes.
4. Reward approved and acceptable behavior and generally ignore unacceptable behavior.
5. In planning lessons, break complex activities into simple components, move from the known to the unknown, let slower children learn through interesting and real experiences.
6. Anticipate. Watch for signs of restiveness, frustration, anxiety, unwillingness to work. Change assignments on an individual basis, if necessary.
7. Provide for as much student success as you can. Handicapped children have not usually experienced much success. Give them activities and experiences that ensure success and some mastery.

Ethnic Differences

Because this is a land of many cultures, you may find in your classes pupils of ethnic origin different from your own. It may be that the class will represent one group, or it may be that several groups are represented. (A teacher in a metropolitan high school found that her fluent Persian was of little help in her class of students speaking five different languages.)

When teaching pupils from different cultural groups, try to become as familiar as possible with their language and culture. Try to incorporate ethnic materials into your classes. Help them to be proud of both their ethnic heritage and their Americanism. Help them make the most of their backgrounds. Try to utilize their taboos, mores, and values in your teaching strategies. If they have come to you speaking a nonstandard English dialect or a foreign tongue, help them to learn standard English, but do not make a fetish of it. Your primary purpose is to help them learn the subject. Do, however, try to learn their language, be it a foreign language or street argot, so that you can understand and communicate with them. In short, treat these students and their cultures with the respect they deserve.

Recapitulation

The individualization of instruction requires that you provide opportunities for pupils to work toward different goals, to study different content, and to work in different ways. Just to vary the rate or amount of work the pupils do is not enough. A list of fifteen techniques and methods you might use follows. Each of these methods or techniques has been described somewhere in this module. As you go through the list, see if you can describe how to carry out each of the techniques.

1. Vary your tactics and techniques in classes according to the abilities and personality characteristics of your pupils.
2. Run your class as a classroom laboratory.
3. Utilize the facilities of the library or resource center.
4. Utilize small-group instruction.
5. Differentiate your classwork and homework assignments.
6. Give special assignments to individual pupils or small groups.
7. Use individual or group projects.
8. Encourage independent study.
9. Use the unit method and unit assignments.
10. Use self-instructional materials such as self-correcting assignments, learning packets, programmed materials, teaching machines, computer-assisted instruction, and correspondence and television courses.
11. Give pupils special help.
12. Use the contract plan.
13. Use a continuous progress scheme. (You can run your course on a continuous progress plan even if the plan has not been adopted schoolwide.)
14. Use minicourses.
15. Use a variety of textbooks, readings, and other materials.[10]

Suggested Reading

Banks, James A. *Teaching Strategies for Ethnic Studies,* 2d ed. Boston: Allyn & Bacon, 1979.

Brockman, Ellen Mary, ed. *Teaching Handicapped Students Mathematics.* Washington, D.C.: National Education Association, 1981.

Charles, C. M. *Individualizing Instruction,* 2d ed. St. Louis, Mo.: C. V. Mosby, 1980.

Corrick, Marshall, ed. *Teaching Handicapped Students Science.* Washington, D.C.: National Education Association, 1981.

Dunn, Rita, and Kenneth Dunn. *Teaching Students Through Their Individual Learning Styles: A Practical Approach.* Reston, Va.: Reston Publishing, 1978.

Fenstermacher, Gary D., and John I. Goodlad. *Individual Differences and the Common Curriculum,* Eighty-second Yearbook of the National Society for the Study of Education, Part I. Chicago: The University of Chicago Press, 1983.

---

[10] Ibid., pp. 124–125.

George, Paul, and Gordon Lawrence. *Handbook for Middle School Teaching*. Glenview, Ill.: Scott Foresman, 1982.

Palomake, Jane, ed. *Teaching Handicapped Students Vocational Education*. Washington, D.C.: National Education Association, 1981.

Stephens, Thomas M., et al. *Teaching Mainstreamed Students*. New York: John Wiley & Sons, 1982.

Tuttle, Frederick B. *Gifted and Talented Students, What Research Says to the Teacher,* revised ed. Washington, D.C.: National Education Association, 1983.

Wehlage, Gary G. *Effective Programs for the Marginal High School Student,* Fastback 191. Bloomington, Ind.: Phi Delta Kappa Educational Foundation, 1983.

Wright, Jill D. *Teaching the Gifted and Talented in the Middle School,* Washington, D.C.: National Education Association, 1983.

Post Test

1. What does true individualization of instruction entail?

2. Give a theoretical justification for homogeneous grouping.

3. Explain "homogeneously grouped classes are not homogeneous."

4. Sometimes homogeneous grouping shortchanges the less academically inclined pupils. How and why?

5. What are the supposed merits of continuous promotion?

6. What is the principal reason for introducing minicourses?

_____

7. What is the advantage of having a learning center?

_____

_____

8. Name at least two ways in which one can differentiate an assignment.

_____

_____

9. What is meant by the term *classroom laboratory?*

_____

_____

_____

_____

10. Why is the unit approach a good method for providing for individual differences?

_____

_____

_____

11. Why is the learning activity package a good instrument for individualizing instruction?

_____

_____

_____

12. What is the essential difference between a learning contract and a learning activity packet or unit?

_____

13. Why are study guides useful in individualizing instruction?

_____

_____

_____

14. For what would you use self-correcting materials?

_____

15. How can you adapt a slide projector for individual viewing?

_____

_____

16. How can you adapt a motion picture projector for individual viewing?

_____

_____

17. How can you make time for working with individuals?

_____

_____

18. What difference in teaching style does homogeneous grouping require of you?

_____

_____

_____

_____

19. What should be contained in an IEP?

_____

_____

20. List five suggestions for teaching the academically talented.

_____

_____

_____

_____

_____

21. List five suggestions for teaching disadvantaged students.

_____

_____

_____

_____

_____

MODULE
13

Measurement and Evaluation

The first edition of this module was written by Isobel L. Pfeiffer of the University of Akron.
It has been somewhat revised and updated by the editors for this edition.

337

Rationale

Evaluation is an integral part of the educational scene. Curricula, buildings, materials, specific courses, teachers, supervisors, administrators, equipment—all must be appraised in relation to student learning, the ultimate goal of the school. When gaps between anticipated results and achievement exist, attempts are made to eliminate those factors that seem to be limiting the educational output, or otherwise to improve the situation. Thus, educational progress occurs.

To learn effectively, students must know how they are doing. Similarly, to be an effective teacher, you must be informed on what the student knows, feels, and can do so that you can build on student skills, knowledge, and attitudes. Therefore you need continuous feedback indicating student progress and problems in order to plan appropriate learning activities. If this feedback tells you that progress is slow, you can provide alternative activities; if it indicates that students have already mastered the desired learning, you can eliminate unnecessary practice. In short, evaluation provides a key for both effective teaching and learning.

The importance of continuous evaluation mandates that you know the principles and techniques of evaluation and measurement. This module will explain some principles of evaluation and show you how to construct and use tests and other evaluative techniques. We define the general terms related to evaluation; consider what makes a good test; relate the criteria to standardized and teacher-made tests; suggest procedures to use in test construction; point out the advantages and disadvantages of different types of test items; and explain the construction and use of other evaluative devices and techniques.

Specific Objectives

At the conclusion of your study of this module, it is expected that you will be able to do the following:

1. Define evaluation and measurement, indicating two specific differences between the terms.
2. Explain the distinction between a norm-referenced test and a criterion-referenced test, and give an example of the appropriate use of each.
3. List five criteria for selecting a test and cite a purpose for each criterion.
4. Set up a table of specifications for a unit test and classify five items in correct cells in the table.
5. Cite five different uses of test results.
6. Give four different types of objective questions, and indicate one advantage and one disadvantage of each type.
7. Specify four guidelines for a teacher preparing an essay test.
8. Define percentile, stanine, and grade equivalence, and explain a use of each.
9. Demonstrate two devices by which one might ensure objectivity in one's evaluation of a product or process.
10. Diagram a teaching model and indicate where evaluation is utilized.

Module Text

A Teaching Model

When Bob Kelly begins his daily trip to his job, his usual route is Lincoln to Main, Main to College, and College to the parking lot beside Central High School. Since construction has started on the new highway, Bob sometimes has to change his route. If the Lincoln-Main intersection is blocked, he goes on Washington to Lake Street, and then over to Main. In the fall, when the family is still staying at the cottage, his drive to work takes him in a southeasterly direction instead of the northwest route he takes from home. Then, occasionally, he has an errand, mailing a package or returning a book to the library. Again his trip is adjusted to the situation. How are such revised routes planned? Often with little conscious effort, since the driver is familiar with the area, knows where he is going, where he is, and what must be accomplished enroute.

If Bob Kelly is driving in a city unfamiliar to him, he plans his route more carefully, using a map or specific directions provided by someone who is acquainted with the area. In such a situation, he may recognize another possibility. Without a street number, sign, or other recognizable clue, he may not know when he reaches his destination. So the final target, which is obvious in a familiar situation (going to work), may not be so easily determined in a strange or unfamiliar setting.

The teacher's plans for the educational journeys of the students in a class require answers to the same basic questions: *Where are we going?; Where are we now?; How do we get where we are going?;* and *How do we know when we get there?*

These are questions that must be considered in educational evaluation. The answers provide the teacher with the basis for working with individuals and with groups. Since, in the never-static educational setting, the answers are ever-changing, the teacher continuously assesses and adjusts flexible plans to the new situation.

The basic question of goals, or where are we going, is in a broad sense determined by society. State requirements and limitations, school board policies, curricula, and courses of study usually evolve with input from all segments of the community. Major factors considered include society, the students, the school, and the future. The purpose and philosophy of the school distilled from the collected efforts of all of these forces provide the broad objectives for the teacher (the where). Guidelines in each course of study provide the framework within which the teacher will make selections of content and strategies (what and how). For those individuals who believe that process is a crucial goal of education, the strategies relate to objectives. If one objective is that the student will be able to demonstrate a rational method of attacking a new problem, then a problem-solving approach must be implemented in the classroom. If, however, the objective is the rote memorization of tribal lore or the accumulation and retention of a wide variety of facts about the world in general, a different approach will be called for. The teacher, in selecting specific objectives and activities appropriate for the situation, exerts considerable influence on the learning environment and helps determine where we are going.

"Start where the student is" is a pedagogical cliché. Nevertheless, the statement emphasizes the need to know where we are before we can make reasonable plans for progress. A student who reads at the third-grade level is not going to be able to cope successfully with a social studies text written on the seventh-grade reading level. A student who does not comprehend percentage is not ready for interest problems. Diagnostic tests are one tool for determining where we are. Other evaluation procedures can also provide information about skills and understanding, such as reading a paragraph and giving an oral summary to indicate comprehension, driving a golf ball to demonstrate the skill, and writing a description of a picture to reveal how well the student can write a paragraph. Students are frustrated and do not progress educationally when they are bored by tasks that they have already mastered, as well as by tasks that require skills or knowledge they do not have. Information about a student's achievement provides a basis for appropriate planning to stimulate further development.

Information about where we are going (objectives) and where we start (achievement and attitude of students) enables the teacher to propose several plans for reaching the goals. Students, for example, may work as individuals or in groups on common goals or on specific individualized objectives. Selection and implementation of a plan and of appropriate learning activities require continuing evaluation to check on progress and to adopt strategies to promote the desired student behavior. When student feedback indicates satisfactory attainment of objectives, the teacher moves to a new unit, problem, or content area, and develops another learning cycle. In the learning cycle (Figure 13-1) evaluation is critical. It establishes the starting point, provides data on progress, and indicates arrival at the destination. A teacher must recognize the need for good evaluation and measurement, and must develop skill in preparing effective instruments.

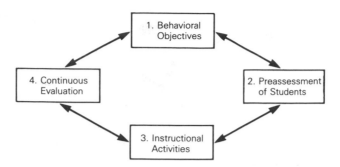

FIGURE 13-1 *Learning Cycle*

Evaluation and Measurement

The terms *evaluation* and *measurement* are related. Measurement refers to quantifiable data and relates to specific behavior. Tests and the statistical procedures used to analyze the results are the emphases in measurement. Evaluation includes measurement data plus other types of information, such as anecdotal records, and written and oral performance ratings. Evaluation also involves a value judgment factor. A teacher may share the information that May Grisso received the top score in East High School on the College Entrance Examination Board Scholastic Aptitude Test (SAT); this statement refers to measurement. However, when the teacher adds that May has not been an outstanding student in the English program at East, evaluation has occurred. Measurement is descriptive and objective, whereas evaluation involves information from varied sources including subjective value input.

Assessment and *appraisal* are two other terms often used. Both of these suggest going beyond the quantifiable information to a personal interpretation or evaluation. The National Assessment of Educational Progress is dealing with measurement in specific content areas for ages nine, thirteen, seventeen, and for adults. Since this testing covers the United States and is expected to provide data to improve the curriculum, the use of assessment as a synonym for evaluation seems appropriate.

Tools for Educational Measurement

Over the years teachers have used four basic approaches for assessing pupil progress: (1) the oral test, which survives as the "orals" given to candidates for advanced degrees and in casual classroom questioning; (2) the observation of pupil performance; (3) the examination of samples of the products of pupil activity; and (4) the written test with which we are all so familiar.

Criterion-referenced and Norm-referenced Instruments

The instruments used in any of these approaches may be criterion-referenced or norm-referenced. *Criterion-referenced* tests, sometimes called mastery tests, are designed to check whether or not the learners have met the basic objectives of a learning segment. Their object is to determine whether or not students can or cannot perform at a set standard. They are, in effect, what the astronauts call "go—no go" instruments. They are not designed to sort out the best from the average or the less than average, but to determine whether or not individuals have met the standard. If students do not meet the standard, presumably they should be given more opportunity to learn the concept or skill, or be failed. They are not particularly tied into age and grade-time-schedules as are other tests because they take into consideration the fact that not all students will progress at the same rate nor be at the same level at the same time. In this kind of testing it is the mastery that is sought and time is a variable instead of the reverse. Programmed materials, continuous progress courses, and some competency-based curricula rely on such instruments.

Norm-referenced tests, on the other hand, are designed to compare pupils with each other and to determine each individual's standing. They are useful when the concern is communication of information about students to parents, colleges, or employing agencies. They reflect the influence of our competitive social structure and because most citizens have been exposed to their *modus operandi,* they are understood fairly well by patrons of the school. They facilitate the process, for example, of selecting the six most accurate math students in a grade or in deciding into which reading group to place a new student when he joins a class. They also are relied upon as predictors of future success, as, for example, when selections are made for admissions after the college aptitude exams have been administered. It is expected that those who score highest will be most likely to succeed in advanced classes. Since some items in norm-referenced tests are easy and some are difficult, by design, it is possible to list students' results in a continuum from highest to lowest and examine specifically where each stands with regard to the other test-takers.

For instance, you might use a norm-referenced test to determine a student's reading level. The individual's score in relation to the group may be expressed in various ways. Percentile rank is commonly used. If George Howe's reading score is at the 35th percentile for tenth-graders, then 35 of 100 tenth-graders who took the test scored below George. Another frequently used system for representing relative performance is stanines. This standard nine-point scale was developed during World War II as a simple and usable norm. A single digit from a low of 1 to a high of 9 indicates where the individual score falls in relation to the group. (See Table 13-1.) George Howe's reading score at the 35th percentile rank can also be described as in stanine 4.

Similarly, grade equivalents are sometimes used to represent the relative performance of students on a test. This method is expressed in two numbers; for example, 9.4 shows the arithmetic average (mean) of students in the fourth month of the ninth grade. The calendar year is divided into ten parts, nine representing the school year and one for summer vacation. George Howe's grade equivalent of 8.2 indicates, according to the test, that as a tenth-grader he reads as well as the average student in the second month of the eighth grade.

These three methods of expressing scores are used to indicate how an individual score compares to the group. Percentile and grade equivalent are perhaps more easily understood by parents and teachers. The stanine and other standard scores are more useful because the difference between steps remains the same. They are all examples of norm-referencing. Techniques for calculating and interpreting such scores will be discussed in a following section of this module.

TABLE 13-1
Comparison of Percentiles and Stanines

Stanine	1	2	3	4	5	6	7	8	9
Percentile	1–4	5–11	12–23	24–40	41–60	61–77	78–89	90–96	97–100

Probably both criterion-referenced and norm-referenced tests have a place in secondary schools today. The teacher, recognizing the differences in purpose and use, must select or construct the appropriate type. As a rule, norm-referenced tests better lend themselves to ordinary school marking systems, whereas criterion-referenced tests are more useful for diagnosis, individualizing instruction, and determining pupil competency.

Types of Tests

Pedagogical tests differ both in form and purpose. Let us look at a sampling of the different types of tests commonly used by classroom teachers. Remember, this list is not an exhaustive study of testing. You will come across other types of tests in your teaching.

Achievement tests are designed to measure the student's level of accomplishment: how much a student has learned about a subject area or a segment of that subject. They are usually commercially prepared and are accompanied by charts and manuals to assist in scoring and interpreting student results.

Teacher-made tests are commonly achievement tests prepared by the teacher to measure student learning in a specific area. A *pretest* is given prior to planned instructional activities. The pretest should provide information about student background that is pertinent to the content and should help the teacher plan more efficiently, in the light of the student strengths and weaknesses revealed by the test. Prerequisite skills and concepts that have not been acquired can be incorporated in the plan. Unnecessary duplication can be eliminated. Students with expertise in the area can be utilized in the instructional program. A *post test* is given at the end of instruction to indicate student achievement at that point. The difference between pretest and post test scores gives an indication of student growth.

A *standardized test* is one prepared with careful research by testing experts so that the instrument represents desirable test characteristics. A test manual that is usually available provides information about administering the test, scoring it, and interpreting results. Norms also are provided as a basis for comparison to a large group or population. These tests are useful for assessing such qualities as students' intellectual abilities, academic achievement, attitudes, interests, and aptitudes. As a rule they give one a single score or measurement level by which one can estimate the differences among individuals and changes in knowledge, behavior, interests, and the like on an individual over a period of time.

An *objective test* is one that can be scored consistently; the answers are either right or wrong. This type of test is probably most frequently used in schools.

True-false, multiple-choice, and matching are examples of types of questions used on objective tests.

Essay tests require original student responses to a question and are considered subjective measures. Different people may react differently when scoring responses in a test of this sort. The same person scoring on two or three occasions could arrive at two or three different scores. Often the answers cannot be considered right or wrong, but involve such value judgment as "more logical," "better evidence," or "more important point."

Speed tests include time as a factor in the test. This should be applied only when the time involved in the performance is critical. Typing tests are commonly timed.

Power tests are those that allow the student sufficient time to respond to the items. A teacher should provide time for 90 per cent of the students to complete a test in which time should not be considered as a part of the test.

A *diagnostic test* is specifically designed to determine the students' deficiencies. A *readiness test* is constructed to find out whether the student has the understanding, skills, and, sometimes, motivation to go to the next level.

A *performance test* is designed to indicate the level at which the student can accomplish a specific skill, usually psychomotor in emphasis. The physical education programs utilize these tests, such as in shooting baskets or in executing a tennis serve. Vocational education uses performance tests frequently, also. To make objective the observation of performance of this sort, teachers frequently turn to *rating scales* or *checklists*.

Standardized Testing

Standardized tests are useful for assessing such qualities as students' intellectual abilities, academic achievement, attitudes, interests, and aptitudes. They are used both to measure the differences among individuals and to determine changes in an individual's knowledge, behavior, interests, emotions, and the like over a period of time. They are common tools for determining a person's mental ability, suitability for employment, special aptitudes, career placement, personality deviation, grade placement, college admission, and so on. They are especially useful for surveying broad areas of achievement. They are called standardized tests because they, after being carefully prepared, have been given to a large presumably representative standardizing group of persons whose test scores have been treated statistically to set up norms by which to judge the meaning of individuals' test scores.

Some standardized achievement tests, for instance, can tell one how the achievement of individual students or classes compares with that of students in the country at large, whereas other standardized achievement tests can be used to point out an individual student's strengths and weaknesses for diagnostic purposes. They are seldom valuable for determining student progress in a particular course, however, for they usually do not sufficiently reflect the objectives and content of specific courses. Personality character, aptitude, and intelligence tests that reflect students' inclinations and potentials are also excellent diagnostic tools.

In general, standardized tests fall into three basic categories: general intelligence and achievement tests, attitude and personality tests (including projective tests), and interest and aptitude tests.

General Intelligence Tests. General intelligence tests are the oldest type of standardized tests. They were invented at the turn of the century in attempts to find ways to identify children's learning potential. Perhaps the most important step in this movement was the development by Binet and Simon of tests by which to identify feebleminded or retarded children for the French government. From these tests and their revisions by Lewis M. Terman come the concepts of mental age and intelligence quotient or IQ. By mental age the testers meant a person's score on a test of mental ability expressed in terms of the average chronological age of persons whose score was the same as his: e.g., if a boy's mental test score is equal to that of the average nine-year-old, his mental score is 9, no matter what his chronological age may be. The intelligence quotient, which was derived from the mental age concept for the Stanford-Binet test (Terman's 1916 revision of the Binet-Simon test), was the ratio of the mental age, as defined by the tests, and the chronological age. Until the 1960s it was indicated by the formula

$$IQ = \frac{MA}{CA} \times 100.$$

Since the 1960s, however, the IQ scores of the Stanford-Binet tests, and many other tests, have been reported as deviation IQs in which the IQ is reported as a standard score whose mean is 100 and whose standard deviation is 16.[1]

The Stanford-Binet test and the Wechsler Intelligence Scale for Children (WISC) and the Wechsler Adult Intelligence Scale (WAIS), which have been widely used in recent years, are individual tests. They are time-consuming to give and require the services of a highly skilled professional to administer, score, and interpret. Since World War I, however, when the U.S. Army invented the pencil and paper Army Alpha group test to test the intelligence of recruits, many group intelligence tests have been published. Among them are such well-known tests as

1. California Test of Mental Maturity.
2. Henman Nelson Tests of Mental Ability.
3. Kuhlmann-Anderson Tests.
4. Lorge-Thorndike Intelligence Tests.
5. Terman-McNemar Test of Mental Ability.
6. School and College Ability Tests (SCAT).
7. Scholastic Aptitude Test (SAT).
8. Graduate Record Examination (GRE—a combination of intelligence and achievement tests).
9. Miller Analogies Test.
10. College Entrance Examination Board tests (CEEB—frequently called the College Boards).

In addition, textbook houses and test publishers have published a great number of group tests aimed at measuring student achievement in various subject fields.

---

[1] Some test developers have used other standard deviations, ranging from about 5 to 20, in defining their deviation IQs.

Interest and Aptitude Tests. Interest and aptitude tests are useful for diagnosis and for counseling students. They include vocational aptitude and interest tests such as the Differential Aptitude Test, the Strong Vocational Interest Blank, and the Kuder Preference Record. These tests can give teachers and counselors insights into the abilities and interests of students and the probabilities of their potential success in various careers and vocations.

Personality Tests. Personality tests are basically tools for school psychologists and counselors, although they can provide valuable information for teachers also. They include paper and pencil tests, drawing tests, and rating scales as well as situational tests and projective techniques for evaluating personality or emotional problems. Among the many well-known personality tests that are ordinarily used in counseling students with serious adjustment and learning problems are the Minnesota Multiphasic Personality Inventory (MMPI), the Rorschach Inkblots, the Thematic Apperception Test (TAT), and the California Psychological Inventory. Administration and interpretation of these tests should be left to experts.

References. Information concerning the various standardized tests can be found in such works as the Mental Measurement Yearbooks[2] and Levy and Goldstein's *Tests in Education*[3], and such journals as *Education Index, Psychological Abstracts, Review of Educational Research* and *Educational and Psychological Measurement.*

What Makes a Good Test?

The teacher who is constructing a test or selecting a test for use must be concerned about some basic characteristics: validity, reliability, objectivity, usability, and discrimination. *Validity,* the most important, refers to whether the test measures what it is supposed to measure. The key questions concerning validity are the following:

1. Does the test adequately sample the content area?
2. Does the test involve the cognitive, affective, and psychomotor skills that are important to the unit?
3. Does the test relate to all the behavioral objectives for the unit?

Standardized tests involve more complex analysis of validity when results are used for prediction.

Reliability refers to the consistency of results (for instance, a scale is reliable if it always records ninety pounds when one weighs a ninety-pound object on it). Test results may not be consistent because of test conditions, poorly designed or worded questions, errors in scoring and a number of other chance variables. Human errors, such as errors in grading or errors in reading questions, are inevitable.

---

[2] O. K. Buros, *Mental Measurement Yearbook* (Lincoln, Neb.: University of Nebraska Press, various cumulative editions).

[3] Philip Levy and Harvey Goldstein, *Tests in Education* (Orlando, Fla.: Academic Press, 1984).

However, instrument-centered errors as well as student-centered errors are taken into consideration by some of the statistical treatments. When you are selecting a standardized test or producing different forms of a test to administer to several sections of a class you should investigate this concept further.

Objectivity refers to freedom from subjective judgments for both the teacher and student. This characteristic implies careful attention in the construction of items and in the selection of the form of items for the test.

Usability refers to the practical aspects of time and resources required for the test, compared to the value of information obtained. An essay test, for instance, may be easily prepared by the teacher, but the time involved in grading the test for twenty-eight students may make such a test impractical. Although the preparation of an objective-type requires more time initially, the grading is relatively quick and easy. Sometimes grading tests involves rather strict time limits because reports on students are due at a specified time, such as at the end of a semester. Cost or equipment required may eliminate the consideration of certain standardized tests.

Discrimination refers to the ability of a test to separate pupils on the basis of how well they perform on the test. Discriminating power is not a factor in a criterion-referenced test. However, in tests given to determine the individual's position in the group, the differentiation ability of the test is crucial. The teacher should make an item analysis of tests to determine the difficulty and discriminatory power of each item as a basis for revising the test. The use of computers in many schools facilitates item analysis, but since the procedure involves only counting and dividing, the teacher untrained in statistics can handle it. Quite specific guidelines for the difficulty and discriminating power of the items in a well-constructed test are available.[4]

Constructing the Instrument

The first step in constructing a measurement instrument is to make an evaluation plan. In this plan, make provisions to

1. Test all desired outcomes. Before the teaching of the unit, determine the objectives of the unit, define them as specific pupil behavior, outline the unit content, and draw up a table of specifications that will show the objectives, the content, and the number or weight of the test items to be given in each area.
2. Build the test when the unit is being constructed.
3. Be sure that you test all objectives in proportion to their importance. Following a table of specifications should ensure that the test has the proper balance.
4. Be sure the items are of the proper degree of difficulty. Include some easy items for the slowest students so they will not give up before even trying.

---

[4] Stanley Ahmann and Marvin D. Glock, *Evaluating Pupil Growth,* 4th ed. (Boston: Allyn & Bacon, 1971), p. 191, for instance.

Arrange the items from easiest to most difficult so as not to discourage the less able.

5. Be sure the instructions give students all the information they need in terms they can understand.
6. Be sure the items are clearly worded. The reading level must not be too difficult; the grammar, vocabulary, and usage must be appropriate for your purpose.
7. Allow time to write good items and criticize the plan. Try it out once.
8. Keep the mechanics simple. For instance, do not mix types of test items.
9. Plan for easy scoring.

Classroom tests and testing programs can and do occasionally have disadvantages or negative side effects. For example, test programs may impede the teaching process by so dominating the school program that instruction becomes totally geared toward tests. This domination is sometimes particularly harmful when standard tests are used as an integral part of the school system's evaluation program. Tests can become, in the eyes of the students, just a series of opportunities to fail, and teachers are likely to corrupt their courses and teach for the test so as to be sure that their students do well. Similarly, passing tests and getting good marks may become so important to students that they are concerned only with marks and not with learning. Cheating and unethical or immoral attitudes often result from overemphasis on testing and test results, too. Sometimes testing can interfere with pupils' wholesome growth in other ways. Tests can be harmful to pupils when they are used to categorize pupils as successes or failures, or when test results are considered the final word on a child's abilities, aptitudes, and prospects, or when they are the only means of communication between the school and the home.

Attaining Validity

Then to be sure that your test measures what is supposed to be measured, you should construct a table of specifications. This two-way grid indicates behavior in one dimension and content in the other (see Table 13-2). In this grid, behavior relates to the three domains: cognitive, affective, and psychomotor. Cognitive domain, involving mental processes, is divided, according to Bloom's taxonomy, into six categories: (1) simple memory or knowledge; (2) comprehension; (3) application; (4) analysis; (5) synthesis (usually involves an original product in oral, written, or artistic form); and (6) evaluation. See Module 3 for a fuller explanation of the domains.

The teacher examining objectives for the unit decides what emphasis should be given to the behavior and to the content. For instance, if vocabulary development is a concern for this class, then probably 20 per cent of the test on vocabulary may be appropriate, but 50 per cent would be unsuitable. This planning enables the teacher to design a test to fit the situation, rather than a haphazard test that does not correspond to the objectives either in content or behavior emphasis. Since knowledge questions are easy to write, tests often fail to go beyond that level even though the objectives state that the student will analyze and eval-

TABLE 13-2
Table of Specifications

CONTENT	BEHAVIORS								TOTAL
World Literature	Cognitive						Affective	Psycho-motor	
Understanding Others	Knowl-edge	Compre-hension	Appli-cation	Analy-sis	Syn-thesis	Evalu-ation			
I. Vocabulary Development		3 (1, 2)	2 (2)						5
II. Individual Selections			1 (8)	2 (7)		2 (7)			5
III. Literary Forms and Style	1 (3)		1 (3)	1 (6)		2 (6)			5
IV. Comparison of Culture	2 (4, 5)			3 (4)					5
V. Comparison of Values	3 (5)			1 (5)		1 (8)			5
TOTAL	6	3	4	7		5			25

uate. The sample Table of Specification for a unit in World Literature on Understanding Others (Table 13-2) indicates a distribution of questions on a test. Since this test is to be an objective test and it is so difficult to write objective-type items to test syntheses and affective and psychomotor behaviors, this table of specifications calls for no test items in these areas. If these categories are included in the unit objectives, some other additional evaluative devices must be used to test learning in these categories. The teacher could also show the objectives tested, as indicated within parentheses in Table 13-2. Then, a check on inclusion of all objectives is easy.

Essay or Objective Tests
Although performance tests are frequently used to test students' skills, written essay and objective tests are the types of tests most frequently used to test students' knowledge. These two types of tests have a number of similarities and differences, and advantages and disadvantages, as shown in Table 13-3. You should bear these characteristics in mind when deciding whether to use an objective-type or essay-type test in a specific situation.

Building Objective-type Tests
To make tests more objective, test builders have invented several types of so-called objective test items,[5] which, when properly used, tend to reduce the amount of subjectivity and human error, particularly in the scoring. The following

[5] Some writers classify all objective-type items as short-answer items. What we call short-answer items they call unstructured free-choice items.

TABLE 13-3
Characteristics of Essay and Objective Tests

Essay	Objective
Student organizes his own responses with minimal restrictions.	Student operates on an almost completely structured task.
Student uses his own phrases, words, and expressions in responding.	Student selects the correct response from a limited number of alternatives, or recalls a very short answer.
Student responds to a very few items.	Student responds to a large number of items.
Student spends most of his time thinking and then writing.	Student spends most of his time reading and thinking.
Quality of test is largely determined by person doing the grading.	Quality of test is determined by the test constructor.
Test is relatively easy to build.	Test is very difficult to build.
Test is very difficult to grade.	Test can be graded quickly and easily.
Test encourages bluffing.	Test encourages guessing.
Test can be to measure the achievement of goals which are measurable by a written test.	Test can be used to measure the achievement of goals measurable by a written test.
Test can be used to encourage pupils to learn (facts, concepts, principles, and so on).	Test can be used to encourage pupils to learn (facts, concepts, principles, and so on).
Test can be used to stimulate either convergent or divergent thinking.	Test can be used to stimulate either convergent or divergent thinking.*

*Joseph F. Callahan and Leonard H. Clark, *Foundations of Education*, 2d. ed. (New York: Macmillan Publishing Co., 1983), p. 238. By permission.

paragraphs give examples of a number of different types of objective test items, with some suggestions that should help you in constructing such items.

Supply (Short or Completion) Items. Supply test items, such as short answer or completion items, require the student to recall the correct answer. They differ from recognition list items, such as true-false or multiple-choice items, in that the pupil must actually supply the answer rather than select one from a set of alternatives.

> Example: Short answer item:
> Give the name of the author of the short story, "The Beggar."
>
> Completion item:
> The name of the author of "The Beggar" is _____
> (Anton Chekov)

The advantages of these items include the reduction of student guessing and ease of construction. Dangers include emphasis on recall of a specific word or factual detail that is not essential; subjectivity in grading when unanticipated responses, legibility, and spelling are involved; neglect of higher cognitive behaviors; and focus on rote memory.

Suggestions for writing short answer items include the following:

1. Design the items so that there is sufficient information to indicate clearly one correct response.
2. Avoid copying statements directly from textbooks.
3. For completion items, put the blank at the end or near the end of the statement.
4. Try to develop items that require the student to go beyond the knowledge level.
5. Avoid ambiguous statements.
6. Provide sufficient space for writing the answer.

True-False Items.   True-False items are declarative sentences that the student marks as true or false statements.

Example: A right triangle is necessarily a scalene triangle. (False)

One advantage of true-false items is the wide sampling of content possible in a short time. The choice between alternate answers is a realistic task for the student since he often must make such decisions in the real world. The items are relatively simple and time-saving to construct. Grading is easy. On the other hand, the fact that guessing is encouraged by the 50-50 chance of success is a disadvantage. Another disadvantage is that there is danger of overemphasis on details and on the lowest level of the cognitive domain when writing true-false items. Further, brief statements that are completely true or false are hard to phrase. Although these items are not suitable for controversial content, they can be useful for stimulative or instructional tests.

Some suggestions for constructing these test items include the following:

1. Use statements related to significant objectives.
2. Write statement clearly and precisely, avoiding ambiguities.
3. Use positive statements; avoid negative statements since they tend to confuse students.
4. Avoid specific determiners, such as never, all, often, or usually, which frequently identify a statement containing them as true or false.
5. Try to develop items that require more than knowledge for responses.
6. Do not use statements directly from the text.
7. Make true and false items similar in length.
8. Do not overload test with either true or false statements.
9. Arrange a random pattern of correct responses.
10. Provide a simple method for indicating responses, so grading is accurate.

Matching Items.   Matching items consist of two sets of terms to be matched to show some indicated relationship. Literary titles may be matched with authors; definitions, with words; geographic names, with locations; dates, with events; statements or examples, with principles; people, with identification; symbols, with terms; causes, with effects; parts, with units to which they belong; short questions, with answers.

Example: In the blank provided, indicate the correct solution for the equation by marking the letter of the answer. Use a letter only once.

____ 1. $2x + 3 = 7$.	A. $x = 9$.
____ 2. $4x = x + 9$.	B. $x = 7$.
____ 3. $6x - 7 = x - 2$.	C. $x = 5$.
____ 4. $9 - 4x = 2 - 3x$.	D. $x = 4$.
____ 5. $\frac{2}{3}x = 6$.	E. $x = 3$.
	F. $x = 2$.
	G. $x = 1$.
	H. $x =$ Correct answer is not listed.

[Correct answers are 1-F; 2-E; 3-G; 4-B; 5-A.]

Another format for matching items is providing a list of terms or phrases that are then applied to a series of items.

Example: Each of the following statements is a sentence. Decide whether the sentence is simple, compound, complex, or compound-complex. Then put the letter corresponding to the correct choice in the blank at the left.
A. Simple.
B. Compound.
C. Complex.
D. Compound-Complex.

____ 1. *During the summer, many families plan vacation trips, and the national parks are crowded.*
____ 2. *If you want a cabin in Yosemite during July, your reservation must be made months in advance.*
____ 3. *Camping is a popular and economical way of traveling.*
____ 4. *A family that camps must plan carefully for a pleasant trip.*
____ 5. *Preparing your own meals is an important economy.*
[Correct answers are 1-B; 2-C; 3-A; 4-C; 5-A.]

The matching of items is a means of checking student recognition of relationships and associations. Many items can be handled in a short period of time. However, the emphasis is usually on knowledge. A teacher may have difficulty finding content that is appropriate and providing plausible incorrect responses.

Suggestions for constructing matching test items include the following:

1. Limit alternatives in a set to ten or twelve; more can be very confusing and time-consuming for students.
2. Each set should be homogeneous.
3. Include two or three extra choices from which responses can be chosen. This practice decreases the possibilities of guessing.

4. Arrange choices in a sequential order, such as alphabetically, or in time sequence.
5. Put all of both sets on the same page so the student does not have to turn from page to page.
6. Make directions clear and specific. Explain how matching is to be done and whether responses are used more than once.
7. Keep the response items short. Otherwise, student time is used in searching through responses.

Multiple-Choice Items. Multiple-choice items provide a statement or question and a number of possible responses. The student selects the correct or best response. There is a possibility of measuring not only knowledge, but comprehension, application, analysis, and evaluation with multiple-choice items. Guessing is substantially reduced with careful construction of responses so that the undesired ones seem plausible. For most test writers this is the preferred type of test item.

Example:

_____ 1. *An individual is most likely to receive a severe sunburn in the middle of the day because*
   a. *we are slightly closer to the sun at noon than at any other time.*
   b. *when the sun's rays fall directly on a surface, more energy is transmitted than when the rays fall obliquely on the surface.*
   c. *when the sun is directly overhead, the rays pass through less filtering atmosphere than when the sun is lower in the sky.*
   d. *the air is warmer at noon than at other times of day.*
   [Correct answer is b.]

Suggestions for constructing multiple-choice items include the following:

1. Arrange the possible responses in a vertical list to help the student see his choices.
2. Provide four or five choices.
3. Be sure all responses would seem plausible to students who do not know the correct response.
4. Be sure every choice has grammatical consistency with the question or incomplete statement.
5. Make the correct answers about the same length and vocabulary level as the others.
6. State the problem or question clearly in the introduction so the choices are as brief as possible.

Situation Items. Situations followed by statements to be checked or classified can be set up to measure various cognitive levels.

Example: Bill Collins planned a large garden to help cut down food expenses for his family. He purchased a quantity of ladybugs and placed

TABLE 13-4
An Overview of Objective-type Items*

Type	Format	Sample Item	Difficulty in Writing	Difficulty in Scoring	Measure of	Recommended Use
Unstructured	Free Choice	What form of economic system is most often instituted in African and Asian countries following independence?	Easiest (6)	Can be difficult	Recall of knowledge	One-time/one-class testing
Completion (Fill-in)	Free Choice	The form of economic system most often instituted in Africa and Asian countries following independence is	5	Can be difficult	Recall of knowledge	One-time/one-class testing
True-False (Yes-No)	Fixed Choice	The form of economic system most often instituted in African and Asian countries following independence is socialism. TRUE FALSE	3	Easy	Recognition of knowledge	Multi-group/repeated testing

		Example				
Other Two-Choice	Fixed Choice	Circle those African and and Asian countries that have introduced social-ism upon achieving independence INDIA GHANA ZAÏRE CHINA SOMALILAND LIBYA	4	Easy for small groups but more difficult for larger ones	Classification of facts	One-time/one-class testing
Multiple Choice	Fixed Choice	Upon achieving independence, the majority of Asian and African countries turned economically to (A) capitalism. (B) laissez-faire. (C) socialism. (D) mercantilism	2	Easy	Recognition of knowledge or comprehension (or occasionally of higher levels)	Multi-group/repeated testing
Matching	Fixed Choice	Match the countries to the economic systems (1) Capitalism (2) Communism (3) Socialism (4) Isolationism a. South Africa b. Srilanka c. Ghana d. Madagascar	Most difficult (1)	Easy for small groups but more difficult for larger ones	Recognition of knowledge or comprehension	Change of pace

*From Measuring Educational Outcomes by Bruce W. Tuckman, © 1975 by Harcourt Brace Jovanovich, Inc. Reprinted by permission of the publisher.

them in the garden area. Check statements that are good reasons for his action.

____ 1. *Ladybugs are colorful insects.*
____ 2. *The ladybug improves the fertilization of tomatoes and squash.*
____ 3. *Ladybugs encourage cross-pollination of sweet corn.*
____ 4. *The ladybug is a natural enemy of aphids.*
____ 5. *Many gardeners want ladybugs in their gardens.*
____ 6. *The garden yield may be increased when ladybugs are in the area.*
____ 7. *Ladybugs help control certain insect pests.*

[*Correct answers are 4, 6, 7.*]

Items of this type are difficult to build. These situations are often difficult to present briefly, and providing appropriate ways for the student to respond may challenge the ingenuity of the teacher.

A summary of formats, difficulties, and recommended uses of the various objective-type items is shown in Table 13-4.

Guidelines for Preparing an Objective-type Test. When building an objective-type test, let the following be your guidelines.

1. Be sure the directions are clear and complete.
2. Be sure your testing emphases are consistent with your teaching emphases.
3. Be sure that the test is neither too long nor too short. Everyone, or nearly everyone, should be able to finish it.
4. Set up a simple, clear system of responses, easy to answer and easy to correct.
5. Put the easiest items first and the most difficult toward the end so that pupils will not get discouraged and give up before finishing.
6. Group items by type; do not intermix true-false, matching, arrangement, multiple choice, and situation questions.
7. Ask only one question at a time. There should be no cross references between questions. Each item should stand alone—independent and unified.
8. Do not provide options; all pupils should take the same test.
9. Ask important questions; avoid trivial questions and trick questions.
10. Keep the items clear.
11. Avoid the use of vague, qualitative terms such as *seldom, often, most, far, near, much, few.*
12. Use correct grammar.
13. Avoid double or triple negatives.
14. Avoid difficult, arcane vocabulary, gobbledygook, and jargon.
15. Consider providing a mix of different types of test items to make the test more reliable.

Building Essay Tests

Since objective questions do not provide students an opportunity to organize ideas or show their creativity, they limit their freedom of response. Essay questions are so named because students respond in an essay form that varies from a sentence or two to many pages in length. Essay questions are suitable for assessing learning at the higher cognitive and affective levels. To reduce the element of student guessing, the questions must be clear and specific. Because writing responses to essay questions is time-consuming, the number of essay questions one can use in a test is severely limited. This fact makes it difficult to cover all the objectives.

Although the essay test takes less time to construct than the objective test because it involves fewer questions, the scoring of essay tests is time-consuming, and consistency of scoring is hard to maintain.

You should prepare your students to take essay tests. In your preparation, you should (1) discuss the meaning of such terms as compare, contrast, and illustrate; (2) develop suitable responses to sample questions; (3) stress the importance of the careful reading of questions; (4) stress the planning of responses; (5) conduct activities in which the students practice how to attack essay questions; and (6) consider such bothersome elements as padding answers, proofreading, and legibility.

Examples of essay questions:

1. *Discuss the essay test as a measure of achievement.*
2. *Compare essay and objective tests in relation to the following factors: (a) validity; (b) reliability; (c) usability; (d) discrimination; and (e) objectivity.*

Suggestions for constructing essay questions include the following:

1. Expected student answers should relate to significant content and behavior, as indicated in the table of specifications and objectives.
2. Phrase the items clearly and specifically so the students know what is expected of them.
3. The number and complexity of the questions should be reasonable for the time limits so the students can demonstrate their achievement.
4. The questions should pose an interesting and challenging problem for the student.
5. If spelling, grammar, and writing style are to be scored, students should be informed about how much these factors will influence the scoring.
6. All students should write on the questions given. This increases reliability.
7. The point value of the questions should be indicated.

Performance Tests, Checklists, and Scales

As you have seen, a performance test consists of observing a learner performing a certain behavior or evaluating the product of the behavior. The test could, of course, include both the process and the product. To set up a performance test you must

1. Specify the performance objective.
2. Specify the test situation.
3. Set the criteria for judging the excellence of the process and/or product.
4. Make a checklist by which to score the performance or product. (This checklist is simply a listing of the criteria you established in step 3. It would

be possible to use a rating scale, but ordinarily a rating scale makes scoring too complicated.)

5. Prepare directions in writing, outlining the situation, with instructions for the pupils to follow.

Example: Checklist for Map Work

Check each item if the map comes up to standard in this particular category.
( ) 1. Accuracy.
( ) 2. Neatness.
( ) 3. Attention to details.

Skillful teachers also use checklists to ensure objectivity in their observation of pupil behavior. Usually a rating scale is more suitable for this purpose. To prepare a rating scale you must

1. Specify just what behavior you wish to observe.
2. Describe the behaviors so that you can recognize and judge them.
3. Decide what weight to give to each behavior.
4. Design the rating scale. Ordinarily, a five-point scale will be most satisfactory. More points tend to make the scale confusing; fewer points are too limiting. An odd number of points makes it possible to record a middle position.
5. Label the points on the scale to make them clear.

Example: Rating Scale for Map Work

(Check the spot on each continuum that is most descriptive of the pupil's work.)

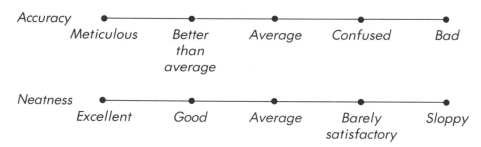

Scoring Tests

Correcting Objective Tests

Objective tests can be designed so that pupils answer the items directly on the test or on answer sheets. In some schools, teachers may have facilities for checking tests by machine. Then, of course, the tests should be set up to use answer sheets. If you do not have machine scoring available, you may still wish to use answer sheets to save time and effort when marking tests. If answer sheets are used, they should be arranged so that the student can move easily from the test to the answer sheet. One way to do this is to make the column on the answer sheet correspond with the pages of the test.

For many teachers, marking on the test paper is an advantage because the test can be returned to the student and used for teaching those areas not mastered. To simplify marking, teachers should have all answers arranged at the left side of the page. Some teachers then simply take an extra copy of the test to make their key and fill in all responses correctly. The key can then be placed against the test and the answers compared. Often, it is easier to cut off the text of the test so that the key will be a strip that can be laid along either side of the answers on the test being corrected. This makes it easier to correct answers listed on the left side of the page if the scorer is right-handed. Some teachers find it easier to score by simply checking all correct items, that is, items that agree with the key. Others prefer to mark the wrong answers.

Keys can also be prepared to fit over the answer section of a test with cutouts for the students' answers. These keys are known as masks.

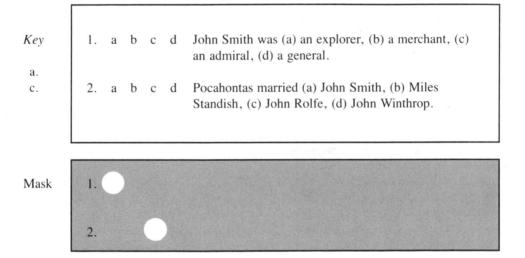

Keys can be prepared either to fit over this section with cutouts for the student's answers or to place beside the student's responses. Keys that indicate correct responses should be accurately prepared and written in colored ink so the key is easily identified. All possible answers should be included in the key. Use of a colored pencil to mark incorrect responses speeds the counting of errors.

Scoring Essay Questions

Scoring essay questions is difficult since it requires much time and involves subjectivity. You can make your handling of this task more effective by following certain procedures.

Write out a model answer when you construct the item. Sometimes, as you attempt to respond to your own questions, you will see some of the ambiguities and can improve the question.

Assign points to the various subparts of the response. In doing so, consider how many points will make an answer excellent, acceptable, or unacceptable.

Score each test anonymously so that the identity of the student is not a factor.

Score the same test questions at the same time for all the students; for example, read and score all answers for question 1 before you start reading the responses to question 2.

Consider the use of a two-step scoring procedure. In this procedure, reading the answers and rating the responses into three categories (excellent, acceptable, poor) is the first step. Rereading and scoring points is the second step. Some teachers prefer to assign points on the first reading. However, sorting followed by scoring gives one a chance to add unpredicted responses to the point array before the actual scoring.

Read each set of answers through without interruption when possible. Fluctuations in the feelings and attitudes of the reader are lessened when no external interference occurs.

Try to disregard irrelevant factors. If neatness is not a criterion, then it should not influence scores. When handwriting is not a part of the objective measured, then handwriting should not be a factor.

Finally, if essay tests are used, teachers are obligated to score the tests with as much reliability and objectivity as possible. The questions that are carefully designed can provide information about students' achievements which helps the teacher plan for students' growth and evaluate the teacher's own instructional activities. Good questions can also stimulate the student to find relationships, synthesize ideas, apply concepts, and evaluate a variety of materials.

Evaluating the Test Instrument

Educational evaluation is not complete unless we evaluate the tests and other instruments we use. Among the questions we should ask ourselves are the following.

Was the Test Valid?

How well does it measure what we wanted to measure? Does the content of the test measure the content of the instruction? Does it cover all of the instructional objectives? Is the emphasis on the objectives in the test proportional to that in the instruction?

Does the Test Have Discriminating Power?

Discriminating power refers to how effectively the item differentiates between the students who did well and those who did poorly on the test. One procedure for determining a test's discriminating power is an item analysis using the upper 25 per cent and lower 25 per cent of the scores.[6] Perfect discrimination of an item would mean that all the students in the upper quarter answered correctly and all in the lower quarter answered incorrectly. Such precise differentiation between groups seldom occurs. The difference between the number of students in the

---

[6] Technically it would be better to use the top 27 per cent and bottom 27 per cent, but for practical purposes in the classroom situation the uppermost and lowest quarters will suffice.

upper group who answer the test item correctly and the number of students in the lower group who answer the item correctly is divided by the number of pupils in both groups.

Example:

Of 100 scores, the top 25 include 20 correct responses on item A; the low 25 include 8 correct responses on the same item.

$$Index\ of\ Discrimination = \frac{20 - 8}{54} = \frac{12}{54} = .22+$$

The index varies from $+1.00$ to -1.00. Positive one indicates complete differentiation in the desired direction. Any negative value indicates the item discriminates in the wrong direction and is therefore unsatisfactory. Any discriminatory values above $+0.40$ are considered good. The range $+0.40$ to $+0.20$ is called satisfactory. Teacher-made tests that are norm-referenced should have more than half of the items with an index discrimination of $+0.40$ or above, and another 40 per cent of the items with a satisfactory index. No items should have a negative index.

How Difficult Were the Test Items?

Another type of item analysis determines item difficulty. Basically, the level of difficulty of an item is determined by the percentage of pupils who have answered the item correctly. It can easily be calculated. First, tabulate the number of students who correctly answered the question and divide by the number of students who tried to answer. Then, multiply by 100 to change the quotient to a per cent.

Example:

Nineteen of the 25 students who responded to a question answered it correctly.

$$Item\ Difficulty = \frac{19}{25} \times 100 = 76.$$

For norm-based tests, the items answered correctly or incorrectly by all or most of the students contribute little to determining the norms. In fact, the level of difficulty should be near 50 per cent. One recommendation is that only items in the 40 to 70 per cent range should be included in a test.

Neither the item difficulty nor discriminating power apply to criterion-referenced tests. Responses on criterion-reference tests will indicate whether or not individual students know or can do what they are supposed to have learned. If the lesson or unit has been well taught, it is possible that 80 per cent or more of the students will have answered all of the items right. Discrimination among students and difficulty factors of items are largely irrelevant for this type of test. If the items show whether or not the objective has been attained, they are good items.

	Rank Order in		
Student	Test I	Test II	Test III
A	1	1	1
B	2	3	2
C	3	4	4
D	4	2	3
E	5	5	6
F	6	6	5

FIGURE 13-2

Does the Test Seem to Be Reliable?

Do the test results concur with the results of other tests and evaluations? One way to check is to rank the performance of the students in your various tests. If the results of the new test are consistent with the other tests, presumably the tests are reliable. In the example (Figure 13-2), presumably Test III is reliable because its results seem to be consistent with those of Test I and Test II.

Is the Test Usable?

Is it too long or too short? Is it too hard or too easy? Is it easy to score? Did the pupils find the directions clear?

General Suggestions

File of Test Items

Tests should be analyzed and revised by the teachers. Reusing the same tests encourages cheating. But using the good questions of a test, eliminating or improving the poor items, and adding new items produce a better test than writing all new items.

Keep a file of your good questions as a convenient way of improving tests. To construct a test item file, put the question on one side of a file card and information about the item on the reverse side. File the question by unit, problem, or other convenient classification. These cards can then be pulled, sorted, and used as a basis for a new test. Since frequent short tests may be important for feedback to both teacher and student, you can use them to develop the test item file rapidly. Then questions for a unit test or semester examination will be readily available. Objective questions and essay questions from your test file may be combined in the same test. If one has the equipment available, test files can be built in a computer data-storage bank as well. The questions could then be pulled from the data bank when it is time to make the test. The computer will randomly select questions from a data bank, or it will make several alternative tests from the data bank using the same data bank of questions.

When Should Tests Be Given?

Since tests can fulfill different purposes, when a test should be given depends on the purpose. Before making realistic plans for instructional activities, a teacher must know the level of student achievement. This information can be obtained through testing. To work with individual students effectively, a teacher needs a diagnosis of the deficiencies of the student. Testing can provide this information. Effective learning requires feedback to the student that testing can provide. Grades or reports on progress of students ordinarily include some test results as a part of the evaluation. Students want information about their capabilities and talents to help them make vocational and educational choices. Testing can provide some data for these decisions. In the appraisal of materials, teaching strategies, and programs, test results are one source of data. Each of the purposes mentioned suggests when the test results can be used. Continuous evaluation means tests are given as the data from the testing are needed.

Cheating

You can discourage cheating by clarifying what the behavioral objectives are and how the objectives will be evaluated. A teacher should give the students information about time allowance for the test, the type of test, its purpose, and general content. Use other means of evaluation to provide more opportunities for students who do not perform well under the pressure of a test situation. Keep alert while the test is given, discourage student communication, and circulate to see how the students are progressing. Such awareness tends to hamper some of the tactics often used in cheating.

If several sections of a class are to take the test, you should vary some of the questions. Perhaps, the multiple-choice sections may remain the same, but you should vary the true-false and essay questions. You might, for instance, prepare three different forms of the test. Sometimes each class could use a different form; other times, one third of each class might use one form. A variety of approaches in different tests will show students that the teacher wants to be fair. In individualized instruction, group tests are eliminated; personal growth becomes a motivation and eliminates the purposes of cheating.

Summary

This module has indicated that testing is an integral part of a teaching model. Criterion-referenced and norm-referenced tests both have a place in the school. Validity, reliability, usability, discrimination and objectivity are discussed as they relate to teacher-made tests. Advantages and disadvantages of types of objective items (supply, true-false, matching, and multiple-choice) are presented. There are suggestions for writing good items of each type. How to construct and score essay questions is also considered. To ensure that the objectives are adequately covered both from the content and behavior dimensions, the use of a table of specifications is recommended. Since tests are such an important part of the teaching-learning situation, as well as the general educational scene, the teacher must purposefully work to develop skills in test construction and utilization. Accountability requires that the responsible teacher collect data on the effectiveness of teaching. Test results are an important part of these data.

Cheating is a persistent problem whenever group testing is done. Teachers can minimize the problem by using tests as an integral part of the instructional program and including other sources of information in grading. Cheating is discouraged by teacher circulating and sensitivity to the problem.

Suggested Reading

Ahmann, J. Stanley, and Marvin D. Glock. *Evaluating Pupil Growth,* 4th ed. Boston: Allyn & Bacon, 1979.

Bloom, Benjamin S., George F. Madaus, and J. Thomas Hastings. *Evaluation to Improve Learning.* New York: McGraw-Hill, 1981.

Ebel, Robert L. *Essentials of Educational Measurement,* 3d ed. Englewood Cliffs, N.J.: Prentice-Hall, 1979, Chaps. 1–11, 13–15.

Gronlund, Norman E. *Measurement and Evaluation in Education,* 5th ed. New York: Macmillan Publishing Co., 1985.

———. *Preparing Criterion-Referenced Tests for Classroom Instruction.* New York: Macmillan Publishing Co., 1973.

———. *Stating Objectives for the Classroom,* 3d ed. New York: Macmillan Publishing Company, 1985.

Hopkins, Charles D., and Richard L. Antes. *Classroom Measurement and Evaluation,* 2d ed. Itasca, Ill: F. E. Peacock, 1984.

Making the Classroom Test, 2d ed. Princeton, N.J.: Educational Testing Service, 1963.

Mehrens, William, and Irving J. Lehmann. *Measurement and Evaluation in Education and Psychology,* 3d ed. New York: Holt, Rinehart and Winston, 1984.

Multiple Choice Questions: A Close Look. Princeton, N.J.: Educational Testing Service, 1963.

Tuckman, Bruce W. *Measuring Educational Outcomes: Fundamentals of Testing.* New York: Harcourt Brace Jovanovich, 1975, Chaps. 1–11.

Weiner, Elliot A., and Barbara J. Stewart. *Assessing Individuals: Psychological and Educational Tests and Measurements.* Boston: Little, Brown, 1984.

Wilhelms, Fred T., ed. *Evaluation as Feedback and Guide.* Washington, D.C.: Association for Supervision and Curriculum Development, 1967.

Post Test

Multiple Choice   Insert the correct answer in the space provided.

 1. A criterion-referenced test is constructed so that
   a. each student will attain a perfect score if he has mastered the objectives.
   b. the student will be compared to other students and his position in the group determined.
   c. the test measures what it is supposed to test or meets the criterion established.
   d. the deficiencies of a student are located in a specific area of behavior.

 2. Evaluation and measurement are defined so that
   a. the terms are synonymous.
   b. evaluation includes measurement.
   c. measurement includes evaluation.
   d. measurement and evaluation are not directly related.

___ **3.** The items on a true-false test are *least* likely to
   a. measure complex cognitive behavior.
   b. encourage guessing.
   c. cover a quantity of material in a short time.
   d. take a reasonable amount of teacher time for constructing and checking.

 4. Supply (completion or short answer) items should be constructed
   a. with the blank at the beginning for easy grading.

b. with hints such as the first letter of the term to limit responses.

c. with several blanks so the student has several chances to respond correctly.

d. with emphasis on important content so item is worthwhile.

___b___ 5. Which teacher comment about scoring easy tests will improve the reliability of the test?

a. "I like to read all the student's answers at one time to get an overview of what he or she knows."

b. "I can do a better job of scoring when I don't know whose paper I'm reading."

c. "The time it takes to separate test papers item by item is time I could use more profitably for other purposes."

d. "I can tell how much a student knows by scanning his paper."

___f___ 6. In a model of teaching, testing is essential in

a. the writing of objectives.

b. preassessment of students.

c. implementation of instructional plans.

d. evaluation of learning.

e. a and b.

f. b and d.

___c___ 7. Multiple-choice items are superior to matching and to true-false items for some purposes because they

a. save teacher time in construction and grading.

b. decrease the number of questions the student can answer in a specified time.

c. measure cognitive processes beyond memory.

d. increase student choices in the test situation.

___d___ 8. Student scores on standardized tests can be expressed in terms of

a. percentile rank.

b. stanine.

c. grade equivalent.

d. all of these.

9–13. *If the following Table of Specifications is set up for a unit in short stories in ninth-grade English, indicate the appropriate placement of the tally for each question listed. Put the letter(s) of the correct cell in the blank. Use the highest cognitive level involved.*

CONTENT	COGNITIVE BEHAVIOR					
	Knowledge	Comprehension	Application	Analysis	Synthesis	Evaluation
Vocabulary	A	D	G	J	M	P
Literary Style	B	E	H	K	N	Q
Elements of the Short Story (Plot, Characters, Setting, Theme)	C	F	I	L	O	R

And ____ **9.** Ten items listing synonyms to be matched with ten of thirteen words given.

✗ *and* **10.** What effect on the reader is expected when the author tells the story in the first person?
   a. The reader is an observer of the action.
   b. The reader identifies with the author.
   c. The reader gets a broad insight into the motivation of all characters.
   d. The reader quickly perceives the theme of the story.

Q ____ **11.** Compare the "Tell-Tale Heart" with "The Fugitive" in regard to
   a. point of view.
   b. setting.
   c. plot.

L ____ **12.** At the end of "Split Cherry Tree," Pa feels that Professor Herbert is a "fine man" because
   a. Professor Herbert had a good education.
   b. Professor Herbert respected the gun Pa carried.
   c. Professor Herbert treated Pa as a worthy individual.
   d. Professor Herbert displayed his intelligence to Pa.

RoQ **13.** Select the best story you read and defend your selection, using four criteria for a good short story.

14–20. *Check the purposes for which teacher-made tests can be appropriately constructed*

✓ **14.** Diagnosing student instructional needs.

✓ **15.** Indicating level of student achievement.

____ **16.** Predicting vocational success.

____ **17.** Indicating psychological problems.

✓ **18.** Determining effectiveness of teaching.

✓ **19.** Showing whether instructional objectives have been attained.

____ (20) Measuring the effectiveness of an experimental program.

21–25. *Match the correct test characteristic (a through h on page 367) with the question asked about the test. Use a term only once.*

h ____ **21.** Does the test measure what is supposed to be measured?

g **22.** Can the test be constructed, administered, and scored conveniently?

f **23.** Are the results consistent?

c **24.** Do the test results show the different achievement levels of the students?

e **25.** Are results affected by the student or the scorer?

a. Comprehensiveness.
b. Correlation.
c. Discrimination.
d. Efficiency.
e. Objectivity.
f. Reliability.
g. Usability.
h. Validity.

c **26.** A student whose test score falls at the fiftieth percentile would be in which stanine band?
  a. 1
  b. 3
  c. 5
  d. 7
  e. 9.

d **27.** To ensure objectivity in your observation of a pupil's performance
  a. use norm-referenced instruments.
  b. use criterion-referenced instruments.
  c. use stanine scoring.
  d. use a checklist.

b **28.** In building an essay test
  a. provide pupils with several choices of questions.
  b. relate the questions to the specifications in a table of specifications.
  c. give equal credit to all items in the essay test.
  d. provide pupils with opportunities for extra credit questions.

29–31. *Short Answer Items* (Please answer in spaces indicated on page 368.) Complete the following model of a learning cycle.

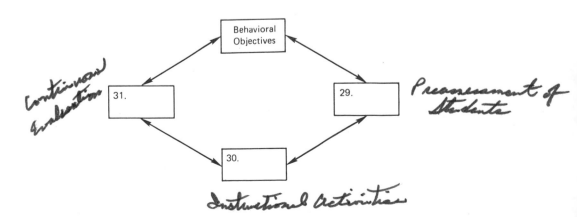

29. _Preassessment of Students_
30. _Instructional Activities_
31. _Continuous Evaluation_

32–35. List four uses of test results.

32. Grading
33. Diagnosis
34. Promotion
35. Setting Goals

MODULE
14

Grading

The first edition of this module was written by Isobel L. Pfeiffer of the University of Akron. It has been somewhat revised and updated by the editors for this edition.

Rationale

Grading is time-consuming and frustrating for most teachers. What should be graded? Should marks represent student growth, level of achievement in a group, effort, attitude, general behavior, or a combination of these factors? What should determine grades—tests, homework, projects, class participation, group work, or all of these? How can individualized instruction be graded? These are just a few of the questions that plague the teacher when decisions about grades must be made.

The report card that records the grades assigned may be one of the few communications left between the school and the student's home. Unless, however, the teacher and the school have clearly determined what grades represent and unless such understanding is periodically reviewed with each set of new parents, the report card may create unrest and dissatisfaction on the part of parents and students and prove to be an alienative device. The grading system then, instead of informing the parents, may separate the home and the school, which have a common concern—the best development of the student.

The development of the student encompasses growth in the cognitive, affective, and psychomotor domains. Consequently, paper and pencil tests provide only a portion of the data needed to indicate student progress. Different methods of evaluation must be utilized to determine how the student works and what he can produce. The teacher needs a repertoire of means of assessing learner behavior and progress.

Although grades have been a part of the secondary school for only one hundred years, they have become entrenched. Both parents and students have come to expect evaluations. Some critics suggest that the emphasis in school is on getting a high grade rather than on learning.

There have been complaints about subjectivity and unfair practices. As a result, a variety of systems for evaluation has evolved. When teachers are aware of alternative grading systems, they may be able to develop grading processes that are fair and effective for particular situations.

Specific Objectives

This module will consider some of the purposes of grading. The differences between criterion-referenced and norm-referenced grading are examined. Some practices in evaluating tests, themes, and other student products and student procedures are suggested. Self-evaluation will be discussed along with pros and cons of peer evaluation. We will scrutinize some of the problems involved in grading in such situations as individualized instruction or contract teaching. Practices in grading will be discussed.

Upon completing the study of this module, you should be able to perform all the following:

1. Indicate purposes accomplished by norm-referenced grading and by criterion-referenced grading.
2. Set up a frequency distribution for a set of test scores and estimate the stanines.
3. Explain three criteria for an effective grading system.
4. Discuss grading in relation to the normal curve, individualized instruction, themes, homework, and class discussion.
5. List and describe instruments for evaluating the behavior and products of secondary students.
6. Indicate specific reasons for helping middle and secondary school students develop self-evaluation skills.
7. Construct a rating scale for some activity or product appropriate to a content area, such as cookies in food class, laboratory procedures in a chemistry class, group discussion in social studies.
8. Explain three means of evaluating affective objectives.
9. Demonstrate how a teacher might set up a point system for grading a class at the end of six weeks.
10. Select appropriate answers to the post test with no more than three errors.

Module Text

Grading and Evaluation

Grading is a tedious task that many teachers dread. The aversive reaction of teachers results from a number of factors including (1) lack of clarity about what grades represent; (2) inability to communicate student behavior—e.g., content mastery in the cognitive domain, study skills, affective response—with a symbol; (3) parent and student confusion about the communication; (4) guilt about subjectivity in determining grades; and (5) concern that grades may adversely influence student behavior, vocational or employment opportunities, and further educational goals.

Evaluation is a requisite in effective learning. Unless learners know how they are progressing, they cannot make the modifications necessary to achieve the goal. They may be practicing incorrect procedures; for example, in spelling a girl may be learning incorrectly a word that she miscopied. Feedback is necessary to keep the learner on target. When a student is performing well, the positive reinforcement facilitates learning.

Evaluation and grading are not synonymous. Evaluation implies the collection of information from many sources, including measurement techniques and observation. These data are then the basis for value judgment for such purposes as diagnosing learning problems, recommending vocational alternatives, and grading. Grades are only one aspect of evaluation and are intended to communicate educational progress to both parents and students. Some questions that must be considered by individual teachers and schools are the following:

1. What should be the criteria for marking—comparison with a group, self-development, or both?
2. What kinds of experiences are involved—academic achievement, attitudes, study patterns, personal habits, or social behavior?
3. What consideration should be given to the psychological effect of grades on students? For instance, will a student who is consistently unsuccessful become convinced that he is worthless or inadequate? Will he give up the ghost and refuse to even try any longer? Will the student who is academically talented, who receives high grades with little effort become satisfied with medocrity?
4. What form of marking is best for communicating—a percentage plan, a letter or number system (A, B, C, D, F; 5, 4, 3, 2, 1; or a modification of this plan), pass/fail, a written description, several grades (one for achievement, one for social skills, and one for study habits), or a combination of these?

The school system or the individual school in which you will teach has, undoubtedly, its own procedure for grades. This procedure is the one that you must use. One of your first professional obligations will be to inquire about, to study, and to adapt your thinking about grading to the procedures already extant in the school and in your department. An example of the approach of one school system can be seen in Table 14-1, which is a copy of a page extracted from the *Program of Studies Handbook of the Fairfax County Public Schools* in Virginia. It serves as a guide for all of the intermediate and secondary teachers in that county school system. However, there are always means of adapting a system; for example, student conferences can always be used to supplement any grades, parent conferences by phone or in person can be individually scheduled, or descriptions of student work and progress can be written as letters to parents to explain grades.

Probably the greatest benefit of any grading system is the fact that teachers must establish criteria and priorities. Someone must decide just what student behavior is important in the teaching-learning situation and what the criteria for effective performance are to be. The decisions may be made by the teacher, by students, or through a cooperative effort. All students should know exactly what the decisions are, and the decisions should be definitely reflected in the learning activities and evaluation. Behavioral objectives must be carefully selected and clearly stated as a basis for effective learning.

Criterion-referenced and Norm-referenced Grading

There are two basic approaches to grading. One is similar to norm-referenced measurement and the other to criterion-referenced measurement, treated in Module 13.

In norm-referenced *grading,* the aim is to reveal how the individual compares to the other students in the group under instruction or with the larger groups who have taken a particular test. It is useful when communicating information about students to parents and colleges or employing agencies. In criterion-referenced *grading* the aim is to communicate information about an individual's progress in knowledge and work skills in comparison to his own previous attainment or in his pursuit of an absolute, such as content mastery. Criterion-referenced grading is featured in continuous-progress curricula, competency-based curricula, and other programs that focus on individualized education.

The philosophy of these two approaches is different. The norm-referenced grading reflects a competitive social structure. The grade is assigned to indicate how a student compares with other students. The top grade, usually A, generally means that the students receiving that grade have learned the content better than most other students in the class. The lowest grade, F or U in many scales, shows that the student has done poorly and has achieved less than others in the class. In general, the system assumes that the group of students approximates a normal distribution or bell-shaped curve. Such a distribution of marks follows a pattern of a similar number of As and Fs and of Bs and Ds. In the curve, shown in Figure 14-1, As and Fs each represent 7 per cent of the students; Bs and Ds each represent 24 per cent, and 38 per cent of the students receive Cs. In other situations, the allocation may be 5 per cent for As and Fs, 15 per cent for Bs and Ds, and 60 per cent for Cs. Many other allocations of grades on the normal curve have been used by teachers to fit certain groups.

One problem that frequently occurs when using norm-referenced grading is what to do with students in the high academic track. Should all receive As and Bs? If a wider grading scale is used for them, does it represent the students' achievement accurately for college entrance? For example, does C in an advanced English class mean the same level achieved by a student getting C in an average class? Probably the achievement in the advanced class represents more complex content and more sophisticated activities by students. To counteract the grade

TABLE 14-1
Guidelines for Report Card Marks*

Mark	Criteria	Percentage
A	—Demonstrates outstanding achievement and mastery of subject area —Goes beyond the goals established for the class in achievement and contribution —Achieves maximum growth in relation to the established objectives —Is self-directed in his/her attainment —Evidences understanding and appreciation of the fundamental concepts of the subject area —Exercises superior ability in problem solving and in arriving at logical conclusions —Shows originality in the preparation of assignments —Expresses ideas clearly both orally and in writing	94–100
B+	—Demonstrates scholarship and achievement well above the class average —Does his/her assignments thoroughly and accurately and occasionally contributes creatively —Is growing into leadership in the development of class and individual goals —Does independent work in addition to the required assignment	90–93
B		84–89
C+	—Achieves the objective developed for the average of the class —Is responsible and participates in class activities —Evidences normal growth at grade level in relation to his/her capacities and skills ✓Frequently requires individual direction and supervision —Achieves sufficient subject matter mastery to enable him/her to proceed to advanced high school work in the subject —Is alert, interested, and participates in class activities —Tries consciously to finish each project or assignment within the time limits allowed	80–83
		74–79

D+	Below-average achievement	—Frequently falls below the level of achievement of which he/she is capable —Seldom completes an undertaking without teacher direction and encouragement —Evidences little growth other than that developed through class association —May be irregular in attendance and generally fails to make up the work he/she has missed —Quality of work is poor, though he/she may have made efforts to improve —Shows little interest in the class and rarely contributes	70–73
D			64–69
F	Poor work, lack of comprehension	—Infrequently completes assignments requiring extended interest and development —Rejects teacher assistance and leadership —Evidences capacity to undertake many of the class activities but refuses to take part —Puts forth no effort though he/she has limited ability —Received an "incomplete" and has done nothing to warrant its change within time allowed —Has excessive unexcused absences. —Fails to meet the minimum requirements of the course	Below 64 No credit
I	Incomplete	—Fails to complete daily work, reports, tests, examinations, assignments, etc.	No credit
P	Pass	—Completes daily work, reports, tests, examinations, assignments, etc., in a satisfactory manner	In lieu of A,B,C,D,F
WP/WF	Withdraw/Pass Withdraw/Fail	—(See Withdraw/Pass-Withdraw/Fail section, page 35)	No credit

*Fairfax (Va.) County Public Schools. Grading and Reporting to Parents: Intermediate and Secondary, pp. 6–8. Reprinted by permission. Note that Fairfax County uses a plus letter system. Other school systems may use either no plus or minus, or both plus and minus letter marking systems.

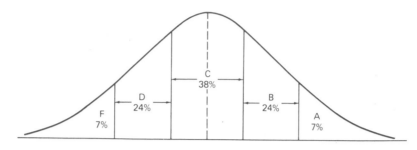

FIGURE 14-1   *Possible Distribution of Marks*

effect of a more difficult curriculum, some schools have special procedures for indicating advanced work on transcripts that are sent to colleges or to prospective employers. The same kinds of difficulties may arise with students from other academic tracks. Employers may interpret grades so that expectations for performance are unrealistic. Then, of course, the school is blamed. Grades often have an effect extending beyond the school.

Criterion-referenced or competency-based grading is based on whether or not a student achieves the specified objectives for the course. The objectives must be clearly stated to represent important student outcomes. This approach implies that effective teaching and learning result in high grades (As) for most students. In fact, when a mastery concept is used, the student must accomplish the objectives before being allowed to proceed to the next learning task. The philosophy of teachers who favor criterion-referenced procedures recognizes individual potential. Such teachers accept the challenge of finding teaching strategies to help students progress from where they are to the designated level. Instead of wondering how Sam compares with Ted, the comparison is between what Ted could do yesterday and what he can do today, and how well these performances compare to the set standard.

Most school systems use both norm-referenced and criterion-referenced grading. In beginning typing classes, for example, a certain basic speed and accuracy are established as criteria. Perhaps only the upper third of the advanced typing class is to be recommended for advanced secretarial courses. The grading for the beginning class might appropriately be criterion-based, but grading for an advanced class might better be norm-referenced. Sometimes both kinds of information are needed. A report card for a junior high student in his eighth year of schooling might indicate how he is meeting certain criteria, such as an A grade for addition of fractions. Another entry might show that this mastery is expected at sixth-grade level. Both criterion- and norm-referenced data may be communicated to the parents and students. Appropriate procedures should be used: a criterion-referenced approach to show whether or not the student can accomplish the task, and a norm-referenced approach to show how well he performs compared to others. Sometimes, one or the other is needed; other times, both are required.

Interpreting Standardized Test Scores

To interpret standardized test scores and to understand other norm-referenced marking systems, one needs a basic knowledge of elementary descriptive statis-

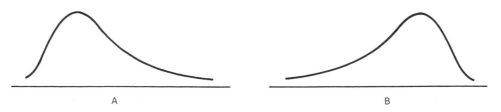

A   B

FIGURE 14-2   *Skewed Curves*

tics. So, as time permits, dig into one or more of the references listed at the end of the module. The statistics that will most concern you, however, are the normal curve, measures of central tendency, measures of variability, and derived scores.

The Normal Curve
The normal curve has already been discussed. It is a bell-shaped curve, bilaterally symmetrical with a single peak in the center, representing a distribution of scores in which most scores cluster in the middle, and other scores are distributed evenly toward the two ends. Such a distribution is typical of physical or behavioral traits and aptitude or intelligence test scores in the general population or large groups. (See Figure 14-1.)

Not all score distributions are normal, of course. If most of the scores are clustered toward one end of the curve, the curve is said to be skewed. (See Figures 14-2 A and B.) Such skewing may indicate that the test was too hard (Figure 14-2A), or too easy (Figure 14-2B) for the group being tested, or that the group was not a really normal one. On the other hand, skewed test score distributions may be useful for discriminating among gifted students or low ability students. Skewed distributions are rather typical of class size groups.

Measures of Central Tendency
The central tendency or "average" of a group of scores can be indicated statistically in three ways.

1. The *mean,* or arithmetical average, is determined by dividing the sum of the scores by the number of scores, i.e.,

$$M = \frac{\Sigma X}{N}$$

when M is the mean, X is the raw score, N is the number of scores, Σ (pronounced sigma) means the sum of or to add, and ΣX is the sum of the scores.

For instance, the mean of 17, 18, 25 would be 20

$$M = \frac{\Sigma X}{N} = \frac{17 + 18 + 25}{3} = 20$$

This measure is important as it is used as the basis for computing other statistical values.

2. The *mode* is the score that occurs most frequently in a distribution. Although it is the easiest to determine (one has only to look at the scores and select

the one that occurs most often), it is likely to be quite misleading, particularly when the distribution of the scores is skewed.

For instance, in the distribution 50, 45, 45, 45, 35, 30, 25, 15, 10, the mode is 45, but the mean is only 33.33.

3. The *median* is the middle point in the distribution, i.e., if there is an odd number of scores, the median is the middle score, or if there is an even number of scores, the median is halfway between the two middle scores. This value is very useful because it is easy to calculate and gives a good indication of the central tendency, particularly when the distribution is skewed. In fact, the median often gives a more realistic indication of central tendency in skewed distributions than the mean does. For the set of scores $X = 10, 15, 20, 25, 80$, for instance, the median is 20, but the mean is 30. In such a situation the unrepresentative high scores causes the mean to be less dependable than mean.

Measures of Variability

Measures of variability indicate how much the scores in a distribution vary. The most obvious one, the *range*, that is the difference between the highest and the lowest scores in the distribution, gives one a rough estimate of the variability of the distribution, but does not help one understand the variability of the scores within the distribution very well. The *standard deviation* corrects that defect, for it gives quite an accurate picture of the variation of the scores within a distribution—the larger the standard deviation the greater the variability.

To compute a standard deviation[1] one uses the following formula

$$\sigma = \sqrt{\frac{\Sigma(X - M)^2}{N}}$$

in which X is one raw score, M is the mean for a set of scores, and N is the number of scores in the set. The procedure is relatively simple. For instance, to calculate the standard deviation of the following set of scores: 20, 22, 33, 18, 21, 28, 24, and 23, one would complete the following steps.

Step 1. Prepare a table with the headings X, M, $(X - M)$, and $(X - M)^2$ as in Table 14-2.

Step 2. List the individual scores under column X.

Step 3. Determine the mean of the scores and place that figure in column M. (In this case the mean will be $189 \div 8$ or 23.6).

Step 4. Subtract the mean from each score and place the result in the column labeled $(X - M)$.

Step 5. Square each entry in column $(X - M)$ and place the results in column $(X - M)^2$.

Step 6. Add the numbers in column $(x - M)^2$ to find $\Sigma(X - M)^2$.

Step 7. Substitute the appropriate values into the formula and solve the equation (as in Table 14-2).

The standard deviation is closely related to the *normal curve*. In a normal distribution about 68 per cent of the scores fall in the area between $+1SD$ and $-1SD$ (i.e., 34 per cent of the scores fall between the mean and $+1SD$ and 34

---

[1] indicated by σ, s, or SD, depending upon the material being used.

TABLE 14-2
Calculation of Standard Deviation

X	M	(X − M)	(X − M)²
33	23.6	9.4	88.36
28	23.6	4.4	19.36
24	23.6	.4	.16
23	23.6	− .6	.36
22	23.6	−1.6	2.56
21	23.6	−2.6	6.76
20	23.6	−3.6	12.96
18	23.6	−5.6	31.36
189 = ΣX			161.88 = Σ(X − M)²

$$M = \frac{\Sigma X}{N} = \frac{189}{8} = 23.6$$

$$\sigma = \sqrt{\frac{\Sigma(X - M)^2}{N}} = \sqrt{\frac{161.88}{8}} = \sqrt{20.24} = 4.5$$

per cent of the score fall between the mean and −1SD), whereas about 13.5 per cent of the scores fall between +1SD and +2SD and another 13.5 per cent fall between −1SD and −2SD and only about 2 per cent fall between +2SD and 3SD or between −2SD and −3SD. (See Figure 14-3.)

Derived Scores

Test scores may be reported either as raw scores or as derived scores. A *raw* score is the number of the student's correct responses on a test. A *derived* score is a raw score that has been modified so as to make interpretation easier. Common types of derived scores include percentile ranks, standard scores (including T scores and stanines), deviation IQ scores, and age-grade scores. These types of scores are particularly useful for reporting the results of standardized tests and assessing the relative achievements, abilities, and aptitudes of students. Figure 14-4 shows how these various scores interrelate.

Percentile Scores. *Percentile* scores indicate the percentage of persons in the distribution whose scores fall at or below a given raw score. For example, a student having a percentile score of 25 scored as well as or better than 25 per cent of those taking the test. The fiftieth percentile is the median and in a normal distribution also the mean.

Percentiles are easy to use and compute. They can be used with any type of test. Since they show where the individual student stands in comparison with the other students in the group, they are excellent tools for comparing a person's performance on different tests.

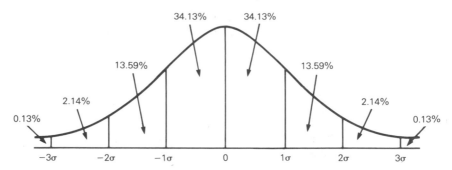

FIGURE 14-3 *Per Cent of Cases Falling within Standard Deviations in a Normal Curve*

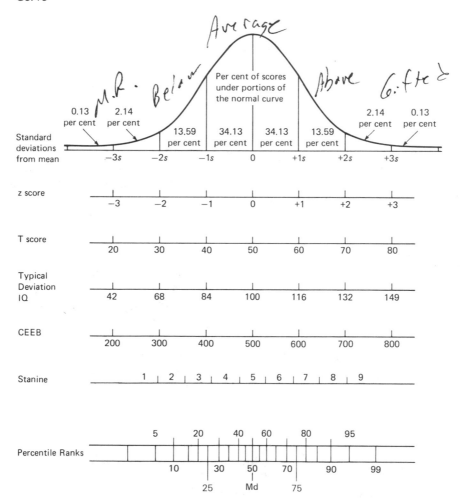

FIGURE 14-4 *A Normal Curve Showing (1) Percentage Distribution of Scores, (2) Standard Deviations, (3) z Scores, (4) T Scores, (5) Deviation IQ Scores, (6) College Entrance Examination Board Scores, (7) Stanine Scores, and (8) Percentile Ranks. *Joseph F. Callahan and Leonard H. Clark,* Foundations of Education *(New York: Macmillan Publishing Company, 1983), p. 235*

Percentage Scores.   Do not confuse percentile ranks with *percentage* scores. Percentage scores are simply raw scores expressed in terms of the percentage of correct responses. Thus, if a student gets 25 items right on a 50-item test, his percentage score would be 50. Fifteen right on a 20-item test would give one a percentage score of 75.

Standard Scores.   *Standard* scores express individuals' scores in terms of their distance, in standard deviations, from the mean. Thus, if a person's score should fall one standard deviation above the mean, his standard score would be $+1$. If it should fall a half standard below the mean, it would be -0.5. Standard scores of this sort are called *z* scores. They are computed by the formula

$$z = \frac{X - M}{\sigma}$$

where X is a particular raw score, M is the mean for a set of scores, and σ is the standard deviation for that set of scores. By substituting in the formula we find that in the example shown in Table 14-2, a student whose raw score was 24, would have a *z* score of .088.

$$z = \frac{X - M}{\sigma} = \frac{24 - 23.6}{4.5} = .088.$$

Note that the positive *z* scores indicate raw scores above the mean, negative *z* scores indicate raw scores below the mean and a *z* score of 0 indicates a raw score at the mean. Sometimes, in order to eliminate numbers and decimal fractions, test workers designate the mean by the value 100 (or 5, or 10) and express the deviation from the mean as a multiple of the standard deviation.

T Score.   The *T score* is an example of the practice of transforming standard scores so as to eliminate negative numbers and decimal fractions. T scores report exactly the same information as *z* scores except that the mean is expressed as 50 and each standard deviation is equal to 10. The formula used to compute a *T* score is

$$T = 10z + 50$$

Therefore, if a *z* score was $+1.5$, the corresponding *T* score would be 65.

$$T = 10 \times 1.5 + 50 = 15 + 50 = 65$$

CEEB Scores.   Other examples of the use of standard scores are the scores reported in the Army General Classification Test, and the College Entrance Examination Board tests. The CEEB scores are computed by the formula

$$CEEB = 100z + 500.$$

The Deviation IQ.   The *Deviation IQ* is also a standard score with a mean of 100 and standard deviations ranging from 5 to 20 depending on the intelligence test used. Because of this fact, when interpreting deviation IQs, one must know not only the IQ reported but also the standard deviation of the test used.

Stanine Scores.   *Stanine* scores that consist of nine one-half standard deviation bands centered on the mean are another example of test scores based on standard deviations. To compute stanine scores one uses the following procedure:

1. Find the mean of the raw scores.
2. Find the standard deviation of the raw scores.
3. Measure one-quarter standard deviation down from the mean and one-quarter standard deviation up from the mean to establish the limits of stanine 5 (the middle stanine).
4. Find the limits of stanine 1 through stanine 4 and for stanines 6 to 9 by measuring down or up one half standard deviation for each stanine.

However, a shortcut method for estimating stanine scores is described later in the discussion of grading techniques.

Age-grade Scores.   *Age-grade* scores are another device for reporting standardized-test results. An age score reports test performance in terms of the typical performance of persons of that age. Similarly, grade scores report test results in terms of the grade level for which this performance is average. Thus an age score of 10 would indicate that a student's achievement is equivalent to that of the average 10-year-old even if he should be 17, and a grade score of 10 would indicate the student's performance to be typical of the average tenth-grader even though he was only in grade 7.

Teacher-made Instruments

Classroom testing serves several purposes. Teachers use classroom tests to determine how well the various students have achieved and how far they have progressed. Teachers also use classroom tests for diagnostic purposes. Class test scores indicate what the students have learned well and what they have not learned. Analysis of test scores may show that some content has not been well taught and so should be reviewed in future lessons or that certain students have not learned well and need remedial help. Teachers also use tests for motivating students, for guidance purposes, and as instructional devices. Tests can also be used to detect and define students' curricular needs and so establish bases for planning and revising course content and curricula.

Unfortunately, classroom tests sometimes have negative side effects. Some schools and classes, for instance, may become too test dominated. As a result, teachers may teach for the test rather than for real pupil learning. Similarly, overemphasis on tests and marks may cause students to aim at grades rather than knowledge. As a result of these emphases they may try to attain high marks by such unethical methods as cheating. Sometimes tests have deleterious effects on student morale, personality, and motivation. Pupils who often fail their tests may so lose self-esteem that they no longer see any point in trying to learn anything. As a result, they may drop out of the class literally or figuratively. Those who remain physically present may no longer attempt assignments, pay attention, study, or, in general, expend energy on what they take to be a useless, impossible waste of time and effort. Failure after failure is no reward. Tests can also be harmful to students when they are used to categorize students as successes or failures, or when test results are considered the final word on a child's abilities, aptitudes, and prospects, or when they are the only means of communication between the school and the home.

Assigning Grades to Tests

After a teacher-made test has been given and scored, it should be used as an instructional tool. Students can be helped to note their errors and discover how to avoid them in the future. In criterion-based situations, successful students are moved onto the next level or sequence while those who have been unsuccessful are recycled for further study and efforts. With norm-referenced results, though, more than a raw score or the number correct will be required to serve your purpose. Further analysis of the data will be necessary to supply the information needed for student evaluation. Table 14-3 illustrates how you might record raw scores from a test so that you will be enabled to make the kinds of judgments required of you.

TABLE 14-3
Frequency Distribution

Unarranged	Arranged	Step Interval of 1		Step Interval of 3		Step Interval of 5	
Column (1)	(2)	(3)		(4)		(5)	
Score	Score	Score	f	Score	f	Score	f
45	97	97	1	96–98	1	95–99	1
76	92	92	1	93–95	0	90–94	2
86	90	90	1	90–92	2	85–89	5
60	89	89	1	87–89	2	80–84	3
80	87	87	1	84–86	3	75–79	3
86	86	86	2	81–83	0	70–74	3
59	86	85	1	78–80	3	65–69	1
49	85	80	3	75–77	3	60–64	2
97	80	77	1	72–74	2	55–59	2
80	80	76	1	69–71	1	50–54	1
73	80	75	1	66–68	1	45–49	2
90	77	73	2	63–65	0	N = 25	
85	76	70	1	60–62	2		
77	75	68	1	57–59	2		
61	73	61	1	54–56	0		
87	73	60	1	51–53	1		
75	70	59	1	48–50	1		
68	68	57	1	45–47	1		
70	61	51	1	N = 25			
51	60	49	1				
80	59	45	1				
87	57	N = 25					
92	51						
57	49						
73	45						
N = 25	N = 25						

Rank, Order, Range, and Mode

Assume, for example, that you have administered a 100-point test to a class of twenty-five students. The number of correct responses on each test paper is looked upon as the *raw* score for that paper. The scores in Column 1 represent the raw scores without regard to any order—just as you finished scoring them. Column 2 contains the same scores that have been arranged in order from highest to lowest *(Rank Order)*. Here you can readily note which was the lowest score and which was the highest, as well as the difference between the two (the *range*), and the most popular score (the *mode,* the score appearing most often). In this test, the mode was 80. (Table 14-3)

Frequency Distribution Table

For some purpose you may have in mind, it may be easier to arrange your data in a *frequency distribution table* by grouping like scores, as in column 3 (Table 14-3). Each score is listed only once. The column headed *f* indicates how many times each score was made.

When the number of cases is large, the data can be arranged with larger step intervals (such as 3 or 5) to make your chart more manageable. In column 4, with a 3-step interval, the interval 45–47 includes the scores 45, 46, 47. In column 5, the interval 45–49 includes the scores 45, 46, 47, 48, 49.

Mean and Median

The *mean* of these scores is the arithmetical average compiled by adding up all the test scores and dividing by the number of test takers. In Table 14-3, the sum of the scores is 1,846; the number of scores is 25; the mean for this test then is 73.84.

To find the *median,* the middle score, take the number of scores (25) add 1 and divide by 2. (The reason you add 1 is to find the pivotal score.) The middle score of this distribution is the thirteenth from either top or bottom. If you count the tallies from either end, you will find the *median score* to be 76.

$$\text{Median} = \frac{(N + 1)}{2} = \text{——th score in order of size}$$

$$\text{when } N \text{ is the number of cases}$$

The *Median* is also the fiftieth percentile. This means simply that one-half or 50 per cent of the scores fall above and one-half or 50 per cent of the scores fall below the median.

Inspection Method

This organization of information will enable you to make some descriptive statements about the entire class and to compare individuals within the group. You may make further use of this arrangement of scores to help you assign grades by the inspection method. Natural breaks in the listing are noted and used in determining letter grades.

In Table 14-3, for example, note that a spread of five points exists between the score of 97 and the score of 92. The score of 92 could thus be used as the upper limit for grade B. The next large gap occurs between the scores of 80 and 85; hence, 80 could be the upper limit of grade C. The next large gap occurs between 61 and 68; and following that, the next large gap is between 51 and 57. This arrangement could produce the following grade distribution:

Grade A	97–up	One score, A
Grade B	85–92	Seven scores, B
Grade C	68–80	Ten scores, C
Grade D	57–61	Four scores, D
Grade F	45–51	Three scores, F

Percentage Method

In some schools the *percentage method* of arriving at grades is used. A predetermined per cent of the possible score for a test, homework, or other assigned material is set up for each grade. For instance, 94 per cent may be set as a matter of schoolwide policy as the lower limit for an A grade, as in Fairfax (Table 14-1). In the same manner 64 per cent may be set as the low limit for a passing grade of D. In a school in which three grades are given (Satisfactory, Unsatisfactory, and Fail) the cutting percentages will be announced by administrative policy. Needless to say, there is a wide variation among school systems in the percentages used because it is relatively easy to standardize. Using the Fairfax County method, the distribution noted above would become:

Grade A	96%	one score of A
Grade B	86%–95%	six scores of B
Grade C	75%–85%	seven scores of C
Grade D	70%–74%	three scores of D
Grade F	69%–Less	eight scores of F

Stanines

Standard scores also can be used for grading. Instead of the 5-point system of letter marks traditionally used to turn raw scores into grades some teachers have begun using a more defensible system known as the Stanine system *(Standard Nine)*. They divide the tested population into nine groups (stanines) instead of five. With the exception of stanine one (the lowest) and stanine 9 (the highest) these groups are spaced in units of half a standard deviation.

Percentages of the class group that fall within each of the nine stanine classifications for a normal population are shown in Table 14-5. A useful characteristic of stanines is the equal distance between steps. Like percentile ranks, stanines report test performance in terms of the student's relative position in some known group. The middle score, the *median,* is the one to start with in setting up a stanine chart.

Note that in Table 14-4 the *median* score is 20. It falls in the stanine 5 category in Table 14-5 and has been labeled average. The other scores are located in stanines by using the percentages provided in this table. In stanines 4 and 6, for example, the percentage of students is seen to be 17 (17% of 25 − 4.25) or 4

TABLE 14-4
Distribution of Scores on English Test

Score	Frequency
25	1
24	3
22	4
20	5
19	2
18	3
15	1
14	2
13	2
10	1
9	1
	N = 25

TABLE 14-5
Approximation of Scores in Each Stanine

	Lowest	Lower	Low	Low Average	Average	High Average	High	Higher	Highest
Stanine	1	2	3	4	5	6	7	8	9
Percentage of Scores	4	7	12	17	20	17	12	7	4

students. In stanines 3 and 7, the percentage is seen to be 12 per cent and the number of students is 3. In stanines 2 and 8 the percentage is seen to be 4 per cent (1 student). Table 14-6 illustrates how letter grades might be allocated to the stanine subgroups. Note that stanines 4, 5, and 6 are designated average; stanines 7, 8, and 9 are designated high categories.

Exercise 14 A

Suppose you gave a unit test to your class of 32 students. Their test raw scores turned out to be 35, 32, 34, 28, 30, 27, 32, 24, 18, 30, 26, 10, 31, 24, 26, 30, 25, 21, 25, 31, 19, 25, 26, 20, 31, 20, 24, 30, 21, 18, 30, 26.

TABLE 14-6
Allocation of Grades to Stanine Subgroups

Distribution Score Frequency	Progress Grade	Explanation
25 – 1 – – Stanine 8 ⎫	A	20% of 25 = 5, 5 scores should be in Stanine 5.
⎬ B or		
24 – 3 – – Stanine 7 ⎭	B	Score 20, the median, has a frequency of 5.
22 – 4 – – Stanine 6 ⎫		17% of 25 = 4.25, 4 scores should be in Stanines 4 and 6.
20 – 5 – – Stanine 5 ⎬ C		Score 22 has a frequency of 4 but we must combine 18 and 19 for a frequency of 5.
19 – 2 ⎫		
⎬ – – Stanine 4 ⎭		12% of 25 = 3, 3 scores should be in Stanines 3 and 7.
18 – 3 ⎭		
15 – 1 ⎫		Score 24 is no problem, but scores 14 and 15 must be combined.
⎬ – – Stanine 3 ⎫		
14 – 2 ⎭ ⎬ D		7% of 25 = 1.75, 2 scores should be in Stanines 2 and 8.
13 – 2 – – Stanine 2 ⎭		Only 1 score remains for Stanine 8.
10 – 1 ⎫		4% of 25 = 1, 1 score should be in Stanines 1 and 9.
⎬ – – Stanine 1	F	
9 – 1 ⎭		Since 2 low scores remain, they would fall in Stanine 1.

Set up a frequency distribution table for this set of scores.

What was the median score on this test?

What per cent of the scores would fall into each of the stanine bands?

What number of scores would you allocate to each band?

What scores would you allocate to each band?

What letter grade would you assign to each stanine band?

Observation Techniques

The learner progresses most efficiently when he knows what his goals are, how he or she is progressing toward those goals, and what behavior changes are needed for their achievement. Continuous evaluation, then, is needed for this process to occur. Tests, if well constructed and appropriately used, provide some of the measurement data. But student performance, in addition to paper and pencil testing, is another source of information about student learning. For example, skill in shooting fouls can be appraised only by an actual demonstration on the gym floor. Threading the sewing machine, preparing a lunch, and making a speech are other competencies that can be appraised only by student activities in real or simulated situations. Sometimes the final result or product is the focal point; at other times the procedure is important. The preparation of the soup, the sandwich, and the dessert for a lunch may each be appraised. But, at some point, there must be coordination of the procedures so that the hot soup and sandwich are ready to serve together, and the dessert available at the appropriate time. The evaluation of products and procedures is an integral part of the teaching-learning situation. Means for such evaluation must be planned and utilized to help the student learn.

Observation techniques are used in evaluating procedures and products. Problems arise in determining the major factors in the appraisal, the distinction of quality levels and establishing, quantifying, or marking steps. When students are presenting speeches to enlist support, for some specific cause, should the basis for evaluation be the logic of the appeal, the speaker's poise and posture, the number of listeners who changed their point of view, the organization of the speech, or all of these? What is to be evaluated depends on the situation and corresponds to the objectives involved. These criteria for evaluation should be established by the teacher, students, or both before the students plan their speeches.

The Rating Scale. Various methods of summarizing observations include rating scales, checklists, and anecdotal records. If, for instance, an oral report is prepared for social studies, the following items might be included in the rating scale:

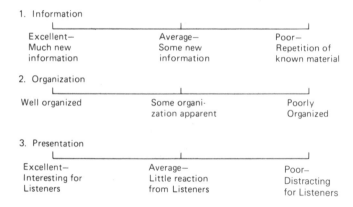

1. Information

Excellent—	Average—	Poor—
Much new	Some new	Repetition of
information	information	known material

2. Organization

| Well organized | Some organi- | Poorly |
| | zation apparent | Organized |

3. Presentation

Excellent—	Average—	Poor—
Interesting for	Little reaction	Distracting
Listeners	from Listeners	for Listeners

The rating scale might be prepared either by students, as they select the major criteria for good reports, or by the teacher. Preparing such an evaluation instrument can be a learning situation in which students analyze behavior and specify desirable aspects of the behavior. The scale might be used by the teacher, by the student presenting the report, or by the class.

Teachers should help students develop self-evaluation skills. Using a rating scale and comparing results with the teacher rating or with the class rating (average) could be a step in developing skills of self-analysis for the student. A student also might do a self-evaluation after reporting to the group, and compare it with one done later after hearing an audiotape of the talk. For instructional purposes, the rating scale provides feedback to the student to help him improve his performance. The evaluation may also be used by the teacher as input for the grading of the student.

The Checklist. The checklist is another method for use in observing student behavior. Use it to note the presence or absence of student skills and understanding. It is particularly useful for recording characteristics of student behavior and for noting down skills that need further development. For some class activities it may be especially necessary that the checklist reflect the sequence of actions performed. If the students are working in small groups, such items as the following might be included:

Behavior	Yes	No	Uncertain
1. Begins work promptly			
2. Explains his point of view			
3. Listens to others			
4. Is a leader sometimes			
5. Is a follower sometimes			
6. Keeps group working on the task			
7. Is pleasant to others in the group			
8. Makes worthwhile contributions			

The checklist not only is a useful device for the teacher in observing behavior but also reminds students about their own activities.

Anecdotal Records. Anecdotal records are simply brief, written statements of what has been observed. The anecdotal record should provide objective evidence about the procedure or product. Each anecdotal record is limited to recording a single situation. It can be useful to a teacher in understanding an individual student and planning for his learning.

When an anecdotal record is used, the teacher indicates that the characteristics of the procedure or product are not well enough defined to organize into a checklist or rating scale. Teachers who use anecdotal records for evaluation are compiling information instead of relying on memory. By regularly collecting and recording this information, they guard against the tendency to recall only recent data and critical incidents that might otherwise make their evaluations unfair and biased. Sometimes, anecdotal records may not present data on all students. Unless one consciously plans to write for different students and include all of them, the anecdotes will usually deal with the excellent or poor students.

Log. A log differs from an anecdotal record in that a log is a daily record. Using a log lends itself to ensuring that one is getting observations of all students. The log also might tend to show development patterns, since it is an ongoing record.

Teachers need to experiment with different ways of collecting information about student learning. When a variety of procedures is used, the teacher and students will be able to develop devices appropriate to specific situations.

Anecdotal records and logs are useful for evaluations of an informal nature. Tests, reports, projects, and products are formally evaluated. Questions asked during or outside of class, explanations to peers, listening, and unassigned contributions to the class (bringing a new book to class or a clipping for the bulletin board) are activities that are informally evaluated. These behaviors can be interpreted as approach (favorable) responses in the affective domain.

Affective Domain Learning in the affective domain is particularly difficult to measure. Whenever a teacher communicates an attempt to evaluate such behavior, students can easily fake the responses. The teacher, however, must be aware of what influence his teaching has on the attitudes of students. Unless students retain or improve their attitudes toward the subject and toward school, the teacher is failing to do an effective job. Some of the student responses that should cause teachers to examine their objectives and learning activities include pain, fear, anxiety, frustration, embarrassment, boredom, and discomfort.[2] Although teachers ordinarily do not try to develop a system of grading these informal areas, they should evaluate the influence of their teaching in this area of feelings. Unsigned questionnaires provide considerable useful information. Course-related student behaviors that are indicators include the incidence of dropping class, absence, tardiness, submitting unrequired papers and projects, evidence of careful work on assignments, and volunteering for special activities.[3]

The interest in value education today forces all teachers to evaluate the affective behavior of the students with whom they work. Ingenuity is needed in developing and using various techniques for collecting data about student reactions. When a considerable amount of cheating takes place, in testing situations, for example, or when intense student animosities are apparent in class discussions or in small-group work, or when assignments are regularly missed or a general lassitude is evident regarding good or poor performance in the class, a careful review and analysis of the total teaching-learning environment is undoubtedly being signaled for.

Grading Themes

English teachers perhaps more frequently than any other group are concerned with the evaluating of student writing. Social studies, health, science, and even mathematics assignments also involve the writing of reports or essays. Probably all teachers at some time evaluate written compositions of students. Many factors are involved in such evaluation and should be specified in accordance with the objectives.

These factors fall into two general categories, content and mechanics. Content encompasses ideas, organization, style, wording, and similar areas. Mechanics deal with grammar, punctuation, spelling, and neatness. Since to some students the two areas seem totally unrelated, teachers may choose to give an evaluation for each category. The symbol A/C on a theme graded by one English teacher indicates the paper to be excellent as far as ideas and style are concerned, but mediocre mechanically; the grade preceding the slash represents content, and the grade following the slash represents mechanics. Some teachers give specific values to mechanical errors to encourage the student to proofread carefully. Reflection upon the tendency of some students to repeat ad infinitum the same mistake in written work has led some teachers to attach penalties to repetition of previous

---

[2] Robert F. Mager, *Developing Attitude Toward Learning* (Palo Alto, Calif.: Fearon Publishers, 1968), pp. 49–57.
[3] Ibid., pp. 79–81.

errors. The goal of this procedure is to encourage proofreading, to cultivate pride in the final product and to magnify the error of letting mediocre efforts suffice. In English classes where this system is followed not all errors are penalized alike. Errors in areas previously studied (and supposedly mastered) like capitalization, for example, are assumed to be due to carelessness. Such errors are penalized moderately as a motivation toward more careful writing. Errors in areas currently under study are penalized more severely in an effort to motivate more study and additional mastery of new concepts. Some teachers work out guidelines with their students similar to the following in their quest for improvement in writing:

Major errors—run-on or fragmentary sentence; muddled sentence.
    (One such error reduces mechanics grade a l er.)
Serious error—nonagreement of subject and ve ; nonagreement of pronoun
    with antecedent; lack of antecedent; incorrect ord.
    (Three of these reduce grade a letter.)
Minor errors—misspelling, errors in capitalizatio punctuation mistakes.
    (Five of these reduce grade a letter.)

These classifications change as students develop mo skill in mechanics. The classifications or penalty may change each semester o ach grading period.

When objectives are improved proofreading and sei ivity to mechanical errors, the teacher may use the themes in proofreading a ities before final evaluation of the themes. For example, a group of students n exchange themes and read them to catch any spelling errors, then exchange ag and read for capitalization and punctuation accuracy. These activities not on provide student opportunities for learning, but assist the teacher in correcting ors.

Since grading content and style is much more subjectiv an checking mechanical errors, the teacher should frequently provide mode f well-organized and interesting writing. The selection of student writing fo e as models is useful to the teacher and is a reward system for students. Stu t judgment of style and content can be cultivated through use of models and th h peer grading of themes (without names, of course). If students read seve themes and rank them as to content, important aspects of writing style can t mphasized and illustrated. Teachers of all content areas can use these same a oaches to improve student writing: models, discussion, peer sharing, and evalua of written work.

Teachers may not evaluate all student themes with the same emp is. On some occasions, a paragraph may be written for a specific purpose—p aps to explain how to do a task. Mechanics may not be graded at all. The teacher should indicate to the class what objectives are involved in the student writing and in the evaluation. Teacher time, student interest, and needs are several factors to be considered. Grading themes is time-consuming. A teacher must determine whether the time required in such effort pays off in student progress. Unless the students get feedback on their writing within a reasonable time and learn from the teacher evaluation, for instance, the teaching is probably inefficient. Sometimes it is wise to set up a system for correcting themes. One system that seems to be advantageous is to ask students to write on alternate lines and then to insert corrections on the blank lines. This arrangement facilitates checking; when a student is required to rewrite the entire theme, the teacher must reread the entire theme, and often finds new errors in the process. Giving a second grade for the correction of mechanical errors may be desirable.

Occasionally, it may be useful to evaluate themes as you circulate around the classroom while the students are writing. By reading as students are producing the composition, the teacher may be able to offer suggestions and correct some errors on the spot. Such a strategy provides variety and utilizes teacher time for individual problems. Help in organizing themes while writing may result in important learning for the student.

Evaluation of Individualized Instruction

Individualized instruction requires individual evaluation and grading. Teachers have found no one way to deal effectively with the variety of starting levels, speed of learning, motivation, distractions, projects, and activities. In a continuous progress curriculum, when diagnostic tests are given and assignments are developed to provide the learning experiences the student needs to progress in the subject area, each student may be doing lessons that are different from those of all other students in the group. How then should the progress of individual students be evaluated?

Sometimes the student and teacher can together establish goals for the individual. These goals may be the basis for a progress grade. The report might also include the norm level of this work. Marvin may be working in general mathematics on basic multiplication facts. Since he is accomplishing the objectives for his learning tasks, his progress is good. However, the task is one that an average fourth-grader masters. Marvin's evaluation should probably include both his learning and the level of the task. The evaluation of a student who works quite slowly should show his growth and give some indication of his work pattern. Can such information be most satisfactorily communicated to students, parents, other schools, and employers by letter grades, written comments, or some other system? Each school using individualized instruction must consider this problem as it evolves its philosophy of grading and each teacher must adapt the procedures he uses in his classroom to that philosophy. Some commercially prepared systems (such as IPI)[4] have totaled the number of concepts involved in the whole math curriculum. When they report, they need merely indicate the current achievement for norm groups such as "20–30 packets completed by successful students. John has completed 25 packets and thus has 5 more to finish before semester's end." Since in these systems progress is continuous, no difficulty is caused by routine slowness. When the current target has been achieved, the student merely goes on to the next. John, above, for example, would start on Packet 26. Even over year-ends and year beginnings if John has not mastered Packet number 30, he will pick up in the new year where he left off and work on that sequence until packet 30 has been mastered.

---

[4] Individually Prescribed Instruction—a program designed to teach arithmetic, reading, and sciences for grades K–6. Subjects are broken into sequences of major cognitive objectives and programmed learning units are provided for each objective. Progress is monitored on the basis of present and past performance.

Contracts

Contracts are another individualized approach that teachers utilize. Contracts may be set up for the class with basic requirements for a passing grade, and options for higher grades. A six-week contract in U.S history might include such options as the following:

D {
Read text assignments.
Attend class.
Get at least 50 per cent on three tests given.

C {
In addition to the previous requirements, participate in class discussion.
Report to class on one current event related to each of three content sections.

B {
In addition to the previous requirements, read a book from the list provided, and participate in a panel discussion to share ideas from the book with the class.

A {
In addition to the previous requirements, plan and carry out an individual project, such as study of a community age, / or investigation of a specific problem. This project must be approv ! by the teacher.

In this approach each student makes a selection of the grade ? aims for and writes a personal contract. The teacher must be aware of qualit n this arrangement. Each contract should include time limits and criteria for sa factory work. The choice by students, as well as timing and quality level, provide or individual differences.

Other uses of contracts may involve more student planning. Grou of students may prepare learning packages that include objectives, resources, ac ities, and tests. Then, individual contracts may be written regarding the use of t se learning packages, their evaluation, or the production of additional packa . Some teachers prefer to use contracts for independent study. The student the will be planning his own objectives, activities, resources, and evaluation. In th situations some teachers establish a range of grades or values that become p sible for those who opt to go this independent route. A maximum number is tablished, 10 points, for example, to be added for acceptable work, or an inc ise of one letter grades for an A/B on the special project. The same cautior of course, applies here regarding judgment of value of work submitted as was ?-viously pointed out. Unless the quality of the work meets the specifications agreed upon at the outset of the activity, full credit will not be awarded to it. The situation to be avoided is permitting students to expect the maximum of reward for spotty or inferior production merely because they have done something extra.

Teacher assistance is important in the contracts that are more student-centered. Guidance in setting reasonable objectives and in selecting appropriate activities helps the student recognize his own strengths and limitations. Students also recognize some of the opportunities and limitations of their environment. Providing for specific evaluation in the contract is important because when the bases for grading are established, misunderstandings are less likely to arise. Usually both self-evaluation and teacher-evaluation should be included in the grading plan for contracts.[5]

Self-evaluation

Self-evaluation is an important goal of the secondary school as well as one aspect of the evaluation process. Effective persons, according to perceptual psychologists, have a positive self-concept. They must think well of themselves, recognizing their capabilities and accepting their limitations. To achieve such self-understanding requires not only having experienced success, but guidance in self-analysis. To meet these needs, teachers should provide opportunities for students to seriously consider what they have learned, how much they have progressed, and what learning styles they have developed. One procedure is the use of rating scales or checklists. These instruments emphasize the criteria for evaluation. They give students a means of expressing their feelings to the teacher, and give the teacher another input of data to use in evaluation. A follow-up conference, in which teacher-and self-ratings are compared and explained, can be mutually beneficial. Probably a joint evaluation should be the final result of such a conference.

Any of the devices developed for evaluating student products and procedures can be utilized for self-evaluation. In addition one can construct specific instruments to encourage self-evaluation. The student may compare responses made early in the school year with those made near the end of the school year. Such comparison may provide the student with information previously not recognized about his or her own growth. Items similar to the following may be used:

1. Check appropriate responses. If other terms should be added, write them in the blanks.
    1. My assignments are turned in
        a. promptly.
        b. late.
        c. on time.
        d. occasionally.
        e. never.
        f. _____ .
    2. My classmates in general consider me
        a. a friend.
        b. a nobody.
        c. a person to ridicule.
        d. an enemy.
        e. _____ .
    3. I consider myself to be
        a. intelligent.
        b. one who has difficulty learning.
        c. average in intelligence.
        d. the smartest in the class.

[5] See Modules 4 and 12 for additional discussion concerning contracts.

     e. the slowest student in the class.

     f. _____ .

   4. My work in school represents

     a. the best I can do.

     b. enough to get by.

     c. my preferences; I do what I enjoy.

     d. as little effort as possible.

     e. whatever will keep the teacher satisfied.

     f. whatever keeps my parents satisfied.

     g. _____ .

Open-ended questions may also provide information to students and teachers. Examples: What have you learned in class this week that you can use outside of school? What have you learned about yourself during this unit?

Some students prefer to let the teacher do the evaluating. The teacher, however, has a responsibility to encourage self-evaluation. Only when individuals recognize their strengths can they utilize their full potential. As human beings they have limitations they should consider realistically as they set their own personal goals. Teachers who accept each student as an individual whose unique capabilities must be encouraged contribute to the development of adolescents. This acceptance, plus successful experiences, gives the student a basis for developing and maintaining self-respect and a feeling of worth. Such a positive self-concept is not only an educational goal in itself but is a prerequisite for maximum learning. Self-evaluation is an essential of the secondary school program and should be implemented by each teacher.

Grading and Reporting

The first step in grading for report cards is to formulate an evaluation plan. This plan should spell out exactly what will be evaluated and what the relative importance of each factor will be. It should be established prior to the teaching so that both the teacher and the students understand the importance of the various activities. A teacher may, for example, in considering plans for six weeks in biology, decide that important activities are (1) class participation; (2) homework assignments; (3) tests (three in number); (4) laboratory performance; and (5) special projects. The importance of these may be established by points, weights, or percentages. The teacher may arbitrarily select a number of points or the appropriate weights as in the following example:

	Points	*Weight*	*Percentage*
1. Class participation	150	3	30
2. Homework assignments	50	1	10
3. Tests	150	3	30
4. Laboratory performance	100	2	20
5. Special projects	50	1	10
	500		100

This decision indicates that tests and class participation will receive equal emphasis; laboratory work is one fifth of the grade; homework and special projects together are considered as important as laboratory work.

Then the teacher must plan the appraisal in each area. Evaluation of class participation cannot be done fairly at the end of six weeks without periodic information. The teacher should sample the class participation throughout the grading period. For example, the discussion on Tuesday of the first week might be evaluated in classes A and B, on Wednesday in classes C and D, and on Thursday in classes E and F. The schedule could be rotated so that the appraisal of discussion would provide a good sample of student behavior. Students who were absent or did not contribute might be deliberately involved in the next evaluation. The teacher should use a system of evaluation that considers the quality as well as the frequency of participation. Marking should be done as soon after class as possible so that the situation is recalled.

Teachers evaluate homework in different ways. Some simply check to see whether the assignment has been done. Others spot-check assigned work. Perhaps question 2 is used as the basis for grading one assignment, and then questions 1 and 6 may be used next time. Sometimes teachers have students check their own work. Since the purpose of discussing assigned work in class is to increase learning, the correcting of papers before they are turned in may have merit. Procedures probably should be varied. However, one should always keep in mind that homework may be the effort of a student, a group of students, a parent, or some other person. Some teachers encourage cooperative study and prefer short, frequent quizzes for the appraisal of daily work by someone. However they arrange it, effective teachers respect the adage that insists on never assigning anything that is not going to be checked.

Evaluating laboratory performance and special projects would involve such evaluation instruments and procedures as ratings, checklists, or logs. Points from these evaluations would necessarily be totaled for each student. Then a frequency distribution could be made and grades assigned by inspection, or by some other procedure, such as using stanines. Teachers should consider the time involved in the procedures and attempt to simplify their work.

Grading Example

Let us consider an example from a biology class. Miss Dougherty, the teacher, has elected to use a five-point scale. She finds that one of her students, Sue Myers, has the following weighted evaluations:

		Evaluation		*Weight*		
1.	Class participation	5	×	3	=	15
2.	Homework	4	×	1	=	4
3.	Tests	3	×	3	=	9
4.	Laboratory performance	5	×	2	=	10
5.	Special projects	2	×	1	=	2
					Total =	40

The frequency distribution for the class follows:

Total Frequency Scores,   *The median is 34*

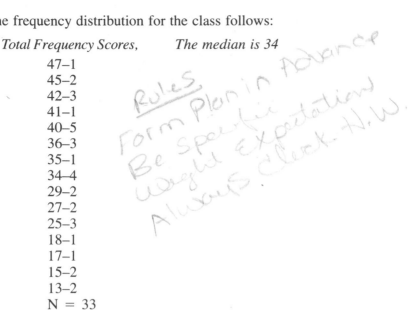

Total Frequency Scores
47–1
45–2
42–3
41–1
40–5
36–3
35–1
34–4
29–2
27–2
25–3
18–1
17–1
15–2
13–2
N = 33

The teacher now applies the grading system of her school to this distribution. There is no absolute way to decide how grades should be allocated. Considering the total situation, the teacher makes the choices that seem most reasonable. Expect to discover that the process of grading is a time-consuming, subjective endeavor.

Exercise 14 B

How would you assign grades A, B, C, D and F to the distribution given in the grading example just cited? Compare your listing with some ideas of experienced teachers (provided at the end of this module).

Grading Systems

The most popular grading system appears to be the use of letter grades in a five-point scale: A, B, C, D, F or U. Some schools use numbers 1, 2, 3, 4, and 5 rather than letters. Often descriptive phrases are used to explain the letter marks, such as A = outstanding achievement or D = minimum achievement. Sometimes letter grades are combined with the percentage system. Then, percentage cutoffs are used for the letter grades, as A, 95–100, or D, 70–76, as noted earlier. In some schools, the five-point scale is modified adding plus (+) or minus (−) to the letters to indicate the upper area or lower area of the letter grade's range. This modification, in effect, changes the five-point scale to a thirteen-point scale.

Percentage grading systems, which were formerly popular, are used less frequently today. It was assumed that teachers could discriminate more clearly the amounts of student progress or differences if they had more specific calibrations to use in their measuring device. Such attempts proved rather futile, however, because few if any teachers could defend the fine distinctions in the schoolwork of students that the percentage system required. It was also assumed that grades of this sort prepared students for the competition they would meet in the adult world because in order to achieve they would have to vie with other students. Motivation to succeed would happen in a natural fashion and serve to augment learning. The failure or disinclination of some students to respond to the stimulus of marks and grading has caused this system of grading to give way to other systems in recent years.

The trend has seemed to be toward a marking system that provides broad areas to indicate general information about individual achievement in comparison to the pattern of the group. However, more schools seem to be trying to develop grading procedures that show the progress of individual students. In general, school marking systems have not provided adequately for the presence of individual differences among students. Students in the typical graded school have been grouped more on a basis of chronological age and time in class than on ability or aptitude. The fact that the manifold differences existing among them is not permitted to modify expectations for each has complicated the teacher's life.

Arriving at the Grade

The following excerpts describe how one school system helps to support each teacher's approach to arriving at marks for work done.

> Teachers provide written instructional objectives and evaluation measures to each student at the beginning of the course. The student is given continual feedback on the quality of work as it relates to the course objectives.
>
> Each teacher develops a percentage based and/or letter based evaluation design best-suited to his or her class for arriving at the quarter grade and the final grade. This design must explicitly indicate how the quarter grade is determined (e.g., the weighting of the tests, assignments, etc.). A copy of this design is placed in the grade book and the information is given to students and parents at the beginning of the course.
>
> Teachers use their judgment on individual tests or assignments in determining the weight of test items and the procedures for scoring tests appropriate for a specific class or subject area.
>
> Grading begins with the individual and with his or her achievement and not with a preconceived pattern. Any system or curve which predetermines the number or distribution of grades tends to be unrealistic and unfair and is not used. Because the art of test making is imprecise at best, this guideline does not preclude teachers' adjusting raw scores or using commercially prepared tests and their results when determining class grades. The county-mandated testing program results are not used in assigning individual student grades. The "curve" of normal distribution should not be used in arriving at grades.
>
> Quizzes, tests, examinations, essays, homework, or papers are evaluated and/or graded, returned promptly, and reviewed with the student before the next related test is administered.
>
> Grades reflect all marks recorded, and each piece of work or each assignment may be valued according to the individual teacher's grading rationale. To emphasize the professional judgment of the teacher in determining quarter, semester and final grades, the following caveat is offered. There may be circumstances in which the collective

quarter marks show a definite trend (ascending or descending) in a student's achievement. When these circumstances occur, a modification of a strictly "numerical" or "letter" average may be a more accurate evaluation of the overall work of the student. For example, students overcoming difficulties during the early part of a grading period should not be penalized for their initial performance; and students enjoying early success and expecting to let this success "average out" should have this "letting down" reported as unsatisfactory performance. The same consideration should be given when determining the final course grade.

A student should be considered to be doing passing work when the marks received indicate a general level of acceptable achievement and a general pattern of acceptable responses. Careful consideration should be given all work. Failure or success on one test or one assigned task (e.g., a book report or notebook) should not be sufficient basis for failing or passing of the course or the grading period.

The teacher conducts frequent and ongoing evaluations in determining a quarter grade. *The teacher is required to use one mark per week in determining a grade, but is encouraged to use at least two marks per week.* These marks can reflect formal or informal tests or quizzes, classroom or lab participation, teacher observation, homework, special assignments, etc. Weekly evaluation encourages class attendance and consistency in study habits.

All nine-week grades and final examination (evaluation activity) grades are used in determining the year's grade. For semester courses, the semester grade is the final grade. For quarter courses, the quarter grade is the final grade. In courses for which the acquisition of a specific skill is the primary terminal objective (e.g., typing) the teacher's grading design will reflect student evaluation in reference to instructional objectives.

The above guidelines are offered to assist teachers in arriving at a grade; however, the grade given reflects the teacher's professional evaluation of student achievement and must be clearly justifiable by the teacher.[6]

Written Evaluations
An alternative calls for written evaluations instead of letter or numerical grades. As utilized by many of the schools today, this plan makes it possible to report not only individual student achievements but also on their strengths, areas needing improvement, social skills, and study habits as well. Such evaluation is more meaningful to parents and students. It also requires careful consideration by the teacher of the individual as a person. However, writing such reports is so time-consuming for the teachers that it may become a vague statement with trite phrases, especially if the teacher tries to write many of these reports at one sitting.

Two-, Three-, Five-Mark Systems
Some schools are using pass-fail grading; they report only if the pupil's work is passing or failing, satisfactory or unsatisfactory. The rationale to support such a system is that it creates a better learning atmosphere. Fewer anxieties and less competition reduce cheating, and yet students work to meet the objectives. Disadvantages include the lack of stimulation for certain students, the possibility that

[6] *Program of Studies Handbook*, Fairfax County Public Schools, Virginia, pp. 7–8.

the evaluation will be neglected, and the fact that excellence goes unrecognized or unrewarded. Because of these disadvantages, some school systems have introduced a three-category system: Honors/Pass/Fail. In an attempt to gain the advantages of both systems, some school systems use both grading systems. In such a plan, for instance, the required courses might be graded with the usual letter grades, but the student might have an option to request pass-fail grading for an elective course.

In addition to subject grades, report cards often include information regarding attitude and habits. A conduct grade to represent social and personal behavior in the school environment has generally been discontinued. Each teacher evaluates the students in regard to their personal and social traits. Frequently, these are reported with coded numbers. The numbers may represent specific behaviors such as (1) study habits are good; (2) assignments are incomplete or unsatisfactory; or (3) improvement in work is evident.

Another way of including evaluation in social and study skills is a five-point scale, ranging from 1—Student initiates opportunities to learn and displays excellent study habits, to 5—Student is apathetic, uncooperative, and disturbs others. All parties touched by this communication system must understand and accept the parameters within which resulting marks are effective. It must be recognized by all that each mark given will be a judgment call and as such is subject to some error. Each interpreter of the grade must accept that a 4 or a 2 on this scale represents an impression by the teacher of the student's participation—not a concise, specific hard number of responses made comparing favorably or unfavorably with the responses from the rest of the class. When separate symbols are used to distinguish achievement from other student behaviors, and all parties accept the guidelines established, communication between the teacher, the student, and the home is facilitated.

Whatever grading system is used, certain essential elements should be included in the evaluation process:

1. Learning objectives should be clearly understood in advance, with criteria for measurement and levels of performance.
2. The teacher should communicate meaningfully, either in written or oral form to the student, in discussing with the student his or her strengths, weaknesses, and suggestions for improvement with respect to the objectives of the course.
3. The student should be involved in self-evaluation of strengths and weaknesses, and should plan improvement in meeting the course objectives as well as personal learning goals.
4. Time is needed for the teacher and student to share perceptions and engage in a discussion of each other's evaluation.[7]

School report systems usually include periodic grading (six or nine weeks), semester grades, and averages for the year. These stipulated marking times necessitate that the planning and use of evaluation procedures be continuous. Interim reports to parents should be used whenever one notes a change in a student's

---

[7] Glenys G. Unruh and William M. Alexander, *Innovations in Secondary Education*, 2d ed. (New York: Holt, Rinehart and Winston, 1974), p. 49.

general behavior. Improved performance, as well as less favorable trends, should be reported to the student and to the home. The school can encourage students greatly by commendations for progress. In some communities, contacts between the home and school always involve problems. Positive reinforcement can help students and help produce amicable school-community relations.

Testing Goals

The tendency to forget the reason for testing or evaluating or grading is ever present for teachers. Busy teachers sometimes can become preoccupied with the process and lose almost complete sight of the product and/or the purpose. They begin to test to get a mark or a grade for reporting purposes, and thus students start giving little thought to the learning that has transpired or that yet remains to be mastered. One of the goals of teaching is keeping the student aware of the goals of teaching so that he can alter his study procedures to fit his needs. When the student is appropriately motivated, he should seek such information in his quest of a learning goal. Teachers can supply such guidance only when they have available the appropriate data on which to base their counsel. The fact that these data can also be used for communicating to parents and others about student progress should be looked upon as a plus but must always be kept in its place as a helping technique rather than as an ultimate purpose.

Since evaluation is an integral factor in the teaching-learning process, you must aim to include the following in your teaching performance:

1. Utilize a variety of instruments to appraise the behavior of students and to focus on the development of the individual. Keep students informed of their standing and progress. Return tests promptly, review the answers to all questions, and respond to inquiries about marks given. Writing the frequency distribution of the scores on the board will enable each student to see where he is and to interpret his score in relation to the rest of the class.

2. Use appraisal procedures continuously so as to contribute to the positive development of the individual student. Such an emphasis requires that the evaluation be important to the student and related to what he considers important. Effective evaluation is helping the student know his competencies and achievement. It encourages further learning and the selection of appropriate tasks. Some teachers give a short quiz every day for this purpose, whereas others achieve the same end by periodic unannounced short tests. Full period tests are reserved for the end of a chapter, or unit, and also the end of a quarter or semester.

3. Adapt the marking system of the school to your situation. When you set your own standard and grade each student in relation to it, you are said to be using an absolute system of grading. When you use the normal curve or a predetermined percentage in each category as the basis for awarding grades, you are said to be using a relative system. Of the two, the absolute system that incorporates your judgment of a student's progress more properly places emphasis on individual evaluation.

4. Avoid using grades as a threat or overstressing them for motivational purposes. It is legitimate to consider as tentative the grade you arrive at after consideration of the factual data you have accumulated. Consideration of extenuating circumstances, such as sudden illness in class, prolonged absence for a serious matter, and so on should then take place before making the grades permanent. Adjusting a borderline mark into the higher alternative in the light of some classroom performance is indeed defensible. Almost never, though, is it prudent to award a lower grade to a student than he has already earned on the basis of the objective evidence at hand.

5. Consider your grading procedures carefully, preplan them, and explain your policies to the students. The various factors to be considered in arriving at a grade and the weight accorded to such things as homework, written assignments, and oral class contributions should all be explained before study is begun.

6. Involve the students, whenever feasible, in setting up criteria and establishing the relative importance of activities. Such cooperative planning is a learning experience for students and encourages self-evaluation. It is important that students understand the directions on any test you give. Before permitting students to begin, make sure to explain any ambiguities that result from the terminology used. Base your tests on the important material that has been taught. Your purpose in giving the test, of course, is not to trap or confuse the student but to evaluate how well he or she has assimilated the important aspects of learning.

7. Incorporate continuous evaluation in your learning activities to be sure that students are aware of their progress. The goals of tests administered should serve as a challenge, but they should be attainable. Goals set too high or made up of questions that are too hard discourage students and so diminish the motivational factor. Goals set too low, with questions that are too easy, encourage disregard of the subject matter that is taught and perpetuation of a lackadaisical approach to study.

8. Strive for objective and impartial appraisal as you put your evaluation plan into operation. Do not allow personal feelings to enter into a grade. Whether you like or dislike a student, the grade you give should represent the student's level of achievement based on the same objective standard used for all.

9. Try to minimize arguments about grades, cheating, and teacher subjectivity by involving students in the planning, reinforcing individual student development, and providing an accepting, stimulating learning environment. Remain alert while students are taking a test. Do not occupy yourself with other tasks at your desk such as reading a book or marking papers while a test is in progress. Circulate, observe, present at least a psychological deterrent to cheating by your demeanor, but be sure not to distract.

10. Keep accurate and clear records of test results so that you will have an adequate supply of data on which to base your judgmental decisions about grades. Sufficient data of this sort are especially helpful when final grades are called into questions or when students or parents require information in depth.

Suggested Reading

Ahman, J. Stanley, and Marvin D. Glock. *Evaluating Pupil Growth: Principles of Tests and Measurement,* 6th ed. Boston: Allyn & Bacon, 1979.

Bellanca, James A. *Grading.* Washington, D.C.: National Education Association, 1977.

Bloom, Benjamin S., George F. Madaus, and J. Thomas Hastings. *Evaluation to Improve Learning.* New York: McGraw-Hill, 1981.

Evaluation and Reporting of Student Achievement, What Research Says to the Teacher. Washington, D.C.: National Education Association, 1974.

Grambs, Jean D., and John C. Carr. *Modern Methods in Secondary Education.* New York: Holt Rinehart and Winston, 1979.

Gronlund, Norman E., *Measurement and Evaluation in Education,* 5th ed. New York: Macmillan Publishing Co., 1985.

———. *Stating Objectives for the Classroom,* 3rd ed. New York: Macmillan Publishing Co., 1985.

Hopkins, Charles D., and Richard L. Antes. *Classroom Measurement and Evaluation,* 2d ed. Itasca Il: F. E. Peacock, 1984.

Mehrens, William, and Irving J. Lehmann. *Measurement and Evaluation in Education and Psychology,* 3d ed. New York: Holt, Rinehart and Winston, 1984.

Milton, Ohmer, and John W. Edgerly. *The Testing and Grading of Students.* New Rochelle, N.Y.: Change Magazine, 1976.

Simon, Sidney B., and James A. Bellanca, eds. *Degrading the Grading Myths: A Primer of Alternatives to Grades and Marks.* Washington, D.C.: Association for Supervision and Curriculum Development, 1976.

Weiner, Elliot A., and Barbara J. Stewart. *Assessing Individuals: Psychological and Educational Tests and Measurements.* Boston: Little, Brown, 1984.

Exercise Answer Key
Exercise 14 A

The frequency distribution table follows.

Raw Score	Frequency
35	1
34	1
32	2
31	3
30	5
28	1
27	1
26	4
25	3
24	3
21	2
20	2
19	1
18	2
10	1

$$N = 32$$

The median is 26.

The percentage of scores and the number of scores to be allocated to each stanine band would be

Stanine	Per Cent		Number of Scores
9	4%	of 32 =	1.28 (or 1)
8	7%	of 32 =	2.24 (or 2)
7	12%	of 32 =	3.84 (or 4)
6	17%	of 32 =	5.44 (or 5)
5	20%	of 32 =	6.40 (or 6)
4	17%	of 32 =	5.44 (or 5)
3	12%	of 32 =	3.84 (or 4)
2	7%	of 32 =	2.24 (or 2)
1	4%	of 32 =	1.28 (or 1)

Allocations of scores to the stanines must be approximated because we cannot use fractions and all the same scores must appear in the same stanine. Following are two sets of possible allocations of scores and corresponding letter marks based on the foregoing data.

Stanine	Possible Score Allocation	Letter Marks	Possible Score Allocation	Letter Marks
9	34–35	A	34–35	A
8	32	B	32	B
7	31		31	
6	27–30		28–30	
5	26	C	25–26–27	C
4	24–25		24	
3	20–21	D	19–20–21	D
2	18–19		18	
1	10	F	10	F

Exercise 14 B

Possible grades for the biology class:

Scores Frequency

47–1	A
45–2	A
42–3	B
41–1	B
40–5	B
36–3	
35–1	
34–4	C
29–2	C
27–2	
25–3	
18–1	
17–1	D
15–2	D
13–2	F
N = 33	

If biology is a course for select students,

40–47 = A
25–36 = B
13–18 = C

_____

If stanines are estimated,

45–47 = A
41–42 = B
25–40 = C
15–18 = D
   13 = F

Post Test

Select the best answer to complete the statement and put the correct letter in the blank at the left.

 b **1.** In setting up a frequency distribution the teacher begins by
 a. listing all scores.
 b. arranging scores from low to high.
 c. finding the middle score.
 d. tabulating scores.

 C **2.** Use of normal curve in grading implies that the teacher
 a. has an average class.
 b. will know how many A, B, C, D, and F grades to give.
 c. will make judgments about assigning grades.
 d. is using a fair and impartial system.

a **3.** If a teacher wants three tests to have equal weight,
 a. the raw scores must be changed to standard scores.
 b. the raw scores are simply added for a total score.
 c. each test score is assigned a letter grade that is translated to points and the points are totaled.
 d. each test score should be expressed as percentage correct and the three should be added.

 c **4.** An advanced class received the following scores on a science test: 29, 16, 20, 23, 28, 25, 11, 15, 26, 17, 20, 23, 27, 25, 23, and 19. What is the median?
 a. 26
 b. 15
 c. 23
 d. 21

a **5.** An effective grading system is *least* likely to
 a. be limited to academic achievement.
 b. include evaluation of a variety of student behaviors.
 c. be able to provide criterion- and norm-referenced grades.
 d. provide information about the achievement of objectives.

 d **6.** Student products and processes are evaluated by
 a. one of the following devices: a rating scale, checklist, anecdotal record, log.
 b. teacher, student, and peers.
 c. the criterion established in the behavioral objective.
 d. the procedure and individuals appropriate to the intent of the objective.

 b **7.** Homework is an important phase of learning activities in many classes and consequently should be
 a. carefully graded by the teacher.
 b. utilized for learning.

    c. occasionally collected and spot-checked.

    d. considered as a major.

 8. When contracts are used in a class, the major purpose of evaluation is to

    a. grade the students.

    b. consider whether the student accomplished the amount of work he selected.

    c. determine the quality of student achievement.

    d. increase self-analysis and development through individual goals and criteria.

 9. Class participation can be graded easily and fairly

    a. at the end of the grading period.

    b. by a plan of daily grading.

    c. by a planned schedule of grading each class.

    d. by keeping anecdotal records.

 10. Students learn best when they are

    a. reminded of their shortcomings so that they are more realistic in setting goals.

    b. accepted as worthy individuals and are encouraged to undertake challenging tasks.

    c. homogeneously grouped and are encouraged to work together on similar tasks.

    d. heterogeneously grouped and are encouragd to work together on similar tasks.

11–15. *A group from the Student Council of Walton High School studied grading systems. Its report to the Advisory Committee included a statement of purpose for grading. Read the following statements and check those that provide valid reasons for grades.*

____ **11.** Teachers can control student behavior with grades.

____ **12.** Colleges and employers can get information about students.

____ **13.** Grades give a student information about his progress.

____ **14.** Grades replace learning as a motivation for students.

____ **15.** Grades encourage continuous evaluation of student learning.

16–19. *Miss Taylor decided to use a weight system for six-week grades. The four items selected were class participation; tests; group project; and assignments. She decided that the most important phase of the learning activities was class participation, which should be half of the grade. The group project and tests were of equal value, but the assignments were half as important as the tests. Set up a system of weights for Miss Taylor to use. Put the appropriate number at the left.*

 16. Class participation.

2

_____ **17.** Tests.

2

_____ **18.** Group projects.

1

_____ **19.** Assignments.

20–25. *Indicate in the blank provided which of the following situations require*
a. *criterion-referenced grades.*
b. *norm-referenced grades.*
c. *both kinds of evaluation.*
d. *neither type of evaluation.*

a

_____ **20.** To select students for continuing the study of French from French II classes.

d

_____ **21.** To find students to do special projects in their special interests for biology.

b

_____ **22.** To assign a transfer student to the appropriate English class in a three-track English program (slow, average, advanced).

b

_____ **23.** To choose students for competition in the state science tests.

d

_____ **24.** To select an appropriate learning package for individualized instruction in geometry.

a

_____ **25.** To decide whether a student should go to the next level of instruction in a continuous progress general science curriculum.

MODULE
15

Instructional Resources

Rationale

Once upon a time, when mankind was young and reading and writing had not yet been invented, men and women taught their children by means of very simple tools. Telling children what they should know was a very important teaching technique. But there were other teaching and learning methods, too. Boys learned to hunt by practicing with spears, by throwing sticks, and by simulated hunts of simulated animals. Parents taught geography by maps drawn in the sand. Religion was taught by pictures drawn on the walls of caves. History, customs, and lore of a group were portrayed by dance and drama. From the very earliest times, teachers have depended on diverse teaching tools to make their teaching effective and interesting.

Today, teachers still depend on teaching tools to make their teaching effective and interesting. In some respects though our modern teaching tools are much more sophisticated than those of old. Yet, we use our new tools for the same purposes and in much the same ways that our forefathers did: to make things clear, to make instruction real, to spice up the teaching-learning process, and to make it possible for pupils to teach themselves. It is impossible to teach without some tools.

This module will focus on how to use effectively the type of teaching tool called audiovisual aids. The aim will not be to teach you how to run the machines and gadgets that make up modern pedagogical technology but to help you to develop a philosophy for using them and to point out some strategies for using these tools in your teaching.[1]

Specific Objectives

By the end of your study of this module you will have command of a general strategy for the use of audiovisual aids, and will be able to recite, in general, something about the various types of audiovisual aids available to you and how to use them.

Specifically, you will be expected to be able to do the following:

1. Explain the benefits of using audiovisual aids.
2. Explain the virtues and uses of overhead projectors, opaque projectors, slide projectors, and filmstrip projectors.
3. Explain how to make and use transparencies, flip-ons, overlays, and masks.
4. Describe how to prepare a slide program.
5. Describe the general procedures for presenting instructional films.
6. Describe how to adapt slide projectors, filmstrip projectors, and moving picture projectors for individual or small-group instruction.
7. Describe how to use commercial and P.B.S. television to enhance classroom instruction.
8. Explain the recommended procedure for conducting instructional television classes.
9. Describe procedures for using taped recordings and records.
10. Describe uses of computers and micro computers, and other teaching machines.
11. Describe ways to mix instructional media.
12. Describe criteria for selecting audiovisual devices.
13. Describe general principles for the effective operation of projectors.
14. Explain ways in which one might make use of commercial films for instruction.
15. Explain the pros and cons of silent and sound films and video tapes.

---

[1] *Technology* is a word with wide meaning. So is the word *medium*. Technology includes machines and techniques. A technique for individualizing instruction is as much a part of educational technology as a teaching machine. Medium refers to any intermediate agency, means, instrument, or channel. A lecture, a movie, a television show, a newspaper, and a picture all are media by which persons can transmit ideas to other people. We should be careful not to confuse technology with gadgetry and medium with the mass media. Each word has wider meaning. Further, we should be careful to remember that *medium* is singular and *media* plural. There is no such thing as a *media*, only a *medium*.

Module Text

Audiovisual Aids

Certain teaching tools that rely upon sight and sound fall into the category commonly known as audiovisual aids. In this category, we can include such teaching tools as films, charts, overhead projectors, filmstrips, models, microscopes, pictures, slides, graphs, phonograph records, maps, mock-ups, audio tapes, globes, terrain boards, radio, opaque projectors, chalkboards, television, and flannelboards.

Exercise 15 A

How many of these teaching tools are familiar to you? How have they been used in classes you have attended? Were they used successfully? That is, did you learn more readily through their usage, or more thoroughly?

These teaching tools are aids to teaching. It is important to remember that their role is to aid you in your teaching. They do not do the teaching. It is you who must select the objectives, orchestrate the teaching plan, evaluate the results, and follow up. If you use these tools prudently as aids, your teaching will benefit.

Uses of Audiovisual Aids

The main effort of any teacher in instruction is to make the message clear—communicate the idea, capture the content, clarify the obscure for the learner. Hence we have the almost universal reliance of teachers upon the spoken word. Most of the day for teachers is filled with periods of explanation and discourse to the point that the teaching profession has been accused of perpetuating verbalism in the schools. We use definitions and recitations and, too often, rote memory in the quest of the goals for the day.

Audiovisual aids can often serve to facilitate understanding and eliminate some of the verbalism. Utilizing the concept that one picture is worth a thousand words, such aids attempt to clarify the presentation and to intensify the image by doubling the number of senses through which the information is communicated to the learner. Instead of mere oral description, the suggestion is to create visual images to accompany the script. In communicating the definition of a word such as *escarpment*, for example, imagine how much more vivid and effective and complete the students' understanding could be when pictures or slides or films are used than if the medium were limited to the spoken word alone. With the visuals added, an empathy for the word can be developed; a "eureka" phenomenon can be induced pertaining to hills and mountains and all outdoors in lieu of the memorization of a bare-bones definition that satisfies only the verbal need for understanding. Consider, too, a presentation of the concept of air pressure in lecture form versus an actual demonstration or a visual presentation of the crushing of a vacuumized can by the power of the atmosphere. Again, weigh a recitation by a teacher about the forces that cause a volcano against a graphic illustration with a model that contains colored and detachable parts.

Evidently, aids not only can facilitate and help clinch the achieving of educational goals but also can be exciting and enhance the lessons being taught. If properly utilized aids can make graphic and thrilling what might have remained pedestrian and routine. They can add color to a presentation, help motivate some students to attend to the instruction, and serve to reinforce the learning that has already taken place.

Sometimes you may hear teachers express the opinion that the use of audiovisual aids sugarcoats learning and so is educationally undignified. Don't be misled. Remember that your job is to teach so that pupils learn something well enough to remember it. Any device that will help you achieve that end is good. The teaching device that will get the idea across is the one you want to use, even though its use may not appear academically rigorous. The use of audiovisual aids is an essential for making teaching effective.

General Audiovisual Teaching Procedures

Like any other boon to progress, audiovisual aids must be worked with if they are to yield as expected. The mediocre teacher who is content to get by without expending any additional effort on his teaching will in all likelihood remain that, just a mediocre teacher, despite the excellent quality of whatever aids he chances to use. Because the mediocre teacher fails to rise to the occasion and hence presents poorly, his lesson will result in being less effective and less impressive than it might have been. The effective teacher will make the inquiry about audiovisual aids and expend the effort needed to implement them well for the benefit of the class. The effective teacher will capitalize on the drama made possible by the shift in presentation method and spice up the quest for knowledge by utilizing vivid materials. Such behavior will involve four steps: (1) selection of the right audiovisual aid; (2) preparing the aid for use; (3) using the aid skillfully; and (4) following up the utilization.

Selecting the Proper Aid. Care must be exercised in the selection of an audiovisual aid for use in the classroom. A poor selection, an inappropriate aid, can turn a heretofore excellent lesson into a disappointing fiasco. An audiovisual aid that projects garbled sound, that presents obscure or shaky images, or that is too profound will certainly not be met with delighted response from the class. An aid that is too difficult to present or takes too long to set up, or that is not suitable for the age level will dampen the enthusiasm of a class as quickly as a boring lesson.

In the selection process, then, the effective teacher follows an inquiry routine similar to this:

1. Is the contemplated aid suitable? Will it help to achieve the objective of the lesson? Will it present an accurate understanding of the facts in the case? Will the aid highlight the points that the teaching has underscored? Will it work with the equipment used in the school?
2. Is the audiovisual aid within the level of understanding of the class? Is it too mature? too embarassing? too dated?
3. Is the audiovidual aid lucid in its presentation? Is it clear in its images and sounds?
4. Is the audiovisual aid readily available?

The best response for most of these questions can come after a careful previewing of the aid. Sometimes because of existing conditions this dry run is not possible. However, the best way to discover how inadequate the catalogue descriptions are of films, filmstrips, videotapes, and records, or the condition in which the product has been left by previous users, is to try them out yourself under practice conditions.

Preparing for the Audiovisual Aid. To use audiovisual aids with maximum effectiveness usually will require preparation of two types: psychological and physical. From the psychological point, students have to be prepped for the utilization of the aid and coached on how best to profit from its presentation. Films, filmstrips, recordings, and pictures will require that you spend some time setting the scene. You will need to make clear the purpose of the activity, suggest points to look for, present problems to solve, and, in general, clue your students about potential dangers that may mislead them.

From the physical point, preparation pertaining to the machine to be used, the equipment involved, and the arrangement of the classroom furniture will have to be attended to. Sometimes, as with the use of the chalkboard, the preparation is minimal. All that may be necessary may be the identification of the aid and a brief recitation concerning the use you intend to make of it other than making sure of a satisfactory supply of chalk and erasers. At other times, however, as when the morning or afternoon sun affects the visibility, each section of the classroom will need to be checked, as well as the focusing dials of the apparatus for appropriate sharpness of images and the amplitude dials for clarity of voice sound. In the absence of preparation, bedlam can ensue. The missing chalk, the borrowing and lending of board erasers among the students, or the absence of an extension cord can spell defeat for even the best audiovisual aid. The double-checking of the action-readiness of the projector, and the arrangement in sequence of the slides to be used are vital to success.

Guiding the Audiovisual Activity. The purpose of audiovisual teaching tools is not to replace teaching, but to make teaching more effective. Therefore, you cannot expect the tool to do all the work. You should, however, make it work for your purposes. You will have to highlight in advance the usage of those things that you want to be remembered most completely. You may have to enumerate the concepts that are developed or to illustrate relationships or conclusions that you wish to be drawn. You may have to prepare and distribute a study guide or a list of questions for students to respond to; to stop the presentation periodically for hints or questions; or maybe even to repeat the entire performance to ensure a more thorough grasp of particulars.

Following Up Audiovisual Activities. Audiovisual presentations that are allowed to just lie there upon completion squander valuable learning opportunities. Some discussion should ensue that is pointed and directed toward closure. The time for such postmortems should have been a vital part of the preparation-for-use-of-aids discussed in the previous paragraph. Upon completion of the use of the aid, students are now permitted to and indeed expected to engage in responding to the sets of questions proposed in the preview activity. Points that were fuzzily made should be clarified. Questions that were not answered should be pursued in depth. Deeper responses that go beyond the present scope of the inquiry should be noted and earmarked for further probing at a later date. Quizzes, reviews, practice, and discussions all can be used to tie loose ends together, to highlight the major concepts, to clinch the essential learnings. The planned, efficient use of the aid helps create the atmosphere that audiovisual presentations are learning opportunities and not purely recreational activities.

Projection and Projectors

Projection machines make it possible to bring into the classroom experiences in a vivid form that otherwise could only be talked about. For example, a film on Egypt can re-create for students aspects of life in a distant land or ancient culture that they might be exposed to in no other way. Such machines also enable a teacher to project the image of an artifact, or of a picture, or of a book page on a screen in such a fashion as to be discernible to all at the same time without interrupting the flow of the class that occurs when pupils must pass realia from hand to hand about the room. Among the most common and most useful kinds of projectors available for teachers' use are the opaque projector, the slide projector, the filmstrip projector, the overhead projector, and, of course, the motion-picture projector. Modern technology has improved these machines so that despite their growing sophistication and multiplicity, they have been almost defanged. Attention has been devoted to making more simple the running procedure for each in order to diminish the risk of error in operation.

Operating Projectors

This module lacks the space to dwell at length on how to run the various machines used as teaching aids. Each has its own idiosyncrasies peculiar to its own make and model. The hands-on approach in which you cultivate a familiarity with a strange machine and develop your dexterity in handling it by actually going through the motions and manipulating its parts is the mode of study recommended by this module of study. However, there are a few general principles that you ought to keep in mind any time you are confronted with a machine with which you are unfamiliar:

1. Handle it. Push its buttons and learn what happens. Dissipate your anxiety about your personal affliction of awkwardness in the presence of such a robotical monster. Gain familiarity with the vernacular about the machine; say the words, and aim to increase your at-easeness when near it. Whatever facility you develop beforehand will stand you in good stead on D-days when the students are present or when mayhem is imminent in a class that is teetering on the brink of boredom while waiting for the show to begin or to continue.
2. One of the first interviews you should conduct in each new school you join after your career has been launched is with regard to the audiovisual equipment possessed by that school. It may be severely dated and mark-

edly different from what you have been exposed to in practice. The generalities that you have collected, however, should see you through to success, especially if you have set aside your awe of the mechanical and strengthened your confidence in yourself.

3. Your first move in greeting audiovisual machines should be to read the directions supplied. The more difficult machines usually have the directions printed somewhere on the casing. These directions will show how the machine's operations differ from others of the same ilk, such as how, specifically, to thread the film, even though the principles are always more or less the same.

4. Projectors all have to be focused. Focusing is done by adjusting the distance from the light source to the lens and/or the lens to the screen. In a slide projector or a movie projector, the light source is in back and the lens in front. In an overhead projector, the light source is on the bottom and the lens is on top. The light passes from the light source through a slide or transparency (frame) and through the lens to the screen. What you have to do is to move the lens back and forth (or up and down in the case of the overhead) until you get a clear picture. Usually the best technique is to move from a blur through a sharp focus until the image starts to blur again and then turn back to the point of sharpest focus. The image can also be brought into focus by moving the projector toward or away from the screen. This fact is important to remember when you find that you cannot move the lens far enough to focus the image sharply.

The point stressed here is that no matter what projection machine with which you have to deal, you focus it by establishing the proper distance between the lens and light source and lens and screen. You look in turn how to plug the set in, how to turn the set on, and how to adjust the distance to get a sharp picture.

Exercise 15 B

Are you ready for a review of what you have just learned? Respond simply to the following:
(1) If you were faced with a new overhead projector you had never seen before, how would you go about focusing it, once you had found out how to turn it on?
(2) If the projector were a filmstrip projector rather than an overhead projector, what difference in focusing would you expect?

The Opaque Projector

The opaque projector (see Figure 15-1) is a most convenient teaching tool. It usually requires a dark room that may be difficult to effect. Since the model used loads from underneath if the size of the object projected should be bulky, it may let light seep out. Bringing the picture into sharp focus can also be tricky. Once you get the hang of focusing it, though, you will find this machine can be used to meet many of your classroom needs. The enlarged image that you desire of a

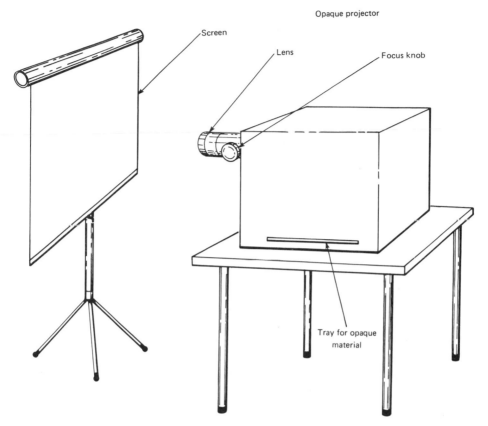

Opaque projector

Screen

Lens

Focus knob

Tray for opaque
material

FIGURE 15-1 *Opaque Projector*

picture or of a printed page, or of a test paper, or of a three-dimensional object can be projected onto a film screen, or on a white wall or even on a chalkboard. A distinctive feature of the opaque projector is the presence of a *platen*—a shelf at the base of the machine that can be lowered or raised on which is placed the item to be projected. A handle or a crank is provided for this operation. When the platen has been returned to its closed position, after loading, it is held by springs to keep the picture or object to be viewed immobilized. When showing pictures from textbooks or the like, a piece of heat-resistant glass can be placed across the open book to flatten its surface and thus improve the focus of the screen picture. Objects that may be damaged by heat should not be used in this projector. In addition, objects made of metal may become hot to handle after they have been in the machine and should be touched with care. In the classroom you use this projector for the following purposes:

1. Project pictures and other opaque materials that are too small for pupils to see easily from their seats. This practice eliminates the necessity for passing such material around the class. It also allows everyone a chance to see the material at once, and gives you a chance to point out details and clear up questions while everyone can see.

2. Enlarge maps and project them on a suitable surface to trace the boundaries, rivers, and other features represented.
3. Project pupils' work so all pupils can see it as you discuss it. This is an excellent device to show pupils good practice, or to allow pupils to react to each other's work.
4. Project illustrative material in pupil reports. Often, shy pupils do well at reporting when they can use projection as a support.
5. Project work on the chalkboard for evaluation and correction.
6. Project illustrative material for lectures and teacher or pupils talks.

The great advantage of the opaque projector is that it projects the image of the real thing. It is not necessary to prepare a slide or a transparency. All that one needs to do is to place the material to be projected on the bed of the projector, turn the projector on, and focus it. Focusing objects such as the pages of a book that will not lie flat may be something of a problem, but usually with patience you will obtain clear images on a screen.

Exercise 15 C

Let us suppose you have never used an opaque projector before. You have loaded a picture on the tray, turned the projector on, and removed the lens cover. You have an image on the screen, but it is not in focus. How do you focus it?

The Overhead Projector

One of the most versatile of teaching tools is the overhead projector (see Figure 15-2). Every classroom should have one just as every classroom should have a chalkboard. It can be used in full daylight. It allows you to point things out or to make notations from the front of the room without turning your back to the class or standing in front of the material you want the pupils to see. It allows you to prepare material ahead of time and save it for use again and again. With the help of flip-ons, it is easy to show development and changes and to compare and contrast. It can be used to record the progress of a discussion. The overhead projector can both make your teaching more effective and reduce the amount of time you must spend on tiresome chores such as copying material on the chalkboard.

A few ways in which the overhead projector may be used follow.

1. Write on the transparency as on a chalkboard while the class proceeds. When the time comes to move on, just roll up the acetate or take a new blank sheet. In this way, you do not have to erase and so can come back to reconsider, if necessary.
2. Emphasize specific points in a lesson by projecting them as they come up in class.
   a. Write points on the transparency as you go along.
   b. Flip-on preprinted materials at propitious moments.
   c. Uncover blocked out preprinted material as the points come up. To keep preprinted material out of sight, simply cover it with opaque material until the proper moment.

Overhead Projector

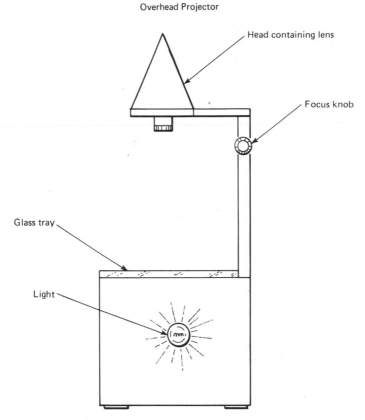

FIGURE 15-2 Overhead Projector. An overhead projector consists of a glass-topped box that contains a light source and a vertical post mounting a head that contains a lens. To use it, place an acetate transparency on the glass top (some overhead projectors are equipped with acetate rolls to use as transparencies), switch on the light, and adjust the focus by moving the head, which contains the lens, up and down

3. Present pictures, drawings, diagrams, outlines, printed matter, and maps.
4. Project an outline form. Fill it in as you go along.
5. Project an outline. Cover it. As you proceed, uncover the points as they are made.
6. Reproduce or enlarge maps.
7. Project grids for graphing.
8. Project silhouettes.
9. Project tests and quizzes.
10. Correct tests, quizzes, and papers. Project the correct answers by writing on the transparency. Transparencies made on spirit duplicators are excellent for this purpose because one can also make duplicate copies. It is then possible for the teacher to go over something projected on the screen or board while the pupils follow along on their own copies.

Preparing Transparencies. Overhead projectors project images in the same way that motion-picture projectors and slide projectors do by shining light through a transparent film or glass. They will not project opaque substances except to make silhouettes. Transparencies may be bought readymade. Many excellent ones are for sale by the various supply houses; however, they are extremely easy to make. Even though the transparencies you make may not be as finished as those commercially made, you will probably find that your own homemade transparencies are more effective for your purposes. After all, when you make your own, you can tailor them to your own needs, something a stranger cannot do, no matter how expert he may be. You can make satisfactory transparencies for overhead projection by the following methods:

1. By using a Polaroid or copy camera. (Polaroid sells a special film for this purpose).
2. By drawing or writing directly on acetate. Usually a frosted acetate, frosted side up, seems to work better for this purpose than smooth, clear acetate. Use India ink, drawing ink, transparent color pencils, felt tipped pens, or grease pencils (china marking pencils) for writing directly on acetate. If you wish to project in color, remember to select an ink or pencil that is translucent. Opaque inks and pencils project only in black, or in silhouette. Grease pencils (china marking pencils) work very well, but the pencils sold by supply houses specifically for making transparencies may be better. If you use felt-tipped pens, check to see whether the ink and the acetate are compatible. Sometimes the ink of the felt-tipped pens will not stick to the acetate.

Impromptu transparencies can be made by writing or drawing while the transparency is on the machine. One can make up a transparency as the class progresses, for instance, by recording on a transparency the important points made in a discussion. For more finished transparencies, the following procedure is recommended:

   a. Sketch the transparency on a sheet of paper.
   b. Cover the paper with the acetate transparency sheet.
   c. Trace the sketch. Use drawing ink.
   d. Add color if you wish. Use translucent colored inks, felt-tipped pens, or transparent color pencils.
   e. Spray with a clear plastic to give permanence.
   f. Mount the transparencies, if you wish.

3. One can also make transparencies on spirit master duplicating machines. If you wish, the machine will make color transparencies. The technique for making such transparencies includes the following:
   a. Make a spirit master as you would for any other duplicating. Use color if you wish to project in color.
   b. Place the spirit master on the duplicating machine and run through two or three sheets of paper to be sure it is working properly.
   c. Take a sheet of frosted acetate, frosted side up, and hand feed it through the duplicator.
   d. Spray the resulting transparency with a clear plastic.
   e. Mount the transparency if you wish. A clear sheet of plastic placed over the transparency face when mounting will give it additional protection.

4. Transparencies may be made on several types of copying machines. With these machines, one can make transparencies from books or from single sheets of printed or typed material. The capabilities of the machines differ according to their design and the copying process used. Consequently, one should become familiar with a machine's capabilities and the technique for operating it before attempting to make transparencies.

5. By lifting pictures from magazines and similar sources if the paper of the magazine is clay-coated. Probably the easiest of several ways to lift a picture is the following method which uses clear Contact paper:

   a. Test the paper to see if it is clay-coated. To do this, wet your finger and rub it along the border of the picture. If greyish white substance rubs off on your finger, the paper is clay-coated.

   b. Cut a piece of Contact paper to fit the picture. Contact can be purchased in any home-center, wallpaper or hardware store, variety or five-and-ten-cent store.

   c. Place the picture face up on a flat surface.

   d. Remove the protective covering from the Contact and place the Contact on the picture, sticky side down.

   e. Bind the Contact to the picture. Rub from top to bottom and left to right. Use a straight edge or a rolling pin. Be sure you get a good bond all over; you should have no air bubbles or creases when you get through.

   f. Place the Contact with the picture bonded to it in a pan of water.

   g. Add a teaspoon of detergent and let soak for at least half an hour.

   h. Remove the picture and Contact from the water. Slowly and easily pull the paper (picture) from the Contact. *Do not rush this step. Be sure to leave the picture and Contact in the water long enough before you try to separate the picture from the paper. If the picture does not come clean, the transparency will be worthless.*

   i. Wipe off any residue of paper or clay with a soft wet rag or a piece of cotton.

   j. Blot off any excess moisture with a paper towel.

   k. Let dry.

   l. Spray with clear plastic.

   m. Mount.

Mounting Transparencies.   If you wish, you can mount your transparencies. Mounting transparencies has certain advantages when it comes to preserving and storing them, although, in some cases, the added length and width makes them difficult to transport and file. Mounts are necessary if one intends to attach flip-ons to the transparency. Otherwise, except for certain machine-made transparencies that are very thin, mounting is not an absolute necessity.

Making a Transparency Overlay.   A transparency overlay is one that you can flip on to another so as to change the detail being presented. Thus, if the basic transparency was an outline map of Europe, for example, one flip-on might show the national boundaries prior to 1914, another the boundaries in 1921, another in 1940, and another in 1980. Or the basic transparency might show the formula: 2

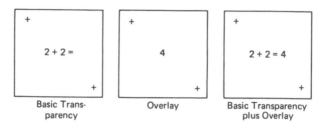

FIGURE 15-3   *Transparency with Overlay*

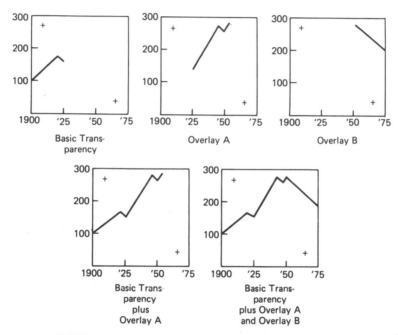

FIGURE 15-4   *Transparency with Several Overlays*

+ 2 = and the overlay shows the answer: 4. By adding the overlay to the basic transparency one can show the complete formula: 2 + 2 = 4. This is illustrated in Figure 15-3. Or if we wish to show the variation of a phenomenon during the first quarters, we could combine overlays of a graph as in Figure 15-4.

You make overlays or flip-ons for transparencies in exactly the same way that you make the transparencies. You can just lay them on top of the basic overlay, if you wish, but usually it is better to hinge them to the basic transparency's mount. Separate overlays tend to get mixed up and to mix you up. Hinges can be purchased or made out of a piece of tape (Figure 15-5).

Use reference marks (+) at the top left and bottom right corners of the basic transparency and each overlay so that you can match them up properly and easily, as shown in Figure 15-6. When the + marks on the overlay fit exactly over the + marks on the basic transparency, the two are properly aligned.

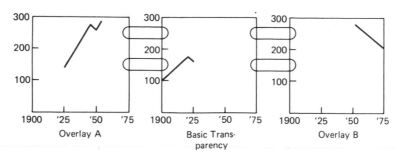

FIGURE 15-5 *Graph Presented with Hinged Overlays*

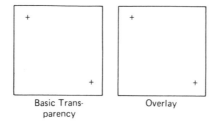

FIGURE 15-6 *Overlay Line-Up Technique*

Masks. Masks are opaque overlays that block out a portion of the transparency so it will not be projected. You can make a mask by laying a piece of paper over the area not to be shown, or you can hinge a piece of light cardboard or plastic so that it will cover the area you wish to block off. The latter procedure is advantageous when one wishes to use the transparency again and again. Masks are useful for heightening the dramatic impact of the information to be shown by the transparency during the class.

Exercise 15 D

Suppose you want to present an outline of a lecture point by point as you proceed through the lecture.
(1) How could you do it with the overhead projector?
(2) How would you go about making an impromptu transparency?
(3) What type of pencil must you use in making a transparency if you wish to project in color?

Slides and Filmstrips

Slides and filmstrips are variations of the same medium. Most of what one says about one of them also applies to the other. As a matter of fact, many filmstrip projectors are also slide projectors and vice versa. In this section, we shall treat them as different media, but remember that they are close relatives.

Using the Slide Projector. Thirty-five millimeter slides are available in great abundance. Commercially produced slides can be purchased through school supply houses and photography and other stores. Others can be obtained from pupils, friends, neighbors, and relatives. It is quite possible to make your own slides. With a little practice, you can learn to copy pictures, book pages, documents, and maps with a 35-mm camera. Pictures you take of scenes and events may be excellent teaching aids. You may even find use for your vacation pictures. Information concerning techniques for use in copying documents and taking other pictures can be found in photographic manuals and works on audio-visual aids and educational technology.[2]

Slides may be used in a number of ways. A most effective technique is to use single slides to illustrate important points or concepts. Another technique is to arrange a series of slides into a slide program, as in a filmstrip. If you wish, you can prerecord your own commentary and sound effects, and synchronize them with the slides, although for most class purposes this really is not necessary. Slide projection can also be adapted for individual or small group use. For individual or small group viewing, the image can be thrown onto a sheet of cardboard no larger than the projector itself. Many teachers place white paper in a cardboard box and project into it. This procedure has the advantage both of shielding the image from outside light and of keeping it from distracting other pupils. Slide projection is excellent for illustrating, clarifying, motivating, summing up, and for introducing study, discussion, or research. Use slides as springboards. Encourage pupils to build slide programs and illustrated reports as individual projects. Projecting two or more pictures at once makes it possible to show comparisons and contrast. This technique is an excellent way to make concepts and facts clear and to stimulate thinking.

Slide-loading Procedures. To load slides into slide carriers or trays, position the slides as follows: (1) Face the screen. (2) Hold the slide so that it reads normally. (In most cases, commercially processed slides will carry the company trademark on the side of the slide that faces the projection screen.) (3) Invert the slide, so that the image is upside down, and insert the slide into the tray slot. Thumb spots help orient slides for projection. Traditionally, the spot is placed in the top right-hand corner of the slide on the side that is away from the screen when the slide is in position for loading.

Preparing a Slide Program. Slide programs are quite easy to prepare. Pupils can and do make excellent programs. Basically, the procedure is to do the following:

1. Decide on your objectives.
2. Decide on the points you want to make.

---

[2] *Copying,* Eastman Kodak Publication M1 (Rochester, N.Y.: Eastman Kodak Co., 1969); *How to Make Good Pictures,* Eastman Kodak Publication AW1 (Rochester, N.Y.: Eastman Kodak Co.); *Producing Filmstrips and Slides,* Eastman Kodak Publication S-8 (Rochester, N.Y.: Eastman Kodak Co., 1969); Jerold E. Kemp, *Planning and Producing Audiovisual Materials,* 3d ed. (San Francisco: Chandler Publishing Co., 1975).

3. Select slides that will make your points. Use slides that are good technically if you can. However, sometimes it may be necessary to use a slide that is photographically less than good to make your point.
4. Arrange these points into an outline or scenario.
5. Arrange the slides in sequence according to the scenario.
6. Make title and commentary slides, and/or prepare an oral or written commentary.
7. Place the slides in the projector tray. Be sure they are in proper sequence. If you will be using a single shot projector, ace the slides in order and number them.
8. If you plan a written commentary, run off the ommentary so all may see it. This type of commentary is good for small up and individual work. If you plan an oral commentary, you or someon lse may read or give the commentary extemporaneously as the slides are own. This procedure is most common. However, if you wish, you can ta record your comments. If you do, be sure to introduce some sort of signa to the tape so that the operator will know when to go to the next slide. you have the proper equipment, it is quite easy to produce a taped prog m in which the slides are changed automatically by an electronic signal, t such sophistication is not really necessary.

Exercise 15 E

Practice building a lesson around one or two illustra e pictures or diagrams. What are the advantages of using this tactic

If you were to make up a slide show, what criteria w ld you use for selecting the pictures? Would you ordinarily prefer t ave it accompanied by an audio-taped commentary, or to supply t commentary yourself as the slides are presented? What are the vantages and disadvantages of both approaches? Compare your mments with those in the following section.

Use of Filmstrips. Filmstrips are, in effect, a series of slides st ng together on a roll of film. They may be used in much the same way as slide grams. In fact, sometimes it may make for more effective teaching if you tre frames as individual slides. Studying an individual frame alone even for an e ire period has much to recommend it. Although presumably filmstrips have the advantage of having been put together by an expert in a ready-made sequence, many filmstrips on the market are deadly. Studying single frames or short sequences may be more interesting and effective. Nowadays many filmstrips come with recorded commentary and sound effects. These may be extremely impressive. On the other hand, perhaps you would rather provide your own commentary as the filmstrip progresses. Usually, to run through an entire filmstrip without stopping for give-and-take and the sharing of ideas makes the class monotonous. For this reason, one should be very careful when selecting sound filmstrips. Unless they are unusually well done, they may be boring. In any case, when using the silent filmstrip, you should try to involve the pupils as much as possible. In slow classes, often, pupils love to be asked to read the captions of silent filmstrips. Stop to discuss the implications of the pictures as you show them. If you let one of the pupils run the projector, it relieves you of this chore and makes at least one pupil interested.

Filmstrips are excellent for small-group and individual work. Use individual screens or screens in boxes. You may, or may not, want to give pupils study guides to use as they view the filmstrips individually. Such study guides make it possible for pupils to study completely on their own. With some filmstrips and slide programs, study guides are not really necessary because directions, problems, and other instructional matter that one would expect in the study guide appear on the filmstrip.

Projection Procedures for Filmstrips. When ready for showing, the filmstrip should be in a roll with the lead end on the outside and the tail of the film in the center of the roll. Face the screen and hold the filmstrip so that the title reads normally. Keep the same surface toward the screen, invert the filmstrip, and insert the end downward into the threading slot, pushing gently while you turn the film-advance knob slowly until the sprocket wheels engage the perforations along the edges of the filmstrip. When the focus frame or title appears, take time to frame it properly by working the framing lever or knob until you see only one complete frame on the screen. Then focus the picture by moving the lens forward or back.

Making a Filmstrip. It is possible to make filmstrips, but to do so requires special equipment or special skills. Ordinarily, what one must do, in effect, is to make a slide program and then have an audiovisual person turn it into a filmstrip with special equipment. If one has good slide projection equipment, making film-strips hardly seems worthwhile. The slide program will do almost everything the filmstrip can do. If you wish to make filmstrips, however, you can find detailed instructions in such texts as Jerold E. Kemp's *Planning and Producing Audiovisual Materials,* or technical manuals such as Eastman Kodak's *Producing Filmstrips and Slides,* Publication S-8.

Film Loops

The single-concept loop film projector is a simple video device that should not be overlooked. It requires no threading or rewinding. Plastic, self-contained cartridges are inserted into a slot in the rear of this unit and the program is viewer ready. The cartridge is foolproof because it can only be inserted in the correct, ready-to-show position. A focus knob, a framer, and an elevation level are the only controls. Three-to-fifteen minute films are available in most subject areas and on most grade levels. Such films illustrate one concept or idea and often are used to introduce a problem without trying to solve it or to demonstrate a technique or procedure for performing some task.

Loops of this type are commercially prepared on 8mm film. Local programs, that is, sequences produced by you or someone in your school on this kind of film are easy to make. All that is needed is an easy to operate 8mm camera, normal classroom lighting, and a self-made plan to follow. You can compose and produce film loops that meet with your specifications and are germane to the topic you are teaching in precisely the way you desire.

Moving Pictures as a Teaching Tool

Moving pictures can be one of the most useful of all the teaching tools currently available. They can be used to arouse interest, to change pupils' attitudes, to clarify students' concepts, to stimulate thinking, to summarize, to reinforce learning, to demonstrate, and to bring into the classroom vividly much that could otherwise only be talked about. They make wonderful springboards for further learning. In this section, we discuss both instructional movies made for use in the classroom, and general purpose or entertainment films.

We have not cited any disadvantages to the use of movies. Can you think of any? There are several. Among the disadvantages you might list are that some movies are irrelevant; many are incorrect and give pupils incorrect notions; pupils treat movies as entertainment rather than as learning features; movies may emphasize elements that you do not want emphasized in your course; movies are not very adaptable because it is difficult to excerpt what you want; movies are difficult to get and to show when you need them; and movies require special provisions for projection.

Procedures for Showing Instructional Films.   As you already know, instructional films are those that are designed for classroom use for instructional purposes. They range from presentations of literary masterpieces to short sequences on how to use a certain piece of equipment. Since they are instructional tools, it is usually important that you select films that are pertinent to your teaching objectives, and use the films when these objectives are the basis of the content to be shown. The biggest hitch in the utilization of films pertains to their availability and your planning. With effective use of long-range planning and early ordering of films, it is to be hoped that you will be able to effect a coincidence of your instruction close to the arrival time of the film requested.

Exercise 15 F

Cite several reasons why it might be better to use only parts of a filmstrip than the whole thing.

How could you adapt a filmstrip projection for individual and small-group work?

If you cannot get the film you want when you want it, it is usually better either to adjust your teaching calendar so that you are teaching the proper content when you can get the film, or to skip it altogether. However, in some cases films are of general enough interest so that they can be used at almost any time during the year. Once selected, the film, if possible, should be previewed. It is important also to order films early.

At the time of the film showing, once the projector has been set up and threaded, it is wise to try it to see that everything is working. Moving-picture projectors are quite rugged, as a rule, but in the school situation they usually get a maximum of use and a minimum of maintenance. Checking the equipment, therefore, is essential.

You would be very wise to learn to troubleshoot the minor difficulties likely to occur in the different machines you have in your school. Many of the common difficulties can be corrected easily and quickly if one is familiar with the equipment. You ought to be able to change the fuses, lamps, and exciter lamps and to determine when a machine is not threaded properly. In older machines, it is important to understand the type of loops and tension required in threading, but in newer machines such matters are not so critical.

Once you are ready to start, introduce the film. Be sure that the pupils know what they are supposed to be doing. Unless you make a point of this, they may think of the movie simply as entertainment. Let them know what they should look for and what questions to think about. In some cases, you may want to give them a study guide to follow. Then as soon as everyone is ready, start the movie and keep quiet. Do not make comments while the movie is running. If you must interrupt for some purpose, stop the machine, say what has to be said, and restart it. To talk while the movie is in progress is silly. All you do is interrupt the film. Besides, no one can hear you. Usually the need for comment can be anticipated and taken care of by your introduction to the film. On the other hand, do not be afraid to stop the film for class discussion or explication if it seems advisable. By so doing, you may make instructional films much clearer. Movies that present a story, however, probably should not be interrupted, because interruptions may destroy the film's impact.

Upon completing the movie, follow it up. Discussion of what was presented is always in order. Written work, tests, problems, or reading on the topic, and practice of a skill demonstrated in the film are also useful. The point is to make sure that the students profit from the showing. If there is no adequate follow-up, films will become mere recreation. Sometimes the follow-up will show the necessity for showing the movie again. This is often true when teaching skills. Then you may want to stop the film, have the student practice, and then show the film again.

Introducing, setting up, and following up films, if done well, are likely to be time consuming. Consequently, you should be careful to allow yourself plenty of time for the introduction, showing, follow-up, and any emergencies that may occur. If a film breaks, wind the film around the takeup reel several times, mark the break with a slip of paper, and continue with the showing. This procedure will allow you to continue with the presentation and yet notify the audiovisual or film library people of just where the break is. Do not try to repair the break yourself. Amateur, extemporaneous, hasty splicing, or attempts to pin, paper clip, or tape broken film together only make it more difficult for the next user of the film.

Silent Film. In this age of sound, one tends to forget how valuable silent films can be. The visual impact may be all that is needed. Sometimes it is better to be able to provide your own commentary. There are times when one would do well to turn off the sound on sound films and use your own or pupil commentary. Furthermore, silent films lend themselves to techniques in which teachers emphasize and clarify by stopping the film and repeating vital sequences as they explain and amplify the film presentation.

Individualizing Instruction. Films can be used for small group and independent study, as was pointed out in Module 12. Single concept films and 8-mm cartridge projectors are excellent for this purpose. Single concept films are excellent because they concentrate on the single concept. The 8-mm cartridge machines are ideal for individual work, because they are so easy to use, as illustrated in Figure 15-7. Any pupil can insert the cartridge and operate the machine. Because the screen is part of the machine, there is no problem of devising a screen for individual projection.

Standard 16-mm. equipment can also be used for small-group and individual work. To prepare a 16-mm machine for small-group work, connect earphones to a junction box plugged into the speaker output. Use a sheet of white paper or a cardboard box for a screen. If you put the group viewing the film in a corner of the classroom and the pupils use earphones, they can watch movies to their hearts' content without disturbing anyone. This is shown in Figure 15-8.

A similar technique can be used to prepare a 16-mm projector for independ   t study:

1. Load the film and thread the projector.
2. Plug carphones into the speaker outlet.
3. Arrange a sheet of paper, or use a box for a screen.
4. Give pupils directions in a written guide. Instruct them about how to t   n on the machine, run it through, and stop it at the end of the film. (A g   d technique is to have the pupils stop the film before it is completely run   t

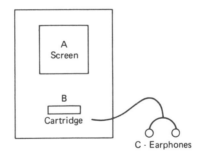

FIGURE 15-7   *8-mm Cartridge Projector Suitable for Individual Viewing*

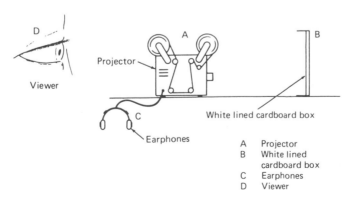

FIGURE 15-8   *16-mm Projector Set Up for Individual Viewing*

and then back it up to the starting point so that the projector will be ready for the next user before the machine is turned off. This technique may not be necessary if the machine is self-threading. However, using it may save some confusion.)[3]

Using General Purpose Commercial Films.   The commercial cinema can be a considerable instructional aid, especially in English, foreign language, and social studies courses. Films playing in local theaters can be used as a basis for oral and written reports. Films that all can see, such as those shown in school or at theater parties, make excellent bases for discussion and other exercises and reports.

To be aware of new films that you might use in connection with your teaching, you ought to scan the notices of coming attractions and read the reviews in newspapers and magazines. Pupils can do much of this type of work for you. Let them tell the class about appropriate films that they have seen or seen reviewed. Theater managers will usually be glad to cooperate with you. They can tell you when they expect to show recommended films. Sometimes, if they have reason to expect a good house, they can arrange for a showing of film classics and other requested films, and for special showings of regularly scheduled films. Film classics are also available in 16-mm for use in schools. These 16-mm films may be either feature length, abridged, or short subject. Showing feature-length films may create something of a schedule problem. This problem can be avoided by scheduling the movie after hours or in episodes. Scheduling movies is not a great problem in schools that have truly flexible schedules. Many excellent films, fit for classroom use, are available from the governmental agencies and from Chambers of Commerce, industry, and travel services. Often these movies are better for your purposes than the usual instructional films. You can find out about them by writing to the agencies concerned. For information about films available, see such references as *Educator's Guide to Free Films.*[4]

Among the tactics and strategies teachers use in order to utilize commercial films are the following:

1. Announce films that are coming to town or on television, and discuss how they might contribute to the course.
2. List films as optional activities. Have on the chalkboard or bulletin board a list of films in local theaters or TV that would be useful for optional activities such as oral or written reports.
3. Arrange theater parties for exceptional movies.
4. Discuss films that all pupils have had a chance to see.
5. Assign exercises and reports, such as the following, based on *The Bridge Over the River Kwai,* a classic movie that reappears on television from time to time: "Map out a route for the railroad from Bangkok to Rangoon, using a large-scale map. Draw a series of map overlays, showing the positions of the various armies in Southeast Asia during the period from the fall of

---

[3] Reprinted by permission from Leonard H. Clark, *Social Studies in Secondary Schools: A Handbook* (New York: Macmillan Publishing Co., 1973), p. 315.
[4] Randolph, Wis.: Educator's Progress Service.

Burma on. Make a terrain map, showing the terrain, vegetation, and principal obstacles. Where did the Japanese actually put their railroad? Would you select the route they did?"[5]

6. Utilize such activities as the following:
   a. Terrain study.
   b. Climate and weather study.
   c. Study of strategy and tactics.
   d. Study of people of the area—religion, economy, social customs.
   e. Map study of campaigns.
   f. Study of important individuals.
   g. Placing of the event into the context of history. Of what importance was it? What led up to it? What resulted from it? What if it had never come off?
   h. Checking the movies against other sources to see if they present the event, period, or characters accurately. For instance, *Becket* presents Thomas Becket as the leader of the Anglo-Saxon cause. Was he really?
   i. Dramatic criticism.
   j. Comparison of the picture with the book.
   k. Study of architecture, art, or customs as shown in the movie.

Television

Everyone in the United States knows that television is a powerful medium. Its use, however, as a teaching aid may present scheduling, curriculum, and physical problems that some school systems have not been able to face up to.

For purposes of professional discussion, television programs can be divided into three categories: instructional television, educational television, and general commercial television. Instructional television refers to programs specifically designed as classroom instruction; educational television, to programs of public broadcasting designed to educate in general, but not aimed at classroom instruction; general commercial television programs include the entertainment and public service programs of the television networks and local stations.

Instructional Television

As we have just noted, television is not always used well in schools. Probably in Utopian circumstances, television should not be used for classroom instruction, but rather should be reserved for supplementing ordinary curricula and instruction. Nevertheless, sometimes instructional television that takes on the role of classroom instruction is necessary in circumstances in which courses cannot be successfully mounted, because they are beyond the capabilities of the local resources, staff, and facilities. By using television well, schools can offer pupils courses that otherwise would be impossible. In other school systems, because of a desire for economy or in an attempt to bring the pupils in touch with master teachers and the very best teaching, instructional television courses have been introduced as substitutes for the regular courses.

---

[5] Adapted from Leonard H. Clark, "Social Studies and *The Bridge Over the River Kwai,*" *School Paperback Journal,* 2:18–20 (Oct. 1965).

Where instructional television courses have been introduced, the fact that the television class is taught by a master television teacher does not relieve the classroom teacher of any teaching responsibilities. He or she must plan, select, introduce, guide, and follow up, as in any other course. Otherwise, the television teaching will leave the pupils with learning gaps and misunderstandings. In spite of the marvels of television and other machines, pupils still need the personal guidance of all teachers. To use instructional television properly, you should follow a procedure similar to the following:

1. Prepare for the telecast.
   a. Study the advance material. If possible, preview the tele st.
   b. Arrange the classroom and warm up the set.
   c. Prepare and distribute materials and supplies as needed.
   d. Discuss the lesson to be viewed. Fill in any necessary backg und. Try to induce a favorable set. Teach any vocabulary necessary.
2. Guide the learning.
   a. Circulate to help pupils, if necessary.
   b. Observe pupil response. Note signs of lack of understanding or i un-derstanding.
3. Follow up.
   a. Question and discuss.
   b. Reteach and clarify as necessary.
   c. Use the telecast as springboard to new experiences involving pupil participation, creativity, problem solving, and critical thinking.
   d. Tie to past and future lessons and experiences.

This same procedure also holds for supplementary programs that are used to fill out, deepen, and enrich the day-by-day instruction.

General and Educational Television Programs

In addition to instructional television programs, there are general and educational programs that you can utilize in your teaching: regular commercial programs, special events, and general cultural, educational, informational, and enrichment programs of the Public Broadcasting System and independent educational television stations. Both public broadcasting stations and commercial stations offer a multitude of programs that can be used to supplement and enrich your teaching. Probably the foremost examples include news programs, news specials, and interview programs such as "Meet the Press" and "Face the Nation." Such programs can be excellent sources of material for use in all sorts of courses, not only, as you might surmise, for courses in the social studies. For example, every day the weather map and the radar patterns shown on the weather report portion of the news give one ammunition for the study of highs, lows, air currents, and the reading of weather maps. Science editors report on new developments in science almost every day and bring to our attention important science knowledge in their science news specials. Stock market reports are basic to the study of business and economics courses.

Ordinary commercial programs may turn out to be the best sources of all. All radio dramas occur in time and place and are subject to dramatic and literary criticism. They can be used to establish historical and literary concepts. We have already seen how movies can be used for such purposes. What would make a better subject for the study of plot or characterization (or lack of it) than many of our television dramas? Music is omnipresent. Even "commercial messages" can be used. They give almost unlimited opportunities for the study of logic, propaganda, and rhetoric.

Educational television courses, such as those given by the public broadcasting stations or by colleges on commercial stations ("Sunrise Semester"), often include lectures, demonstrations, and background information that is usable for high school courses. Although these courses may be aimed at adults taking the courses for college credit, they are usually not too difficult for many high school pupils.

To find what programs that you might use will be telecast locally, you can consult such references as your local newspaper, news and television magazines, your local television guide, professional journals such as *Today's Education,* and television station and network publicity releases. Sometimes you can obtain helpful information about future programs suitable for school use by writing to the stations or networks.

Exercise 15 G

Look at the television news and commentaries. How many programs can you find that might be useful as supplementary material for a course in science, business, mathematics, foreign language, art, or music? Do you find any that might prove useful to a course you might teach?

Unfortunately, perhaps, television studios do not ordinarily adapt their schedules to those of the secondary schools. This problem may be met in several ways. One solution is to tape the programs for replaying during the class period. Recent advances in videotape technology have made it possible to record programs relatively easily. Attention should be paid, however, to copyright laws, although presumably videotaping single programs for classroom use but not for rebroadcasting should be interpreted as falling under the fair use clause. In spite of the desirability of videotaping programs, audiotaping of talk programs such as "Close-Up" or "Meet the Press," or a press conference, should be adequate for most classroom use. Another solution is to ask the pupils to view the telecast at home. This solution is fraught with problems because not everyone will be able to watch the television program. Some may not have television sets available (they may not own one, or it may be preempted at that hour. If Father plans to watch the Monday night football game, he may not take kindly to an assignment of ballet viewing in the middle of the second period), and others may not have the time available. Consequently, it may be that you should make such assignments selectively to certain individuals or committees who will report what they have seen and heard. Sometimes, when a major event is to be telecast on several channels, you might do well to ask different pupils to watch different channels so that they can compare the coverage. The difference in opinions of various commentators on a presidential message might be quite revealing, for instance. In any case, the assignments made to the pupils must be clear and followed up.

Some teachers find it helpful to list the assignments, questions, and projects on the bulletin board.

Physical Arrangements for Television Classes

When using television in the classroom, one should, of course, try to be sure that everyone can see and hear sufficiently well. The following are guidelines for the physical arrangement of the classroom that should make the use of television most effective:

1. Use 21- to 24-inch screen television sets with front directional speakers.
2. Place the sets so that each pupil has an unobstructed line of sight.
3. The screen should not be more than thirty feet from any pupil.
4. The set should be about five and one half feet from the floor (that is, about the same height as the teacher's face).
5. The vertical angle of sight from any pupil to the set should never be more than 30°; the horizontal angle, never more than 45°.
6. The room should be kept lighted so that pupils can see to take notes.
7. No glare should reflect from the screen. To reduce glare one can
   a. Move the set away from the windows.
   b. Tilt the set downward.
   c. Provide the set with cardboard blinders.
8. The sound should come from front directional speakers. If several sets are in use in one room, it may be better to use the sound from only one set than to have it come from several sources. In large rooms for large-class instruction it may be more satisfactory to run the sound from one set through a public address system.
9. Pupils should have adequate surface space for writing.
10. To allow for quick, easy transition from the telecast, television class-rooms should be fitted out with adequate audio-visual equipment, display space, filing and storage space.[6]

Tape Recorders and Record Players

Audio Recordings

You will find that audio-tape recordings and records are excellent media for many purposes. In addition to bringing music, speeches, plays, and other dramatic devices to the class, they can be used to support other media. (What would movies and television do without the background of the sound track?) Audio-tape can also be used to record one's own performance so that one can criticize his own work. Such recording is essential in the study of language and speech.

In using audial activities in your classes you would do well to follow the suggestions made by Haney and Ullmer.

---

[6] Reprinted by permission from Leonard H. Clark and Irving S. Starr, *Secondary and Middle School Teaching Methods*, 4th ed. (New York: Macmillan Publishing, Co., 1981), p. 272.

1. Develop a utilization plan. Preview audio materials, listening to them carefully and critically, and identify the learning outcomes for which they are appropriate. Identify the important terms and concepts contained in the program and make plans to ensure that prerequisite concepts are understood by the pupils. Decide on a presentation technique. You may wish to play the audio materials once and then have a follow-up activity; to play them in segments with activity interspersed; to play them through once and then again with frequent stopping for discussion or practice; or to provide some kind of handout that guides pupil participation. Also, an important part of developing a utilization plan is to decide on test items that will be used to measure learning that results from the listening experience.

2. Prepare the students for listening. Try to stimulate interest in the program by making introductory comments. Explain the program and the reason for using it. You might list key words or concepts on the chalkboard or employ a handout to guide pupil participation. The important thing is that they be given a good idea of what will be expected of them in terms of learning from the listening experience.

3. Play the program. Encourage pupils to listen quietly and carefully. Some method of evoking their participation should be employed, whether the participation is to be overt or implicit. Overt participation might be in the form of taking notes, recording observations, completing statements, or answering questions. Implicit or overt participation can be improved by encouraging the children to concentrate on what they are hearing, to analyze what is being said, to arrange facts or concepts in their minds, to react to different points of view, or to devise solutions to problems presented.

4. Engage in follow-up activity. After most media presentations, it is a good idea to have some type of activity to ensure that learning has taken place, to fill in the gaps where the presentation fell short of expectations, to clarify misunderstandings, or to extend the learning to new but related areas. The discussion is a popular form of follow-up, but there are other activities, such as pupil projects, reports, panel discussions, a game or simulation, or a field trip. The presentation and the follow-up activity together should constitute an integrated and total learning experience.

5. Evaluate learning from the listening experience. Evaluation of the outcomes of a media event is really no different from evaluating outcomes of conventional events. The important thing is to confirm that desired learning has taken place and that the teacher's utilization strategy has been effective.[7]

These suggestions are similar to those we have made for other media. Used as recommended, these principles should make your use of audio media much more effective.

The tape recorder comes in two basic designs, reel-to-reel and cassette units. Regardless of their configuration, all reel-to-reel tape recorders have essential

---

[7] John B. Haney and Eldon J. Ullmer, *Educational Media and the Teacher* (Dubuque, Ia.: William C. Brown Co., 1970), p. 50.

features in common. There are two reels, a supply reel and a take-up reel. There are also buttons or keys which are to be touched or pushed depending upon the use you are making of the machine: Rewind, Record, Pause, STOP, PLAY, FAST FORWARD. There are also controls: sound and power and an off-on switch. Your procedure should be to examine the machine that will be available to you. Look for special instructions which indicate how this machine may differ from other typical recorders. The newer form of recorder, the cassette, adds the dimension of ease of operation and facility in storage to the realm of tape. Winding and threading, and loading and rookie mistakes which result in erasures of programs are simplified to the extreme. Audiotapes or cassettes can be easily used as supplements to workbooks and textbooks in any classroom or as powerful primary sources of information within a course. It is possible, for example, to build a language laboratory around a storage and retrieval system of cassette tapes. Stored tapes can also be used as learning resources in literature or drama courses, as detailed instruction for laboratory experiments, as exciting supplements in the progress of a lesson where opinions of experts in the field under study are needed for decision making, and, of course, as a revelation of the treasures of our musical heritage through the efforts of recorded artists who have presented them best.

On almost all cassette recorders the following items will be found:

—a power supply. It will run on batteries, an AC power cord, or a receptacle for connecting external DC power.
—a cassette compartment. When opened, the cassette is inserted for play with the open side of the tape facing downward.
—Controls. Essentially the same as in the reel to reel, above.
—Features: The small size, ease in use. The cost and availability of machines and tapes is the attractive feature with cassettes. Commonly they are available in uninterrupted playing times of 15, 30, 45, and 60 minutes. They are designated by the playing time of both sides, that is, a C 60 plays 30 minutes on each side. Cassette machines are easily adapted to individualized instruction and to class presentations for small groups.

Video Recordings

Videotaped programs can do about everything films can do and should be treated in the same manner as films. The procedures that apply for film in the classroom apply equally to video tapes except, of course, the viewing area should be set up as for television viewing. In addition, video tape makes it possible to record pupil activities, practice, special projects, and the like. It gives pupils a marvelous opportunity to see and hear themselves in action.

Multimedia

You should use different media to reinforce each other. You will do so naturally some of the time, such as when you write on the chalkboard to illustrate a problem you are discussing. But you ought to make an effort to combine media in ways that will make your teaching more effective and exciting. You can do so by using different media in sequence or by using them simultaneously. The essential ingredient is that the media support each other and the objectives of your lessons.

For instance, you might want to show a picture of a scene, then a map of the area, and then a taped narrative describing what travel was like. Or you might present all three simultaneously; as the taped narrative plays, you could point out features referred to by the narrative on both the map and the picture. In teaching the westward movement, for instance, one might project a map of the West on the chalkboard, and then with colored chalk trace routes west on the board as you project pictures of the terrain and other features on an adjacent screen. Techniques using two or more screens can be very interesting and informative. For instance, while you hold a picture on one screen, you can flash a series of closeups on another. Or you could put up two pictures side by side and compare and contrast them. Or you could present a schematic on one screen and a picture of the real thing on another, or a picture on one screen and pictures about it on another. Similarly, such presentations could be combined with the use of models, realia, or sound tracks. There is no limit to what you can do if you are ingenious and venturesome. Almost anything will serve as long as the media used support each other and the objectives of instruction. If the media are not compatible and do not complement each other, they may confuse rather than clarify, however.

Computers and Microcomputers

Recently educational technology has expanded to include teaching machines and computers. Basically, these are machines that present teaching-learning programs to pupils. They can assist instruction by carrying out instructional chores such as drill, or practice activities in which they can not only present the drill exercise, but also correct it immediately and prescribe corrective exercises when necessary. They can also prescribe individualization by preassessing pupils' knowledge, presenting them with the information they need and evaluating their progress. With the advent of the new microcomputers that are becoming popular, it seems that there is almost nothing that the machine cannot do if the teacher is aware of its potential and has good software (programs) available.

Computer-Assisted Instruction (CAI)

Computer-assisted instruction (CAI) is the most popular term used to describe the use of computers for instructional tasks. CBI (computer-based instruction) and CMI (computer-managed instruction) are also commonly used descriptive terms. CAI can be purchased in the form of diskettes, cassette tapes, or cartridges.

Several distinct types of CAI exist: drill and practice, tutorial, simulation, and computer-managed instruction. No programming knowledge is necessary to use these "canned" software packages. The method for transferring the programs on disk, tape, or cartridge into the computer's memory is usually a simple procedure which can be learned in just a few minutes.

In general, *drill and practice* software allows learners to come in contact with facts, relationships, problems, and vocabulary until the material is committed to memory. Good software of this type possesses an interesting format that encourages reuse by students, thus ensuring mastery of the skill or establishment of the stimulus-response association required for memorization of certain facts.

Software of the *tutorial* type utilizes written explanations, descriptions, questions, problems, and graphic illustrations for concept development, much like a private "tutor." Often traditional pretests are included with tutorial software to determine the most appropriate beginning lessons for a particular student or whether certain lessons should be skipped. After the tutorial part of the lesson has been presented, drill and practice exercises are offered and finally a post test for each objective to determine degree of mastery.

As can be guessed, tutorial courseware is more sophisticated and requires more complicated programming technique than the drill type. The author must anticipate all possible correct responses and allow for spelling and capitalization errors. In the simplest design, tutorials progress in a *linear* fashion that presents a series of screen displays to all users, regardless of individual differences among the students. *Branching* tutorials do not require all to follow the same path but will direct students to certain lessons or parts of lessons according to results of pretests and posttests or student responses to embedded questions within the tutorial.

Software of the purely drill and practice variety should not be used until some conceptual development has taken place. Tutorial software is most effective when students show varying levels of conceptual understanding, and it can provide for individual tutoring needs that may be difficult to satisfy through traditional instructional arrangements.

Computer-Managed Instruction (CMI)

In its purest form, computer-managed instruction (CMI) does not offer instruction of any type, but rather *manages* instruction in a classroom through computer-assisted testing and record keeping which indicates students' mastery or nonmastery of specific objectives. The computer does the tedious record-keeping work, which is especially helpful when attempting individualized instruction, and provides reports that can be used when grouping students for instruction leading to mastery of specific objectives.

Simulation

Educational simulation provides situations for students to live through, as it were, that would be difficult to duplicate in a classroom setting. Simulations allow students to become involved in some enterprise, for example, to select certain options or risks and then to witness the results of the decision. They can be prepared for almost any subject where a simulated experience for a certain real-life situation would contribute to increased learning.

Languages

Computer users must learn a *computer language* of symbols and commands in order to activate and interact with their machine. Like students of a foreign language, they must study and practice the terminology if they wish to become proficient. Among those languages most widely used in educational settings are *BASIC, LOGO,* and *PASCAL.* Each language possesses certain qualities that make it more suitable for some applications than for others.

In all probability the language with which you will be interacting first will be BASIC (Beginners All Purpose Symbolic Instruction Code). Designed originally for use in teaching beginner programmers to write instructions for computers, it is a relatively simple language to learn. It is made up of approximately twenty commands that instruct the computer to perform various functions. It is especially popular with microcomputer users because it requires less space in the computer's memory than do other high-level languages.

LOGO is a language that allows even young children to interact with computers without extensive training beforehand. It permits users to manipulate images on a video screen or command actual computerized objects. Perhaps its greatest advantage is that it lays the foundation for the assimilation of increasingly complex computer languages while providing children with a positive and reinforcing early computer experience with its turtle graphic displays possibility.

PASCAL is the language of choice for computer science education. It is a highly graphics-oriented language, which is simple in structure and provides an excellent foundation for learning other more complex languages.

The growth of interest in the computer in recent years has been truly phenomenal. In 1980, for example, in Montgomery County in Maryland there were 40 microcomputers scattered throughout the 165 elementary and secondary schools in the system. These units were used only by identified gifted and talented students. By 1983 the number of microcomputers in the system had grown to 400 to which all students and teachers in the system had some access. The attitude of students, teachers and administrators about the uses and value of the computer in the classroom had changed radically in just that short period of time.

This phenomenon has been mirrored in school districts nationwide with varying degrees of success. Parents and teachers and educational leaders who follow the trends have become convinced that the schools must teach students to use computers if they are to survive and thrive in an information-based, computer-dependent society such as ours.

Consequently, if you are to prepare yourself adequately to play an effective part in the classrooms of the future, you will need to become "computer-literate." You will in all probability be called upon to have recourse to computers in your instruction as they are utilized in the real world so that your students will have recourse to them as students of previous generations resorted to books and encyclopedias.

If at all possible, schedule a course or two for yourself while you are still on the college campus to ensure an up-to-date orientation to the state of the art in the area in which you will be teaching. Subsequently, expect to receive invitations and/or requirements to attend in-service courses sponsored by your school system on the uses of computers in instruction. Participate willingly in them and learn what you can so that you make your contribution in this important area.

Suggested Reading

Refer to Module 16 for a list of suggested readings.

Exercise Answer Key
Exercise 15 B

Appropriate answers:
(1) Look for some method of moving the lens of the overhead projector up and down.

(2) For the filmstrip projector, look for some way to move the lens back and forth. Once you have located the method of adjusting the lens, you load a transparency or filmstrip on the machine and adjust the lens. If you cannot move the lens far enough up or down (or back and forth) to get a sharp focus, move the machine or the screen to adjust the distance between lens and screen.

Exercise 15 C

The answer, of course, is to find some way to move the lens back and forth. Assuming that the axis of the machine is horizontal, you adjust the lens back and forth until the focus is as sharp as can be.

Exercise 15 D

(1) In your answer you should mention (a) writing the points out on the transparency as you lecture, or (b) preparing the transparency beforehand, covering it with a mask, and uncovering the points one by one as you lecture.
(2) One method is to write or draw on the acetate with a grease pencil or similar pencil.
(3) A translucent pencil.

Exercise 15 F

There are many reasons that should pop into your head on this score in addition to those previously mentioned: expeditious use of time, focusing all attention on the single issue selected, editing out all of the filler in order to concentrate only on the most relevant, or effective frames, escape the boredom of unnecessary repetition of previously learned material, and so on.

Adaptation is quite simple. Set up a projector with a small screen or cardboard box. Use earphones for sound, or supply a study guide or write out a commentary of your own to accompany in readable form the sequence of the frames.

Post Test

1. How can audiovisual aids help to reduce verbalism?

_____

_____

_____

2. In selecting an audiovisual device what should you consider?

_____

_____

3. What is the basic principle about focusing that has to be taken into account when focusing a projector?

_____

_____

4. If you had a series of small prints that you wanted pupils to look at and study, what is probably the most efficient method of presenting them to the pupils?

_____

_____

5. What would be an advantage of running off a transparency and a ditto sheet of an exercise on a spirit master?

_____

_____

6. Can it be done?

_____

7. What is the essential, practical difference between an opaque projector and an overhead projector?

_____

_____

_____

8. A supervisor was heard to say that the overhead projector was the teacher's best friend. What is so good about this kind of projector?

_____

_____

_____

9. How would you go about making a hand-drawn colored transparency?

_____

_____

_____

_____

_____

10. How is a transparency overlay or flip-on used?

_____

_____

11. What is the purpose of a mask when used with an overhead projector?

_____

_____

12. How can you adapt a slide projector for individual or small group viewing?

_____

_____

13. How does one prepare a slide program?

_____

_____

14. What should you do if a motion picture film breaks?

_____

_____

15. What can you do to make pupils understand that films are instruction, not entertainment?

_____

_____

_____

16. Many people seem to think that movies are the audiovisual aid par excellence, but they have many disadvantages. What are three of them?

_____

_____

_____

_____

_____

17. Once the film is completed and the machine turned off, what should you, the teacher, do?

_____

18. How might you utilize in your instruction commercial films showing at local theaters or on television?

_____

_____

_____

19. How do Haney and Ullman recommend that one prepare the pupils for listening to taped or recorded audio materials?

_____

_____

_____

20. Give at least one example of a multimedia presentation.

_____

_____

_____

21. Describe two uses of the microcomputer.

_____

_____

22. When might it be preferable to use a silent film or filmstrip for instruction?

_____

23. What advantage does a slide program have over a filmstrip?

_____

24. Name two ways that one might utilize Public Broadcasting or commercial television programs for classroom use.

_____

_____

25. Which audiovisual devices can be used to individualize instruction?

_____

26. Describe CAI.

_____

_____

_____

_____

27. How does CMI work?

_____

_____

_____

_____

28. What is the value of simulation?

_____

_____

_____

_____

29. How does branching work in programmed instruction?

_____

_____

_____

_____

MODULE
16

Materials of Instruction

Rationale

This module continues our study of teaching tools. We start with a discussion of textbooks. Although the most ubiquitous of all teaching tools used in American schools, textbooks are not always chosen wisely or used effectively. Neither are other printed materials such as workbooks, which when well used can be a medium for awakening thought and interest, but when poorly used can be a source of tedium. Sometimes the most useful of printed materials are teacher-made exercises, study guides, and supplementary reading matter.

How to get the most out of the various printed materials available will be one of the most pressing problems for you to solve, if you are to teach effectively. Similarly, you should master the use of display materials. Often, bulletin boards, pictures, charts, flannel boards, and similar displays make the difference between pupils' understanding and not understanding.

Self-instructional materials and devices such as teaching machines and teaching programs make it possible for teachers to lift their teaching from the humdrum dishing out of information to creating and experimenting with ideas. Their potentials have seldom been realized in the classroom. Finally, the module ends with suggestions about where and how to procure materials of instruction. After all, if you don't have it, you cannot use it!

Specific Objectives

Specifically, it is expected that you will be able to do the following:

1. Explain the pros and cons of textbook use.
2. Describe recommended procedures for using textbooks.
3. Describe how to teach with multiple readings.
4. Describe criteria to consider when selecting textbooks.
5. Describe how other printed matter and duplicated materials, such as paperbacks, workbooks, study guides, newspapers, periodicals, and springboard materials, may be used in your teaching.
6. Explain how to use display devices including the chalkboard, bulletin board, flannel board, and flip chart.

7. Explain how to use pictures, illustrations, charts, graphs, and posters.
8. Explain how the teaching machine works.
9. Tell what procedures a teacher should use in teaching by machine.
10. Describe several sources of procuring free art, inexpensive teaching materials, and references for finding what materials are available.

Module Text

Textbooks

Of all the materials of instruction, the textbook has had the most influence on teaching content and method. For many teachers, it has been the "be all and end all" of their instructional life. This is unfortunate because, properly used, the textbook is merely one of many teaching tools. It is not supposed to be revered as the ultimate word. As a tool, it is an aid; a means to an end. Do not let it dominate you. You, not the textbook, are supposed to be the master.

Although textbooks are only teaching tools, they can be of great value, particularly to beginning teachers. You will find them very helpful in your planning, because they (1) provide an organization or structure for the course; (2) provide selection of subject matter that can be used as a basis for determining course content and determining emphases; (3) provide a certain number of activities and suggestions for teaching strategies and tactics; and (4) provide information about other readings, sources of information, audiovisual and other aids, and other teaching materials and teaching tools.

You will also find that a textbook can make an excellent base for building interesting, high-order learning activities (discussion, inquiry, research activities) that call forth critical thinking and other higher mental processes. On the other hand, textbooks are far from being the ideal tool some teachers take them to be. They have many faults. As used by many teachers, they assume too large a place in the classroom teaching and in curriculum making. Their construction is often too rigid to allow them to fit in easily in today's enlightened classroom situation: they are sometimes dull, they discourage the reading and studying of more profitable materials; they are often superficial and above all they do not allow for differences in students' talents, interests, and goals. Uncritical utilizers have a tendency to build their whole course around their text, modifying class activities to conform to the time needed for text analysis.

To get the most out of your textbooks and to avoid their weaknesses, it is recommended that you do the following:

1. Become really familiar with the textbook before you use it.
2. Use the textbook in your planning as a source of structure if it seems desirable to do so, but do not let yourself become chained to the book.
3. Use the text as only one of many materials and activities. Use other readings, simulation, role playing, discussion, films, and pictures.
4. Use problem-solving approaches in which the text is but one source of data.
5. Use only those parts of the book that seem good to you; skip the other

parts; rearrange the order of topics if you think it desirable. In other words, adapt the text to your pupils and their needs.

6. Use additional or substitute readings to allow for differences in pupils.
7. Provide help for pupils who do not read well.
8. Teach pupils how to study the text and to use the parts of the text, such as table of contents, index, headings, charts, graphs, and illustrations.
9. Use the illustrations, charts, graphs, and other aids included in the textbook in your teaching. Build lessons around them; study them.
10. Encourage critical reading. Compare the text to source materials and other texts. Test it for logic and bias.
11. Teach vocabulary.
12. Incorporate the textbook into a multiple-text teaching strategy.

Introducing the Text

Because pupils seldom know how to use their texts efficiently and effectively, Cartwright has suggested that on the first day before they begin to read, you introduce the pupils to the textbook in a lesson in which you and they discuss the following:

1. The title page.
   What information does it give?
   When was the book written? Has it been revised?
   Who is the publisher? Where was it published? Do these indicate any likelihood of bias?
2. The preface.
   What does the author claim he intended to do?
   What was his purpose?
3. Table of contents.
   How much weight is given to various topics? How can we use the information contained in the table of contents to help us study the text?
4. The list of maps, charts, and illustrations.
   What is the importance of these devices? How can one use them to aid study?
   Choose examples of each—maps, charts, tables, graphs, illustrations—and have pupils find essential information in them.
5. Appendix.
   What does appendix mean? What is it for?
6. Index.
   Use drill exercises to give pupils practice in using the index. These can be made into games or contests.
7. Glossary.
   What is a glossary? Why is it included? Utilize exercises that call for looking up words and then using them in sentences.
8. Study the aids at the ends of chapters.
   How can study questions be used? Which are thought questions? Which are fact questions?

9. Chapter headings, section headings, paragraph leads, introductory overviews, preliminary questions, and summaries.
   What are the purposes of each of these? Use exercises that call for getting meaning from aids such as these without reading the entire text.[1]

Selecting the Textbook

Because textbooks play such a large part in most classes, they should be selected carefully. In many schools, textbook selection is made by a committee of teachers. In some, teachers select their own texts. No matter what selection process is used, the text should be tested for such criteria as the following:

1. What is the date of the copyright? Is the information and interpretation presented up to date?
2. Who is the author? Is he competent in the field? Does he write clearly and well?
3. Is the book suitable for the objectives of your course? Does it cover the proper topics with the proper emphases?
4. Are the topics arranged in a desirable sequence? If not, can the sequence be altered or portions omitted without disrupting the usefulness of the book?
5. Is the content accurate and accurately presented? Is the book free from bias?
6. Are the concepts presented clearly? Are they adequately developed with sufficient detail or is there a tendency to attempt to jam in too many ideas too compactly?
7. Are the vocabulary and language appropriate for the pupils of the class?
8. Does it presume background knowledge and experiences that the pupils do not yet have?
9. Does the author make good use of headings, summaries, and similar devices? Does he give opportunity for the readers to visualize, generalize, apply, and evaluate the content?
10. Are the table of contents, preface, index, appendices, and glossary adequate?
11. Does the book provide suggestions for use of supplementary materials?
12. Does it provide a variety of suggestions for stimulating thought-provoking instructional activities?
13. Are these suggestions sufficiently varied both as to level and to kind?
14. Does the author document his sources adequately?
15. Is the book well illustrated? Are the illustrations accurate, purposeful, and properly captioned? Are they placed near the text they are designed to illustrate?
16. Does the book have suitable maps, charts, and tables? Are they clear and carefully done? Does the author refrain from trying to cram too much data onto his maps and charts?
17. Is the book well made? Does it seem to be strong and durable?
18. Does the book look good? Is the type clear and readable? Do the pages make a pleasant appearance with enough white space?[2]

---

[1] William H. Cartwright, *How to Use a Textbook,* How to Do It Series, No. 2, rev. ed. (Washington, D.C.: National Council for the Social Studies, 1966).

Item seven of this list of criteria refers to the reading level of the textbook. Sometimes this information is supplied by the textbook publishers. But in any case, a simple method for discovering whether a textbook is too difficult for the pupils is to ask them to read selections from it aloud. If they can read them without stumbling over many of the words and can tell you the gist of what the selections said, you can be quite sure the selections are not too difficult.

Multitext Approaches

More and more modern teachers are expressing dissatisfaction with the single textbook approach to teaching. Some of them have substituted a strategy in which they use one set of books for one topic and another set for another. This strategy provides some flexibility, but it is really only a series of single texts. Others, usually more knowledgeable and more proficient teachers, utilize a strategy that incorporates the use of many readings for the same topic at the same time. This multiple-reading strategy gives the pupils a certain amount of choice in what they read. The various readings allow for differences in reading ability and interest level. By using a study guide, all the pupils can be directed toward specific concepts and information, but they do not have to all read the same selections.

To carry out this type of multiple-reading approach, do the following:

1. Select your instructional objectives.
2. Select a number of readings that will throw light on these objectives. Be sure that there are several readings for each goal. Try to provide for variations in pupils' reading level and interests when you make your selections.
3. Build a study guide that will direct the pupils toward the goals and suggest readings appropriate to the goals.
4. Let the pupils select the readings that they will pursue to carry out the provisions of the guide.

Other Print Materials

The number and amount of printed materials suitable for instruction is almost infinite. Besides textbooks, there are other books, periodicals, pamphlets, and brochures. Many of these are available without cost or for only a small fee. Newspapers and magazines are excellent sources of reading matter for every one of the subject fields. They are also excellent sources of materials for bulletin boards. You should start now making a collection of things you might use, if you have not already done so. Once you have begun teaching, pupils and pupil committees can be utilized to do the gathering. Gathering materials is discussed later in the module.

Paperbacks

The paperback revolution of several decades ago opened up a great reservoir of fairly inexpensive reading matter for use in our classes. Paperbacks make the multiple-reading approach practicable. They also "make it possible to read pri-

---

[2] Reprinted by permission from Leonard H. Clark and Irving S. Starr, *Secondary and Middle School Teaching Methods,* 4th ed. (New York: Macmillan Publishing Co., 1981), pp. 237–238.

mary sources rather than snippits, and both extensively and intensively rather than being exposed only to a single textbook account. With inexpensive paperbacks it is much easier to provide pupils with opportunities to analyze and compare works, a practice which is almost impossible if one uses only the ordinary textbook or anthology."[3]

Workbooks

Many schools use workbooks in their classes. Sometimes educators scoff at workbooks on the grounds that they encourage rote learning and discourage creative thought. These allegations hold true when the workbooks are limited to narrow fact questions and when the learning exercises require only that pupils search the text for pat answers like dogs sniffing about the yard for a bone. Nevertheless, well-made workbooks can be useful tools. The learning activity packets that are so highly recommended by modern theorists are really a variation of the workbook. So are the duplicated exercises that are so often prepared by teachers. Well-written workbooks in the hands of skillful teachers can prove most effective as aids to learners. They are susceptible, to be sure, to abuse from the lazy teacher who uses them as a replacement for teacher imagination and leadership. Even the best of aids loses its effectiveness when it is thoughtlessly overused and no one bothers to follow-up or check for the accuracy of written-in responses requested. Conscientious teachers in their utilization of workbooks,

1. Try to find workbooks that emphasize thinking and problem solving rather than simple rote learning.
2. Follow up the workbook assignments. They correct them. They use their exercises as bases for next steps.
3. Use workbook assignments as a springboard for higher learning.
4. Let pupils work on different exercises or different workbooks. There is no advantage in everyone's doing the same workbook exercises at the same time. However, if pupils are using workbooks not designed to accompany their text or syllabus, then cut and edit the workbook exercises so that they do match the course.

Duplicated Materials

The teaching tools used most by teachers are perhaps the duplicated materials they run off and give out to their pupils. These materials may be dittoed, mimeographed, or "xeroxed." Often they are prepared from commercially produced masters. More frequently perhaps they are teacher made, typed up, or even written in longhand by the teacher and then reproduced. No matter what mode of production you use, you should make every effort to be sure that the copy given to the pupils is clear, attractive, and free from errors.

One of the most common types of duplicated material consists of duplicated exercises prepared by the teacher. All that has been said about workbooks applies to these exercises as well. When using them, you should consider the advisability of using answer sheets so that you can save the duplicated material and use it again. Sometimes teachers require pupils to retain their exercises and answer

[3] Ibid., p. 275.

sheets in a notebook. The result is a sort of combination workbook and review book that can be helpful to both teacher and pupils. It has the advantage of being written for the class and course being taught and so contains material the teacher wants included.

Exercise 16 A

Try your hand at creating some exercises that could be duplicated and distributed. Think in terms of using an answer sheet to accompany these handouts and visualize how you might implement the exercise. To avoid the stigma of mediocre or inferior creation, strive for the stimulation of high-level mental activity in your exercises, and the avoidance of simply rote memory in performance. You may need to refer to Module 3 to refresh your memory on taxonomies and objectives.

As you have probably already learned, in pedagogical circles, we have given the name of springboard to materials or activities that, it is hoped, will be jumping-off places for pupil inquiry, investigation, or discussion. Among the materials used for springboards are films, filmclips, and videotapes. Most consist of duplicated or printed reading matter, sometimes purchased from commercial sources, but more often homemade. Among the types of homemade springboard material you can make are descriptions of real or imagined situations that should arouse the curiosity of the pupils, case studies, historical accounts, news items, stories, and anecdotes. When you select material to be duplicated as a springboard, keep in mind the objective of arousing the pupils' interest and stirring up open-ended questions.

Among the most common uses of duplicated materials for instruction is the study guide (also discussed in Modules 4 and 12). Study guides are especially useful for students who are working alone or in small groups in individualized, laboratory-type classes, for students involved in special assignments, independent study, research activities, or supplementary assignments, and for such special activities as field trips and movie or TV watching. Their purpose is to provide students with directions and suggestions for carrying out the activity, and to pose questions and problems that will provoke thought along the lines of the designated study. As self-instructional devices they tend to free students to inquire without the constriction of marking time until teacher has an opportunity to attend to their status or achievement. Among the elements that may be found in a study guide are a statement of purpose, directions to follow, questions to answer, problems to solve, things to do, answer sheets, suggested reading, and suggested follow-up activities. An example of a special study guide follows.

Specimen Activity Guide or Job Breakdown

Project: *Screwdriver—Wooden handle*
Part: *Handle—Hard maple*
              Size 1¼″ sq. × 4″

   1. *Layout diagonals both ends.*
   2. *Drill center holes.*

3. *Drill one end* $^{3}\!/_{64}$ *diameter* $\times$ *1 $^{11}\!/_{16}$ deep.*
4. *Assemble ferrule and wood.*
5. *Turn 1 $^{1}\!/_{16}$ diameter entire length.*
6. *Turn $^{1}\!/_{4}$-inch radius knurled end.*
7. *Mill six grooves equidistant .050 deep.*
8. *Turn $^{1}\!/_{2}$-inch radius.*
9. *Sandpaper wooden surfaces only.*
10. *Get instructor's approval.*

Exercise 16 B

Review the material on springboards and study guides in Modules 4 and 10. Prepare a springboard and a general study guide for a unit you might teach. What would you include in them? How would you organize them to make them clear, attractive, and useful?

Display and Display-type Devices and Materials

There are ever so many ways of displaying information and materials for pupils to see. We have already discussed projectional techniques in a previous module. We shall now present some more prosaic devices and materials. In using all of them, the following general rather obvious principles apply. They should be clearly visible, be attractive, catch the eye, be simple, be clear, make a point, have a center of interest, and avoid clutter and confusion.[4]

Chalkboards

Chalkboards are so ubiquitous that we tend to forget them when we speak of teaching tools. That is probably one reason why so many of us fail to get the most out of them. Yet, chalkboards are about the most useful and versatile of the visual aids that we have available. They are useful for presenting subject matter, for reinforcing oral explanations and presentations, for clarifying difficult concepts, for illustrating, for pupil presentations of their work, and for practice activities. They are very flexible instruments; just a swipe of the eraser and you are ready for something new. This flexibility is also a cause of one of its disadvantages. Chalkboard work is impermanent and transitory. The swipe of the eraser that makes it ready for something new also destroys the old material. One cannot save material placed on a chalkboard without rendering the chalkboard useless for anything else. In this respect, the flannel board and overhead transparencies are much more useful.

Because the chalkboard is potentially a powerful instrument and is so often used thoughtlessly, it is not inappropriate to suggest to you a few pointers that may make your use of it more efficient and effective.

1. The material on the chalkboard must be visible and legible if it is to do any good. When you are using the chalkboard, be sure that the pupils can see easily. Stand out of the way. Use a pointer or a yardstick. The old expression about making a better door than a window applies to teachers, too.

[4] Leonard H. Clark, *Teaching Social Studies in Secondary Schools: A Handbook* (New York: Macmillan Publishing, Co., 1973), pp. 303–304.

2. A clean, neat, orderly board improves the impact of the presentation. Use the eraser. Take off material you no longer need as soon as you are finished with it. Cluttered boards not only detract from the appearance of the room, but they also tend to confuse students.
3. If the board work is simple and tasteful, it will be more effective. Leave plenty of "white space" so that the material you want to emphasize shows up.
4. Judicious use of color, underlining, and boxes will make important points stand out. Diagrams, rough drawings, and stickmen are also useful for emphasizing and clarifying.
5. When possible, boardwork that is to be used later should be covered until you are ready to use it. One way to do this is to pull a map or screen down over it. Another way is to cover it with wrapping paper taped to the board, although this technique may be difficult in the rush of ordinary classes.

Bulletin Boards

Bulletin boards are, or should be, instructional tools. You should treat them as such, not as classroom decorations. They can be used to motivate, interpret, supplement, and reinforce. To be useful teaching tools, they must be kept up to date and aimed at the objectives of the unit being taught. Following are a number of suggestions for effective use of bulletin boards:

1. Bulletin boards should be carefully planned. In planning the board, select one of the instructional aims of the unit and gather material suitable for that aim. Pick out the most desirable materials until you have only what seems to be the best of the lot. Resist the temptation to use too much material. Then sketch out a plan for presenting the material you have selected. In your plan try to do the following:
   a. Make the display tell a story.
   b. Have a center of interest. (Only one central idea or theme to a board.)
   c. Use lines or arrows to draw the viewer to the center of interest.
   d. Be sure it is visible and eye-catching. Be sure captions and pictures are large enough to strike the eye. Keep captions brief and clear.
   e. Utilize questions, action, and drama to attract attention.
   f. Provide for plenty of white space. There should be no solid blocks of material and no clutter. Again, resist the temptation to use too much. A few well-selected items will have more impact than a large hodgepodge.
   g. Consider using unusual materials, such as three-dimensional objects, combining the bulletin board with a table display, or other devices to give the bulletin board zip. Color, variety, and humor add spice. To build a mood, coordinate the colors to the ideas or atmosphere you wish to present.
2. Turn the planning and preparation of the bulletin boards over to a pupil committee. You might have a competition to see who prepares the best board.
3. Be sure the materials are secured firmly and neatly. Consider the use of invisible fastening, such as bulletin board wax or adhesive plastic, or loops of masking tapes with the adhesive side out. Fasten one side of the loop to the material and the other to the wall. Or use double-faced adhesive tape,

or tape tack units. These consist of a thumbtack stuck through a piece of adhesive tape with the adhesive side out. Fasten the tape to the material and fasten it to the bulletin board. Sometimes, fastening with brightly colored thumbtacks makes the display more interesting.

4. To be sure that the bulletin board stays up to date, keep a calendar or schedule for changing it.
5. Start a collection of bulletin board materials. Encourage pupils to bring in materials for your collection.

Charts

Charts can be used for displays just as bulletin boards are, but, as a rule, they are better suited for explaining, illustrating, clarifying, and reinforcing points in specific lessons. Among the many types of useful charts are lists, graphs, organizational charts, flow charts, pictorial charts, diagrammatic presentations of cause and effect and other relationships, multicolumned lists showing contrast or comparison, and time charts and time lines. In general, the principles previously mentioned concerning the use of chalkboards and bulletin boards also apply to the use of charts. Clarity, simplicity, and dramatics are essential considerations. At the risk of a certain amount of repetition, we list the following suggestions:

1. Most of the charts used in classrooms should be the work of pupils who have found out the information, planned how to represent it, and executed the plan themselves.
2. Charts should be planned ahead. Sketch out the chart on a piece of paper before beginning the chart itself. Pencil in the details of the chart lightly before inking them in.
3. Make the chart simple. One major point is quite enough for a chart.
4. Make the chart clear. Avoid confusing detail. Do not crowd it. Use symbols one can understand.
5. Make charts eye-catching. Use colors and pictures.
6. Make charts forceful. Emphasize a central idea.
7. Be sure charts are visible. Make letters and symbols large enough. Leave plenty of white space so the message stands out.
8. Keep everything in proportion. Be careful of spacing.
9. Avoid too much printing and writing. Let the chart tell its own story. To avoid too much printing on the chart, use a legend and keyed symbols.

Tips on Graphs

Since graphs are a specialized type of chart, the suggestions for making and using graphs follow those for constructing and using charts. In addition the following tips may prove valuable:

1. Keep the graph in proportion. This is particularly important.
2. Don't try to show too much on the same graph. If you wish to show several phenomena, use several graphs.
3. Be sure to select units that fit your idea and your paper. In making pie graphs (circle graphs), note that one percent = $3.6°$ ($100\% = 360°$).
4. Be sure there is a common baseline for all phenomena represented. Have the baseline start at zero.
5. Be sure the total to which individual items are compared is shown.

6. Use color coding to show contrast, comparisons, or growth. Be sure the key tells exactly what each symbol represents.
7. Be sure to credit your sources.
8. Be sure the title is brief but clear.

Flip Charts

Flip charts are used frequently in schools, sales meetings, and television studios. They are really series of charts, set on a tripod, to illustrate points in the lesson. Certain map sets and series of biological charts are examples of commercially prepared flip charts. Homemade flip charts can be made on large pads such as those artists use for sketching. All one does is to prepare a series of charts on the pages of the pad so that you can flip the pages over as you need them. They should be used more in middle and secondary schools.

The simplicity of the flip chart's design makes it possible to move back and forth easily from chart to chart as one desires. Separate charts, arranged in order on top of each other and mounted on an easel or even stood on a chalk tray, can be used in exactly the same way although they are usually a little more difficult to manage physically.

Flannel Boards

Flannel boards and their close relatives, felt boards, hook and loop boards, and magnetic boards have many of the advantages and uses of chalkboards. They are best used for immediate presentations rather than for displays over a long period of time. In some ways, they are not as flexible or useful as chalkboards; in others they are more so. They do have several advantages.

1. One can prepare the material to be presented in advance.
2. The material to be presented can be saved to be used again.
3. They can be used very dramatically. Just slap the material up for all to see at the propitious moment and drive home your point. It is probably this feature that makes its advocates claim that flannel boards are 50 per cent more effective than chalkboards.
4. They are especially useful for showing change and development, because it is so easy to add or to subtract from the display without the disturbance that erasing creates. This also makes them excellent for reinforcing points. Just put up or take off the appropriate word, caption, or picture to make your point.

Making a Flannel Board. To make a flannel board is very easy. Simply cut a piece of plywood or similar board to the desired proportions. Then cover the plywood with suede, or long napped flannel, nap side out. Stretch it tight, and tack or staple it to the board. The result should give you a smooth, tight, nappy surface to which light sandpaper-backed paper figures and the like will adhere.

Making Flannel Board Display Materials. To prepare flannel board display materials is also easy.

First, select the materials you wish to display. These might be pictures cut out of magazines, student drawings, homemade graphs, diagrams, captions, figures or letters made of flannel cloth, felt, or some similar material. Strips of yarn may be used to make letters, to show relationships, or simply for decoration. Whether construction paper, cardboard, or cloth, the material used should be lightweight. If too heavy, it will fall off the board. It may be necessary to back flimsy material with construction paper to give it body.

Next, prepare the materials so they will stick to the board. You can do this by any of the following procedures.

1. Glue, not paste, pieces of sandpaper, sand side out, to the back of the picture or figure. It is not necessary to cover the entire back. Sandpaper at the corners, or strips crossed on the center of the back will usually do, but don't be too stingy.
2. Cover the back of the material with rubber cement. Sprinkle sand on the rubber cement while it is still wet. Let dry.
3. Using a brush and long strokes, cover the back of the material with water glass (sodium silicate). Sprinkle with sand while still wet.
4. Paint the back of the letter or figure with oil-based paint. Spray or sprinkle the wet paint with flocking.

   If the letters or figures are made from felt, flannel, roughened construction paper, oilcloth, blotting paper, or light sponge, they do not need any sandpaper backing. Just press them on the flannel board as is.

When laying out the design for your flannel board, keep in mind the suggestions for the effective use of bulletin boards listed in the preceding section.

Felt Board and Hook and Loop Boards

Felt boards are simply flannel boards made with felt rather than flannel. Stiff felt-backed dining room table pads make excellent felt boards. Hook and loop boards are the commercially prepared boards used by speakers, salespersons, and television studios. They are made of the type of materials used for Velcro fasteners. They are somewhat more dependable than homemade flannel boards. They are used in exactly the same manner as flannel boards.

Magnetic Boards

Magnetic boards are also used in the same manner as flannel boards. These boards are made of thin sheets of iron or steel-based metal to which materials are attached by means of small magnets. To make a magnetic board, one simply cuts the sheet of metal to the desired size, paints it with automobile enamel or blackboard paint, and either nails it to a wooden frame or tapes the sharp edges so that they will not cut the fingers. Galvanized iron screening, stapled or tacked to a wooden frame, also makes a satisfactory magnetic board. Materials for displaying on a magnetic board can be made simply by gluing materials to small magnets with heavy-duty glue or mending cement. If the magnetic board is enameled, you can write on it with a grease pencil; if painted with chalkboard paint, with chalk. Many families use magnetic boards to post notices and reminders.

Exercise 16 C

Make a flannel board or a magnetic board. What size would be best for your purpose, do you think?

List and compare the advantages and disadvantages of the chalk-board, flannel board, and overhead projector.

Pictures and Posters

A picture is worth a thousand words, it is said, so let's use them effectively and save ourselves some breath. They make excellent tools for clarifying and illustrating what one wishes to teach. They make good springboards for inquiry. They can be used for sparking interest in the topic. Sometimes an entire lesson can be built around a single picture.

In using pictures, there are no special techniques necessary. As in any other teaching, the teacher should try to guide the pupils. One of the best ways to do so is to ask questions that will guide pupils into interpreting. Another is to point out what pupils should look for and to explain its significance. The teacher must also be careful to use only pictures that are pertinent and useful. One must avoid showing pupils pictures just for the sake of showing them. Also, avoid passing pictures around the room while the class is in progress. When the pupils are looking at the pictures, they are no longer paying attention to the class instruction. It is better practice to use the opaque projector.

Finally, don't forget that most pictures in textbooks were put there because the author thought they shed light on the content being studied. Detailed study of the pictures in the texts, using controlled discussion, or openended questioning techniques may prove to be very rewarding.

When selecting a picture to show to the class, keep in mind the following criteria:

A picture should be suitable for the purpose, make an important contribution to the lesson, be accurate as to authenticity, be easy to understand, be interesting, and should be easily visible to the entire class.

Exercise 16 D

Find a picture, poster, or other illustration. Build a lesson plan around it.

Look at some of the illustrations in a high school text. How might you use them to give impact to your teaching?

If you have not done so, begin to gather pictures and other illustrative material you might be able to use in your teaching.

Posters have somewhat of an advantage over other pictures for display and instructional purposes. They are usually large and striking. Commercially printed or prepared posters can be used in the same manner as other pictures. Making posters can be an interesting, worthwhile pupil activity. If you wish to use poster-making as one of your activities, do the following:

1. Discuss the possibilities with pupils.
2. Discuss the criteria of good poster-making.
   a. Aim at getting one idea across.
   b. Use as few words as possible.
   c. Make key words stand out. Use contrast, size, or color for this purpose.

    d. Keep the design simple.

    e. Leave plenty of white space.

3. Have pupils block out their designs on a sheet of paper, and get teacher approval of the design.

4. Let the pupils execute their own designs.

Teaching Machines and Programs

The teaching machine acts as a sort of mechanical tutor that meets pupils in a one-to-one relationship. The machine does not teach, but rather presents a teaching program to the pupil. It is the teaching program that really does the teaching. The machine is just the delivery system, whether it is a high-powered computer or a simple programmed book.[5]

The teaching program, which really does the teaching, is made up of the subject matter content arranged into a system so that it can be presented in a manner that will, supposedly, best utilize the principles of behavioristic psychology. Basically, there are two types of programs: *linear programs* and *branching (or extrinsic) programs.*

The difference between these types of programs is that the linear program consists of a series of very easy frames or steps—steps so easy that the pupil progresses through the program without ever making a mistake. In the linear program, every pupil goes through exactly the same process (see Figure 16-1). The branching program is made up of much larger and more difficult steps. If a pupil completes a frame successfully, he moves on to the next one. If he does not, then the program or machine reteaches him until he can answer the same or similar question or problem again. In effect, the pupil with the machine's aid builds himself an individual program as he goes along. In a sophisticated branching program, it is quite possible that no two pupils will complete exactly the same sequence of frames.

The procedures in both types of program have much in common:

1. The machine presents the pupil with some content and then asks him a question or puts a problem to him.

2. The pupil answers the question or solves the problem.

3. The machine corrects the pupil's answer and then tells him what to do next.

4. In the case of the linear program, the pupil always moves on to the next step. In the case of the branching or extrinsic program, if the pupil response is incorrect, the machine reteaches him and then either returns to the original question (or problem), or moves on to a different question calling for the same knowledge.

As a teaching strategy, programs have several real advantages. They have clearly defined objectives; they follow a carefully planned learning procedure; they keep the pupil actively involved in his own learning; they give the responsibility for learning and the rate of learning to the pupil, and they give the pupil immediate feedback concerning his progress.

---

[5] B. F. Skinner, "Programmed Instruction Revisited." *Phi Delta Kappan*, (October 1986), 68:103–110.

1. If you have not read the article, "Interaction Analysis in the Classroom," do so now before you continue.	1. When you have completed your reading, go to the next question.
2. The Flanders system of interaction analysis assumes that 　a. the verbal behavior of an individual is an adequate sample of his total behavior. 　b. nonverbal behavior is the only important index of classroom interaction. 　a. ☐　　　　　b. ☐	2. "a" is correct.
3. In this system, all teacher statements are classified as either _____ or _____	3. restrictive or encouraging
4. Restrictive or encouraging behavior indicates the amount of _____ the teacher gives the student.	4. freedom
5. The teacher has a _____ regarding behavior.	5. choice
6. If the teacher is restrictive, he _____ the freedom of the student to respond.	6. minimizes or limits
7. If the teacher is encouraging, he _____ the freedom of the student to respond.	7. maximizes
8. All of the statements which occur in the classroom are categorized in one of three major sections. These sections are: 　1. _____ 　2. _____ 　3. _____	8. teacher talk, student talk, and silence or confusion

FIGURE 16-1　*An Excerpt from a Linear Program.* [*Source:* Miles C. Olson. *Learning Interaction Analysis: A Programmed Approach* (Englewood, Colo.: Educational Consulting Associates, Inc., 1970).]

Because they are flexible tutoring devices, teaching machines are ideally suited to individualizing instruction, and they relieve the teacher of some of the more tedious and mechanical teaching chores so that they can spend more time working at high-level activities. For instance, while some pupils are drilling on essential skills or learning basic content on the machine, teachers can work with other pupils individually or in small groups, or teachers can delegate the teaching of information to the machine in order to concentrate on teaching the higher cognitive and thinking skills and processes that are likely to be neglected in ordinary classes.

Use teaching programs, teaching machines and computers to individualize instruction, to teach basic skills and information, to provide pupils with the background necessary for discussion, inquiry, and problem-solving activities, and to free yourself for giving pupils individual attention and teaching them at the higher levels. When teaching with machines, it will be necessary for you to do the following:

1. Guide and supervise the pupils.
2. Continually check the pupils' progress.
3. Select suitable programs for individual pupils and see to it that the pupils go through these programs correctly.
4. Provide follow-up activities. (Programmed activities make good springboards, but teachers must provide the follow-up).
5. Provide other types of instruction. (Programmed teaching should not be overused. Some pupils find it boring.)
6. Evaluate pupil progress. (Programmed material is learning and practice material. It is not a test. It should never be graded. Teachers must provide other criteria—tests, papers, class discussion—to use as a basis for evaluation and reporting.)

Other kinds of self-administered, self-correcting materials are discussed in Module 12.

Sources of Teaching Materials

Ingenious teachers can find almost limitless supplies of teaching materials available from a host of sources. Much of this material is free for the asking, and other material is available for a small fee. To find out what is available, turn to your local curriculum guides and resource units and to those of other schools and communities. You will also find other publications, such as the bulletins of your state department of education and professional organizations, very helpful. Many educational periodicals list and review new materials. In addition, there are a number of reference works that specialize in listing instructional materials. Among the reference works that you might find useful are the following:

The American Film Review. St. Davids, Pa.: The American Educational and Historical Film Center, Eastern Baptist College. Annual
An Annotated Bibliography of Audiovisual Materials Related to Understanding and Teaching the Culturally Disadvantaged. Washington, D.C.: National Education Association.
Annual Paperbound Book Guide for High Schools. New York: R. R. Bowker Company.
Aubrey, Ruth H. *Selected Free Materials for Classroom Teachers*, 6th ed. Belmont, CA: Fearon-Pitman Publishers, 1978.
Bibliography of Free and Inexpensive Materials for Economic Education. New York: Joint Council on Economic Education.
Civil Aeronautics Administration, *Sources of Free and Low-Cost Materials*. Washington, D.C.: U.S. Department of Commerce.
Educational Film Guide. New York: The H. W. Wilson Company.
Educators' Guide to Free Audio and Visual Materials. Randolph, Wis.: Educators' Progress Service.
Educators' Guide to Free Films. Randolph, Wis.: Educators' Progress Service.
Educators' Guide to Free and Inexpensive Teaching Materials. Randolph, Wis.: Educators' Progress Service.

Educators' Guide to Free Social Studies Materials. Randolph, Wis.: Educators' Progress Service.
Educators' Guide to Free Teaching Aids. Randolph, Wis.: Educators' Progress Service.
Feature Films on 8mm and 16mm. New York: R. R. Bowker Company.
Film Guide for Music Educators. Washington, D.C.: Music Educators National Conference.
Free and Inexpensive Learning Materials. Nashville, Tenn.: Division of Surveys and Field Services, George Peabody College for Teachers.
Freedom, Florence B., and Esther L. Berg. *Classroom Teachers' Guide to Audio-Visual Material*. Philadelphia: Chilton Book Company, 1971.
Horn, Robert E. *The Guide to Simulations/Games for Education and Training,* 3d ed. Cranford, N.J.: Didactic Systems, Inc., 1977.
Index to Multi-Ethnic Teaching Materials and Teaching Resources. Washington, D.C.: National Education Association.
Materials List for Use by Teachers of Modern Foreign Languages. New York: Modern Foreign Language Association.
Mathies, Lorraine. *Information Sources and Services in Education*. Bloomington, Ind.: The Phi Delta Kappa Educational Foundation, 1973.
National Tape Recording Catalog. Washington, D.C.: National Education Association.
New Educational Materials. Englewood Cliffs, N.J.: Citation Press.
Rufshold, Margaret. *Guides to Educational Media*. Chicago: American Library Association.
Sources of Free and Inexpensive Pictures for the Classroom. Randolph, Wis.: Educators' Progress Service.
Sources of Slides and Filmstrips (S-9). Rochester, N.Y.: Eastman Kodak Co.
Taggart, Dorothy T. *A Guide to Sources in Educational Media and Technology*. Metuchen, N.J.: Scarecrow Press, 1975.
Textbooks in Print. New York: R. R. Bowker Company.
U.S. Government Films for Public Education Use, Superintendent of Documents. Washington, D.C.: Government Printing Office.
U.S. Government Printing Office. Thousands of publications. Catalogs available.
Using Free Materials in the Classroom. Washington, D.C.: Association for Supervision and Curriculum Development.
Wegner, Hart. *Teaching with Film,* Fastback 103. Bloomington, Ind.: Phi Delta Kappa Educational Foundation, 1977.
Wittich, Walter A., and Charles F. Schuller. *Instructional Technology: Its Nature and Use,* 5th ed. New York: Harper & Row, Publishers, 1973.
Woodbury, Marda. *Selecting Instructional Materials,* Fastback 110. Bloomington, Ind.: Phi Delta Kappa Educational Foundation, 1978.

The following periodicals are a sampling of those that carry information about instructional materials and how to procure them:

Audio-Visual Guide: The Learning Media Magazine.
Educational Technology.
The English Journal.
Journal of Business Education.
Journal of Home Economics.
Journal of Physical Education and Recreation.
Learning.
The Mathematics Teacher.
Media and Methods.
Music Educators' Journal.
School Arts.
The Science Teacher.
Social Education.
Social Studies.

Exercise 16 E

Browse through the list of materials included in some of the sources listed. Select free or inexpensive material that would be suitable for your courses. Write for it. Prepare a list of more expensive materials that seem to you highly promising.

Community as a Resource

The community itself may be the best of all the resources available to you. It can provide places and things to see first-hand in the field, and it can provide speakers and materials of instruction for use in the classroom. To take advantage of the many community resources available, every school needs a community resource file. If your school does not have one, you should collect information about resources yourself and record it on 5 × 8 cards. A central file would be more efficient, but a file of your own is usually well worth the effort. In it there should be such information as the following:

1. Possible field trips.
   a. What is there?
   b. How is location reached?
   c. Who handles arrangements?
   d. Expense involved?
   e. Time required?
   f. Other comments?
2. Resource people.
   a. Who are they?
   b. How can they help?
   c. Addresses?
3. Resource material and instructional materials obtainable locally.
   a. What is it?
   b. How is it procured?
   c. Expense involved?
4. Community groups.
   a. Names and addresses?
   b. Function and purpose?
   c. Type of thing with which they can help?
5. Local businesses, industries, and agencies.
   a. Name?
   b. Address?
   c. Key personnel?

Making One's Own Materials

Many teachers enjoy making their own teaching materials. Besides the duplicated materials so common in elementary and secondary school classes, teachers make slides, transparencies, tapes, and all sorts of audio and visual teaching aids. Doing so can be great deal of fun and satisfaction. It also has the advantage of giving you the material you want, not what some professor or publisher thinks you want. Suggestions for making teaching aids are presented elsewhere in this volume and in a number of references. Following is a sampling of publications on the production and use of such materials.

Anderson, Ronald H. *Selecting and Developing Media for Instruction.* New York: Van Nostrand Reinhold Company.

Brown, James W., and Richard B. Lewis. *AV Instructional Technology Manual for Independent Study,* 5th ed. New York: McGraw-Hill Book Company, 1977.

Bullard, John R., and Calvin E. Mether. *Audio-Visual Fundamentals: Basic Equipment Operation and Simple Materials Production,* 2nd ed. Dubuque, Ia.: William C. Brown Company, Publishers, 1979.

Eastman Kodak Publications, Rochester, N.Y.
   Adapting Your Tape Recorder to the Kodak Carousel, SC-1.
   Applied Color Photography Indoors, E-76.
   Audio-Visual Projection, S-3.
   Basic Copying, AM-2.
   Basic Developing, Printing, and Enlarging, AJ-2.
   Color Photography Outdoors, E-75.
   Composition, AC-11.
   Copying, M-1.
   Effective Lecture Slides, S-22.
   Good Color Pictures—Quick and Easy, AE-10.
   Making Black and White Transparencies for Overhead Projection, S-17.
   Planning and Producing Visual Aids, S-13.
   Producing Slides and Filmstrips, S-8.

Goudket, Michael. *Audiovisual Primer,* rev. ed. New York: Teachers College Press, 1974.

Green, Lee. *Teaching Tools You Can Make.* Wheaton, Ill.: Victor Books, 1978.

Kemp, J. E. *Planning and Producing Audio-Visual Materials,* 4th ed. New York: Harper & Row, Publishers, 1980.

McClure, Larry, Sue Carol Cook, and Virginia Thompson. *Experience-Based Learning: How to Make the Community Your Classroom.* Portland, Oregon: Northwest Regional Educational Laboratory, July 1977.

Minor, Edward O. *Handbook for Preparing Visual Media,* 2nd ed. New York: McGraw-Hill Book Company, 1978.

Minor, Edward O., and Harvey R. Frye. *Techniques for Producing Instructional Media,* 2nd ed. New York: McGraw-Hill Book Company, 1977.

Oates, Stanton C. *Audio Visual Equipment: Self Instructional Manual,* 4th ed. Dubuque, Iowa: William C. Brown Company, 1979.

University of Texas at Austin, Instructional Media Center (VIB), Austin, Texas.
   Better Bulletin Boards.
   Designing Instructional Visuals.
   Educational Displays and Exhibits.
   Instructional Display Boards.
   Models for Teaching.
   The Overhead System.
   The Tape Recorder.
   Using Tear Sheets.

Free and Inexpensive Materials

As we have pointed out, much material is available without cost. Pictures are available in a multitude of magazines. Commercial houses and government agencies have reams of printed material they would like to give you, and sometimes also samples, filmstrips, and other audiovisual materials. All that is required to obtain these materials is a letter of request. In your letter, state who you are, what you are asking for, and why you want it. Write your letter on official school stationery. Sometimes, it is useful to have pupils write the letter. If you have pupils do this, be sure to check over the letters to see that they meet the standards of good letter writing, and countersign it so that the recipients will know the request is valid.

Once you get the material, you must examine it carefully before using it with pupils. Some items will turn out to be useless and others so overladen with bias or sales pitch that they are impossible to use. In evaluating materials, use such criteria as the following:

1. Will the material really further educational objectives?
2. Is it free from objectionable advertising, propaganda, and so on?
3. Is it accurate, honest, free from bias (except when one wishes to illustrate dishonesty and bias, of course)?
4. Is it interesting, colorful, exciting?
5. Does it lend itself to school use?
6. Is it well made?

Reading on Computers in Teaching

Bitter, Gary G., and Ruth A. Camuse. *Using a Microcomputer in the Classroom.* Reston, Va.: Reston Publishing Co., a Prentice-Hall Company, 1984.

Brumbaugh, Ken, and Don Rawitsch. *Establishing Instructional Computing: The First Steps.* St. Paul, Minn.: Minnesota Educational Computing Consortium, 1982.

Coburn, Peter, et al. *A Practical Guide to Computers in Education.* Reading, Mass.: Addison-Wesley, 1982.

DeVault, M. Vere. "Computers," in Elizabeth Fennima, ed., *Mathematics Education Research: Implications for the 80s.* Alexandria, Va.: Association for Supervision and Curriculum Development, 1981, Chap. 8.

Grady, M. Tim, and Jane D. Gawronski. *Computers in Curriculum and Instruction.* Alexandria, Va.: Association for Supervision and Curriculum Development, 1983.

Graham, Neill, *The Mind Tool,* 4th ed. St. Paul, Minn.: West Publishing, 1986.

Hunter, Beverly. *My Students Use Computers.* Reston, Va.: Reston Publishing Company, a Prentice-Hall Company, 1983.

Hofmeister, Alan. *Microcomputer Applications in the Classroom.* New York: Holt, 1984.

Taylor, Robert P. *The Computer in the School: Tutor, Tool, Tutee.* New York: Teachers College Press, 1980.

Vockel, Edward L., and Robert H. Rivers. *Instructional Computing for Today's Teachers.* New York: Macmillan, 1984, Particularly Chaps. 1–5, 12.

Suggested Reading

Brown, James W., and Shirley N. Brown, eds. *Educational Media Yearbook.* Littleton, Colo.: Libraries Unlimited, 1983.

————, Richard B. Lewis, and Fred R. Harclerod. *A V Instruction: Technology, Media, and Methods,* 5th ed. New York: McGraw-Hill, 1977.

Bumpass, Donald E. *Selected A V Recipes: Materials, Equipment Use and Maintenance.* Dubuque, Ia.: Kendal Hunt Publishing, 1981.

Gerlach, Vernon S., and Donald P. Ely. *Teaching & Media,* 2d ed. Englewood Cliffs, N.J.: Prentice-Hall, 1980.

Heinrich, Robert, and M. Molenda. *Instructional Media: The New Techologies of Instruction.* New York: Wiley, 1982.

Kemp, Jerrold E. *Planning and Producing Audio-Visual Materials.* 4th ed. New York: Harper Row, 1980.

Klein, M. Frances, *About Learning Materials.* Washington, D.C.: Association for Supervision and Curriculum Development, 1978.

Krepel, Wayne J., and Charles R. DuVall. *Field Trips: A Guide for Planning and Conducting Educational Experiences.* Washington, D.C.: National Education Association, 1981.

Leifer, Aimee Dorr. "Teaching with Television and Film," in N. L. Gage, ed. *The Psychology of Teaching Method.* The Seventy-fifth Yearbook of the National Society for the Study of Education. Chicago: The University of Chicago Press, 1976, Chap. 9.

Locatis, Craig N., and Francis D. Atkinson. *Media and Technology for Education and Training.* Columbus, Oh.: Charles E. Merrill, 1984.

Potter, Rosemary Lee. *Using Television in the Curriculum,* Fastback 208. Bloomington, Ind.: Phi Delta Kappa Educational Foundation, 1984.

Siminson, Michael, and Roger P. Volker. *Media Planning and Production.* Columbus, Oh.: Charles E. Merrill, 1984.

Woodbury, Marda. *Selecting Instructional Materials,* Fastback 110. Bloomington, Ind.: Phi Delta Kappa Educational Foundation, 1978.

Exercise Answer Key
Exercise 16 C

The chalkboard is an ever present, flexibile visual aid that you can easily adapt to the situation. It can be used to make things vividly clear. Unfortunately it is not as dramatic a tool as some others, and the material it presents cannot be saved.

The flannel board is also versatile and can be quite dramatic. By changing the display, it is easy to show changes and development. Display materials must be prepared in advance, however, but they can be saved and reused.

The overhead projector is another versatile instrument. Every classroom should have one. Display material can be made in advance or fashioned at a moment's notice. The displays can be quite dramatic and colorful. By the use of flip-ons, or changing transparencies, one can show changes, developments, and make comparisons. Transparencies can be reused for review and clinching purposes, or filed away for future classes. They are very useful for presenting details.

Post Test

1. The textbook should not dominate your teaching. How should you use it?

_____

2. In selecting a textbook, what should you look for?

_____

_____

_____

_____

3. How does one conduct a multitext approach?

_____

_____

_____

_____

_____

_____

_____

_____

_____

_____

4. What has been the great advantage of the paperback?

_____

5. In selecting a workbook, what particularly should you look for?

_____

_____

_____

6. What sort of things can you use for springboard material?

_____

_____

7. What is the purpose of a study guide?

_____

_____

8. In speaking of chalkboards and bulletin boards, it is recommended that one leave plenty of white space. What is meant by white space? Why should you leave plenty of it?

_____

_____

9. Flannel boards are supposedly much more effective than chalkboards. Why?

_____

10. How do you make the material to put on a flannel board?

_____

_____

_____

11. How can you get the most benefit out of a bulletin board?

_____

12. How can you make a bulletin board or chart forceful?

_____

_____

_____

_____

13. What is a flip chart?

_____

_____

14. How do you use it?

_____

_____

15. Why use pictures in your teaching? Why not pass them around the room during a class?

_____

_____

_____

16. What is the difference between a linear program and a branching (extrinsic) program?

_____

_____

_____

_____

17. What would you include in a community resource file?

_____

_____

_____

18. Teaching machines and programs should make it possible for teachers to concentrate on higher learning in their teaching. Why?

_____

_____

_____

19. Experts warn against overuse of the single textbook. Give two reasons why.

_____

_____

20. Where might you turn to find out about teaching material that might be suitable for your courses?

_____

MODULE
17

Becoming a Professional

Rationale

To become a truly professional teacher you must cultivate a wide repertory of teaching skills and an understanding of when and how to use them in the teaching-learning situations you encounter.

To master this type of know-how, it will be necessary to learn much more of the theory behind the various methods than we have been able to discuss in these modules. To become more proficient, teachers take many different routes, such as graduate study, workshops, independent study, curriculum committee work, action research, and professional conferences. The essential point is that all of them are working to improve teaching competencies. One is never too old to learn in the teaching profession. And one is never old enough to let oneself become locked into a rigid teaching style. You should always be ready to renew and revamp your style. Who knows, you may find a revised style more comfortable, and new strategies and tactics may make you more interesting. While you are still in training, it would be helpful for you to observe as many different teachers as you can to note the many different styles and strategies in action. You should also avail yourself of every opportunity which presents itself to try out various techniques and examine your performance in them.

Professional laboratory experiences provide an opportunity for you to become familiar with various teaching methods and life in school by actually observing and working with pupils and teachers in classrooms. It is this portion of the program that gives reality to teacher education.

In a sense, the professional laboratory experiences—particularly student teaching—are the culmination of one's teacher education. But teacher education does not stop when one begins to teach. In addition to learning from experiences in school and classroom, one should also upgrade one's skills and understandings by professional growth activities of various sorts. It is not too early to become familiar with these opportunities now.

This module will briefly examine professional laboratory experiences and suggest ways to make them profitable. It will also discuss ways by which you may examine and evaluate your own teaching, both in your laboratory experiences and later in your own classes, so that you can correct your shortcomings and build on your strengths. Finally, the module examines some of the methods you can use to grow professionally, starting now.

Specific Objectives

Specifically, upon completion of the module you should be able to do the following:

1. Explain the purposes of laboratory experiences.
2. Describe the characteristics and role in teacher education of the three types of professional laboratory experiences.
3. Explain what student teachers can do to make their student teaching experience pleasant and profitable.
4. Describe procedures for analyzing and evaluating your lessons and teaching procedures.
5. Describe the suggestions made in this module for growing in the profession.

Module Text

Professional Laboratory Experiences

Professional laboratory experiences include the portions of your college program in which you observe classroom teachers in the act of teaching, participate in the conducting of classes, teach simulated classes and minilessons, microteach, and teach real classes in the student teaching or internship experience. This module considers observation, participation, and student teaching experiences that occur in secondary and middle schools.

Unless you are greatly different from most student teachers preparing to be teachers, your professional laboratory experiences will have the greatest impact of all your college experiences. They are real, often exciting, and full of opportunities for creative learning. They provide a milieu in which you can experiment with different styles and strategies and develop skills in the various teaching techniques.

Observation

Most college teacher education programs provide opportunities to observe teachers and pupils in the public schools. They may also allow students to observe other students as they teach. They may also provide demonstration lessons for students to observe. Such observations can give you insights into teacher-pupil relations, the effects of certain types of teaching strategies and techniques, different kinds of materials and media available, and various types of teaching styles. The more different styles you observe, the better you will understand the potentials of the various approaches.

Some ways to make your observation profitable include the following:

1. Concentrate on watching the pupils. Note the range of differences in appearances, abilities, and interests that appear in a single class. Note how pupils react to different teaching approaches. What types of teaching techniques and materials excite their interest and what engender boredom? Follow a pupil's schedule all day long. How does it feel to go through the routine? (It may be worse or better than you remember your own student days to have been.) Try to think of ways that you as a teacher could make the classes more enjoyable and profitable.
2. Observe the ways different teachers handle their classes. How do they get their classes started? How do they bring their classes to a conclusion? How do they bring out the important points? How do they create interest? How do they get pupils involved? How do they provide for differences in pupils?

What techniques for motivation, probing, inquiry, discovery, closure, and reinforcement do they use? How do the pupils respond to the various tactics? What procedures do the teachers use to maintain control of the class?

3. What is the climate in each class you observe? What seems to be the cause of the climate? Is the class teacher-centered or pupil-centered? Is the class diffusely structured or centrally structured? Is the morale high or low? What seems to be the cause for the state of the morale?

4. Most particularly, pay attention to the manner in which the teachers carry out various strategies and tactics and the pupils' responses to each of the strategies and tactics and the teachers' manner of carrying them out.

Participation

Participation refers to the type of experiences in which college students actually perform teaching tasks in the schools, although they do not actually teach classes. It includes such activities as tutoring, working with small groups, conducting exercises, supervising tests, correcting tests and papers, preparing tests, taking attendance, filling out forms, and generally acting as a teacher aide.

These types of activities can be very helpful because they provide opportunities to become accustomed to handling routines, to get to know pupils, and to acquire skill in various techniques under supervision. Enter into them willingly and wholeheartedly even though they may sometimes seem onerous. Try to share in as many different types of experiences as possible. The more you can learn from them, the easier your student teaching and beginning teaching will be. Therefore, try to get feedback from your pupils, other teacher trainees, and classroom teachers so that you can perfect your techniques.

Student Teaching and Internship

In student teaching, after a period of observation and participation, the teacher trainee gradually takes over the classes and other duties that make up a teacher's load, under the supervision of cooperating or critic public school teacher and college supervisor. The experience is expected to develop into a genuine simulation of reality. Although the cooperating teacher is the professional of record and that person cannot escape ultimate responsibility for what transpires in the classrooms, the intent is for the intern to assume as much responsibility as he is capable of and to perform within indicated parameters, as though the class were fully his to lead. The legal and instructional and pedagogical ramifications of this activity are such that only a simulation of reality is possible. However, the greater the effort made to approximate the real thing and the greater the sensitivity to the goals of the activity on the part of the cooperating teacher, the intern, and the college supervisor, the more rewarding the student teaching experience should be.

Internship is often nothing more than student teaching by another name, although it may refer to a longer or to a more independent apprenticeship period. In this module, we use the term *student teaching* to refer to both concepts from this point on.

For most teacher candidates, student teaching is the capstone of their teacher education program. It can be most exciting and rewarding. It can also be most difficult and trying. In this section of the module we shall try to point out ways to make your student teaching experience profitable and satisfying.

Perhaps the first thing to remember about student teaching is that, like observation and participation, it is intended to be a learning experience. It is in student teaching that the beginning teacher first applies the theories and techniques learned in college classes to real teaching situations. Here you will have an opportunity to try out various strategies and techniques so as to begin to build a wide repertoire of teaching skills and to develop an effective, comfortable teaching style.

Student teaching is also a time of trial and error. Do not be discouraged if you make mistakes or your lessons do not go well at first. If you were already a skilled teacher, you would not need the practice. Making mistakes is part of the learning process. Use them as a means for improvement. With the help of your cooperating teacher and supervisor, try to analyze your teaching to find what steps to take to do better next time. Perhaps your execution of the strategies and techniques was faulty; perhaps you used a strategy or technique inappropriate for the particular situation. Such errors can be quite easily remedied as you gain experience.

As a general rule, errors of omission are often more culpable than errors of commission. The latter generally reflect faulty judgment or inexperience. They do, however, just as often, confirm an indication of good will, commendable effort, and a willingness to try. Omission errors that are censorable most often stem from lack of zeal: failure to devote enough time to planning adequately, neglect of previewing audiovisual equipment, lack of research on the topic of presentation and the like.

In this connection, do not be quick to reject a teaching strategy or technique that fails for you. As you become more skilled in using various strategies and techniques, you will find that all have their uses. Do not allow yourself to become one of those boring teachers who can teach in only one way. Instead, if a strategy or technique does not work for you, examine the teaching-learning situation to see what went wrong. Then try it again in a new situation after brushing up your technique and correcting your faults.

Since student teaching is a time for learning and for getting one's mistakes out of one's system, it is important not to become discouraged. Many student teachers who do miserably for the first weeks blossom forth into excellent teachers by the end of the student-teaching period. On the other hand, if things seem to go well at first, do not become overconfident. Many beginners, too soon satisfied with the seeming success of early classes, have become complacent and doomed themselves to mediocrity. In any case, examine your classes to see what went well and what went wrong. Then try to correct your faults and capitalize on your strengths.

After your initial anxiety and nervousness wear off, use your student teaching as an opportunity to try out new strategies and techniques. Avoid becoming a clone of the cooperating teacher or a replica of the old-time teacher who gave lectures, heard recitations, and sometimes did very little else. Work out the new approaches and techniques you wish to try with your cooperating teacher before you try them, however. Usually the cooperating teacher can show you how to get the most out of your new ventures and warn you of pitfalls you might encounter.

Make haste slowly as you try new methods and approaches. Things will go more smoothly if you continue with the same strategies and tactics to which the class is accustomed. Students used to a particular style may not readily adapt to innovations. This reluctance is especially virulent when one confronts students with quick changes in the length and difficulty of homework assignments or an abrupt switch from prescriptive, didactic methods to discovery and inquiry approaches.

Sometimes the cooperating teacher may think it necessary to veto what seem to you to be your best ideas. Usually there is a sound basis for the veto. It may be, in the cooperating teacher's view, that these ideas will not serve the objectives well, or they may require time, money, or equipment not available to you, or violate school policy, or seem unsuited to the age and abilities of the pupils. Sometimes your ideas may be rejected because they conflict with the cooperating teacher's pedagogical and philosophical beliefs or prejudices. Whatever the objection, you should accept the decision gracefully and concentrate on procedures the cooperating teacher finds acceptable. After all, the classes and the instruction are the cooperating teacher's responsibility.

Furthermore, you need to become a master of many techniques. If you master the techniques and style your cooperating teacher recommends now, you will have begun to assemble a suitable repertoire of teaching skills. Later, when you are teaching your own classes, you can expand your repertoire by trying out other strategies and styles you find appealing.

To be successful in student teaching requires more study and preparation than most students think possible. To do the job, you must know what you are doing, so pay particular attention to your planning. Bone up carefully on the content of your lessons and units and lay them out carefully step by step. Leave nothing to chance. Check and double check to be sure you have your facts straight, that your teaching strategies and tactics will yield your objectives, that you have the necessary teaching materials on hand, that you know how to use them, and so on. It is most embarrassing when you find you cannot solve the problems you have given to the pupils, or cannot answer the pupils' questions, or cannot find the equipment you need, or cannot operate the projector. So try to be ready for any contingency. As a rule, you should ask your cooperating teacher to approve your plan before you become committed to it. If the cooperating teacher suggests changes, incorporate them into the plan and try to carry them out.

Planning lessons and units for student teaching is no easy task. To become really sure of your subject matter and to think out how to teach it in the short time available during your student teaching is asking a lot of yourself. Therefore, prepare as much as you can before the student teaching period begins. Try to find out what topics you will be expected to teach and master the content before you report for your student teaching. Then when you start student teaching you can concentrate on planning and teaching, confident that you have a firm understanding of the content. Many students have botched their student teaching because they had to spend so much time learning the content they never had time to learn how to teach! Remember, middle and secondary school classes are not replicas of college classes. The content of what you must teach will probably be quite different from what you have been studying in college lately. You will need time to master it. If you take the time before your student teaching starts, you will have a considerable advantage.

Because student teaching is difficult and time demanding, most teacher education institutions recommend that student teachers not combine student teaching with other courses or outside work. If you have to work to eat, you must, but very few people are able both to hold down a job and perform creditably in their student teaching. Outside jobs, additional courses, trying to master inadequately learned subject content, and preparing classes are just too much for one ordinary person to do well at the same time. It is true that many successful teachers have moonlighted on outside jobs or on course work for advanced degrees. It is also true that many undergraduate students have maintained high grades with a full load of college courses and at the same time have worked full time in the evenings. But the student teaching experience is so unique in the plethora of demands that it makes on a student teacher's time as to be virtually impossible to perform in a superior fashion if one bogs oneself down with outside responsibilities at this crucial early part of one's career.

Usually one's student teaching starts with a few days of observing. This gives you a few days to get ready for actually teaching. Use this time to become familiar with the classroom situation. Get to know the students. Learn their names. Borrow the teacher's seating chart and study it and the students as the class proceeds. In this way you will learn to associate names with faces and also have some inkling of the sort of persons with whom you will soon be dealing. Learn the classroom routines and other details of classroom management. Familiarize yourself with the types of teaching, activities, and assignments that the class is used to so that you can gradually assume the classroom teaching responsibility without too much disruption. Remember, pupils are likely to resent too much deviation from what they have come to expect, at first.

In your observation of the efforts of your cooperating teacher in the act of teaching, keep in mind the following topics and questions:

1. **Aims.** What were the aims of the lesson? How did the teacher make the students aware of them? Were the aims achieved?
2. **Homework.** Did the teacher make a homework assignment? At what point in the lesson was the assignment made? How did the assignment relate to the day's work? How was the assignment from the previous day handled? How did the teacher deal with students who failed to submit completed work? How much time did the teacher spend on the assignment for the next day? Did the students appear to understand the assignment?
3. **Review.** How much of the period was devoted to review of the previous lesson? Did the teacher make any effort to fit the review into the day's lesson? How did the teacher conduct the review—question and answer, student summarization of important points?
4. **Methods.** What various methods were used by the teacher in the day's lesson? Did the teacher lecture? For what length of time? How did the teacher shift from one method to the next? How did the teacher motivate the students to attend? Was any provision made for individual differences among the students? Was any provision made for student participation in the lesson? Were the students kept busy during the entire period? Did any disciplinary problems arise? How did the teacher dispose of them?
5. **Miscellaneous.** Was the teacher's voice pleasant enough to listen to? Did the teacher have any distracting idiosyncratic habits? Were lighting and

ventilation adequate? What system did the teacher use for checking attendance?

6. Evaluation. How could this lesson have been improved?

Relations in Professional Laboratory Experiences

When you take part in professional laboratory experiences in school, you are in a rather anomalous position. In a sense, you are neither teacher nor student; yet, in another sense, you are both teacher and student. Many college students have found this position trying. Therefore we are including here a number of suggestions that may make your life a little more pleasant during your laboratory experiences. Although these suggestions apply to observation, participation, and student teaching experience, they are somewhat loaded toward student teaching, the most difficult of the professional laboratory experiences. These suggestions are not meant to be preachy. Rather, they are conclusions drawn from years of observing and trying to help student teachers. It is hoped that they will point out some of the pitfalls in student teaching and ways to make this experience a success.

In professional laboratory experiences your relationship with your cooperating teacher is critical. You should concentrate on keeping these relationships amicable and professional.

Whether you like it or not, student teaching—and to a lesser degree, observation and participation—is a job as well as a learning experience, and the cooperating teacher and college supervisor are your bosses. Ordinarily, you can expect them to be nice bosses who will not only strive to help you in every way they can but will also be tolerant of your mistakes. They are bosses, however, and must be treated as such.

They will have pretty high expectations of you. Not only will they expect you to have an adequate command of the subject to be taught, they will also expect you to have the following:

1. A basic understanding of the nature of learners and learning.
2. A repertoire of teaching skills and some competence in them.
3. A supply of instructional materials.
4. An adequate understanding of the process of evaluation and some skill in its techniques.

Do not disappoint them. You should check yourself in each of these areas. If you believe yourself deficient in any of them, now is the time to bring yourself up to par. Student teaching is too hectic to take time out for learning and collecting what you already should have learned and collected.

Your colleagues in the school will also expect you to be a professional—a beginning professional, it is true, but a professional just the same. You will be expected to do your job carefully without carping, criticizing, or complaining. Carry out instructions carefully. Hew to the routines of the school. If next week's lesson plans are due at the department head's office before the beginning of school Friday morning, make sure that they are there. Be prompt with all assignments. Never be late or absent unless previous arrangements have been made. Pay attention to details. Fill out reports, requisitions, and so on accurately and on time. Be meticulous in the preparation of your unit and lesson plans. Never approach a class unprepared. Be sure you know your content and exactly how you plan to teach it. Nothing upsets cooperating teachers more than classes that do not go because the student teacher was not sufficiently prepared.

Build a reputation for being responsible and dependable by carrying out your assignments faithfully and accurately. Sometimes student teachers fail because they do not understand what their responsibilities are or how to carry them out. Study the teacher's handbook, observe the cooperating teacher, and heed the cooperating teacher's instructions so that you will know just what to do, and when and how. If you are uncertain about what to do or how to do it, ask, even though it may embarrass you to admit ignorance. It is much better to admit you do not understand than to keep quiet and reveal it.

Be a self-starter. Teachers, principals, and college supervisors are impressed by evidences of initiative. Volunteer to do things before you have to be asked. Willingly take on such tasks as reading papers and correcting tests. Take part in cafeteria supervision, extracurricular activities, attendance at PTA meetings, and the like. Participating in such activities will give you experience and expertise in these areas of the teacher's job and will also indicate to your colleagues that you are a professionally minded person who does not shun the nitty gritty.

Remember that you are being evaluated all the time that you are student teaching, so try to be just a little more accurate, a little more prompt, a little more precise, a little more dependable, and a little more willing than in other college activities.

During your professional laboratory experiences you are a guest of the school in which you are observing, participating, or student teaching. Your tenure in the school is not a right, but a privilege. Behave in a way that will make you and succeeding student teachers welcome. As quickly as you can, adapt yourself to the culture of the school and conform to the mores of the school as they apply to teachers. Do not stand on your rights—as a guest of the school you may not have many—but concentrate on your responsibilities. Try as soon as possible to become a member of the school staff and to set up pleasant relationships with your cooperating teacher and other colleagues.

Refrain from criticizing the school, its administration, or its teachers. Be particularly careful about what you say to teachers and other student teachers. If some things in a situation bother you, seek the advice of your college supervisor before you do anything drastic. If there is to be any friction, let the college supervisor absorb the sparks. It is his or her job to see that everything runs smoothly and that you get the best learning experience possible in your laboratory experience.

Do not under any circumstances discuss school personnel with the pupils. Often pupils tell student teachers how much better they are than their regular teachers. Do not respond to such bait. To allow yourself to discuss a teacher's performance and personality with a pupil can lead only to trouble.

Professional laboratory experiences, particularly student teaching, throw students and cooperating teachers into proximity that can be greatly rewarding and also extremely difficult. From the point of view of the cooperating teacher, the student teaching period presents a threat in several ways. To allow a neophyte to interfere in the smooth running of one's class is risky. More than one teacher has had to work extra long hours to repair the damage done to a class by an incompetent student teacher. Teachers who are insecure may find the presence of any other adult in their classes threatening; the presence of a student teacher critically observing the teacher's work can be particularly disturbing. So avoid any appearance of opposing or competing with the cooperating teacher. Consult with him or her before you undertake anything and follow his or her advice and instructions carefully. If you believe those instructions or advice are wrong, your only recourse is to consult with the college supervisor.

Above all, listen to what the cooperating teacher tells you! Many teachers (and college supervisors as well) complain that student teachers do not listen to what they are told. Often student teachers do not listen because they are so caught up in their problems that they find it difficult to concentrate on anything else. They may be too busy justifying their behavior or explaining away what has gone amiss in their classes to hear someone else's criticism. Although it may require some effort, try to hear what the cooperating teacher has to say and follow through on the suggestions. Teachers find it exasperating when student teachers carry on in unwanted ways in spite of the teacher's long and detailed instructions or explanations of what should be done.

As with any public figure in the community you can expect that you and your performance will be discussed by students as well as the parents in the community. Usually, the students' comments are far removed from the teacher's ears but sometimes chance remarks are caught as you walk through the halls or as students are leaving the room. Let them not turn your head because often these remarks are quite flattering. At the same time, guard against that feeling of annihilation which usually follows derogatory statements about your efforts or intentions. Whether you are praised or denigrated try to assume an objective attitude and use the comments for the inherent value they may possess. Remind yourself that you cannot always be all things to all people nor should you even try to be. Your personality, the school regulations, and the classroom procedures will not let you be equally appealing to nor effective with all of your students. You must expect that in the process of upholding your standards you will leave an occasional student dissatisfied. Only by keeping your reactions under control will you be able to preserve your mental equilibrium and zest for your job.

Relationships with Students

Your relationships with students may make or break you in a laboratory situation, so try to make them as amicable and purposeful as possible. Boys and girls like teachers who treat them with respect and whom they can respect. Therefore, treat them courteously and tactfully but at the same time require of them standards of behavior and academic productivity reasonably close to those established by the regular teacher. Show that you have confidence in them and expect them to do well. Let them know you are interested in them and in their activities.

The best way to earn the students' respect and liking is to do a good job of teaching and to treat all students fairly and cordially. Do not, however, become overfriendly. Be friendly, not chummy. Your role is not to be a buddy, but to be a teacher. Seek respect rather than popularity. Remember that you are an adult, not a kid. The students will respect and like you more if you act your age and assume your proper role.

Analysis of Teaching

The examined life is always better than the unexamined life, philosophers tell us. If one knows oneself, there is little doubt that the knowledge is beneficial to him or her as a teacher. Therefore, those who wish to become really professional should examine themselves and their teaching every once in a while. By so doing, it may be possible to detect weaknesses in your classroom behavior and teaching techniques that you can remedy and to discover unrealized strengths on which you can capitalize. This section of the module discusses a number of methods by which to examine your own teaching behavior in the classroom. Most of the procedures you will study here are rather simple methods of analyzing or evaluating teaching. It is hoped that they will not only give you a basis for examining your own teaching but will also serve as a means for reviewing some of the strategies and tactics discussed in earlier modules.

Analyzing Your Lessons

To make the most of your student teaching, you should occasionally stop to examine your lessons. The simplest way to do this is to stop and think back over a lesson and ask yourself how it went and why. Usually, it is best to pick good lessons to examine so that you can see what you are doing well. The practice is good for the ego and tends to reinforce your good traits. From time to time, you will want to examine classes that failed, to see if you can figure out why they did not go well. If you are having trouble with a class, such an analysis may help you spot the difficulty and correct the errors that you may have been making.

In this type of analysis, as you review your lesson, ask yourself such questions as, What went well? What went badly? Why? What could I have done to improve the lesson? Next time, how should I handle this type of class? A questionnaire, such as that portrayed in Figure 17-1, should prove very helpful in this reviewing

Use this form to analyze the class you thought went best this day.

1. Do you feel good about this class? Why, or why not?

2. In what way was the lesson most successful?

3. If you were to teach this lesson again, what would you do differently? Why?

4. Was your plan adequate? In what ways would you change it?

5. Did you achieve your major objectives?

6. Was the class atmosphere pleasant, productive, and supportive?

7. Were there signs of strain or misbehavior? If so, what do you think was the cause?

8. How much class participation was there?

9. Which pupils did extremely well?

10. Were there pupils who did not learn? How might you help them?

11. Were the provisions for motivation adequate?

12. Was the lesson individualized so that pupils had opportunities to learn according to their abilities, interests, and needs?

13. Did the pupils have any opportunities to think?

FIGURE 17-1 *Self-analysis of a Lesson.*

of your procedures. Rating scales and checklists are also useful, but probably not as useful as the open-ended questionnaire. Figure 17-2, is an example of a rating scale used in rating the teaching experiences of teaching interns and student teachers. Figure 17-3 is a rating scale devised by a group of prospective student teachers as a means of rating their teaching during student teaching. Perhaps you could develop a better one yourself.

Another way to check on your teaching is to consider at what level your students have learned. According to Bradfield and Moredock, there are five levels of performance. These levels are set forth in Figure 17-4. Ideally, the pupils should attain the highest levels of learning in your units. Examine your teaching. Is it the type that should bring pupils to this high level of learning? Or does it handcuff them to the lower levels?

Another way to upgrade your teaching is to examine your lesson plans. Pre-

1. What intellectual experiences were involved?
   a. Information-getting (fact-finding and compiling)?
   b. Organizing facts into own patterns (reasoning)?
   c. Judging, evaluating, applying criteria?
   d. Problem-solving (inventing criteria)?
   e. Creative thinking?
      (cf. also item 9 below)

2. Did the learning experience utilize emotional powers?
   a. Wholesome and self-expressive interest in the ideas or end-product of the work?
   b. Wholesome and self-expressive interest in the activity?
   c. Wholesome and self-expressive interest in the persons or group?

3. Did the learning experience give opportunity for realistic relating by each child?
   a. to individual peers?
   b. to peer groups?
   c. to teacher and other adults?

4. Did the learning experience promote realistic self-esteem?
   a. Awareness of own feelings?
   b. Recognizing own purposes or goals?
   c. Finding ways to effectively fulfill "a" or "b"?
   d. Realistic awareness of effect of powers and limitations?
   e. Realistic awareness of effect of own words and behavior upon others?
   f. Increased awareness of what he wants from situation to situation (i.e., of own self-expressive interest)?
   g. Realistic viewing of own competences (present and in near future)?
   h. Realistic, independent ideas of self-worth?
   i. Realistic awareness of learnings needed next?

5. Did the learning experience promote improved behaviors in significant life situations?
   a. Family?
   b. Social groups?
   c. Civic competences?
      (1) Voting
      (2) Study of public problems
      (3) Organizing action groups

6. Did the learning experience involve choosing?
   a. Ability to make critical choice?
   b. Ability to explain and support choice?
   c. Consideration of the consequences of own decision upon self and upon others?

FIGURE 17-2 *Criteria for an Educational Experience [Source: J. A. Vanderpol, Jersey City State College, unpublished manuscript.]*

FIGURE 17-2 *(Continued)*

	*	┼	X
7. Did the learning experience improve understanding of how own mind works?			
a. Such mind-needs as 'who, how, what, why, when, where, so what'?			
b. Basic outlines or structures of ideas (peg ideas) into which many future ideas will be organized?			
c. Logical reasoning patterns such as 'if. . ., then. . .' thinking; or of 'Are there any alternative answers?'			
d. Examining evidence or making careful generalizations or asking for needed 'date'?			
e. Recognizing own bias or error or mistaken idea?			
f. Considering what thoughts, feelings, and actions will be changed in the future?			
g. Applying the new learning or idea to many situations or kinds of ideas?			
h. Increased readiness for 'more of same' ideas or activities			
8. Did the learning experience promote realistic concepts of others?			
a. Awareness of others' feelings?			
b. Recognizing others' purposes or goals?			
c. Finding ways to effectively fulfill 'a' or 'b'?			
d. Realistic awareness and acceptance of others' powers and limitations?			
e. Realistic expectations from others?			
f. Realistic awareness of effect on own words and behaviors upon others?			
g. Increased awareness of what he 'wants' from situation to situation?			
9. What intellectual skills or competences have been forwarded?			
a. Speaking skills?			
b. Writing skills?			
c. Reading skills?			
d. Arithmetical skills?			
e. Eye-hand muscular coordination?			
f. Discriminating discussion skills?			
10. Did each child experience a feeling of achievement?			
11. Did the experience provide for teacher pupil conferences and constant re-evaluations?			

* Insert M for much; or S for some; or L for little; or N for none.
+ Insert A for all children; M for most children; F for few children; N for no children;
X List specific next steps the teacher will take to improve the learning experience.

Rate yourself   5, 4, 3, 2, 1   5 is best

1. Did I look O.K.?

2. Did I sound O.K.?

3. Did I make my point?

4. Was I clear?

5. Did I make them think?

6. Is my questioning technique O.K.?

7. Is my blackboard work O.K.?

8. Is my audio-visual O.K.?

9. Did the lesson develop logically?

10. Overall rating

FIGURE 17-3 *Rating Scale Designed by Teaching Internes*

Level   Performance

I.   Imitating, duplicating, repeating.

     This is the level of initial contact. Student can repeat or duplicate what has just been said, done, or read. Indicates that student is at least conscious or aware of contact with a particular concept or process.

II.   Level I, plus recognizing, identifying, remembering, recalling, classifying.

     To perform on this level, the student must be able to recognize or identify the concept or process when encountered later, or to remember or recall the essential features of the concept or process.

III.   Levels I and II, plus comparing, relating, discriminating, reformulating, illustrating.

     Here the student can compare and relate this concept or process with other concepts or processes and make discriminations. He can formulate in his own words a definition, and he can illustrate or give examples.

IV.   Levels I, II, and III, plus explaining, justifying, predicting, estimating, interpreting, making critical judgments, drawing inferences.

     On the basis of his understanding of a concept or process, he can make explanations, give reasons, make predictions, interpret, estimate, or make critical judgments. This performance represents a high level of understanding.

V.   Levels I, II, III, and IV, plus creating, discovering, reorganizing, formulating new hypotheses, new questions, and problems.

     This is the level of original and productive thinking. The student's understanding has developed to such a point that he can make discoveries that are new to him and can restructure and reorganize his knowledge on the basis of his new discoveries and new insights.

FIGURE 17-4   *Levels of Performance* [*Source: James M. Bradfield and H. Stewart Moredock,* Measurement and Evaluation in Education *(New York: Macmillan Publishing Co., 1957), p. 204.*]

sumably, the better your lesson plans, the better your teaching will be. Perhaps the form included as Figure 17-5 will help you to evaluate your plans. With a little adjustment, it could be used to evaluate unit and course plans. When using this form, remember that all the characteristics may not be necessary for every lesson plan, but in the long run teachers whose lessons do not meet these criteria cannot be fully effective.

Audio and Video Feedback

Both audio- and videotapes of your classes can be a great help to you as you examine your teaching and personality. Although at first the presence of the tape recorder or camera may make you nervous and self-conscious, the feeling will soon wear off. Then the camera or recorder can get a good record of how you look and sound as you teach. You can and should use this record as a basis for detailed analysis of your teaching, but just listening to and seeing yourself may give you important insights into your own teaching behavior. If your self-observation is done thoughtfully and critically, it will, of course, be more rewarding than if it is superficial. Using a simple questionnaire in which you ask yourself such questions as the following may make your self-observation more useful: What are my best points? What points are fairly good? What points are not so good? Are my explanations clear? Do I speak well and clearly? Do I speak in a monotone? Do I slur my words? Do my sentences drop off so that ends are difficult to hear? Do I involve everyone in the class or do I direct my teaching only to a few? Are my questions clear and unambiguous? Do I dominate class discussion? Do I allow certain pupils to dominate the class?

1. The Objective

   a. The objective is clearly stated.

   b. The objective is measurable.

   c. The objective is pertinent to the unit and course.

   d. The objective is worthwhile.

   e. The objective is suitable to the pupils' age and grade level.

   f. The objective can be achieved in the time alloted.

   g. The objective can be attained in different degrees and/or amounts.

   h. The objective is relevant to the pupils' lives.

2. The Procedure or Suggested Activities

   a. The suggested activities will stimulate pupils' thinking.

   b. The suggested activities will produce the objectives.

   c. The procedure is outlined in sufficient detail to be followed easily.

   d. The procedure allows for individual differences.
      (1) choice in required work
      (2) optional work for enrichment
      (3) encouragement of initiative

   e. The activities in the procedure are interesting and appealing enough to arouse pupil motivation.

   f. The activites relate to
      (1) the aims of the pupils
      (2) the needs of the pupils
      (3) work in other courses
      (4) extracurricular life
      (5) out-of-school life
      (6) community needs and expectancies.

FIGURE 17-5 *Form for Evaluating Lesson Plans*

Exercise 17 A

Make a list of check questions that you might use to evaluate your own teaching.

According to one analysis, there are seven major types of teaching operations: motivating, planning, informing, leading discussion, disciplining, counseling, and evaluating. One way to evaluate your teaching would be to check on a form, such as that shown in Figure 17-6, the type of teaching you were doing every five seconds in one of your classes. In this form an eighth category has been added for operations that do not seem to fit into any of the seven listed.

A usually more profitable use of the recording device is to apply interaction analysis techniques to recording of your own teaching. Such self-evaluation may be more illuminating than simple critical listening to your recordings or hearing the criticisms and comments of an observer.

Interaction Analysis

There are a number of methods by which one can analyze the student-teacher interaction in a class. All of these methods require the services of either an observer or an audio- or video-recorder. Interaction analysis is valuable because it gives one an indication of just who is doing the talking in the class. From it one

Motivating

Planning

Informing

Leading discussion

Disciplining

Counseling

Evaluating

Other

FIGURE 17-6 *Types of Teaching Activities Checklist (Five-second Interval Tallies)*

can learn whether or not the class is teacher-dominated or pupil-dominated, free and open or repressive, and whether the teaching style is direct or indirect—in short, the general tenor of the classroom atmosphere and type of learning that is going on. As a rule of thumb, one can safely assume that when classes are satisfactory, the following take place:

1. The interaction will show that pupils actively participate at least half of the time. (Teachers who find themselves to be talking more than half the time should check their procedures.)
2. As far as possible, every pupil participates in some way. (Classes that are dominated by a few pupils are not satisfactory.)
3. A good share of the class time is given over to thoughtful, creative activity rather than to mere recitation of information by either teacher or pupils.

Interaction analysis schemes vary from the simple to the complex. Some, such as the Flanders system, require that the observation be done by trained observers and that upon completing the observation, the observer arranges findings into a matrix from which one can tell not only what happened but what the atmosphere of the class was. Such systems can give you an excellent picture of the interaction in the classroom that may lead to important insights into your own teaching. If you tape record the class, it is possible to apply the analysis to the class without the use of an outside observer. Therefore, it would be advantageous for you to learn how to use this system of interaction analysis. Unfortunately, we do not have the space to go into the procedure in detail in this module.

Even though they are not so useful as the more sophisticated methods, simple interaction analysis techniques can be truly helpful. The picture they give is not as clear, but it will show up glaring faults and give indications of more subtle elements of the classroom interaction and atmosphere.

Probably the simplest type of classroom interaction analysis is for an observer to mark down on a sheet of paper every time the teacher talks and every time a pupil talks, as T P T T T P T T T P P T T. This record shows how much the teacher talks as compared to how much the pupils talk, although it will not show how long they talk. If you tape record your class, you can do this analysis yourself.

Exercise 17 B

If a classroom analysis of one of your typical classes consists almost entirely of T's, what would it show about your teaching? Does this analysis indicate that perhaps you should consider changing your style?

A more complex refinement of this technique is for an observer to sit at the back of the class and to record the number of times each person speaks. This technique gives you a much clearer picture of what is happening in the class. The disadvantage of this technique is that it requires an outside observer. Neither audio- nor videotapes of the type we could procure in the ordinary classroom situation would be usable for such an analysis. Figure 17-7 is an illustration of the tallying by this method of interaction analysis. In this figure, the teacher is represented by a circle, and the pupils by squares.

Exercise 17 C

Do the tallies in Figure 17-7 give you any inkling about the style of the teacher in this class? How about the class participation? In general, what does the chart tell you about this class?

Another version of the form of analysis just described is for the observer to record who is talking every five seconds. This variation of the tallying approach has the advantage of showing what persons are interacting and how much they talk, although it does not give as complete a picture as the Verbal Interaction Category System (V.I.C.S.) or Flanders analysis system.

Some supervisors use a simplified version of the Flanders system which does

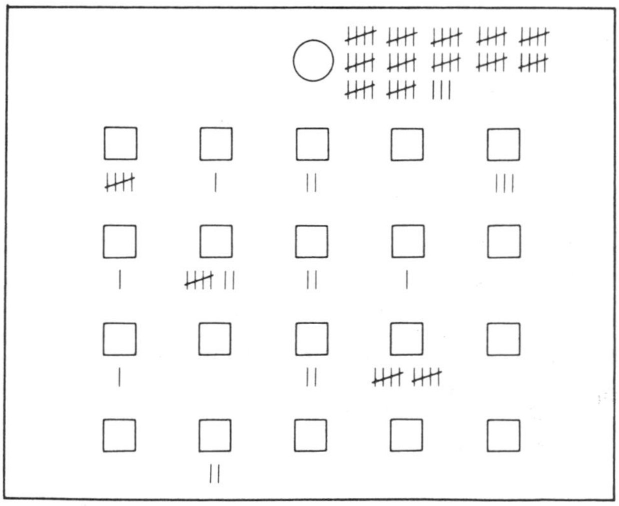

FIGURE 17-7 *A Form for Interaction Analysis*

Category	Tallies
Teacher Talk	
Accepts Feeling	
Praises or Encourages	
Accepts or Uses Ideas of Students	
Asks Questions	
Lectures	
Gives Directions	
Criticizes	
Student Talk	
Student Response	
Student Initiation	
Silence or Confusion	

FIGURE 17-8   *Interaction Analysis Check Sheet*

not require the use of a matrix. In this version of the system the observer simply records, at regular intervals, whether the teacher or a student is talking, and the nature of the talk. Flanders has divided the talk into 10 categories. Teacher talk he has divided into talk designed to influence students indirectly and talk designed to influence students directly. Under indirect influence teacher talk he includes 4 sub-categories:

1. Talk in which the teacher accepts the student's feelings in a non-threatening manner.
2. Talk in which the teacher praises or encourages the student's performance or behavior.
3. Talk in which the teacher accepts, uses or builds on the student's ideas.
4. Talk in which the teacher asks questions designed to elicit ideas.

In direct influence teacher talk Flanders includes:

5. Lectures and teacher talks in which the teacher presents information and ideas.
6. Orders, commands, and gives directions which students are expected to follow.
7. Criticizes student behavior, reprimands, and gives explanations justifying class procedures.

Student talk in this type of instruction analysis is limited to two categories:

8. Student responses to the teacher.
9. Student initiated talk.

This type of interaction analysis also provides for a tenth category for times when no one is speaking or if there is a confusing Babel as at the beginning or end of a class period or during laboratory or small group discussion sessions.[1]

To record the interaction according to this simplified version of the Flanders system use a form such as that shown in Figure 17-8.

---

[1] Edmund J. Amidon and Ned A. Flanders, *The Role of the Teacher in the Classroom* (Minneapolis, Minn.: Paul S. Amidon and Associates, 1963), p. 15.

Evaluating Specific Teaching Techniques

Evaluating One's Discussions

To improve your skill in using class discussions, you should analyze the discussions that you lead. It is possible to do this in armchair fashion, but it would be more productive to react to a tape recording of the discussion. A self-evaluation form, similar to the one presented as Figure 17-9, should be very helpful for spotting one's weaknesses and building one's strengths in leading discussions. Flow charts that depict the course of the discussion may be even more useful. Preparing the flow chart can be entrusted to a pupil observer since the technique for preparing one is so simple. If the class is arranged in a circle, preparing the flow chart is easier; it is slightly less so if the class is arranged as a hollow square; but when the class is arranged in rows, making the chart becomes quite difficult. (Discussions are difficult to conduct when the pupils are in rows, too.) All the observer does is to make an arrow from the speaker to the person to whom he is speaking each time anyone speaks. A direct reply to a speaker can be noted by a double-headed arrow. Comments or questions that are directed to the group rather than to an individual are indicated by arrows that point to the center of the circle or square. An example of a flow chart showing a portion of a class discussion appears as Figure 17-10.

Figure 17-11 shows another device used to analyze class discussions. In this technique, a recorder simply tallies the number of times each person talks. There is no indication of the conversational interchanges so this type of record does not give one as complete a picture as the flow chart does.

A.

1. Did I have a legitimate objective?

2. Were the objectives suitable for the discussion technique?

3. Did I get good participation?

4. Did I encourage participation or did I tend to cut people off?

5. Did I keep from letting people dominate?

6. Did I encourage the shy, timid, etc.?

7. Did I keep the group to the subject?

8. Did I domineer or dominate?

9. In what did I best succeed?

10. In what was I least successful?

11. Did I solicit evocative questions and tentative solutions?

12. Did I summarize conclusions or positions so as to follow through and tie the discussion together?

B.

1. Identify the techniques that seemed to make the discussion effective.

2. Identify the techniques that seemed to detract from the effectiveness of the discussion.

FIGURE 17-9 *Self-evaluation Form for Discussion Leaders*

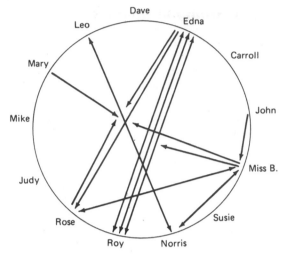

FIGURE 17-10

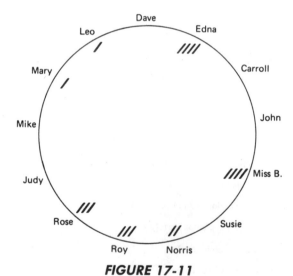

FIGURE 17-11

Questions

Questions are among the teacher's most important tools; it is important to learn how to use them well. To check on your questioning technique, you might record and observe yourself. Among the things you might observe are the following:

1. What sorts of questions do I use?
2. Are my questions clear?
3. Do I ask one question at a time or do I confuse pupils by asking two or more questions as one?
4. Do I ask real questions, or are my questions whiplash questions that start out as statements and then suddenly convert into questions, such as "The

point that the author was trying to get across is what?" Whiplash questions are not really fair because they give pupils the wrong set.

5. Do my questions require pupils to use their knowledge, information, and ideas?
6. Do I direct my questions to pupils or to the class as a whole?
7. Do I wait until I have finished asking my question before calling on someone to answer it?
8. Do I follow up my questions with probing questions to ferret out ideas, understandings, and thinking?

Exercise 17 D

List other questions you might use to check your questioning technique. Refer to Module 8.

Construct a questionnaire and use it to analyze the use of questions in one of your own lessons or a lesson you observe.

Most questions in a typical class are aimed at eliciting memorized facts and information. When teachers ask high-order questions, the questions are likely to be convergent questions rather than divergent or evaluative questions. See Module 8 if you cannot remember what these are. To find out what type of questions you and your pupils use, a form similar to that presented as Figure 17-12 can be helpful. To use the form, an observer simply checks the appropriate column each time the teacher asks a question.

Probing Questions

Probing questions are used to follow up questions that originally elicit only superficial answers. According to Dwight Allen and his associates, this can be done in five ways: (1) asking pupils for more information or more meaning; (2) re-

	Cognitive Memory Questions	Convergent Questions	Divergent Questions	Evaluative Questions
Teacher Questions				
Student Questions				

FIGURE 17-12 *A Form for Analyzing Questions*

Objective	Item	Joe	Julia	Jim	Jane	Jean	Josie
1.	1	+	+	+	+	+	+
	2	+	0	+	+	+	+
	3	+	0	0	+	+	+
2.	4	+	0	0	0	0	+
	5	+	+	+	0	0	0
	6	0	+	0	+	0	0

+ correct answer
0 incorrect answer

FIGURE 17-13   *Example of Test Item Analysis Form*

quiring the pupil to rationally justify his response; (3) refocusing the pupil's or class's attention on a related issue; (4) prompting the pupil or giving him hints; and (5) bringing other students into the discussion by getting them to respond to the first student's answer.[2]

Exercise 17 E

To check your use of probing questions, listen to a tape of one of your classes to observe whether or not you actually do follow up and what type of probing tactics you use. Ask yourself if these tactics were the best under the circumstances. Why, or why not?

Analysis of Test Results

Analysis of pupils' test results can give one an inkling of the success of one's teaching, providing the tests are properly designed and written. For test results to be of value for the analysis of one's teaching success, the teaching objectives must be carefully defined and each test item must be aimed at a teaching objective. Once you have given and corrected the test, to analyze the test you must set up a chart that indicates what objective each test item tests, and what items each pupil got right, as in Figure 17-13. Such a chart would show you how effectively you taught by indicating how well you achieved each of your objectives. In the example, for instance (Figure 17-13), if our small sample is any indicator, the teacher evidently was quite successful with objective 1; not so successful with objective 2. This type of analysis is also an excellent tool by which to diagnose the progress of the various pupils in the class.

Exercise 17 F

Problem: A test was given to a 10th grade class. Figure 17-14 shows the results for items 1 to 23. In this test items 1, 2, 21, 22, 23 test objective A; items 3, 4, 7, 18, 20 test objective B; items 5, 6, 8, 9, 13 test objective C; items 10, 11, 14, 15, 16 test objective D; items 12, 17, 19 test objective E. Interpret the test results.

[2] Dwight W. Allen, et al., *Technical Skills of Teaching*, rough draft proposal, Stanford University School of Education, July 24, 1967 (Mimeographed).

Key: + = correct response; 0 = incorrect response.

Pupil	Total score	1	2	3	4	5	6	7	8	9	10	11	12	13	14	15	16	17	18	19	20	21	22	23
																		Test Item						
Pat	95	+	+	+	+	+	+	0	0	+	+	+	0	+	+	+	+	+	0	0	0	+	+	+
Al	93	+	+	0	0	+	0	0	+	+	+	0	+	+	+	+	+	+	0	0	+	0	+	+
Carol	88	+	+	+	0	+	+	0	+	+	+	+	+	0	+	+	+	+	+	0	+	0	+	+
Lee	85	+	+	0	0	+	0	0	+	+	+	+	0	+	+	+	+	0	0	+	0	+	+	+
Tina	83	+	+	0	0	+	+	0	0	+	+	+	0	+	+	+	+	+	0	0	0	+	+	+
Linda G.	83	+	+	0	0	+	+	0	0	+	+	0	0	+	+	+	+	+	+	0	0	0	+	+
Tom	81	+	+	0	0	+	+	+	0	+	0	+	+	+	+	+	+	+	0	+	0	+	+	+
Ed	80	+	0	0	+	+	0	0	0	+	+	+	0	+	+	0	+	+	+	+	+	+	+	+
Barbara	80	+	+	0	0	+	0	0	0	+	+	0	+	0	0	0	0	+	0	0	0	+	+	+
Alfred	80	+	+	0	0	+	+	0	0	+	+	0	+	+	+	+	+	+	+	0	+	0	+	+
Linda B.	79	+	+	+	0	0	0	+	0	0	+	0	+	+	+	+	+	+	0	0	0	+	+	+
Mary	77	+	0	+	0	0	+	0	0	+	0	+	+	+	+	+	+	0	0	0	0	+	+	+
Vance	77	+	+	0	+	+	+	+	0	0	0	0	+	+	+	+	+	0	0	+	0	+	+	0
Mike	77	+	+	0	0	+	+	0	0	+	+	+	+	+	+	+	+	+	0	+	+	+	+	+
Fred	74	+	0	0	0	+	0	0	0	0	0	0	+	+	0	0	+	+	+	0	0	+	+	+
Bill	73	0	+	0	0	+	0	+	+	0	+	0	+	+	+	+	+	+	0	+	0	+	+	+
Joe	72	+	+	+	+	0	0	0	0	+	+	+	0	+	+	+	+	+	0	+	0	+	+	+
Tim	72	+	+	0	+	+	+	0	0	+	+	0	0	+	0	+	0	+	0	0	0	+	+	+
Steve	71	0	0	0	+	+	+	+	+	+	+	+	+	+	+	+	+	0	0	+	0	+	+	+
Bea	65	+	+	0	+	+	0	0	0	+	0	+	+	+	+	+	0	+	0	0	+	0	+	+
Joe	64	+	0	0	+	+	0	+	0	+	+	+	+	0	+	0	+	0	0	0	+	+	+
Carl	63	+	+	0	0	+	0	0	0	0	+	0	+	+	0	+	+	0	0	0	+	+	+

FIGURE 17-14 *Test Item Analysis*

Pupil Evaluation

You can learn much from the pupils' opinions of your teaching. Just watching their reactions will be enlightening. An eager, enthusiastic, attentive class is a good sign; an apathetic, inattentive, antagonistic class is not. Another method by which to gather pupil evaluations is to use a simple questionnaire or opinion sampling. Some teachers make a practice of collecting such data at the end of the school year, but if you are to capitalize on the information, perhaps it would be better to collect it earlier in the year. Whenever you do it, make sure that the evaluations are entirely anonymous. To preserve anonymity, use check sheets rather than handwritten comments. Sometimes, however, pupils will react well to open-ended, free response questions if the questions ask for constructive criticism concerning ways to make the course more effective.

Growing in the Profession

Surveying Employment Prospects

Early in your teacher preparation program you should start thinking about your first job and your career in teaching. If you have not done so already, you should investigate the job market. At the moment this is being written, there appears to be a change settling in regarding the availability of jobs. The decline in student enrollments of the 1970s and early 1980s precipitated a drastic reduction in the number of candidates interested in a teaching career. Of late, however, it appears that the demand has caught up with and in many cases has surpassed the supply of teachers that had seriously dwindled. Salaries in teaching are rising. Several states have made teaching and teacher preparation items of immediate concern. It also appears that teacher openings are occurring where previously there were none.

Similarly, you should try to pick courses that will prepare you for the subject matter you are likely to have to teach in middle or secondary schools. Courses in writing, composition, and American literature are more likely to be useful to beginning English teachers than is Gothic literature, for instance.

In times of tight employment it may be wise to consider the advisability of seeking a graduate degree or working as a substitute teacher for a year or two. Both of these experiences will make you more hirable. Being a substitute teacher has the added advantage of giving you an inside track when opportunities in the system open up. If you are headed toward a crowded field, perhaps you should reconsider your goal. There are many teaching jobs in business, industry, or government you might want to investigate.

Take advantage of the facilities of your college placement service early. You will probably find them anxious to coach you on ways to find, apply for, and obtain jobs, and also to tell you how you can best prepare for the jobs that are becoming available. Similarly, education professors are usually anxious to coach students on such matters as finding job opportunities, writing letters of application, securing favorable recommendations, job interviewing, preparing for the types of jobs available, and so on. The sooner you become knowledgeable in these areas, the better chances you will have of finding congenial employment when the time comes.

You should, as soon as you can, become familiar with the certification requirements of the state or states in which you hope to teach, just as you should become familiar with the college graduation requirements. Usually you can be confident that your college program will meet the local certification requirements for your major. Studying the certification requirements may show you how to become certifiable in more fields and in other parts of the country.

Professional Memberships

Become familiar with the teacher associations in your field as early as you can. Organizations such as The National Council of Teachers of English, The National Council for the Social Studies, and the National Council of Teachers of Mathematics, publish journals and monographs that can help you become familiar with what is going on in the teaching field. They also provide opportunities for fellowship with leading teachers and supervisors. As a rule, local affiliates of these organizations welcome teacher education students to their meetings. These meetings provide opportunities to meet important professionals and to learn about the most recent developments in the teaching field.

The local affiliates of the teachers' unions (The American Federation of Teachers and the National Education Association) also provide opportunities for students to become involved in professional activities. You may find joining the union's student affiliate or attending the state or national meetings especially profitable. State and regional conventions in particular can give beginners a superb view of new professional materials and technology available. There is hardly a supplier of educational materials or equipment that does not exhibit at these conventions.

Keeping Up

Once you have begun to teach, do not become complacent. After a period of teaching some teachers become bored, frustrated, and discontented. This phenomenon attacks teachers who do not grow with the profession and so atrophy. Teaching is interesting and exciting if you approach it that way. Try to keep it so by keeping up with what is going on and by becoming active in the professional organizations. Attend workshops, institutes, and conventions, which present the new methods and materials of your profession. Take graduate courses that will help you better to understand your subject, your pupils, and methods of teaching. Take interest in the students and their activities. Involve yourself in curriculum revision. In short, keep yourself professionally and personally alert and active. You should begin this process now!

Try to grow as a person as well as professionally. Keep your mind sharp by interesting yourself in many things and by becoming more expert in your field. Deepen your appreciation for your work and guard against letting it become a secondary occupation. You may find it necessary to combine your teaching with other work—either part-time work or homemaking—but do not let the other work take away from your teaching. Keep abreast of developments in your field through refresher courses, professional reading, or advanced graduate study. No matter how you do it, keep moving forward with your development of your own personality and your mastery of professional skills. Arrange to visit other teachers and interact with them about what accounts for their success. Keep yourself on the alert for new ways of doing things, new approaches to your students and your subject. Therein lies the excitement of your new profession—reaching a point of competency in your teaching, engaging in activities that bring about successful learning, and finding outlets for your creative juices that will benefit your students. Thus equipped, involve yourself in curricular revision and in short keep yourself professionally alert and alive.

Hail and Farewell

Working through these modules may have made it seem that teaching is a difficult, arduous profession. Maybe so, but it is also rewarding. Teaching done well is never dull. It can be great fun. Besides, it is important. Working with young minds will keep you on your toes. It also gives you an opportunity to influence the shaping of the future.

Teaching is a profession to be proud of. We welcome you to it!

Suggested Reading

Britt, Samuel, S., and Daniel C. Walsh. *The Reality of Teaching.* Dubuque, Ia.: Kendall Hunt Publishing, 1979.

Cooper, James M. *Classroom Teaching Skills: A Handbook.* Lexington, Mass.: D. C. Heath, 1977, Chap. 9.

Emmens, Amy Puett. *After the Lesson Plan: Realities of High School Teaching.* New York: Teachers College Press, 1981.

Goddard, Roger E., Ed.D. *Teacher Certification Requirements: All Fifty States.* 4th ed. Sarasota, Fla.: Teacher Certification Publications, 1986.

Henson, Kenneth T. *Secondary Teaching Methods.* Lexington, Mass.: D. C. Heath, 1981, Chap. 16.

Highet, Gilbert. *Immortal Profession: The Joys of Teaching and Learning.* New York: Weybright and Talley, 1976.

Hoover, Kenneth H. *The Professional Teacher's Handbook: A Guide for Improving Instruction in Today's Middle and Secondary Schools,* 3d ed. Boston: Allyn & Bacon, 1982.

House, Ernest R., and Stephen D. Lapan. *Survival in the Classroom. Negotiating with Kids, Colleagues, and Bosses,* abridged ed. Boston: Allyn & Bacon, 1981, Part I, III, and IV.

Kelley, James L. *The Successful Teacher: Essays in Secondary School Instruction.* Ames, Ia.: Iowa State University Press, 1982.

Levin, Thamar, with Ruth Long. *Effective Instruction.* Alexandria, Va.: Association for Supervision and Curriculum Development, 1981.

Lorton, Eveleen, et al. *The Teacher's World.* Special Current Issues Publication No. 9. Washington, D.C.: ERIC Clearinghouse on Teacher Education, 1979.

Ryan, Kevin, et al. *Biting the Apple: Accounts of First Year Teachers.* New York: Longman, 1980.

Travers, Robert M. W., and Jacqueline Dillon. *The Making of a Teacher: A Plan for Professional Self-Development.* New York: Macmillan, 1975.

Troisi, Nicholas F. *Effective Teaching and Student Achievement.* Reston, Va.: National Association of Secondary School Principals, 1983.

Exercise Answer Key

Exercise 17 B

Probably you talk too much and should consider ways in which to involve more student participation.

Exercise 17 C

The Teacher is a talker who tends to involve only a few of the students.

Exercise 17 F

Objective A was well learned. Almost everyone answered the pertinent items correctly.

Objective B was not learned well at all. Probably this should be retaught. Three quarters of the pertinent answers were wrong.

Objective C was fairly well learned. Three fifths of the answers were correct.

Objective D was fairly well learned. Three quarters of the answers were correct.

Objective E was fairly well learned. Three fifths of the answers were correct.

Post Test

Checklist   In the following, check the appropriate answers according to the module text.

1. Check those of the following that the cooperating teacher will expect you to have when you come to do your student teaching.
   ( ) **a.** A command of the subject to be taught.
   ( ) **b.** Expertise in many teaching skills.

( ) **c.** A supply of instructional materials.
( ) **d.** An adequate understanding of the evaluation process.
( ) **e.** A well-developed teaching style.

2. To make a favorable impression on your cooperating teacher and supervisor,
( ) **a.** Prepare very carefully.
( ) **b.** Go right ahead with your plans without asking advice.
( ) **c.** Show your expertise by criticizing the school's procedures.
( ) **d.** Learn and follow the school routines.
( ) **e.** Be prompt at all assignments.
( ) **f.** Listen to what you are told.
( ) **g.** Study the content before the class period begins.

Multiple Choice   Write the letter of the most appropriate answer in the space provided.

( ) 3. When you get right down to it, college supervisors and cooperating teachers are your
a. colleagues.
b. assistants.
c. bosses.
d. collaborators.

( ) 4. As a student teacher, you are
a. a member of the school staff.
b. only a student.
c. a guest of the school.
d. on your own.

( ) 5. Most college teacher education students find that the most difficult part of their teacher education program is
a. Theory courses.
b. Microteaching.
c. Participation (Practicum).
d. Student Teaching.

( ) 6. To make your participation experience profitable, you should
a. engage in as many types of experiences as you can.
b. spend the entire period conducting classes.
c. spend the entire period observing.
d. focus on getting to know the pupils.

( ) 7. Basically, student teaching is supposed to be
a. a testing experience.
b. a learning experience.
c. a trial experience.
d. a full-fledged teaching experience.

Free Response—Short Answer

8. Suppose you should try out a new teaching technique and it fails miserably for you. What should you do, according to this module?

   _____

   _____

9. According to Bradfield and Moredock, what is the highest level of teaching?

   _____

   _____

   _____

   _____

10. List four of the eight criteria for the objective included in the form for evaluating lesson plans.

    _____

    _____

    _____

11. What is the purpose of recording and playing back your lessons?

    _____

    _____

12. An interaction analysis shows that most of the class consisted of teacher-initiated talk in which the teacher gave pupils information and asked narrow memory questions. If this class is typical of this teacher's style
    a. is she a direct or indirect teacher?
    b. is her style a most effective one?

    _____

    _____

    _____

13. A simple interaction analysis tally shows the following: T T T T T P T P T P T T T P T T P T T P T P T P T P T P.
    a. What does this show about the class?
    b. Is the class good or bad?

    _____

    _____

    _____

14. List six things you would look for in evaluating a discussion.

_____

_____

_____

_____

_____

_____

15. The flow chart of a discussion shows that there are only a few arrows from the teacher's position and all of these point to the center of the diagram. How would you interpret this phenomenon?

_____

_____

16. Why should you avoid using whiplash questions?

_____

_____

_____

17. In what ways are cognitive memory questions, convergent questions, and divergent questions different?

_____

_____

_____

_____

_____

18. In an item analysis, we find the following:

Objective	Item	Pupil					
		A	B	C	D	E	F
	1	+	+	+	+	+	+
1	2	+	+	+	+	+	+
	3	+	+	0	+	+	0
	4	0	0	+	0	0	0
2	5	0	0	0	0	0	0
	6	+	0	+	0	+	0

Assuming that this excerpt is typical of the entire test item analysis, what does it tell you?

_____

_____

_____

19. Give three ways that you can become more hirable.

_____

_____

_____

20. Why does the module recommend that you join the professional organization in your field?

_____

_____

_____

Post Test Answer Keys

Module 1

1. b, h, c	**11.** √	**21.** c	**31.** a
2. a, f	**12.**	**22.** a	**32.** c
3. e	**13.** √	**23.** c	**33.** d
4. b	**14.** √	**24.** b	**34.** c
5. d, g	**15.**	**25.** c	**35.** a
6. √	**16.** √	**26.** b	**36.** c
7. √	**17.** √	**27.** d	**37.** a
8.	**18.** c	**28.** b	**38.** d
9. √	**19.** a	**29.** b	**39.** d
10. √	**20.** a	**30.** c	**40.** a

Module 2

1. a. Teachers have not really thought through what they are trying to do.
    b. Teachers have not thought about how they ought to do it so their teaching becomes inconsequential, irrelevant, and dull.

2. a. What should my objectives be?
    b. How should I try to achieve these objectives?

3. a. What do I want to accomplish?
    b. How can I accomplish it?
    c. Who is to do what?
    d. When and in what order should things be done?
    e. When will things be done?
    f. What materials and equipment will I need?
    g. How will I get things started?
    h. How shall I follow up?
    i. How can I tell how well I have accomplished my goals?
    j. Why?

4. Teachers do not ask themselves: why should the pupils have to study and learn this?

5. a. The curriculum.
    b. Nature of the learners.
    c. What do you have to work with?
    d. Nature of the community.
    e. What the community expects.
    f. The nature of the subject matter.

6. Will it contribute to the achievement of the objectives?

7. Does it contribute to the objectives?

8. a. Suggested objectives.
    b. Suggested content.
    c. Suggested learning activities.
    d. Suggested reading.
    e. Suggested audio-visual and other materials of instruction for a course or curriculum.

9. It makes the coordination of teaching and learning activities easier.

10. It provides not only content, but a basis for organizing the course units and sequence.

11. The only real difference is that the team must plan together. This may cause some difficulty as you may have to give in to the group's wishes even when you do not want to and you must execute your part of the group plan even when it does not please you.

12. Probably the best argument is that it seems to promote favorable motivation and attitudes.

13. A resource unit lists objectives, teaching procedures, materials and so on that a teacher might use when building a plan for a particular teaching unit.

14. A textbook can be used to give your course its basic outline and to form the basis of various units and lessons. It should not be the be-all and end-all of one's teaching, however.

15. **a.** It produces well-organized classes.
    b. It helps to produce a purposeful class atmosphere.
    c. It helps to reduce discipline problems.
    d. It ensures that you know the subject.
    e. It tends to make classes more effective.

Module 3

1. a. C	**b.** B	**c.** D	**d.** X
e. X	**f.** C	**g.** X	**h.** B

2. a. A	**b.** A	**c.** B	**d.** B
e. B	**f.** B	**g.** B	**h.** A
i. A*	**j.** B	**k.** A	**1.** B

3. a. G	**b.** G	**c.** S	**d.** G
e. S	**f.** S	**g.** G	

4. a. C	**b.** C	**c.** B	**d.** B

5. a. ( )	**b.** (√)	**c.** (√)	**d.** (√)

6. a. 4	**b.** 3	**c.** 2	**d.** 5
e. 1	**f.** 6		

7. c

8. d

9. b

10. a

11. a. B C A S X R	**b.** B C A S X R
c. B A S X R	**d.** B A S X R
e. A	

*If one predicts or realizes without indicating to someone else one's prediction or realization, the activity is covert; if one writes down or tells the prediction or realization, it is behavioral.

12. A criterion-referenced behavioral objective is one that specifies the standards of behavior required.

13. a. They prepare a clear objective for one's teaching.
   b. They provide definite bases for evaluation.

14. Terminal behavior is the behavior of the learner at the completion and as a result of the instruction.

15. A covert objective is one in which the learner activity cannot be observed directly.

16. The taxonomies give a framework by which to structure your teaching so that it covers the more important types of learning.

17. a. Who?
   b. Does what?
   c. Under what conditions?
   d. How well?

18. For what purpose?

19. It is impossible to observe activity in the affective domain directly.

20. Descriptive objectives that describe the result of learning are most useful to describe general aims and goals. Since they represent covert activity they are not really useful as specific objectives except perhaps in the affective domain.

21. Specific objectives should support the more general objectives and goals.

22. A general objective, or educational goal, aim, or purpose.

23. Behavioral objectives usually make the best specific objectives.

24. Level 5, Perfection and Maintenance of the psychomotor domain.

25. Level 3, Valuing of the affective domain.

26. Level 4, Analysis of the cognitive domain.

27. Level 2, Comprehension of the cognitive domain.

28. Level 3, Valuing of the affective domain.

29. Level 2, Comprehension of the cognitive domain.

30. Level 3, Application in the cognitive domain.

Module 4

1. a	**2.** a	**3.** d	**4.** d
5. d	**6.** a	**7.** b	**8.** c
9. b	**10.** c	**11.** d	**12.** a

13. Both.

14. Of course.

15. Yes, if you think it advisable.

16. Either. It's up to you. The trend at the moment is to favor behavioral objectives for everything.

17. Any four from the following:
  a. It is pertinent to the course.
  b. It centers on some major underlying issue, problem, or theme.
  c. It is not too difficult, too big, or too demanding of time or resources.
  d. It is relevant to pupils' lives and to the community.
  e. It is suitable to pupils' interests and abilities.

18. Pick four from the following:
  a. They really contribute to the larger (general) objectives of the course or unit.
  b. They should be clear to you and to your pupils.
  c. They should be specific enough.
  d. They should be achievable in the time and with the resources available.
  e. They should be worthwhile and seem worthwhile.
  f. They should allow for individual differences, that is, attainable in different amounts and in different ways.

19. **a.** Activities that motivate.
  b. Activities that tie in with past units and other course work.
  c. Planning activities.

20. **a.** No. They can schedule themselves during the laboratory sessions.
  b. No. They do not all have to read the same material to solve the problems, for instance.

21. The learning packet is designed more for independent, individual self-study.

22. None, really.

23. Note the requirements for 1, 2, 3, and 4 on the study guide. Then have the pupil indicate which level he intends to shoot for.

24. **a.** Problems to be solved.
    b. Activities to do.
    c. Directions for finding information needed to solve problems and for doing the activities.
    d. Optional, related activities from which to select.
    e. Information concerning readings and materials.

25. **a.** Rationale including overall objectives and reasons that this learning is worth study.
    b. Specific objectives.
    c. Directions for carrying out the activities to be included in the module.
    d. Materials needed for the module or directions for obtaining them.
    e. Measuring devices, such as pretests, progress tests, and post test.

26. **a.** The course should be psychologically organized.
    b. The course should be compatible with the available resources.
    c. The course plan should lend itself to retention and transfer.
    d. The course content, organization and instruction should contribute to the achievement of the course objective.
    e. The course content, organization, and teaching strategies should reflect the nature of the discipline.

27. **a.** Determine the objectives.
    b. Determine the course content including topic, sequence, and emphasis.
    c. Decide on the time allotment.
    d. Determine basic strategies, major assignments, and materials.

28. There are more than three possibilities. Your module text mentions the following. Take your pick.
    a. The value of the learning needs to be pointed out.
    b. The ways the learning can be used needs to be pointed out.
    c. The learning should be thorough. It is better to learn a lesser amount thoroughly than a lot superficially.
    d. The student should have occasion to draw generalizations and apply them.
    e. There should be many opportunities for renewal of the learning.

29. The steps are
    a. Prepare overall course objectives.
    b. Determine the sequence of modules.
    c. Prepare general and specific objectives for the modules.
    d. Select content and learning procedures for the modules.
    e. Prepare learning packet for the modules.

30. **a.** Introduce course and planning.
    b. Set up limits.
    c. Set up criteria for topic selection.
    d. Select topics.

e. Select problems to be studied in each unit.

f. Make final decisions by discussion and consensus procedures.

Module 5

1. F. "The best laid plans of mice and men gang aft agley."

2. T. Not necessarily detailed written plans, but plans. Otherwise how do they know what to do and how to do it.

3. F. You must have more than subject matter in your head. The lesson plan outlines what and how to teach. In the beginning you had better have both a written objective and procedure.

4. T. You will develop your own style anyway. It would be nice if it should be appropriate to you.

5. F. Why not?

6. F. Not after several years.

7. T. Bring them up to date and smooth out the wrinkles.

8. F. Not really. There is no single most important element. If your overall conception is no good, the lesson plan will not save it.

9. T. Course or unit goals are usually general. Lesson plan objectives should be specific.

10. F. That is a class period. A lesson begins when you begin it and ends when you end it.

11. F. If it is a good one, why not?

12. T. Use the one that suits you and your purposes best.

13. F. This one is iffy. Probably you could find something better to do as a follow-up, but studying in class under supervision is an excellent thing.

14. T. If you have made a careful plan, it is usually best to stick with it, but you should never marry a set plan until death do you part.

15. T. It may make all the difference.

16. F. Not every lesson needs one, but most of them do.

17. F. Usually not. They are usually general unit objectives.

18. F. An outline is much more usable.

19. T. Absolutely. That's one reason for writing out plans.

20. T. A strong conclusion can clinch closure.

21. F. You ought to have an outline of the content, but it does not necessarily have to appear here.

22. F. There may not be one.

23. T. It is often easy to forget details in an interesting class, even more so in a difficult one.

24. F. Some classes need only a simple outline, e.g., classes featuring a movie or laboratory work sessions.

25. F. A written plan shows that you are prepared.

26. T. Most plan books are just that—layout sheets.

27. T. In some schools plans for the week must be submitted the previous Friday. Those may be only layouts.

28. F. As a rule you should; the procedure should outline just what you plan to do.

29. F. General or affective objectives particularly might be stated in descriptive terms.

30. T. Absolutely. Why would anyone want to throw away a good thing?

31. F. Not necessarily. There are several acceptable formats.

32. F. Ordinarily, there is not room for your plan in the planbook. Just indicate what the lesson will be.

33. F. Most plans do need introduction, development, and conclusion sections, but some lessons are simply parts of units or long term plans.

34. T. It is much easier to follow an outlined plan than one written in text form.

35. T. Of course. Lest you forget.

36. The method should be such that it helps achieve the objective.

37. Use it to give focus to your lesson. It can be featured in the introduction, the body, or conclusion of the lesson, but wherever it is located, it should be the central idea that binds the lesson together.

38. The reasons include:
    a. To form a firm base for your lesson, i.e., by clarifying what you hope to do and how you hope to do it.
    b. To give yourself security during the lesson.
    c. To have a reminder in case you forget or are distracted.
    d. To inform a substitute teacher what was planned for the lesson.

39. Review, introduce the next lesson.

40. At the most propitious moment, i.e., when it fits in best. Giving it at the beginning of the class may keep you from forgetting it or rushing it, but it may be more logical to give it at the end of class sometimes.

Module 6

1. R	6. R	11. R	16. X
2. R	7. X	12. R	17. R
3. R	8. R	13. X	18. X
4. X	9. R	14. R	19. X
5. X	10. R	15. R	20. R

21. All sorts of information. Test scores, academic record, home information, extracurricular activities, and health information.

22. Open ended.

23. To find out the pupil's interests, of course.

24. Looks like a clique.

25. M. is popular, maybe a natural leader.

26. Reward.

27. Immediate.

28. A list of rewards that a person can choose if he does well.

29. Plutarch was pretty modern; his method is still theoretically sound.

30. As soon as you finish the conference.

31. Set up behavioral objectives. Then write test items that test those objectives.

32. Before starting a new learning activity, e.g., lesson, unit, discussion, question and answer session, assigning homework, student report, assigning reports, film or film-strips.

33. An agreement in which the student agrees to do something in return for a certain reward.

34. Betty did not achieve Objective 1. The other kids did.

35. They might provide you with information which would help you adjust your teaching to their needs, interests, goals, etc.

Module 7

1. X	**8.** R	**15.** X	**22.** R
2. X	**9.** X	**16.** R	**23.** X
3. R	**10.** R	**17.** R	**24.** R
4. X	**11.** X	**18.** R	**25.** R
5. R	**12.** R	**19.** R	
6. R	**13.** R	**20.** X	
7. X	**14.** R	**21.** X	

26. Classes need order, quiet, and discipline. When anything goes (which is what the French phrase means), discipline, order, quiet, and learning go too.

27. Make the pupils aware of the advantages of high standards and the disadvantages of low standards. Value-clarifying techniques may help.

28. Tiresome, boring, irrelevant teaching and courses.

29. Sounds ridiculous to me. Try to be firm, businesslike, but pleasant.

30. No. Rigid rules may cut down on your options too much. A few simple ones would be much better.

31. It is much easier to relax after being strict than to try to become strict after being relaxed. Start off being quite strict and you will usually do better.

32. Making life miserable for a student while he is misbehaving and then removing the aversiveness the minute his behavior improves.

33. You set up an alternative behavior that is so rewarding the pupil gives up his misbehavior.

34. Relaxed.

35. Motivation.

36. Permissive teaching is supportive teaching that helps pupils learn and think. It is not repressive; neither is it a free-for-all. All pupil behavior must be correct and within the limits set down by the rules. In laissez-faire teaching anything goes. The result is usually chaos, not learning.

37. Harsh, never. Strong and impressive, yes.

38. Basically, the idea is to plan well and thoroughly. Here are some points you might use.
  a. Provide purposeful activities.
  b. Provide for differences.
  c. Provide motivation.
  d. Eliminate dead spots.
  e. Give good, clear assignments so pupils know what to do and how to do it.
  f. Keep pupils busy. Not too much lecture.
  g. Make lessons seem worthwhile.
  h. Keep lessons to the point.

39. a. Ask pupil what happened.
  b. Try to find out the central issue.
  c. Ask pupil what he thinks should be done.
  d. If it is not resolved, discuss with the student what is likely to happen if such behavior continues.
  e. Find out from the pupil how he thinks he may be helped and how you may help him.
  f. Develop a follow-through with the pupil.

40. Movement management is a process of keeping the class moving forward smoothly without interruption and digressions.

Module 8

1. c, d, e, g	**2.** a, c, f	**3.** a, b, c, e, f
4. b, c, e, f, g	**5.** b, c, d	**6.** a, c, d
7. c, d, e, g, h	**8.** a, b, d, e, f	**9.** d
10. a	**11.** c	**12.** a
13. b	**14.** c	**15.** b
16. d	**17.** a	

18. For several reasons (check the module), but principally because pupils are receivers rather than doers and, as a result, seldom learn as well by this method as by others.

19. The module suggests the following:
   a. State purpose.
   b. Be logical.
   c. Include clues to development.
   d. Avoid attempting too much.
   e. Begin with an interest catcher.
   f. Provide for repetition.
   g. Provide for real and rhetorical questions.
   h. Be as short as reasonably possible.
   i. Include humor.
   j. Give examples.
   k. Summarize at end.
   l. Tell what you are going to tell them, tell them, and tell them what you told them.

20. Give pupils a chance to think before you give the answers. Use questions. Bring in challenging questions.

21. The module mentions the following:
   a. Establish a general point of view.
   b. Present facts quickly.
   c. Arouse interest.
   d. Fill in background information.
   e. Introduce new units.
   f. Summarize.
   g. Provide information.

22. Cognitive memory questions are those that test one's memory for facts or information; convergent questions are narrow-range questions that require a correct answer; divergent questions are open-ended, broad questions that have no correct answer; evaluative questions are divergent questions that ask one to put a value on something.

23. Reword, rephrase, come back again.

24. Of course.

25. To lead the pupil to discover the desired answers or come to the desired conclusions.

26. Of course. The open text recitation is one of the best techniques.

27. Ordinarily, if we can use the regular materials, the pupils' learning will be more beneficial.

28. It depends on what you want to do. Narrow questions tell whether pupils know specifics; broad questions are more likely to be thought questions.

29. No, you should use both. Unless pupils understand at the lower levels, there is not much point in asking high-level questions.

30. Any of the following may help. Make questions interesting, use thought-provoking questions, carefully plan your questions, deemphasize rote learning, keep the content meaningful, follow questions with discussion of implications, and the like; use open-text recitations.

31. In this method the student tries to learn by running through the entire procedure, then concentrating on different difficult parts, and finally practicing the whole procedure.

32. There are many ways to do it. Perhaps the best is to utilize discussion based on upper level questioning in which pupils may, and should, refer to the text for arguments and confirmation of facts.

33. Utilize repetition of the main points in various ways. Hammer at the points. Tell them what you are going to tell them; tell them; tell them what you told them.

34. Whenever you want to arouse original thinking. They are good for starting discussions.

35. When pupils' answers are superficial or when you want pupils to expand or dig deeper into the concepts.

36. The teacher may be tempted to talk too much. The teacher may think that because he has told it, the students may know it.

37. An advance organizer is a brief presentation, either written or not, describing the main ideas of the lecture, talk, or lesson.

38. Use interesting thought questions (and a mix with other activities).

39. He asked a series of questions—largely leading questions—by which he helped students to examine their beliefs, upset their preconceptions, and draw new conclusions.

40. Yes. Why not?

Module 9

1. d	**2.** d	**3.** b	**4.** c
5. a	**6.** d	**7.** c	**8.** a
9. c	**10.** b	**11.** a	**12.** b
13. c	**14.** d	**15.** c	**16.** b
17. a	**18.** a	**19.** d	**20.** d

Module 10

1. a. Good motivating qualities.
   b. Teaches and offers practice in intellectual skills.
   c. Results in more thorough learning.
   d. Involves pupils.

2. a. Costly in time.
   b. Costly in effort.
   c. Sometimes lead to mislearning.
   d. Not very efficient.

3. Of course.

4. Why not?

5. Check back to the text for the answer. Basically, the steps are as follows:
   a. Become aware of the problem.
   b. Look for a solution.
   c. Test out solution to see if it will work.

6. a. Is it pertinent to course objectives?
   b. Is it relevant to pupils' lives?
   c. Is it feasible (time, materials, abilities)?
   d. Is it worthwhile?

7. a. Provide lists.
   b. Class discussion.

    c. Describe past projects.
    d. Bring in former pupils.

8. No.

9. a. Rating scales.
    b. Checklists.
    c. Standardized directions for observing.

10. a. Set procedure required of all interviews.
    b. Standard list of exactly worded questions used by all interviewers.

11. Turn back to the module and check your answers against the explanations.

12. Turn back again. Socratic dialogue is mostly a matter of asking leading questions until you get the pupil to arrive at the conclusion you wanted him to reach.

13. Basically that it is controlled by the teacher and so teacher-dominated. True discussions are free and open ended.

14. Value-clarifying discussions are very open, free from leading questions, preaching, or teacher judgments.

15. Refer to module text to see if your answer checks with it. Basically the procedure is
    a. Pick the situation.
    b. Select the cast.
    c. Be sure pupils understand the situation.
    d. Brief the audience.
    e. Stage the role playing.
    f. Repeat with reversed roles or different players if it seems desirable.
    g. Follow up.

16. They are fun. They make clear difficult concepts and procedures. They give practice.

17. Again, see the module text and compare your answer with it. Basically the procedure is
    a. Decide on goals or problem.
    b. Define problem.
    c. Allocate tasks.
    d. Gather materials and equipment.
    e. Gather the data.
    f. Review and analyze the data.
    g. Draw inferences.
    h. Report findings and conclusions.

18. The pupil arrives at the conclusion or generalization rather than having it told to him.

19. Present the pupils with a dilemma.

Conduct a discussion about the dilemma in which you use thought-provoking and probing questions if necessary to stimulate thought but keep the discussion open, nonjudgmental, and nonauthoritative.

20. Pick from the following.

Example (modeling).

Persuasion.

Limiting choice.

Inspiration.

Citing dogma and religion.

Appeal to conscience.

Exhortation (telling them what to believe).

21. Use it to clarify pupils' values and beliefs about issues. Present the issue; have pupils fill out value sheet; follow up by class discussion, small group discussion, reading selected sheets or portions of sheets to class, read them privately with comments but no grade, have committee select sheets representing various positions to be read to the class.

22. Select from the following:

Is the topic relevant to the course?

Are the students knowledgeable and neutral enough?

Is it worth the time and effort?

Do we have sufficient material?

Can the topic be discussed without upsetting the pupils or the community?

Module 11

The most accurate statements are as follows:

1. b	**2.** c	**3.** b	**4.** d
5. b	**6.** a	**7.** a	**8.** b
9. d	**10.** a	**11.** d	**12.** b
13. c	**14.** c	**15.** a	

For supporting reasons and for explanations of the limitations or inaccuracy of the other statements, reexamine the module at appropriate points.

Module 12

1. True individualization entails a tailor-made curriculum for each pupil, not just a change of pace or varying amount of content to be covered. It narrows the span of ability or achievement in a class so that everyone is able to profit from the same presentation. It diminishes the need for so much remedial instruction and individual attention.

2. Theoretically, it makes it easier to pick content and methods suitable for everyone.

3. There is always a spread of characteristics in a homogeneously grouped class. Besides, all the characteristics, other than those reduced by the grouping process, run the entire gamut found in the population.

4. They tend to be written off. Teachers give up on them. Teachers concentrate on the uninteresting and unchallenging content and presentation, because they conclude that poor students can't keep up. Missing is the spark of vitality from student responses often supplied by the brighter students.

5. Everyone can move through the curriculum at his own pace. No one is forced to move on before he is ready or to wait for others to catch up.

6. To provide for more variety, and to circumvent the failure attributed to long periods of time spent on units that fail to capture the imagination of the student.

7. It provides a place for pupils to work on their own with all the materials they need readily available.

8. **a.** Give some pupils more work, and others, less.
   b. Give some pupils more difficult work, and others, easier.
   c. Use committees and small-group work.
   d. Individualize.
   e. Give totally different assignments.

9. A classroom laboratory is arranged so that the materials and equipment are readily available for pupils to work individually and in groups, or on a variety of assignments or projects, under guidance.

10. The bulk of the work is done in a laboratory situation in the true unit. Not all students are expected to attend at the same time to what the teacher is saying. Not everyone does the same thing in the same way.

11. It allows pupils to work individually on different units at the same time as well as allowing for laboratory-type procedures. It is a self-teaching instrument that frees the student to establish his own pace of learning.

12. The feature of *quid pro quo*. In the contract the student specifies the scope and depth of his inquiry. In the packet the student demonstrates mastery of the content in the fashion requested.

13. They give the pupil direction and structure so that he can work without constant recourse to the teacher for direction.

14. Practice, diagnosis, and study, but not for marks.

15. Focus it on a small sheet of paper or into a box. Attach earphones if it is a sound program.

16. Same way. Arrange it so that pupils do not run out the film, but reverse it for the next pupil or group of pupils.

17. Use study guides, self-correcting materials, student tutors and proctors, and laboratory teaching.

18. Not much, just that you adapt the content, materials, and methods to the group. The basic approach should be about the same, but adapted to pupils' talents, interests, abilities, and goals.

19. Pupils' present educational levels. Year's educational goals. Specifications for services to be provided; extent pupils should be in regular programs. Type, direction, and criteria for the services.

20. Take your pick from the following:
  a. Encourage the talented to think. Use problem solving, inquiry, and open-ended assignments. Insist that pupils dig into the subject. Hold them to a high level of analysis and critical thinking.
  b. See to it that the talented keep to high academic standards. Do not accept sloppy thinking or sloppy work. Force them to discipline themselves and their thinking.
  c. Don't hold them back. Give them a chance to move on to the new, the interesting, and the challenging. Don't make them repeat what they already know.
  d. Be sure they become well grounded in the academic skills.
  e. Give them lots of responsibility for their own work. Let them plan and evaluate. Encourage independent study and research.
  f. Use high-level materials: original sources, college textbooks, and adult materials.
  g. Use the seminar discussion strategy in which pupils present and criticize original papers or reports and discuss topics in depth. Be sure that their discussions hew to a high level of criticism and thinking.

21. Take your pick from the following:
  a. Respect the pupils as people.
  b. Give students opportunity to succeed
  c. Use laboratory techniques and help on basic skills
  d. Use role playing and dramatization techniques
  e. Use a variety of reading materials
  f. Use inductive approaches
  g. Use Socratic questions
  h. Adjust subject content to the needs of the students.

Module 13

1. a	**2.** b	**3.** a	**4.** d	**5.** b
6. f	**7.** c	**8.** d	**9.** A or D	**10.** K
11. O	**12.** L	**13.** R or Q	**14.** √	**15.** √
16.	**17.**	**18.** √	**19.** √	**20.**
21. h	**22.** g	**23.** f	**24.** c	**25.** e
26. c	**27.** d	**28.** b		

29. Preassessment of students.

30. Instructional activities.

31. Continuous evaluation.

32–35. Pick from the following:
Placement.
Determine readiness.
Grading.
Diagnosis.
Promotion.
Setting goals.
Determine what to do next.
Judge the effectiveness of one's teaching.

Module 14

1. b	**2.** c	**3.** a	**4.** c	**5.** a
6. d	**7.** b	**8.** d	**9.** c	**10.** b
11.	**12.** √	**13.** √	**14.**	**15.** √

16. 5
17. 2 } any other numbers in same relationship, such as { 10 4 4 2 or { 50 20 20 10
18. 2
19. 1

20. a	**21.** d	**22.** b
23. b	**24.** d	**25.** a

Module 15

1. By showing pupils the real thing or representation of the real thing, the pupils see or hear it rather than words about it.

2. Is it suitable to do the job you want it to do? Other considerations pale before this one.

3. The distance between the lens and light source must be properly adjusted.

4. Use the opaque projector. With it you can blow up the pictures so all can see and study them.

5. You can show the material on the screen or board while pupils work with copies at their seats.

6. Of course.

7. Overhead projectors project only transparent (translucent) material. An opaque projector projects the image of opaque materials.

8. It is versatile, can be used in a lighted room, takes only a second to prepare, can be used as a chalkboard, and for many things.

9. That depends upon how fancy one wants to make it. A quick, temporary transparency can be made by drawing on the frosted plastic with a grease pencil or felt-tipped pen. To draw a more finished project, follow the procedure outlined in the module text.

10. Lay it on top of the basic transparency to add new information, or take it off to subtract information.

11. It blocks out part of the transparency you do not want pupils to see now.

12. Run it on a small screen or box. Use earphones if it is a sound program.

13. To do a good job is quite a lengthy process. Check your answer against the module text.

14. Wrap the film around the take-up reel a few times, mark the break with a slip of paper, and continue with the show. *Do not* try to tape or pin the film together.

15. Lots of things. Require notes, give quizzes, introduce it well, use study guide, follow-up, discussion, and assignments, for example.

16. Some movies are pretty awful—boring, irrelevant, or incorrect. Pupils tend to think of them as entertainment. Movies may emphasize what you would rather not emphasize. They are not very adaptable. They require special arrangements and are generally awkward to use. They are expensive and often difficult to get when you need them.

17. Follow up. What else?

18. See special films. Use them as optional activities, assign activities for theater parties, bases for committees, or individual reports.

19. Introduce. Explain. List key words, use a handout (study guide). Be sure pupils know what is expected of them.

20. Music plus pictures, maps plus pictures, tape plus pictures, board plus screen, or two screens. Or any other combination you think of.

21. The microcomputer can be used to individualize instruction, conduct drill and practice, give immediate feedback, present learning programs, and the like. It can provide both computer-assisted instruction and computer-managed instruction, if the software is available.

22. If you want to explain things yourself or stop the film to go into detail on a particular point, or when the sound film is incorrect, distracting, or boring.

23. In slide programs the sequence can be varied to suit your needs, if you do not use canned commentary. It is much easier to put together a slide program than it is to construct a filmstrip.

24. One could assign viewing for homework, videotape progress, assign different channels to different students, use viewing as an extra or optional activity, or if the occasion permits, watch the program in class.

25. Most of them. Slides, filmstrips, 8mm and 16mm films, overheads, audio- and videotapes, records (with earphones), are all easily adapted for individual viewing and listening even if one does not have individual equipment.

26. CAI (Computer-Assisted Instruction) is programmed software that puts the student in contact with pretests, facts, instruction, and responses. It provides drill and practice exercises, or tutors, under the control of the student until the point of mastery has been reached.

27. CMI (Computer-Managed Instruction) is software that does all the record keeping when attempting individualized instruction. It manages the instruction, i.e., keeps track of test gains made, indicates next sequential step to take, and provides reports that can be used when grouping students for instruction.

28. Simulation provides experiences and activities that are realistic. It encompasses the vicarious living through a real situation, and calls for students to make important decisions at critical points in problem solving that determine the outcome of the problem.

29. Branching is a technique in programming that directs the course of the study by the student. When students' answers are accurate, the direction is to continue to the next step. When the answer is wrong, the student is re-routed back through the material he has just studied until he is ready for another mastery-test-attempt.

Module 16

1. The textbook should be just one of many tools.

2. The module lists eighteen items. Basically, it should present the relevant content interestingly, logically, and accurately at a reading level that is compatible with that of the pupils.

3. Select a number of readings that will lead to the instructional goals. Let the pupils under guidance read those things that will best suit them. Although they read different things, since the readings all lead to the goals, the pupils should emerge with the concepts. A study guide will help the pupils in their study. The readings should have as much spread in interest, reading level and so on as feasible to provide for the pupils' differences.

4. The greatest advantage has been their inexpensiveness, which allows one to use multitexts, introduce original pieces, and mark up books, and so on.

5. Most important, try to find something that encourages thinking. Avoid workbooks that are cut and dried. Otherwise, use the same criteria as for other books and materials.

6. Almost anything, including anecdotes, stories, case studies, pictures, films, filmstrips, histories.

7. To guide pupils so that they can study alone without being tied to the teacher's apron strings.

8. White space is blank space. Leave white space so what you want to stress will stand out.

9. They are more dramatic.

10. Attach sandpaper, felt, or flannel, or Velcro fasteners to light material such as paper. See the module text for the details.

11. Use it as a teaching tool.

12. Have a central focus without clutter that draws the eye toward what you want to show off. Use eye catchers and lines to draw attention to the center of interest. There should be plenty of white space and no clutter.

13. A flip chart is a big pad of charts that one can flip back and forth as needed.

14. You flip the pages to the proper place, talk about it, and then flip to the next page.

15. Pictures give life to dull classes and reality to abstract descriptions, but when you pass them around the room, they distract the pupils from the lesson.

16. In a linear program, the pupils all progress in order through the program in small steps. In a branching program, the pupils take large steps. If they make mistakes, the program branches to reteach them.

17. People, places, things, directions, persons to contact, and any other information on local resource persons, materials, and places to visit.

18. Theoretically, the machine can teach the facts and leave the teacher free to individualize, give additional help, and teach the higher mental skills and processes.

19. Among the reasons you might cite are: they have only a single point of view, they have only a single reading level, they are too rigid, they are too dull, they do not allow for pupils' individual differences, they are likely to be superficial, and they discourage pupils from reading more profitable works.

20. Among the many sources of information are curriculum guides, resource units, curriculum bulletins, educational periodicals, and the reference works listed in this module.

Module 17

1. **a, c, d.** Expertise in many teaching skills is asking too much at this stage; you have not had a chance to start developing teaching style yet.

2. **a, d, e, f, g.** Ask advice to keep from making unnecessary blunders; criticizing the school shows not your expertise, but your boorishness.

3. c

4. c

5. d

6. a

7. b

8. Examine the incident to see what went wrong and then try again.

9. One that includes all the lower level plus creating, discovering, reorganizing, and formulating new hypotheses, new questions and problems; in short, the level of original and productive thinking.

10. The objective should be clearly stated, measurable, pertinent to unit and course, worthwhile, suitable to age and grade level, achievable, attainable in different degrees and/or amounts, and relevant to the pupils' lives.

11. So you can get a picture of what you and your teaching are like.

12. **a.** Direct
    b. Probably not as effective as it would be if it were more indirect.

13. **a.** Teacher did most of the talking.
    b. Can't tell. Probably the teacher talks too much.

14. Select from good objectives, objectives obtainable by discussion techniques, good participation, teacher drew pupils out, teacher did not let anyone dominate, teacher kept group on the topic, teacher did not dominate, teacher used evocative questions and tentative solutions, teacher summarized well when needed, and teacher tied the discussion together in summary.

15. Teacher runs a good discussion, does not dominate, and draws out the class.

16. Whiplash questions are really incomplete sentences. They tend to confuse. They do not induce the proper set for answering questions.

17. Cognitive memory questions are narrow memory questions calling only for recall of information. Convergent questions are narrow thought questions that call for coming to a correct solution. Divergent questions are broad, open-ended thought questions for which there are probably no single correct answers.

18. The pupils seem to have achieved objective 1 but missed objective 2. If objective 2 is important, it probably should be retaught.

19. Choose from (a) become certifiable in more than one subject, (b) pick courses that will prepare you to teach middle and high school courses, (c) seek a graduate degree, (d) do substitute teaching, (e) take advantage of the college or university placement service, (f) learn the skills of job procurement.

20. Basically so you can learn about new developments in the field at meetings or by reading their journals and monographs and so you can meet leaders and knowledgeable practitioners in your teaching field.

Index